# the political ecology of the metropolis

Edited by
Jefferey M. Sellers, Daniel Kübler,
Melanie Walter-Rogg, and R. Alan Walks

**ecpr**PRESS

First published by the ECPR Press in 2013

The ECPR Press is the publishing imprint of the European Consortium for Political Research (ECPR), a scholarly association, which supports and encourages the training, research and cross-national cooperation of political scientists in institutions throughout Europe and beyond.

ECPR Press
University of Essex
Wivenhoe Park,
Colchester
CO4 3SQ,
UK

Typeset by AnVi
Printed and bound by Lightning Source

British Library Cataloguing in Publication Data
A catalogue record for this book is available from the British Library

Hardback ISBN: 978-1-907301-37-7

Paperback ISBN: 978-1-907301-44-5

www.ecpr.eu/ecprpress

ECPR – *Studies in European Political Science*
Series Editors:
Dario Castiglione (University of Exeter)
Peter Kennealy (European University Institute)
Alexandra Segerberg (Stockholm University)
Peter Triantafillou (Roskilde University)

ECPR – *Studies in European Political Science* is a series of high-quality edited volumes on topics at the cutting edge of current political science and political thought. All volumes are research-based offering new perspectives in the study of politics with contributions from leading scholars working in the relevant fields. Most of the volumes originate from ECPR events including the Joint Sessions of Workshops, the Research Sessions, and the General Conferences.

**Books in this series:**

**Europeanisation and Party Politics**
ISBN: 9781907301223
*Edited by Erol Külahci*

**Interactive Policy Making, Metagovernance and Democracy**
ISBN: 9781907301131
*Edited by Jacob Torfing and Peter Triantafillou*

**Perceptions of Europe**
ISBN: 9781907301155
*Edited by Daniel Gaxie, Jay Rowell and Nicolas Hubé*

**Personal Representation: The Neglected Dimension of Electoral Systems**
ISBN: 9781907301162
*Edited by Josep Colomer*

**Political Participation in France and Germany**
ISBN: 9781907301315
*Oscar Gabriel, Silke Keil, and Eric Kerrouche*

**Political Trust: Why Context Matters**
ISBN: 9781907301230
*Edited by Sonja Zmerli and Marc Hooghe*

**Please visit www.ecpr.eu/ecprpress for up-to-date information about new publications.**

# | Contents

# | List of Figures and Tables

*Figures*

*Tables*

# | Contributors

HENRY BÄCK is emeritus Professor of Public Administration at the University of Gothenburg. He has co-edited *The European Mayor: Political Leaders in the Changing Context of Local Democracy* (VS Verlag, 2006) and *Urban Political Decentralisation: Six Scandinavian Cities* (VS Verlag, 2005). The author of numerous books, articles and book chapters on local government and politics.

DANIEL ČERMÁK is PhD student in Sociology at Faculty of Arts of Charles University in Prague. He works as a junior researcher at the Institute of Sociology of Academy of Sciences. He is an author of scholarly articles and book chapters related to local democracy, electoral geography and institutional trust.

ANNA HAZAN teaches at the Administration and Public Policy Department of the Sapir College, Israel. She served for many years as the director of the Local Development Department of Israel's Ministry of Interior and coauthored numerous publications on Israel's local government, mainly in Hebrew, such as *Personal Liability in Local Government in Israel* (Floersheimer Studies, 2008). She has several English and French publications in books and scientific journals, such as Geografiska Annaler, Political Geography, and Environment and Planning.

VINCENT HOFFMANN-MARTINOT is Professor of Political Science and Director of Sciences Po Bordeaux. He is the author of *Le gouvernement des villes. Une comparaison internationale* (L'Harmattan) and editor of *Metropolitanization and Political Change* (VS Verlag, 2005; French edition, CNRS Press 2007) as well as numerous articles and book chapters.

TOMÁŠ KOSTELECKÝ is Director of the Institute of Sociology of the Academy of Sciences of the Czech Republic in Prague. He is author of *Political Parties after Communism: Developments in East-Central Europe* (Woodrow Wilson Center Press, 2002) and numerous articles and book chapters dealing with comparative politics, local government and housing.

DANIEL KÜBLER is Professor of Political Science at the University of Zurich and co-director of the International Metropolitan Observatory Project. He has co-edited *Metropolitan governance: capacity, democracy and the dynamics of place* (Routledge, 2005) and authored numerous articles and book chapters related to metropolitan governance, urban democracy and public policy analysis.

CLEMENTE J. NAVARRO is Professor of Sociology and head of the Centre for Local Political Sociology and Policies at the Pablo de Olavide University. He is author of scholarly articles and book chapters related with urban governance and political participation.

ERAN RAZIN is director of the *Institute of Urban and Regional Studies*, head of *Floersheimer Studies*, and Associate Professor of Geography at the Hebrew University of Jerusalem. He specialises in local government and urban development. He has coauthored/edited several books, such as *Employment Deconcentration in European Metropolitan Areas, Market Forces versus Planning Regulations* (Springer, 2007), and *Metropolitan Governance, Different Paths in Contrasting Contexts: Germany and Israel* (Campus, 2011), and numerous journal articles.

PHILIPPE ROCHAT is a Political Scientist. He works at the University of Zurich and at the GfS research institute in Berne. He is co-author of book chapters and analysis related to Swiss politics, federal referenda and urban development.

JEFFEREY M. SELLERS is Professor of Political Science and Public Policy at the University of Southern California. The author of *Governing From Below: Urban Regions in the Global Economy* (Cambridge University Press, 2002) and editor of *Metropolitanization and Political Change* (VS Verlag, 2005; French edition, CNRS Press 2007) as well as numerous articles and book chapters, he is co-founder and co-director of the International Metropolitan Observatory Project.

PAWEŁ SWIANIEWICZ is Professor of Economics at University of Warsaw, Department of Local Development and Policy, Faculty of Geography and Regional Studies. He is an author of numerous books and articles on local politics, regional policies and local government finance in Poland and other countries of Central and Eastern Europe.

URS SCHEUSS was a postdoctoral fellow at the Centre for Democracy Studies (ZDA) in Aarau, Switzerland, until 2010 when he became a political secretary of the Swiss Green Party. He is the author of a PhD thesis on political divisions and cleavages in metropolitan areas of Switzerland that will be published in 2013.

JANA VOBECKÁ is a Researcher at the Vienna Institute of Demography of the Austrian Academy of Sciences and the Institute of Sociology of the Academy of Sciences of the Czech Republic. Her research combines sociology and demography and focuses inter alia on spatial population dynamics and its effects on social inequalities, local governance, and historical demography. She has published in journals such as *Population, Space and Place*, *Czech Sociological Review* and *Central European Journal of Public Policy*.

R. ALAN WALKS is Associate Professor of Geography at the University of Toronto. He is the author of a number of scholarly articles and book chapters related to electoral geography, urban inequality, and the relationship between suburbanisation and ideology.

MELANIE WALTER-ROGG is Professor of Political Science and Methodology at the University of Regensburg. She is author of a number of scholarly articles and book chapters related to metropolitan governance, urban democracy as well as political culture and political behaviour.

# Preface

This volume, the product of a ten-year endeavour, presents the second set of results from the International Metropolitan Observatory (IMO) research programme. The current work represents in many respects the culmination of this initiative to establish the politics of metropolitan regions as a new frontier of research in political science and such allied disciplines as geography and sociology.

We would like to thank all the contributors to this ambitious comparative enterprise for their constant efforts and their patience since this collaborative undertaking first took shape in September 2002 in Stuttgart.

Successive meetings organised around the project over 2002–9 were made possible through the support of several institutions. We express in particular our deep gratitude to the Center for International Studies, the Center for Religion and Civic Culture, the Dornsife College of Letters, Arts and Sciences and the Office of the Provost at the University of Southern California, the University of Stuttgart (Institute of Social Sciences), the French Ministries of Research (PIR-Villes and ACI-Ville Programs) and Education (DRIC – ACCES Program), the CNRS (SHS Department) and the GRALE in Paris, Sciences Po Bordeaux, the European Consortium for Political Research, and the Thyssen Foundation.

Several mechanisms for cooperation have contributed decisively to the strengthening of the IMO network: the CODE (*Comparing Democracies in Europe*) Associate European Laboratory of the CNRS at Sciences Po Bordeaux and the Institute of Social Sciences of the University of Stuttgart; the Marie Curie Research Fellowship and the Fulbright-Masaryk Program, which enabled Tomáš Kostelecký to spend a year in Bordeaux and a year in Los Angeles; the Maison des Sciences de l'Homme, which supported a three-month research stay by Eran Razin in Bordeaux; the Joint Sessions of the European Consortium for Political Research; the Social Sciences and Humanities Research Council of Canada (SSHRC), which funded the research discussed in the Canadian and UK-based chapters; and the National Centre of Competence in Research *Challenges to Democracy in the 21st century* at the University of Zurich, which funded crucial work related to the construction of the pooled dataset.

This project could not have been completed successfully without the intensive and dedicated participation of numerous additional collaborators beyond contributors to the country chapters. We are especially indebted to Philippe Rochat for his outstanding work piecing together and analysing the pooled dataset, to Deniz Kuru for help with construction and analysis of the survey-based indexes for several chapters, and to Julia Bischoff for her tireless endurance and meticulousness during the formatting and proofreading of the final manuscript. Each played an indispensable role in the realisation of this project. We also thank Hanspeter Kriesi for incisive feedback at a crucial stage.

*Jefferey M. Sellers, Daniel Kübler, Melanie Walter-Rogg and R. Alan Walks*
Los Angeles/Zürich/Regensburg/Toronto, March 2012

# Chapter One | Introduction – The Metropolitanisation of Politics

*Jefferey M. Sellers and R. Alan Walks*

Metropolitanisation and the changing shape of metropolitan regions are respon-sible for global parallel shifts in the conditions of everyday life. As metropolitan areas have emerged as the predominant form of human settlement, extended urban regions increasingly shape national economies and cultures. Comparative analysis of the ways urban regions shape political behaviour has advanced little beyond the traditional distinctions between urban and rural localities. Most accounts of contemporary changes in political culture focus on survey analysis of individu-als or on the macro analysis of global change. These approaches fail to account sufficiently for the new patterns of politics emerging across the developed world. Patterns of consumption, production and settlement within urban regions are cru-cial to understanding the new politics of the twenty-first century. This volume undertakes a pioneering investigation into the role these metropolitan shifts have played in the changing politics of nations across the developed world and beyond.

Until recently, it was commonly held that as nation states industrialised and urbanised, political behaviour and values would form around national institutions and countrywide groups. This nationalisation thesis, put forward by scholars of 'political modernisation' (Campbell *et al.* 1966; Hoffbert and Sharkansky 1971; Lipset and Rokkan 1967), held that national political cleavages rooted in social class would come to dominate political contests and party structures at every elec-toral scale. Regional and locally-based political parties would wither. Localities would no longer serve as a basis for political engagement, value formation and po-litical party strength (Agnew 1987). Caramani's analysis of nineteenth and twenti-eth century elections in national legislative districts across Europe (2005) demon-strates the continued relevance of this thesis for explaining earlier transformations. His analysis of partisan allegiances shows a growing territorial uniformity within countries throughout Europe that extends into the post-war era.

From the late 1960s onward, however, party systems have fragmented, and partisan attachment and membership have declined (Dalton and Wattenberg 2000). As the territorial arrangements and settlement patterns of developed and transitional countries have shifted, metropolitan and local contexts have become more rather than less important in shaping national political ideologies and be-haviour. Analyses of these changes have thus far remained focused on regional economies and regional concentrations of particular cultural or language groups (e.g. Caramani 2005; Gimpel and Shuknecht 2004). New regional parties and se-cessionist movements have emerged in industrial countries such as the United Kingdom, Spain, Italy, Belgium, Japan, and Canada. Elsewhere, such as in the United States, France and Germany, regional cleavages in party support have in some respects become more pronounced (Agnew 1987).

The metropolitan dimension of contemporary territorial shifts, however, is both more pervasive and in many ways more important for politics. In 1968, Henri Lefebvre announced a coming 'urban revolution'. Global capitalism, he argued, was in the midst of a transition away from a mode of production grounded in industrialisation, which posed rural existence against modern industrial cities. Instead, as the countryside was swept up into the accelerating process of urbanisation, the social and political divisions of the future would run between different forms and levels of urbanisation. Throughout the developed world today, as contemporary theorists such as Hayward (2001) suggest, this revolution has already taken place. The everyday experiences of production, consumption, social life, and politics within urban regions form the building blocks upon which regional and national politics develop. The argument of this volume is that metropolitanisation is contributing to a re-territorialisation of politics.

The thesis of metropolitanisation developed in this volume not only directly counters the thesis of nationalisation, but offers a refined approach to transnational political change. Global shifts in culture and the spread of political ideologies, norms, and behaviour in many countries often appear to be imposed from the outside. We argue that social, economic and political conditions within metropolitan regions are central to these shifts and that they have decisively influenced patterns of political participation and partisan competition at a wider level. In doing so, influences rooted in local and regional settings interact with the more familiar social structures of class, age, and ethnicity. How metropolitan influences take place differs with the political institutions and pre-existing legacies of settlement in different countries. Yet overall, metropolitanisation has re-territorialised politics under a new set of configurations and conditions.

## Why metropolitan political ecology?

Several far-reaching shifts in the political economies and cultures of contemporary societies are restructuring the spaces of politics. These changes highlight the need for new analytical approaches to take into account the local and metropolitan contexts of political behaviour. We have adopted a multilevel political-ecological approach to the study of electoral behaviour. This approach utilises a quantitative empirical examination of contextual and spatial effects on the collective political behaviour of voters within bounded electoral communities (districts, cantons, communes, constituencies, municipalities), rather than individual level electoral or survey responses. This well-established methodological approach to political ecology (going back to Siegfried 1913; Dogan and Rokkan 1969) thus differs from the less formalised qualitative analysis of ecological and environmental politics that has recently also gone by the name 'political ecology'.

The vast majority of people in developed countries and emerging majorities in transitional countries, such as those of Eastern Europe, Latin America and South Africa, now live in urbanised settings (see Table 1.1). Throughout most of the developed world, the settlements that have accompanied growing affluence bear only a limited resemblance to the concentrated nineteenth century European city that stood out so clearly from its surrounding rural region. Forms of settlement that, in the mid-twentieth century, were mostly identified with the Anglo-American countries have evolved and since grown to dominate the lives of a majority of urban citizens. In most developed countries, metropolitan regions have replaced dense cities as the main articulation of urbanisation (see Figure 1.1). More households have moved outside urban centres, to new green fields, to former villages on the urban periphery, or to high-rise concentrations of cheap housing on the outskirts (see Figure 1.2). In Europe and Asia as well as North America, and increasingly in transitional and developing countries as well as settled democracies, a growing diversity in the economies, social composition and lifestyles of places within metropolitan regions has reinforced this process. In the few developed countries where this metropolitan transformation remains limited to less than half of the population, such as the Nordic countries, it continues apace.

This shift in settlement is only part of a wider transformation in the political economies of developed countries that has broad implications for political behaviour. New issues, technologies and social distinctions, and shifting political cleavages around them, have increasingly complicated the settled lines of division that have for a long time characterised the political parties of developed countries (Lipset and Rokkan 1967). As the nature of capitalism has shifted, mass

*Table 1.1: Urban population, 1950–2000 (%)*

|  | 1950 | 1960 | 1970 | 1980 | 1990 | 2000 |
|---|---|---|---|---|---|---|
| Canada | 61 | 69 | 76 | 76 | 77 | 79 |
| Czech Republic | 41 | 46 | 52 | 75 | 75 | 74 |
| France | 54 | 62 | 71 | 73 | 74 | 76 |
| Germany | 72 | 76 | 80 | 83 | 85 | 88 |
| Hungary | 39 | 43 | 49 | 57 | 62 | 64 |
| Israel | 65 | 77 | 84 | 89 | 90 | 92 |
| Netherlands | 54 | 54 | 56 | 58 | 60 | 64 |
| Norway | 50 | 50 | 65 | 71 | 72 | 76 |
| Poland | 39 | 48 | 52 | 58 | 61 | 62 |
| South Africa | 43 | 47 | 48 | 48 | 49 | 56 |
| Spain | 52 | 57 | 66 | 73 | 75 | 76 |
| Sweden | 66 | 73 | 81 | 83 | 83 | 83 |
| Switzerland | 44 | 51 | 55 | 57 | 68 | 68 |
| United Kingdom | 79 | 78 | 77 | 88 | 89 | 89 |
| United States | 64 | 70 | 74 | 74 | 75 | 79 |

*Note:* Urban population defined as those living in places with populations over 2,000 (in the United States, over 2,500).

*Source:* United Nations Population Division, *World Urbanization Prospects 2003* (New York: United Nations, 2004).

consumption and the boundaries of welfare states have taken their place alongside production modes and practices as sources of social divisions and political cleavages. The growing transnational dimensions of economic production and immigration have created new lines of division between regions, places and types of workers. With the shifts in the economic and social order, new divides have emerged over nationhood and ethnicity, as well as religion and values. As a result, new determinants of political behaviour have consistently altered and sometimes wholly replaced the old divisions of class and religion that moulded the electoral patterns and party systems of the early and mid-twentieth century.

Shifts in the localities of metropolitan regions are closely linked to these wider spatial, economic and social changes. As the metropolitan regions of developed countries have grown, clear commonalities among them have emerged (Hoffmann-Martinot and Sellers 2005). Everywhere, urban centres have maintained analogous concentrations of businesses, advanced business services, and recreational activities. At the same time, these centres have continued to attract well-to-do residents with interests in urban lifestyles, and they have harboured concentrations of immigrants, minorities and the poor. Out from central cities, whether in the arid deserts of southern California or the rural networks of ancient villages in southern Europe, middle-class residents have sought the amenities and lifestyles of suburban residence. In other metropolitan regions, from Germany to parts of the United States, marginalised citizens, including immigrants and the unemployed, have found cheap housing at the fringes of cities. Fragmented and uneven local government systems often reinforce existing spatial divisions. As transitional countries have developed market institutions and prosperity has grown, similar metropolitan dynamics of spatial fragmentation and differentiation have become increasingly apparent there.

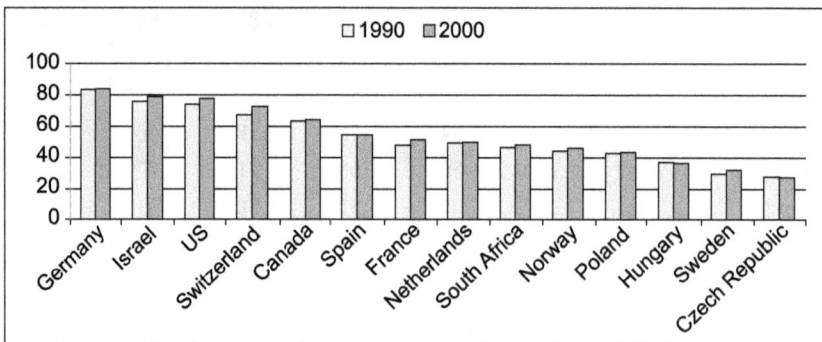

*Figure 1.1: Proportion of national population living in metropolitan areas with over 200,000 inhabitants, 1990–2000 (%)*

*Note:* Canada: 1996, 2001; Czech Republic: 1991, 2001; France: 1990, 1999; Germany: 1989, 2002; Hungary: 1990, 2001; Israel: 1989, 2002; Poland: 1993, 2001; Spain: 1996, 2001; South Africa: 1996, 2001; Sweden: 1990, 2002; US: 1990, 2000.

*Source:* Hoffmann-Martinot and Sellers 2005, p. 427.

Metropolitan shifts like these have profound implications for the widely observed changes under way in the political behaviour of developed and transitional
societies. Through parallel analyses in eleven advanced industrial and transitional
countries, this volume will show how the communities and metropolitan regions
where people live have emerged as important determinants of how often they vote,
of their ideology, and of which political parties they support. The resulting theory
of political behaviour, rooted in the context and dynamics of localities and metropolitan regions, is essential to fill an increasingly apparent gap in the study of
place, parties and elections.

We thus build this analysis on a community-centred or 'ecological' approach
to political behaviour that was one of the first to emerge in professional political
science (Siegfried 1913; Dogan and Rokkan 1969). This differs from the more
qualitative analysis of environmental and ecological politics that in some quarters
has recently been termed 'political ecology'. Existing comparative analyses of
political behaviour generally employ two different techniques. Macro level
approaches to comparative politics have generally examined parties and political
behaviour from the standpoint of national party leaders and aggregated electoral
patterns at the national scale. Survey analysis has offered powerful tools to
supplement these approaches with attention to how individuals behave at what is
often termed the micro level.

Yet even the combination of these two techniques is often insufficient to find
out how local and metropolitan settings of politics affect voting and elections.
Our argument here resonates with the arguments of political geographers (e.g.
Agnew 1987, 1995; Johnston et al. 1988, 2004) and calls of such comparativists
as Tarrow (2006) and Kocher and Laitin (2007) for renewed attention to the spatial
determinants of politics. What is needed are ways to better understand the multiple
local influences that flow from, and at the same time, define a 'place'.

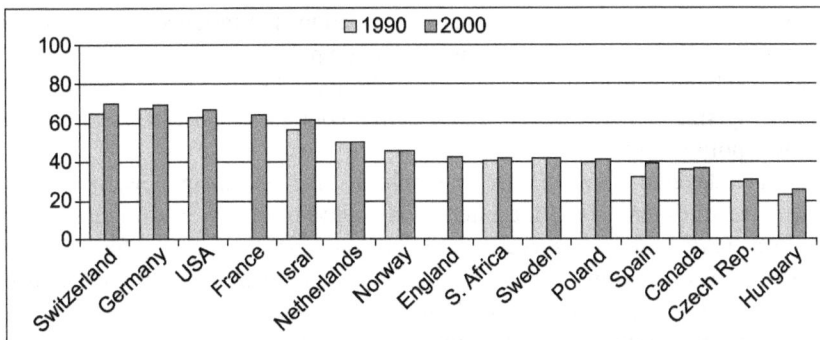

*Figure 1.2: Proportion of metropolitan population living in suburbs, 1990–2000 (%)*

*Notes:* South African percentages for low-density wards within metropolitan governments.
Canada: 1996, 2001; Czech Republic: 1991, 2001; France: 1999; Germany: 1989, 2002; Hungary:
1990, 2001; Israel: 1989, 2002; Poland: 1993, 2001; Spain: 1996, 2001; South Africa: 1996, 2001;
Sweden: 1990, 2002; US: 1990, 2000.

*Source:* Hoffmann-Martinot and Sellers 2005, p. 429.

Place can partly be understood in terms of effects from the context of a community on the political behaviour of individuals. The economic interests of homeowners, the cultural norms of a neighbourhood, the social status of residential location, the quality of life in a locality for its residents all establish individual and collective interests that are rooted in the production and consumption of place. At the same time, the term also encompasses collective dynamics of communities and social mobilisation. Political competition in local elections, the infrastructure of civic associations, dynamics of conflict and the relations between communities are also important in understanding the effects of places on behavioural patterns.

The metropolitan dimensions of places pose additional questions that centre largely on relations within and between localities. Continued suburbanisation and decline in the share of residents living in the urban cores have brought about shifts in the national locus of political power in favour of the interests of residents in the urban periphery. As larger and more globally connected metropolitan regions have accumulated economic power and influence, new political cleavages have emerged at wider regional scales. One of the most important unanswered questions about places is how much and under what circumstances they matter in any of these ways. The importance of place varies systematically between countries, between types of elections, and even between types of political formations in a single election.

This focus on places departs from a view of political activity as a national-level – or individual-level – process, or as constituted solely by classes or other groups. Instead of a dichotomy, we propose a layered, territorially-scaled view of the collective choices that the citizens make. On this view, localities and metropolitan regions – and increasingly countries themselves – comprise at best partial collectivities. Collective dynamics at each scale nest both in wider and in more localised patterns of interests and actions. A place in which voting follows nation-wide patterns in a national election, for instance, could vote in distinctive local ways in elections at the municipal scale. A contextual (place-based) mechanism that works one way at the local level, such as the effect of community size on participation, could exert a contrary effect when scaled up to the metropolitan level.

Such a layered view of electoral politics also opens up new, previously unexplored questions about the interactions between effects at different scales. Previous work based on surveys or on national political elites, for instance, has given little attention to the vertical dimensions of political mobilisation in elections at different scales. This volume demonstrates that national political systems differ significantly in how much the dynamics of participation in local and national elections are integrated or follow divergent logics. Changing power relations among parties or regions at the national scale can be rooted in distinctive metropolitan and local patterns of politics. Similarly, different metropolitan contexts can contribute to distinctive variations in local political behaviour.

A long tradition of political geography has maintained the importance of place and its dynamics (Diamanti 1993; Agnew 1987, 1995; Barnett and Low 2004; Johnston et al. 2004). Political cleavages established during early agrarian and industrial periods counterposed a rural periphery against a modernising urban centre (Lipset and Rokkan 1967). Parties organised around rural places represented agrarian interests in primary production, cultural traditionalism, and parochialism. Parties organised in urban places asserted commercial economic interests, cultural elites and cosmopolitanism. The nationalisation thesis held that with industrialisation, class interests would come to dominate political discourse and partisan competition. Comparative analysis of political behaviour in Europe and North America has generally regarded rural places as more and more marginal, if disproportionately influential. Little attention has been given to the role of places within metropolitan regions as an influence on politics.

The new metropolitan bases of politics differ profoundly from these older cleavages rooted in place. Divergences in politics among metropolitan places trace to consumption, property, public services and lifestyle, as much as to production. They grow out of complex interdependencies between the economies of bedroom communities and workplaces, between communities with commercial centres and inflows of consumers, and between metropolitan centres of finance, innovation and culture and the smaller metropolitan regions in their shadow. They are also the consequences of conscious and unconscious choices, both by the residents who select places to live, work and shop and by the governments and businesses that plan the shape and function of metropolitan regions.

A layered understanding of the divergences within and between metropolitan regions is critical to comprehending the patterns that have resulted. Table 1.2 outlines the possible combinations of effects at different scales. When place has strong influences on political behaviour both within and between metropolitan regions, a society is fully differentiated by metropolitanisation. When most of the differences are located at the neighbourhood or municipal (sub-metropolitan) level, segregation, consumption and local places are the driving factors. On the other hand, if place is important mainly for differentiating politics between metropolitan areas, then globalisation and regionalism (economic and cultural) are the major determinants. Even if nationalising effects persist along with these others, the result is a multi-scalar rather than uniformly national process of political differentiation. Only if place has little effect, either among or within metropolitan areas, can the hypothesis of nationalisation hold. A true understanding of the importance of metropolitanisation thus requires the separation and controls for

*Table 1.2: Scales of place effects and political processes*

| Between metro areas<br>Within metro areas | Low | High |
|---|---|---|
| **High** | Segregation and suburbanisation | Multi-scalar spatial differentiation |
| **Low** | Nationalisation | Regionalisation |

place effects at each of these scales.

The metropolitanisation of politics poses a challenge to national party systems and democratic traditions. Its place-based dynamics portend a re-territorialisation of ideology, civic engagement and partisanship that will reconfigure the politics of most developed countries. This re-territorialisation is not patterned on old cleavages between agrarian and industrialised regions, but on new territorial cleavages within and between metropolitan areas. It presents a challenge to a view of political systems as organised around nationalised parties and de-territorialised dynamics, as well as to a view of electoral mobilisation that discounts the effects of place. National parties seeking to cope with metropolitan spatial fragmentation find themselves forced to appeal to particular segments of metropolitan populations. In doing so, they must also take into account the clear differences in electoral mobilisation and interests among various metropolitan constituencies. This opens up new possibilities for place-based political mobilisation, and helps explain ideological shifts witnessed among electorates and party platforms in the metropolitan era.

## Metropolitanisation and the context of electoral participation

Participation in local and national elections is a fundamental political act. Voter turnout provides one of the best examples of how the effects of metropolitan and local contexts have altered national political behaviour. While electoral turnout represents only one indication of the nature and overall quality of participation in a democracy, it is the most systematically available indicator at the local level, and has implications for much wider patterns. Political scientists frequently rely on aggregate election turnout as one gauge of the overall health of democratic systems (e.g. Dahl and Tufte 1970; Verba and Nie 1972; Verba, Nie and Kim 1978). Disparities in turnout among groups and places can reinforce inequities in representation and policy. The relationship between turnout at the local and the national level can also have implications for the character of democracy at both levels of the state.

Studies of electoral participation in national elections have generated a substantial comparative literature (e.g. Verba, Nie and Kim 1978; Powell 1986; Jackman 1987, 1995). Most often, these comparisons employ turnout statistics or survey results that are aggregated by countries. Such an approach is entirely in keeping with the thesis of nationalisation. It presumes what Caramani (2005) has gone to great lengths to demonstrate: national parties mobilise in uniform ways regardless of the setting. Social, economic and cultural groupings organise and mobilise similarly regardless of where they are located. Local political mobilisation occurs in parallel ways in contexts across the country. National media exert the same effects on mass publics independent of place.

To assess the nationalisation of politics more fully, however, requires acknowledgement of the layered dimension of elections themselves. Local elections and parties and the dynamics of competition within municipal arenas are intrinsic to national patterns of participation and party competition (Saiz and Geser 1999).

Many national politicians had their start in local government. Even in countries where local government is non-partisan, national parties often recruit candidates within municipalities. Local elections may also contest national agendas. For voters, local elections often represent the best opportunity to influence the actual workings of government. For all these reasons, voter turnout at the local level provides critical insights both into the character of turnout at higher levels and the wider patterns of politics in a country. Yet, up to now, only a small number of studies have compared how voter mobilisation at the local level relates to electoral participation in national elections (Morlan 1984; Hoffmann-Martinot, Rallings and Thrasher 1998).

The strongest version of the thesis of nationalisation implies that widespread engagement in the political process will produce high, uniform rates of participation in national elections and corresponding patterns of participation in local elections. Uniformities in partisan performance such as those analysed by Caramani (2005) should contribute to this effect. The widespread electoral engagement that Verba, Nie and Kim (1978) found in countries with strong party systems should translate into greater spatial uniformity in national turnout, as national party competition and national media engage voters across the country. It might be assumed that the transformations in parties and elections since the 1960s would reinforce tendencies toward nationalised political participation. As parties have become more professionalised and national media campaigns have grown in significance, national campaign organisations have in important respects become more centralised (Dalton and Wattenberg 2000).

There are several analytical alternatives to this uniform mobilisation (see Table 1.3). One would be a widespread disengagement from electoral participation at either the local or the national level. Although turnout in developed democracies has until recently been considered to be in long-term decline (Gray and Caul 2000), recent surges in national election turnout in the United States and other countries suggest that this may no longer be the case.

Two other possibilities have rarely been investigated systematically. If local turnout is high while national turnout is low, electoral participation is localised: citizens engage more consistently in local than in national elections. Conversely, where voters participate intensively in national elections but not in local elections, political engagement is *delocalised*. Such a community can be fully mobilised in

*Table 1.3: Varieties of relations between national and local electoral participation*

| National<br>Local | Low | High |
|---|---|---|
| **High** | Localised participation | High, integrated participation |
| **Low** | Low participation | Delocalised participation |

elections at the national level but disengaged from politics at the level of government closest to the citizenry.

Nationalising effects should be more likely to appear in national elections than in local elections. For this reason, national turnout should prove higher or more uniform than local turnout. But analyses of the recent transformations in the political life of both North America and Europe have been especially critical of the dangers from delocalisation. In the United States, Skocpol (2003) has analysed how middle- and upper middle-class Americans have turned to issue-oriented mass membership organisations with lobbies at the national level, and away from general civic associations rooted in communities. In Europe, parallel shifts may also be at work. Electoral constituencies oriented toward national and transnational economic and cultural concerns have mobilised over controversies over European integration and national politics, but have shown less engagement in local politics.

The thesis of metropolitanisation holds that national and local turnout will vary within and between metropolitan regions. Nationalisation will be confined at the most to certain kinds of places rather than remain uniform and high. The other three quadrants of Table 1.3 will predominate. Closer examination of national and local election turnout show them to vary in significantly divergent ways within different countries (e.g. Flanagan 1980; Gabriel 1997; Oliver 2002; Campbell 2006). For the first time, the systematic metropolitan data of this study make it possible to compare national and local patterns in ways that control for the contextual effects of different regions and localities.

Our analysis assimilates numerous hypotheses that have already been adduced to account for the ways national and local electoral participation differ among places. The survey literature has identified a number of demographic characteristics that make individuals more likely to vote than others. Communities with high incomes and high levels of education should turn out to vote more frequently (Verba, Nie and Kim 1978; Oliver 2000). Places where people face the greatest social disadvantages like poverty or unemployment generally vote less frequently than others. Communities with more disadvantaged ethnic or racial groups and immigrants also tend to vote less regularly (Hill and Leighley 1999). Places with older citizens characteristically vote more consistently than those with younger citizens (Gimpel, Morris and Armstrong 2004; Goerres 2005).

Accumulating evidence shows many such demographic effects to be bound up with the characteristics of metropolitan communities. Even when individuals or households choose their places of residence, sorting through housing markets produces differences among neighbourhoods that correspond to demographic composition. The friendship networks and social contacts that residential proximity helps to support and have been shown to enhance the propensity to vote (Huckfeldt 1979; Huckfeldt and Sprague 1995). Community ties among affluent, educated citizens can reinforce connections to the national and international media, as well as to the national political process.

The strongest case for place as an influence on patterns of turnout stems from independent effects linked to the character of places themselves. Here metropolitanisation reinforces a number of variations between the localities of urban regions that make significant differences for political participation.

The institutions and political dynamics of a community can raise or lower rates of participation. Local political dynamics can exert effects at either the local or metropolitan level. Competition among different political formations within a community could raise turnout (Campbell 2006: 19–49). Alternatively, solidaristic mobilisation in more homogenous communities could prompt stronger electoral mobilisation (*ibid.*). In countries with a variety of local institutions, differences in electoral rules, such as proportional representation and first-past-the-post systems or the timing of local elections, have been demonstrated to make important differences for rates of electoral participation (Wolfinger and Rosenstone 1980).

In most developed countries, residents in search of the assets and amenities linked to property, and in particular to ownership of single-family houses, have largely driven processes of metropolitanisation. Studies in both Europe and North America show that homeowners are more involved in political activities within their localities (Alford and Scoble 1968; Kingston *et al.* 1984), make more contacts with elected officials (Coulter 1992), register more for voting (Bréchon and Cautrès 1987), and participate more in elections (Clanché 2003; Eagles and Erfle 1989; Gilderbloom and Markham 1995; Hoffmann-Martinot, Rallings and Thrasher 1996). Such effects have persisted even with controls for income, education or occupational status.

The ties residents have to the place where they live within a metropolitan area also influence patterns of electoral participation. Several lines of work dating back to Merriam and Gosnell (1924) demonstrate that the more attenuated the ties to a local community, the lower participation rates will be. In the United States, most analyses have found that higher rates of commuting and longer commutes lead to lower rates of political participation and engagement (Putnam 2000; Oliver 2001). There is also ample reason to presume that newer, faster growing and more transient communities generate lower levels of civic and political engagement (Alford and Lee 1968; Wolfinger and Rosenstone 1980; Squire *et al.* 1987; Brown 1988).

Little of this work has considered either the differential effects on national and local elections or the metropolitan context of local mobility. Mobility among closely adjacent metropolitan localities need not weaken all social ties or political engagement. Recent research in Sweden suggests that commuters there may be more politically engaged than other voters (Lidström 2006). The citizens who move to a new place or between places may in fact be unusually active in politics just as they are more active in their daily routines or the search for residence. They may also have more experience with which to assess and compare local policy proposals, services and tax rates. New development in a community can also raise new issues that induce citizens to participate.

Metropolitan regions further affect electoral participation through the variety of size and population densities among metropolitan places. Kelleher and Lowery (2004) have summarised the large and diverse US literature on these issues under two broad hypotheses:

- What might be termed the 'small is beautiful' hypothesis is a long-standing fixture in the literature on political participation that dates back to ancient and early modern political theory. Smaller, less densely populated places provide for less anonymous forms of social life and governance that promote higher rates of electoral and civic participation.
- Adherents of the contrary 'large is lively' hypothesis point to the diversity, social contestation and broader political agendas in larger, more diverse communities as a stimulus to stronger political participation.

A number of more specific hypotheses are bound up in these two broad propositions (Frandsen 2002). Oliver (2001), in an analysis focused on the United States, found smaller community size to be one of the main inducements to higher rates of electoral and civic participation in suburbs. Controlling for size, however, diversity among social and economic interests in a community can also promote higher levels of participation. In Oliver's study, diverse economic interests fostered greater political engagement and participation than in more socially and economically homogenous 'bedroom' communities.

Earlier work on urbanisation found a straightforward relationship between urban density and lower turnout (Verba and Nie 1972). Metropolitanisation imposes a further layer of differentiation on these local effects. Kelleher and Lowery, whose analysis focused on US metropolitan counties, found that both the geopolitical fragmentation of local governments within a metropolitan area and the concentration of population in a central jurisdiction affected levels of local election turnout. Concentration of population at the metropolitan level generated the highest turnout, they concluded, so that 'large' means 'lively'. Metropolitan governmental fragmentation also promoted higher turnout, but its effects remained more limited.

Finally, metropolitanisation has entrenched regional cultures that have been shown to produce differences in participation within countries (e.g., Hoffmann-Martinot 1992; Putnam 2000). Participation rates in most mid-sized to larger countries, and even in diverse, if smaller, countries like Switzerland, differ significantly among regions with distinctive historical trajectories and contemporary cultures.

These local and metropolitan influences on participation need to be considered alongside the national and subnational institutional differences that have been shown to influence turnout rates (Blais et al. 2003). As might be expected, place-linked influences often have stronger consequences for municipal voter turnout than for national turnout. But the relationship between local and national turnout depends on whether political parties, the media and government institutions are highly integrated between the national and the local level (see Table 1.4).

Where this integration between levels is less strong, we expect to find not simply reduced turnout, but also delocalisation and localisation in turnout rates. Delocalised electoral mobilisation should be especially strong when communities mobilise in the absence of a strong local party system or intergovernmental integration between the national and local levels. Across the developed world, and increasingly in transitional countries, we expect delocalisation to be a feature of metropolitan regions and local communities made up of high earning, well educated and informed citizens. Other influences on delocalisation and localisation of participation should operate within as well as between metropolitan regions. Delocalised places in the larger, more cosmopolitan metropolitan regions, for instance, should emerge in locations linked to transnational economic and cultural networks.

Localised places, like those with generally lower electoral participation, might be expected to exhibit fewer ties to these networks. Where land use markets and policies have made it possible over time for residents to sort into distinct residential communities with distinctive economic assets, ethno-racial composition and consumption patterns, delocalised and localised places will emerge. Local

*Table 1.4: Factors favouring different relations between national and local electoral participation*

| National<br>Local | Low | High |
|---|---|---|
| **High** | (Localised participation)<br><br>*National*<br>Locally weak national parties and media<br>Local clientelistic attachments<br><br>*Metropolitan/local*<br>High spatial disparities<br>Social and economic disadvantage<br>Limited local integration into global economy<br>Strong local social ties | (High, integrated participation)<br><br>*National*<br>Locally strong national parties and media<br>Integrated national and local policymaking<br><br>*Metropolitan/local*<br>Limited spatial disparities<br>(Limited local disparities or variation) |
| **Low** | (Low participation)<br><br>*National*<br>Locally weak national parties and media<br><br>*Metropolitan/local*<br>High spatial disparities<br>Social and economic disadvantage<br>Limited local integration into global economy<br>Weak local social ties | (Delocalised participation)<br><br>*National*<br>Locally weak national parties and media<br>Top-down national partisan mobilisation<br><br>*Metropolitan/local*<br>High spatial disparities<br>Social and economic privilege<br>Local integration into global economy<br>Local integration into national culture and media<br>Weak local social ties |

conditions that detract from civic activity within communities, such as commuting and residential mobility, are also expected to foster delocalised forms of political engagement.

### Metropolitan sources of partisan cleavages

The era of metropolitanisation also corresponds to the emergence of new patterns of political party allegiance throughout the developed world. While party systems in Western Europe and North America remained largely stable until the 1960s, a flurry of new parties has since emerged on both the left and right. Many traditional parties have lost support and splintered, to be replaced by regional or secessionist parties. Established parties on both sides of the political spectrum have been forced to compete with these new stalwarts to attract supporters while simultaneously trying to maintain their traditional constituencies. In the transformed politics that have emerged, metropolitan places have played a major and at times a decisive role. The shifting new patterns of support and opposition correspond not just to differences among social groups, but to contrasts in lifestyles and values that are embedded in, and emerge from, the places where people live. Especially where suburbanisation has predominated, the local context can be a decisive factor how citizens vote.

Post-war work on comparative political behaviour, buttressed by the newly-refined techniques of survey analysis, has outlined long-standing influences on partisanship. The class cleavages that have largely defined the political spectrum since the 1930s grew out of basic features of Fordist political economy. Keynesian domestic economic policies, manufacturing growth and the construction of post-war national welfare states helped fashion the national party systems that emerged. The traditional left depended for support on the industrial working class; the traditional right relied on bourgeois and petty-bourgeois interests, and on an affluent middle class. In countries with larger concentrations of ethnic and racial minorities, like the United States under the New Deal coalition, these groups often furnished traditional bases of support for the left. Throughout the developed world, a diverse array of religious and ethnic cleavages reinforced divergent tendencies based on regional histories and traditions (Caramani 2005).

Since the 1970s, the party systems of developed countries have undergone massive transformations that are still ongoing. On the left, various new 'green', 'pink' and social democratic parties appealing to professional middle-class fractions emerged out of an array of social and environmental movements to challenge the dominance of established working class parties. On the right, utopian neoliberal parties have sought to dismantle the Keynesian welfare state, while simultaneously new ethnocentric and racist parties have gained support with appeals to nationalism, religious and family values, and anti-immigration stances. Regional and secessionist parties have formed to contest national policies and decentralise national states. Increasingly the established parties have had to compete for the support of groups that were once taken for granted as core supporters, such as working-class and middle-class constituencies, or particular ethnic groups. In order to appeal to middle-class professionals and compete with new 'green' parties, traditional parties on the left have thus adopted some neoliberal and environmental policies. Nationalist and populist appeals have won parties on the right of the working class vote despite neoliberal economic policies (such as privatisation) that mostly cut against working class economic interests. In transitional countries like those of Eastern Europe, where new party systems remain fragmented and unstable, the social bases for left and right support have been even more up for grabs.

The established wisdom of the Columbia and Michigan schools of political science holds that socio-economic status, education, age, family status and relationship to the dominant ethnic or national group (i.e. ethnicity, race or immigration status) are the primary determinants of partisanship. If the United States' suburbs were more likely to vote Republican, it was because they were wealthier and whiter, for instance (Wirt *et al.* 1972). Since the publication of this early research, however, closer examination has demonstrated that place plays an important role influencing the level and direction of partisanship (Gainsborough 2001; Johnston *et al.* 1988, 2004; Walks 2004a, 2004b, 2005).

A wide array of analysts link the growth of new forms of partisanship and their concretisation in new political parties to the emergence of neoliberalism as a widespread economic and social policy agenda (Hackworth 2007; Harvey 2005; Peck and Tickell 2002). This neoliberal agenda favours trade liberalisation, privatisation, inter-local competition, and cutbacks to social support. We contend that the territorial shifts associated with metropolitanisation have played a critical role in both the changing landscape of party competition and these wider transnational shifts in policy agendas. These effects result from transformations in post-industrial structures of work, ownership and consumption, from new challenges of cultural diversity and immigration, and from shifts in norms and value orientations within metropolitan regions.

Early on, Tingsten (1937) found that concentrations of voting for working-class parties often exceeded levels that could be predicted from the class background of local residents. He concluded that concentrations in a community produced a social and organisational environment that made it more likely that any resident there would vote for the party. Likewise, Butler and Stokes (1974) argued that once the concentration of a particular class surpassed a particular threshold in a given place, it became the 'core' class that shaped local political attitudes and behaviours. Miller (1977) assumed the mechanism by which political leanings were transferred between core classes and others is 'conversion by conversation', since one is statistically more likely to come across neighbours expounding the majority view than the other way around. MacAllister *et al.* (2001) demonstrate that the way one's neighbours vote is at least as important, and may be even more important, than the social demographics for determining how that person votes. Huckfeldt and his collaborators have contributed greatly to our understanding of the importance of social networks and social interaction in influencing individuals' political proclivities (Huckfeldt 1984; Huckfeldt, Plutzer and Sprague 1993; Huckfeldt and Sprague 1995; Braybeck and Huckfeldt 2002a, 2002b). Parallel work suggests that ethnic and racial diversity, by reinforcing inter-ethnic networks within communities, can reinforce support among all ethnic or racial groups for parties representing minority interests (Carsey 2001; Braybeck and Huckfeldt 2002a, 2002b).

Residential segregation and concentration affect political preferences in other ways as well. As Iris Marion Young noted (1999), segregation makes privilege blind to the privileged 'in a double way', as it not only conceals the true extent of poverty, but also makes privilege appear 'normal'. Both effects work to reduce support for redistributive policies and parties. If inner cities and suburbs remain segregated, as in many Anglo-American urban regions, residents of the more distant suburbs may oppose any spending intended for low-income neighbourhoods in the inner cities or for new public goods in general, and thus may vote for parties advocating neoliberal cutbacks and reforms (Gainsborough 2001; Sellers 1999; Walks 2004b). Similarly, suburban residents may adopt a politics of exclusion in order to keep property taxes low and protect privileged access to sought-after local collective resources such as schools, parks, and other high-quality public amenities (Danielson 1976). Concentration of professional middle-class supporters of the 'new left' within the inner cities works to reinforce ideological distinctions between inner city and suburb through its effects on local organising, social interaction, and through increasingly segregated spatial bases of party representation (Walks 2004b, 2006). As these differences in urban form and political ideologies congeal, they in turn influence local identities, ideological dispositions and discourses of what is 'normal', or 'in' and 'out of place' in a given setting (Walks 2008).

Through these effects, we contend that metropolitan transformations have laid the territorial foundations for a general shift toward neoliberal policies. At the same time, such transformations account for much of the unexplained variation and volatility that has come to characterise partisan competition and policy throughout North America, Europe and beyond.

Metropolitanisation has entrenched new divisions in economic interests, lifestyles and local political subcultures. These divisions increasingly have become the fault lines of contemporary politics and policy, and the touchstones of partisan competition. As such recent overviews as Kriesi *et al.* (2006) have observed, the spectrum of political competition has since the 1970s separated out into several domains that are analytically distinct and potentially at odds. Alongside the longstanding economic dimension of preferences for markets or the state, cultural values and positions on globalisation have increasingly shaped voter preferences and party positions. Effects from metropolitan places have shaped each of these dimensions.

### *Metropolitan transformation and the economic bases of partisanship*

How local residents perceive their party choices or merits of neoliberal policies that restructure the welfare state and undercut the power of unions depends in part on their economic interests. Accounts of party formation in the nineteenth and early twentieth century pointed to the divergence between urban and rural economic interests as an important source of partisan cleavages (Lipset and Rokkan 1967). Attempts to account for the shifts in political cleavages since Europe and North America became urbanised have adopted the thesis of nationalisation. Instead of territorial economic interests, these analyses focus on class structures at the national scale. The thesis of metropolitanisation sets forth two types of new territorial economic interests that such an account neglects:

- on the one hand, the economic interests of occupations are tied to the interests of the cities and regions where workers carry out their jobs;
- on the other hand, new interests in economic assets and consumption linked to places have increasingly shaped the economic interests of voters.

Kitschelt (1994; Kitschelt and Rehm 2004) contends that a growing, highly educated cosmopolitan stratum of new knowledge workers now opposes a less educated working class threatened by global manufacturing competition. Such a cleavage could oppose the economic interests of different places as well as different jobs. In the uneven territorial geography of the global economy, post-industrial development has concentrated, in particular, metropolitan centres of high technology, advanced services and culture. Centres of rising economic sectors, such as information technology, finance or cultural services, face new opportunities as a result of post-industrial economic transformations. Local economies rooted in more traditional forms of production, such as manufacturing industries, face new threats.

Table 1.5 shows a limited (and schematised) set of possibilities for places depending on their position within the global economy and their predominant economic activities. The old Fordist centres of primary and secondary production, located in the lower-left quadrant, face the biggest disadvantages. Their residents can least appreciate the benefits of neoliberalism and globalisation. Within the old economy, however, a stratum of higher level managers, providers of business services and research and development experts has often benefited from globalisation and technological change even when other workers have not. Meanwhile, contemporary, private residential construction, most of which has occurred in growing metropolitan areas, has operated according to market forces and is generally antithetical to state intervention or regulation. Concentrations of such workers in urban centres of globalising business services produce places that can instead be expected to support neoliberal parties and policies.

The new economy of high technology, innovation and services contains a largely analogous class divide. Those with less secure jobs, with lower wages, like clerks, restaurant workers and programmers, share many of the same needs for the welfare state and limits on markets as workers in older, declining industries. Higher salaried professionals in information industries, professional services and creative industries have as much interest in neoliberal policy as their counterparts in the old economy. However, for activities provided by or closely related to the state, such as education, health or welfare, in many countries, these higher status workers share an obvious interest in stronger direct provision or at least funding by the state.

*Table 1.5: Industry and occupational clustering and political restructuring*

| Production base / Economic liberalism | Traditional economy (manufacturing, mining, construction) | 'New' economy (information, high tech, advanced services) |
|---|---|---|
| **Positive (supports market liberalism)** | Management<br>Producer services<br>Research and development<br>Residential construction | Private management<br>Financiers<br>Designers<br>Information-based entrepreneurs<br>Advertising<br>Entertainment |
| **Negative (supports state intervention)** | Mining<br>Agriculture<br>Heavy industry | State-provided services (education, health, administration, research)<br>Telemarketers<br>Clerks, data processing<br>Programming |

In the increasingly affluent societies of advanced industrial countries, economic assets and consumption supply a crucial component of economic interests beyond occupations and industries (cf. Kitschelt 1994; Iversen 2005). Consumption interests link voters directly to the places where they live. More than just matters of consumer choice, they shape lifestyles that in turn reinforce preferences for parties and policies.

Perhaps the best established example of this influence is homeownership. Owning a home has long been associated with fiscally conservative politics, since homeowners have a long-term stake in protecting their property values (Fischel 2001; Saunders 1978; Thorns 1981). Likewise, tenants, particularly those who stay for only short durations in any given place, have fewer stakes in the local community and are less likely to cast their vote based on local concerns. Saunders (1990) argues that homeownership among factions of the British working classes provided the basis for working-class support for Margaret Thatcher. Among the professional middle classes, there is reason to expect that supporters of 'new' left parties may be self-selecting into particular inner-city communities out of a desire for an urban lifestyle and search for 'community' (Walks 2006), while more traditional families with children at home are likely to prefer the private lifestyle associated with more distant suburbs.

Dunleavy (1979) points to emerging lines of political cleavage between places where consumption is mostly restricted to the private sector and those where voters benefit from collectively-subsidised forms of consumption such as public transit, social housing, public education and public health. The inner cities provide greater opportunities for the efficient delivery of these collective services because of higher population density, more urbanised settlement and, in

*Table 1.6: Consumption interests and metropolitan political restructuring*

| Economic interests \ Location | Suburbs | Inner city |
|---|---|---|
| **Middle and upper class** | *Consumption interests* Homeownership Private amenities Limited need for social services <br><br> *Economic preference* Markets (strong) | *Consumption interests* Limited homeownership Public amenities Public infrastructure Limited need for social services <br><br> *Economic preference* State (moderate) |
| **Working class and poor** | *Consumption interests* Homeownership Limited private amenities Need for social services <br><br> *Economic preference* Markets (moderate) | *Consumption interests* Little homeownership Public amenities Public infrastructure Need for social services <br><br> *Economic preference* State (strong) |

many cases, concentrations of low-income populations. As a result, more of these residents use and benefit from collective services of this kind. The more dispersed, more residentially exclusive and more auto-dependent nature of many suburbs encourages more of their residents to turn for the same services to the private sector.

Following this analysis, we expect consumption interests rooted in differences between metropolitan places to alter traditional class cleavages (see Table 1.6). Homeowners and residents of suburban areas will be more likely to support neo-liberal (fiscally-conservative) parties, particularly those advocating privatisation. Although affluent and distant suburbs will be more likely to share these preferences, working and middle-class suburbs with large homeowner constituencies will also share them. Inner-city residents and tenants can be expected to prefer left-leaning parties advocating subsidised collective consumption and expansion, or at least maintenance, of the welfare state.

### *Cultural orientations*

In nineteenth century Europe and North America, as in many developing countries today, a cultural divide reinforced the divergence between agrarian and urban interests. Rural areas embraced traditional values such as religion, patriarchal families, social order and respect for authority. Cities, where cultural elites congregated, fostered modernist values of secularism, gender equality and tolerance of difference. If the thesis of nationalisation was to hold, then full urbanisation should have eliminated the territorial bases for this cleavage and diminished the cleavage itself. In fact, the metropolitan transformation has helped give rise to new partisan cleavages rooted in social and cultural values. Consumption patterns rooted in the divergent lifestyles and values of metropolitan regions and places have fostered a set of cultural divides that since the 1970s have played a growing role in partisan competition.

Inglehart (1990, 1997) and Clark and Hoffmann-Martinot (1998) show how increasing education and affluence have given rise to new cultural issues that cut across the established left-right divide on state and market issues. One dimension of the new cultural politics, similar to earlier divides between tradition and modernity, revolves around challenges to such forms of authority as the state, religion, patriarchy and other social traditions. In addition, Inglehart (1990, 1997) points to a 'post-modern' cultural divide that emerged out of unsurpassed levels of economic security that resulted from the long post-war boom. He argues that the generations that grew up after this era internalised more 'post-materialist' values of fulfilment, moral purpose and idealism, in opposition to older 'materialist' values centred on economic survival and success.

Metropolitanisation has helped generate and reinforce these new divergences in values. As affluence has enabled greater choices among lifestyles, metropolitan regions have given residents choices among a variety of residential environments and communities with different lifestyles. When residents select a community or region, the values of a community's civic associations, neighbourhoods and services comprise part of the consumption interests that affect their choices. The clustering of residents with similar values, along with the local practices of communities, reaffirms the values of individual residents. Divergences in values thus become rooted in the subcultures of particular types of places.

As modernisation theory first emphasised, the traditional and materialist values located in the lower-left quadrant of Table 1.7 are most likely to be found in rural agrarian communities. Although many of these communities have become absorbed into the economies of metropolitan regions, the strongest adherence to traditional values and social order persists in peripheral regions and communities. At the same time, in the largest metropolitan regions as well as in regional centres of administrative and educational services, areas in and around inner cities have emerged as centres of the post-materialist, libertarian culture, as shown in the upper-right quadrant of Table 1.7. As concentrations of residents with liberal, secular cultural orientations have gravitated toward these settings, clusters of younger, post-materialist residents have supported environmentalist and social movements, and artistic communities.

As metropolitan regions have expanded into more differentiated landscapes of residential consumption, other subcultures with value orientations between these two quadrants have often grown to predominate (Clark and Hoffmann-Martinot 1998). One value orientation portrayed schematically in the upper-left quadrant of Table 1.7 combines rejection of authority with an emphasis on materialism over idealism. In these regions or communities, we expect economic interests to dictate political choices. Many affluent suburbs and fast-growing suburbs have harboured subcultures of strong individualism, conspicuous consumption and exclusivity joined to cultural liberalism. An alternative orientation, in the lower-right quadrant, incorporates elements of post-materialism, like civic engagement and communitarian values, with a moderately conservative embrace of traditional religious

*Table 1.7: Cultural bases of metropolitan political restructuring: value orientations in local political subcultures*

| Materialism / Traditionalism | Materialism (survival/security) | Post-materialism (fulfilment/idealism) |
|---|---|---|
| | *Orientations*<br>Social Darwinism<br>Financial success<br>Exclusion and privilege<br>Fiscal populism<br>Civic apathy | *Orientations*<br>Social responsibility<br>Social movements<br>Personal autonomy<br>Openness and tolerance<br>Creativity |
| **Low**<br>**(Rejection of**<br>**authority)** | Cultural liberalism (moderate)<br><br>*Places*<br>(M) Rapidly-growing regions<br>(M) Global metro regions<br>Affluent suburbs<br>High-growth suburbs | Cultural liberalism<br><br><br>*Places*<br>(M) Administrative and<br>Educational service centres<br>Inner cities<br>Singles/childless couples<br>Student concentrations |
| | *Orientations*<br>Family values<br>Patriarchy<br>Fatalism<br>Social order<br>Trust in business/unions | *Orientations*<br>Local/private<br>Communitarianism<br>Personal spiritualism<br>Family values<br>Civic engagement |
| **High**<br>**(Acceptance of authority)** | Cultural conservatism<br><br><br>*Places*<br>(M) Peripheral metro regions<br>(M) Smaller metro regions<br>Older residents<br>Peripheral suburbs | Cultural conservatism<br>(moderate)<br><br>*Places*<br>(M) Most metro regions<br>Middle-class suburbs<br>Families with children |

*Source:* Adapted from various works by Inglehart (1990, 1997) and Adams (2003)
*Note:* (M) = metropolitan effects

and family values. In middle-class suburbs, families often seek child-friendly surroundings, community values and elements of traditional rural lifestyles.

The landscape of metropolitan subcultures thus varies along two distinct but
related dimensions. The suburban communities in the upper-left and lower-right
quadrants share with the rural metropolitan peripheries a resistance to the cultural
liberalism and collective orientations of the post-materialist concentrations. The
sources of this resistance differ. Suburban value orientations may reaffirm neoliberal ideology directly or reinforce support for some form of traditional values.
In the emerging metropolitan political geography, anti-traditional, post-materialist
orientations have remained a minority subculture that only predominates in circumscribed local contexts. The intra-metropolitan bases of differentiation along
these lines have not received sufficient attention, partly due to the difficulties in
operationalising and measuring such attitudes. Indeed, the limited data currently
available (particularly that which is comparable across national contexts) force us
to restrict our analysis to only a partial examination of these hypotheses.

### *Globalisation and multiculturalism*

A final difference between traditional urban and rural settings involves issues of
cultural diversity, immigration and trade. In nineteenth century Europe and North
America, cities were centres of cosmopolitanism and culture and often experienced higher levels of immigration than rural areas. In the last two decades, divides over immigration and transnational economic integration have increasingly
shaped partisan competition, potentially even more than social and cultural issues
(Kriesi *et al.* 2006).

Metropolitan and community contexts have also shaped positions on these issues. Value orientations associated with types of metropolitan places differ along
an axis that opposes cosmopolitanism at one end and ethnonationalism at the other.
The value orientations on this axis, and the types of places associated with them,
vary in ways that depend on related preferences for collective, state-supported
services or for market provision. Pre-existing ethnic and cultural diversity within
the metropolitan area or community, and the presence of global economic and cultural influences, comprise one set of influences on this axis. Immigration creates
pressures on job and housing markets and on services like schools and hospitals
that also influence local and regional orientations, but in ways that depend on these
previous legacies.

Table 1.8 presents, again in an idealised form, the various alternative scenarios
that follow. In regions with a high level of diversity, and stronger links to the
global economy, local orientations should favour pluralism and cosmopolitanism.
Where the community is already highly diverse, pressures produced by high local
levels of immigration will likely reinforce preferences for incorporation and en-
couragement of difference. In places with a strong orientation toward transnational markets, this cosmopolitanism will centre more on the values of global markets.
In places with stronger support for collective, state-supported goods and services,
social cosmopolitan communities will actively support such transnational norms

as human rights and local practices to incorporate local immigrant and minority groups. The 'global' cities of the United States, Canada, and the United Kingdom, but also large established immigrant cities in Western Europe, belong either in the upper-right quadrant or, in some cases, the upper-left quadrant of Table 1.8. Educational and administrative centres linked to international cultures of activism, policy and culture belong more to the upper-right quadrant (Sellers 2002). Especially in these metropolitan settings, affluent suburbs and fast-growing localities will attract residents with orientations in the upper-left segment.

*Table 1.8: Cultural bases of metropolitan political restructuring: ethnonationalism and cosmopolitanism*

| Economic \ Cosmopolitanism | Market | State |
|---|---|---|
| **High (Support for Globalisation, diversity)** | *Orientations* <br> Market cosmopolitanism (Support for globalised markets) <br> Tolerance of diversity <br> Acceptance of immigrants, spatial sorting <br><br> *Places* <br> (M) Global metro regions <br> (M) High immigration regions with spatial sorting <br> (M) Rapidly-growing regions <br> Affluent suburbs <br> Growing suburbs | *Orientations* <br> Social cosmopolitanism (Support for globalised policies, e.g. human rights) <br> Support for diversity <br> Minority and immigrant political incorporation <br><br> *Places* <br> (M) Large, global metro regions <br> (M) Diverse, high immigration regions <br> (M) Administrative and Educational service centres <br> Central cities <br> Poor minority/immigrant Suburbs |
| **Low (Ethnonationalism)** | *Orientations* <br> Ambivalence toward global markets <br> Cultural regionalism or Isolationism/nationalism <br> Low tolerance of immigrants, minorities <br><br> *Places* <br> (M) Homogenous, low immigration regions <br> (M) Regions with distinctive cultural traditions <br> Homeowners <br> Growing suburbs <br> Peripheral, low density suburbs | *Orientations* <br> Opposition to globalisation <br> Cultural vulnerability <br> Isolationism/nationalism <br> Racism/anti-immigrant Backlash <br><br> *Places* <br> (M) Homogenous, high immigration regions <br> (M) Peripheral and economically vulnerable metro regions <br> (M) Smaller metro regions <br> Poor nonminority suburbs <br> Peripheral, low density suburbs |

*Note:* (M) = metropolitan effects

The low diversity characteristic of an ethnically and nationally homogenous population is most likely to give rise to protectionist, isolationist and ethnocentric attitudes. In metropolitan regions where the local host population is largely homogenous and remains culturally distinct from communities elsewhere within the larger nation, local populations often resent the success of distant regions, and may in turn form regionalist or secessionist movements, as has occurred in Wales, Scotland, the Basque region, and Quebec. Where a homogenous region or community is confronted with an influx of immigrants or pressures from other international forces, the resulting cultural and economic vulnerabilities will generate the strongest local ethnonationalist or racist backlash. Older manufacturing or mining centres and peripheral outlying suburbs will thus typically be located in the lower-left or lower-right quadrant in Table 1.8. Smaller and economically peripheral or vulnerable metropolitan regions, and poor suburbs facing threats from immigrant or minority workforces, are most likely to provide strong support to anti-immigrant and anti-globalisation parties.

As Table 1.8 suggests, these three analytically distinct dynamics often reinforce each other. The relationship between economic preferences and internationalism provides some of the best examples of this dynamic. The large metropolitan centres identified as global cities, for instance, are becoming more culturally diverse, while at the same time they are increasingly tied into the global economy. In these settings, support for parties advocating internationalisation of markets and culture will be stronger than elsewhere. Conversely, centres of declining economic sectors like heavy industry and mining have often also experienced large influxes of immigrant workers. There, both economic and intercultural dynamics could converge to promote support for parties opposed to internationalisation and immigration.

By producing an urban space that is divided in these ways, metropolitanisation has played an important and, at times, a critical role in determining new patterns of partisanship and political behaviour. The communities and metropolitan regions where people live are redefining established determinants of political behaviour such as class and ethnicity with new dynamics of spatial differentiation. Where extensive sorting of lifestyles and communities has taken place within and among metropolitan regions, these dynamics have altered the political orientations of communities in ways that go far beyond demographics.

## The approach to metropolitanisation

To date, there has been no comparative account of what the widespread shifts toward metropolitanisation and suburbanisation mean for politics. This volume undertakes a first mapping of political participation and partisanship in relation to the emerging metropolitan political economies and political cultures of contemporary developed and transitional countries. At the same time, the analysis probes how far the character of places in metropolitan regions can account for aspects of collective life that up to now have been understood as consequences of demography and culture. In challenging the nationalisation thesis, it outlines the patterns of political cleavages and engagement that are emerging as a consequence of metropolitanisation. We argue that the rise of neoliberal political ideologies and parties is intimately tied to these growing intra-metropolitan social, cultural and economic divisions.

The study builds on the phased research program of the International Metropolitan Observatory (IMO), a fifteen-country collaborative study of metropolitan areas as sites of politics and governance founded in 2002 by Jefferey Sellers of the University of Southern California and Vincent Hoffmann-Martinot of the University of Bordeaux. In the first phase (Hoffmann-Martinot and Sellers 2005, 2007), contributors demonstrated the general patterns of metropolitanisation and suburbanisation and their aggregate political consequences in the 4,500 metropolitan areas with populations over 200,000 in each country. This project established common procedures for adjudicating between definitions of metropolitan areas (see Chapter 14, the Methodological Appendix to this volume) and identified basic patterns of politics and governmental fragmentation in all the countries, but also demonstrated the need for closer attention to the variations within as well as between the metropolitan areas of each country.

Several choices framed the more in-depth study that follows. This volume focuses on variations in voting within metropolitan areas. Although the analyses draw on findings from established survey literature about individuals, the account adopts places, and specifically municipalities, electoral districts and metropolitan regions, as units of analysis. Alongside the inherent value in understanding the collective properties and dynamics of metropolitan communities, several methodological reasons ground this choice. The accuracy of actual official voting results eliminated any caveats about response bias. Community-level results lent themselves in every country to thorough, detailed statistical analysis using census data and supplemental sources. The data enabled detailed, nuanced analysis of spatial and temporal patterns that sampling techniques in survey research would have been unable to match. Techniques centred on generating ecological inferences from this data about individuals, such as King's (1997), would also have sacrificed the rich possibilities this data offered for drawing conclusions about community patterns and the multilevel interplay of influences.

For Germany and the United States, the dataset represents a controlled sample of metropolitan areas with populations over 200,000. For other countries it includes the universe of all metropolitan localities with significant populations. The analysis in each country framed the overarching issues through a typology of different types of metropolitan places that owes a great deal to the work of Myron Orfield (2002). A common protocol based on census data enabled participants to designate several parallel types of localities (see Chapter 14, the Methodological Appendix to this volume):

- urban concentrations;
- poor communities with high proportions of immigrants or minorities;
- poor communities with lower proportions of immigrants or minorities;

- low-density peripheral localities;
- affluent suburbs; and
- middle-class suburbs.

To probe the relationships further, each national analysis estimates correlations and regression models with continuous variables. We employ systematic survey data from the World Values Survey, the International Social Survey Program, and other surveys as well as party manifestos (Budge *et al.* 2001) to locate parties in relation to the left-right scale and its cultural and economic dimensions. Each analysis then uses patterns of partisan voting to locate communities on each scale (Gross and Sigelman 1984), and analyse the demographic and spatial sources of the variations. A second analysis examines sources of national and local voter participation.

To take into account the multicollinearity between demography and geography, alternative tests compare explanations of partisanship and participation based on the demographic composition of localities with models based on the institutional, social, political and geographic attributes of places. Comparison of alternative and combined models enables a systematic examination of the strength and direction of how metropolitan places matter for politics.

The regression techniques used to carry out these models necessarily differ with the number of cases and data available in each country. A central methodological challenge for most national analyses has been to take simultaneous account of both the variations between places within metropolitan regions and the parallel variations at the metropolitan and wider regional scales. Where the number of local and metropolitan units and the amount of inter-metropolitan variation in a country permitted, the analyses employed multilevel modelling to take account of variations at both levels and examine the relations between them (Bryck and Raudenbush 2001; Snijders and Bosker 1999; Kreft and DeLeuw 2001). Because this procedure made it possible at a minimum to control for the influence of metropolitan and regional differences, it generally enabled more encompassing and accurate models than ordinary least squares regressions. Where multilevel modelling gave unclear or insignificant results due to a small number of metropolitan regions, authors have relied on ordinary least squares or supplemented the multilevel models with additional visual evidence (Bowers and Drake 2005).

The following two chapters analyse metropolitan influences on voter participation and partisanship in the United States and Canada, where metropolitan effects were first analysed extensively. Subsequent chapters trace the variations on these patterns in the emerging metropolitan political ecologies of Western Europe. In France and Switzerland, two of the most territorially fragmented countries in the developed world, metropolitan places now operate in ways partly similar to North American patterns as important influences on partisanship and voter turnout. In Britain, similar configurations of places have played a decisive role in the swings between Conservative and New Labour majorities. In Germany, despite different trajectories in the East and West, a clear metropolitan divide runs between central cities and other metropolitan localities. In Spain, divergences among metropolitan places have increasingly shaped voter turnout, and have played a surprising role in reinforcing the position of regional parties. Even Sweden, a country with less metropolitanisation and suburbanisation than the other European cases, has increasingly come under the sway of metropolitan influences. There, the first centre-right government in the post-war era to be re-elected has benefited from strong support in some suburbs and defections from the left in others.

Further chapters turn to examples of societies beyond Western Europe and North America. There, metropolitan dynamics are newer and often operate in different ways, but have no less significant consequences for political change. In Poland and the Czech Republic, a growing divide separates political behaviour in the larger central cities and near suburbs from the patterns in their surroundings. In Israel, the deep social divisions between ethnic and religious communities are in large measure tied to metropolitan divides.

The concluding chapter draws on three-level models of the integrated eleven-country dataset to undertake an overall assessment of metropolitanisation and its consistent or contingent effects. This analysis points to accumulating effects from metropolitanisation on election turnout and on axes of partisan competition that have major implication for policy agendas across the developed world. The clearest consequences are an array of political challenges for the Left, and for the welfare statist agendas it has traditionally advocated. Metropolitanisation has given rise to new suburban territorial constituencies supportive of neoliberal economic policies and new geographies of electoral mobilisation that favour these constituencies. In altering territorial patterns inherited from previous industrial eras, metropolitan influences have thus become a driving force behind global shifts in policy and political culture.

## Bibliography

Adams, M. (2003) *Fire and Ice: The United States, Canada and the myth of converging values*, Toronto: Penguin.

Agnew, J. A. (1987) *Place and Politics: The geographical mediation of state and society*, London: Allen and Unwin.

— (1995) 'The rhetoric of regionalism: the Northern League in Italian politics, 1983-1994', *Transactions of the Institute of British Geographers* 20: 156–72.

Alford, R. R. and Lee, E. C. (1968) 'Voting turnout in American cities', *American Political Science Review*, 62(3): 796–813.

Alford, R. R. and Scoble, H. M. (1968) 'Sources of local political involvement', *American Political Science Review*, 62(4): 1192–206.

Barnett, C. and Low, M. (2004) *Spaces of Democracy: Geographical perspectives on citizenship, participation and representation*, London: Sage Publications.

Blais, A., Massicotte, L. and Dobrzynksa, A. (2003) *Why is Turnout Higher in Some Countries Than in Others*, Ottawa, Elections Canada.

Bowers, J. and Drake, K. (2005) 'EDA for HLM: visualization. When probabilistic inference fails', *Political Analysis*, 13 (2005): 301–26.

Braybeck, B. and Huckfeldt, R. (2002a) 'Urban contexts, spatially dispersed networks, and the diffusion of political information', *Political Geography*, 21: 195–220.

— (2002b) 'Spatially dispersed ties among interdependent citizens: connecting individuals and aggregates', *Political Analysis*, 10: 261–75.

Bréchon, P. and Cautrès, B. (1987) 'L'inscription sur les listes électorales: indicateur de socialisation ou de politisation', *Revue Francaise de Science Politique*, 37(4): 502–25.

Brown, T. A. (1988) *Migration and Politics: The impact of population mobility on American voting behavior*, Chapel Hill: University of North Carolina Press.

Bryk, A. S. and Raudenbush, S.W. (2001) *Hierarchical Linear Models: Applications and data analysis methods*, Newbury Park, CA: Sage.

Budge, I., Klingemann, H. -D., Volkens, A. (2001) *Mapping Policy Preferences*, Oxford: Oxford University Press.

Butler, D. and Stokes, D. E. (1974) *Political change in Britain: the evolution of electoral choice*, London: Macmillan.

Campbell, A., Converse, P. E., Miller, W. E., and Stokes, D. (1966) *Elections and the Political Order*, New York: Wiley.

Campbell, D. (2006) *Why We Vote*, Princeton: Princeton University Press.

Caramani, D. (2005) *The Nationalization of Politics*, Cambridge: Cambridge University Press.

Carsey, T. (2001) 'Racial context and racial voting in New York City mayoral elections revisited', paper presented at the Annual Meeting of the Southern Political Science Association, Atlanta, Retrieved October 2,

2004 at garnet.acns.fsu.edu/~tcarsey/research/workingpapers/Carsey-Southern2001.pdf.

Clanché, F. (2003) 'La participation électorale au printemps 2002. De plus en plus de votants intermittents', *INSEE-Première*, janvier, n°877: 1–4.

Clark, T. N. and Hoffmann-Martinot, V. (eds) (1998) *The New Political Culture*, Boulder: Westview.

Coulter, P. B. (1992) 'There's a madness in the method', *Urban Affairs Review*, 28: 297–316.

Dahl, R. A. and Tufte, E. R. (1973) *Size and Democracy*, Stanford, Calif., Stanford University Press.

Dalton, R. I and Wattenberg, M. (eds) (2000) *Parties Without Partisans*, Oxford: Oxford University Press.

Danielson, M. D. (1976) *The Politics of Exclusion*, New York: Columbia University Press.

Diamanti, I. (1993) *La Lega: Geografia, storia e sociologia di un nuovo soggetto politico*, Rom: Donzelli.

Dogan, M. and Rokkan, S. (eds) (1969) *Quantitative Ecological Analysis in the Social Sciences*, Cambridge, MA: MIT Press.

Dunleavy, P. (1979) 'The urban basis of political dealignment: Social class, domestic property ownership, and state intervention in consumption processes', *British Journal of Political Science*, 9(4): 409–43.

Eagles, M. and Erfle, S. (1989) 'Community cohesion and voter turnout in English parliamentary constituencies', *British Journal of Political Science*, 19(1): 115–25.

Fischel, W. (2001) *The Homevoter Hypothesis*, Cambridge: Harvard University Press.

Flanagan, S. (1980) 'National and local voting trends: cross-level linkages and correlates of change' in Steiner, K., Krauss, E. S. and Flanagan, S. (eds) *Political Opposition and Local Politics in Japan*, Princeton: Princeton University Press, 131–84.

Frandsen, A. G. (2002') 'Size and electoral participation in local elections', in *Environment and Planning C: Government and policy*, 20(6): 853–69.

Gabriel, O. W. (1997) 'Kommunales Wahlverhalten: Parteien, Themen und Kandidaten' in Gabriel, O. W., Brettschneider, F. and Vetter, A. (eds) *Politische Kultur und Wahlverhalten in einer Großstadt,* Opladen: Westdeutscher Verlag, 147–68.

Gainsborough, J. (2001) *Fenced Off: The suburbanization of American politics*, Washington, DC: Georgetown University Press.

Gilderbloom, J. I. and Markham, J. P. (1995) 'The Impact of Homeownership on Political Beliefs', *Social Forces*, 73(4): 1589–1607.

Gimpel, J. and Shuknecht, J. (2003) *Patchwork Nation*, Ann Arbor: Michigan University Press.

Gimpel, J. G., Morris, I. L. and Armstrong, D. R. (2004) 'Turnout and the local age distribution: examining political participation across space and time', *Political Geography*, 23(1): 71–95.

Goerres, A. (2005) 'Grey voting power on the rise? How the transition from middle to old age influences turnout in Europe', paper presented at the 55th Political Studies Association Annual Conference, 4–7 April 2005, University of Leeds.

Goldsmith, M. and Rose, L. (2002) 'Size and democracy', *Environment and Planning C: Government and policy*, 20(6): 791–92.

Gray, M. and Caul, M. (2000) 'Declining voter turnout in advanced industrial democracies, 1950 to 1997', *Comparative Political Studies*, 33: 1091–122.

Gross, D. A. and Sigelman, L. (1984) 'Comparing party systems. A multidimensional approach', *Comparative Politics*, 16: 463–479.

Hackworth, J. (2007) *The Neoliberal City: Governance, ideology and development in American urbanism*, London: Routledge.

Harvey, D. (2005) *A Brief History of Neoliberalism*, Oxford, UK: Oxford University Press.

Hayward, C. R. (2003) 'The difference states make: democracy, identity, and the American city', *American Political Science Review*, 97: 501–14.

Hill, K. Q. and Leighly, J. E. (1999) 'Racial diversity, voter turnout, and mobilizing institutions in the United States', *American Politics Quarterly*, 27: 275–95.

Hofferbert, R. I. and Sharkansky, I. (1971) 'The nationalization of state politics' in Hofferbert, R. I. and Sharkansky, I. (eds) *State and Urban Politics*, Boston: Little and Brown.

Hoffmann-Martinot, V. (1992) 'La participation aux élections municipales dans les villes françaises', *Revue Francaise de Science Politique*, 42(1): 3–35.

Hoffmann-Martinot, V., Rallings, C. and Thrasher, M. (1996) 'Comparing local electoral turnout in Great-Britain and France: More similarities than differences?', *European Journal of Political Research*, 30 September 1996: 241–57.

Hoffmann-Martinot, V. and Sellers, J. M. (eds) 2005, *Metropolitanization and Political Change*, Wiesbaden: Verlag für Sozialwissenschaften.

—— (2007) *Politique et métropole: une comparaison Internationale*, Paris: CNRS Editions.

Huckfeldt, R. (1979) 'Political participation and the neighborhood social context', *American Journal of Political Science*, 23: 579–92.

—— (1984) 'Political loyalties and social class ties: The mechanisms of contextual influence', *American Journal of Political Science*, 28(2): 399–417.

Huckfeldt, R. and Sprague, J. (1995) *Citizens, Politics and Social Communication: Information and Influence in an Election Campaign*, Cambridge: Cambridge University Press.

Huckfeldt, R., Plutzer, E. and Sprague, J. (1993) 'Alternative contexts of political behaviour: Churches, neighbourhoods and individuals', *Journal of Politics*, 55(2): 365–81.

Inglehart, R. (1990) *Culture Shift in Advanced Industrial Society*, Princeton, NJ: Princeton University Press.

— (1997) *Modernization and Postmodernization: Cultural, economic and political change in 43 societies*, Princeton, NJ: Princeton University Press.

Iversen, T. (2005) *Capitalism, Democracy, and Welfare*, Cambridge: Cambridge University Press.

Jackman, R. (1987) 'Political Institutions and Voter Turnout in Industrial Democracies', *American Political Science Review*, 81: 405–23.

Jackman, R. and Miller, R. A. (1995) 'Voter turnout in the industrial democracies during the 1980s', *Comparative Political Studies*, 27: 467–92.

Johnston, R. J., Jones, K., Sarker, R., Propper, C., Burgess, S. and Bolster, A. (2004) 'Party support and the neighbourhood effect: Spatial polarization of the British Electorate 1991–2001', *Political Geography*, 23(3): 367–402.

Johnston, R. J., Pattie, C. J., and Allsopp, G. (1988) *A Nation Dividing? The Electoral Map of Great Britain 1979–1987*, Harlow, UK: Longman.

Kelleher, C. and Lowery, D. (2004) 'Political participation and metropolitan institutional contexts', *Urban Affairs Review*, 39(6): 720–57.

King, G. (1997) *A Solution to the Ecological Inference Problem*, Princeton, NJ: Princeton University Press.

Kingston, P. W., Thompson, J. L. P. and Eichar, D. M. (1984) 'The politics of homeownership', *American Politics Quarterly*, 12(2): 131–50.

Kitschelt, H. (1994) *The Transformation of European Social Democracy*, Cambridge: Cambridge University Press.

Kitschelt, H. and Rehm, P. (2004) *Socieconomic Group Preferences and Partisan Alignment,* Paper presented at Conference of Europeanists, Chicago. Retrieved June 15, 2005 from http://0-cas.uchicago.edu. luna.wellesley.edu/workshops/cpolit/papers/kitschelt.pdf.

Kocher, M. and Laitin, D. (2007) 'On Tarrow's Space', *CP-APSA* 17(2): 25–8.

Kreft, I. G. and De Leeuw, J. (1998) *Introducing Multilevel Modeling*, Newbury Park, CA: Sage.

Kriesi, H., Grande, E., Lachat, R., Dolezal, M., Bornschier, S. and Frey, T. (2006) 'Globalization and the transformation of the national political space: six European countries compared', *European Journal of Political Research*, 45: 921–25.

Lefebvre, H. (2003, org 1968) The *Urban Revolution*, Minneapolis: University of Minnesota Press, translated by Robert Bononno.

Lidström, A. (2006) 'Commuting and citizen participation in Swedish city-regions', *Political Studies*, 54(4): 865–88.

Lipset, S. M. and Rokkan, S. (1967) 'Cleavage structures, party systems and voter alignments: an introduction', Lipset, S. M. and Rokkan, S. (eds) *Party systems and voter alignments*, New York: The Free Press: 1–64.

MacAllister, I., Johnston, R. J., Pattie, C. J., Tunstall, H., Doorling, D. and Rossiter, D. J. (2001) 'Class dealignment and the neighbourhood effect: Miller revisited', *British Journal of Political Science*, 31(1): 41–59.

Merriam, C. E. and Gosnell, H. F. (1924) *Non-Voting, Causes and Methods of Control*, Chicago, Ill.: The University of Chicago Press.

Milbrath, L. W. and Goel, M. L. (1977) *Political Participation: How and why do people get involved in politics?*, Chicago: Rand McNally College Pub. Co., 2nd edn.

Miller, W. L. (1977) 'Social class and party choice in England: a new analysis', *British Journal of Political Science*, 8(3): 257–84.

Morlan, R. L. (1984) 'Municipal vs. National Election Voter Turnout: Europe and the United States', *Political Science Quarterly*, 99(3): 457–70.

Oliver, J. E. (2000) 'City size and civic involvement in metropolitan America', *The American Political Science Review*, 94(2): 361–73.

— (2001) *Democracy in Suburbia*, Princeton, NJ: Princeton University Press.

Orfield, M. (2002) *American Metropolitics*, Washington, DC: Brookings Institution Press.

Peck, J. and Tickell, A. (2002) 'Neoliberalizing space', *Antipode*, 34(3): 380–404.

Powell, G.B. (1986) 'American voter turnout in comparative perspective', *American Political Science Review*, 80: 17–43.

Putnam, R. (2000) *Bowling Alone*, New York: Touchstone.

Rosenstone, S. J. (1982) 'Economic adversity and voter turnout', *American Journal of Political Science*, 26(1): 25–46.

Saiz, M. and Geser, H. (1999) *Local parties in political and organizational perspective*, Boulder, CO: Westview Press.

Saunders, P. (1978) 'Domestic property and social class', *International Journal of Urban and Regional Research*, 2 (2): 233–51.

Saunders, P. (1990) *A Nation of Homeowners*, London: Unwin Hyman.

Sellers, J. M. (1998) 'Place, post-industrial change and the new left', *European Journal of Political Research*, 33 (2): 187–217.

— (1999) 'Public goods and the politics of segregation: an analysis and cross-national comparison', *Journal of Urban Affairs*, 21(2): 237–62.

— (2002) *Governing from Below: Urban regions and the global economy*, New York: Cambridge University Press.

Siegfried, A. (1913) *Geographie de la Troisieme Republique*, Paris.

Skocpol, T. (2003) *Diminished Democracy: From Membership to Management in American Civic Life, Norman*, OK: University of Oklahoma Press.

Snijders, T. and Bosker, R. (1999) *Multilevel Analysis*, London: Sage.

Squire, P., Wolfinger, R. E. and Glass, D. P. (1987) 'Residential mobility and voter turnout', *The American Political Science Review*, 81(1): 45–66.

Tarrow, S. (2006) 'President's letter: space and comparative politics', *APSA-CP* 17(1): 1–4.

Thorns, D. C. (1981) 'Owner-occupation: its significance for wealth transfer and class formation', *Sociological Review*, 29(6): 705–28.

Tingsten, H. (1937) *Political Behavior: Studies in election statistics*, London: King.

Verba, S. and Nie, N. H. (1972) *Participation in America: Political democracy and social equality*, New York: Harper & Row.

Verba, S., Nie, N. H. and Kim, J. (1978) *Participation and Political Equality*, Chicago: University of Chicago Press.

Walks, R. A. (2004a) 'Place of Residence, Party Preferences, and Political Attitudes in Canadian Cities and Suburbs', *Journal of Urban Affairs*, 26(3): 269–95.

— (2004b) 'Suburbanization, the vote, and changes in federal and provincial political representation and influence between inner cities and suburbs in large Canadian urban regions, 1945–1999', *Urban Affairs Review*, 39(4): 411–40.

— (2005) 'City-suburban electoral polarization in Great Britain, 1950–2001', *Transactions of the Institute of British Geographers*, 30(4): 500–17.

— (2006) 'The causes of city-suburban political polarization? A Canadian case study', *Annals of the Association of American Geographers*, 96(2): 390–414.

— (2008) 'Urban form, everyday life, and ideology: support for privatization in three toronto neighbourhoods', *Environment and Planning A*, 39(2): 367–93.

Wirt, F. M., Rabinowitz, F., Walter, B. and Hensler, D. (1972) *On the City's Rim: Politics and policy in suburbia*, Lexington, MA: DC Heath.

Wolfinger, R. E. and Rosenstone, S. J. (1980) *Who Votes?* New Haven: Yale University Press.

Young, O. R. (1999) *Governance in world affairs*, Itahca, NY: Cornell University Press.

# Chapter Two | Place, Institutions and the Political Ecology of US Metropolitan Areas

*Jefferey M. Sellers*[1]

As the first nation with a suburban electoral majority, the United States has come to exemplify how metropolitan places matter for politics (Sellers 2005). Up to the 1960s, large-scale regional divides dominated the political geography of the United States. With metropolitanisation and suburbanisation now predominant across the country, national political divides run between places in metropolitan areas and between varieties of metropolitan areas within the same regions (*Ibid*). As the International Metropolitan Observatory (IMO) dataset reveals systematically for the first time, differences among metropolitan places are crucial to the cultural and social sources of partisanship. To date, the growing literature on geographic differences in the sources of support for the political left and right (Gimpel and Shuknecht 2004; Bishop 2007; Bartels 2008; Gelman *et al.* 2009) has employed geographic units too large to fully capture these variations in communities and places of residence. Examination of localities demonstrates clear metropolitan patterns of electoral division and contestation. In supplanting older regional divergences, metropolitanisation has contributed to the nationalisation of US voting behaviour. At the same time, it has brought about new territorial divides within metropolitan regions across the country, and contributed to the rise of new regional differences.

A full understanding of the consequences of metropolitanisation must take into account the corresponding effects on voter participation. The layered dataset of the IMO project also casts new light on the recent, growing mobilisation of voters in US presidential elections. The average turnout gap between national and local elections in the United States is more dramatic than in any other older democracy in this study. This gap is especially pronounced in the affluent suburbs that

---

1. Versions of this chapter were presented at meetings of the International Metropolitan Observatory and at the American Political Science Association Annual Meeting in 2008. The author would like to thank Melissa Marschall and the IMO participants for comments on an earlier version; Evan Bacalao, Simrata Batra, Crystal Becker, Ben Beezy, Damien Carlson, Joelle Emerson, Anne Gervais, Doreen Grosvirt-Dramen, Minna Jia, Galia Kirsanova, Deniz Kuru, Wenyu Li, Kumkum Maheshwari, Boris Melnikov, Parth Shah and Lea Smith for invaluable research assistance; Michael Latner and Lilyanne Ohanesian for major contributions to the supervision of data collection as well to data collection, processing and analysis; Robert Wilkes for assistance with data collection; the High Performance Computing Center at the University of Southern California for use of their facilities; and the hundreds of state and local officials who assisted with the process of data collection. Support for this research has been provided by the University of Southern California Provost's Urban Initiative, the Provost's Undergraduate Research Program, the Center for International Studies, and the College of Letters, Arts and Sciences, and the METRANS Center for Transportation Research.

have mobilised with growing intensity in US presidential elections. To date, the expanding literature that has sought to account for the sources of US local voter participation (Oliver 2001; Hajnal and Lewis 2003; Kelleher and Lowery 2004a; Campbell 2006) has paid little attention to this turnout gap. Its origins trace to differences in subnational institutions, community practices, and the characteristics of metropolitan places, as well as the composition of local electorates. Its consequences have increasingly shaped the national balance of power between the left and the right.

This chapter begins with an overview of the US dataset and the types of towns that make up the US metropolitan areas. Subsequent sections will analyse the sources of voting participation, then the patterns of partisan voting in these settings.

### Dataset and research design

The analysis here draws on an original dataset of voting data collected from the incorporated municipalities of twelve United States metropolitan areas with populations of 450,000 or more. The analysis focuses on presidential voting for Democratic or Republican candidates in 1996, 2000, and 2004; on the proportion of the local voting age population voting in these elections; and on turnout in municipal council elections from 1996 through 2003.[2]

Municipal-level electoral data had to be assembled from county and often from individual municipal elections records around the country. To date, the extensive demands of primary data collection have made it impossible to construct a dataset of local election data below the county level for the entire universe of US metropolitan areas. Instead, a stratified sample was constructed from those metropolitan areas with sufficient numbers of localities to enable a multilevel analysis. The sample encompassed the main dimensions of variation among large US urban regions (see Table 2.1). They include the two US cities most often classified as global cities or megacities (Los Angeles and New York), a selection of regional centres, and a sample of smaller metropolitan areas with populations as low as 450,000. Each of the four types of US metropolitan areas classified by Sellers (2005) is represented (Older, New Service, Traditional and Latino Working Class). The metropolitan areas are distributed across all the major regions of the country (East, South, Midwest, Southwest and Northwest). Politically, the sample is also representative. It includes several metropolitan areas that are predominantly Republican (Atlanta, Cincinnati, Kalamazoo and Wichita), two that vote mostly Democratic (Philadelphia and Seattle), and several largely split between

---

2. Because voter registration is not universal in the United States and varies widely among different states, rates based on registration figures could not be compared with those in the other IMO countries. Instead, turnout rates were imputed based on census estimates of the voting age native born and naturalised population. To correct for additional ineligible populations, such as prisoners, all turnout models included a control for the institutionalised adult population.

Democratic and Republican municipalities (Detroit, Fresno, Los Angeles and Syracuse).[3] The sample was also stratified to enable examination of the relationship between state and metropolitan influences. The twelve states encompassed the wide variety of institutional frameworks that state governments have authorised for municipal governments across the country. Three metropolitan areas (New York, Philadelphia and Cincinnati) included localities in more than one state, while two of the states sampled (Michigan and New York) contained more than one metropolitan area.

To maintain comparability with other national datasets, many of which encompassed all or most of the metropolitan communities in other countries, the analyses did not incorporate weights by metropolitan size or numbers of localities. The results that follow therefore reflect a bias in the sample towards the largest metropolitan areas, especially those with more municipalities. The sample nonetheless encompasses a diversity of regions, size and other characteristics that captures the distinctive breadth of variation in US metropolitan regions (Sellers 2005).

To assure parallel units for comparison with the other IMO countries, data collection and analysis centred on incorporated municipalities, or other units of government with equivalent general authorities to the local governments in other countries. Although the dataset excluded populations living in unincorporated areas, the municipalities included captured the full variety of place types within US metropolitan areas. In a number of states with several varieties of municipalities, overlapping jurisdictions or limited data access required municipal units to be excluded. Table A2.1 in the Appendix to this chapter lists which units were included in each state with multiple types of municipal governments.

A typology of metropolitan towns provides an overview of general patterns of variation in demographic, spatial and other characteristics (Orfield 2002). Analysis of demographic characteristics revealed largely common clusters of characteristics among towns throughout metropolitan areas across the United States. The five types of towns in the IMO typology generally corresponded to these clusters.[4]

---

3.  Within each metropolitan area, the coverage rate by town was 70 per cent or more for Presidential elections, and 57 per cent or more for municipal election results.

4.  Following Orfield (2002), the process of classification began with k-means cluster analysis to explore relationships among compositional and place-linked variables. The final classification of municipal types employed the hierarchical, factor analytic procedure prescribed in the IMO protocol (see Chapter 14, the Methodological Appendix to this volume). The resulting categorisation nonetheless bore a close resemblance to results from the previous cluster analyses.

*Table 2.1: Metropolitan areas included in dataset*

| Metropolitan area | States | Total population (2000) | Number of general govern- ments | Govern- ments /100,000 inhabit- ants | Central city popula- tion (%) | Geopo- litical fragmen- tation index | Type of metropol- itan area (Sellers 2005) | Region |
|---|---|---|---|---|---|---|---|---|
| New York CMSA | Connecticut, NY, New Jersey[a] | 21,199,865 | 1268 | 6.5 | 37.8 | 1.7 | Older | East |
| Los Angeles CMSA | California | 16,373,645 | 303 | 1.9 | 22.6 | 0.8 | New Service | West |
| Philadelphia CMSA | Pennsylvania, New Jersey[a] | 6,234,765 | 869 | 13.9 | 24.3 | 5.7 | Older | East |
| Detroit MSA | Michigan | 5,456,428 | 659 | 12.1 | 17.4 | 6.9 | Older | Midwest |
| Atlanta MSA | Georgia | 4,112,198 | 230 | 5.6 | 10.9 | 26.1 | Trad. Southern | South |
| Seattle MSA | Washington | 3,554,760 | 190 | 5.3 | 15.8 | 3.4 | New Service | West |
| Cincinnati CMSA | Ohio, Kentucky[a] | 1,979,202 | 455 | 23.0 | 16.7 | 13.7 | Older | Midwest |
| Fresno MSA | California | 922,516 | 36 | 3.9 | 46.4 | 0.8 | Lat. work. Cl. | West |
| Birmingham MSA | Alabama | 921,106 | 98 | 10.6 | 26.4 | 4.0 | Trad. Southern | South |
| Syracuse MSA | New York | 732,117 | 260 | 35.5 | 20.1 | 17.7 | Older | East |
| Wichita MSA | Kansas | 545,220 | 223 | 40.9 | 63.1 | 6.5 | Older | Midwest |
| Kalamazoo MSA | Michigan | 452,851 | 163 | 36.0 | 17.0 | 21.1 | Older | Midwest |
| Average | | 3,753,164 | 317 | 17.2 | 25.5 | 9.7 | | |
| National average[b] | | 2,070,750 | 194 | 12.7 | 31.1 | 6.7 | | |

[a]Additional metropolitan municipalities in other states were too few to be included.
[b]Average of all 91 metropolitan areas with greater than 450,000 population.

Table 2.2: Characteristics of municipal types

| | | Poverty (%) | Per capita income in ($) | Foreign born (%) | African-American (%) | Latino American (%) | Housing built since 1980 (%) | Population density (per km²) | Population | N |
|---|---|---|---|---|---|---|---|---|---|---|
| Urban concentrations | Mean | 20 | 19.657 | 24 | 26 | 27 | 17 | 3,111 | 875,529 | 22 |
| | S.d. | 5 | 6.636 | 17 | 24 | 22 | 9 | 2,146 | 1,770,875 | |
| Poor minority communities | Mean | 16 | 17.325 | 17 | 20 | 22 | 20 | 2,088 | 31,398 | 237 |
| | S.d. | 7 | 4.276 | 16 | 21 | 25 | 16 | 2,724 | 42,850 | |
| Poor non-minority communities | Mean | 11 | 19.562 | 5 | 4 | 6 | 26 | 721 | 11,794 | 245 |
| | S.d. | 6 | 4.408 | 7 | 6 | 10 | 15 | 810 | 32,822 | |
| Middle-class communities | Mean | 6 | 25.183 | 11 | 7 | 8 | 21 | 1,411 | 23,434 | 385 |
| | S.d. | 4 | 6.888 | 11 | 11 | 13 | 16 | 1,168 | 50,492 | |
| Low-density suburbs | Mean | 6 | 26.500 | 7 | 5 | 6 | 39 | 389 | 15,759 | 423 |
| | S.d. | 4 | 7.087 | 7 | 7 | 9 | 15 | 391 | 22,726 | |
| Affluent suburbs | Mean | 3 | 46.134 | 9 | 3 | 3 | 33 | 764 | 14,793 | 251 |
| | S.d. | 2 | 17.915 | 7 | 4 | 4 | 23 | 730 | 17,500 | |
| Total | Mean | 8 | 26.753 | 10 | 7 | 9 | 28 | 1,049 | 31,346 | 1563 |
| | S.d. | 6 | 12.895 | 11 | 13 | 15 | 19 | 1,467 | 231,613 | |

The urban concentrations included 20 cities (see Table 2.2), of which nine were located in the polycentric Los Angeles Consolidated Metropolitan Statistical Area. These cities had high poverty rates and population density, and lower than average home values and per capita incomes. The low-density suburbs were also the fastest growing places, with nearly half of all housing built since 1980 and with average socio-economic status. Affluent suburbs stood out everywhere, except in the smaller metropolitan areas of Fresno and Wichita. Distinguished primarily by high overall income and housing prices twice the level of any other type, these places also featured lower density, higher rates of new housing and higher proportions of foreign-born residents than the middle-class and low-density suburbs. Poor minority communities were present in each of the metropolitan areas, and registered the lowest incomes and the second highest poverty rates. Low minority, high hardship suburbs also averaged lower income levels and had less new growth than middle-class suburbs, but had lower poverty rates and much lower density than the other high hardship communities. These were often communities on the rural outskirts of metropolitan regions.

### Electoral turnout in the United States

By comparison with other advanced industrial democracies, the rate of voter participation in the United States is low. The recent rise in national turnout of the eligible population from a historic low of 52 per cent in 1996 to 54 per cent in 2000, 60 per cent in 2004 and 62 per cent in 2008 has only partly reversed this. A more dramatic contrast with other democracies marks US rates of municipal election participation. Some estimates have put local turnout rates as low as 20 per cent of the eligible population (Hajnal and Trounstine 2005). The relationship between patterns of voter participation at the local and national levels has important implications for the wider integration between these two levels of governance and politics, and ultimately for the state of democratic practice in the United States.

Since local government itself is the product of fifty different state systems, and often varies considerably even within these states, even the most consistent local government rules are rarely uniform in the United States. Several frequent features of local government and municipal elections nonetheless could contribute to the low rates of voter turnout:

- In many states, general purpose local governments receive comparatively limited powers and fiscal resources, as state governments or functional special districts take on more responsibilities for governance. Local governments with fewer responsibilities or capacities give citizens less reason to participate in municipal elections.
- Local elections frequently take place on different days and years from the biennial general elections for national office.
- National parties are seldom organised in local politics. Non-partisan municipal electoral rules throughout most of the country discourage local party formation. Local political parties have long been suspect in the

United States for their association with 'political machines' that supplant grassroots democracy.

- The large number of elected offices at the local level, including multiple votes for council seats, can bring about voter fatigue and ballot roll-off.

Beyond institutional differences, previous studies have found divergent effects from local social, economic and political diversity on voter turnout. While some studies show local economic diversity to boost turnout (e.g. Oliver 2001), others have pointed to higher voter participation in more homogenous districts (e.g. Campbell 2006). No study has examined variations in these effects between national and local elections, or spillover effects between national and local political competition.

Studies based mainly on surveys have also established a variety of demographic determinants of turnout rates in the United States (Powell 1986; Jackman 1987; Rosenstone and Hansen 1993; Verba et al. 1995). Those citizens that are better educated, more affluent and older vote more frequently than those that are less educated, poorer and younger. The characteristics of places have also been shown to influence voter turnout rates. Long-settled residents, fewer commuters, and more homeowners generate higher turnout (e.g. Oliver 2001). The effects of city size and urban density are more disputed. A 'small is beautiful' hypothesis emphasises the beneficial effects of smaller scale for participation (Rose 2002; Oliver 2001; Verba et al. 1978); an opposed 'large is lively' hypothesis stresses greater opportunities for political mobilisation in larger, more urban settings (Oliver 2001).

Whether these hypotheses and findings apply in the same way to national and to local voter turnout has thus far escaped systematic scrutiny. In a country where national and local elections follow distinct rules, however, there is ample reason to expect divergent dynamics at the two levels. Analyses of the rising turnout in US presidential elections have pointed to new modes of mobilisation-based voter contacts that bypass local governments, along with increased motivation among voters themselves (e.g. Bergan et al. 2005). This nationalised mobilisation has almost certainly added to the divergence between presidential and municipal participation. However, as long as national electoral mobilisation remains linked in some way to local communities, some basis for linkages between the two levels persists.

## Typological analysis

The typology of metropolitan towns reveals several striking patterns in local electoral participation and partisanship (see Figure 2.1). Across the board, the 20 to 40 per cent gap between turnout for elections to the highest national office and municipal elections is more pronounced than in any other country in the IMO dataset. Especially in presidential elections, the disparities of 20 per cent between the different types of communities are also remarkably high. Both patterns have persisted despite the surge in presidential turnout from its historic low in the Clinton

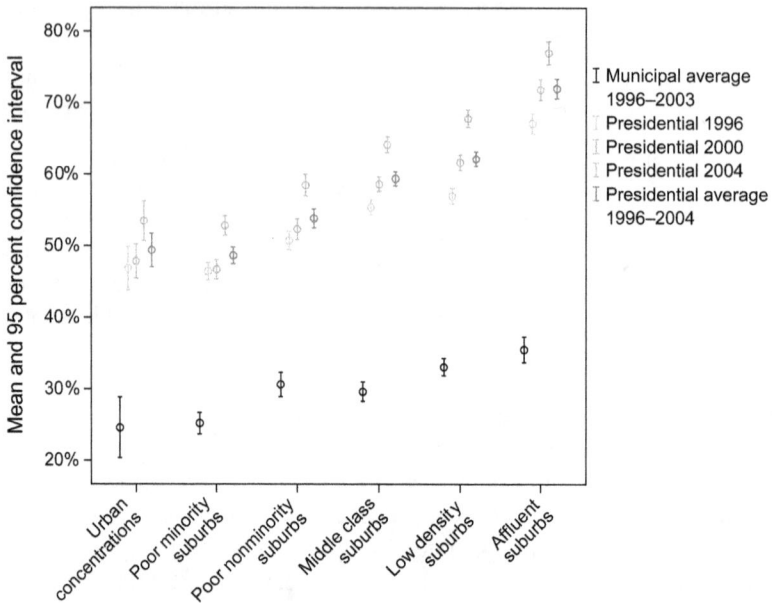

*Figure 2.1: Presidential and municipal turnout, by municipal types*

re-election of 1996 to the 2000 race between Bush and Gore, to the intensified mobilisation in the Bush-Kerry contest of 2004.

In presidential elections, the disparities in turnout between the minority and urban concentrations and the other types are especially pronounced. In 1996 and 2000, fewer than half of eligible citizens in these two types voted, compared to 70 per cent in affluent suburbs and 60 per cent in low density, high growth towns. Even in 2004, as voter participation in urban and minority concentrations rose above 50 per cent, the rate climbed to 74 per cent in the affluent suburbs. In municipal elections the disparities between the highest and lowest average rates were smaller. Thirteen per cent more of the eligible voters participated in the affluent suburbs than in the high hardship minority communities. As in most other countries, turnout in the central cities remained among the lowest.

Delocalisation concentrates most in the affluent and low-density suburbs. There the turnout gap approached 40 points in 2000, compared to just less than 20 per cent in the poor minority suburbs. The five types of towns nonetheless capture only a fraction of the overall variation in turnout rates. An ordinary least squares regression model based on the five types explains only 8 per cent of the variance in municipal turnout (Table A2.3 in the Appendix), and 37 per cent of the variance in average presidential election turnout over 1996–2004 (Table A2.4 in the Appendix). More fine-grained methods of multivariate ecological analysis offer the means to probe more deeply into these patterns, and ultimately to account for more of the variation in turnout rates.

## Multivariate and multilevel analyses

Beyond the ethnic, racial, generational and socio-economic composition of places, multivariate regressions enable an examination of the roots of community political behaviour in local spatial structures, political cultures and institutional contexts. Alternative multivariate regressions compared the explanatory power of demographic variables with features of the local socio-spatial context. To account for various effects from wider contextual differences among metropolitan areas and states necessitated multilevel regression models that could overcome the limits of ordinary least squares regression.

Ecological analysis of this kind demands special sensitivity toward the relations among the independent variables. Although the level of multicollinearity was generally not high, several variables captured theoretically distinct dimensions of the same or related phenomena. Latinos correlated at 0.75 with foreign-born residents and at 0.549 with a general hardship index combining unemployment, crowded housing and poverty.[5] The hardship variable also correlated at −0.53 with a separate index measuring socio-economic status, composed of indicators for per capita income and proportion of adults with college or higher education. Local economic diversity, measured by a Simpson index based on three occupational categories, also correlates at −0.789 with the socio-economic status index.[6] In the US, a higher value for this index mainly reflects a larger proportion of the resident workforce in manufacturing. The proportion of people under age eighteen correlated at −0.606 with the proportion aged sixty or more. Negative correlations between 0.5 and 0.6 also linked the proportion of homeowners to hardship, to population density and to residential mobility. Commuters in a town also correlated at 0.64 with density.[7] Following tests for multicollinearity in the multivariate regressions, the variables for the population under eighteen and for manufacturing occupations were excluded from final models. Other intercorrelated variables, notably the Simpson Index, the hardship and socio-economic status indexes, and homeowners, were retained due to their distinct effects in the multivariate models or the need to capture all relevant dimensions of demographic composition.

A second threshold issue for multivariate analysis concerns the proper levels at which to measure the variation. Analysis of variance confirmed that a significant portion of the variance is between states, regions or metropolitan areas. Seventeen per cent of the average variation in presidential turnout over 1996–2004 was between metropolitan areas; an alternative test showed that interstate differences accounted for an equivalent proportion. States made more of the difference in municipal turnout rates. Interstate variance accounted for 17 per cent of overall

---

5. Construction of this and the index for socio-economic status followed procedures from Nathan and Adams (1976).

6. The Simpson index included classes based on census data for manufacturing occupations, professional and managerial occupations, and lower status service occupations.

7. Principal components analysis (with varimax rotation using Kaiser normalisation) confirmed most of these relationships.

*Table 2.3: Multilevel models of municipal turnout*

| | Compositional | | Contextual | | Full model | | Full with Cross-level effects | |
|---|---|---|---|---|---|---|---|---|
| | **B** | **t** | **B** | **t** | **B** | **t** | **B** | **t** |
| Constant | *0.30* | *20.29* | *0.30* | *6.25* | *0.26* | *8.91* | *0.24* | *10.25* |
| *Metropolitan or state level* | | | | | | | | |
| Municipal capacity (state) | | | | | 0.0004 | 1.75 | *0.0006* | *3.41* |
| *Compositional variables* | | | | | | | | |
| Foreign born | *−0.18* | *−3.83* | | | 0.02 | 0.53 | 0.03 | 0.66 |
| African Americans | *−0.09* | *−3.31* | | | −0.03 | −1.09 | −0.03 | −1.29 |
| Latino Americans | 0.05 | 1.18 | | | −0.01 | −0.29 | −0.01 | −0.36 |
| Age 60 or more | *0.18* | *3.32* | | | *0.19* | *4.18* | *0.19* | *4.15* |
| Hardship | *−0.13* | *−2.51* | | | −0.04 | −0.95 | −0.03 | −0.60 |
| Socio-economic status | *0.13* | *4.57* | | | *0.15* | *5.53* | *0.16* | *5.94* |
| *Contextual and cross-level variables* | | | | | | | | |
| Township | | | *0.03* | *3.29* | *0.04* | *4.21* | *0.13* | *5.39* |
| Special district activity (state) | | | | | | | *−0.001* | *−4.39* |
| Elected mayor | | | 0.01 | 0.80 | 0.01 | 1.22 | *0.020* | *1.92* |
| Partisan competition, US House (state) | | | | | | | *−0.380* | *−3.31* |
| Partisan municipal elections | | | *−0.05* | *−2.36* | *−0.04* | *−1.96* | *0.51* | *2.53* |
| State centralisation | | | | | | | *−0.01* | *−2.69* |
| General election year | | | *0.16* | *17.47* | *0.15* | *17.71* | *0.13* | *15.08* |
| General election month | | | 0.01 | 1.17 | *0.02* | *1.82* | *0.03* | *3.03* |
| District magnitude | | | −0.002 | −0.99 | −0.002 | −1.05 | −0.004 | −1.82 |
| Municipal political diversity | | | *0.08* | *13.75* | *0.08* | *14.68* | *0.08* | *15.46* |
| National partisan diversity | | | −0.02 | −1.02 | −0.03 | −1.77 | −0.03 | −1.65 |
| Homeowners | | | *0.21* | *8.25* | *0.14* | *5.13* | *0.12* | *4.52* |
| Commuters | | | *−0.07* | *−4.53* | *−0.07* | *−4.90* | *0.27* | *4.40* |
| Metropolitan commuters | | | | | | | *−0.66* | *−5.15* |
| Mobility | | | −0.03 | −0.76 | −0.05 | −1.15 | −0.08 | −1.79 |
| Housing since 1980 | | | *−0.08* | *−4.24* | *−0.07* | *−3.35* | *−0.07* | *−3.32* |
| Occupational diversity | | | *−0.07* | *−7.02* | −0.01 | −0.73 | −0.01 | −0.95 |
| Population (log) | | | *−0.05* | *−9.50* | *−0.05* | *−9.26* | *−0.05* | *−8.97* |
| Population density (log) | | | 0.01 | 1.35 | *0.01* | *1.65* | 0.01 | 0.84 |
| *Controls* | | | | | | | | |
| Institutionalised population | *−0.34* | *−4.23* | *−0.32* | *−5.00* | *−0.30* | *−4.59* | *−0.26* | *−4.13* |
| Uncontested seats (Alabama) | *0.37* | *2.06* | *0.29* | *1.96* | *0.26* | *1.82* | *0.25* | *1.78* |
| Uncontested seats (quadratic) (Alabama) | *−0.57* | *−2.31* | *−0.49* | *−2.45* | *−0.45* | *−2.32* | *−0.44* | *−2.31* |
| Chi-square: Local/metro | | 27.96 | | 130.9 | | 118.8 | | 64.12 |
| State | | 242.3 | | 314.2 | | 71.68 | | 61.54 |
| N: Local | | 1432 | | 1432 | | 1432 | | 1432 |
| Metropolitan | | 12 | | 12 | | 12 | | 12 |
| State | | 12 | | 12 | | 12 | | 12 |
| p: rows (metropolitan & local) | | 0.004 | | 0 | | 0 | | 0 |

| | Compositional | Contextual | Full model | Full with Cross-level effects |
|---|---|---|---|---|
| p: columns (state) | 0 | 0 | 0 | 0 |
| Variance explained | | | | |
| Metropolitan/state | 21% | (negative) | (negative) | 45% |
| Local | 11% | 44% | 46% | 49% |
| Total | 13% | 14% | 36% | 48% |
| Deviance | −2208 | −2856 | −2923 | −2994.6 |

*Notes*: Coefficients are full maximum likelihood estimates using HCM2 module in HLM. For italicised coefficients, $p<0.10$; for boldface coefficients, $p<0.05$; for boldface italicised coefficients, $p<0.01$.

variance in these, compared to 11 per cent between metropolitan areas. Each of these patterns of variance between groups is important enough to demand explanation. To fully account for both types of turnout, and ultimately for the gap between them, requires models than can address these metropolitan and state level variations as well as the local ones.

To capture how both state and metropolitan contexts affected local variation, the multilevel models employed the cross-classified nested modelling procedure (HCM2) in HLM (Bryk and Raudenbush 2001). This method represents a step beyond a two-level hierarchical linear model that treated all variation between metropolitan areas the same. Since state and metropolitan effects on the local variations partly diverged, the cross-classified models allowed each set of influences to be modelled as an independent effect at the same time. Because these models enabled the most probing examination of hierarchical and cross-level effects, the account here will focus mainly on the results from them, rather than on the ordinary least squares and the two-level models. All of these multivariate models accounted not only for nearly all of the variations explained by the municipal types, but for much of the remaining variance as well. Places and the institutions and processes linked to them proved indispensable to a full account of both national and local turnout.

## *Municipal turnout*

As might be expected in a country with multiple local government systems, municipal turnout proved most susceptible to explanations based on local, state or metropolitan contexts. Effects from place-linked local factors were especially important to account for municipal turnout. Effects from institutional, community and other contextual factors confirmed a number of hypotheses from the survey literature, but also revealed several surprising results.

Neither the demographic composition of communities nor the municipal types account for a large portion of the variation in municipal voter participation. In both the ordinary least squares regressions and the maximum likelihood regressions used for the multilevel models, the municipal types explain 10 per cent or less of the variation in municipal turnout (see Table A2.3 in the Appendix to this chapter). Even adding the municipal types to the full multilevel model provides only 1 per cent additional explanation in the ordinary least squares models, and none in the maximum likelihood models. The compositional variables also accounted for only 15 per cent of the total variation in the ordinary least squares model, and only 11 per cent of local variation in the maximum likelihood model (see Table 2.3). In the purely compositional models, foreign-born residents, African American residents, and socio-economic hardship all depress municipal turnout. With the full panoply of contextual and multilevel effects included, however, only older residents and average socio-economic status register significant coefficients. Multivariate analysis thus confirms limits to the effects of social and economic composition.

Local institutional, political and contextual differences clearly comprise the most decisive influences on municipal turnout. The municipal government activity associated with the distinct local government systems of different states predicted a significant proportion of the variation in local turnout rates. A measure of municipal activity taken from Stephens and Wikstrom (2000: 138) averaged three fiscal and personnel measures from the US Census of Governments to compare municipal government activity under different state systems.[8] Although the limited number of states in the present sample necessitated caution about any inference about effects at this level, examination of the state by state patterns showed this effect to be part of a general, if not entirely uniform, tendency (see Figure 2.2). In both greater Atlanta (Georgia) and greater Philadelphia (Pennsylvania), lower local government activity corresponds to lower average municipal turnout rates. In states with comparatively high municipal activity, such as Connecticut, Alabama, Kansas and Kentucky, municipal turnout averages are higher.

Concurrence between local and other national and state elections proved the most powerful single predictor of higher local turnout (cf. Hajnal and Lewis 2003). Where local elections take place in the same year as the biennial US general elections for federal office, and to a lesser extent when they occur on the day of the general election in November, the higher national election turnout boosts municipal voter participation.

Other institutional effects stem from other features of state systems of local government. The traditional township form established by a number of Midwestern and Eastern states to deliver local services (see Table A2.1 in the Appendix) registers significantly higher voter participation than municipalities formed through independent locally initiated incorporation. The larger scale and greater capacities for administration in active township governments help to explain this effect.[9] A cross-level variable measuring the activity of the functional special districts active

8.   This measure was based on the average of statewide municipal direct expenditures per person, own source municipal revenues per person, and full time equivalent employees per person from 1992 (Stephens and Wikstrom 2000).

9.   Note that types of townships lacking strong responsibilities and accompanying administrative capacities, like those in Ohio, were excluded from the dataset.

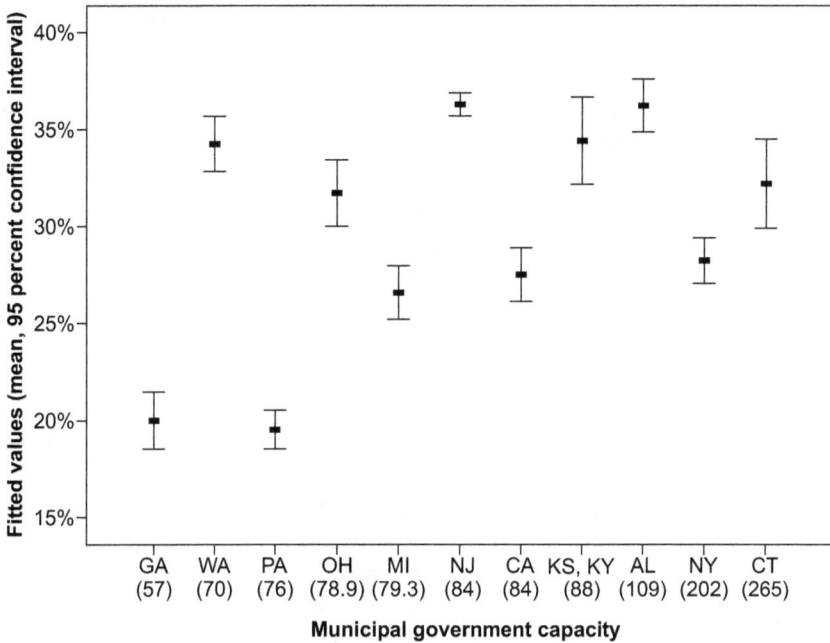

*Figure 2.2: State-level differences in municipal turnout, by municipal government capacity*

at the local level in many states shows that these can influence this effect.[10] In states where special districts take more responsibilities away from townships, the boost to turnout from township institutions is less pronounced.

Effects from partisan municipal elections vary with other aspects of local government systems; on their own, partisan elections lower municipal turnout. As Stephens and Wikstrom's indicator of overall state centralisation reveals, however, this effect depends on the extent of devolution to municipal government. This cross-level variable measures how much the state government takes on the delivery of local services itself rather than delegate them to local governments.[11] Where centralisation is low, local institutions are charged with more of local services, and the negative cross-level effect shows that partisan elections actually promote local turnout. The depressive effect of partisanship on municipal turnout is therefore centred in states that allow less local control.

Other institutional variables exert small, but significant effects. Election of the mayor contributes to higher turnout at a rate just short of $p=0.05$, once the level

10. Stephens and Wikstrom (2000: 131) based this metric on per capita direct expenditures, per capita revenues and full-time equivalent employees in special districts in 1992.

11. This indicator averages three distinct indexes based on the state proportion of state and local direct expenditures, the distribution of state activity across fifteen separate functions, and the state proportion of personnel (Stephens 1974; Stephens and Wikstrom 2000: 125ff.).

of partisan competition is controlled. Higher levels of statewide partisan competition, as measured by the average overall margin in U.S. House elections, swamp this effect from local institutions. The ordinary least squares models suggest that a higher number of seats per district, or district magnitude, produces significant ballot roll-off. This effect falls to a significance of $p<0.10$ in the multilevel models.

Electoral competition has different effects at the national and local level. Municipal electoral competition, measured by a local candidate fractionalisation index, exerts one of the strongest, most consistent effects on local turnout. Consistent with Campbell (2006), however, diversity in national partisan voting emerges in the multilevel models with a slight ($p<0.10$) depressive effect on local turnout. Competitive dynamics of voter mobilisation in local elections coexist with solidaristic effects from concentrations of partisanship in national elections.

Finally, spatial characteristics beyond demographic composition exercise some of the strongest influences on municipal voter participation. Consistent with theories that stress the greater stake of property owners in a community (Fischel 2001, 2005), higher homeownership promotes higher municipal turnout more strongly and consistently than any variable except socio-economic status. City size has almost as sharp and consistent a negative effect (cf. Oliver 2001: 42-47).[12] As expected, all three indicators of lesser community attachment – commuting, residential mobility, and new housing – also depress local turnout. Putnam (2001) and Oliver (2001: 147) have argued that commuting is one of the main ways that the US suburban context depresses voter participation. A cross-level variable for metropolitan commuting, however, shows this effect to be concentrated in larger metropolitan areas with higher overall commuting rates. In other metropolitan areas, local commuting is instead linked to higher rates of voting participation.

Municipal election turnout remains highly contingent on local, metropolitan or state-level influences. The contextual models of place-linked effects do a much better job of accounting for variation than does the demographic composition of communities. Multilevel models, especially those including cross-level effects, capture much more of the variation between metropolitan areas and states than typological or ordinary least squares models. Overall, the multilevel and ordinary least squares models accounted for just under half (48 or 49 per cent) of the variance in municipal voting rates.

### Presidential turnout

Over 1996–2008, a broad, consistent rise in voter turnout marked elections to the nation's highest office. In a country like the United States, with a wide variety of local arrangements and much higher levels of voter mobilisation in national elections, national turnout might be expected to follow more nationalised patterns

---

12. Although population density exerts a positive effect alongside population size in the ordinary least squares models, no such effect is evident in the multilevel models.

than local election turnout. Individual-level survey analyses, which have mostly focused on elections at the national level, demonstrate the importance of citizenship, age, race and socio-economic status to US voter turnout (Verba *et al.* 1978; Oliver 2001; Campbell 2006). Even in presidential elections, however, there is evidence of metropolitan and local influences on participation. Local government, local electoral institutions and spatial characteristics of places account for variations in turnout that the demographic composition of places cannot explain.

The types of towns made more of a difference for national election turnout than for municipal turnout. Compositional models of average presidential turnout, however, show that demographic characteristics accounted for more of the variance in presidential election turnout than the municipal types. The same compositional model that explained 11 per cent of the variation in municipal turnout accounted for 54 per cent of the variance in presidential turnout in the ordinary least squares model, compared to 37 per cent for the municipal types (see Appendix Table A2.4). A maximum-likelihood version of the same compositional model accounted for 51 per cent of the total variance (see Table 2.4), which is far more than the 27 per cent explained by the municipal types.

As the municipal types themselves suggest, stronger mobilisation among more privileged communities by comparison with disadvantaged ones has produced a much more systematic socio-economic bias in presidential elections than in municipal elections. General socio-economic status boosts presidential voting more than any other attribute of communities. Socio-economic hardship depresses presidential turnout the most of any explanatory variable. Residents over age sixty exert a similarly strong, positive influence on turnout as in municipal elections; foreign-born residents show a similarly significant negative influence. With both socio-economic status and the proportion of immigrants controlled, the proportion of Latino residents switches from negative to a significant positive influence on turnout.

If the institutional and spatial features of localities account for less of the variance than in municipal elections, these influences still add significant explanatory power. A separate ordinary least squares model of place-linked variables accounts for 2 per cent more of the variance than the municipal types (or 39 per cent) (see Appendix Table A2.4). Adding local contextual variables to the compositional model also raises the explained variance by 7 per cent to 61 per cent. Institutional and spatial variables supplant part of the explanatory power of hardship, socio-economic status and immigrants. In the multilevel maximum likelihood models (see Table 2.4), state and metropolitan level variables add further to these effects. These models explain 78–80 per cent of the metropolitan and state variance, compared to only 27 per cent for the compositional model, as well as 4–5 per cent more of the local variance. The total explained variance, at 63 per cent, rises to 11 per cent higher than for the compositional variables alone.

Local government institutions, though almost entirely neglected in the literature on presidential election turnout, prove one of the strongest state-level influences. Municipal government activity has a similarly significant effect on the much higher, more varied turnout rates in presidential elections to its effect on

*Table 2.4: Multilevel models of presidential turnout*

| | Compositional | | Contextual | | Full model | | Full, cross-level effects | |
|---|---|---|---|---|---|---|---|---|
| | **B** | **t** | **B** | **t** | **B** | **t** | **B** | **t** |
| Constant | *0.60* | *49.04* | *0.62* | *18.84* | *0.54* | *39.73* | *0.55* | *38.07* |
| *State level variables* | | | | | | | | |
| Municipal capacity (state) | | | | | **0.00** | **3.96** | **0.00** | **3.74** |
| Battleground states, 2000–4 | | | | | **0.08** | **5.07** | **0.08** | **4.90** |
| *Compositional variables* | | | | | | | | |
| Foreign-born | −0.22 | −7.02 | | | **−0.12** | **−3.54** | **−0.09** | **−2.75** |
| African Americans | 0.02 | 0.98 | | | 0.03 | 1.37 | 0.02 | 1.07 |
| Latino Americans | *0.13* | *4.74* | | | *0.09* | *3.38* | *0.08* | *2.93* |
| Age 60 plus | *0.23* | *6.41* | | | *0.20* | *5.37* | *0.19* | *5.23* |
| Hardship | *−0.49* | *−14.16* | | | *−0.34* | *−9.38* | *−0.33* | *−9.18* |
| Socio-economic status | *0.40* | *21.25* | | | *0.36* | *17.65* | *0.36* | *17.42* |
| *Contextual and cross-level variables* | | | | | | | | |
| Partisan local elections | | | −0.04 | −1.78 | **−0.03** | **−2.09** | **−0.03** | **−2.14** |
| Local elections in general election year | | | **0.02** | **2.62** | *0.02* | *3.08* | *0.02* | *3.03* |
| Local elections in general election month | | | 0.00 | 0.18 | 0.01 | 1.15 | *0.01* | *1.90* |
| Local political diversity | | | 0.00 | -0.07 | **0.01** | **2.15** | **0.03** | **2.80** |
|   Local government capacity (state) | | | | | | | **0.00** | **−1.98** |
| National political diversity | | | 0.00 | 0.13 | −0.03 | −1.63 | **−0.11** | **−2.95** |
|   Local government capacity (state) | | | | | | | **0.00** | **2.32** |
| Homeowners | | | *0.33* | *14.31* | *0.13* | *5.92* | *0.12* | *5.52* |
| Commuters (local) | | | 0.00 | 0.20 | 0.01 | -0.68 | *0.14* | *3.29* |
|   Commuters (metropolitan) | | | | | | | −0.30 | −3.50 |
| Residential mobility | | | −0.05 | −1.19 | *−0.10* | *−2.90* | *−0.12* | *−3.56* |
| Housing since 1980 | | | 0.00 | 0.17 | 0.02 | 1.20 | 0.02 | 0.95 |
| Occupational diversity (Simpson index) | | | *−0.16* | *−17.84* | **−0.02** | **−2.23** | **−0.02** | **−2.24** |
| Population (log) | | | *−0.02* | *−3.27* | *−0.02* | *−3.42* | 0.08 | 1.56 |
|   Metropolitan population (log) | | | | | | | *−0.01* | *−1.90* |
| Population density (log) | | | **0.01** | **2.04** | **0.01** | **2.35** | *0.01* | *1.67* |
| *Control* | | | | | | | | |
| Institutionalised population | *−0.60* | *−11.47* | *−0.54* | *−9.28* | *−0.54* | *−10.36* | *−0.53* | *−10.26* |
| Chi-square: Local & metro | | 91.814 | | 69.428 | | 44.696 | | 45.386 |
|   State | | 89.92 | | 1191.8 | | 30.273 | | 32.808 |
| N: Local | | 1432 | | 1432 | | 1432 | | 1432 |
|   Metropolitan | | 12 | | 12 | | 12 | | 12 |
|   State | | 12 | | 12 | | 12 | | 12 |
| p: rows (metropolitan and local) | | 0 | | 0 | | 0 | | 0 |
| p: columns (state) | | 0 | | 0 | | 0.001 | | 0 |
| Variance explained | | | | | | | | |
|   Local | | 55% | | 46% | | 59% | | 60% |
|   Metro/state | | 27% | | (negative) | | 80% | | 78% |
|   Total | | 51% | | (negative) | | 63% | | 63% |
| Deviance | | -3420 | | -3130 | | -3570 | | -3599 |

*Notes:* Coefficients are full maximum likelihood estimates using HCM2 module in HLM. For italicised coefficients, p<0.10; for boldface coefficients, p<0.05; for boldface italicised coefficients, p<0.01.

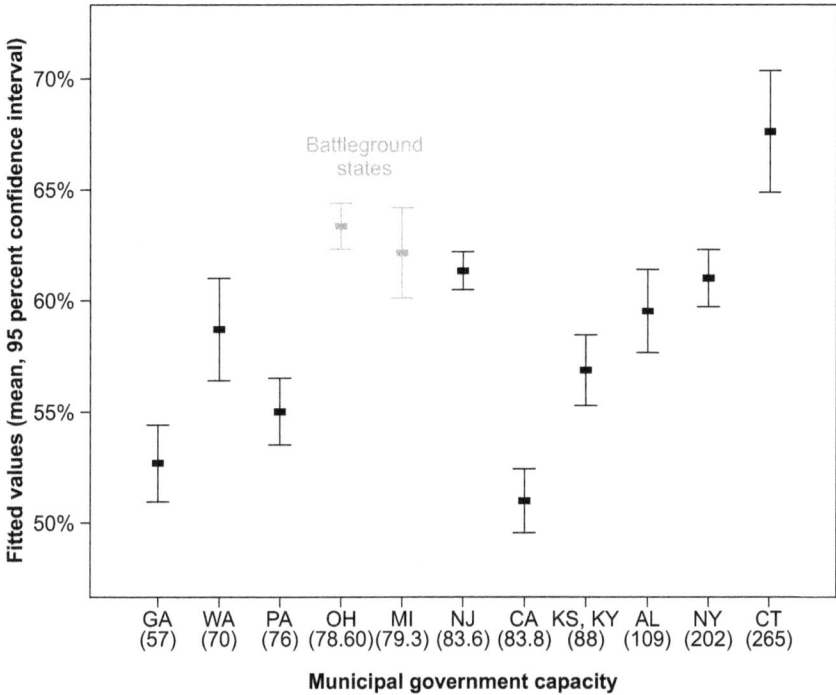

*Figure 2.3: State-level differences in presidential election turnout, by differences in municipal government capacity*

municipal turnout rates. State-by-state examination showed this to be a result of a general pattern (see Figure 2.3).[13] More active local governments may simply make it easier for citizens to vote, or municipal participation may promote political cultures more supportive of participation in any kind of elections. In the state of Connecticut, where municipal government is strongest, presidential turnout is highest. In Georgia and Pennsylvania, the states with two of the three weakest municipal governments, presidential turnout lags the levels elsewhere.

The competitiveness of presidential elections at the state level had one of the most systematic influences on presidential turnout. Presidential elections in the United States are won in the Electoral College, where votes are allocated by state on a winner-take-all basis. National parties and campaigns have therefore found it advantageous to focus voter mobilisation on highly competitive states like Ohio and Michigan, which averaged generally higher turnout (see Figure 2.4). Other states with less municipal government activity and higher average turnout, such

---

13. Further analysis of presidential turnout in all fifty states confirmed significant correlations with local government capacity in 1996 (0.32, $p < 0.05$), but weakening relationships in 2000 (0.27, $p < 0.10$), and 2004 (0.17). Since Stephens and Wikstrom's measure of capacity dates from 1991, this may be the result of changing capacity as well as other factors.

as Washington state, Pennsylvania and New Jersey, also had been considered battleground states for at least part of the campaign in one or more of the three presidential elections.

Other local institutional influences and political dynamics that promote turnout in municipal elections also appear to have spillover effects on presidential turnout. Where local elections take place in the same year as national general elections and, to a lesser degree, when they occur at the same time, the resulting local mobilisation raises national as well as municipal turnout rates. Partisan local elections detract almost as much from national turnout as from municipal turnout. Local political competitiveness raises presidential turnout significantly, although the effect is less pronounced than on turnout in municipal elections. Partisan homogeneity also exerts a similarly weak positive effect on presidential and municipal elections. Stronger state-level patterns of municipal activity limit these effects from national and local political diversity.

In elections to the highest national office, national party and media campaigns and widespread voter attention might be expected to create a more attenuated relationship than in municipal elections between turnout and spatial features of metropolitan places. The only measure of ties to the local community that depresses presidential turnout is residential mobility, indicated by the proportion of residents who moved in the last five years. Unlike in municipal elections, neither commuting nor new housing in a community has a negative linear effect. A cross level variable reveals negative influences from local commuting in those larger metropolitan areas with higher commuting rates. Elsewhere, however, commuting actually promotes higher presidential turnout. Ties to the locality where voters live clearly make less of a difference for voter mobilisation in presidential elections than in municipal elections.

The size of communities also has different consequences. The negative effects of larger city size for voter participation, although still significant, are considerably lower than in municipal elections ($B=-0.02$ versus $B=-0.05$). A cross-level variable shows this effect to be especially limited in smaller metropolitan areas. With the control for population size included, population density even bears a significant positive relation to presidential voter turnout. Clearly, urbanised communities have turned out in presidential elections to a degree that is nowhere evident in local elections.

In presidential elections, the much higher turnout is also much more skewed in favour of metropolitan communities with greater socio-economic advantages. Spatial features of metropolitan communities that US analysts have generally found to suppress participation matter less for presidential elections than for municipal elections. Some aspects of places that discourage municipal turnout, such as urban density, may even help promote higher turnout in the most salient national elections. Features of local politics with no direct relation to national elections, such as competitive local political cultures and stronger local governments, also account to a surprising degree for national as well as local turnout. In all these ways, metropolitanisation remains a significant influence on voter mobilisation in even the most nationalised US elections.

### Sources of delocalisation: comparing presidential and local turnout

Models of the turnout gap offer a clear view of the contrasts in mobilisation between the two levels, and reconfirm the importance of local, state and metropolitan contexts (see Table 2.5).

Compositional variables account for 18 per cent of the variation in the turnout gap within metropolitan areas, and 17 per cent of overall variation. Class rather than race or immigration accounts for most of these compositional effects. National elections mobilise the most privileged communities most consistently and poor communities significantly less than others. Because immigrant communities vote less in both types of elections, their presence reduces the turnout gap. Controlling for class, African American and Latino communities both mobilise significantly more in national than in local elections.

The contextual variables account for most of the explained variation. Concurrent elections and local political competition, by raising levels of participation in local elections, reduce the turnout gap. Variables for partisan elections, townships and election of the mayor confirm effects already evident in the municipal models. Attributes of metropolitan communities clearly affect mobilisation in national elections in different ways from in local elections. As the indicator for municipal population demonstrates, urbanised communities participate more intensively in national elections, and remain more demobilised in municipal contests. Commuting, rather than impede all voter participation, contributes to delocalisation. It disengages citizens more from municipal politics than from national election campaigns and media coverage. Similarly, newly-settled communities with large proportions of recent construction remain more actively engaged in national elections than in local elections.

Place matters for both local and presidential electoral participation, but in ways that are both distinct and interrelated. For voting in municipal elections, state and local institutions and community characteristics matter the most. Even in national elections these factors help to account for variations in turnout that correlate with demographic composition, and also explain a significant amount of additional variation. The growing mobilisation in presidential elections, especially among affluent and middle-class suburban communities, contrasts with the persistent widespread disengagement in the elections within urban and suburban communities. This delocalisation is a consequence of weak, fragmented local government, of limited local political contestation, of urban anonymity, and of attenuated ties among metropolitan residents to their local communities. Despite this growing disjuncture between national and local participation, mobilisation at the two levels remains interrelated. Local institutions and electoral dynamics that promote higher levels of electoral participation within a community have frequently contributed to higher levels of presidential election turnout at the same time.

*Table 2.5: Multilevel models of presidential-municipal turnout gap*

| | Compositional | | Contextual | | Full model | | Full with cross-level | | Significant only | |
|---|---|---|---|---|---|---|---|---|---|---|
| | B | t | B | t | B | t | B | t | B | t |
| Constant | 0.30 | 17.09 | 0.31 | 14.28 | 0.30 | 14.76 | 0.32 | 15.05 | 0.31 | 19.30 |
| *Metropolitan or state-level variables* | | | | | | | | | | |
| Municipal capacity (state) | | | | | -0.0001 | -0.97 | -0.0002 | -1.87 | | |
| Battleground states, 1996-2004 | | | | | 0.06 | 2.85 | 0.06 | 2.34 | 0.05 | 2.20 |
| *Compositional variables* | | | | | | | | | | |
| Foreign born | -0.05 | -1.08 | | | -0.15 | -3.56 | -0.13 | -3.27 | | |
| African Americans | 0.10 | 3.97 | | | 0.05 | 1.97 | 0.06 | 2.18 | 0.06 | 2.90 |
| Latino Americans | 0.09 | 2.29 | | | 0.10 | 3.05 | 0.10 | 3.04 | 0.05 | 1.87 |
| Age 60 plus | 0.05 | 1.00 | | | -0.01 | -0.20 | 0.01 | -0.19 | | |
| Hardship | -0.34 | -6.88 | | | -0.31 | -6.69 | -0.32 | -7.14 | -0.37 | -8.92 |
| Socio-economic status | 0.28 | 10.17 | | | 0.20 | 7.71 | 0.20 | 7.79 | 0.20 | 9.16 |
| *Contextual and cross-level variables* | | | | | | | | | | |
| Township | | | -0.05 | -5.31 | -0.05 | -5.30 | -0.15 | -6.31 | -0.18 | -9.26 |
| Special district activity, by state | | | | | | | 0.00 | 4.74 | 0.00 | 6.84 |
| Mayor elected | | | -0.01 | -2.17 | -0.01 | -1.91 | -0.04 | -3.53 | -0.04 | -3.99 |
| Partisan margin, US House | | | | | | | 0.51 | 4.31 | 0.52 | 4.97 |
| Partisan elections | | | 0.00 | -0.04 | 0.01 | 0.29 | -0.41 | -2.16 | -0.38 | -2.11 |
| State centralisation | | | | | | | 0.01 | 2.13 | 0.01 | 2.05 |

| | Compositional | | Contextual | | Full model | | Full with cross-level | | Significant only | |
|---|---|---|---|---|---|---|---|---|---|---|
| | B | t | B | t | B | t | B | t | B | t |
| Local election in general election year | | | -0.13 | -14.34 | -0.13 | -16.27 | -0.11 | -12.80 | -0.12 | -14.02 |
| Local election in general election month | | | -0.02 | -1.72 | -0.01 | -0.75 | -0.02 | -1.42 | | |
| District magnitude | | | 0.00 | -0.64 | 0.00 | 0.26 | 0.00 | 0.47 | | |
| Local political diversity | | | -0.08 | -14.29 | -0.07 | -13.88 | -0.07 | -5.61 | -0.08 | -14.40 |
| Municipal capacity, by state | | | | | | | 0.00 | -0.90 | | |
| National political diversity | | | 0.01 | 0.66 | 0.00 | 0.23 | -0.04 | -0.84 | | |
| Municipal capacity, by state | | | | | | | 0.00 | 0.91 | | |
| Homeowners | | | 0.13 | 5.12 | 0.00 | -0.10 | 0.01 | 0.20 | | |
| Commuters | | | 0.07 | 4.60 | 0.06 | 4.00 | -0.11 | -1.69 | | |
| Commuters (metropolitan) | | | | | | | 0.28 | 2.13 | | |
| Residential mobility | | | -0.01 | -0.19 | -0.04 | -0.93 | -0.04 | -0.82 | | |
| Housing since 1980 | | | 0.09 | 4.43 | 0.09 | 4.20 | 0.08 | 3.92 | 0.07 | 4.73 |
| Occupational diversity (Simpson index) | | | -0.08 | -8.39 | -0.02 | -2.27 | -0.01 | -1.13 | | |
| Population (log) | | | 0.05 | 7.86 | 0.04 | 7.42 | 0.02 | 0.25 | 0.03 | 7.31 |
| Metropolitan population (log) | | | | | | | 0.00 | 0.36 | | |
| Population density (log) | | | 0.00 | -0.16 | 0.00 | 0.13 | 0.00 | 0.46 | | |

| | Compositional | | Contextual | | Full model | | Full with cross-level | | Significant only | |
|---|---|---|---|---|---|---|---|---|---|---|
| | *B* | *t* | *B* | *t* | *B* | *t* | *B* | *t* | *B* | *t* |
| *Controls* | | | | | | | | | | |
| Institutionalised population | *-0.26* | *-3.42* | *-0.22* | *-3.33* | *-0.24* | *-3.79* | *-0.27* | *-4.22* | *-0.28* | *-4.62* |
| Unopposed seats, Alabama | **-0.40** | **-2.30** | **-0.31** | **-2.02** | **-0.30** | **-2.11** | **-0.31** | **-2.17** | **-0.28** | **-1.98** |
| (quadratic variable) | *0.68* | *2.89* | *0.53* | *2.64* | *0.55* | *2.85* | *0.55* | *2.92* | *0.53* | *2.77* |
| Chi-square: Local & metro | 49 | | 123 | | 375 | | 191 | | 174 | |
| State | 313 | | 114 | | 14 | | 34 | | 23 | |
| N: Local | 1422 | | 1422 | | 1422 | | 1422 | | 1422 | |
| Metropolitan | 12 | | 12 | | 12 | | 12 | | 12 | |
| State | 12 | | 12 | | 12 | | 12 | | 12 | |
| p: rows (metro & local) | 0 | | 0 | | 0 | | 0 | | 0 | |
| p: columns (state) | 0 | | 0 | | 0.12 | | 0 | | 0.01 | |
| Variance explained | | | | | | | | | | |
| Local | 18% | | 40% | | 45% | | 47% | | 46% | |
| Metropolitan/State | 16% | | (negative) | | 16% | | 40% | | 46% | |
| Total | 17% | | 25% | | 38% | | 45% | | 46% | |
| Deviance | -2355 | | -2795 | | -2926 | | -2980 | | -2953 | |

*Notes*: Coefficients are full maximum likelihood estimates using HCM2 module in HLM. For italicised coefficients, $p<0.10$; for boldface coefficients, $p<0.05$; for boldface italicised coefficients, $p<0.01$.

## Partisanship in US metropolitan areas

For the first two centuries of US political history, the main geographic divides in partisan allegiances ran between large-scale regions (e.g. Sundquist 1983; Bensel 1984). Rural regions like the Midwest and West developed distinctive political cultures from the urban, industrialised regions of the East. Well into the twentieth century, legacies from the divide over slavery and the Civil War perpetuated a distinctive party regime in the Jim Crow South (Key 1949). Metropolitanisation and suburbanisation have converged with such developments as the establishment of civil rights for African Americans to reduce these traditional regional divergences. In their place, new lines of territorial political contestation between places within metropolitan areas have arisen. New regional divides rooted partly in metropolitan geographies have also emerged.

A number of recent works have documented significant geographic patterns in partisan voting, especially in presidential elections (Gimpel and Schuknecht 2004; Gelman 2008; Gelman et al. 2009; Chinni and Gimpel 2010), or different relations between demographic patterns and political ideologies in different parts of the country (Bartels 2008). Popular accounts of recent shifts in US political geography contend that voters are sorting themselves increasingly into separate communities and regions on the basis of distinct political cultures (e.g. Bishop 2008; Brooks 2004). Systematic work on these patterns has so far relied on geographic units too large to capture the full dimensions of partisan variations at the metropolitan and community levels. The IMO dataset thus provides the first clear national picture of how partisan cleavages and patterns of partisan competition are rooted in metropolitan as well as regional geographies.

Since the bitterly contested presidential race of 2000, polarisation between 'red' (Republican) and 'blue' (Democratic) Americas has emerged as the central feature of US electoral politics (Klinkner and Hapanowicz 2005; McCarty et al. 2006). One strand of work on this divide points to metropolitan divisions as a primary source. A number of analysts point to a growing partisan polarisation between cities and suburbs, or between the cities of different regions (Sellers 1999; Dreier et al. 2001; Bishop 2007). Survey evidence indicates that the metropolitan segregation typical of many US urban regions has fostered more sceptical suburban attitudes toward the welfare state and toward government in general (Gainsborough 2001; Kaufman 2005). Another survey analysis by Bartels (2008) finds regional differences between red and blue states in the relationship between class and ideology. An ecological analysis of local and metropolitan voting can further illuminate the sources for each of these patterns, and the relationship between them.

The increasingly clear partisan divide between Republican and Democratic electorates in the United States of the 1990s and 2000s (Fiorina et al. 2005) has made preferences between the two major US parties a straightforward, if blunt, test of community preferences for the right or the left. While the ideological spectrum of the US party system remains somewhat truncated relative to European liberal democracies (Budge et al. 2007), more recent polarisation among party elites has reinforced the left-right divide. Both the survey-based IMO classifications of party ideology and the party manifestos' data for 1996 and 2000 placed the Democratic Party around the centre of the left-right spectrum, and the Republican Party significantly to the right (see Table 2.6). In the absence of multiple parties appealing to different dimensions of the ideological spectrum, the shifts in party campaigns from 2000 to 2004 also enable a longitudinal test of distinct ideological dimensions of partisanship. Over this period, as the party manifestos' codings show, the economic differences between the parties converged significantly. In their place, differences over traditional morality, national security and the Iraq War gained in salience.

Analysis of these patterns shows the red-blue divide to be chiefly the result of consistent divergences between different types of localities. The spatial features as well as the social composition of places explain their partisan orientations. Although the effects from local socio-economic composition differ markedly between red states and blue states, these contrasts are also rooted in metropolitan political ecologies.

## Typological analysis

The municipal types reveal distinct partisan orientations of voters in different types of communities (see Figure 2.4(a)). In the urban concentrations and the high hardship minority suburbs – and to a lesser degree in the other high hardship suburbs – the Democratic advantage is decisive. In the affluent suburbs, Republicans enjoy an analogous, if less dramatic, advantage. Middle-class suburbs have become the central battlegrounds of US presidential and Congressional elections. During 1996–2004, these suburbs shifted gradually towards the Republican Party. The trend would shift back toward the Democrats in 2006–2008 and 2012, but back toward the Republicans in 2010.

As the national Republican campaign turned to nationalistic and traditionalist themes in 2004 (Langer and Cohen 2005), the low-density and high hardship non-minority suburbs emerged as the communities most supportive of President Bush. In these types of towns, the Republican margin rose to an average of 16–20 per cent in 2004. This represented a shift from previous years, when affluent communities furnished the strongest Republican support. In 1996, Republican candidate Bob Dole had enjoyed his greatest margin on average (just under 10 per cent) in affluent communities. Over the next two elections, the margin in these settings remained largely stable even as the overall margin for the party rose substantially and turnout in these communities rose. Between 2000 and 2004, surges in turnout in the affluent suburbs of Detroit, Philadelphia and Seattle contributed to falling support for President Bush. Democratic mobilisation in the affluent suburbs would culminate in even stronger support for the Obama campaign of 2008.

*Table 2.6: Ideological positions of main US political parties and their voters*

| | Party manifestos | | | | Voter preferences | | | |
|---|---|---|---|---|---|---|---|---|
| | Left (0 to -50) – Right (0 to + 50) | Economic (Left (0 to -50) – Right (0 to + 50)) | Cultural (Left (0 to -50) – Right (0 to + 50)) | Globalization (Left (0 to -50) – Right (0 to + 50)) | Voter Self-Placement (2004) | Economic Index (1998-2000) | Cultural Index (1998-2002) | Globalization Index (2003) |
| Democratic [1996] | 8 | -1.25 | 6.08 | -0.36 | 4.69 | 5.78 | 4.68 | 4.74 |
| [2000] | -3.6 | -1.52 | 3.65 | -0.08 | | | | |
| [2004] | 8.6 | -1.04 | 4.24 | 0.04 | | | | |
| Republican [1996] | 24 | -0.23 | 5.60 | 0.65 | 6.87 | 6.75 | 5.24 | 5.16 |
| [2000] | 33 | -0.16 | 3.51 | 0.98 | | | | |
| [2004] | 25.6 | -0.40 | 6.70 | 0.59 | | | | |

*Notes:* Party manifesto items. Economic index: free enterprise, market regulation, economic planning, social justice, welfare state expansion/limitation, controlled economy, economic orthodoxy, anti-growth. Cultural index: traditional morality (positive/negative), law and order. Globalisation index: Foreign special relationships (negative), anti-imperialism, military (positive/negative), peace, internationalism (positive/negative), protectionism (positive/negative), multiculturalism (positive/negative).

*Source:* Party manifesto codings from party manifestos' dataset (Budge *et al.* 2007); Voter self-placement and party placement from Comparative Study of Electoral Systems; Indexes from World Values Survey and International Social Survey results (see Chapter 14, the Methodological Appendix to this volume, for specific survey questions and methods).

**(a) All metropolitan areas**

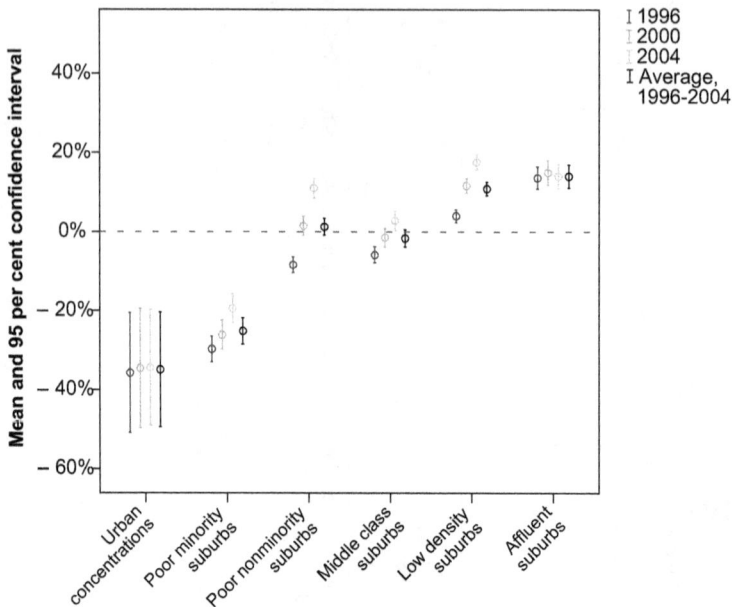

**(b) Red states**
(with adjacent part of Cincinnati metro)

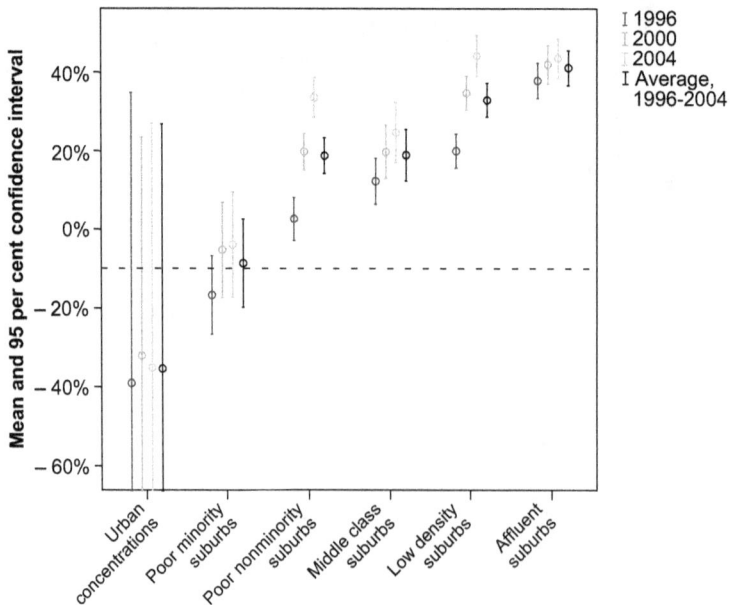

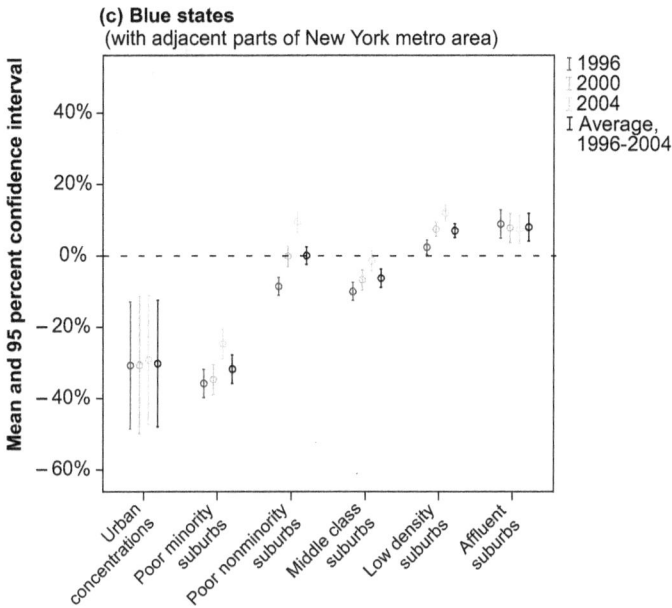

*Figure 2.4: Partisanship (Republican percentage minus Democratic percentage) by type of town, 1996–2004*

Reflecting the blue-red state divide, fully 18 per cent of the variation in partisanship in 2004 occurred between regions and metropolitan areas rather than within metropolitan units. This proportion represented a significant rise of 5 per cent from 1996, but only 1 per cent from 2000. Whether in red states or blue states, the order of partisan preferences among similar types of towns remained largely the same (see Figures 2.4(b) and 2.4(c)). But regional differences in partisanship, combined with a number of regionally-specific local divergences, brought about important ecological variations. In the red states, the affluent and middle-class metropolitan communities maintained a suburban culture of virtually hegemonic Republican support (see Figure 2.4(b)). Affluent suburbs led this trend most consistently. The Republican margin there averaged just under 40 per cent for all three elections, and rose with each election. In the other types of non-minority suburbs, the margin averaged 18 per cent or more and had risen more rapidly. Only the poor minority suburbs and the largest urban centres with the largest minority populations (Atlanta and Birmingham, but not Wichita) voted consistently Democratic.

In the blue states, urban centres and minority communities also provided the only consistently strong margins for Democratic Party candidates (on average, 28 and 30 per cent) (see Figure 2.4(c)). In these states, the suburban vote was split much more evenly. Blue-state, middle-class suburbs gave an edge to Democrats Clinton in 1996 and Gore in 2000, but divided almost evenly in 2004. Affluent suburbs there gave a small, but progressively diminishing advantage to Republican candidates. More clearly than in the red states, the low-density and poor non-minority suburbs stood out in 2004 as the biggest bastions of support for George W. Bush.

Regressions of the municipal types against local partisan voting confirmed their predictive power (see Appendix Table A2.5). With partisan preferences in the middle-class suburbs as a baseline, all the municipal types except for poor minority suburbs registered significant relationships in the expected direction. As with turnout, however, the municipal types themselves account for only a modest proportion of the variation in partisanship (26 per cent in ordinary least squares models and only 19 per cent in maximum likelihood models). Multivariate analysis that can take account of the multilevel patterns of variation is essential for a full explanation.

## Multivariate and multilevel analysis

As the examination of the regional variations has already suggested, state and metropolitan, as well as local contexts, make a difference for local partisanship. The relationship between these contextual effects requires a different form of multilevel analysis from the cross-classified design for analysis of turnout. In partisan voting, influenced by metropolitan media and other common cultural factors, divergent effects from different state contexts within the same metropolitan areas matter less. Within all three split metropolitan areas, the Democratic or Republican margins in different states closely correspond (see Figure 2.5). This continuous pattern enables hierarchical linear models to capture both state and metropolitan variations within a single second-level model based on a total of sixteen units of analysis.

Both ordinary least squares models and these hierarchical models account for more of the local variation than the types of towns alone (see Table 2.7 and, Appendix Table A2.5). As the extensive survey literature on the social and economic determinants of voting in the United States suggests, the demographic composition of communities accounts for considerably more of the variations in local partisanship than the typology of towns. Together, these compositional variables explain 43 per cent of the variation in the ordinary least squares model, and 41 per cent in the multilevel model. High socio-economic status, low hardship and, above all, fewer African Americans and fewer foreign-born residents contribute to a bigger Republican margin in a community. Latinos emerge in the multilevel model as a significant source of Democratic preferences. Only the proportion of older residents is of limited significance.

Local partisanship is much more than simply a reflection of the social and economic composition of communities. In the ordinary least squares and the multilevel models, contextual variables linked to the physical structure and cultural characteristics of places accounted for just as much of the partisan variance as the five compositional variables. In a multilevel model, combined with a dichotomous regional variable for 'red' or Republican states, contextual factors explained fully 51 per cent of the variance.[14] Addition of these contextual and regional variables

---

14. Although a similar ordinary least squares model explained 67 per cent of the variation, this result

**a) Presidential election turnout, 1996–2004**

**b) Presidential partisan voting, 1996–2004**

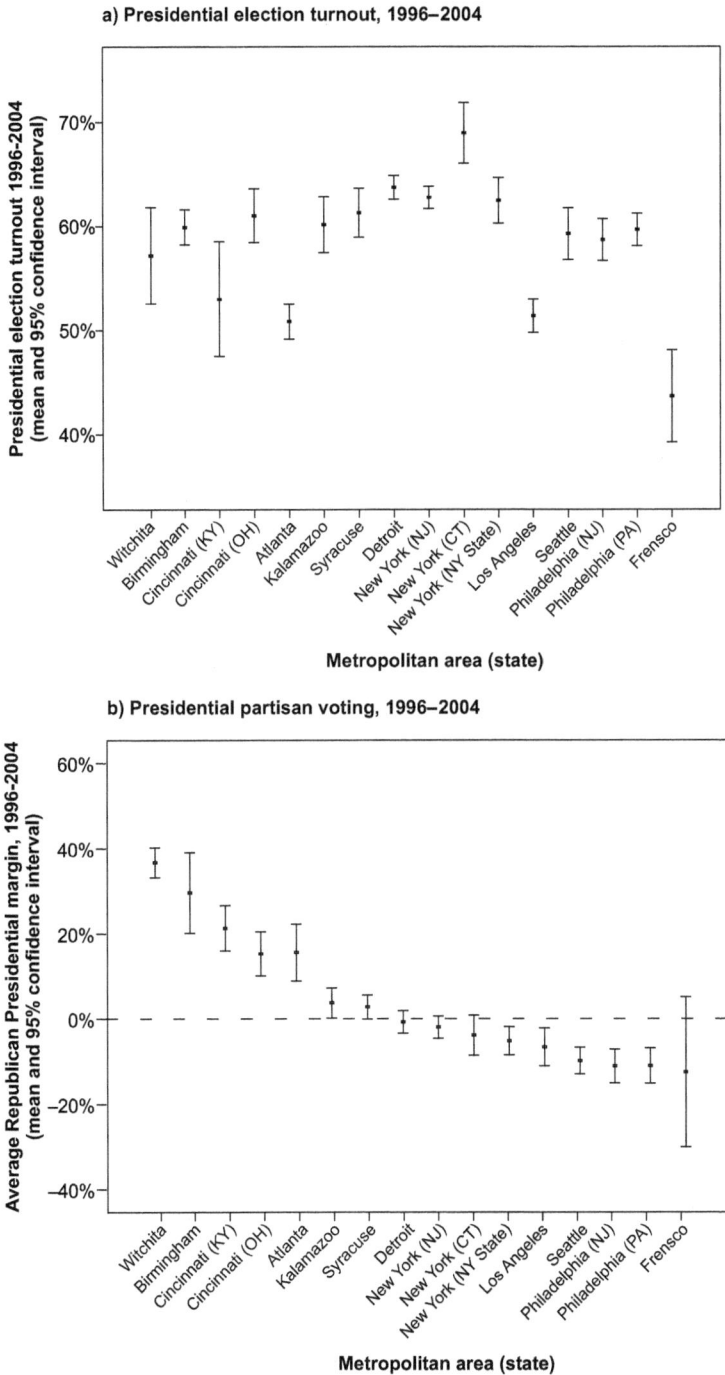

*Figure 2.5: Metropolitan and state variations in presidential election turnout and partisanship*

Table 2.7: Multilevel models of average partisan voting, 1996–2004

| Fixed effect | Compositional | | Contextual | | Full with cross-level | | Full randomised | | Final randomised | |
|---|---|---|---|---|---|---|---|---|---|---|
| | B | t | B | t | B | t | B | t | B | t |
| Constant | 0.04 | 1.03 | -0.05 | -9.28 | -0.05 | -2.54 | -0.06 | -2.93 | -0.06 | -2.94 |
| *Metropolitan/state level* | | | | | | | | | | |
| Red states | | | 0.26 | 22.01 | 0.29 | 7.58 | 0.31 | 9.85 | 0.31 | 9.91 |
| *Compositional and cross-level variables* | | | | | | | | | | |
| Foreign born | -0.76 | -12.28 | -0.47 | -7.41 | -0.44 | -6.91 | -0.36 | -5.79 | -0.36 | -5.86 |
| African Americans | -0.98 | -28.14 | -0.87 | -25.40 | -0.86 | -25.46 | -0.91 | -27.33 | -0.91 | -27.45 |
| Latino Americans | -0.20 | -3.85 | -0.25 | -4.98 | -0.35 | -6.77 | -0.30 | -5.54 | -0.29 | -5.54 |
| Age 60 or more | -0.08 | -1.24 | 0.12 | 1.76 | 0.10 | 1.53 | 0.02 | 0.30 | 0.02 | 0.32 |
| Hardship | -0.43 | -6.37 | -0.32 | -4.61 | -0.17 | -2.33 | -0.22 | -1.28 | -0.18 | -1.08 |
| Red states | | | | | -0.46 | -4.09 | -0.50 | -1.77 | -0.64 | -2.57 |
| (Random coefficient, p) | | | | | | | 0.00 | | 0.00 | |
| (Reliability estimate) | | | | | | | 0.78 | | 0.78 | |
| Socio-economic status | 0.20 | 5.52 | 0.28 | 6.59 | 0.51 | 7.94 | 0.51 | 3.75 | 0.37 | 3.06 |
| Blue states | | | | | -0.29 | -4.54 | -0.32 | -1.72 | | |
| (Random coefficient, p) | | | | | | | 0.00 | | 0.00 | |
| (Reliability estimate) | | | | | | | 0.73 | | 0.77 | |
| *Contextual and cross-level variables* | | | | | | | | | | |
| Homeowners | 0.66 | 13.81 | 0.07 | 1.60 | 0.07 | 1.73 | 0.09 | 2.24 | 0.09 | 2.19 |
| Commuters | 0.03 | 1.29 | 0.02 | 0.86 | -0.20 | -1.96 | -0.42 | -2.84 | -0.46 | -3.16 |

| Fixed effect | Compositional B | Compositional t | Contextual B | Contextual t | Full B | Full t | Full with cross-level B | Full with cross-level t | Full randomised B | Full randomised t | Final randomised B | Final randomised t |
|---|---|---|---|---|---|---|---|---|---|---|---|---|
| Metropolitan commuting | | | | | | | 0.45 | 2.18 | 0.79 | 2.61 | 0.88 | 3.01 |
| (Random coefficient, p) | | | | | | | | | 0.00 | | 0.00 | |
| (Reliability estimate) | | | | | | | | | 0.55 | | 0.56 | |
| Mobility | | | 0.35 | 4.25 | 0.18 | 2.84 | 0.18 | 2.97 | 0.20 | 3.29 | 0.20 | 3.29 |
| Housing since 1980 | | | 0.24 | 5.92 | 0.18 | 5.98 | 0.15 | 4.81 | 0.14 | 4.62 | 0.14 | 4.65 |
| Occupational diversity | | | -0.08 | -4.00 | 0.07 | 3.47 | 0.11 | 5.21 | 0.13 | 5.79 | 0.13 | 5.72 |
| Population (log) | | | -0.07 | -6.25 | 0.00 | 0.30 | 0.00 | -0.04 | -0.01 | -1.40 | -0.01 | -1.33 |
| Population density (log) | | | -0.07 | -4.49 | -0.07 | -5.69 | -0.10 | -4.59 | -0.06 | -1.19 | -0.06 | -3.09 |
| Metropolitan density | | | | | | | -0.03 | -1.85 | 0.00 | -0.01 | | |
| (Random coefficient, p) | | | | | | | | | 0.00 | | 0.00 | |
| (Reliability estimate) | | | | | | | | | 0.67 | | 0.65 | |
| Chi-square: | 1049.1 | | 161 | | 278.32 | | 285.52 | | 352.15 | | 352.66 | |
| N: Metro/state | 16 | | 16 | | 16 | | 16 | | 16 | | 16 | |
| Local | 1717 | | 1691 | | 1686 | | 1686 | | 1686 | | 1686 | |
| p | 0 | | 0 | | 0 | | 0 | | 0 | | 0 | |
| Reliability estimate | 0.985 | | 0.897 | | 0.94 | | 0.942 | | 0.95 | | 0.95 | |
| Variance explained: Metro/state | — | | 79% | | 79% | | 79% | | 79% | | 79% | |
| Local | 59% | | | | | | 66% | | 71% | | 71% | |
| Total | 41% | | | | | | 70% | | 73% | | 73% | |
| Deviance | -1539 | | | | | | -1786.4 | | -1958 | | -1963 | |

Notes: Coefficients are restricted maximum likelihood estimates using HLM2 module in HLM. For italicised coefficents, p<0.10; for boldface coefficients, p<0.05; for boldface italicised coefficients, p<0.01.

to the compositional model raised the explained variance to 69 per cent, or 28 per cent beyond what the demographics alone could explain. Addition of cross-level random effects raised the amount explained still further to 73 per cent.

Several of the place-linked variables contributed particularly strong effects linked to local economic assets and associated cultural attributes. Voting for the pro-market Republican candidates, as both multilevel and ordinary least squares models confirm, has concentrated among places with the most dynamic housing markets and the most mobile residents. Communities where more residents possess the economic assets of homeownership and where lower-density settlement indicates larger residential plots for suburban land owners have also voted consistently more Republican.

In contrast, Democratic presidential candidates performed better in more urbanised, more stable and older metropolitan communities with more rental housing. The full multilevel models also identify a Democratic propensity in communities with more occupational homogeneity. This characteristic is generally a consequence of the predominance of higher-status service workers in the resident workforce, as opposed to manufacturing or lower-status service workers. The ordinary least squares and contextual multilevel models show these post-industrial communities to vote more Republican. Controls for the social and economic composition of communities and regional effects reveal significant Democratic preferences analogous to those in European post-industrial communities (Sellers 1998).

The multilevel models also reveal a non-linear relationship between commuting and partisanship. Although commuter towns tend to vote significantly more Democratic, this effect disappears in the metropolitan regions with high overall levels of commuting.

In addition, the multilevel models demonstrate a cross-level relationship between the large regional differences suggested in Figure 2.4 and the local compositional variables measuring socio-economic status and hardship. In an analysis of survey data, Bartels (2008) has shown that more affluent, better educated US voters tend to vote more Republican in red states and more Democratic in blue states. Modelling of the metropolitan ecological variations enables a clearer understanding of both how and why this occurs. A regional predictor of the slope for socio-economic hardship shows that this variable has a significantly stronger effect in predicting Democratic orientations in the red states. As Figure 2.4(b) suggests, localities with greater hardship in these metropolitan areas amount to isolated hotspots of Democratic voting in a largely uniform suburban culture of Republicanism. A randomised version of this predictor, by allowing the slopes to vary, demonstrates a consistent steep slope in all the red-state metropolitan regions (see Figure 2.6(a)). In other metropolitan regions, the mixed slopes manifest a variety of relationships between hardship and partisan voting.

In the blue-state metropolitan areas of Syracuse, Seattle and New York, the

---

reflected distortions due to correlations among standard errors that the multilevel models are designed to correct.

high hardship communities have trended more Republican than other localities. In these same blue state metropolitan areas, a randomised indicator for general socio-economic status shows the affluence of communities to have a contrary effect on local partisanship from that in other regions (see Figure 2.6(b)). Rather than embrace Republican candidates like most other affluent suburbs, the more affluent communities of these metropolitan areas vote more Democratic than elsewhere.

As these cross-level variations show, the regional differences between blue and red states are rooted in distinct but partly parallel metropolitan political ecologies. In red states as well as some of the blue state metropolitan areas, the more affluent suburbs endorse the majority preferences of the wider region. A similar parallel between the regions marks metropolitan communities with more socio-economic hardship. The most disadvantaged metropolitan communities of the red states have diverged most from the Republican preferences of the wider region. The most disadvantaged communities of the blue states have responded more than other communities there to Republican appeals. Within the more general national patterns, these cross-level variations in socio-economic influences follow analogous regional and local logics.

The two-party results in the United States provide more limited analytical leverage than in multiparty systems to assess different dimensions of partisan ideology in metropolitan communities. However, the shift between elections in the agendas framed by the national party campaigns enables a roughly equivalent test. In 2004, the Republican Party under George W. Bush mobilised voters around support for the Iraq War, opposition to terrorism, and traditionalist positions on such issues as abortion, same-sex marriage and religious values. As Table 2.6 has suggested, the Bush victory of that year turned more on these issues than on the economic issues that dominated the previous two elections (Langer and Cohen 2005).

Although most local effects on presidential preferences remained consistent in 2004 with those in previous years (see Table 2.8), socio-economic cleavages between localities clearly declined in salience. Low-density suburbs and disadvantaged non-minority suburbs replaced affluent suburbs as the Republican strongholds. The linear coefficient for hardship fell to statistical insignificance. The coefficient for socio-economic status fell by half. Commuting and residential mobility also disappeared as significant predictors of Republican voting. In their place, new housing emerged as the strongest contextual predictor, and homeownership gained in significance. These results are consistent with a shift in the basis for Republican mobilisation among suburban communities to traditional values, to the security of semi-rural lifestyles and to ethnonationalist sentiment rather than economic opportunities. The shift in Republican campaign agendas from economic ideology to issues of nationalism and cultural traditionalism enabled George W. Bush to appeal effectively to communities that had favoured Bill Clinton in 1996, and split their vote in 2000.

In the two-party struggle for national electoral dominance in the United States, metropolitan territories now define the main lines of division. As the suburbs have grown to absorb the majority of the electorate, they have become the central

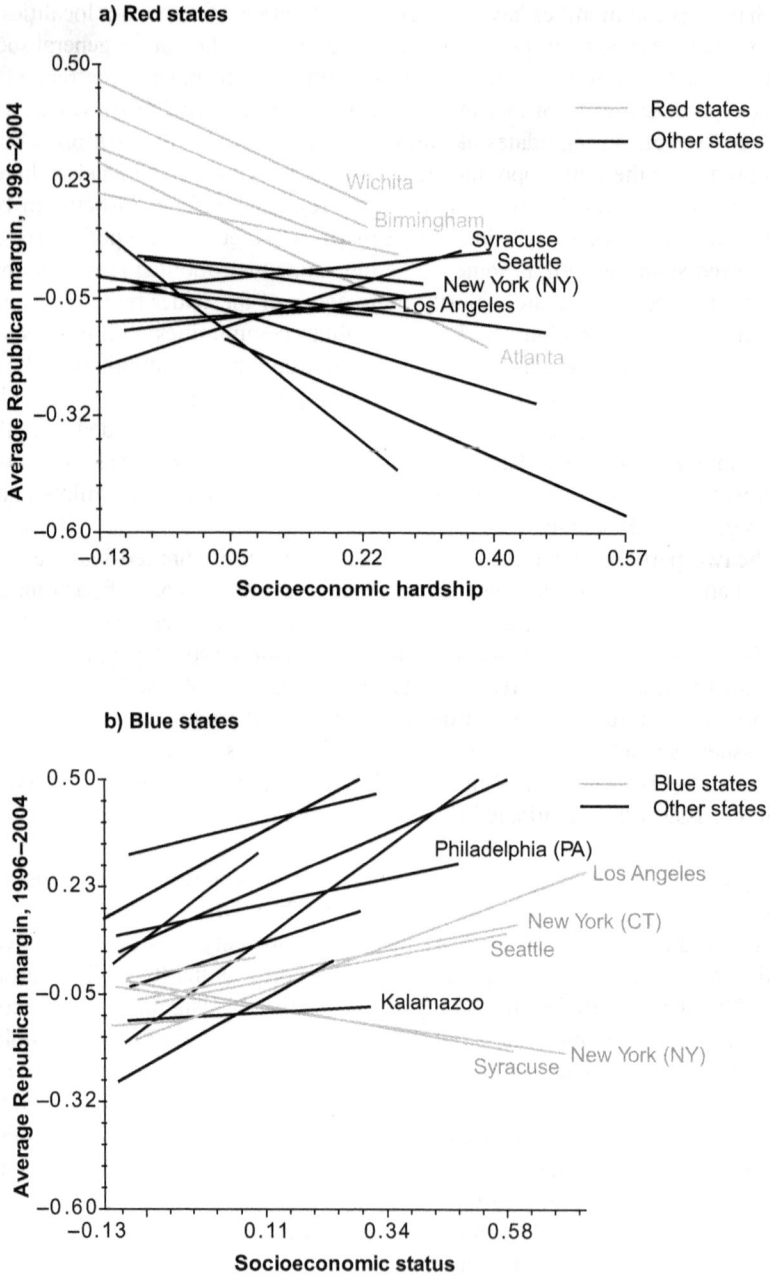

*Figure 2.6: Partisanship, socio-economic hardship and socio-economic status in red and blue states*

*Table 2.8: Multilevel models of partisan presidential voting, 1996–2004*

| | 1996 | | 2000 (Economic index) | | 2004 (Culture, Globalisation index) | |
|---|---|---|---|---|---|---|
| | **B** | **t** | **B** | **t** | **B** | **t** |
| Constant | *−0.10* | *−4.41* | **−0.06** | **−2.59** | −0.01 | −0.25 |
| *Metropolitan/state level* | | | | | | |
| Red states | *0.25* | *6.06* | *0.30* | *7.72* | *0.32* | *7.44* |
| *Compositional and cross-level variables* | | | | | | |
| Foreign born | *−0.37* | *−5.40* | *−0.46* | *−6.53* | *−0.48* | *−6.94* |
| African Americans | *−0.70* | *−19.17* | *−0.88* | *−23.36* | *−1.01* | *−27.42* |
| Latino Americans | *−0.32* | *−5.65* | *−0.38* | *−6.47* | *−0.37* | *−6.64* |
| Aged 60 or more | *0.13* | *1.77* | 0.07 | 0.89 | 0.11 | 1.52 |
| Hardship | **-0.20** | **−2.44** | **−0.25** | **−2.98** | −0.08 | −0.97 |
| Red states | *−0.66* | *−5.35* | *−0.31* | *−2.48* | *−0.41* | *−3.31* |
| Socio-economic status | *0.67* | *9.55* | *0.59* | *8.11* | *0.31* | *4.40* |
| Blue states | *−0.26* | *−3.64* | *−0.33* | *−4.61* | *−0.32* | *−4.52* |
| *Contextual and cross-level variables* | | | | | | |
| Homeowners | **0.09** | **1.97** | **0.04** | **0.92** | *0.08* | *1.68* |
| Commuters | *−0.29* | *−2.59* | *−0.22* | *−1.95* | −0.05 | −0.50 |
| Metropolitan commuters | *0.61* | *2.68* | 0.47 | 2.06 | 0.20 | 0.88 |
| Residential mobility | *0.25* | *3.72* | *0.23* | *3.26* | 0.06 | 0.81 |
| Housing after 1980 | *0.10* | *3.13* | *0.15* | *4.33* | *0.20* | *6.08* |
| Occupational diversity | *0.07* | *3.05* | *0.12* | *5.39* | *0.13* | *6.05* |
| Population (log) | 0.01 | 1.15 | 0.00 | −0.51 | 0.00 | -0.49 |
| Population density (log) | *−0.11* | *−4.47* | *−0.10* | *−4.09* | *−0.09* | *−3.72* |
| Metropolitan density (avg. log) | **−0.04** | **−2.39** | −0.02 | −1.19 | −0.02 | −1.14 |
| Chi-square: | | 220.73 | | 275.83 | | 324.59 |
| N: Metro/state | | 16 | | 16 | | 16 |
| Local | | 1681 | | 1638 | | 1659 |
| p | | 0 | | 0 | | 0 |
| Reliability estimate | | 0.939 | | 0.933 | | 0.946 |
| Variance explained: Local | | 60% | | 63% | | 65% |
| Metro/state | | 70% | | 79% | | 78% |
| Total | | 63% | | 68% | | 69% |
| Deviance | | −1511 | | −1418 | | −1496 |

*Notes:* Coefficients are restricted maximum likelihood estimates using HLM2 module in HLM. For italicised coefficients, p<0.10; for boldface coefficients, p<0.005; for boldface italicised coefficients, p<0.01.

battleground in this struggle. Close analysis of the patterns from 1996–2004 points to common metropolitan ecological trends that will also be apparent in other countries. Democratic voting has concentrated increasingly in urban communities, in diverse, minority suburbs, in older areas and centres of post-industrial services. These are some of the same places where the analysis of turnout showed lower levels of participation in presidential elections. Republican voting has concentrated in suburban areas in transition, in areas of low-density settlement, and in affluent communities throughout most of the country. These places have also recorded some of the most consistent national turnout rates and the highest levels of delocalisation. Even contemporary regional variations between blue and red states reflect the dominant position that one party or the other has established in affluent and middle-class suburbs.

The shift in the Republican campaign strategy in 2004 occurred partly in response to the growth of constituencies in disadvantaged and low-density suburbs, which were susceptible to nationalist and conservative cultural appeals. Some of these same tendencies have furnished new sources of support for the right in Europe and beyond. The shift of these suburbs back to Obama in 2008 gave way to a renewed Republican wave in 2010, and a partial shift back in 2012. The national contest between left and right in the United States thus continues to be rooted in metropolitan patterns.

## Conclusion

In the United States, as early twentieth century regional political divisions have partly converged, metropolitanisation has created parallel territorial patterns of partisan division and shifting loyalties across the country. Compared with earlier divides between large-scale regions dominated by distinct economies and political cultures, the divisions of this national metropolitan political ecology embody a new type of territorial pattern. Even metropolitan municipalities with persistent, starkly opposed partisan loyalties remain interrelated and often closely proximate communities within an intricately interconnected metropolitan space. Moreover, as the focus of political competition in national elections has shifted to the suburbs, many metropolitan communities have maintained divided, shifting and contingent partisan attachments. Characteristics of metropolitan places themselves are often critical to these territorial patterns, and to the closely related local divergences in national and municipal voting participation. Even the persistent contemporary divergences in regional partisan allegiances are rooted partly in distinctive metropolitan patterns. As a final analysis of residuals from the multilevel regressions showed, the multilevel models of these influences captured nearly all the variance reflected in the place classifications and a large amount of additional variation as well.[15]

---

15. The only regression of residuals with more than one significant coefficient for the municipal types or a significant adjusted R squared (0.01) was the model for presidential election turnout. Both

For local electoral participation, the characteristics of places within metropolitan areas are especially decisive. Local institutions, local communities, and ties to the community affect municipal turnout the most. A number of these influences shape national electoral turnout as well. They contribute to a widespread delocalisation of electoral participation that centres in the affluent suburbs.

Characteristics of metropolitan communities have also increasingly defined the divisions between Democratic and Republican constituencies. A pervasive divide separates the Republican low-density areas of metropolitan peripheries from the Democratic urban centres and minority suburbs. Outside the red states, middle-class and growing suburbs have emerged as the central battleground for votes in national elections. The political ecologies of poorer and richer suburbs in the blue and red states have also diverged. Our analysis of these patterns points to the relations between electoral patterns at multiple scales, from local to metropolitan to regional, as an exciting new frontier in the study of electoral behaviour.

The combined findings about partisanship and turnout highlight major electoral challenges for the Democratic Party, and embedded electoral disadvantages for its core urban and underprivileged constituencies. The lower voter participation in disadvantaged communities and urban concentrations has left the strongest cores of Democratic support significantly – at times dramatically – under-represented in the presidential electorate. In the absence of mobilisation among these constituencies, the higher turnout among low-density and affluent suburbs favouring neoliberal and conservative agendas has assured the right an entrenched advantage in US national elections. To counter the resulting Republican advantage, Democratic presidential campaigns have most often succeeded through appeals to middle-class suburbs. The need for suburban votes remains a primary source of the persistent political constraints on the left agenda of Democratic Presidents, from Carter to Obama.

---

minority and nonminority suburbs had significantly lower turnout than elsewhere (p<0.05). This result suggests additional barriers to presidential election turnout in poorer suburbs that are not reflected in the multilevel models, but that have been alleged in some post-election accounts (e.g., US House of Representatives Committee on the Judiciary, 2005). The only other coefficient with a level of 0.05 significance indicated a stronger Democratic margin in 1996 in poor non-minority communities.

## Bibliography

Bartels, L. M. (2008) *Unequal Democracy: The political economy of the new gilded age*, Princeton: Princeton University Press.

Bensel, R. E. (1984) *Sectionalism and American Political Development*, Madison, WI: University of Wisconsin Press.

Bergan, D. E., Gerber, A. S., Green, D. P. and Panagopoulos, C. (2005) 'Grassroots mobilization and voter turnout in 2004', *Public Opinion Quarterly*, 69(5): 760–77.

Bishop, B. and Cushing, R. G. (2008) *The Big Sort: Why the clustering of like-minded America is tearing us apart*, Boston: Houghton Mifflin.

Brooks, D. (2004) *On Paradise Drive: How we live now (and always have) in the future tense*, New York *et al.*: Simon & Schuster.

Budge, I., Klingemann, H. -D., Volkens, A. and Bara, J. (2007) *Mapping Policy Preferences II*, Oxford: Oxford University Press.

Campbell, D. (2006) *Why We Vote*, Princeton, NJ: Princeton University Press.

Chinni, D. and Gimpel, J. (2010) *Our Patchwork Nation*, New York: Gotham.

Dreier, P., Mollenkopf, J. H. and Swanstrom, T. (2001) *Place Matters: Metropolitics for the twenty-first century*, Lawrence: University Press of Kansas.

Fiorina, M., Abrams, S. and Pope, J. (2005) *Culture War? The myth of a polarized America*, London: Longman Press.

Fischel, W. A. (2001) *The Homevoter Hypothesis*, Cambridge: Harvard University Press.

— (2005) *The Homevoter Hypothesis: How home values influence local government taxation, school finance, and land-use policies*, Cambridge: Harvard University Press.

Flanigan, W. and Zingale, N. (1974) 'Measures of electoral competition', *Political Methodology*, 1: 31–60.

Gainsborough, J. (2001) *Fenced Off: The suburbanization of American politics*, Washington, DC: Georgetown University Press.

Gelman, A. (2008) *Red State, Blue State, Rich State, Poor State*, Princeton, NJ: Princeton University Press.

Gelman, A., Park, D. and Shor, B. (2009) *Red State, Blue State, Rich State, Poor State: Why Americans vote the way they do*, Princeton: Princeton University Press.

Gimpel, J. and Shuhknecht, J. (2004) *Patchwork Nation*, Ann Arbor, MI: University of Michigan Press.

Hajnal, Z. and Lewis, P. (2003) 'Municipal institutions and voter turnout in local elections', *Urban Affairs Review*, 38(5): 645–68.

Hajnal, Z. and Trounstine, J. (2005) 'Where turnout matters: the consequences of uneven turnout in city politics', *The Journal of Politics*, 67(2): 515–35.

Jackman, R.W. (1987) 'Political institutions and voter turnout in the industrial democracies', *American Political Science Review*, 81: 405–23.

Kaufman, K. (2005) *The Urban Voter*, Ann Arbor, MI: University of Michigan Press.

Kelleher, C. A. and Lowery, D. (2004) 'Political Participation and Metropolitan Institutional Contexts', *Urban Affairs Review*, 39 (6): 720–57.

Key, V. O. (1949) *Southern Politics in State and Nation*, New York: Vintage Press.

Klinkner, P. and Hapanowicz, A. (2005) 'Red and blue déjà vu: measuring political polarization in the 2004 election', *The Forum*, 3(2), Article 2. Available at: http://www.bepress.com/forum/vol3/iss2/art2.

Laakso, M. and Taagepera, R. (1979) 'Effective number of parties: a measure with application to Western Europe', *Comparative Political Studies*, 12: 3–27.

Langer, G. and Cohen, J. (2005) 'Voters and values in the 2004 election', *Public Opinion Quarterly*, 69(5): 744–59.

Lijphart, A. (1997) 'Unequal participation: democracy's unresolved dilemma', *American Political Science Review*, 91(1): 1–14.

McCarty, N., Poole, K. T. and Rosenthal, H. (2006) *Polarized America: The dance of ideology and unequal riches*, Cambridge, MA: MIT Pres.

Nathan, R. and Adams, C. (1976) 'Understanding central city hardship', *Political Science Quarterly*, 91(1): 47–62.

Oliver, J. E. (2001) *Democracy in Suburbia*, Princeton, NJ: Princeton University Press.

Orfield, M. (2002) *American Metropolitics*, Washington, DC: Brookings Institution Press.

Powell, G. B. (1986) 'American Voter Turnout in Comparative Perspective', *American Political Science Review*, 80: 17–37.

Raudenbush, S. W. and Bryk, A. S. (2001) *Hierarchical Linear Models: Applications and Data Analysis Methods*, Thousand Oaks, California: Sage Publications.

Rose, L. E. (2002) 'Municipal size and local nonelectoral participation: findings from Denmark, the Netherlands, and Norway', *Environment and Planning C: Government and Policy*, 20: 829–51.

Rosenstone, S. J. and Hansen, J. M. (1993) *Mobilization, Participation, and Democracy in America*, New York: Macmillan Publishing Company.

Sellers, J. M. (1998) 'Place, post-industrial change and the New Left', *European Journal of Political Research*, 33(2): 187–217.

— (1999) 'Public goods and the politics of segregation: an analysis and cross-national comparison', *Journal of Urban Affairs*, 21(2): 237–62.

— (2005) 'Re-placing the nation', *Urban Affairs Review*, 40: 419–45.

Stephens, G. R. (1974) 'State centralization and the erosion of local autonomy', *Journal of Politics*, 36(1): 44–76.

Stephens, G. R. and Wikstrom, N. (2000) *Metropolitan Government and Governance*, Oxford: Oxford University Press.

Sundquist, J. L. (1983) *Dynamics of the Party System: Alignment and realignment of political parties in the United States*, Washington, DC: Brookings Institution.

United States House of Representatives Committee on the Judiciary (2005) *What went wrong in Ohio: The Conyers report on the 2004 presidential election*, Chicago: Academy Chicago Publishers.

Verba, S., Nie, N. H. and Kim, J. -O. (1978) *Participation and Political Equality: A seven nation comparison,* New York: Cambridge University Press.

Verba, S., Schlozman, L. K. and Brady, H. E. (1995) *Voice and Equality: Civic voluntarism in American politics,* Cambridge, MA: Harvard University Press.

# Appendix

*Table A2.1: Selection criteria for units of analysis (for all other states, dataset includes all incorporated municipalities)*

| State | Unit Type | Criteria | | | | | Selected |
|-------|-----------|----------|---|---|---|---|----------|
| | | Legally incorporated | 'Minor civil division' in US census | Service functions | Tax, Other Autonomy | Nesting with other units (elections or functions) | |
| **Michigan** | Township | no | yes | limited | limited | (village inside) | yes |
| | Charter Township | no (but equivalent) | yes | some | some | (village inside) | yes |
| | City | yes | no | yes | yes | no | yes |
| | Village | yes | no | some | yes | (inside township) | no |
| **New Jersey** | Township | yes | yes | yes | yes | no | yes |
| | Town | yes | no | yes | yes | no | yes |
| | City | yes | no | yes | yes | no | yes |
| | Borough | yes | no | yes | yes | no | yes |
| | Village | yes | no | yes | yes | no | yes |
| **New York** | Town | yes | yes | varies | yes | (village inside) | yes |
| | Village | yes | no | yes | yes | (inside township) | no |
| | City | yes | no | yes | yes | no | yes |
| **Ohio** | Township | no | yes | limited | limited | no | no |
| | Village | yes | no | yes | yes | no | yes |
| | City | yes | no | yes | yes | no | yes |
| **Pennsylvania** | First-class township | no, but town decides | yes | limited/some | some | (boroughs overlap) | yes (where no overlap) |
| | Second-class township | usually not | yes | limited | limited | (boroughs overlap) | no |
| | Boroughs | yes | yes | yes | yes | no | yes |
| | Cities | yes | yes | yes | yes | no | yes |

*Table A2.2: Definition of variables*

| Variable | Description | Source |
|---|---|---|
| Voting eligible population (for turnout) | Native-born population over 18 plus foreign-born naturalised citizens over 18 | US Census 2000 |
| *Metropolitan or state level variables* | | |
| Municipal capacity (state) | Normalised index based on expenditures and personnel per capita for municipal governments (Census of Government, 1991) | Stephens and Wikstrom, 2000 |
| Special district activity (state) | Normalised index based on expenditures and personnel per capita for special districts (Census of Government, 1991) | Stephens and Wikstrom, 2000 |
| State centralisation (state) | Index based on state proportion of all state and local expenditures and personnel (Census of Governments, 1996) | Stephens and Wikstrom, 2000 |
| Battleground states, 1996–2004 | Metros in states with partisan margin under 5 per cent in two or more Presidential elections (1,0) | Statistical Abstracts of the United States |
| Vote margin in US House of Representatives races, 1996–2004 | Average partisan margin by state in House elections | Statistical Abstracts of the United States |
| Red states, 1996–2004 | Metros in states with an average Republican advantage of 10 per cent or more in Presidential and U.S. House elections (1,0) | Statistical Abstracts of the United States |
| Blue states, 1996–2004 | Metros in states with an average Democratic advantage of at least 8 per cent in Presidential and 10 per cent in U.S. House elections (1,0) | Statistical Abstracts of the United States |
| *Compositional variables* | | |
| Foreign-born | Per cent of residents born outside the United States | US Census 2000 |
| African Americans | Per cent African American residents | US Census 2000 |
| Latino Americans | Per cent Latino Americans | US Census 2000 |
| Age 60 plus | Per cent residents aged 60 or more | US Census 2000 |
| Hardship | Index of per cent of residents in poverty and per cent of workforce unemployed | US Census 2000 |
| Socio-economic status | Index based on per capita income, per cent with higher education, and value of owner-occupied housing | US Census 2000 |
| *Contextual and cross-level variables* | | |
| Township | Township form of government (1, 0) | State and local government offices |

| Variable | Description | Source |
|---|---|---|
| Mayor elected | Chief executive elected (1, 0) | State and local government offices |
| Partisan elections | Partisan affiliations of council candidates appear on ballot (1, 0) | State and local government offices |
| Local election in general election year | Local election in even numbered year (1, 0) | State and local government offices |
| Local election in general election month | Local elections the same day as general elections (first Tuesday in November) (1, 0) | State and local government offices |
| District magnitude | For district systems, number of council members elected from a district; for at large systems, number of ballots each voter casts | Local government offices |
| Local political diversity | Effective number of candidates per seat (Laakso and Taagepera 1981) | State and local government offices |
| National political diversity | Effective number of candidates (based on Democratic and Republican votes) (Laakso and Taagepera 1981) | State and local government offices |
| Homeowners | Per cent of households owned by occupants | US Census 2000 |
| Commuters | Per cent of residents in workforce who commute to work outside their municipality of residence | US Census 2000 |
| Residential mobility | Per cent of residents in 2000 who changed residence since 1995 | US Census 2000 |
| Housing since 1980 | Per cent of housing in 2000 built since 1980 | US Census 2000 |
| Occupational diversity (Simpson index) | Three-component index of diversity: High end professional services, low-end services, and manufacturing | US Census 2000 |
| Population (log) | Population | US Census 2000 |
| Population density (log) | Persons per square kilometre | US Census 2000 |
| *Controls* | | |
| Institutionalised population | Per cent of residents institutionalised in group quarters | US Census 2000 |
| Unopposed seats, Alabama | Council seats unopposed | Local government offices |

Table A2.3: Ordinary least squares models of municipal election turnout, 1996–2003

| | Town types only | | Compositional | | Contextual | | Full model | | Full with types | |
|---|---|---|---|---|---|---|---|---|---|---|
| | B | t | B | t | B | t | B | t | B | t |
| (Constant) | 0.30 | 48.56 | 0.26 | 20.29 | 0.11 | 2.21 | 0.13 | 2.13 | 0.13 | 2.11 |
| Municipal government capacity | | | | | | | 0.00 | 5.23 | 0.00 | 5.15 |
| Affluent suburbs | 0.05 | 5.62 | | | | | | | -0.01 | -1.14 |
| Urban concentrations | -0.05 | -1.91 | | | | | | | 0.04 | 1.76 |
| Poor minority suburbs | -0.04 | -3.94 | | | | | | | 0.02 | 2.39 |
| Poor nonminority suburbs | 0.00 | 0.48 | | | | | | | 0.01 | 1.57 |
| Low-density suburbs | 0.04 | 4.25 | | | | | | | 0.00 | 0.13 |
| Foreign-born | | | -0.13 | -2.74 | | | 0.02 | 0.49 | 0.00 | 0.05 |
| African Americans | | | -0.12 | -4.57 | | | -0.05 | -1.93 | -0.06 | -2.09 |
| Latino Americans | | | 0.06 | 1.53 | | | -0.06 | -1.85 | -0.05 | -1.49 |
| Age 60 or more | | | 0.30 | 5.73 | | | 0.17 | 3.53 | 0.17 | 3.54 |
| Hardship index | | | -0.17 | -3.26 | | | -0.03 | -0.73 | -0.10 | -1.85 |
| Socio-economic status | | | 0.15 | 5.70 | | | 0.19 | 7.52 | 0.23 | 6.96 |
| Townships | | | | | 0.03 | 3.17 | 0.06 | 6.07 | 0.06 | 5.91 |
| Mayor elected | | | | | 0.01 | 0.80 | 0.01 | 1.12 | 0.01 | 0.90 |
| Partisan elections | | | | | -0.04 | -3.91 | -0.05 | -5.26 | -0.05 | -5.23 |
| Local election in general election year | | | | | 0.12 | 17.00 | 0.13 | 18.28 | 0.13 | 18.38 |
| Local election on general election day | | | | | 0.00 | 0.20 | 0.02 | 2.70 | 0.03 | 2.94 |
| District magnitude | | | | | 0.01 | -4.13 | -0.01 | -4.88 | -0.01 | -4.76 |
| Local political diversity | | | | | 0.06 | 10.62 | 0.06 | 11.99 | 0.06 | 11.95 |

| | Town types only | | Compositional | | Contextual | | Full model | | Full with types | |
|---|---|---|---|---|---|---|---|---|---|---|
| | B | t | B | t | B | t | B | t | B | t |
| National political diversity | | | | | 0.03 | 1.78 | -0.01 | -0.73 | -0.02 | -0.75 |
| Homeowners | | | | | 0.26 | 9.79 | 0.14 | 4.58 | 0.14 | 4.55 |
| Commuters | | | | | -0.04 | -2.49 | -0.06 | -3.74 | -0.05 | -3.58 |
| Residential mobility | | | | | 0.02 | 0.38 | -0.03 | -0.63 | -0.03 | -0.74 |
| Housing since 1980 | | | | | -0.08 | -3.85 | -0.06 | -2.73 | -0.05 | -2.31 |
| Occupational diversity | | | | | -0.02 | -3.83 | 0.00 | 0.44 | 0.00 | 0.64 |
| Population (log) | | | | | -0.03 | -5.87 | -0.05 | -8.28 | -0.05 | -8.25 |
| Population density (log) | | | | | 0.01 | 1.28 | 0.03 | 3.60 | 0.03 | 3.63 |
| Institutionalised population | -0.41 | -5.10 | -0.37 | -4.71 | -0.37 | -5.12 | -0.29 | -4.11 | -0.29 | -4.09 |
| Unopposed seats, Alabama | 0.57 | 3.81 | 0.66 | 4.54 | 0.04 | 0.26 | 0.07 | 0.56 | 0.09 | 0.70 |
| (quadratic variable) | -0.75 | -3.15 | -0.86 | -3.73 | -0.25 | -1.21 | -0.27 | -1.40 | -0.29 | -1.51 |
| N | 1602 | | 1598 | | 1435 | | 1432 | | 1432 | |
| F | 19 | | 32 | | 56 | | 53 | | 53 | |
| p | 0.00 | | 0.00 | | 0.00 | | 0.00 | | 0.00 | |
| Adj. R squared | 0.08 | | 0.15 | | 0.41 | | 0.47 | | 0.48 | |

*Note*: For italicised coefficients, p<0.10; for boldface coefficients, p<0.05; for boldface italicised coefficients, p<0.01.

Table A2.4: Ordinary least squares models of presidential election turnout, 1996–2004

| | Town types only | | Compositional model | | Contextual model | | Full local model | | Full model with state | | Full model with types | |
|---|---|---|---|---|---|---|---|---|---|---|---|---|
| | B | t | B | t | B | t | B | t | B | t | B | t |
| (Constant) | 0.60 | 132.52 | 0.55 | 68.24 | 0.29 | 6.15 | 0.50 | 11.13 | 0.49 | 10.87 | 0.48 | 10.66 |
| Municipal capacity | | | | | | | | | 0.0004 | 7.11 | 0.00 | 7.27 |
| Battleground states | | | | | | | | | 0.06 | 8.85 | 0.06 | 8.61 |
| Affluent suburbs | 0.12 | 16.38 | | | | | | | | | 0.02 | 2.73 |
| Urban concentrations | -0.10 | -5.01 | | | | | | | | | 0.03 | 1.50 |
| Poor minority suburbs | -0.10 | -13.61 | | | | | | | | | -0.02 | -2.26 |
| Poor non-minority suburbs | -0.06 | -8.04 | | | | | | | | | -0.02 | -3.49 |
| Low-density suburbs | 0.03 | 4.77 | | | | | | | | | 0.01 | 1.09 |
| Foreign born | | | -0.29 | -9.39 | | | -0.14 | -4.24 | -0.10 | -3.14 | -0.08 | -2.40 |
| African Americans | | | -0.02 | -0.90 | | | 0.01 | 0.51 | 0.03 | 1.62 | 0.03 | 1.44 |
| Latino Americans | | | 0.06 | 2.46 | | | 0.03 | 1.23 | 0.04 | 1.49 | 0.02 | 0.76 |
| Age 60 or more | | | 0.23 | 7.12 | | | 0.19 | 5.09 | 0.19 | 5.23 | 0.20 | 5.40 |
| Hardship index | | | -0.42 | -12.37 | | | -0.31 | -8.39 | -0.31 | -8.85 | -0.25 | -6.36 |
| Socio-economic status | | | 0.38 | 21.47 | | | 0.39 | 19.61 | 0.37 | 19.01 | 0.30 | 12.23 |
| Partisan local elections | | | | | 0.02 | 2.75 | 0.03 | 4.14 | -0.01 | -1.60 | -0.01 | -0.99 |
| Local election in general election year | | | | | -0.01 | -1.32 | 0.00 | 0.87 | 0.01 | 2.02 | 0.01 | 1.97 |
| Local election on general election day | | | | | -0.01 | -0.85 | 0.01 | 1.86 | 0.01 | 1.48 | 0.01 | 1.18 |
| Local political diversity | | | | | -0.01 | -2.48 | 0.01 | 1.55 | 0.01 | 2.51 | 0.01 | 2.58 |

| | Town types only | | Compositional model | | Contextual model | | Full local model | | Full model with state | | Full model with types | |
|---|---|---|---|---|---|---|---|---|---|---|---|---|
| | B | t | B | t | B | t | B | t | B | t | B | t |
| National political diversity | | | | | 0.01 | 0.36 | -0.04 | -2.63 | -0.03 | -2.05 | -0.02 | -1.33 |
| Homeowners | | | | | 0.43 | 17.32 | 0.13 | 5.51 | 0.13 | 5.76 | 0.13 | 5.93 |
| Commuters | | | | | 0.04 | 2.71 | -0.01 | -0.54 | -0.01 | -1.31 | -0.01 | -0.82 |
| Residential mobility | | | | | 0.04 | 1.01 | -0.11 | -3.10 | -0.10 | -3.02 | -0.10 | -2.81 |
| Housing since 1980 | | | | | -0.03 | -1.63 | 0.01 | 0.38 | 0.03 | 1.88 | 0.02 | 1.31 |
| Occupational diversity | | | | | -0.02 | -5.07 | 0.02 | 4.89 | 0.00 | -0.75 | 0.00 | -1.04 |
| Population (log) | | | | | 0.00 | 0.56 | -0.01 | -2.53 | -0.02 | -4.57 | -0.02 | -5.11 |
| Population density (log) | | | | | 0.00 | 0.49 | 0.01 | 1.39 | 0.01 | 2.43 | 0.02 | 2.51 |
| Institutionalised population | -0.62 | -10.81 | -0.64 | -12.78 | -0.63 | -9.41 | -0.54 | -9.91 | -0.54 | -10.09 | -0.55 | -10.32 |
| R squared | 0.37 | | 0.54 | | 0.39 | | 0.61 | | 0.63 | | 0.64 | |
| f | 179 | | 309 | | 72 | | 118 | | 119 | | 99 | |
| p | 0 | | 0.00 | | 0 | | 0 | | 0 | | 0 | |
| N | 1826 | | 1821 | | 1438 | | 1435 | | 1435 | | 1435 | |

*Note:* For italicised coefficients, p<0.10; for boldface coefficients, p<0.05; for boldface italicised coefficients, p<0.01.

*Table A2.5: Ordinary least squares models of average local presidential partisan voting, 1996–2004*

| | Town typology | | Compositional model | | Contextual model | | Full model | | Full with typology | |
|---|---|---|---|---|---|---|---|---|---|---|
| | B | t | B | t | B | t | B | t | B | t |
| (Constant) | -0.01 | -1.23 | 0.18 | 8.56 | 0.00 | 0.06 | 0.01 | 0.14 | 0.03 | 0.39 |
| Red states | | | | | | | 0.28 | 21.93 | 0.28 | 21.18 |
| Affluent suburbs | 0.15 | 8.71 | | | | | | | 0.00 | 0.01 |
| Urban concentrations | -0.34 | -6.85 | | | | | | | 0.00 | -0.06 |
| Poor minority suburbs | -0.24 | -13.77 | | | | | | | -0.02 | -1.16 |
| Poor non-minority suburbs | 0.03 | 1.47 | | | | | | | -0.02 | -1.57 |
| Low-density suburbs | 0.12 | 8.12 | | | | | | | 0.00 | -0.26 |
| Foreign-born | | | -0.89 | -11.87 | | | -0.37 | -5.70 | -0.36 | -5.46 |
| African Americans | | | -0.82 | -19.84 | | | -0.84 | -24.60 | -0.85 | -23.28 |
| Latino Americans | | | 0.04 | 0.63 | | | 0.03 | 0.57 | 0.02 | 0.32 |
| Age 60 or more | | | -0.08 | -1.00 | | | 0.27 | 3.76 | 0.26 | 3.70 |
| Hardship index | | | -0.40 | -4.87 | | | -0.23 | -3.33 | -0.18 | -2.34 |
| Socio-economic status | | | 0.16 | 3.51 | 0.59 | 12.78 | 0.25 | 6.77 | 0.23 | 4.63 |
| Homeowners | | | | | 0.18 | 8.23 | 0.14 | 3.19 | 0.14 | 3.21 |
| Commuters | | | | | 0.32 | 3.93 | 0.02 | 0.80 | 0.02 | 0.92 |
| Residential mobility | | | | | 0.25 | 6.31 | 0.15 | 2.37 | 0.16 | 2.43 |
| Housing since 1980 | | | | | -0.03 | -3.84 | 0.21 | 6.65 | 0.20 | 6.24 |
| Occupational diversity | | | | | -0.08 | -8.44 | -0.01 | -2.38 | -0.02 | -2.53 |
| Population (log) | | | | | | | 0.01 | 0.92 | 0.01 | 0.77 |
| Population density (log) | | | | | -0.10 | -6.85 | -0.07 | -6.44 | -0.07 | -6.51 |

|  | Town typology | | Compositional model | | Contextual model | | Full model | | Full with typology | |
| --- | --- | --- | --- | --- | --- | --- | --- | --- | --- | --- |
|  | **B** | **t** | **B** | **t** | **B** | **t** | **B** | **t** | **B** | **t** |
| F-test | 123 |  | 219 |  | 180 |  | 247 |  | 182 |  |
| p | 0 |  | 0 |  | 0 |  | 0 |  | 0 |  |
| Adj. R squared | 0.26 |  | 0.43 |  | 0.43 |  | 0.67 |  | 0.67 |  |
| N | 1729 |  | 1717 |  | 1692 |  | 1687 |  | 1686 |  |

*Note:* For italicised coefficients, $p<0.10$; for boldface coefficients, $p<0.05$; for boldface italicised coefficients, $p<0.01$.

# Chapter Three | Metropolitan Political Ecology and Contextual Effects in Canada

*R. Alan Walks*

The importance of urban life in articulating political behaviour in Canada has only recently begun to receive attention in the literature. Canadian political discourse and literature has traditionally been preoccupied with understanding regional differences, which are very marked due to the distinct geographies of language, immigration, class, industrial production, the history of ethnic and loyalist settlement across the country, and the vast distances between population centres (Blake 1972; Schwartz 1974; Erikson 1981; Gidengil 1989; Leuprecht 2003). From a country once characterised by its longest-serving Prime Minister, William Lyon McKenzie-King, as having 'too much geography', have emerged countless regional and/or separatist political parties, thirteen distinct provincial and territorial political cultures (and seven distinct provincial party structures), and a host of federal political traditions devised in order to share political power in ways that appease regionalist aspirations. Regionalism has been at the heart of Canadian political culture from the very first federal election in 1867 and, in recent times, has produced two close referenda on the secession of the province of Quebec (in 1980 and 1995). Because of the dominance of regionalist perspectives, intra-metropolitan place effects have received insignificant attention in the literature examining local-level contextual processes in Canada (Eagles 1990; Cutler 2007).

Nonetheless, there is evidence of significant political contextual effects operating within Canadian metropolitan areas. Notably, the residents of suburban areas as a whole, and the outer suburbs in particular, have diverged from their inner-city counterparts in both their political attitudes and their partisanship during elections (Walks 2004a, 2004b, 2005). Residents of the outer suburbs have been increasingly drawn toward the main parties of the right, which in 2004 merged together to form a new Conservative Party. The stark exception is in Quebec, where the suburbs have been more likely to vote for other parties, often for reasons related to language and culture. Until 1993, the citizens of Quebec provided the bulk of their votes to the Liberal Party, followed by the Bloc Quebecois between 1993 and 2008, and the New Democratic Party (NDP) in the 2011 federal election. Meanwhile, residents of the inner cities have disproportionately favoured the Liberal Party (the traditional party of the centre), and the NDP.

The divergence in partisanship that has developed between voters in the outer suburbs and the inner cities is a phenomenon that emerged only since the early 1980s (Walks 2004b, 2005). Such spatial political divergences have occurred alongside the growth and transformation of Canada's metropolitan areas, and the continued metropolitanisation of the country. Between 1981 and 2006, the proportion of Canada's population residing in metropolitan areas (as defined by Statistics Canada) increased from 57 per cent to over 68 per cent, while the proportion living in any sort of urban area rose from 76 per cent to 81 per cent, revealing stagnation and even decline in many smaller urban places. Similar to their southern neighbour, Canadian metropolitan areas are characterised by widespread and increasing 'sprawl' and automobile use, and by growing income inequality between both households and neighbourhoods (Walks 2010). They also reveal a cleavage based on homeownership, like their US counterparts (Pratt 1986; Verberg 2000; Gainsborough 2001). However, unlike most US cities, Canadian metropolitan areas do not tend to exhibit high degrees of racial segregation, nor significantly poor or declining inner cities (the important exception is Winnipeg). Many Canadian cities are instead developing what might be called a 'Parisian' pattern of income decline and filtering of housing within a number of early post-war 'inner' suburbs characterised by above-average levels of social housing, while the outer suburbs continue to attract middle- and upper-income households and the inner cities witness gentrification of varying intensity (Walks 2001, 2008, 2010; Walks and Maaranen 2008). New immigrants are locating in all three zones, however, and as in Paris the poorest immigrants are increasingly concentrating in the declining inner suburbs.

The emergence of new spatial and contextual factors at the neighbourhood level are important in explaining growing political divergences in electoral behaviour, particularly in relation to support for parties defining the left and right of the spectrum (Walks 2005). Spatial political divergences are not due to increasing city-suburban segregation by class, ethnicity or race, which in fact have largely been declining over time at this scale – although not necessarily at smaller scales (Walks and Bourne 2006). Instead, evidence from the Toronto region suggests the main mechanisms producing such a divergence are conversion effects stemming from different everyday life experiences in the two different settings, and the self-selection of residents based on their political sympathies into different communities (Walks 2006). Those with preferences on the left of the spectrum are selecting the inner cities in search of 'community' with others with similar values and/or out of a desire to synchronise their lifestyles to their political values. Those on the right, on the other hand, are moving into the suburbs out of a preference for private space. To this end, it is differences in urban form and lifestyle, related to concepts such as 'habitus' and identity, that increasingly articulate political discrepancies between urban zonal areas, rather than municipal tax rates, municipal policies, or racial or class segregation (Walks 2007).

The research described above provides much insight into potential neighbourhood effects operating on political preferences in metropolitan Canada. However, that research has been focused on a smaller set of the largest metropolitan regions, while important shifts occurring since the year 2000 have yet to be explored. It is not yet clear whether neighbourhood effects remain strong after controlling for socio-economic differences between metropolitan areas, or how electoral behaviour might vary across different types of communities within the same zones. Furthermore, we do not yet know how place of residence might effect electoral turnout, and very little research has dealt with place effects in the context of municipal elections, partly because the data is very difficult to compile and most municipal elections in Canada remain officially non-partisan.

This chapter fills these gaps through analysis of eleven of the largest metropolitan areas representing each major region in Canada. The chapter analyses the effects of contextual factors on differential levels of electoral turnout and compares the relative importance of social composition and spatial effects between federal and municipal elections. It then examines changes in the importance of compositional and contextual factors operating on partisanship and ideological positions related to globalisation, economic policy, and sociocultural attitudes, in federal elections. The focus is on results from the 1980 and 2006 federal elections across the eleven major metropolitan areas at the level of the electoral district/ constituency – called 'ridings' in Canada – and on municipal elections across the three largest metropolitan regions in 2005/2006. Socio-demographic and contextual data are derived from the 1981 and 2006 censuses of Canada. The results demonstrate that Canada fits the pattern of delocalisation in electoral participation, while contextual factors operating at the intra-metropolitan scale are growing in importance in accounting for shifts in partisanship across the urban landscape.

## Political parties and ideology in Canada

Canada's Westminster-based electoral system has traditionally been dominated at the federal level by three main political parties: the right-of-centre Progressive Conservative (PC) Party (Canada's oldest federal party); the nominally centrist Liberal Party, which has won the majority of federal elections since 1896; and the New Democratic Party (NDP), Canada's left-of-centre social democratic party, dating from 1961 (their predecessor was the Cooperative Commonwealth Federation, or CCF, which formed in 1944). Since the early 1990s, however, this party structure has been transformed. In the 1993 election, the PC Party, in power since 1984, was reduced to a rump of only two elected Members of Parliament (MPs) after much of their support defected to two new regional parties. One of these, the Bloc Quebecois (BQ), was formed as a federal vehicle to advocate for the separation of Quebec. The other, the right-wing populist Reform Party, began as a voice for western-Canadian alienation in the late 1980s and evolved into the Canadian Alliance (CA) in an attempt to become a national (farther-) right wing alternative to the PC Party in time for the 2000 election. However, vote-splitting on the right (between the PC and CA parties) continued and, in early 2004, these two parties merged into a single Conservative Party under the leadership of the former CA leader, Stephen Harper, who was subsequently elected Prime Minister of Canada in 2006.

Ideologically, each of Canada's main political parties draws significantly on variants of liberalism. The Liberal Party is associated with a utilitarian and Keynesian welfare-oriented liberalism, although it has by now fully embraced neoliberal policies not dissimilar to those of 'New Labour' in the United Kingdom, while under Tony Blair. Meanwhile, Fabian socialism competes with welfare liberalism and trade unionism within the NDP (not dissimilar to 'old' Labour in the UK) (Christian and Campbell 1990). From the beginning, the PC ('Tory') Party combined traditional British conservatism (and Canadian nationalism) with classical liberalism, and has been Canada's political voice for 'big business'. Indeed, the original name of the party until the late 1870s was the Liberal-Conservatives, but this officially changed to the Progressive Conservatives after it merged with the Progressive Party in 1942. The Reform and Canadian Alliance parties followed the US Republican Party in mixing religious fundamentalism and a focus on 'family values' with Thatcher- and Hayek-inspired anti-state neoliberalism, and this has remained the main ideological focus within the merged Conservative Party. The Bloc Quebecois, leaning towards social democratic policy during parliamentary votes and reflecting Quebecers' more liberal social attitudes, has shared with its provincial sister, the Parti Quebecois, a primary focus on separation and a big-tent philosophy (i.e. work with anyone in pursuit of mutually-shared goals) toward representing Quebec's social and business interests.

Figure 3.1 locates the four main parties contesting the 2006 federal election in relation to their positions on four indices as adjudicated by their supporters in electoral surveys: self-placement on a left-right scale, index of economic policy, index of attitudes towards globalisation, and an index of sociocultural attitudes (lower scores identifying policy preferences on the left and higher scores on the right). Clearly the Conservatives distinguish themselves from each of the other parties with their position lying far to the right of the other parties on each index. Based on the attitudes of their supporters, the NDP is positioned farthest to the left on the economic and left-right indices, while the Bloc is the farthest left on the sociocultural scale, and the Liberals are farthest to the left on the globalisation index.

It might be noted that despite a number of popular political parties vying to occupy the right of the spectrum in both federal and provincial politics, it has been rare for them to promote on a natalist/nationalist or racist platform, and reported levels of xenophobia have remained low overall. Indeed, in a survey conducted in the mid-2000s Canada, ranked as the most welcoming nation for immigrants in the developed world with 74 per cent agreeing that immigration is good for the country (Bramham 2006). While there is some evidence of racial discrimination in the housing and labour markets, and in urban segregation between whites and visible minorities (Galabuzi 2006; Walks and Bourne 2006), political realities have required all political parties to support high rates of immigration and compete for the votes of immigrants. This is despite traditionally low rates of electoral participation among immigrants (Black 2001; Chui et al. 1991). On the whole, parties of the right in Canada have kept to a neoliberal fiscal platform, officially intent on reforming (or eliminating) the welfare state, privatising public assets and services, and reducing public spending and taxation levels, although occasionally also making a scapegoat of 'illegal' immigrants and refugees for taking advantage of Canadian generosity.[1]

---

1. An example of the latter can be seen in the official Conservative Government response to the arrival of a boat of Sri-Lankan refugees in the autumn of 2010. The response has been to blame the refugees, invoke punitive detention for the migrants, and to promise tougher immigration legislation (Youssef and Leblanc 2010).

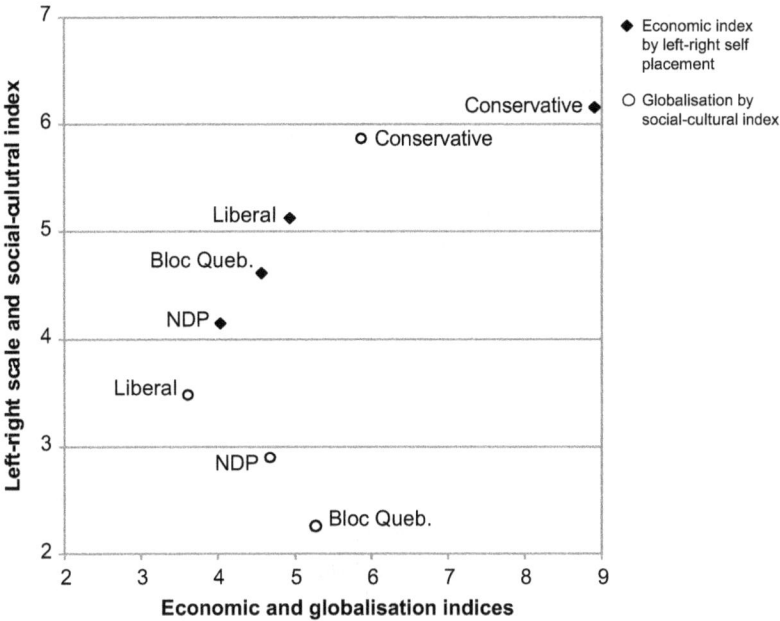

*Figure 3.1: Location of Canadian political parties on the left-right, economic, globalisation, and sociocultural indices*

*Notes*: Each index is calibrated such that higher values indicate higher propensity to lean to the right on the issue, while lower values indicate left-leaning positions. Higher values of the economic index indicate support for neoliberal policies such as privatisation, tax and spending cuts, two-tier health care, support for the private sector, and the idea that the welfare state makes people lazy. Lower values of the economic index indicate support for the welfare state, public health care, public daycare, higher public spending, and the idea that government should reduce income inequality. Higher values of the globalisation index indicate support for free trade, nationalism and tighter links with the United States, as well as the idea that there are too many immigrants, that immigrants take away jobs from Canadians, and that people born in Canada should be taken care of first. Lower values of the globalisation index indicate disdain for free trade, but support for immigration and cosmopolitan identity with the world as a whole. Higher values on the sociocultural index indicate support for traditional family types and values, the death penalty, and confidence in organised religion. Lower values indicate tolerance for children out of wedlock, same-sex marriage, support for women's rights to an abortion, and opposition to the death penalty.

## Measuring electoral behaviour in Canadian core and suburban areas

With a population of just over thirty-one million in 2006 – roughly half the size of European countries such as France, Italy, or the United Kingdom, and about one tenth the size of its North American neighbour, the United States – 81 per cent of whom live in urban areas, Canada is a highly urbanised nation. This chapter analyses participation and partisanship at the federal level in eleven key metropolitan areas (see Table 3.1). These represent eleven of the thirteen largest metropolitan areas across all regions of the country, and are the only eleven

*Table 3.1: Canadian metropolitan regions under study*

| Urban region | Metro population (2006) | Core municipalities | Electoral districts | Municipalities (2006) |
|---|---|---|---|---|
| Toronto (includes Oshawa, Barrie) | 5,620,804 | Pre-1998 Cities of Toronto, York, East York | 46 | 29 |
| Montreal | 3,635,571 | Cities of Montreal, Outremont, Westmount, & Verdun (pre-merger) | 32 | 186 |
| Vancouver (includes Abbotsford) | 2,275,601 | City of Vancouver | 20 | 26 |
| Ottawa | 1,130,761 | Pre-1998 City of Ottawa | 8 | 1 (Ontario side) |
| Calgary | 1,079,310 | City of Calgary* | 10 | 3 |
| Edmonton | 1,034,945 | City of Edmonton* | 10 | 10 |
| Quebec City | 715,515 | Pre-2002 City of Quebec | 10 | 15 |
| Winnipeg | 694,668 | City of Winnipeg* | 8 | 5 |
| Hamilton | 692,911 | Pre-1998 City of Hamilton | 5 | 2 |
| Halifax | 372,858 | Pre-1996 City of Halifax | 4 | 1 |
| Victoria | 330,088 | City of Victoria | 3 | 11 |
| Total | 17,583,031 | | 156 | 282 |

*Notes*: (*) These central cities make up over 90 per cent of the total regional population. In these cities, it is only those parliamentary constituencies covering areas built up before the end of the Second World War that here are represented as the 'core'/urban concentrations. Municipalities do not include Indian Reservations.

metropolitan areas for which there are a sufficient number of electoral districts (ridings) in both core and suburban areas, and for which these constituencies are bounded appropriately to facilitate intra-metropolitan analyses of spatio-political differences.[2] Unfortunately, data for upper-level governmental elections in Canada are not collected, released, nor aggregated at the level of the municipality. Until very recently, the only spatial scale that one could attain aggregate election results for federal and provincial elections is the parliamentary constituency (riding), of which there were 308 across the country in 2006. The eleven metropolitan areas examined here contain 156 ridings, just over 50 per cent of all federal electoral constituencies in the country, and are home to over 55 per cent of Canada's total population.[3]

---

2.  In smaller metropolitan areas, including those of London and Kitchener, there are very few parliamentary constituencies and they bound the region in a sectoral fashion, such that portions of both the inner city and its suburbs are included within the same constituency. This prevents analysis of community and zonal effects in these metros.

3.  The federal parliamentary constituencies (ridings) are designed such that they encompass similar communities, and ideally should hold roughly equal populations. However, federal legislation implemented with the Constitution Act 1982 allows the populations of federal ridings to vary by up to 25 per cent within provinces, and significantly more than this across the entire country.

Because of the existence of very distinct provincial political histories and cultures, the municipal structure of Canadian metropolitan areas differs significantly across regions and provinces. At one extreme are metropolitan areas that contain very few municipalities. This is true of all the cities in the Prairie Provinces, as well as Ottawa and Hamilton in Ontario, and Halifax in Nova Scotia (NS). These involve 'unicity' municipal governments that control all the territory within the region; alternatively, they are typically dominated by one very large 'central city' municipality that houses over 90 per cent of the total regional population, including those living in the traditional suburbs.

In contrast, metropolitan areas in the province of Quebec have always had a large number of smaller municipalities, and thus high levels of fragmentation. The Montreal and Quebec City regions have undergone a series of restructurings involving multi-tiered governance, forced municipal amalgamations and, in 2004, a referendum that produced a number of 'demergers', which amongst other things reinstituted fifteen of the older municipalities as they previously existed on Montreal Island. The greater Montreal region went from containing over 330 municipalities before 2001, to 186 in 2006, making it (still) the most municipally-fragmented metropolitan region in Canada. The Toronto and Vancouver regions, currently containing twenty-nine and twenty-six municipalities, respectively, reveal moderate levels of municipal fragmentation. Many metropolitan regions also contain upper-tier regional districts or regional municipal governments ('regional municipalities' in the Canadian terminology), which have control over a portion of local-area revenues and programme spending.

In a number of the smaller municipalities, particularly in Quebec, many electoral contests proceed uncontested. This diversity of municipal structures and contexts complicates analysis of municipal electoral behaviour in urban Canada, and because most provinces do not collect information on municipal elections but leave this up to the whims of the municipalities, it is often very difficult to obtain data at this scale, particularly outside the central cities (Kushner *et al.* 1997; Hicks 2006). In this chapter, municipal electoral participation is examined and compared among municipalities in the three largest urban regions: Toronto, Montreal and Vancouver – Canada's 'global' cities. It is in these metropolitan areas, containing 83 per cent of our total potential municipal sample, that a sufficient number of municipalities are located for modelling place-based political effects at this scale and across community types.[4]

This analysis uncovers the importance of effects resulting from social composition and spatial/contextual factors in determining and predicting the electoral

---

This results in lower representation ratios for Canada's metropolitan areas. Re-districting occurs roughly every ten years or so, after publication of the decennial census.

4. The Edmonton, Calgary, and Hamilton regions contain municipalities of only two of the six community types being examined in this volume (a central-city 'urban concentration', and low-density exurbs), while the Winnipeg region contains three (urban concentration, low-density suburbs, and an affluent suburb). The Halifax and Ottawa regions are governed by a single municipality that includes all residents, including all those residing in low-density and rural exurban areas beyond the urban fringe (only the Ontario side of the Ottawa region is examined herein).

participation and partisanship at the local level, after controlling for differences among metropolitan areas and the effects of variables at the upper-level. Multilevel modelling (MLM) methods provide for further investigation of cross-level effects between variables at the upper (metro) and lower (riding/municipal) levels on, and these are important in the Canadian case for understanding how contextual effects operate on participation and partisanship. Unfortunately, the eleven metropolitan areas available for analysis in Canada are too few for the MLM methods to produce robust standard errors, likelihood estimates or tests for significance. Thus, in this chapter, linear models are primarily estimated using ordinary least squares (OLS) regression and then compared with the randomised models estimated using MLM. Upper-level variables in the models include dichotomous variables for province of residence, important continuous metropolitan-wide variables and in the MLM models, cross-levels effects. This method allows for the OLS results to be qualified by the MLM estimates, as strictly speaking the OLS method assumes independence between the upper and lower levels.

Electoral turnout and partisanship variables at the district level are regressed on the set of compositional and contextual independent variables that make up the protocol methodology employed in this volume, with the addition of two important variables that have been found to be particularly relevant to the Canadian scene:

- the proportion of residents who speak French at home (in light of Canada's history of two 'founding' peoples and its importance for understanding regional differences); and

- transportation mode share – the proportion of workers who drive to work.

As discussed below, this latter variable has the greatest explanatory effect on partisanship across Canadian communities. At the upper (metropolitan) level, four continuous variables are employed to get at the underlying differences in production bases, level of complexity, population growth and city-suburban disparities among metropolitan areas in the eleven-metro analysis. The variables and their definitions are described in Table A3.1 in the Appendix of this chapter.

Federal ridings and local municipalities can be sorted into the typological categories of core and suburban areas used to classify communities throughout this volume (see Table 3.2). Of the 156 districts in the sample, thirty-two (just over 20 per cent) are defined as urban concentrations. These areas have higher levels of hardship and population density, coupled with lower levels of manufacturing employment, detached and owner-occupied housing, and far fewer commuters who drive to work. In Canada, relatively few suburban communities reveal high levels of disparity. There are thirteen (8.3 per cent) high-minority, high-disparity suburbs identified, most of which are found in the post-war 'inner' suburban areas located within the largest metros where immigration is strongest. In addition to having more immigrants, these areas have higher densities than in other suburban communities (but not higher than the inner cities), higher levels of hardship and the highest levels of manufacturing employment. Although these areas are home to larger populations of immigrants (44 per cent) than the metro average (28 per cent), it might also be noted that only the low-density suburbs have significantly below average proportions of those born abroad than the other categories. There is no statistically significant difference between the urban cores, the middle-class suburbs or the affluent suburbs, in their proportions of immigrants. High-disparity but low-minority suburbs, meanwhile, are more likely to be found in metropolitan areas with lower levels of immigration and in areas suffering from de-industrialisation. Of this type of community, there are only six (3.8 per cent of the total) and their characteristics fall between those of high-minority and middle-class suburbs.

The rest of the districts in the study, more than two-thirds of the sample, fall into one of the last three suburban categories, and all exhibit similar tendencies toward owner-occupied housing, high levels of inter-municipal commuting, the use of the automobile for getting work and low levels of hardship. Middle-class suburbs, with fifty-six districts, make up the largest proportion of communities examined here. They exhibit average levels of immigration, socio-economic status, detached housing, and manufacturing employment. The affluent suburbs reveal very high socio-economic status and few manufacturing workers, but average levels of many other variables. Low-density suburbs are all located at the suburban fringe, and as we might expect, have higher levels of owner-occupied detached housing and are the most auto-dependent locales.

## The shifting spatial ecology of electoral behaviour in Canada

The 1980 and 2006 elections examined here present insightful contrasts. The post-war period lasting from the 1960s through to the early 1980s is often perceived in Canada as a time of stability and consolidation within the party structure, when party-based regionalism had largely subsided and national governance came to the fore. The 1979 and 1980 elections were a contest between three main nationally-representative political parties,[5] and because they were held before both the unsuccessful 1980 Quebec referendum on secession and the patriation of the constitution in 1982, the Liberal party (then led by Pierre Trudeau) still enjoyed significant popularity in Quebec (Prime Minister Trudeau's actions during these latter episodes are still today seen as a betrayal of Quebec by many Quebecers). By 2006, the federal political landscape had undergone significant transformation. The Bloc Quebecois had emerged at the federal level as a vehicle for separation and commanded upwards of half the votes of Quebecers during the 1990s and 2000s, while after a tumultuous fifteen-year experiment with multiple regionally-based right-wing parties, the newly merged Conservative Party had come to be led by those who previously had advocated for western regionalism.[6]

---

5. The fourth largest party, Social Credit, was still somewhat active in British Columbia, Alberta and Quebec, in the 1980 federal election. However, it had largely faded from popular consciousness, did not contest a majority of seats, only attained 1.7 per cent of the vote, and did not win any seats.

6. The Green Party also contested the 2006 federal election, and was able to run candidates in every riding in the country. However, it only attained 4.6 per cent of the vote and did not win any seats in this election.

*Table 3.2: Means of selected variables by community district typology, 2006*

| District types | | Urban concen- trations | High dispar- ity, high minor- ity | High dispar- ity, low minor- ity | Mid- dle- class sub- urbs | Af- fluent sub- urbs | Low- density sub- urbs | Total |
|---|---|---|---|---|---|---|---|---|
| Number of districts | | 32 | 13 | 6 | 56 | 20 | 29 | 156 |
| Proportion of urban districts (%) | | 20.5 | 8.3 | 3.8 | 35.8 | 12.8 | 18.5 | 100 |
| Foreign born (%) | | 31.5 | 44.6 | 23.5 | 29.2 | 28.7 | 12.9 | 27.7 |
| | (s.d.) | (13.3) | (14.1) | (11.8) | (19.1) | (11.7) | (11.5) | (17.4) |
| Employed in manufacturing industry (%) | | 8.3 | 14.5 | 13.1 | 11.9 | 8.8 | 12.2 | 11.1 |
| | (s.d.) | (4.1) | (6.1) | (4.7) | (4.5) | (3.4) | (5.6) | (5.0) |
| SES (socio-economic status) | | 0.91 | 0.80 | 0.85 | 1.06 | 1.53 | 1.06 | 1.04 |
| (Canada = 1.00) | (s.d.) | (0.24) | (0.11) | (0.11) | (0.16) | (0.23) | (0.22) | (0.26) |
| SES Hardship Index (Canada = 1.00) | | 1.56 | 1.66 | 1.31 | 0.98 | 0.83 | 0.68 | 1.09 |
| | (s.d.) | (23.5) | (14.8) | (1.5) | (16.8) | (19.1) | (13.4) | (32.9) |
| Density/km$^2$ | | 6,053 | 4,247 | 2,847 | 1,756 | 1,838 | 288 | 2,625 |
| | (s.d.) | (3,526) | (2,141) | (1,037) | (1,462) | (1,678) | (435) | (2,844) |
| Detached housing (%) | | 21.2 | 29.4 | 28.3 | 51.2 | 59.3 | 70.4 | 49.0 |
| | (s.d.) | (20.5) | (14.2) | (23.1) | (16.8) | (13.1) | (10.6) | (25.3) |
| Owner-occupied housing (%) | | 44.1 | 48.6 | 58.9 | 73.4 | 75.4 | 79.9 | 66.2 |
| | (s.d.) | (12.3) | (11.7) | (14.1) | (10.7) | (13.9) | (6.3) | (17.7) |
| Apts/multi-unit housing (%) | | 61.9 | 51.6 | 54.3 | 30.0 | 25.6 | 14.8 | 34.6 |
| | (s.d.) | (23.2) | (9.0) | (25.9) | (16.0) | (14.8) | (7.5) | (24.2) |
| Population growth 2001–2006 (%) | | 1.3 | 1.5 | 4.9 | 8.7 | 11.8 | 8.9 | 6.9 |
| | (s.d.) | (4.5) | (4.6) | (4.3) | (9.5) | (13.4) | (7.1) | (9.2) |
| Commute to other municipality (%) | | 13.8 | 20.9 | 25.3 | 36.6 | 30.9 | 46.7 | 31.3 |
| | (s.d.) | (10.4) | (14.1) | (23.1) | (21.9) | (23.7) | (7.1) | (9.2) |
| Drive to work (%) | | 47.1 | 56.9 | 66.1 | 72.8 | 69.9 | 81.2 | 67.2 |
| | (s.d.) | (11.6) | (6.2) | (6.4) | (8.3) | (8.4) | (4.6) | (14.5) |
| Moved in last five years (%) | | 49.2 | 44.6 | 41.9 | 42.9 | 42.4 | 38.5 | 43.4 |
| | (s.d.) | (6.3) | (4.1) | (3.6) | (6.9) | (6.7) | (5.6) | (6.9) |

In view of this history, it is surprising, yet telling, that regionalism is clearly more important for explaining variation in electoral support in 1980 than in 2006, and that intra-metropolitan differentiation had grown to explain such a large proportion of the variation in electoral choices (see Table 3.3). In 1980 roughly 41 per cent of the variation in turnout is explained at the regional (between metro) level, but this drops to only 15 per cent by 2006. Likewise, regional differences explain on average 75 per cent of the variation in partisanship in 1980, but this drops to 55 per cent in 2006. The corollary is that the importance of intra-metropolitan (within-group) variation has almost doubled over this period, from explaining roughly 25 per cent of the variation in partisanship to over 45 per cent. Despite twenty years of growing regional political tensions and the addition of a separatist party to the mix, intra-metropolitan differentiation is the most salient growth trend explaining electoral behaviour. The discussion below first examines the factors determining electoral turnout in Canadian federal and municipal elections. The second section analyses the changing metropolitan ecology of partisanship and ideological orientations within Canada's metropolitan regions.

## Electoral participation in federal and municipal elections

Among the indicators of political participation, the act of voting is the easiest to measure. Turnout in federal elections has been dropping from an average of 74.6 per cent over the 1945–1993 period, to an average of only 61.4 per cent through the 2000s. Most Canadian analyses of the reasons for the decline in electoral turnout do not examine any spatial or contextual factors, but highlight the importance of social capital and lack of education, age (youth), citizenship, and the role of democratic institutions (Blais *et al.* 2004; Hicks 2006; Milner 1997; Nakhaie 2006). In Canada, participation is not compulsory and there is no direct enumeration of electors. Instead, enumeration lists at the federal level are constructed from tax filer records and from property tax records at the municipal level. Uneducated young people in particular are less likely to make the effort to get on the enumeration list and in turn to vote. Unlike the United States and some other countries, federal elections in Canada are conducted in a uniform way across the country by Elections Canada. All ballots are counted by hand and municipalities play no role in helping conduct federal or provincial elections. This contrasts with municipal elections, which vary according to the whims and resources of municipal authorities, and there is no standard or universal method by which municipal votes are counted and registered.

The 1980 election is notable for taking place only nine months after the previous (1979) election. Turnout declined substantially between these two elections, from 75.7 per cent (the norm since 1945), to 69.3 per cent, with the drop popularly blamed on the fact that the election took place so soon after the previous election and the fact it was held in the middle of a February cold snap. The 2006 election registers a similar turnout rate at 64.7 per cent of eligible voters. It was conducted at the end of January and followed the collapse of an eighteen-month Liberal minority government beset by a government 'sponsorship' scandal (on the latter, see Gidengil *et al.* 2006; Pammett and Dornan 2004). Analysis of the two federal elections suggests that many more factors affected electoral participation in 1980 than in 2006, with far more of the variation in turnout explained in the earlier election (see Table 3.4). Areas with more children, immigrants, French speakers, tenants, population growth, and higher rates of turnover, were all less likely to participate, as were Albertans, as many in Alberta were disenchanted and stayed away from the ballot boxes after the PC leader at the time, Prime Minister Joe Clark, broke a promise and imposed a gasoline tax.

Unlike in 1980, there is only one contextual variable – homeownership – op-

*Table 3.3: Analysis of within and between-metro variance in turnout and partisanship in federal elections*

| | 1980 Federal election | | | | | 2006 Federal election | | | | |
| --- | --- | --- | --- | --- | --- | --- | --- | --- | --- | --- |
| Turnout | Sum of Squares | df | % Vari-ance | F | Sig. | Sum of Squares | df | % Vari-ance | F | Sig. |
| Between groups | 3487.565 | 10 | 40.9 | 8.308 | 0.000 | 592.054 | 10 | 15.2 | 2.599 | 0.006 |
| Within groups | 5037.486 | 120 | 59.1 | | | 3302.696 | 145 | 84.8 | | |
| Total | 8525.052 | 130 | | | | 3894.750 | 155 | | | |
| **Partisanship** | | | | | | | | | | |
| *NDP* | | | | | | | | | | |
| Between groups | 11586.228 | 10 | 64.8 | 22.096 | 0.000 | 11132.22 | 10 | 46.6 | 12.640 | 0.000 |
| Within groups | 6292.199 | 120 | 35.2 | | | 12770.56 | 145 | 53.4 | | |
| Total | 17878.427 | 130 | | | | 23902.79 | 155 | | | |
| *Liberal* | | | | | | | | | | |
| Between groups | 44950.763 | 10 | 83.7 | 61.679 | 0.000 | 22252.69 | 10 | 51.2 | 15.241 | 0.000 |
| Within groups | 8745.446 | 120 | 16.3 | | | 21171.37 | 145 | 48.7 | | |
| Total | 53696.209 | 130 | | | | 43424.06 | 155 | | | |
| *Conservative/ PC* | | | | | | | | | | |
| Between groups | 36076.105 | 10 | 75.4 | 36.819 | 0.000 | 27680.16 | 10 | 66.2 | 28.414 | 0.000 |
| Within groups | 11757.944 | 120 | 24.6 | | | 14125.31 | 145 | 33.7 | | |
| Total | 47834.050 | 130 | | | | 41805.47 | 155 | | | |
| *Bloc Quebecois (BQ)* | | | | | | | | | | |
| Between groups | n/a | | | | | 125.84 | 1 | 1.6 | 0.73526 | 0.386 |
| Within groups | | | | | | 8200.61 | 43 | 98.4 | | |
| Total | | | | | | 8326.45 | 44 | | | |

erating on the propensity to participate in 2006. Other effects involve the negative coefficient for immigrant concentration and for residing in the province of Quebec (where many Liberals stayed home out of disenchantment with politics due to the scandal). However, there are significant positive upper-level effects related to population size and city-suburban disparity, and negative effects associated with manufacturing employment, while significant cross-level effects of the latter two also affect the slopes of the lower-level manufacturing and population density variables. The randomised slopes presented in Figure 3.2 demonstrate the relationship between electoral participation and both population density and immigrant concentration. Interestingly, population density has a dampening effect on turnout in Quebec (where higher-density areas are more likely to house both immigrants and the aforementioned disenchanted Liberal supporters) and in de-industrialising cities with declining inner cores. Density has the largest positive effects meanwhile in Toronto, Vancouver, and Ottawa, three cities experiencing extensive gentrification of their inner cores (Figure 3.2a). Figure 3.2(b), meanwhile, demonstrates that while the presence of those born abroad reduces the local propensity to participate, the effect is weaker in those metropolitan areas containing the largest immigrant communities, Toronto and Vancouver.

In this chapter, the strength and direction of both compositional and contextual effects on electoral participation in federal elections is compared with those in municipal elections held in 2005 and 2006 in the three largest cities: Montreal, Toronto, and Vancouver (MTV). Turnout in Canadian municipal elections is notably low, rarely attracting the same level of attention as their federal or provincial counterparts. The literature suggests one reason for this is found in the lack of institutional continuity between electoral systems at upper levels of government and the municipal level, where most elections are non-partisan and even when they are, municipal party structures are completely different from those at upper levels (Milner 1997). In only 39 per cent of municipal contests (in our MTV sample) is the level of turnout above 50 per cent, and all but three of these took place in municipalities within the Montreal region. The average municipal turnout in the Toronto and Vancouver regions is 32 per cent, while in the Montreal region it is 52 per cent. Meanwhile, in a full seventy-one of the municipal elections in the Montreal region, or 43 per cent, the candidates were acclaimed.

It might be seen as ironic that Quebec province has such a low degree of local-level electoral competition but the highest municipal turnouts. Higher electoral participation at all levels of government, but particularly at the municipal scale, is part of the political culture in the province of Quebec, and has been explained in relation to higher levels of social capital in that province (Nakhaie 2006). It is notable that residents of the Montreal region hardly differ from their Toronto and Vancouver counterparts in their levels of federal participation, but significantly in their propensity to vote in municipal elections.

Table 3.5 suggests that when it comes to electoral participation, a much larger number of compositional and contextual factors operate at the local scale in municipal elections than in national elections. Indeed, there are only two local-level variables that remain significant in the OLS models estimating turnout in the

Table 3.4: Models of electoral turnout, Canadian national elections

| | 1980 | | | | | 2006 | | | | |
|---|---|---|---|---|---|---|---|---|---|---|
| | Composition | Contextual | Full linear | Backward linear | Full randomised | Composition | Contextual | Full linear | Backward linear | Full randomised |
| Constant (A) | **149.88** | 107.62 | **110.137** | **116.077** | 123.72 | −128.739 | −107.167 | −241.74 | −12.993 | −613.063 |
| *Lower level variables: (B)* | | | | | | | | | | |
| *Compositional:* | | | | | | | | | | |
| Age under 18 (%) | *0.505* | | −0.383 | **−0.332** | −0.345 | 0.137 | | 0.296 | | 0.299 |
| Age 65+ (%) | *1.066* | | 0.132 | | 0.259 | 0.095 | | 0.466 | | 0.481 |
| Foreign born (%) | **−0.370** | | **−0.419** | **−0.467** | −0.156 | **−0.102** | | **−0.131** | **−0.094** | **−0.126** |
| French at home (%) | 0.028 | | −0.032 | −0.044 | 0.036 | −0.011 | | −0.023 | | −0.022 |
| Manufacturing (%) | 0.039 | | 0.063 | | −0.293 | −0.103 | | −0.083 | | −0.086 |
| SES General Index (Ave = 1.00) | 0.004 | | 0.037 | 0.038 | 0.038 | 1.304 | | 0.612 | | 0.346 |
| SES Hardship Index (Ave = 1.00) | **−13.737** | | **−9.743** | −8.896 | **−9.132** | 0.857 | | 0.837 | | 0.405 |
| *Spatial/contextual:* | | | | | | | | | | |
| Log population density | | −0.001 | 0.001 | | −0.001 | | −0.089 | 0.312 | | 2.098 |
| Population change previous 5 years (%) | | **−0.256** | **−0.218** | **−0.220** | **−0.213** | | −0.115 | −0.133 | | −0.128 |
| Owner-occupied housing (%) | | **0.129** | **0.224** | **0.208** | **0.255** | | 0.082 | **0.190** | | **0.184** |
| Movers in last 5 years (%) | | −0.086 | −0.231 | **−0.256** | −0.269 | | 0.152 | 0.282 | | 0.275 |
| Commute to another municipality for work | | −0.022 | −0.006 | | 0.024 | | 0.024 | 0.034 | | 0.038 |
| Drive to work | | 0.164 | 0.003 | | −0.047 | | | | −0.128 | −0.128 |
| Distance to centre (tri-zone) | | 1.440 | 0.537 | | 0.796 | | −0.015 | −0.127 | | −0.016 |
| Simpson Index (occupational diversity) | | −1.611 | −7.05 | | −9.221 | | 0.13 | 0.124 | | −3.018 |

| | 1980 | | | | | 2006 | | | | |
|---|---|---|---|---|---|---|---|---|---|---|
| | Composition | Contextual | Full linear | Backward linear | Full randomised | Composition | Contextual | Full linear | Backward linear | Full randomised |
| *Upper Level Variables: (G)* | | | | | | | | | | |
| Region – Nova Scotia | -3.718 | -1.895 | -4.757 | **-4.896** | -0.933 | 5.302 | 4.715 | 10.901 | | 28.886 |
| Region – Quebec | -4.349 | -2.676 | 0.124 | **-4.661** | -5.532 | **-14.547** | **-13.374** | **-19.282** | **-11.876** | **-46.558** |
| Region – Manitoba | 2.859 | -1.686 | -7.14 | | 3.325 | 2.93 | 2.492 | 7.775 | | 31.081 |
| Region – Alberta | **-24.912** | **-11.298** | **-13.379** | **-15.579** | **-20.495** | **-11.947** | **-9.801** | **-14.824** | | -30.716 |
| Region – British Columbia | -2.067 | -0.775 | -2.264 | | -0.413 | **-4.352** | **-6.953** | **-7.126** | | 2.445 |
| *Upper–level variables (effect on A):* | | | | | | | | | | |
| Log population (metro size) | -4.879 | -2.626 | -1.15 | **-1.728** | -1.188 | 10.184 | 8.587 | 14.723 | 7.227 | 36.583 |
| Population change previous 5 years | 0.561 | -0.224 | -0.194 | | 0.536 | 1.188 | 0.834 | 1.639 | 0.725 | 4.706 |
| Employed in manufacturing (%) | 0.775 | 0.050 | -0.236 | | 0.057 | -1.372 | -1.475 | -2.134 | -1.056 | -3.581 |
| City–Suburban Disparity Index* | -0.290 | -0.123 | 0.043 | | -0.130 | 0.372 | 0.351 | 0.580 | 0.245 | 1.094 |
| *Cross–level effects on slope of (B):* | | | | | | | | | | |
| Foreign born (on foreign born %) | | | | | **-0.008** | | | | | 0.016 |
| Manufacturing % (on manufacturing %) | | | | | **0.018** | | | | | **-0.036** |
| Population size (on pop density) | | | | | 0.009 | | | | | -0.026 |
| City–Sub. Disparity Index (on pop density) | | | | | -0.001 | | | | | **-0.030** |
| R Square | 0.758 | 0.710 | 0.879 | 0.871 | | 0.215 | 0.180 | 0.252 | 0.197 | |
| Adj R Square | 0.724 | 0.667 | 0.852 | 0.858 | | 0.125 | 0.079 | 0.114 | 0.153 | |
| S.E. | 4.247 | 4.674 | 3.110 | 3.0435 | | 4.688 | 4.809 | 4.717 | 4.614 | |
| Sigma Squared | | | | | 8.864 | | | | | 22.229 |

*Notes:* For boldface coefficients, p<0.05. Cross–level effect of upper level variable on slope of the lower–level variable (B). Higher values of CHSI indicate higher levels of city–suburban disparity (parity = 100).

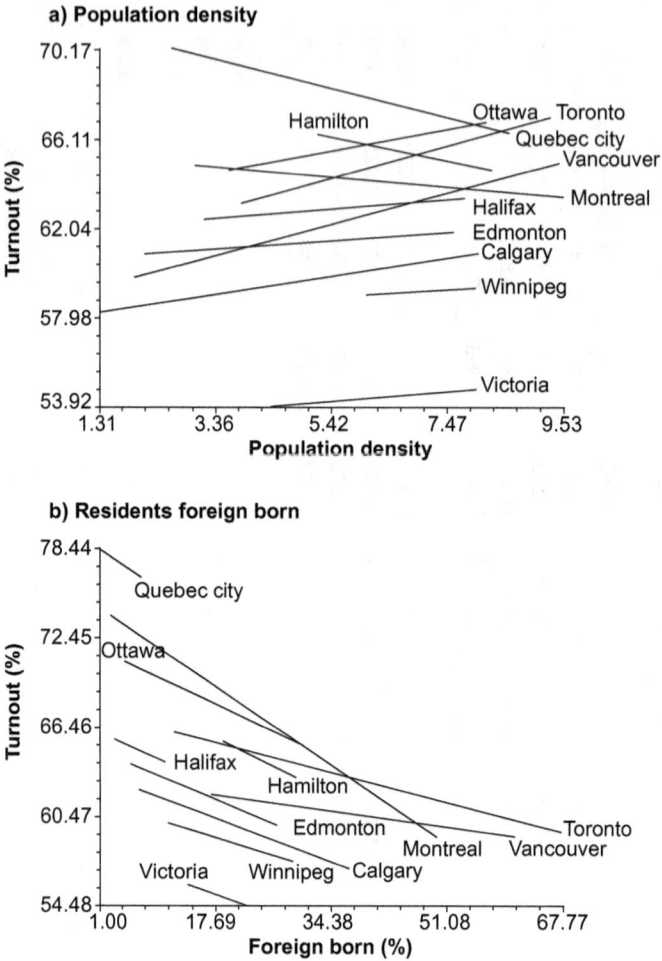

*Figure 3.2: Metropolitan variation in effects on federal electoral turnout, 2006 (randomised slopes by metropolitan area)*

2006 federal election: the proportion of foreign-born residents, which has a weak negative effect, and socio-economic status, which has a strong positive effect on participation. There are no significant contextual effects at all, except for the minor positive effect of residing in the Toronto region. The picture painted here is that of a fairly uniform national mobilisation of the vote, at least across the largest cities.

This is contrasted with the models for municipal participation, which have far greater explanatory power (r squares greater than 0.6, in contrast with 0.25 and under for the federal election models). In addition to the strong negative effect of hardship, significant contextual effects operate in municipal elections. The latter include a strong negative effect of population density (this contrasts with the positive but insignificant effect of density in federal elections), as well as strong nega-

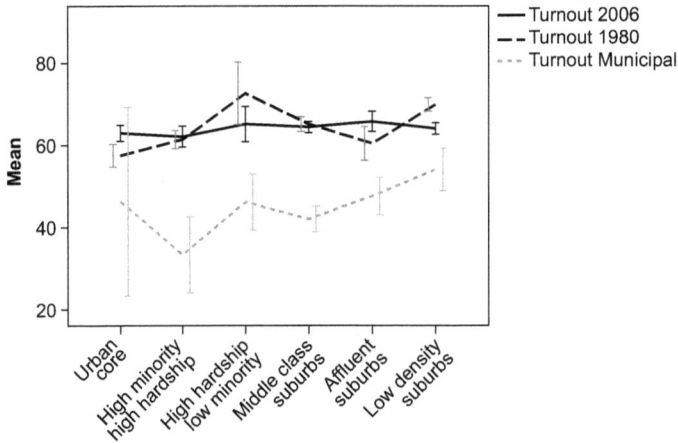

*Figure 3.3: Turnout in federal and municipal elections, by community type*

tive effects for lengthy commuting, driving to work, and income diversity. These findings conform to an explanation suggesting that commuting long distances, particularly by car, impacts on local community political engagement and participation, with obvious implications for continued metropolitanisation.

The significantly lower level of turnout at the municipal scale is evident in comparison with those at the federal level (see Figure 3.3). The Canadian context provides a good example of delocalisation, with much higher levels of participation at the national scale and with participation declining even faster over time at the municipal than at the national scale (Milner 1997; Nakhaie 2006). There is, notably, very little variation in levels of turnout across different types of communities in federal elections, while there is a clear bias towards higher turnouts in affluent and low-density communities in municipal elections (and significantly lower participation in high-minority, high-hardship communities, where minorities would appear particularly disenfranchised). While the gap between national and local participation is clearly smaller among communities that are lower density and display more rural characteristics, there is little evidence that this gap is higher in more affluent communities (Oliver 2001; Sellers and Walks, this volume).

## Metropolitanisation and shifting contextual effects on partisanship

The way that partisanship has become re-spatialised over time within the Canadian metropolis is evident when support for each party is mapped on to the typology of intra-urban community types in both 1980 and 2006 (see Figure 3.4). While certain features remain consistent – higher levels of support for the Liberals in minority suburbs and the strong support for the Conservatives in affluent communities – it is also clear that the gradients have become steeper across community types for both the NDP and Conservative Party. In 1980, for instance, there is very little variation in support for the NDP across different communities, and

Table 3.5: Comparison of municipal and federal turnout, Montreal, Toronto, and Vancouver regions

| Dependent variable = Turnout % | 2005/2006 Municipal elections | | | | 2006 Federal election | | | |
|---|---|---|---|---|---|---|---|---|
| | Composition | Contextual | Full linear | Backwards linear | Composition | Contextual | Full linear | Backwards linear |
| (Constant) | **87.450** | **122.63** | **197.82** | **157.74** | **62.285** | **63.927** | **47.071** | **60.660** |
| *Socio-demographic/compositional variables* | | | | | | | | |
| Age under 18 (%) | **-1.025** | | -0.621 | | -0.133 | | 0.059 | |
| Age 65+ (%) | -0.342 | | -0.564 | | 0.083 | | 0.491 | |
| Foreign born (%) | -0.125 | | -0.160 | | -0.060 | | -0.123 | **-0.067** |
| Employed in manufacturing (%) | -0.116 | | 0.032 | | 0.155 | | 0.306 | |
| SES general | 0.053 | | 0.064 | | **4.118** | | **3.885** | **4.499** |
| SES Hardship Index | **-10.429** | | **-10.257** | **-11.858** | -1.551 | | -0.555 | |
| *Spatial/contextual variables* | | | | | | | | |
| Log population density | | **-5.815** | **-4.928** | **-6.246** | | -0.428 | 0.259 | |
| Pop growth 1996–2001 (%) | | 0.011 | 0.044 | | | 0.011 | -0.007 | |
| Owner-occupied housing % | | 0.084 | -0.052 | | | 0.043 | 0.165 | |
| Moved in last 5 years (%) | | -0.236 | -0.233 | | | -0.028 | 0.091 | |
| Commute to different municipality for work | | -0.032 | -0.115 | **-0.128** | | 0.048 | 0.054 | |
| Drive to work (%) | | -0.189 | **-0.506** | **-0.427** | | -0.084 | -0.245 | |
| Distance to centre (tri-zone) | | 0.398 | 1.035 | | | 0.153 | 0.133 | |
| Simpson Index (income diversity) | | **-43.504** | **-52.371** | **-40.310** | | 3.472 | 0.771 | |
| *Dichotomous regional variables* | | | | | | | | |
| Toronto region (vs. Montreal) | **-15.961** | **-18.670** | **-17.555** | **-21.270** | **3.131** | **2.347** | **2.506** | **2.219** |
| Vancouver region (vs. Montreal) | **-13.845** | **-13.364** | **-9.850** | **-14.056** | **2.006** | 0.346 | 2.093 | |
| R Square | 0.529 | 0.569 | 0.623 | 0.600 | 0.207 | 0.166 | 0.251 | 0.158 |
| Adjusted R Square | 0.500 | 0.539 | 0.579 | 0.581 | 0.135 | 0.070 | 0.103 | 0.140 |
| Std. Error of the Estimate | 10.004 | 9.605 | 9.181 | 9.157 | 4.422 | 4.586 | 4.505 | 4.410 |

*Notes:* For boldface coefficients, p<0.05. Coefficients in model 4 are those resulting from backwards OLS regression.
*Source:* Municipal data for the Toronto region is from 2006. Municipal data for the Vancouver and Montreal regions are from 2005.

both the NDP and Conservatives received roughly the same level of support in the low-density communities as they did in the urban concentrations. By 2006, the trajectory of support for the Conservatives had shifted and now rose in virtually monotonic fashion with increasing spatial and social distance from the city core. The trajectory of Liberal support is less clear, but the party remained more dominant in the urban cores and minority suburbs. Only the vote for the Bloc Quebecois shows few and insignificant place effects across the community types (except for their low levels of support in affluent suburbs, which are far more likely to house Anglophones and 'allophones' (a resident, usually an immigrant, whose mother tongue or home language is neither English nor French) and their greater support in low-minority, high-hardship suburbs, which in Quebec are far more likely to be Francophone).

Table 3.6 compares OLS and multilevel models estimating support for each of the three main political parties in the 1980 and 2006 federal elections. To produce the most effective model of support for the three main national parties, a number of cross-level interactions were added to the multilevel models. Statistically significant cross-level effects were uncovered for variables related to the presence of immigrants, manufacturing workers, population size/density, and for the effects of the city-suburban disparity index on the slope of homeownership at the lower level. Additionally, cross-level effects of residing in Quebec were found to influence the slope for the lower-level variables for manufacturing employment and owner-occupation. The latter were necessary to control for differential effects operating within and outside of Quebec related to the different political culture and party structure there.[7] Finally, as already noted, two additional variables were added to the protocol at the lower level, the proportion who spoke French at home, and the proportion of those who drove to work (instead of using some other mode of transport).

In both 1980 and 2006, fairly similar proportions of the vote across the entire country went to the Conservatives (32.4 per cent in 1980, 35.4 per cent in 2006), and to the NDP (19.7 per cent in 1980, 17 per cent in 2006). What differed dramatically was the proportion of the vote going to the Liberal Party (44.4 per cent in 1980, 31.9 per cent in 2006), with the vote for the Bloc Quebecois in Quebec (10.2

---

7.   The presence of the separatist Bloc Quebecois on the ballot only in Quebec presents somewhat of a challenge for modelling national support for the other parties in 2006. The inclusion of upper-level variables, including dummy variables indicating province of residence, allows for the effects of the Bloc to be accounted for when modelled at the regional and metropolitan levels. However, the intra-urban geography of support for the Bloc within Quebec's cities also needs to be understood. Importantly, middle- (and lower-) income suburbs of Quebec cities are far more likely to contain Francophones, who were more likely to vote for the Bloc than other parties in 2006. Also, homeowners within the Montreal region were disproportionately more likely to vote for the Bloc in the suburbs, while elsewhere in Canada homeowners are more likely to vote for the Conservatives in the suburbs (and the NDP within the inner cities). Finally, while those employed in manufacturing were more likely to vote for the NDP outside of Quebec, within Quebec they were more likely to vote for the Liberals (and not the Bloc) in 2006. See Table A3.2 in the Appendix for the OLS models estimating support for the Bloc Quebecois in the 2006 federal election.

a) Per cent of the vote, by party, 1980 federal election

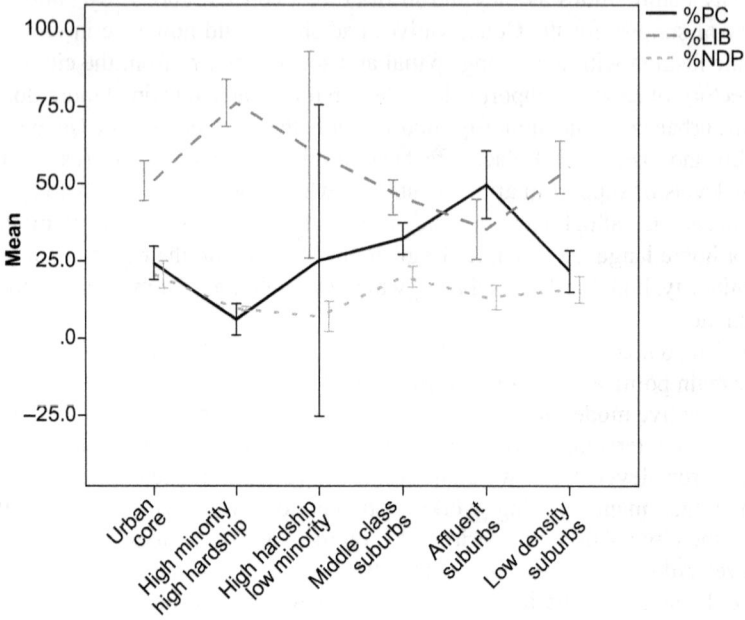

b) Per cent of the vote, by party, 2006 federal election

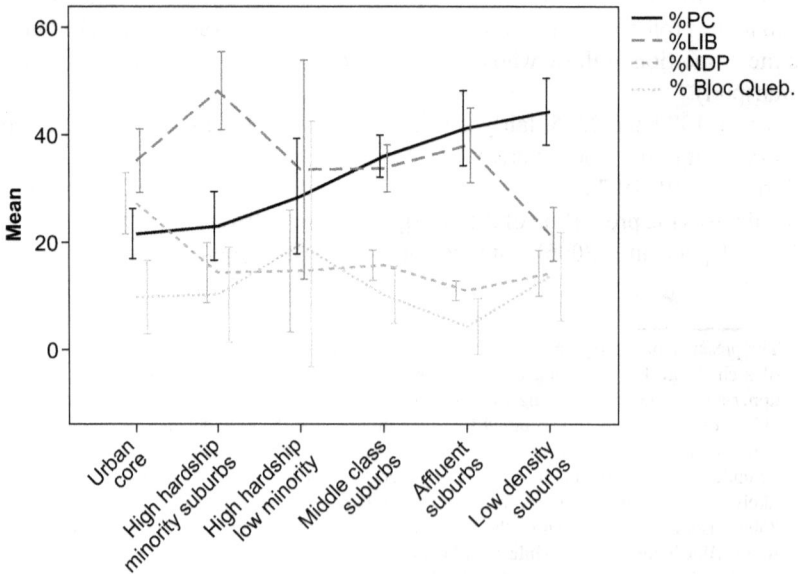

Figure 3.4: Partisanship by community type, 1980 and 2006

per cent) making up for most of the national difference (hence the Conservative minority government of 2006). This shift in regionalist sentiment represents only one small part of the re-territorialisation of partisanship revealed by the models. In the case of each of the main political parties, contextual variables at both upper (between metro) and lower (within metro) levels explain a greater portion of the variation in partisanship in 2006 than in 1980.

This is particularly true for the Conservatives, which are located as ideologically most removed from the positions of the other parties. Compositional effects have largely remained the same for this party over time – it traditionally attracts a greater proportion of the vote from the affluent and seniors, and receives disproportionately low levels of support from immigrants, Francophones and poor neighbourhoods. The contextual variables, on the other hand, have grown in importance (see Table 3.6). In 1980, only two of the contextual variables are shown to exhibit any significant effects (in the OLS models): homeownership and distance to the centre (zone). Both are factors fuelling the suburban shift to the right in Canada in the early 1980s (Walks 2004a, 2005). By 2006, the number and strength of contextual effects on Conservative partisanship had increased substantially. Not only had their vote become more intensely regionalised (taking almost all seats in the Prairie Provinces, while losing much of their Atlantic support, for instance), but place-based variation in their support widened significantly across the largest metros, with metro growth rates and city-suburban disparities boosting suburban support for the party. Even more importantly, a series of contextual effects are now operating on Conservative support at the lower level. Population density, population growth and lengthy commuting now predict reduced support for the Conservatives and their policies, while higher levels of turnover, and most importantly, automobile use, increase it.

Most saliently, the latter variable – the proportion residing in a district who drive to work – has become the single most important variable in predicting the vote for the Conservatives (and is a very strong predictor of lack of support for the other parties as well). Despite having virtually no effect in 1980, by 2006 this variable reports the highest standardised coefficient among the lower-level variables included in the OLS models, and when modelled separately (i.e. in an OLS model with no other independent variables included) explains fully 30.6 per cent of the variation in Conservative support in 2006 on its own (r square = 0.306). This is much higher than the r square for a model solely containing the next strongest predictor of Conservative support, general socio-economic status (r square of 0.197). As might be expected, driving to work is highly correlated with both homeownership (r = 0.804) and zonal distance to the centre (r = 0.630). However, when added to the OLS and multilevel models, it is the drive mode variable that shows up as statistically significant, while the significance of the other two variables is greatly reduced.[8]

---

8.  Interestingly, commuting to another municipality for work is shown to have a negative effect on Conservative support (in the OLS models), a result which appears opposite to that in the United States. This discrepancy between the Canadian and US results is likely related to the fact that

*Table 3.6: Models of partisanship, 1980 and 2006*

| | 1980 NDP | | NDP 2006 | | 1980 LIBERAL | | LIBERAL 2006 | | 1980 CONSERVATIVE | | CONSERVATIVE 2006 | |
|---|---|---|---|---|---|---|---|---|---|---|---|---|
| | Linear | Randomised | Linear | Randomised | Linear | Randomised | Linear | Randomised | Linear | Randomised | Linear | Randomised |
| Constant (A) | -156.10 | -231.90 | 48.765 | 171.80 | 105.27 | 279.57 | 163.22 | -24.347 | 47.710 | 35.337 | -128.71 | -569.67 |
| *Lower-level variables: (B)* | | | | | | | | | | | | |
| *Compositional:* | | | | | | | | | | | | |
| Age under 16 (%) | 0.056 | 0.020 | -0.201 | -0.217 | 0.200 | 0.361 | 0.091 | 0.218 | -0.086 | -0.214 | -0.309 | 0.185 |
| Age 65+ (%) | -0.236 | -0.231 | -0.949 | -0.798 | -0.254 | 0.064 | 0.423 | 0.210 | 0.598 | 0.423 | 0.079 | 0.606 |
| Foreign born (%) | -0.032 | 0.645 | -0.485 | -0.505 | 0.621 | 0.306 | 0.693 | 0.883 | -0.547 | -0.937 | -0.117 | -0.174 |
| French at home (%) | -0.108 | 0.001 | -0.155 | -0.186 | 0.314 | 0.375 | -0.188 | -0.118 | -0.303 | -0.452 | -0.139 | -0.176 |
| Manufacturing (%) | 0.286 | -0.257 | 0.300 | 1.518 | -0.147 | -0.862 | 0.022 | -1.431 | -0.302 | 0.098 | 0.227 | 0.771 |
| SES General Index (Ave = 1.00) | -0.069 | -0.074 | -8.556 | -7.224 | -0.014 | 0.006 | 1.120 | 1.740 | 0.073 | 0.065 | 13.921 | 7.594 |
| SES Hardship Index (Ave = 1.00) | 5.893 | 6.956 | 14.030 | 14.650 | -3.882 | -4.218 | -10.681 | -12.736 | -4.528 | -5.616 | -1.162 | -4.693 |
| *Spatial/contextual:* | | | | | | | | | | | | |
| Log population density | 0.000 | 0.008 | 0.619 | 0.521 | 0.000 | -0.005 | 0.167 | -9.559 | 0.002 | 0.002 | -1.189 | -0.489 |
| Population change previous 5 years (%) | 0.047 | 0.064 | -0.016 | 0.077 | 0.043 | -0.004 | 0.433 | 0.423 | -0.132 | -0.101 | -0.306 | -0.410 |
| Owner-occupied housing (%) | -0.001 | 0.343 | 0.289 | 0.140 | -0.220 | -0.497 | -0.379 | 0.299 | 0.185 | 0.401 | -0.088 | -0.147 |
| Moved in last 5 years (%) | 0.293 | 0.311 | -0.135 | -0.284 | -0.031 | -0.095 | -0.597 | -0.732 | -0.027 | 0.008 | 0.304 | 0.836 |

| | 1980 NDP 2006 | | | | 1980 LIBERAL 2006 | | | | 1980 CONSERVATIVE 2006 | | | |
|---|---|---|---|---|---|---|---|---|---|---|---|---|
| | Linear | Randomised | Linear | Randomised | Linear | Randomised | Linear | Randomised | Linear | Randomised | Linear | Randomised |
| Commute to another municipality for work | 0.048 | 0.069 | 0.088 | 0.051 | 0.004 | 0.059 | 0.051 | 0.016 | −0.006 | −0.055 | **−0.216** | −0.056 |
| Drive to work (%) | 0.073 | −0.039 | **−0.515** | **−0.424** | 0.104 | 0.123 | **−0.166** | −0.284 | −0.096 | −0.051 | **0.844** | **0.642** |
| Distance to centre (tri-zone) | −3.020 | −2.002 | −0.569 | −0.570 | −0.551 | −1.018 | 1.012 | 1.034 | **3.242** | 3.037 | −0.048 | −0.037 |
| Simpson Index (income diversity) | **47.080** | **57.850** | 12.044 | 1.668 | 12.881 | −7.578 | 14.118 | 19.577 | −25.767 | −21.970 | −8.620 | −12.326 |
| *Upper-level variables: (G)* | | | | | | | | | | | | |
| Region: | | | | | | | | | | | | |
| Region – Nova Scotia | −6.518 | −0.408 | 10.249 | 4.562 | 5.274 | 11.032 | −1.136 | 7.137 | −0.064 | −5.002 | **−21.381** | 7.589 |
| Region – Quebec | −4.642 | −12.362 | −11.530 | 14.876 | **12.462** | 6.878 | 1.442 | −29.533 | **−10.726** | 0.440 | −12.040 | −16.375 |
| Region – Manitoba | −5.219 | 1.728 | −1.876 | −8.487 | 3.820 | 35.955 | −7.324 | 1.090 | −4.049 | −15.638 | −0.975 | **30.649** |
| Region – Alberta | −4.869 | −16.140 | −4.483 | −1.485 | −3.076 | −3.509 | 0.795 | −0.293 | **16.770** | 23.206 | **11.129** | 2.281 |
| Region – British Columbia | 7.141 | 9.162 | **11.820** | **12.672** | −11.660 | −3.543 | **−15.898** | **−11.856** | 2.283 | 0.421 | 6.239 | **−13.185** |
| *Upper-level variables:* | | | | | | | | | | | | |
| Log population (metro size) | 5.207 | 8.943 | −0.597 | −6.672 | −2.585 | −8.840 | −3.813 | 4.134 | 0.629 | −0.140 | 7.759 | **29.942** |
| Population change previous 5 years (%) | −0.577 | 0.338 | −0.599 | −1.181 | −0.662 | 0.139 | **−2.577** | −1.759 | 0.468 | −0.286 | **2.665** | **6.643** |
| Manufacturing (%) | −1.495 | −1.366 | 1.003 | 2.315 | 0.637 | 1.460 | −0.600 | −2.049 | 0.532 | 0.307 | **−2.476** | **−5.037** |

| | 1980 NDP 2006 | | | | 1980 LIBERAL 2006 | | | | 1980 CONSERVATIVE 2006 | | | |
|---|---|---|---|---|---|---|---|---|---|---|---|---|
| | Linear | Randomised | Linear | Randomised | Linear | Randomised | Linear | Randomised | Linear | Randomised | Linear | Randomised |
| City-Suburban Disparity Index (CSHI) | 5.599 | 6.461 | 4.612 | -16.839 | -4.130 | -1.200 | -1.521 | 5.371 | -3.303 | 2.462 | **2.793** | **9.980** |
| *Cross-level effects on slope of (B):* | | | | | | | | | | | | |
| Foreign born (on foreign-born %) | | **-0.024** | | -0.001 | | 0.013 | | -0.004 | | 0.011 | | 0.003 |
| Manufacturing % (on manufacturing %) | | 0.025 | | -0.184 | | **0.040*** | | **0.237*** | | -0.020 | | **-0.167** |
| Pop.size (log) (on population density) | | -0.005 | | 0.786 | | 0.003 | | 0.653 | | -0.007 | | **-1.365** |
| City-Sub. Disparity Index (on owner-occ.) | | -0.002 | | -0.112 | | 0.002 | | -0.522 | | -0.001 | | **0.488** |
| Region – Quebec (on manufacturing %) | | | | -0.981 | | | | **0.752*** | | | | **0.582** |
| Region – Quebec (on owner-occ. %) | | | | 0.373 | | | | 0.141 | | | | **-0.433** |
| R Square | 0.746 | | 0.741 | | 0.907 | | 0.826 | | 0.909 | | 0.856 | |
| Adj R Square | 0.691 | | 0.693 | | 0.886 | | 0.794 | | 0.889 | | 0.832 | |
| S.E. | 6.518 | | 6.879 | | 6.858 | | 7.590 | | 6.390 | | 6.729 | |
| Sigma Squared | 39.200 | | 44.117 | | 42.839 | | 56.177 | | 42.091 | | 27.467 | |

*Notes:* bold values are sig. = $p < 0.05$. Cross-level effect of upper level variable on slope of the lower-level variable (B). Higher values of CHSI indicate higher levels of city-suburban disparity (parity = 1.00).

Thus, auto-dependent commuting patterns and lifestyles are demonstrated to profoundly link different forms of suburbanism to recent support for neoliberal policies and political parties like the Conservatives. Growing social distance represented by distinct modes of everyday life, and the very different political consumption interests that this brings about and reinforces, is a core product of metropolitanisation. An initial argument was made by Dunleavy (1979) in relation to the implications of new cleavages based on modes of collective consumption, which included political divergence between public transit riders and drivers of private automobiles. More recently, Henderson (2006) writes about the growth of 'secessionist automobility' in the United States, which simultaneously provides the means to exit the city into private urban spaces and to secure the social exclusion of strangers. For Urry (2004), automobility constitutes a coherent economic, social, and cultural system, which then can be expected to generate political interests geared to its survival and dominance.

Rajan (2006) notes the strong match between the political ethos of liberalism on the one hand, with its emphasis on freedom and individual choice, and on the other hand the materiality and practice of automobility/driving, which reinforces the feeling of the freedom of movement by autonomous individuals in control of their own private space, but within a quasi-democratic auto-realm containing other autonomous individuals each of whom is in competition for space. The evidence presented here suggests that diverging consumption and lifestyle interests related to mode of transportation are helping drive the growth of ideological cleavages in Canada.[9]

Cross-level interactions estimated in the randomised multilevel models provide further insight into the bases of Conservative support. Most importantly, higher levels of city-suburban disparity have a strong positive and significant effect on the slope of homeownership at the lower level, while residence in the province of Quebec has a strong negative effect on the slope of the homeownership variable. In those cities with poorer inner cores and wealthier suburbs, homeownership has a stronger and more positive effect on Conservative support (except in Montreal, where the Bloc received more support from homeowners). Meanwhile, where the inner cities are gentrifying the fastest, the NDP is more likely to win the votes of homeowners. The relationship between homeownership and Conservative partisanship in Canadian metropolitan areas can be seen in Figure 3.5a, which graphs the randomised slopes at the lower level. The slopes are steepest and more positive

---

much less commuting in US cities is enacted via public transit or other non-auto modes, and that the factors leading to lengthier commutes in Canada are far more likely to be related to the geography of housing affordability, with the affluent most able to afford to live close to the main employment districts.

9. In another example, the 2010 municipal election in Toronto quickly evolved into a contest between downtown-living mayoral candidates who would invest in public transit and maintain city programs, and a suburban-resident mayoral candidate (Rob Ford) who won by promising to 'stop the war on cars' and privatise city services, while suggesting that the city's treasured light-rail streetcars be replaced by buses (see Paperny 2010).

in manufacturing cities and the smaller cities with poorer inner cores, but flatter in the larger cities, and outright negative in Montreal.

The contextual bases of support for the NDP have also undergone transformation over time (see Table 3.6). The party has always relied on support from the working class and this is reflected in the support it continued to receive from areas of greater disadvantage, and the negative relationship with general socio-economic status. Yet, the NDP went from attracting disproportionate support from the foreign born in 1980 (when the largest immigrant groups were still the Portuguese, Italians, and other Europeans), to a strongly negative likelihood of receiving immigrants' votes in 2006 (by which time the vast majority originated in Asia), as well as receiving little attention from Francophone voters (within Quebec, French speakers who favour social democracy were far more likely to support the Bloc in 2006). The NDP has also largely lost support from places experiencing high levels of turnover (which now are more likely to vote Conservative). Despite this, the NDP has largely become, and in Canada is increasingly perceived as, a party representing the inner cities. As in the case of support for the Conservatives, the proportion who drive to work has emerged as one of the most important variables predicting support for the NDP at the lower level: places with more car drivers are far less likely to support the party than those commuting via public transit, walking or bicycling, all of which are far more likely to occur within the inner cities. If the drive mode variable is removed from the model, then the zonal variable (distance to the centre) becomes highly significant and rises in strength (to $-0.829$), but the coefficient for the homeownership variable remains largely unaffected.

The nationalisation thesis suggests that local differences should subside over time with the growth of industrialisation and the integration of regional and national economies. As the party of the working class, the NDP should be expected to increasingly mobilise support from industrial workers across the national landscape. To a certain extent this was true from the 1960s until the early 1990s, and the NDP was itself formed in order to give unions a vehicle for influencing politics directly and electing their own candidates. However, ironically, there appears to be little relationship between manufacturing employment and support for the party in the earlier (1980) election, when union membership was at its peak in Canada and the NDP was winning many blue collar seats, including those in the suburbs. By 2006, the NDP had largely lost these ridings (the exception is Burnaby in British Columbia). Yet strong and significant results are still reported for manufacturing employment when the differential effects in Quebec are factored into the multilevel model. Figure 3.5b shows how the relationship between manufacturing employment and NDP support varies across Canadian metropolitan areas. Importantly, the slopes are positive everywhere except in the province of Quebec, where they reverse and become negative (where those votes went to the Liberals instead).

The Liberal Party typically receives disproportionate support from visible minorities and new immigrants to Canada, the vast majority of who live in the largest cities. Over the study period examined here, contextual effects clearly have become more important determinants of their support. Areas of population growth

**a) Home ownership and Conservative partisanship**

**b) Employment in manufacturing and NDP partisanship**

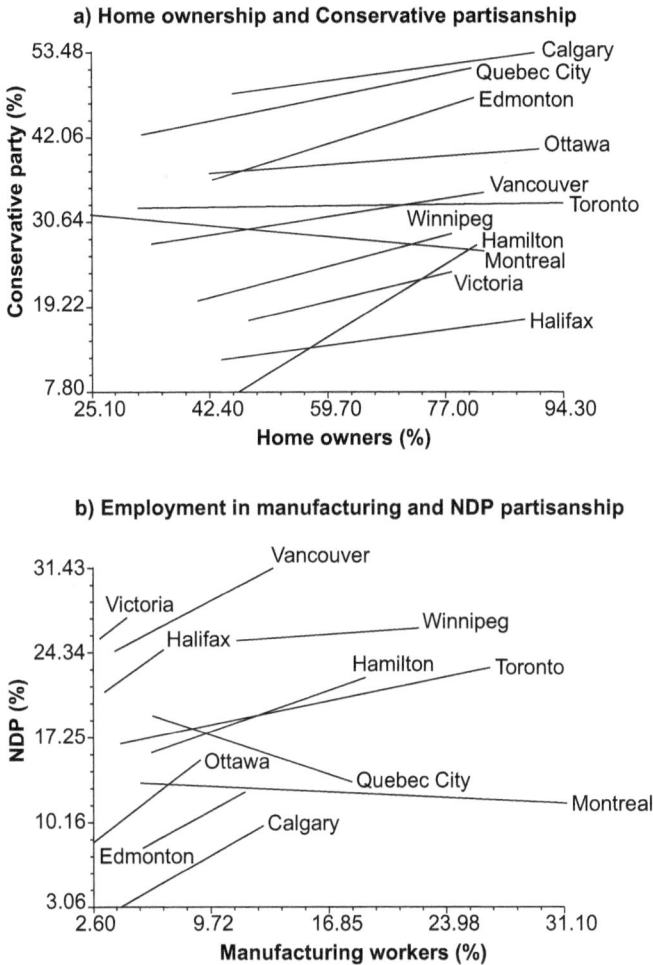

*Figure 3.5: Metropolitan variation in effects on partisanship, 2006*

(which are also more likely to house new immigrants), tenants, lower turnover, and fewer drivers, were more likely to support the Liberals in 2006. Only the positive association with tenants has carried over from 1980 (if the drive mode variable is removed from the models, the negative coefficient for homeowners increases in strength to −0.503, and becomes statistically significant in the multilevel models as well).[10]

Shifts in partisanship analysed above have implications for the relationship between metropolitanisation and changing policy preferences in Canada. Figure

---

10. Regressing the residuals onto the typology does not provide many further insights and all result-ing coefficients are statistically insignificant.

3.6 maps the economic, globalisation and sociocultural indices on to a common ten-point scale in which left-leaning tendencies are indicated by lower scores (support for welfare-state redistribution, tolerance toward minorities, cosmopolitanism and international cooperation, and opposition to patriarchy and openness to alternative family forms), while right-leaning tendencies receive higher scores (support for neoliberal policies, anti-immigrant sentiment, nationalism, and support for traditional family values). In the case of each index, there is a clear shift toward right-leaning policy preferences with each increase in social and spatial distance from the inner cores.

Estimates of compositional and contextual effects in relation to the economic, globalisation and cultural indices arising from OLS and multilevel models are reported in Table 3.7. Some of the main compositional determinants of such indices follow from expectations: affluence and hardship largely determine opposite positions on the economic index related to taxation and welfare-state spending, while the presence of immigrants and of Francophones, who are more likely to support separatism or cultural nationalist positions, have opposite effects on the direction of the globalisation/cosmopolitanism index.

However, as might be expected given the virtually monotonic slopes evident across the community types in Figure 3.6, contextual factors tied to community characteristics also loom large. Importantly, areas with higher levels of income diversity are less likely to lean to the right on the economic index, suggesting that spatial proximity among different classes has an effect in educating them to the plight of others, and population growth is associated with leaning to the left across each index. In contrast, the opposite sign of the coefficient for population density suggests that local competition for space might spur appreciation for individualism and competitive markets in the economic policy realm, once growth and diversity are controlled for. Commuters that have to travel far for work are less likely to lean to the right in their policy preferences, particularly in terms of economic policy, but this effect is overpowered by the strong inclination of areas with higher proportions of automobile drivers to lean to the right across both the economic and sociocultural indices. Interestingly, driving to work has little to no effect on positions with respect to the globalisation index, while homeownership has statistically significant effects in moving residents to the right on this index.

At the metropolitan level, significant effects result from manufacturing employment, which has a strong general effect on influencing policy preferences to the left, and city-suburban disparity, which has the opposite effect. The latter is instructive, as it suggests that suburban residents will be much more likely to lean to the right in their policy preferences if the inner cities concentrate and segregate the poor. The political effects of metropolitanisation would therefore appear to be augmented by the presence of high rates of segregation.

These secondary models provide some insight into the evolution of Canadian federal politics since the early 1980s. After establishing a base among homeowners in the suburbs with promises of mortgage interest deductions (in the 1979 and 1980 elections), Conservative policies supporting free trade (1988), and then, in the 1990s, of reducing welfare-state support for collective consumption items,

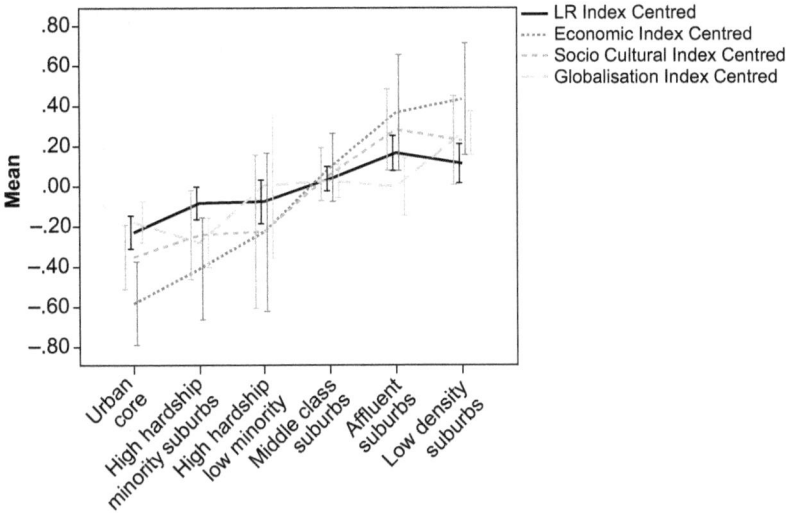

*Figure 3.6: Ideological orientations, by community type, 2006*

further divided metropolitan populations. Many among the suburban populations, feeling vulnerable due either to recession, globalisation, and/or fast growth and the influx of newcomers, identified with either the populist right-wing messages of the Reform and Canadian Alliance parties or, in Quebec Francophone suburbs, with the collectivist/nationalist message of the Bloc.

As suburban communities split their votes among the new parties through the 1990s and early 2000s, this allowed the Liberals to maintain their dominance nationally for a time (allowing the Liberals to win the majority of suburban seats, while splitting the inner cities with the NDP). But the merging of the right into a single Conservative Party at the same time that the Liberals were tainted by scandal allowed populist sentiments to be channelled effectively into Conservative electoral victories. The Conservatives maintain a focus on the populist angst and vulnerabilities of 'regular' Canadians, who are increasingly found within the auto-dependent suburbs surrounding the largest metropolitan areas, including some working-class suburbs. In both tailoring their policies to the desires and needs of this population and in directing their efforts to convincing this population of the merits of their neoliberal approach, the Conservatives have been cultivating and deepening their bases of support; in turn driving wedges within and between metropolitan communities. The match between ideological structures and policy platforms, and the objective conditions of existence in such places makes voting for the Conservatives (and for neoliberal policies and parties at the provincial level) seem like 'common sense' (Keil 2002). Such is the way that Canadian political discourse, practice, and party strategies have evolved reflexively alongside the spatial and social transformations begat by metropolitanisation.

Table 3.7: Models of economic, globalisation, and cultural indices, 2006 federal election

| | Economic | | | | Globalisation | | | | Cultural/Social | | | |
|---|---|---|---|---|---|---|---|---|---|---|---|---|
| | | | Full | | | | Full | | | | Full | |
| | Compos. | Contextual | linear | Randomised | Compos. | Contextual | linear | Randomised | Compos. | Contextual | linear | Randomised |
| Constant (A) | −25.155 | −8.705 | −20.401 | −58.795 | −2.022 | −8.705 | −2.172 | −28.071 | −19.287 | −5.547 | −16.130 | −35.404 |
| *Lower-level variables: (B)* | | | | | | | | | | | | |
| *Compositional:* | | | | | | | | | | | | |
| Age under 16 (%) | 0.037 | | 0.012 | 0.000 | 0.014 | | 0.003 | 0.000 | 0.022 | | 0.009 | 0.001 |
| Age 65 + (%) | 0.040 | | 0.029 | 0.020 | 0.000 | | 0.002 | 0.001 | 0.027 | | 0.018 | 0.012 |
| Foreign born (%) | −0.007 | | 0.000 | −0.006 | −0.010 | | −0.008 | −0.015 | −0.003 | | 0.000 | −0.001 |
| French at home (%) | −0.007 | | −0.008 | −0.010 | 0.005 | | 0.004 | 0.002 | −0.010 | | −0.010 | −0.011 |
| Manufacturing (%) | 0.014 | | 0.004 | 0.091 | 0.003 | | −0.001 | 0.037 | 0.011 | | 0.006 | 0.068 |
| SES General Index (Ave = 1.00) | 0.394 | | 0.482 | 0.413 | 0.053 | | 0.091 | 0.063 | 0.252 | | 0.303 | 0.254 |
| SES Hardship Index (Ave = 1.00) | −0.379 | | −0.419 | −2.605 | 0.020 | | 0.056 | −0.604 | −0.262 | | −0.309 | −1.666 |
| *Spatial/contextual:* | | | | | | | | | | | | |
| Log population density | | −0.030 | −0.031 | 0.974 | | 0.103 | −0.007 | 0.263 | | −0.009 | −0.020 | 0.642 |
| Population change previous 5 years (%) | | 0.001 | −0.012 | −0.014 | | −0.011 | −0.008 | −0.009 | | 0.005 | −0.006 | −0.008 |
| Owner-occupied housing (%) | | −0.004 | −0.004 | −0.004 | | 0.007 | 0.005 | 0.005 | | −0.005 | −0.004 | −0.004 |
| Moved in last 5 years (%) | | −0.001 | 0.020 | 0.025 | | 0.004 | 0.013 | 0.015 | | −0.009 | 0.010 | 0.013 |
| Commute to another municipality for work | | −0.006 | −0.005 | −0.004 | | −0.007 | −0.002 | −0.002 | | −0.002 | −0.003 | −0.002 |
| Drive to work (%) | | 0.031 | 0.027 | 0.035 | | 0.024 | 0.009 | 0.012 | | 0.018 | 0.015 | 0.020 |
| Distance to centre (tri-zone) | | −0.007 | −0.008 | −0.008 | | −0.007 | −0.013 | −0.001 | | −0.005 | −0.005 | −0.002 |
| Simpson Index (income diversity) | | −0.024 | −0.709 | −0.629 | | −0.024 | −0.372 | −0.346 | | 0.078 | −0.351 | −0.288 |

| | Economic | | | | Globalisation | | | | Cultural/Social | | | |
|---|---|---|---|---|---|---|---|---|---|---|---|---|
| | | | Full | | | | Full | | | | Full | |
| | Compos. | Contextual | linear | Randomised | Compos. | Contextual | linear | Randomised | Compos. | Contextual | linear | Randomised |
| *Upper-level variables: (G)* | | | | | | | | | | | | |
| *Region:* | | | | | | | | | | | | |
| Region – Nova Scotia | **0.709** | -0.199 | 0.316 | 1.517 | 0.152 | -0.196 | 0.104 | 1.056 | **0.570** | -0.053 | 0.330 | 0.863 |
| Region – Quebec | **-1.747** | **-1.048** | **-1.168** | **-3.796** | **-0.516** | **-1.011** | -0.250 | **-2.182** | **-1.366** | **-1.10** | **-1.032** | -2.323 |
| Region – Manitoba | **1.864** | **0.889** | **1.462** | **4.000** | **0.493** | **0.812** | **0.357** | 2.047 | **1.366** | **0.611** | **1.131** | 2.393 |
| Region – Alberta | **-1.076** | **-0.648** | **-1.138** | -2.945 | -0.076 | **-0.603** | -0.126 | -1.300 | **-0.981** | **-0.44** | **-1.004** | -1.940 |
| Region – British Columbia | **-0.383** | -0.278 | **-0.452** | 0.249 | **0.140** | -0.201 | **0.146** | 0.692 | **-0.361** | -0.135 | **-0.393** | -0.070 |
| *Upper-level variables:* | | | | | | | | | | | | |
| Log population (metro size) | **1.488** | **0.655** | **1.228** | 3.386 | **0.288** | **0.322** | **0.279** | 1.762 | **1.130** | **0.453** | **0.966** | 2.038 |
| Population change previous 5 years (%) | **0.326** | **0.236** | **0.285** | 0.659 | **0.093** | **0.112** | **0.079** | 0.312 | **0.237** | **0.158** | **0.213** | 0.407 |
| Manufacturing (%) | **-0.297** | -0.164 | **-0.250** | -0.368 | **-0.049** | **-0.354** | **-0.033** | -0.123 | **-0.231** | **-0.10** | **-0.201** | -0.246 |
| City-Suburban Hardship Index (CSHI) | **0.067** | **0.030** | **0.053** | 0.107 | **0.015** | **0.027** | **0.011** | 0.048 | **0.051** | **0.021** | **0.043** | 0.069 |
| *Cross-level effects on slope of (B):* | | | | | | | | | | | | |
| Foreign born (on foreign born %) | | | | 0.0002 | | | | 0.0002 | | | | 0.0001 |
| Manufacturing % (on manufacturing %) | | | | **-0.008** | | | | **-0.003** | | | | **-0.006** |
| Population size (on population density) | | | | **-0.069** | | | | -0.018 | | | | **-0.045** |
| R Square | 0.856 | 0.838 | 0.889 | | 0.852 | 0.838 | 0.883 | | 0.893 | | 0.911 | |
| Adj R Square | 0.840 | 0.818 | 0.869 | | 0.835 | 0.818 | 0.862 | | 0.881 | | 0.895 | |
| S.E. | 0.286 | 0.305 | 0.254 | | 0.135 | 0.305 | 0.124 | | 0.183 | | 0.171 | |
| Sigma Squared | | | | 0.052 | | | | 0.014 | | | | 0.023 |

*Notes:* For boldface values, p<0.05. Cross-level effect of upper level variable on slope of the lower-level variable (B). Higher values of CHSI indicate higher levels of city-suburban disparity (parity = 100).

## Conclusion

Metropolitan areas are the fastest growing settlements in Canada and home to the majority of the Canadian population. As the metropolis has grown in importance, what is traditionally a highly-regionalised Canadian polity is being transformed. New political cleavages based on intra-urban differences have risen in importance along with the emergence of new regional dynamics, while old cleavages based on production or agrarian economies, or religious settlements, wither. Metropolitanisation has meant a re-territorialisation of the ideological and cultural bases of partisanship, and of political mobilisation, within the Canadian polity.

The Canadian context provides an example of the delocalisation of electoral participation. Municipal elections in English Canada in particular have drawn significantly lower turnouts, to a level close to half that of federal elections. Participation in municipal elections is, however, more dependent upon local context than is participation in federal elections, and it varies far more across different localities. Localised characteristics, both at the scale of the municipality and the entire metropolitan region, matter more for determining participation in local elections and thus factor large in producing delocalisation. Such shifts are occurring alongside the declining salience of not only municipal elections, but also municipal policies, at a time when the relative power and resources of municipal governments have been declining.

The nationalisation thesis, which posits that industrialisation, urbanisation and the growing power of the nation state should lead to more uniform and universal class-based cleavages supplanting regional or place-based ones, is not demonstrated in the Canadian case, at least not in the way it was originally formulated. Not only have provincial/regional cleavages become increasingly fortified and institutionalised within the party structure over time, but new intra-urban cleavages based on consumption and lifestyle have arisen to challenge those based on production and social class. Industrial/materialist suburbs that once voted for the left now elect Conservatives, while in the post-materialist gentrifying communities within the central cities that had traditionally elected Conservatives, the NDP wins.

Intra-urban spatial and contextual variables have emerged as important determinants of electoral behaviour in Canada. Metropolitanisation, by fashioning new cleavages based on lifestyle and consumption interests, has shaped the evolution of ideological orientations, party structures and the mobilisation of voters. Most salient is the rising importance of automobility as a delimiter of metropolitan space, consumption and lifestyle, and in turn as a predictor of partisanship and ideology. Economic interests rooted in a differential urban space, coupled with the way that urban lifestyles are increasingly politicised at the level of state policy, have worked to dominate and reframe political interests, leading to a re-territorialisation of politics. Metropolitanisation is thus implicated in the rise of support for neoliberal policies and parties in Canada.

## Bibliography

Black, J. H. (2001) 'Immigrants and ethnoracial minorities in Canada: a review of their participation in federal electoral politics', *Electoral Insight*, 3(1): 8–13.

Blais, A., Gidengil, E. and Nevitte, N. (2004) 'Where does turnout decline come from?' *European Journal of Political Research*, 43(2): 221–36.

Blake, D. E. (1972) 'The measurement of regionalism in Canadian voting patterns', *Canadian Journal of Political Science*, 5(1): 55–81.

Bramham, D. (2006) 'How countries welcome newcomers', *The Vancouver Sun*, June 17: 5.

Christian, W. and Campbell, C. (1990) *Political Parties and Ideologies in Canada*, 3rd edn, Toronto: McGraw-Hill Ryerson.

Chui, T. W. L., Curtis, J. E. and Lambert, R. D. (1991) 'Immigrant background and political participation: examining generational patterns', *Canadian Journal of Sociology*, 16(4): 375–96.

Cutler, F. (2007) 'Context and attitude formation: social interaction, default information, or local interests?' *Political Geography*, 26(5): 575–600.

Dunleavy, P. (1979) 'The urban basis of political dealignment: social class, domestic property ownership, and state intervention in consumption processes', *British Journal of Political Science*, 9(4): 409–43.

Eagles, M. (1990) 'Political ecology: local effects on the political behaviour of Canadians', in Gagnon, A. G. and Bickerton, J. P. (eds) *Canadian Politics*, Toronto: Broadview Press: 285–307.

Erikson, B. H. (1981) 'Region, knowledge, and class voting in Canada', *Canadian Journal of Sociology*, 6(2): 121–44.

Gainsborough, J. (2001) *Fenced Off: The suburbanization of American politics*, Washington, D.C.: Georgetown University Press.

Galabuzi, G. -E. (2006) *Canada's Economic Apartheid: The social exclusion of racialized groups in the New Century*, Toronto: Canadian Scholars Press.

Gidengil, E. (1989) 'Class and region in Canadian voting: a dependency interpretation', *Canadian Journal of Political Science*, 22(3): 563–87.

Gidengil, E., Blais, A., Everitt, J., Fournier, P. and Nevitte, N. (2006) 'Back to the Future? Making sense of the 2004 Canadian election outside Quebec', *Canadian Journal of Political Science*, 39(1): 1–25.

Henderson, J. (2006) 'Secessionist automobility: racism, anti-urbanism, and the politics of automobility in Atlanta, Georgia', *International Journal of Urban and Regional Research*, 30(2): 293–307.

Hicks, B. M. (2006) *Are marginalized communities disenfranchised? Voter turnout and representation in post-merger Toronto*, Montreal: Institute for Research and Public Policy. IRPP Working Paper series no. 2006-03.

Keil, R. (2002) '"Common-sense" neoliberalism: Progressive conservative urbanism in Toronto, Canada', *Antipode*, 34(3): 578–601.

Kushner, J., Siegel, D. and Stanwick, H. (1997) 'Ontario municipal elections: voting trends and determinants of electoral success in a Canadian province', *Canadian Journal of Political Science*, 30(3): 539–53.

Leuprecht, C. (2003) 'The Tory fragment in Canada: endangered species?' *Canadian Journal of Political Science*, 36(2): 401–16.

Milner, H. (1997) 'Electoral systems, integrated institutions and turnout in local and national elections: Canada in comparative perspective', *Canadian Journal of Political Science*, 30(1): 89–106.

Nakhaie, M. R. (2006) 'Electoral participation in municipal, provincial and federal elections in Canada', *Canadian Journal of Political Science*, 39(2): 363–90.

Oliver, J. (2001) *Democracy in Suburbia*, Princeton: Princeton University Press.

Pammett, J. H. and Dornan, C. (eds) (2004) *The Canadian General Election of 2004*, Toronto: Dundurn Press.

Paperny, A. M. (2010) 'Ford would scrap streetcars in favour of buses', Globe and Mail, September 9. Online. Available /www.theglobeandmail.com/news/national/toronto/ford-would-scrap-streetcars-in-favour-of-buses/article1700695 (accessed 9 May 2011).

Pratt, G. (1986) 'Housing tenure and social cleavages in urban Canada', *Annals of the Association of American Geographers*, 76(3): 366–80.

Rajan, S. C. (2006) 'Automobility and the liberal disposition', *Sociological Review*, 54(s1): 113–29.

Schwartz, M. (1974) 'Canadian voting behaviour', in Rose, R. (ed.), *Electoral Behaviour: A comparative handbook*, London: Collier Macmillan: 543–617.

Urry, J. (2004) 'The 'System' of automobility', *Theory, Culture, and Society*, 21(4/5): 25–39.

Verberg, N. (2000) 'Homeownership and politics: testing the political incorporation thesis', *Canadian Journal of Sociology*, 25(2): 169–95.

Walks, R. A. (2001) 'The social ecology of the post-Fordist/global city? Economic restructuring and socio-spatial polarisation in the Toronto urban region', *Urban Studies*, 38(3): 407–47.

—— (2004a) 'Place of residence, party preferences, and political attitudes in Canadian cities and suburbs', *Journal of Urban Affairs*, 26(3): 269–95.

—— (2004b) 'Suburbanization, the vote, and changes in federal and provincial political representation and influence between inner cities and suburbs in large Canadian urban regions, 1945 –1999', *Urban Affairs Review*, 39(4): 411–40.

—— (2005) 'The city-suburban cleavage in Canadian federal politics', *Canadian Journal of Political Science*, 38(2): 383–413.

—— (2006) 'The Causes of City-Suburban Political Polarization? A Canadian Case Study', *Annals of the Association of American Geographers*, 96(2): 390–414.

—— (2007) 'The boundaries of suburban discontent? Urban definitions and neighbourhood political effects', *The Canadian Geographer*, 51(2): 160–85.

—— (2008) 'Urban form, everyday life, and ideology: support for privatization in three Toronto neighbourhoods', *Environment and Planning A*, 40(2): 258–82.

— (2010) 'New divisions: social polarization and neighbourhood inequality in the Canadian city', in Bunting, T. E., Filion, P. and Walker, R. (eds), *Canadian Cities in Transition: New directions in the twenty-first century*, Oxford: Oxford University Press, 170–90.

Walks, R. A. and Maaranen, R. (2008) 'The timing, patterning and forms of gentrification and neighbourhood upgrading in Montreal, Toronto, and Vancouver', 1961–2001, Toronto: University of Toronto Cities Centre, Research Report 211.

Walks, R. A. and Bourne, L. S. (2006) 'Ghettos in Canada's cities? Racial segregation, ethnic enclaves and poverty concentration in Canadian urban areas', *The Canadian Geographer*, 50(3): 273–97.

Youssef, M. and Leblanc, D. (2010) 'Harper vows to toughen laws as Tamils zip through hearings', Globe and Mail, Wednesday, August 18. Online. Available /www.theglobeandmail.com/news/politics (accessed 9 May 2011).

## Appendix

*Table A3.1: Variable definitions*

| Concept | Variable | Definition |
|---|---|---|
| *Socio-demographic/compositional variables:* | | |
| Presence of families/ family values | Age: under 18 | % of total population under age 18 |
| Aging, aged, greying, seniors | Age: 65+ | % of total population age 65 or older |
| Immigrant enclaves | Foreign born | % of total population born outside Canada |
| Secondary sector, production workers | Employed in manufacturing | % of labour force employed in manufacturing occupations |
| Socio-economic status | SES General index | Average location quotient values for: <br> • % w/managerial/professional occupation <br> • % households w/income one standard deviation above the local metro average. |
| Disadvantage/ marginalisation | SES Hardship Index | Average location quotient values for: <br> • % unemployed (of total labour force) <br> • % with less than high school education <br> • % female single-parent households <br> • % of persons in households with income below the low-income cut-off (i.e. in poverty). |
| *Spatial/contextual variables:* | | |
| Urbanity, crowding | Log population density | Log of persons/km square |
| New/revitalised vs. declining areas | Pop growth | % change in population 1981–6, 2001–6 |
| Security of tenure/res. investment | Owner-occupied housing | % total dwellings owner-occupied |
| Areas with high turnover, migrants* | Migrant last 5 years | % of total population who lived outside the municipality 5 years earlier* |
| Commuter areas* | Commute to different municipality for work | % of the employed labour force commuting outside of their municipality for work* (all transportation modes) |
| Transport mode share* | Drive to work | % of employed who drive to work (regardless of where they are employed)* |
| Fringe settlement/ distance to core/CBD | Distance to centre (tri-zone) | Three-zonal categorisation based on proximity to central city (zone 1) (higher values = further away) |
| Economic 'diversity', mixing | Simpson Index | Calculated from % of households in four income categories roughly corresponding to: <br> • less than 50% of the metro median income <br> • from 50% of the median to the median <br> • from the median to twice the median <br> • more than twice the metro median income. |

| Concept | Variable | Definition |
|---|---|---|
| *Upper-level variables:* | | (Base for regional variables = Ontario) |
| Region (dichotomous) | Region – Nova Scotia | Province of Nova Scotia (Halifax Metro) |
| | Region – Quebec | Province of Quebec (Montrea & Quebec City) |
| | Region – Manitoba | Province of Manitoba (Winnipeg Metro) |
| | Region – Alberta | Province of Alberta (Calgary & Edmonton metros) |
| | Region – B.C. | Province of British Columbia (Vancouver & Victoria Metros) |
| Metropolitan size/ complexity | Log population (metro size) | Log of total metro population |
| Metro growth/decline | Population change 1976–1981 and 2001–2006 | % change in metro population 1976–1981 and 2001–2006 (negative values = decline) |
| Production centres | Employed in manufacturing | % labour force employed in manufacturing industry |
| City-suburban differences | City-Suburban Hardship Index | Ratio of the SES hardship index for the central city to the SES hardship index for the rest of the metro, *100 |

*Notes:* *Variable is not present in the raw census data for 1981. In these cases, it is estimated using data from the 1986 or 1991 census, and the 1982 Survey of Family Expenditures. All variables are present in the 2006 census.

*Table A3.2: OLS regressions – support for the Bloc Quebecois in the 2006 federal election*

|  | Model 1 | Model 2 | Model 3 | Model 4 |
|---|---|---|---|---|
| (Constant) | **−8.087** | −157.491 | **2.687** | **−28.885** |
| *Lower level – compositional variables* | | | | |
| Age under 18 (%) | −0.217 | | −0.405 | |
| Age 65+ (%) | −0.348 | | −0.282 | |
| Foreign born (%) | 0.233 | | 0.414 | **−0.398** |
| French spoken at home | 0.781 | | 0.910 | 0.905 |
| Employed in manufacturing (%) | **−0.781** | | **−0.956** | **−0.876** |
| SES General (1.00=average) | −13.641 | | −1.263 | **0.321** |
| SES Hardship Index (1.00=average) | −1.866 | | 1.615 | |
| *Lower level – spatial/contextual variables* | | | | |
| Log population density | | −0.265 | 0.415 | |
| Pop growth 1996–2001 (%) | | **−2.348** | 0.215 | |
| Owner-occupied housing (%) | | 0.462 | 0.292 | |
| Movers last 5 years (%) | | **3.227** | −0.432 | |
| Commute to different municipality for work | | 0.056 | 0.061 | |
| Drive to work | | 0.843 | −0.076 | |
| Distance to centre (tri-zone) | | 8.710 | −4.661 | **−6.143** |
| Simpson Index (Class Diversity) | | −40.058 | −10.376 | |
| *Upper level – regional variables (Montreal = base)* | | | | |
| Quebec City | **−26.949** | −82.140 | **−73.442** | **−89.236** |
| R Square | 0.962 | 0.532 | 0.944 | 0.936 |
| Adj R Square | 0.908 | 0.400 | 0.907 | 0.923 |
| Std. Error of the Estimate | 4.652 | 11.877 | 4.663 | 4.246 |

*Notes:* For boldface coefficients, p<0.05. The Bloc only contested elections in the province of Quebec, and so the above model only covers electoral districts in Quebec. Coefficients in model 4 are those for variables remaining in the model after backwards regression.
*Source:* Census data from the Census of Canada, 2006. Election results for the 2006 Federal election.

# Chapter Four | The Political Ecology of Metropolitan Great Britain

*R. Alan Walks*

There is an extensive range of literature examining the importance of place and contextual effects for understanding electoral behaviour in Great Britain, with traditional emphases on regional effects and/or differences between urban and rural areas. Ecological research conducted using local authorities or constituencies as the units of analysis has typically been concerned with uncovering the importance of social class and social composition or, in the case of turnout, seat marginality, for understanding geographic patterns. While geographic unevenness in British electoral behaviour has often been the problem to be explained, this is usually executed by way of the distribution of classes and local party competition, or through the use of broad economic 'placeless' categories defined by class or industrial composition, rather than to geographic attributes of the places. While we now know much about the politics of, say, mining regions, resort areas, council housing estates and whole conurbations (Johnston 1986; Johnston *et al.* 1988), the relative importance of place and context for determining political behaviour within urban areas remains underexplored.

This chapter sheds light on the relationship between place-based attributes and electoral behaviour in British metropolitan areas. In part, this research is concerned with understanding the importance of post-war forms of suburbanisation for the emerging political ecology of the metropolis. While remaining a minor subset of the vast British electoral literature, interest in the effects of suburbanisation dates back to the 1960s debates around the 'embourgeoisement' of the working class (Goldthorpe *et al.* 1968), and was further influenced by the literature on 'class dealignment' in the 1970s (Crewe *et al.* 1977). Importantly, contextual factors related to suburbanisation were said to portend a decline in working-class loyalties to the left (and thus 'class dealignment'). Low-density suburban lifestyles were linked to materialistic and individualist beliefs on behalf of the new 'suburban workers', who were thus expected to be less partisan and more instrumentalist in their political behaviour (Abrams 1960; Nordlinger 1967). Such debates were again prominent in the 1980s, with the 'two-cars attitude' of suburban residents (particularly in the south-east region around London) blamed for Thatcher's rise and keeping Labour out of power (Clapson 2003: 182). Rasmussen (1973) found strong independent effects for low-density housing and homeownership (producing disproportionately low support for Labour), while Curtice and Steed (1982, 1986) demonstrated that 'class dealignment' was accompanied by a virtually monotonic effect of population density (the higher the density, the greater the support for Labour and the lower the support for the Conservatives). The link between suburban location and voting for the Conservatives (and support for

Labour in the inner cities) was confirmed by Walks (2005). Spatial polarisation in partisanship is strongest for the Tories, for which city-suburban distinctions became increasingly predictive of electoral support over the post-war period. By the 2001 national election, the Conservatives had lost virtually all of their traditionally-held inner-city seats, yet maintained disproportionately high levels of support in outer suburban and rural areas, while Labour's safest seats were, at least until 2010, to be found in the inner cities. Why this should be the case, however, remains to be answered. Is it a result of increasing class segregation, or suburban 'embourgeoisement' as early commentators expected, or might something else be at play?

More recently, MacAllister *et al.* (2001) compared the predictive power of British voters' socio-demographic characteristics to their neighbours' partisanship (thus employing a strictly spatial definition), while Johnston *et al.* (2001) explored the effect of the 'lifestyle environment' in different neighbourhoods on individual voter proclivities (mostly, however, based on 'placeless' variables not tied to any particular location, denoted by the presence of families and the form and age of housing, in addition to occupational/class differences). These studies found that British voters' 'spatial location' had a greater influence over their partisanship than did their 'social location' – at least in the 1992 and 1997 national elections (see also Johnston *et al.* 2004). Each of these studies, however, uses different data sets and variables, and it is not known whether the same variables have an effect in local elections. In Britain, turnout in local elections hovers at under 40 per cent, compared with over 60 per cent in national elections. Furthermore, despite the presence of partisan elections at the local level, surveys suggest that approximately 20 per cent of British voters select candidates from different parties in municipal and national elections (Rallings and Thrasher 1997: 154). Thus, it might be expected that different factors are responsible for driving electoral behaviour at the local and national levels.

This chapter sets out to examine and compare the factors underlying the geography of political partisanship and participation in national and local elections in Great Britain (England, Wales, and Scotland).[1] The first section analyses electoral turnout in Westminster and Scottish parliamentary constituencies for all metropolitan regions ('conurbations') in the 1992 and 2001 national (general) elections, and examines the factors driving national and municipal participation using a case study of Greater London. In the latter case, the 2004 Greater London Authority (GLA) municipal (borough) election results are compared with those from the 2001 national election. The second section examines the compositional and contextual effects operating on partisanship in the 1992 and 2001 national elections. Many of the same elements animate municipal elections as in their national counterparts at this scale, although often to different degrees. While socio-demographic composition is the strongest element in predicting both turnout

---

1. Although part of the United Kingdom, Northern Ireland has a completely different party structure and political culture than found in Great Britain. It is thus left out of this analysis.

and partisanship, a number of key spatial/contextual factors also play a role. Importantly, while the effects of social composition are similar across the different local and national contests, different sets of spatial/contextual variables emerge as important for understanding partisanship at different times.

## Party ideology and the party structure

Since the ascendance of the first Labour government in 1924, the government of the United Kingdom has passed between successive Labour and Conservative administrations. The Labour Party, the main party of the left, has traditionally garnered the greatest electoral successes in manufacturing and mining areas, places with a long history of working-class mobilisation. The Conservative Party (or 'Tory' party), the primary party of the right, has been strongest in resort towns and areas dependent upon either agriculture or higher-order services (including financial services, which are concentrated in London), sectors typically demonstrating low levels of unionisation (Butler and Stokes 1974; Norris 1997). Despite losing its status as the official opposition to Labour in 1924, the Liberal Party and its descendents have maintained a strong presence as Britain's third party, typically sandwiched ideologically between Labour and the Tories.[2] The Liberals, and the Liberal Democrats that followed, are not particularly strong in any region, relying mostly on local contests and by-elections for their electoral successes, although they often draw protest votes from both Labour and Conservative supporters. Nonetheless, they have had more success in the rural south, where they tend to take Labour's place as the main opposition to the Tories. This is somewhat ironic because in the urban north-east and north-west (and Yorkshire) they have had more success supplanting the Tories as the main opposition to Labour, for example in places such as Liverpool and Sheffield (Dorling et al. 1998; Fisher 2002).

Meanwhile, a number of regionally-based quasi-separatist parties have arisen and won seats in Wales and Scotland. The most successful of these are the two regional parties that have gained prominence since the onset of Thatcherism, the Plaid Cymru (in Wales) and the Scottish National Party (SNP). Remaining marginal, but nonetheless fielding candidates in most English (and some Scottish and Welsh) seats are the natalist/nationalist parties the UK Independence Party (UKIP), committed to withdrawal from Europe and more restrictive immigration policies, and even farther to the right, the racist British National Party (BNP).

British parties have undergone ideological shifts over time, although the general structure with Labour on the left, the Tories on the right, and the Liberals/ Liberal Democrats in the 'centre', continues largely intact. Labour's version of

---

2. In 1981, a number of disgruntled Labour MPs, unhappy with Labour leader Michael Foot's shift of the party to the left, formed the Social Democratic Party (SDP). While identifying itself as a centre-left party, the SDP distinguished itself by its commitment to Europe, to the free market, and its opposition to nuclear disarmament (policies antithetical to Foot's Labour at the time). The SDP thus positioned itself ideologically much closer to the Liberals, and the 1983 and 1987 elections were contested as the Liberal-SDP Alliance. After 1987, the two parties formally merged and changed their name to the Liberal Democratic Party.

Fabian socialism has remained open, moderate, democratic and reform-minded. The progression of first Neil Kinnock and then Tony Blair as leaders and the emergence of 'New Labour' are factors often considered to have brought about the 'modernisation' of Labour policies, which typically means a shift toward the centre and the acceptance of market-based policies first introduced under Thatcher. In recent times, meanwhile, the Liberal Democrats are largely seen as having moved to the left since their inception, becoming particularly critical of New Labour's management of the two-tier health system and advocating increased income taxes to improve the public health and education infrastructure (Heath *et al.* 2001). The most distinct ideological shift among the main political parties is associated with Thatcherism – the neoliberal revolution that Thatcher installed in the Conservative party. Since the time of Benjamin Disraeli, the Conservatives had been associated with a peculiar mix of both pro-business orientation and anti-unionism on the one hand, and on the other a collectivist orientation towards maintaining social peace and order, and improving the lives of the poor. This mix of apparently contradictory politics has been called the essence of Toryism. Thatcher turned away from traditional Toryism, instead advocating individualism and neoliberal policies which subjected the rules of society to those of the market (indeed, she is widely quoted for saying 'there is no such thing as society', in Keay 1987). Many in her own party rebelled, but were marginalised. Under Thatcher, the Conservatives largely ceased being traditional Tories, and became neoliberals although tinged with an anti-Europe nationalism ('authoritarian populism', in Stuart Hall's memorable phrase), and begun the process of dismantling the significant welfare state that previous Tory administrations helped construct.[3]

Differences in ideological orientations on behalf of the four most popular political parties are evident when measured using the positions of their supporters on the left-right self-placement index, and the economic, globalisation, and social-cultural indices examined throughout this volume (see Figure 4.1). The Conservatives clearly lean farthest to the right on each dimension and are particularly distinct from the other parties on the left-right and economic indices. Labour leans farthest to the left on both of these counts, but it is the SNP and Liberal Democrats that lean farthest left in their positioning in relation to the globalisation and cultural indices, respectively (but by small margins).

## Measuring electoral behaviour in British conurbations

This chapter analyses election data collected at the level of the Westminster and Scottish parliamentary constituency for national elections, and at the level of local authorities (boroughs) for the Greater London election. In the United Kingdom, aggregate electoral data for national elections and referenda is only released

---

3.   A key issue of Thatcherism was the Poll Tax, which did away with the traditional property tax and replaced it with a straight per-capita tax unrelated to level of wealth or income (and thus, an incredibly regressive form of taxation). The unpopularity of the Poll Tax, among other things, forced the party to remove Thatcher as leader, replacing her with John Major.

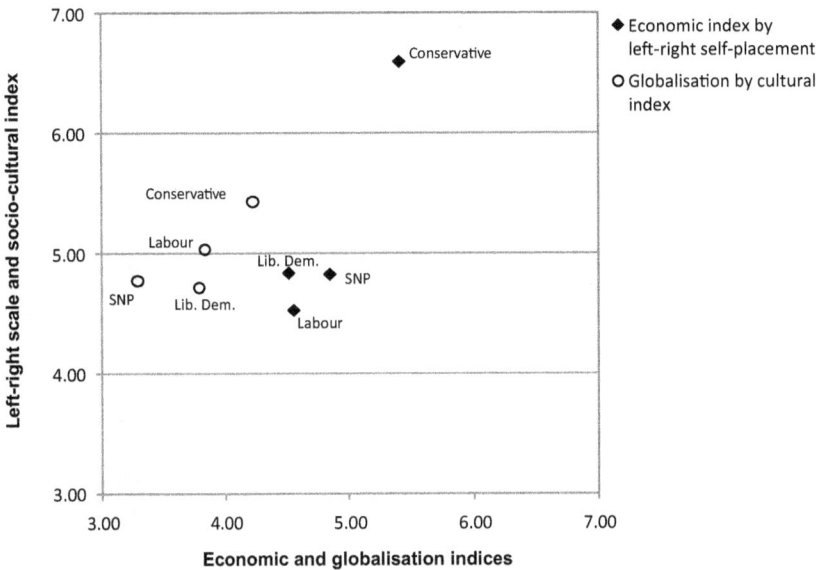

*Figure 4.1: Party placements on the left-right, economic, globalisation, and cultural indices*

*Note:* Each index is scored from lower (left) to higher (right). Higher values for the economic index indicate more support for competition, privatisation, tax reduction, individualism and economic freedom generally. Higher values for the globalisation index indicate reduced support for immigration, the rights of immigrants, and higher levels of nationalism and reduced feelings of cosmopolitanism. Higher values for the social-cultural index indicate greater degrees of religiosity and pro-family values, coupled with reduced support for same-sex marriage and divorce.

at the level of parliamentary constituencies; these are spatial units designed to encompass communities with populations of similar size and composition.

In 2001, Westminster parliamentary constituencies in England contained an average population of roughly 92,890, while those in Wales averaged 72,577 people, and Scottish parliamentary constituencies held 70,305 people on average.[4] Redistricting occurs every ten years, after publication of the decennial census and the recommendations of the Boundary Commission. While local authorities (municipalities, i.e. metropolitan councils, counties, boroughs and unitary districts) provide the basic building blocks of parliamentary constituencies, the boundaries of the latter often diverge from the municipal boundaries because of the requirement for similar populations. Many large (central) cities are themselves divided into a number of constituencies. The use of constituencies thus allows for a more fine-grained

---

4.  The difference in population sizes between the three 'nations' is partly due to national provisions introduced by the Labour Government under Blair to devolve part of the responsibility for the redistricting of parliamentary constituencies to Scotland and Wales, and with it, changes to the requirements for roughly equal populations among constituencies.

analysis of ecological associations, and in turn increases the statistical significance of the results. This is particularly important in British metropolitan areas, in which the central cities are typically large and contain a diversity of neighbourhoods, including typically both the richest and poorest metropolitan residents.

The analysis of national turnout and partisanship is conducted for the twenty largest metropolitan regions in England, Wales and Scotland (see Table 4.1). The method for categorising the inner city and suburban areas differs slightly from that employed in another study by Walks (2005). Herein, the inner cores are defined in relation to municipal boundaries, and not the era of development as in that earlier study. Thus, all parliamentary constituencies contained within the central city (or central cities, in those conurbations with more than one old core) are defined as urban concentrations, while all constituencies located outside the boundaries of the central cities are classified as suburban communities. Six of the conurbations under study are defined as having more than one central city municipality, including London, where, following tradition, the inner city is defined here as the Inner London boroughs (Cox 1968; Johnston 1986; Walks 2005). While parliamentary constituencies do not always follow municipal lines in the suburban areas, there are very few cases in which they will overlap the boundary of the central city. On average, this method categorises about a third of metropolitan residents as living in the central cities, although this varies significantly between conurbations.

Analysis of municipal elections in the United Kingdom is fraught with difficulties. Local authorities (municipalities) can take a number of different forms: metropolitan councils/authorities, metropolitan boroughs, counties, shire districts, unitary authorities, regional districts, and Scottish or Welsh districts. In some cases, urban areas are governed by two tiers, at other times, by a single tier. In many of the metropolitan councils (including London), as well as all non-metropolitan district or regional councils, a proportion of council members are elected at-large, making comparisons with district councils that do not follow this practice problematic, particularly in regards to sorting out spatial effects. While there are municipal elections in every year in the United Kingdom, in many municipalities only a third, and sometimes half, of candidate positions are filled, with the remainder filled in a different year.[5] Simplest are the 'whole elections', which take place in Greater London, in the Scottish or Welsh districts, and in many of shire counties. In such places, a single election takes place once every four years, filling all positions at once.

The lack of significant levels of political fragmentation at the municipal level

---

5. In most municipal elections, multiple members at different scales, and the number of councillors elected varies by ward. In London boroughs, for instance, while fifteen wards elect a single member, 330 elect two, and another 414 wards election three members. This structure has been reformed many times over the years, including the late 1990s. Yet, as Rallings and Thrasher (1997) note, each successive system appears equally complex. Part of the complexity involves the municipal electoral schedule, making it difficult to compare trends between different types of municipalities. 'Partial' elections are held for one third of the council members in each of the first three years of every four-year term in all metropolitan councils and many metropolitan boroughs, and in about one third of shire counties and unitary authorities. In some metropolitan areas, this means electing a single member every year in three-member wards. In other cases, only one third of the wards hold elections. In a small number of local authorities holding 'partial' elections, half of the council is elected every other year, thus completing the cycle every two years.

*Table 4.1: British conurbations/urban regions under study*

| Conurbation | Conurbation population | Core municipalities | Population change, 1991–2001 (%) | Foreign born (%) | Disad-vantage/ hardship | Employed in manu-facturing (%) |
|---|---|---|---|---|---|---|
| London | 10,916,053 | Inner London Boroughs | 14.5 | 24.6 | 105 | 4.2 |
| Manchester | 3,133,127 | Manchester, Bolton, Oldham | 4.2 | 7.3 | 105 | 7.5 |
| Birmingham | 3,033,133 | Birmingham, Wolverhampton | 4.0 | 10.7 | 133 | 8.9 |
| Leeds | 1,979,211 | Leeds, Bradford | 7.3 | 8.1 | 111 | 8.0 |
| Newcastle | 1,744,658 | Newcastle, Sunderland | 2.2 | 3.7 | 120 | 7.1 |
| Glasgow | 1,619,806 | Glasgow | 2.6 | 3 | 135 | 5.9 |
| Sheffield | 1,425,394 | Sheffield | 4.0 | 4.2 | 111 | 7.7 |
| Liverpool | 1,390,096 | Liverpool | 1.5 | 3.8 | 130 | 5.8 |
| Edinburgh | 791,288 | Edinburgh | 12.5 | 5.2 | 89 | 5.4 |
| Bristol | 744,163 | Bristol | 10.3 | 7.1 | 75 | 6.2 |
| Nottingham | 727,978 | Nottingham | 6.6 | 7.1 | 1.07 | 7.5 |
| Leicester | 724,494 | Leicester | 10.4 | 13.4 | .97 | 10.1 |
| Cardiff | 671,435 | Cardiff | 10.4 | 6.4 | 1.03 | 5.9 |
| Portsmouth/ Southampton | 670,716 | Portsmouth/ Southampton | 13.0 | 9.0 | 83 | 5.9 |
| Teeside | 625,458 | Middlesbrough | 1.6 | 3.6 | 1.34 | 7.0 |
| Coventry | 489,502 | Coventry | 6.8 | 11.2 | 1.02 | 9.1 |
| Stoke | 468,491 | Stoke-on-Trent | 3.8 | 3.8 | 98 | 10.6 |
| Hull | 438,121 | Kingston-upon-Hull | 4.9 | 3.9 | 1.16 | 8.0 |
| Bournemouth | 421,939 | Bournemouth | 11.9 | 7.9 | 73 | 5.8 |
| Plymouth | 278,074 | Plymouth | 5.7 | 5.7 | 89 | 6.5 |

*Notes:* Conurbation data are calculated from parliamentary constituency data. Values for the socio-economic disadvantage and hardship index are calculated against the total level for the UK (1.00). Higher values indicate more hardship.

presents another obstacle to systematic comparative research. In some cases, there is one very large central city governed by a metropolitan district council surrounded by a small number of contiguous counties or boroughs, which together produce only a small number of potential electoral contests. For simplicity's sake, this chapter focuses on the 2004 Greater London Authority (GLA) election results and compares them with the 2001 national election results for Greater

London. The GLA is a metropolitan district assembly led by a mayor with one assembly member elected from each of fourteen large wards, the latter which are aggregations of the thirty-two boroughs. The original Greater London Council is notorious for being abolished by the Thatcher Tories in 1986, with all of its responsibilities at that time downloaded to the individual borough municipalities. The Labour Government under Blair re-established the council as the GLA after a referendum in 1999, with the first elections held in 2000. This chapter analyses the 2004 election. Ken Livingstone, mayor at time of abolition in 1986, won the 2000 election as an independent when Labour refused to endorse his candidacy, in turn skewing significantly the party totals in that election. Livingstone won again in 2004 by a smaller margin, but this time under the Labour Party endorsement (for more information, see Travers 2004). For this reason, the 2004 elections have been selected for this analysis.

Electoral turnout – the proportion of the total electorate that cast a vote – and partisanship – the proportion of the total vote for the main national parties – are the dependent variables in both the national and municipal analyses. In keeping with established practice (Johnston *et al.* 2002), the proportion of the total vote going to the three main national political parties is used here to define partisanship, so that partisanship can be measured without having the results skewed by regional support for separatist parties, namely the Plaid Cymru and the SNP. This method effectively factors out support for the regional/separatist parties, as well as other marginal parties. Separate independent regional variables are also included for both Wales and Scotland. In addition to drawing out regional bases of support, these variables have the advantage of controlling for the effects of the regional parties on the electoral structure.

The independent variables derive from the 1991 and 2001 censuses, (see Table A4.1 in the Appendix to this chapter for description). A series of compositional and contextual variables were entered at both the lower-local level and the upper (metropolitan) level, with significant cross-level variables included in the final models reported herein. As some of the variation at the lower level is accounted for by variation at the upper level, the determinants of electoral behaviour were modelled using randomised multilevel modelling (MLM) techniques, and these are reported upon in this chapter.[6] Determinants of the variables influencing elec-

---

6.  As MLM allows for simultaneous estimation of regression slopes at both the lower and upper levels, cross-level interaction effects between the two levels could also be examined. A series of different models were estimated for each of the electoral phenomenon under study. However, in this chapter, the models that are reported include only the full model (with all variables input but without cross-level interactions) and separate models for composition and contextual effects on turnout, as well as a final MLM model estimated using only those variables and effects, including cross-level effects, that were found to be significant in of the exploratory models. This final model is then manually fine-tuned by re-estimating it in iterative fashion to maximise the log likelihood with variables removed in turn from the analysis that are revealed as statistically insignificant (at p<0.10), and by experimenting with the placement of the upper-level variables (i.e. their effects on both the constant and slopes). This iterative process mimics the backwards regression process of OLS (ordinary least squares) regression, and produces models that provide the most

toral behaviour in Greater London were modelled using ordinary least squares (OLS) linear regression, however, since in this case the effects are all occurring within the same single region. The variables chosen at each level were selected in accordance with the requirements of the protocol agreed upon by contributors to this volume.[7]

British metropolitan areas can be divided into distinct types of communities based on shared characteristics, as determined by the collaborative protocol of this study (see Table 4.2).[8] Urban concentrations, which represent one third of all metropolitan constituencies, refer to those districts located within the boundaries of the central cities. Areas located outside the central city municipalities with population densities significantly lower than the metropolitan average, all located at the fringes of the study conurbations, are categorised as low-density suburbs (11 per cent of the sample). Such areas have approximately twice the British average proportion of detached housing. They are districts largely containing newer suburbs and exurban areas, as well as small towns and rural areas now found within commuting range of the expanding metropolis. Affluent suburbs (about 10 per cent of the total sample) are notable for having levels of socio-economic status at least 20 per cent higher than the metropolitan average (which represents approxi-

---

parsimonious picture of the factors shaping electoral behaviour. These MLM models estimated using the entire national data set were compared to those estimated using OLS linear regression for the purposes of sensitivity testing. Since the latter did not yield any notable discrepancies, and since there are enough observations at each scale for the MLM method to permit calculation of robust standard errors, likelihood estimates, and tests for significance, only the MLM models are reported here. (For more detail, contact the author.)

7.   Most of these variables are self-explanatory, but there are some important exceptions, and one variable – the proportion commuting more than 20 km to work – is not available in 1991. As is the case in many European nations, income is not recorded in the British census. Socio-economic status is therefore determined via educational attainment and occupational status. A hardship index is calculated using variables for the lack of qualifications, unemployment, and female single-parent family households. This index correlates highly with the presence of council housing (rented from a public authority), population density, and tenants more generally. There is, on the other hand, little correlation between the hardship index and the presence of immigrants, which instead correlates moderately with high levels of population growth and residential turnover. Distance to the centre is here determined through a three-zonal classification (corresponding roughly to the central city, contiguous suburbs and non-contiguous outer suburbs/exurbs). The city-suburban hardship index consists of a ratio of the central-city hardship index value relative to the hardship index in the remainder of the metropolitan region multiplied by 100 (a value of 100 thus suggests parity between city and suburban levels of hardship). There is no variable representing fragmentation, since the units of analysis for national elections examined here are parliamentary constituencies, whose populations are meant to vary only slightly. Four regional variables are included in the analysis as dichotomous variables. Previous analyses (Johnston and Pattie 1992; Norris 1997; Walks 2005) have shown these regions to vote significantly differently than elsewhere in Great Britain.

8.   Admittedly, the use of parliamentary constituencies to represent communities here is not ideal, since they were constructed merely for the purpose of conducting national elections, and as such there are no historical or political bases for characterising them as constituting the features of community. However, as they are the only units for which electoral data is collected, they have to act as a proxy for political community.

mately one standard deviation), and levels of hardship approximately 20 per cent below the average. They also have above-average concentrations of immigrants and average proportions of visible minorities. There are many urban core districts within the central cities that mimic their affluent suburban counterparts, although many of such areas within the central cities will have somewhat higher densities and higher levels of economic diversity, and in some places, such as Greenwich, Woolwich, and Islington in London, high levels of hardship as well.

Meanwhile, twenty-eight suburban constituencies (approximately 8 per cent of the total sample) reveal levels of disadvantage and hardship greater than 25 per cent higher than the metropolitan average. The latter can be further subdivided into areas with above- or below-average proportions of visible minorities and/or immigrants (the former represents 3.3 per cent and the latter 4.4 per cent of the total sample).[9] Such areas have high proportions of council (social/subsidised) housing estates (similar in proportion to the urban concentrations), very little detached housing and, in the case of high-minority high-hardship suburbs, even higher average densities than found in the inner cities. The 38 per cent of districts not otherwise classified above fall into the category of middle-class suburbs. The latter areas typically have higher concentrations of detached and owner-occupied housing and lower proportions of immigrants and visible minorities than the metropolitan average, but otherwise middling values on most indices (see Table 4.2).

## Metropolitanisation and contextual effects in British conurbations

Great Britain has witnessed a shift in the geography of electoral behaviour over the post-war period. Urban and rural political distinctions, varying with population density, had been growing since the 1950s (Curtice and Steed 1982). The rise of Thatcher and the Tories' neoliberal approach, which largely benefited the south at the expense of the industrial (and de-industrialising) north, Scotland and Wales, had the effect of significantly polarising the electorate by region (Mohan 1999). The late 1980s also saw rapid growth of intra-metropolitan divergence in partisanship as the effects of Thatcher's policies were unevenly felt across urban areas, and inner-city populations began voicing their discontent (Johnston *et al.* 2004). The shift to the right on behalf of the Labour Party, and the subsequent election of Labour Governments from 1997 until 2010 with increased support from the south, have been accompanied by reduced levels of regional polarisation in partisanship overall. Yet city-suburban differences, particularly in support for the Conservatives, continued to increase (Walks 2005).

---

9. For districts located within the Greater London conurbation, the London average proportion foreign born was used as the base for such calculations. In other conurbations, the base was determined via the metro average excluding London. This method controls for the very high concentration of minorities and immigrants in London.

*Table 4.2: Means of selected variables by district typology (2001 census)*

| District types | Core districts Urban concentrations | Suburban districts High disparity, high minority | High disparity, low minority | Middle-class suburbs | Low-density suburbs | Affluent suburbs | Total |
|---|---|---|---|---|---|---|---|
| Number of districts | 121 | 12 | 16 | 138 | 39 | 35 | 361 |
| Proportion of urban districts (%) | 33.5 | 3.3 | 4.4 | 38.2 | 10.8 | 9.7 | 100 |
| Proportion of urban population (%) | 33.3 | 3.4 | 4.1 | 38.2 | 10.6 | 10.4 | 100 |
| Density/km$^2$ | 4,621 | 5,014 | 2,474 | 1,846 | 299 | 1,898 | 2,747 |
|  | (2,852) | (1,921) | (1,380) | (1,201) | (105) | (1,386) | (2,485) |
| Detached housing (%) | 8.3 | 6.5 | 10.0 | 19.0 | 28.6 | 23.7 | 16.1 |
|  | (7.0) | (4.2) | (4.4) | (10.0) | (8.4) | (12.7) | (11.3) |
| Owner-occupied housing (%) | 54.1 | 59.2 | 56.3 | 71.5 | 73.9 | 72.5 | 64.9 |
|  | (13.5) | (7.3) | (8.0) | (7.3) | (7.0) | (8.8) | (13.1) |
| Rent from council (%) | 30.0 | 24.8 | 33.9 | 19.3 | 17.8 | 14.7 | 23.1 |
|  | (11.7) | (6.7) | (6.3) | (7.5) | (7.5) | (6.2) | (10.8) |
| Visible minorities (%) | 17.2 | 37.5 | 5.1 | 7.2 | 1.8 | 10.7 | 11.2 |
|  | (15.8) | (13.9) | (5.7) | (9.6) | (1.7) | (12.3) | (13.9) |
| Foreign born (%) | 16.2 | 28.0 | 4.8 | 8.2 | 3.7 | 15.4 | 11.6 |
|  | (13.5) | (14.1) | (3.9) | (7.8) | (1.9) | (13.0) | (11.7) |
| Employed in manufacturing (%) | 5.4 | 5.5 | 6.8 | 6.9 | 8.7 | 5.8 | 6.4 |
|  | (2.3) | (2.8) | (2.4) | (2.1) | (2.0) | (2.4) | (2.5) |
| Population growth 1991–2001 (%) | 10.5 | 9.6 | 1.1 | 6.5 | 6.9 | 10.2 | 8.1 |
|  | (11.7) | (8.0) | (7.8) | (5.4) | (4.5) | (5.6) | (8.5) |
| SES Hardship Index (Britain = 100) | 135.7 | 148.4 | 151.2 | 95.5 | 88.3 | 79.8 | 101.9 |
|  | (40.9) | (39.1) | (13.0) | (21.7) | (19.5) | (22.0) | (37.4) |

*Note*: standard deviation in parentheses.

Such shifts have meant that intra-urban divergences in partisanship have increased relative to regional/metropolitan-level disparities. This is borne out in Table 4.3, which compares levels of within and between-group variance in electoral participation and partisanship in both the 1992 election (which resulted in a Conservative majority) and the 2001 election (Labour majority). Alongside overall declines in spatial differentiation (as indicated by the lower sums of squares and F statistics), the share of the total variance accounted for by between-group differences (i.e. between metropolitan areas and thus also between regions) declined for all three of the main national political parties. Only one third of the variation in Labour and Conservative support is explained by between-group (metropolitan-level) differences in 2001, down from over 40 per cent in 1992. Meanwhile, the proportion of the variation explained at the intra-metropolitan level rose by approximately 8 per cent, accounting for two-thirds of the variation

*Table 4.3: Analysis of within and between metro variance in turnout and partisanship in national elections, 1992 and 2001*

| | 1992 | | | | | 2001 | | | | |
|---|---|---|---|---|---|---|---|---|---|---|
| **Turnout** | **Sum of squares** | **df** | **% variance** | **F** | **Sig.** | **Sum of squares** | **df** | **% variance** | **F** | **Sig.** |
| Between groups | 1440.8 | 19 | 9.2 | 1.91 | 0.013 | 1823.3 | 19 | 11.6 | 2.36 | 0.001 |
| Within groups | 14263.9 | 340 | 90.8 | | | 13891.7 | 341 | 88.4 | | |
| Total | 15704.6 | 359 | | | | 15715.0 | 360 | | | |
| **Partisanship** | | | | | | | | | | |
| *Labour* | | | | | | | | | | |
| Between groups | 48891.8 | 19 | 42.0 | 13.68 | 0.000 | 31010.2 | 19 | 33.5 | 9.03 | 0.000 |
| Within groups | 67549.6 | 340 | 58.0 | | | 61426.0 | 340 | 66.5 | | |
| Total | 116441.4 | 359 | | | | 92436.2 | 359 | | | |
| *Liberal Democrat* | | | | | | | | | | |
| Between groups | 3888.0 | 19 | 15.7 | 3.53 | 0.000 | 3285.1 | 19 | 11.1 | 2.24 | 0.002 |
| Within groups | 20801.2 | 340 | 84.3 | | | 26294.5 | 340 | 88.9 | | |
| Total | 24689.2 | 359 | | | | 29579.7 | 359 | | | |
| *Conservative* | | | | | | | | | | |
| Between groups | 28871.2 | 19 | 40.7 | 12.99 | 0.000 | 17614.6 | 19 | 32.5 | 8.63 | 0.000 |
| Within groups | 42006.2 | 340 | 59.3 | | | 36531.0 | 340 | 67.5 | | |
| Total | 70877.3 | 359 | | | | 54145.6 | 359 | | | |

in support for the two main parties in 2001. While still an important factor structuring politics in Britain, regionalism has nonetheless declined in importance.

The same is true for the Liberal Democrats. However, very little of the variation in support for the Liberal Democrats is accounted for at this upper level anyway, as this party has traditionally relied on attracting local personalities and on protest and strategic voting in by-elections for its ability to win elections (thus at least 84 per cent of the variation in support for the Liberal Democrats rests at the lower level). Electoral participation, in contradistinction to the trends uncovered for partisanship, would appear far less affected by shifts in regional power bases. The proportion of the total variation in electoral turnout explained at each level changed little over the study period, with approximately 90 per cent of the variance in turnout accounted for at the lower-district (within-group) level. The next sections examine in detail the determinants of electoral participation and partisanship.

## Electoral participation in British conurbations

Over most of the post-war period, participation in national elections across the entire United Kingdom averaged approximately 76 per cent. However, that dropped in the 2000s to an average of just over 60 per cent (rising again to 65.5 per cent in the 2010 national election). Municipal elections, meanwhile, attract a far lower proportion of electors, averaging less than 40 per cent over the post-war period. Figure 4.2 compares the rates of electoral turnout between national and municipal elections across the typology of different urban and suburban communities that make up metropolitan Britain. The trajectory is one of a gentle increase in participation in the move from the central cities to the low-density communities at the edges. Municipal turnout in the 2004 Greater London election, averaging 35.9 per cent, is roughly half that for the 1992 national election. In keeping with the falling rates of participation through the 2000s noted above, turnout in the 2001 national election is roughly 18 per cent lower than recorded only nine years before. Urban concentrations and high-hardship but low-minority suburbs reveal the lowest recent levels of participation.

The factors influencing turnout in national elections have remained fairly consistent over time (see Table 4.4). However, in some cases the direction of the coefficients has reversed, and the extent of cross-level interactions has grown. Place effects are clearly evident across the whole study period: areas with growing populations and with owner-occupied housing are more likely to vote, whereas higher population densities are associated with lower turnouts. There are also a number of differences. Family status and age variables are important in 2001, but not 1992, while employment in manufacturing (which, it might be noted, has been in the process of shifting from the north to the south) ceased having any noticeable effect. Socio-economic status (SES) in both its guises would appear the most important factors driving turnout in both elections, although the precise nature of the relationship shifts. In 1992, in addition to the effect of class at the lower level, there is also a linear positive effect of socio-economic status at the upper level –

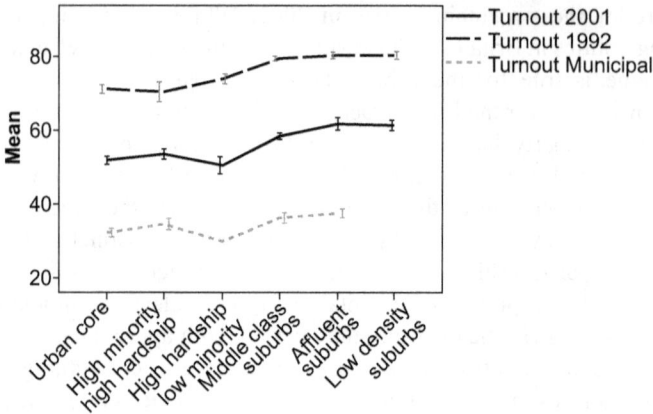

*Figure 4.2: Turnout in national and municipal elections, by community type*

the better-off conurbations, and the better-off areas within all conurbations, were more likely to vote. Hardship, on the other hand, reveals a non-linear association. The negative coefficients at the lower level coupled with the positive (though low) coefficients at the upper level suggest that the dampening effect of SES hardship on electoral turnout was somewhat exacerbated in the better-off conurbations (where, perhaps, those experiencing hardship felt more marginalised and less efficacious politically), but reduced in the conurbations with high levels of hardship. Class differences between metropolitan areas became less important over time, yet the effects at the lower level remained similar.

What is perhaps most interesting is the apparent shift in the direction of the effect of immigrant concentration and the increasingly complex interplay between immigration and population growth. In 1992, districts with large proportions of foreign born were significantly associated with lower likelihood of voting, while districts with a growing population had higher turnout rates. By 2001, areas containing more immigrants had become more, rather than less, likely to turn out to vote by a strong margin, but this effect was reduced in conurbations (particularly in London) with high levels of overall immigration. Similar, albeit weaker, effects are found for population growth in 2001. Growing areas were more likely to vote, but the strength of the effect of population shifts on national turnout was reduced in conurbations that were growing. The opposite set of effects is revealed for residential turnover, however. Districts with high rates of turnover are less likely to vote, but this effect is somewhat reduced in conurbations with greater levels of residential turnover. It might be noted here that high turnover rates are highly correlated with private rental areas, so this suggests areas containing concentrations of private rental tenants are less likely to vote. Together, these results suggest possible discrepancies between immigrant streams.

Urban and suburban growth fuelled by immigration in slower-growing conurbations (which also tend to have lower rates of residential mobility) is tied to higher turnouts, while areas of high turnover (which may also have relatively

**a) Effect of immigrant concentration**

**b) Effect of manufacturing employment**

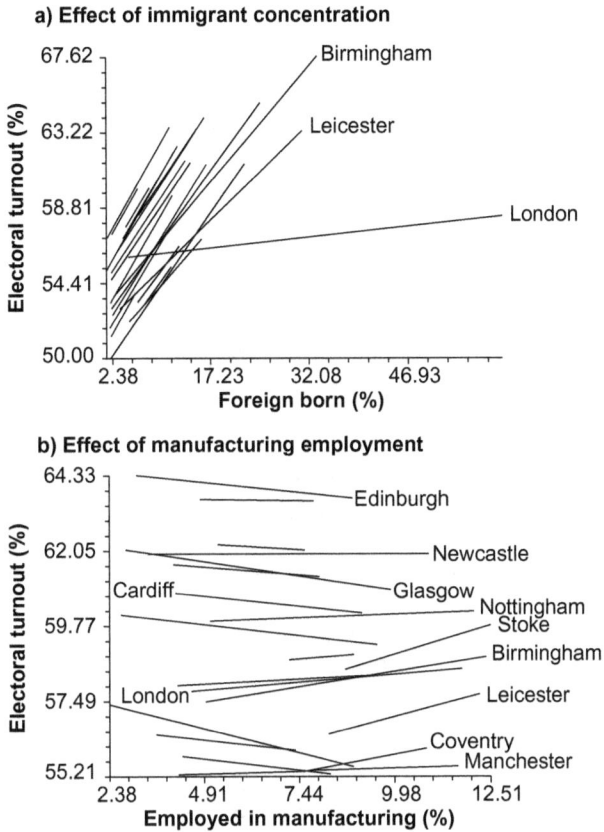

*Figure 4.3: Effects on turnout, by conurbation, 2001 national election (randomised slopes)*

high immigrant concentration) in such cities show lower turnouts. The effect of immigrant concentration, turnover, and population growth, however, is reduced in high-immigrant, high-growth and high-turnover cites (such as London), where such variables are perhaps overshadowed by class and hardship effects.

Randomised slopes relating electoral participation and the presence of immigrants and of manufacturing workers are presented in Figure 4.3. The strong positive correlation between concentrations of immigrants and high turnout is evident, as is the much weaker, almost flat, relationship in Britain's immigrant metropolis, Greater London. The lack of an overall relationship between manufacturing employment and participation across all metropolitan areas, meanwhile, is shown to mask how the relationship varies across different types of conurbations. Importantly, while there is a negative relationship between manufacturing employment and turnout in Scotland, Wales, and large conurbations with lower dependence on manufacturing (particularly London, where the relationship is

*Table 4.4: Models of electoral turnout, UK national elections*

| | 1992 | | | | 2001 | | | |
|---|---|---|---|---|---|---|---|---|
| | Composition | Contextual | Full randomised | Final randomised | Composition | Contextual | Full randomised | Final randomised |
| Constant (A) | 91.514 | 43.137 | 66.117 | 66.836 | 75.582 | 49.261 | 65.564 | 59.368 |
| *Lower-level variables: (B)* | | | | | | | | |
| *Compositional:* | | | | | | | | |
| Age under 16 (%) | 0.166 | | −0.086 | | 0.899 | | 0.655 | 0.429 |
| Age 65+ (%) | −0.032 | | 0.155 | | 0.270 | | 0.277 | 0.236 |
| Foreign born (%) | −0.194 | | −0.146 | −0.147 | 0.196 | | 0.117 | 0.438 |
| Manufacturing (%) | −0.021 | | 0.157 | 0.157 | −0.210 | | −0.039 | |
| SES General Index (Ave = 100) | −0.131 | | 0.027 | 0.030 | 0.031 | | 0.075 | 0.077 |
| SES Hardship Index (Ave = 100) | 0.004 | | −0.062 | −0.165 | −0.173 | | −0.091 | −0.094 |
| Migrants % last 3 years | −0.878 | | −0.812 | −0.884 | −0.501 | | −0.214 | −1.185 |
| *Spatial/contextual:* | | | | | | | | |
| Owner-occupied housing (%) | | 0.251 | 0.102 | 0.086 | | 0.364 | 0.174 | 0.128 |
| Population Change 1991–2001 (%) | | 0.084 | 0.076 | 0.079 | | 0.133 | 0.037 | 0.202 |
| Log population density | | −0.167 | −1.027 | −1.079 | | −4.394 | −2.345 | −1.761 |
| Simpson Index (occupational diversity) | | 0.056 | 0.088 | 0.112 | | −0.020 | −0.134 | −0.193 |
| Commute 20+ km to work | | n/a | n/a | | | −0.112 | −0.028 | |
| Distance to centre (tri-zone) | | 0.329 | 0.670 | | | −0.202 | −0.282 | |
| *Upper-level variables: (G)* | | | | | | | | |
| *Region:* | | | | | | | | |
| Region – North/Yorkshire | −0.078 | −1.296 | −1.303 | | −2.458 | −2.055 | −1.776 | −0.981 |
| Region – South E/W | 1.730 | −0.093 | 0.875 | | −1.367 | 1.702 | 0.087 | |
| Region – Wales | 4.680 | 1.588 | 3.127 | | 1.508 | 0.331 | 0.608 | 1.601 |
| Region – Scotland | 2.076 | 2.510 | 1.247 | | 1.185 | −0.217 | 1.060 | |

| | 1992 | | | | 2001 | | | |
|---|---|---|---|---|---|---|---|---|
| | Composition | Contextual | Full randomised | Final randomised | Composition | Contextual | Full randomised | Final randomised |
| *Upper-level variables:* | | | | | | | | |
| Log population (metro size) | -0.022 | 0.397 | 0.943 | | **-3.014** | 0.870 | -1.555 | |
| Population change 1991–2001 | -0.190 | -0.165 | -0.242 | | **-0.264** | 0.012 | -0.184 | |
| Employment in manufacturing (%) | 0.019 | 0.095 | -0.069 | | -0.164 | -0.291 | -0.344 | |
| City-Suburban Hardship Index* | 0.016 | 0.002 | 0.002 | | -0.003 | 0.004 | 0.004 | |
| *Cross-level effects:* | | | | | | | | |
| Upper-level effect on slope of (A) or (B) | | | | | | | | |
| Foreign born | | | | | | | | **-0.013**\*\* |
| Migrants % last 3 years | | | | | | | | **0.093**\*\* |
| SES General | | | | **0.075**\*\* | | | | |
| Population change 1991–2001 (%) | | | | | | | | **-0.016**\*\* |
| R square | 0.706 | 0.687 | | | 0.752 | 0.729 | | |
| Std. error of the estimate | 3.5663 | 3.675 | | | 3.362 | 3.508 | | |
| Random coefficient reliability+ | | | 0.713 | 0.615 | | | 0.752 | 0.778 |
| Log Likelihood (x - 1)~ | | | 1008.91 | 1008.41 | | | 929.06 | 926.7 |

*Notes:* For boldface values, p<0.05. Only those cross-level effects with coefficients to report have been reported above. (\*) Cross-level effect of upper level variable on slope of (A) (constant). (\*\*) Cross-level effect of upper level variable on slope of the lower-level variable (B). (+) Higher values indicate greater reliability. (–) Lower values indicate greater likelihoods. Higher values of CHSI indicate higher levels of city-suburban disparity (parity = 100).

*Table 4.5: Comparison of municipal and national turnout, Greater London*

| Dependent variable = Turnout (%) | 2004 Municipal election | | | | 2001 National election | | | |
|---|---|---|---|---|---|---|---|---|
| | Model 1 | Model 2 | Model 3 | Model 4 | Model 1 | Model 2 | Model 3 | Model 4 |
| | Composition | Contextual | Full linear | Backwards linear | Composition | Contextual | Full linear | Backwards linear |
| (Constant) | **39.178** | 33.384 | 52.770 | **36.135** | **67.380** | 78.002 | 87.673 | 52.164 |
| *Socio-demographic/compositional variables* | | | | | | | | |
| Age under 16 (%) | 0.718 | | **0.945** | **0.662** | 0.589 | | −0.081 | |
| Age 65+ (%) | −0.026 | | 0.098 | | −0.118 | | −0.314 | |
| Foreign born (%) | 0.073 | | **0.196** | | 0.030 | | −0.085 | −0.116 |
| Employed in manufacturing (%) | 0.131 | | −0.376 | | −0.245 | | −0.467 | |
| SES General | −0.042 | | 0.106 | | 0.003 | | **0.116** | **0.102** |
| SES Hardship Index | **−0.132** | | **−0.141** | **−0.095** | **−0.157** | | −0.017 | |
| Migrant last 3 years (%) | 0.0005 | | 0.030 | | −0.427 | | −0.392 | |
| *Spatial/contextual variables* | | | | | | | | |
| Log population density | | 0.413 | 0.844 | | | −5.338 | −3.944 | |
| Owner-occupied housing (%) | | 0.066 | −0.107 | | | **0.317** | **0.239** | **0.289** |
| Pop growth 199–2001 (%) | | −0.088 | **−0.152** | **−0.070** | | −0.005 | −0.023 | |
| Commute > 20km to work | | 0.058 | 0.215 | | | −0.139 | 0.014 | |
| Simpson Index (Occupational diversity) | | **−10.916** | **−19.013** | | | −0.161 | **−0.378** | **−0.340** |
| Distance to centre (tri-zone) | | 1.455 | 1.385 | | | −2.581 | −0.113 | |
| R Square | 0.708 | 0.624 | 0.786 | 0.699 | 0.706 | 0.713 | 0.798 | 0.786 |
| Adjusted R Square | 0.626 | 0.537 | 0.639 | 0.667 | 0.675 | 0.687 | 0.754 | 0.774 |
| Std. Error of the Estimate | 1.874 | 2.085 | 1.840 | 1.766 | 3.511 | 3.445 | 3.056 | 2.930 |

*Notes*: For boldface coefficients, $p<0.05$. Coefficients in model 4 are after backwards OLS regression.

negative and very strong), there is a positive (albeit mild) relationship with manufacturing throughout the industrial heartland of middle England (Birmingham, Leicester, Stoke, Coventry, Nottingham). The geography and history of working class and immigrant mobilisation across different regions clearly matters here.

Greater London provides an opportunity to examine differences between the factors responsible for producing spatial patterns in electoral participation between municipal and national elections. Both the mayor and assembly members for the Greater London Authority (GLA) are elected in whole-council elections every four years, with the inaugural GLA election held in 2000.[10] The levels of turnout in the 2004 GLA mayoral election are here compared to those for constituencies within Greater London for the 2001 national election. Four sets of OLS models are estimated and compared between the municipal and national elections: the compositional and contextual models, the full linear model, and one that utilises backward regression to select the most parsimonious model. This fourth set of models provides the most accurate fit and predictive power, as indicated by the higher adjusted R square coefficients and the lower standard errors of the estimate (see Table 4.5).

Although the 2004 mayoral election in Greater London drew significant media and public attention, partly due to Mayor Ken Livingstone's high level of popularity and charisma, the overall turnout rate (at 35.9 per cent) remained low and with-in the standard range for British municipal elections. This compares with the rate of 59.2 per cent in the 2001 national election for Greater London (still one of the lowest turnout rates for national elections in the history of the United Kingdom). Most of the factors affecting electoral participation in Greater London would appear similar in both municipal and national contexts, although the importance and direction of a number of the variables does change. While the presence of children/families is positively associated with turnout in the 2004 municipal election, this variable has virtually no effect in the 2001 national election. Socioeconomic status is clearly important in both cases, but it is the level of hardship that factors more strongly in the municipal elections. Immigrant concentration is associated with higher rates of voting in the 2004 municipal election, but not in the 2001 national election (indeed, the backwards regression suggests a mild insignificant negative effect – note how this fits in with the discussion of the MLM results above).

Only a few spatial/contextual variables appear important, and the effects differ between the two types of electoral contest. In national, but not municipal elections, owner-occupation is associated with greater turnouts, while population change is more important in the municipal context. Economic diversity would appear to have a significant negative effect on turnout, although this variable stays in the backwards regression models only in relation to the national election. The municipal and national contexts are seen to mobilise different constituencies, even within the same large metropolitan region.

---

10. This also marked history with Greater London's first directly-elected mayor (in the past, the mayor was elected by council members). Ballots for mayor employ the Supplementary Vote (SV) system, which asks voters to mark a first and second choice, and if no candidate gets a majority of first-choice votes, the discrete second choice votes for the top two candidates are added to the first (this is referred to as the second ballot, even though the choices were made simultaneously on the same ballot). Turnout rates apply to any mark on the ballot.

## Shifting contextual effects on partisanship in metropolitan Britain

Metropolitanisation has led to a reorganisation of partisanship within the United Kingdom. The Conservative party under Thatcher was able to win a number of middle-income but working-class suburban areas through the 1980s, partly by selling off many of the more desirable state-owned council estate units to their residents (some of whom then resold for significant profits). However, after Thatcher restructured property taxation with the poll tax, and with the onset of recession in the early 1990s (and the bottom falling out of the real estate sector), the Conservatives began to lose support. The 1992 national election saw John Major lead the Conservatives to a weaker majority victory, but it would be the last time the Conservatives would form the government again until 2010. This section contrasts the factors predicting support for the three main parties in Britain in the 1992 election, and the 2001 election won decisively by 'New' Labour under Tony Blair.

There are some clear trends linking social composition and local context to consistent bases of partisanship (see Table 4.6). When moving from areas of higher disparity to areas of affluence and/or with lower densities, support for the Conservative increases and the proportion voting Labour decreases. The main exceptions concern disadvantaged areas in the suburbs, which are more likely than urban concentrations to vote for Labour (and less likely to vote for the Liberal Democrats). High hardship areas with few minorities, which also contain the highest concentrations of council housing, are particularly more likely to vote for Labour and less likely to vote for the Tories. Suburban areas with low levels of hardship disproportionately voted Conservative, although only in affluent suburbs did the Tories consistently out-poll Labour (though they did win a number of middle-class and low-density suburban seats). The Liberal Democrats, on the other hand, are strongest in the inner city areas and affluent suburbs, and weakest in highly disadvantaged areas with few minorities. Note that middle-class and low-density suburban districts reveal almost identical patterns of partisanship, particularly in 2001. This is despite the fact that low-density suburbs contain fewer minorities, lower levels of hardship, and less detached housing (but similar levels of homeownership).

The MLM models confirm the evidence of significant contextual/place effects on partisanship at the district scale, even after controlling for social composition and a host of metropolitan-level factors (see Table 4.7). Furthermore, while most of the socio-demographic compositional variables have remained relatively constant in their effects over time (with some exceptions), the importance of place-based contextual variables has both increased and shifted in importance over the period. In the case of Labour, positive effects of manufacturing employment, and strong negative effects of owner-occupied housing, as well as for the presence of children and the elderly, are present in both periods. Yet, 2001 saw the replacement of an effect of distance (suburban areas less likely to support Labour), with effects for population decline (which are further augmented by population change at the conurbation level) and population density, as well as an increased effect of occupational diversity. As the inner city gentrifies, it is increasingly areas

*Table 4.6: Mean partisanship, by district typology*

| | Core districts | Suburban districts | | | | | |
|---|---|---|---|---|---|---|---|
| | Urban concentra-tions | High disparity, high minority | High disparity, low minority | Middle-class suburbs | Low-density suburbs | Affluent suburbs | Total |
| **2001** | | | | | | | |
| Number of districts | 121 | 12 | 16 | 138 | 39 | 35 | 361 |
| Proportion of urban districts | 33.5 | 3.3 | 4.4 | 38.2 | 10.8 | 9.7 | 100 |
| Labour (mean %) | 56.6 | 60.2 | 66.6 | 49.5 | 50.2 | 35.5 | 51.7 |
| | (12.5) | (5.6) | (6.8) | (16.7) | (16.0) | (15.3) | (16.0) |
| Liberal Democrat (mean %) | 17.2 | 13.2 | 12.0 | 16.5 | 16.4 | 19.3 | 16.7 |
| | (9.0) | (7.4) | (2.7) | (9.4) | (6.2) | (11.8) | (9.1) |
| Conservative (mean %) | 21.6 | 22.2 | 17.8 | 31.4 | 31.5 | 39.0 | 28.0 |
| | (9.5) | (6.0) | (6.1) | (12.0) | (12.4) | (10.3) | (12.3) |
| **1992** | | | | | | | |
| Number of districts | 133 | 12 | 34 | 115 | 39 | 42 | 375 |
| Proportion of urban districts | 35.4 | 3.2 | 9.0 | 30.6 | 10.4 | 11.4 | 100 |
| Labour (mean %) | 50.7 | 48.3 | 62.1 | 40.0 | 42.0 | 23.5 | 44.2 |
| | (14.0) | (7.9) | (10.5) | (16.2) | (16.8) | (12.4) | (17.5) |
| Liberal Democrat (mean %) | 13.9 | 17.0 | 10.6 | 15.6 | 16.0 | 20.6 | 15.2 |
| | (7.6) | (16.4) | (2.6) | (7.5) | (7.0) | (7.9) | (8.0) |
| Conservative (mean %) | 33.4 | 30.1 | 26.8 | 43.8 | 41.4 | 54.6 | 39.1 |
| | (11.8) | (11.6) | (9.0) | (12.2) | (11.7) | (7.5) | (13.7) |

*Notes:* Means for partisanship concern proportions of the three-party vote only (Labour, Liberal Democrats and Conservatives). Standard deviation in parenthesis. This method factors out partisanship for the nationalist parties in Wales and Scotland, as well as minor national parties.

containing higher-density council housing, as well as a few important gentrifying neighbourhoods housing the left-leaning professional middle-classes (Butler and Robson 2001) that, by and large, still vote Labour. Joining such areas, however, would appear to be the (mostly inner-) suburban areas to which those displaced by gentrification are likely to be moving (thus perhaps explaining the reduced effect of distance from the centre).

The relationships evident between partisanship and the social composition variables have become more complex and in some cases shifted over time, often revealing non-linear effects. Hardship is associated with a strong tendency to

*Table 4.7: Multilevel randomised models of partisanship*

| | Labour | | | | Liberal Democrats | | | | Conservatives | | | |
|---|---|---|---|---|---|---|---|---|---|---|---|---|
| | 1992 | 1992 | 2001 | 2001 | 1992 | 1992 | 2001 | 2001 | 1992 | 1992 | 2001 | 2001 |
| | Full | Final | Full | Final | Full | Final | Full | Final | Full | Final | Full | Final |
| Constant (A) | 103.29 | **105.55** | **173.705** | **116.799** | −10.24 | −10.60 | −0.149 | −5.436 | 16.15 | −39.58 | −53.16 | −7.94 |
| *Lower-level variables: (B)* | | | | | | | | | | | | |
| *Compositional:* | | | | | | | | | | | | |
| Age under 16 (%) | **−1.548** | **−1.655** | **−1.765** | **−1.248** | **0.800** | **0.739** | **0.895** | **0.732** | **0.502** | **0.580** | **0.942** | **0.949** |
| Age 65 + (%) | **−1.731** | **−1.706** | **−2.480** | **−2.030** | **1.081** | **1.061** | **0.751** | **0.586** | **0.635** | **0.691** | **1.703** | **1.480** |
| Foreign born (%) | **0.337** | **0.343** | **0.196** | **−0.732** | **−0.223** | **−0.236** | **−0.179** | **0.313** | −0.073 | −0.095 | 0.012 | |
| Manufacturing (%) | **0.278** | **0.297** | −0.229 | **0.917** | −0.0009 | | −0.254 | | −0.263 | −0.245 | −0.022 | |
| SES General Index (Ave = 100) | −0.040 | −0.041 | **−0.192** | **−0.176** | **0.033** | **0.047** | 0.056 | **0.045** | −0.009 | | **0.059** | **0.074** |
| SES Hardship Index (Ave = 100) | **0.232** | **0.244** | 0.085 | **0.383** | **−0.069** | **−0.051** | −0.088 | **−0.189** | **−0.175** | **−0.171** | −0.073 | −0.087 |
| Migrants % last 3 years | **−1.609** | **−1.557** | **−2.123** | **−0.906** | 0.462 | | 0.987 | **0.791** | 1.038 | **−2.280** | 1.167 | 1.046 |
| *Spatial/contextual:* | | | | | | | | | | | | |
| Owner-occupied housing (%) | **−0.192** | **−0.174** | **−0.357** | **−0.156** | −0.018 | | 0.006 | | 0.227 | **0.224** | **0.312** | **0.287** |
| Population change 1991–2001 (%) | −0.748 | | **−0.323** | **−0.318** | **0.144** | **0.154** | 0.226 | −0.135 | −0.055 | | 0.062 | |
| Log population density | 1.015 | | **3.128** | **2.717** | −1.076 | | −0.533 | | −0.853 | | **−3.569** | **−4.528** |
| Simpson Index (occupational diversity) | **0.158** | **0.163** | **0.333** | **0.309** | −0.033 | | −0.063 | | −0.170 | −0.145 | −0.134 | −0.167 |
| Commute 20km or more to work | n/a | | −0.082 | | n/a | | −0.107 | | n/a | | | |
| Distance to centre (tri-zone) | −0.890 | **−1.409** | 1.085 | | −0.403 | | −1.329 | **−1.586** | 0.850 | **1.121** | −0.022 | **−0.488** |
| *Upper-level variables: (G)* | | | | | | | | | | | | |
| *Region:* | | | | | | | | | | | | |
| Region – North/Yorkshire | 5.015 | **8.154** | 2.308 | | 0.735 | | 1.112 | 2.039 | −4.623 | −8.628 | −3.441 | −6.170 |

| | Labour | | | | Liberal Democrats | | | | Conservatives | | | |
|---|---|---|---|---|---|---|---|---|---|---|---|---|
| | 1992 | 1992 | 2001 | 2001 | 1992 | 1992 | 2001 | 2001 | 1992 | 1992 | 2001 | 2001 |
| | Full | Final | Full | Final | Full | Final | Full | Final | Full | Final | Full | Final |
| Region – South E/W | -3.731 | | -4.877 | | 3.706 | **4.077** | 2.131 | **4.212** | 0.559 | | 0.427 | |
| Region – Wales | **17.250** | **20.559** | **10.927** | **12.258** | **-7.263** | **-7.508** | -2.164 | | **-7.204** | **-15.974** | **-4.575** | **-9.516** |
| Region – Scotland | **13.360** | **20.853** | **11.232** | **12.689** | **-3.399** | **-3.161** | 0.741 | | **-7.761** | **-13.306** | **-8.881** | **-9.147** |
| *Upper-level variables:* | | | | | | | | | | | | |
| Log population (metro size) | -2.040 | | -2.935 | | 0.586 | | -0.189 | | 1.768 | | **2.488** | |
| Population change 1991–2001 | -0.540 | | -0.401 | **-1.363** | 0.083 | | -0.170 | | 0.390 | | 0.303 | |
| Manufacturing (%) | 0.136 | | 0.191 | | -0.193 | **-0.213*** | -0.679 | | -0.038 | | 0.074 | |
| City-Suburban Hardship Index (CSHI) | -0.058 | | -0.078 | **-0.065** | -0.003 | | 0.006 | | 0.069 | | **0.079** | |
| *Cross-level effects:* | | | | | | | | | | | | |
| *Upper-level effect on slope of (A) or (B)* | | | | | | | | | | | | |
| Age under 16 | | | | | | | | | | **3.375*** | | |
| Foreign born | | **-3.623*** | | **0.036**** | | | | **-0.019**** | | **0.503**** | | |
| Migrants % last 3 years | | | | **-0.092**** | | | | | | | | |
| SES Hardship | | | | **-0.002**** | | | | **0.0007*** | | | | |
| Population change 1991–2001 | | | | | | | | **0.036**** | | | | |
| Commute 20+ km to work (%) | | | | | | | | | | | | **0.048**** |
| Random coefficient reliability+ | **0.753** | **0.710** | **0.369** | **0.570** | **0.011** | **0.004** | 0.179 | 0.368 | **0.825** | **0.572** | **0.702** | **0.795** |
| Log likelihood (x -1)~ | 1254.1 | 1247.6 | 1257.88 | 1262.88 | 1255.6 | 1257.4 | 1257.77 | 1250.75 | 1205.8 | 1200.4 | 1138.8 | 1139.1 |

*Notes*: For boldface values, p<0.05. Only those cross-level effects with coefficients to report have been reported above. (*) Cross-level effect of upper level variable on slope of (A) (constant). (**) Cross-level effect of upper level variable on slope of the lower-level variable (B). (+) Higher values indicate greater reliability. (~) Lower values indicate greater likelihoods. Higher values of CHSI indicate higher levels of city-suburban disparity (parity = 100).

support Labour at the lower level, but this tendency diminishes in conurbations with higher levels of hardship. While regional effects remained strong, they nonetheless were diminished from the levels in 1992 (for instance, a location in Wales or Scotland gave Labour roughly a 21 per cent lead in 1992, but a 12 per cent lead in 2001, over the other three parties). Importantly, the relationship between immigration and Labour support changes significantly over time and between different conurbations. In 2001, there is a new negative effect of immigrant concentration on Labour support at the local level (it was positive in 1992), but this reverses in the conurbation with the greatest concentration of immigrants (London). This is evident in Figure 4.4a, which charts the randomised slopes for the effect of immigrant concentration on the vote for Labour. There is a strong negative association between the presence of immigrants and labour support in every conurbation except London, where the relationship is strongly positive.

Cross-level interaction effects are also present in the relationship between manufacturing employment and Labour support. In keeping with the strong class bases of British political culture and institutions, there is a very strong positive relationship between local manufacturing employment and Labour support in 1992. In 2001, while a positive effect at the lower level is still present, there is now a negative coefficient at the upper level for the proportion employed in manufacturing. Thus, while local districts containing manufacturing workers are more likely to vote Labour, this relationship is stronger in areas with fewer manufacturing workers (such as in London, the capital cities, and a number of smaller cities), while cities where manufacturing employment remains strong (such as Stoke, Leeds, Birmingham, and Leicester), local levels of manufacturing employment predict fewer votes for Labour. This is evident in Figure 4.4b.

Conservative partisanship, as might be expected, is predicted by many of the same variables as Liberal support, but with the coefficients pointing in mostly opposite directions (see Table 4.7). Stable socio-demographic variables include the presence of children (reinforced in 1992 by the strong positive relationship for this variable at the upper level) and, particularly, the elderly, as well as high socio-economic status and low levels of hardship. The importance of the five sub-national regions remains in 2001, though, as in Labour support, the strength of the coefficients declined overall by about one third over the early 1990s. Stable contextual/place effects result from concentrations of owner-occupied housing and low levels of the Simpson index (i.e. occupational diversity). On the other hand, the presence of immigrant concentrations or manufacturing workers no longer had much of an effect on Tory partisanship in 2001, while high turnover rates went from having a strong negative effect at the lower level (albeit one that diminished as the overall turnover rate increased at the upper level) to a positive one (effectively the flipside of the trends for Labour reported above).

Important changes among those spatial/contextual variables reveal an effect on partisanship. While there is a clear and consistent positive relationship between homeownership and Conservative support (see Figure 4.5a), distance to the centre (zone) ceases to be significant, whereas population density has become a very strong and significant predictor of Conservative partisanship (of course, both

**a) Effect of immigrant concentration**

**b) Effect of manufacturing employment**

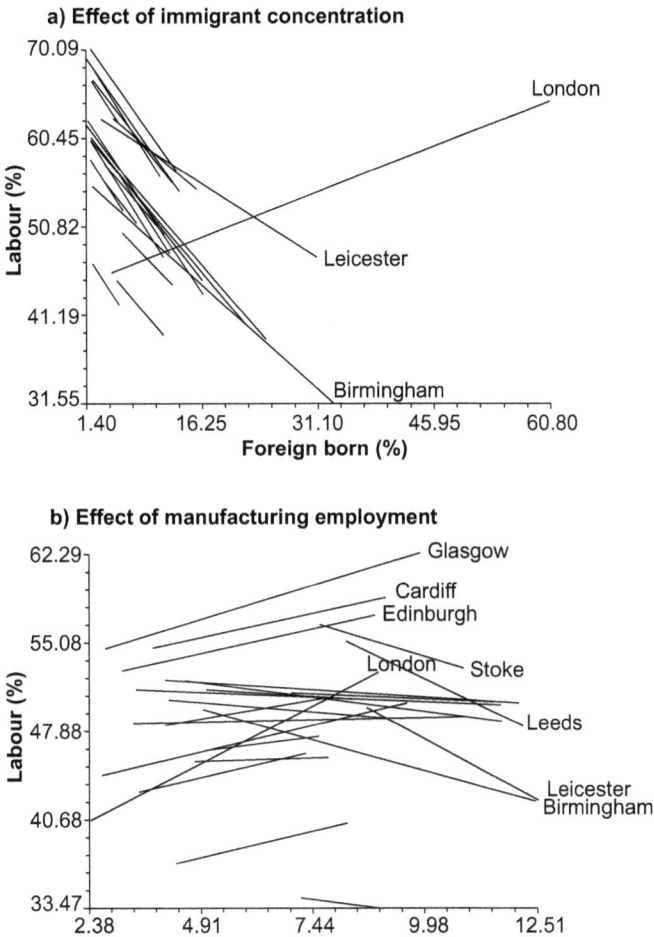

*Figure 4.4: Contextual effects on Labour partisanship, by conurbation, 2001 (randomised slopes)*

reflect different forms of city-suburban differentiation and are correlated with each other). Commuting (more than 20 km to work) also becomes important for understanding Tory support in 2001 – the only time in any of our models this variable shows a significant affect. However, the relationship is not linear. At the lower level commuting has a negative effect within metropolitan areas, while the effect at the upper level is positive on the slope of the intrametropolitan relationship (though only slight). At first glance this result might appear contradictory, but can be understood if we remember the link between long distances spent commuting, economic vibrancy, and housing markets. In economically-stagnant areas, once homeownership, density and other markers of affluent suburbanism are controlled for, long distance commuting is likely to indicate marginality and inability to afford housing costs closer to the centre. Furthermore, cross-

**a) Effect of homeownership**

**b) Effect of commuting**

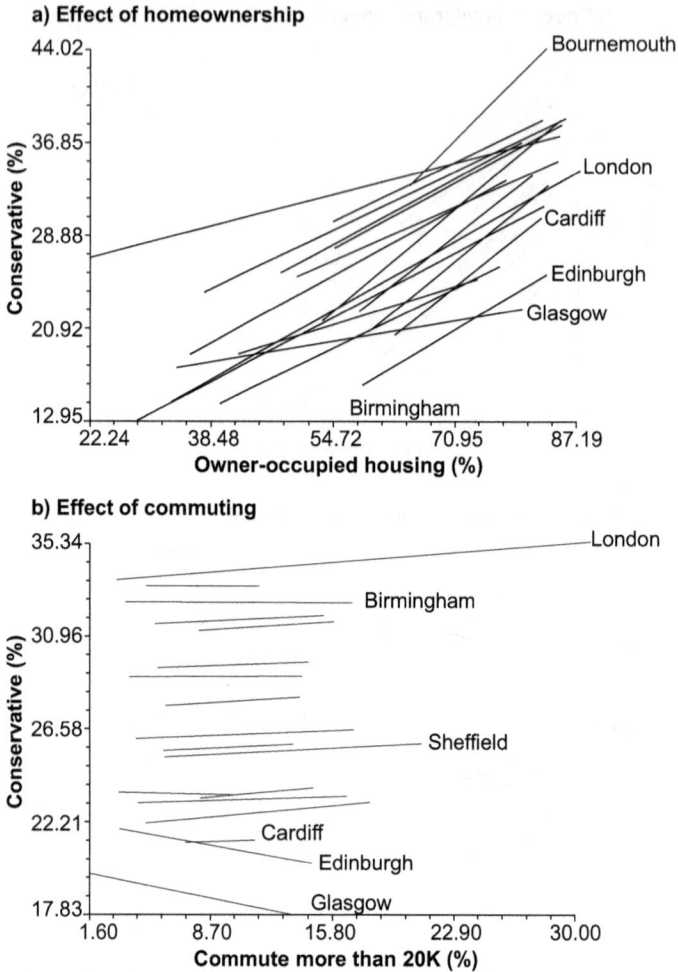

*Figure 4.5: Contextual effects on Conservative support by conurbation, 2001 (randomised slopes)*

level effects demonstrate that the effect of commuting changes with increasing size and thus the proportion commuting long distances (see Figure 4.5). Areas with very long commutes, particularly into London, show a positive relationship between commuting and Conservative support, whereas poorer cities and metropolitan areas in Scotland show a negative relationship (see Figure 4.5b).

Support for the Liberal Democrats (and their predecessors) has always been difficult to predict. The reliability estimates are very low, many models do not achieve statistical significance, and the log likelihoods suggest lower probabilities of accuracy for this party. On the one hand, Liberal Democrat partisanship would appear driven by many of the same socio-demographic factors as support for the Conservatives: the presence of children/families, the elderly, high socio-economic

*Table 4.8: Proportion of within-unit and between-unit variance explained*

| | Level 1 – Constituency (within-unit) | Level 2 – Metropolitan (between-unit) |
|---|---|---|
| **1992 National Election** | | |
| Turnout | 64.17 | 100.00* |
| Labour Party | 83.03 | 10.86 |
| Conservative Party | 74.38 | 23.51 |
| Liberal Democratic Party | 37.73 | 15.44 |
| **2001 National Election** | | |
| Turnout | 75.54 | 45.84 |
| Labour Party | 76.28 | 60.13 |
| Conservative Party | 76.02 | 16.19 |
| Liberal Democratic Party | 24.42 | 41.39 |

*Notes:* Calculated by the author using the method proposed by Snijders and Bosker (1999).
* This method can produce situations in which more than 100 per cent of the variance is explained by the model. In such cases, the results are rounded to 100.00 per cent

status and low rates of hardship (except that the strength of the negative relationship between hardship and the Liberal Democrats vote declines in conurbations with higher levels of hardship, probably reflecting the fact that over the study period this party has replaced the Conservatives as the main opposition in a few of the northern cities).

Few spatial/contextual variables show up as having any importance for understanding the geography of support for this party. Population growth changes from having a positive to a negative effect (but in 2001, the strength of this negative effect declines in conurbations with higher growth rates). Likewise, immigrant concentration goes from having a negative to a positive effect on the party's electoral fortunes. This latter positive effect diminishes the higher the immigrant population in a given conurbation. This is the flipside of the pattern for Labour, suggesting that the Liberal Democrats were able to capitalise on lax support for Labour outside of London, but within London Labour was able to mobilise the immigrant vote.

It is possible to calculate the proportion of the total variation in support that is accounted for at the within-unit (constituency/municipality) and between-unit (metropolitan) levels (for details on the method see Snijders and Bosker 1999). The results are presented in Table 4.8. First, in most cases, the models do a much better job at explaining variance in electoral behaviour within metropolitan areas (at the lower level). The MLM models explain between 64 and 76 per cent of the variation in turnout, and between 74 and 83 per cent of the variance in partisanship for the two main political parties, at the local level. The results are generally weaker (and less consistent) in explaining variation between metropolitan regions, suggesting that upper-level variables missing from the models are also important in determining regional effects. Secondly, the MLM models do a better job at explaining variation between metropolitan areas in 2001 than in 1992. This period witnessed a marked decline in regionalism among the main parties, so there is less between-unit variation to explain in the latter election. Running counter to this trend, however, in 2001 only a very small proportion (16 per cent, down from 23 per cent) of the difference in Conservative support between metropolitan areas is explained by the MLM model. On the whole, the MLM models do a very good job explaining spatial variation in electoral participation and support for the Labour Party, a decent job capturing the geography of the vote for the Conservatives, but only a moderate job in explaining support for the Liberal Democrats. Few further insights are gained by regressing the residuals of the MLM models on the typology of communities employed throughout the chapter.

The picture painted by these analyses is that of a set of fairly consistent predictors of partisanship for the two largest political parties, Labour and the Conservatives, with changes in their support explained by shifts among a small set of variables. Many of the predictors that remain consistent over time reflect socio-demographic composition or regional effects. Homeownership effects, on the other hand, change over time, as does the role of immigrant concentration, which was found to reverse its effects on partisanship outside of Greater London. Meanwhile, the effects of density, distance to the centre and population change all show shifts in strength and direction. This research thus suggests that the change in government between 1992 and 2001 can at least be partly explained by the shifting importance of these contextual variables, as Labour was able to mobilise support across a broader terrain, penetrating into denser suburban areas feeling the strain of recession. The effects of economic restructuring had a differential effect on the suburbs across metropolitan Britain. Many of the working-class suburbs voted for the Conservatives during the 1980s (Walks 2005) and switched to Labour in the late 1990s and through the 2000s.

These shifts in partisanship largely occurred because of the changing abilities of each of the two main parties to mobilise support in key suburban areas. This is evident when the index scores for the typology of communities is examined in relation to their placement on the left-right scale, their economic policy preferences, social-cultural attitudes, and position with regards to globalisation (see Figure 4.6). What is particularly remarkable is how little change is evident in the pattern of differentiation across community types in regards to these basic ideological orientations over time. Whether with regard to the 1992 Conservative majority or the 2001 Labour majority, patterns of support for the largest political parties indicate that ideological orientations remained fairly consistent. For each index there is a pattern whereby the urban concentrations, high-hardship minority suburbs and high-hardship, low-minority suburbs (particularly on the economic and left-right indices), lean to the left, while middle-class suburbs and affluent suburbs have similar leanings to the right, followed by low-density communities that fall much further to the right than the others.

Variation is starker for the left-right index and, to a lesser degree, the index of economic policy preferences, while the social-cultural and globalisation indices follow each other very closely and change more gradually between community types. Nonetheless, what is striking is the strong temporal continuity to these patterns. They provide evidence that the underlying ideological orientations of

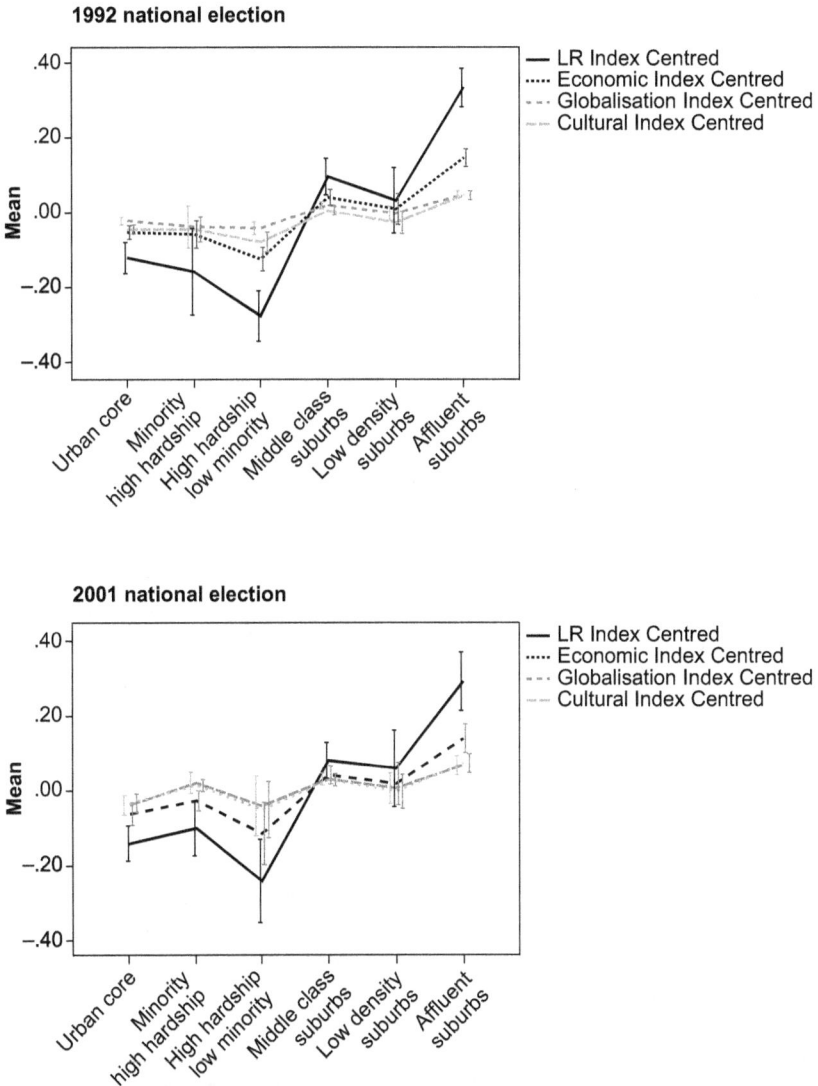

**1992 national election**

**2001 national election**

*Figure 4.6: Ideological orientations by community type*

British communities are not what are changing. Instead, it is the ability of the different political parties to mobilise voters on the basis of such attitudes and orientations that has changed. The shift to the right by Labour is particularly important in this regard. In order to win over working-class and middle-class suburbs, Labour swung to the right and embraced many of the neoliberal policies that the Conservatives had introduced thus gearing their strategy to the suburban vote. Metropolitanisation was thus partly responsible for producing New Labour, and the 'third-way' neoliberalism it reflected.

## Conclusion

This analysis has illuminated the factors and processes most important for understanding the geography of turnout and partisanship within metropolitan areas in Great Britain. In doing so, it identifies a number of elements most important for producing levels of intra-metropolitan differentiation earlier uncovered by Walks (2005). This chapter presents evidence for the existence of substantial place (or contextual) effects on political behaviour. Such place/contextual effects do not always operate in a similar fashion over time, nor are they strictly comparable between municipal and national contexts. Indeed, one of the main findings of this research is that variables related to place have largely changed in their effects, while most variables related to social composition have produced consistent effects over time (the exception being immigrant concentration). Shifts and divergences among British polities at both the local and national scales would thus appear to derive mainly from discrepancies in the relationships between contextual/ spatial factors and the likelihood of voting in elections among subgroups of the population. In addition, the main ideological orientations associated with different types of communities have not changed noticeably, even though many such areas shifted their votes from the Conservative Party to Labour. The implication of this research is that it is spatial/contextual factors that increasingly facilitate the mobilisation of voters, even when political positions associated with different groups do not change. Labour was thus able to steal seats from the Conservatives and win the 1997 and 2001 elections by mobilising votes on the basis of place-based differences and disparities.

A number of the spatial/contextual factors would appear key to understanding geographic differentiation in British electoral participation and partisanship. The link between homeownership and both higher turnout and Conservative strength supports the hypotheses concerning the specific interests that 'homevoters' have regardless of their class or socio-demographic background (Fischel 2001; Thorns 1981). When coupled with the similarly strong relationship between high turnover (which correlates with private apartment housing) and Conservative support, such results also acknowledge a role for collective consumption and public subsidies in influencing political partisanship. Areas of population growth consistently reveal both higher participation rates and Conservative leanings (while areas of slow growth and/or decline show support for Labour and reduced turnout), even after controlling for class/socio-economic status. Thus, the fortunes and trajectories of places would also seem to impart impressions related to the efficacy of electoral behaviour and party policy, in addition to – or perhaps even regardless of – the class makeup of such areas (see also Savage 1987). Economic restructuring, for instance, can thus be seen to influence perceptions of party platforms through place-based mechanisms.

Coupled with the growing and reinforcing effects of population density on partisanship, this research suggests that British voters who live in more urban environments and among greater population diversity are more likely to favour the inclusive policies of parties on the left, while suburban communities and lower-density communities at the urban fringe identify with policies and parties that place them to the right. On the other hand, population density is found here to consistently dampen levels of participation, which may be explained by the sociological theories of urbanism and anomie, and/or the potential lack of identification with a local community that this may produce in urban societies (Wirth 1964; Oliver 2001). Yet, the precise mechanisms translating place-effects into ideological orientations and patterns of participation and partisanship remain underexplored in the British context. (For a review of potential mechanisms, see Johnston *et al.* 2004; Walks 2006.) This research thus sets the stage for further and deeper future analyses of the relationship between local context, spatial mechanisms and social composition in producing the variegated electoral landscape in evidence in Great Britain. What is clear is that metropolitanisation has produced new political cleavages with significant staying-power, but at the same time new avenues for political mobilisation. New Labour, by shifting to the right and mobilising working-class and middle-class suburban communities in metropolitan areas with vulnerable economies, was able to use such cleavages to its benefit for a time.

## Bibliography

Abrams, M. (1960) 'The future of the left: new roots of working-class conservatism', *Encounter*, 80(1): 57–90.

Butler, D. and Stokes, D. (1974) *Political Change in Britain: The evolution of electoral choice*, 2nd edn, London: Macmillan.

Butler, T. and Robson, G. (2001) 'Social capital, gentrification, and neighbourhood change in London: a comparison of three south London neighbourhoods', *Urban Studies*, 38(12): 2145–62.

Clapson, M. (2003) *Suburban Century: Social change and urban growth in England and the U.S.A.*, New York: Berg.

Cox, K. (1968) 'Suburbia and voting behaviour in London Metropolitan Area', *Annals of the Association of American Geographers*, 58(1): 111–27.

Crewe, I., Sarlvik, B. and Alt, J. (1977) 'Partisan dealignment in Britain, 1964–1974', *British Journal of Political Science*, 7(1): 129–90.

Curtice, J. and Steed, M. (1982) 'Electoral choice and the production of government: the changing operation of the electoral system in the United Kingdom since 1955', *British Journal of Political Science*, 12: 249–98.

—       (1986) 'Proportionality and exaggeration in the British electoral system', *Electoral Studies*, 5(3): 209–28.

Dorling, D., Rallings, C. and Thrasher M. (1998) 'The epidemiology of the Liberal Democrat vote', *Political Geography*, 17(1): 45–70.

Fischel, W. (2001) *The Homevoter Hypothesis*, Cambridge, Mass.: Harvard University Press.

Fisher, J. (2002) 'The Liberal Democrats', in Geddes, A. P. and Tonge, J. (eds) *Labour's Second Landslide: The British General Election of 2001*, Manchester: Manchester University Press, 65–83.

Goldthorpe, J. H., Lockwood, D., Bechhofer, F. and Platt, J. (1968) *The Affluent Worker: Political attitudes and behaviour*, Cambridge: Cambridge University Press.

Heath, A. F., Jowell, R. M., and Curtice, J. K. (2001) *The Rise of New Labour: Party policies and voter choices*, Oxford University Press: Oxford.

Johnston, R., Forrest, J. and Poulsen, M. (2002) 'Are there ethnic enclaves/ghettos in English cities?', *Urban Studies*, 39(4): 591–618.

Johnston, R., Rossiter, D., Pattie, C. and Dorling, D. (2002) 'Labour electoral landslides and the changing efficiency of voting distributions', *Transactions of the Institute of British Geographers*, 27(3): 336–61.

Johnston, R. J., Pattie, C. J., Dorling, D. F. L., MacAllister, I., Tunstall, H. and Rossiter, D. J. (2001) 'Social locations, spatial locations and voting at the 1997 British general election: evaluating the sources of Conservative support', *Political Geography*, 20(1): 85–111.

Johnston, R. J. (1986) 'Places and votes: the role of location in the creation of political attitudes', *Urban Geography*, 7(2): 103–17.

Johnston, R. J. and Pattie, C. J. (1992) 'Class dealignment and the regional polarization of voting patterns in Great Britain, 1964–1987', *Political Geography*, 11: 73–86.

Johnston, R. J., Jones, K., Sarker, R., Propper, C., Burgess, S. and Bolster, A. (2004) 'Party support and the neighbourhood effect: spatial polarization of the British electorate 1991–2001', *Political Geography*, 23: 367–402.

Johnston, R. J., Pattie, C. J. and Allsopp, G. (1988) *A Nation Dividing? The electoral map of Great Britain 1979–87*, Harlow, Essex: Longman.

Keay, D. (1987) 'Aids, education and the year 2000!', *Woman's Own*, October 31, 8–10.

MacAllister, I., Johnston, R. J., Pattie, C. J., Tunstall, H., Doorling, D. and Rossiter, D. J. (2001) 'Class dealignment and the neighbourhood effect: Miller revisited', *British Journal of Political Science*, 31(1): 41–59

Mohan, J. (1999) *A United Kingdom? Economic, social and political geographies*, London: Oxford University Press.

Nordlinger, E. A. (1967) *The Working Class Tories*, London: MacGibbon and Kee.

Norris, P. (1997) *Electoral Change Since 1945*. London: Blackwell.

Oliver, J. E. (2001) *Democracy in Suburbia*. Princeton, NJ: Princeton University Press.

Rallings, C. and Thrasher, M. (1997) *Local Elections in Britain*, London: Routledge.

Rasmussen, J. (1973) 'The impact of constituency structural characteristics upon political preferences in Britain', *Comparative Politics*, 6(1): 123–45.

Savage, M. (1987) 'Understanding political alignments in contemporary Britain: Do localities matter?', *Political Geography Quarterly*, 6(1): 53–76.

Snijders, T. and Bosker, R. (1999) *Multilevel Analysis: An introduction to basic and advanced multilevel modelling*, London: Sage Publications.

Thorns, D. C. (1981) 'Owner-occupation: its significance for wealth transfer and class formation', *Sociological Review*, 29(6): 705–28.

Travers, T. (2004) *The Politics of London: Governing an Ungovernable City*, London: Palgrave.

Walks, R. A. (2005) 'City-suburban electoral polarization in Great Britain, 1950–2001', *Transactions of the Institute of British Geographers*, 30(4): 500–17.

—  (2006) 'The causes of city-suburban political polarization? A Canadian case study', *Annals of the Association of American Geographers*, 96(2): 390–414.

Wirth, L. (1964) *On Cities and Social Life*, Chicago: University of Chicago Press.

## Appendix

*Table A4.1: Variable definitions*

| Concept | Variable | Definition |
|---|---|---|
| *Socio-demographic/compositional variables:* | | |
| Presence of families/ family values | Age under 16 (%) | % of total population under age 16 |
| Aging, aged, greying | Age 65+ (%) | % of total population age 65 or older |
| Immigrant enclaves | Foreign born (%) | % of total population born outside UK |
| Secondary sector, proletariat | Employed in manufacturing (%) | % of labour force employed in manufacturing industry |
| Socio-economic status | SES General index | Average Location Quotient values for:<br>• % with university degree (of pop. aged 20)<br>• % employed in managerial or professional occupation (of labour force). |
| Disadvantage/ marginalisation | SES Hardship Index | Average Location Quotient values for:<br>• % unemployed (of total labour force)<br>• % permanently unemployed, never worked and/or disabled (of pop. aged 20+)<br>• % with no educational qualifications (of pop. aged 20+)<br>• % female single-parent households (of total households). |
| Areas with high turnover, migrants | Migrant last 3 years % | % of total population who lived outside the constituency 3 years earlier |
| *Spatial/Contextual Variables:* | | |
| Commuter areas (*2001 only) | Commute 20 km+ to work % | % of employed labour force commuting 20 km or greater to work |
| Security of tenure/ res. investment | Owner-occupied housing (%) | % total dwellings owner-occupied |
| New/revitalised vs. declining areas | Population growth 1991–2001 (%) | % change in population 1991–2001 |
| Urbanity, crowding | Log population density | Log of persons/km square |

| Concept | Variable | Definition |
|---|---|---|
| Mixing, economic diversity | Simpson Index | Calculated from % of labour force in four broad occupational categories:<br>• managers/owners of large corporations<br>• professionals, skilled technicians<br>• intermediate, semi-skilled, small-scale self-employed<br>• routine and unskilled. |
| Fringe settlement/ distance to core/CBD | Distance to Centre (tri-zone) | Three-zonal categorisation based on proximity to central city (zone 1) |
| *Upper-level variables:* | | |
| Region (dichotomous) | Region – North/ Yorkshire | Northeast, Northwest, Yorkshire |
| | Region – South | Southeast, Southwest |
| | Region – Wales | Wales |
| | Region – Scotland | Scotland |
| Production centres | Employment in manufacturing (%) | % labour force employed in manufacturing industry |
| Metropolitan size/ complexity | Log population (metro size) | Log of total metro population |
| Metro growth/ decline | Population change 1981–1991 and 1991–2001 | % change in metro population 1981–1991 and 1991–2001 |
| City-suburban differences | City-suburban Hardship Index | Ratio of the SES hardship index for the entire central city to the SES hardship index for the rest of the metro, *100 |

# Chapter Five | The Emerging Metropolitan Political Ecology of France

*Vincent Hoffmann-Martinot and Jefferey M. Sellers*

In France, as in other European countries, the metropolitan transformation poses a challenge to generations of analyses of political behaviour and culture. Through most of the twentieth century, from the analyses of politics under the Third Republic (Siegfried 1913), accounts of territorial influences on voting have centred on either long-standing regional traditions or the divide between urban and rural. At the same time, peri-urban development has absorbed more and more of the countryside surrounding the largest urban concentrations such as Paris and Lyon, and even smaller regional cities across the country (Julien 2003; Cavailhès *et al.* 2002; Péguy 2000). A growing majority of the French electorate now lives in extended, interconnected regions divided into localities with distinctive patterns of consumption, employment, social homogeneity and cultural practices (Hoffmann-Martinot 2005). This transformation has immense implications for patterns of electoral participation and explains much of the new patterns of partisanship that have emerged in France since the 1980s.

In this chapter, we examine metropolitan and local sources of the patterns of voter turnout and partisanship that have emerged. The analysis focuses on results at the communal level from the first-round presidential election of 2002, and the first-round results from municipal elections the previous year. As multilevel analyses reveal, the local and metropolitan contexts of voting account for variations in both turnout and partisanship beyond what demographic composition can explain. Interests, values and cultural orientations linked to metropolitan places help to account for the success of the right in national elections under Jacques Chirac and Nicolas Sarkozy, and the surprise second-place showing of the extreme right under Jean-Marie le Pen in 2002. Similar local and metropolitan influences have shaped turnout in elections at the municipal and national levels, and the relation between them.

## French metropolitan areas: demographic and spatial dimensions

Since the 1970s, metropolitan areas in France have grown continuously. In France, state intervention played a direct role in the shaping of mid-century suburbanisation, as the French state directed new development outwards from central cities into high-rise housing estates (*grands ensembles*) and new cities created in the Paris region (Zones à Urbaniser en Priorité (ZUP)). From the 1980s, metropolitanisation proceeded predominantly from private inputs and individual choices. As in the United States, subsidies for homeownership and public programmes, such as the construction of new highways, offered incentives for middle-class families to move out of the central cities into the urban periphery.

The resulting flight of middle- and upper-class urban residents from the central cities has departed in significant ways from the US example. From the 1950s, the redevelopment of historical and cultural amenities in French central cities has reinforced their economic drawing power for well-to-do residents. As a result, cross-national comparisons have shown that socio-economic disparities between central cities and their suburbs in France remain more limited than in the United States, and that concentrations of disadvantage are often most dramatic in the near-suburbs that have built high-rise housing estates (Hoffmann-Martinot 2005). In the metropolitan periphery, following a pattern of 'rurbanisation' (Julien 2003; Cavailhès *et al.* 2002), new housing continues to cluster around the networks of small villages that have long characterised rural France.

New data sources since 2000, including the first publicly-available electronic database with wealth indicators by commune, have made it possible to investigate metropolitan spatial patterns and their electoral consequences systematically. This analysis employs a new categorisation of municipalities by the French National Statistical Office (INSEE) that uses commuting and labour market patterns rather than built-up areas to designate metropolitan regions. The resulting forty-two 'urbanised areas' (*aires urbaines*) with populations over 200,000 provide the first definitions of metropolitan regions comparable to those in the United States, Canada and other developed countries. In 1999, 77 per cent of the French population lived in these areas, up from 73 per cent in 1990.

The unusual geopolitical fragmentation of French local governments has made municipalities especially helpful units for capturing the variations in political participation and partisan mobilisation within these metropolitan areas. With few exceptions, the boundaries between municipalities have remained fixed since the commune was established as a unit of municipal government in the eighteenth century. Following metropolitanisation, central cities generally encompass only a small proportion of the metropolitan area. The remaining local governments are among the most fragmented in the world (Hoffmann-Martinot 2005). Many communes on the periphery of metropolitan regions number only a few hundred residents, or fewer. These variations ensure that communal ecological data will capture a large portion of the variation in residential contexts within French metropolitan areas, and may even promote patterns of residential sorting that correspond to municipal boundaries.

Despite the particularities of French metropolitanisation, communes in these metropolitan regions sort into types broadly comparable to those in other developed countries. Cluster analysis confirmed the categories from the hierarchical procedure of the IMO protocol.[1] The types are set out in Table 5.1 and below.

*Urban concentrations* combine high social hardship and immigrant populations with attraction for higher status groups, housing the second highest proportion of

---

1.    For the precise procedures used, see Chapter 14 (the Methodological Appendix to this volume).

*Table 5.1: Characteristics of municipal types*

| Type of commune | | Population 1999 | Inhabitants / km$^2$ | Post-secondary education (%) | Median income/ person | Home owners (%) | Unemployed (%) | Population born abroad (%) | Workers working & residing in same commune (%) | N |
|---|---|---|---|---|---|---|---|---|---|---|
| Urban | Mean | 187,546 | 3,900 | 35 | 9,017 | 36 | 18 | 11 | 65 | 50 |
| concentrations | S.d. | 308,749 | 2,978 | 9 | 1,486 | 8 | 4 | 6 | 14 | |
| Affluent | Mean | 6,992 | 1,407 | 50 | 13,575 | 73 | 7 | 10 | 15 | 539 |
| suburbs | S.d. | 11,797 | 3,044 | 8 | 1,745 | 14 | 2 | 6 | 6 | |
| Poor | Mean | 18,956 | 2,420 | 28 | 8,561 | 54 | 16 | 18 | 26 | 331 |
| minority | S.d. | 20,844 | 3,149 | 7 | 1,454 | 16 | 4 | 5 | 10 | |
| Poor non- | Mean | 4,398 | 558 | 24 | 8,438 | 67 | 15 | 6 | 21 | 843 |
| minority | S.d. | 6,412 | 891 | 8 | 1,182 | 15 | 4 | 4 | 9 | |
| Middle-class | Mean | 2,822 | 354 | 31 | 10,135 | 78 | 8 | 6 | 17 | 2,298 |
| suburbs | S.d. | 4,361 | 725 | 7 | 1,185 | 11 | 2 | 4 | 7 | |
| Low-density | Mean | 441 | 35 | 27 | 9,152 | 80 | 9 | 5 | 20 | 2,713 |
| suburbs | S.d. | 450 | 16 | 9 | 1,552 | 9 | 4 | 4 | 9 | |
| Total | Mean | 4,548 | 463 | 30 | 9,760 | 75 | 10 | 6 | 19 | 6,774 |
| | S.d. | 31,609 | 1,409 | 10 | 1,919 | 13 | 4 | 5 | 10 | |

adult residents with a post-secondary education among the types (35 per cent).

*Low-density suburbs* – the most numerous type of commune – exemplify the 'rurbanised' pattern on the fringe of metropolitan regions.[2] Communes of this type have maintained the high homeownership of agrarian communities, modest average incomes and low percentages of foreigners.

*Middle-class suburbs* – the second largest group of metropolitan communes – have comparatively high average incomes and high rates of commuting. They also retain aspects of traditional village character, including the second- lowest population densities, the second-highest rate of homeownership and the second-lowest proportion of foreign residents.

*Poor minority suburbs* correspond most closely to the popular image of the French *banlieux*, with the biggest immigrant concentrations, the lowest average incomes and among them the highest population densities.

*Poor non-minority suburbs* possess high average unemployment like their more ethnically-diverse counterparts, and even lower average income as well as a

---

2.   In contrast to the United States, low-density suburbs have not generally been the fastest growing. For this reason, density alone, rather than a combination of density and growth rates, was used to classify this group.

lower proportion of adults with secondary education. Located largely on the rural metropolitan fringes, however, they exhibit population densities only one-fourth or lower those of poor minority suburbs.

*Affluent suburbs* are overwhelmingly dormitory suburbs, with 85 per cent of workers commuting outside communal boundaries to work. Predominately located within a short distance of the central city, they possess high homeownership, high rates of post-secondary education, and low unemployment.

Along with broad resemblances to parallel types in North America and other European countries in the process of metropolitanisation, this classification also reflects various patterns of clustering among the demographic indicators used in this analysis. Relations among these variables at the community level evince some of the same correlations that demographic analysis at the individual level has shown. Post-secondary education and median income correlate closely (0.76, p<0.001). However, ecological relationships between each of these variables and other features of communities suggest divergences that will ultimately be shown to have political consequences.[3] Place-linked characteristics of communities bear more limited relations to these measures of demographic composition. Only the Simpson Index, a three-category indicator of economic diversity, manifests correlations higher than 0.50 with the indicators for income (0.70, p<0.01) and post-secondary education (0.64, p<0.01).[4]

### Examining the political ecology of French metropolitan areas

The growth of metropolitan areas into the predominant form of settlement in France has made the characteristics of metropolitan places increasingly decisive both for national patterns of political participation and for national partisan affiliations.

Our analysis of these effects focuses on the presidential election of 21st April 2002 and the communal elections of 11th March 2001. In each instance, the elections under scrutiny represent the first round of a two-round majoritarian electoral

---

3. Rates of post-secondary education correlate significantly more positively with foreign-born populations, residential mobility, and with unemployment. Median income correlates negatively with the presence of children and with homeownership, while education rates bear no significant relation to these indicators. Although similar variations mark the two highly-correlated age categories (−0.72, p<0.001), the indicator for young children was eliminated after regressions showed it to have no independent effect alongside the indicator for residents over 60 years old.

4. Homeownership correlated at −0.48 (p<0.01) with foreign-born populations and −0.45 (p<0.01) with unemployment. As the typology suggests, denser communities feature smaller proportions of homeowners (−0.56, p<0.01) and more foreign-born residents (0.44, p<0.01). Indicators of mobility and new housing correlated significantly but usually modestly with each other and with the other indicators. Finally, communes with populations fewer than 3,500 and fewer than 2,500 were governed by distinctive rules for local elections that affect participation. Although dichotomous indicators for these contextual effects inevitably correlated with population density (−0.71, p<0.01), further analysis will show additional effects from these rules that density alone cannot explain.

process.[5] The first round of the 2002 presidential election marked the first of two successive presidential elections in which the candidate of the centre-right dominated candidates of the left; it was also a high watermark of support for anti-immigrant, ethno-nationalist parties on the right. In the first round of voting, Jean-Marie Le Pen of the right-wing National Front unexpectedly edged out Socialist Party candidate Lionel Jospin to win second place in the balloting. Although Le Pen lost decisively in the second round to President Jacques Chirac of the conservative Union for a Presidential Majority (UMP), the first ballot holds special interest as a window on the sources of support for the conservative formations that have dominated French politics since the 1990s, and on patterns of electoral mobilisation that contributed to a surge in support for the extreme right. Metropolitan and local influences provide much of the explanation for both of these results.

### Election turnout and delocalisation

The data released by the Ministry of the Interior for this study offer a comprehensive overview of election turnout as a proportion of registered voters in metropolitan areas throughout France. Turnout in both national and local elections remained high in low density and middle-class suburbs, but averaged lower in urban concentrations and poor minority suburbs. Turnout gaps that fit the pattern of delocalised electoral participation were present in the affluent suburbs and central cities, and in larger metropolitan regions. In the most rural parts of French metropolitan regions and in certain regions of the country, local turnout still exceeds national turnout. Multilevel statistical analysis disclosed these relationships at various levels and the relations between them.

Up until the 2007 presidential election, when national turnout surged, participation of registered voters in French elections had been in decline since the 1970s (Clanché 2003). In the first round of the 2002 presidential elections, the abstention rate of 28.4 per cent represented a historical low for the Fifth Republic. In municipal elections, the decline in turnout has been more continuous, reaching an abstention rate of 32.6 per cent nationwide in 2001 and 33.5 per cent in 2008.

The analysis in this volume, along with international literature on electoral turnout and a more circumscribed body of research on French voter participation (Hoffmann-Martinot 1992; Blais 1994), points to several clear, expected findings with regard to how patterns of turnout are likely to vary between places. The nationally-uniform electoral system, the national party system and the tightly integrated national media in France give reason to anticipate uniform patterns of turnout among localities in both types of elections. If the ecology of communities reflects the individual propensities evident from survey analysis, then the demographic composition of communities should predict participation. Higher participation rates should result from more educated and affluent residents (Dalton 2008:

---

5. In the first round, all candidates appear on the ballot. Should no candidate win a simple majority in this round, a second round pits the leading candidates from the first round against each other.

63), a greater number of older residents (Dalton 2008; Niemi and Barkan 1987; Gimpel *et al.* 2004; Goerres 2005), fewer unemployed residents (Rosenstone 1982), and more native French residents as a proportion of the population (Tiberj 2004).

Contextual predictors of participation have rarely been tested in France. There is ample reason to suspect that the growing population of suburban homeowners, like their counterparts in the United States or Britain, will vote more often (Fischel 2001; Kingston *et al.* 1984). The 'decline of community' argument states that the low-density and middle-class communes should give rise to stronger solidaristic tendencies and more personal motivation to vote (Verba and Nie 1972; Hoffmann-Martinot 1992; Frandsen 2002). In rural France, local clientelism and village social networks have traditionally fostered high participation rates, particularly in the south (Kesselman 1967; Hoffmann-Martinot *et al.* 1996). Socio-economic diversity, measured here by the tripartite Simpson Index based on occupational categories, has been shown to promote greater local mobilisation to vote in the United States (Oliver 2000). Various dimensions of social mobility, including the day-to-day mobility of commuters and frequent changes in residence, can undermine participation as well (Squire *et al.* 1987; Putnam 2000).

Political effects on turnout have received virtually no attention. Either local political competition (Oliver 2000, 2001) or local solidarity effects (Bréchon and Cautrès 1987; Campbell 2006) could induce voters to participate more regularly. In small communes, rules for local elections provide additional incentives for participation and voter choice. In communes with populations under 3,500, voters may choose individual candidates from the lists of candidates for council seats. In communes with populations under 2,500, the lists need not include candidates for every seat and even individual candidacies are permitted. Both rules could encourage stronger ties between voters and individual local candidates, supporting the local mobilisation that has maintained high electoral participation in rural France (Hoffmann-Martinot 1992; Nevers 2002).

The relations between participation in national and local elections have received even less scrutiny. Overall, participation in national elections has generally ranged higher than in local elections (Flanagan 1980; Abrial *et al.* 2003). The news media and political parties should have stronger nationalising effects in national elections than in local ones. We might also expect the gap between national and local turnout to be greater among affluent communities (Oliver 2001; also see Chapter 1 in this volume) and weaker or even reversed for metropolitan communities that retain rural characteristics.

### Overall patterns of electoral participation

An initial comparison of the first round presidential and municipal elections points to a consistently high turnout in the most 'rurbanised' metropolitan communities, and a significant but limited turnout gap in other types. The lowest overall turnout rates and the most significant turnout gaps appear in the most urbanised places and the largest urban regions.

Although both municipal and national elections were administered uniformly across the country, the presidential election clearly mobilised the electorate at more uniform rates. The median turnout for the presidential election was 76.8 per cent; for municipal elections it was only slightly lower at 74.9 per cent. In presidential elections, however, turnout diverged much less among metropolitan municipalities. The standard deviation (5.5 per cent) was lower by nearly half of that for the municipal ballot (9.8 per cent). Means for the distinct town types also varied by only 10 per cent for the presidential election, compared to 25 per cent for the municipal elections (see Figure 5.1)

The municipal types revealed significant variations across French metropolitan areas in the relationship between national and local turnout. The low density communes on the outskirts of metropolitan regions manifested the same intense, localised pattern of participation noted in previous analyses (Hoffmann-Martinot 1992; Nevers 2002). Turnout for both types of elections was highest in these municipalities. Local electoral turnout clearly and consistently exceeded national turnout. In the middle-class suburbs and poor non-minority suburbs that shared 'rurbanised' tendencies with the low-density suburbs, turnout also proved to be higher than in the remaining types.

In both the most advantaged and the most disadvantaged communities, and even more in the urban concentrations that harboured both affluence and disadvantage, tendencies toward delocalisation appeared. The gap between national and municipal turnout averaged from 7 per cent in the affluent suburbs and poor minority communities to 13 per cent in the urban concentrations. The

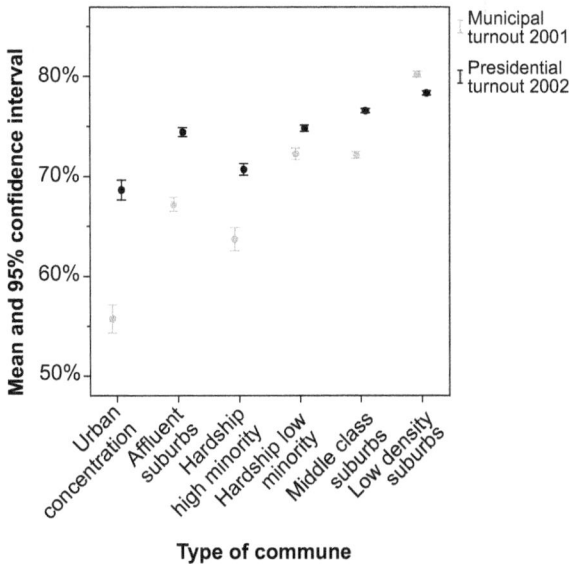

*Figure 5.1: Turnout in presidential and municipal elections, by type of metropolitan commune*

main source of these bigger gaps was the fall-off of turnout in municipal elections. Although national turnout rates averaged 12 per cent lower in urban concentrations than in the low density suburbs, turnout in municipal elections averaged 34 per cent lower. A less dramatic gap of 10 per cent in national elections and 13 per cent in municipal elections separated turnout in poor, high minority suburbs from the low-density suburbs. In affluent suburbs, national election turnout fell off only slightly (1 to 4 per cent) from the averages in low density, middle class, or poor, low minority suburbs. However, average municipal election turnout dropped to 13 per cent below the average for high density suburbs, and 5 per cent below the other two types. Despite a more standardised national electoral context than in the United States, these patterns demonstrate a delocalisation of voter participation among affluent, disadvantaged and urbanised communities.

Seventy-five per cent of the variance in presidential turnout and 79 per cent of variance in municipal turnout occurred within metropolitan areas. Comparison of the mean local turnout by metropolitan areas also pointed to systematic regional and metropolitan differences (see Figure 5.2).

Studies of French local politics have consistently shown that local participation ranges particularly high relative to national participation in the southern regions where clientelism has persisted (Kesselman 1967; Hoffmann-Martinot 2005). Localised participation consistent with this pattern predominates in such metropolitan areas as Pau, Nimes, Perpignan and Bayonne. A similar pattern of high local participation also appears in a number of metropolitan regions along the eastern border with Italy, Switzerland, Germany and Belgium. Clientelism seems less likely as an explanation for the patterns in Annemasse along the Swiss border, or Nancy and Mulhouse in Alsace-Lorraine. The local mobilisation there may derive more from engagement in cross-border issues at the local level, or stronger regional and local identity in these border regions.

Regardless of wider regional differences, local election turnout in the largest French metropolitan areas falls below levels elsewhere. The diverse theories that have linked larger urban size to lower participation clearly apply in some combination to this contrast. Local electoral participation is especially low in the biggest metropolitan areas. Two of the four largest, Paris and Lyon, register the lowest metropolitan average rates of local election turnout. Rates for the Lille and Marseille metropolitan areas are the lowest or second lowest in their respective regions.

Ordinary least squares regressions confirmed the lower turnout rates in urban concentrations, affluent suburbs and poor minority suburbs, and the higher turnout in high-density suburbs (see Table A5.1 in the Appendix to this chapter and Table WA.5.1 in the Web Appendix[6]). The town types can account for 29 per cent of the variation in municipal election turnout, but only 14 per cent of the variation in presidential turnout.

---

6.    See this table and all other Web Appendixes WA05, http://press.ecpr.eu/resources.

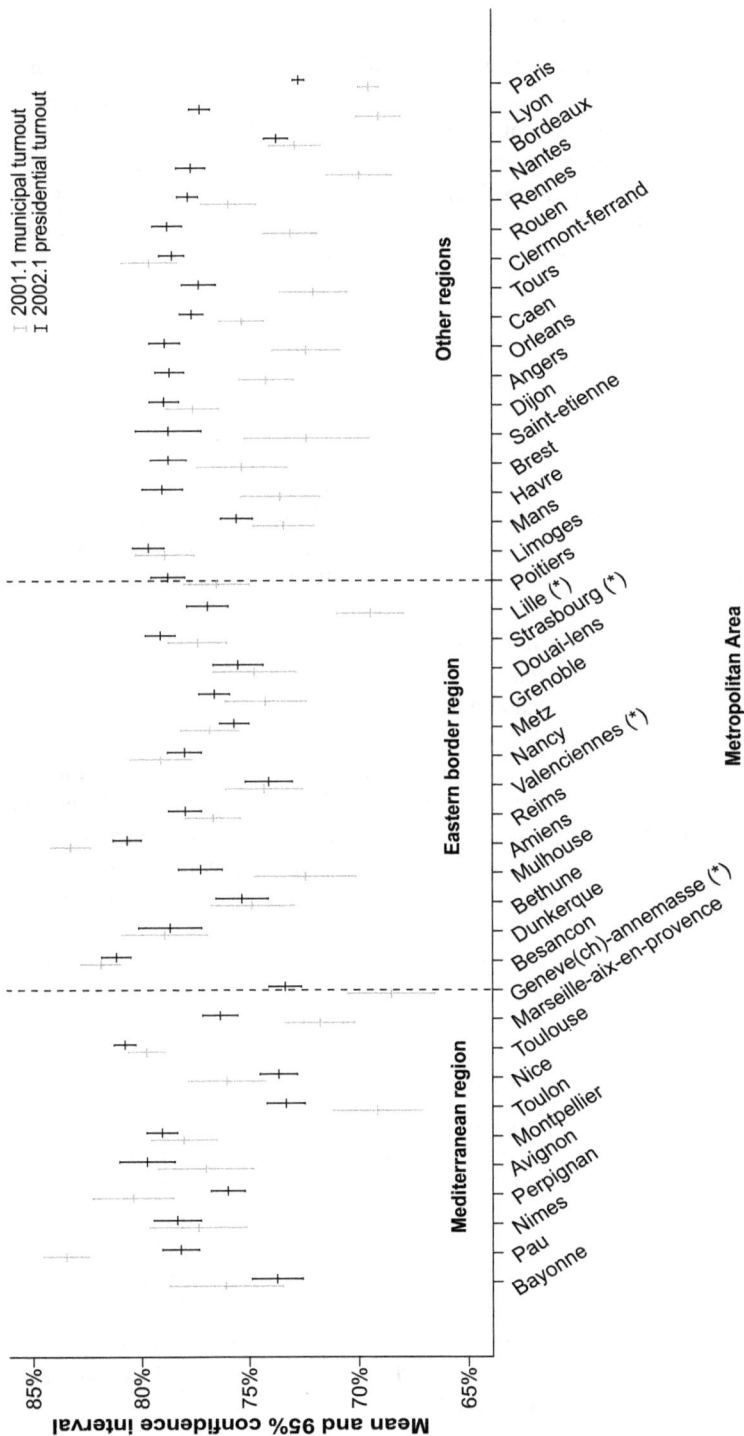

Figure 5.2: Turnout in presidential and municipal elections, by region and metropolitan population

### Examining multilevel variation

Multivariate analysis enabled examination of the specific sources for the variations among the town types and a fuller account of the variations. Although ordinary least squares regressions confirmed numerous hypotheses, they did not allow full exploration of the clear regional and metropolitan variations. Hierarchical linear models provided a way to explain these effects at different scales and to examine the relations between them. Because multilevel analyses provided the most complete accounts, the discussion will focus on these results.

Models of continuous demographic and contextual variables generally account for much more of the variation in turnout than the town types alone. The complex ecological relationships among these variables made it more helpful to examine alternative models than to base the analysis on a single model (see Table 5.2). Alternative models enabled tests of whether the variations in turnout grew out of the demographic composition of municipalities or can be traced to differences rooted in the metropolitan spatial context of municipalities.

Metropolitan level contextual variables include dichotomous indicators for the southern and eastern border regions, along with the significant variables that emerged from a backwards regression with the full array of communal level variables. A combined model tested these compositional and contextual variables alongside each other. Finally, multilevel analysis with randomised variables at the metropolitan and regional levels permitted closer examination of the often complex relationships between local and metropolitan variations.

Both the contextual and the compositional variables explain significant portions of the variation in presidential election turnout. In hierarchical linear models, which included the metropolitan context, a spatial contextual model of presidential election turnout accounted for nearly as much of the local variance as a compositional model (28 per cent compared to 35 per cent). The combination of these contextual variables with compositional ones explained 8 per cent or more local variance than in either separate model, for a total of 43 per cent.

The compositional variables generally performed consistent with established hypotheses, but several had metropolitan as well as local effects. As expected, more adult residents with higher education led to higher turnout. More local residents born abroad brought about lower turnout. Ordinary least squares regressions showed that parallel effects at the metropolitan level accompanied each of these local effects (see Table WA.5.1). Multilevel analysis demonstrates a relationship between the communal and metropolitan variations. In metropolitan areas with more educated adult residents or more residents born abroad, the local effects from both education and foreign-born populations proved significantly stronger. When levels of education were controlled, the median income of a community proved to be a significant predictor of lower rather than higher turnout at both local and metropolitan scales. Multilevel analysis confirmed that the comparatively low presidential turnout in affluent suburbs was part of a wider disengagement among higher income regions that had contributed to the breakthrough of Le Pen in the first-round presidential election of 2002.

*Table 5.2: Presidential election turnout, first round 2002*

| | Compositional | | Contextual | | Full linear | | Full randomised | |
|---|---|---|---|---|---|---|---|---|
| | **B** | **t** | **B** | **t** | **B** | **t** | **B** | **t** |
| Intercept | 89.09 | 24.14 | 89.01 | 18.69 | 89.08 | 19.00 | 77.64 | 155.20 |
| *Metro level* | | | | | | | | |
| Eastern border region | −0.53 | −1.11 | −0.42 | −0.70 | −0.53 | −0.91 | −0.90 | −1.23 |
| South | 0.93 | 0.94 | 1.01 | 1.10 | 0.92 | 1.02 | −0.72 | −0.86 |
| Post-secondary education | **0.24** | **3.83** | **0.25** | **3.13** | **0.24** | **3.10** | | |
| Foreign-born | **−0.36** | **−5.43** | **−0.37** | **−4.05** | **−0.36** | **−3.94** | | |
| Population (log) | **−2.96** | **−4.61** | **−2.95** | **−3.29** | **−2.96** | **−3.36** | | |
| *Cross-level* | | | | | | | | |
| Post-secondary education | | | | | | | **0.00** | **−2.86** |
| Foreign-born | | | | | | | **0.01** | **3.08** |
| Population (log) | | | | | | | **−0.71** | **−5.67** |
| *Local level* | | | | | | | | |
| Post-secondary education | **0.07** | **4.53** | | | **0.06** | **5.14** | **0.18** | **4.34** |
| Foreign born | **−0.42** | **−7.23** | | | **−0.17** | **−9.62** | **−0.24** | **−6.83** |
| Age 60 or more | −0.01 | −0.19 | | | 0.00 | 0.22 | 0.01 | 0.67 |
| Median income | **−0.0003** | **−2.14** | | | **−0.0003** | **−2.68** | **−0.0003** | **−3.24** |
| Unemployment | **−0.38** | **−7.95** | | | **−0.24** | **−13.11** | **−0.25** | **−13.19** |
| Homeowners | | | **0.05** | **8.83** | **0.03** | **4.14** | **0.02** | **3.25** |
| Non-commuters | | | **−0.02** | **−2.96** | **−0.03** | **−4.18** | **−0.04** | **−5.33** |
| Residential stability | | | **−0.04** | **−4.87** | **−0.02** | **−2.24** | −0.01 | −1.19 |
| Housing after 1975 | | | **0.02** | **4.63** | 0.01 | 1.30 | 0.00 | 0.75 |
| Occupational diversity | | | **5.20** | **10.14** | **1.84** | **2.49** | 1.23 | 1.63 |
| Population density (log) | | | **−2.10** | **−14.95** | **−1.27** | **−8.61** | **3.11** | **3.97** |
| Political diversity | | | **−0.33** | **−6.31** | **−0.26** | **−4.95** | **−0.25** | **−4.74** |
| Population 2,500–3,500 | | | **0.63** | **2.43** | **0.55** | **2.39** | **0.51** | **2.20** |
| Population under 2,500 | | | **1.85** | **9.06** | **1.81** | **9.66** | **1.79** | **9.60** |
| Chi-square | | 926 | | 928 | | 1046 | | 4854 |
| D.f. (Metropolitan) | | 36 | | 36 | | 36 | | 39 |
| (Local) | | 6304 | | 6766 | | 6295 | | 6295 |
| p-value | | 0 | | 0.00 | | 0.00 | | 0.00 |
| Reliability est. | | 0.943 | | 0.94 | | 0.95 | | 0.97 |
| Total variance explained | | 37% | | 30% | | 42% | | 36% |
| Metro variance explained | | 43% | | 41% | | 42% | | 1% |
| Local variance explained | | 35% | | 28% | | 43% | | 43% |
| Estimator | | −1.75 | | −1.91 | | −1.72 | | −1.71 |

*Notes: For boldface coefficients, p<0.05.*

**a) Education, by communes and metropolitan areas**

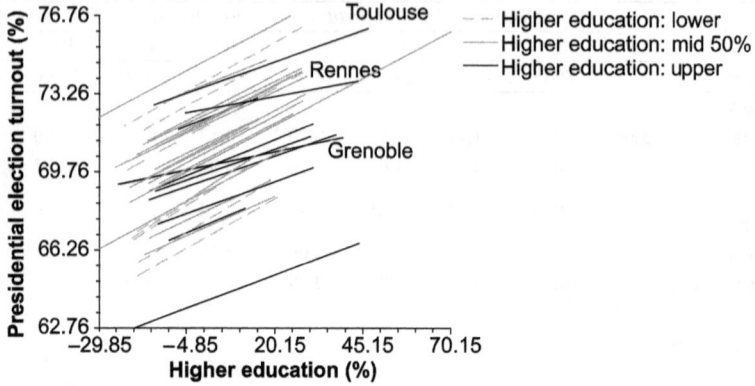

**b) Residents born abroad, by communes and metropolitan areas**

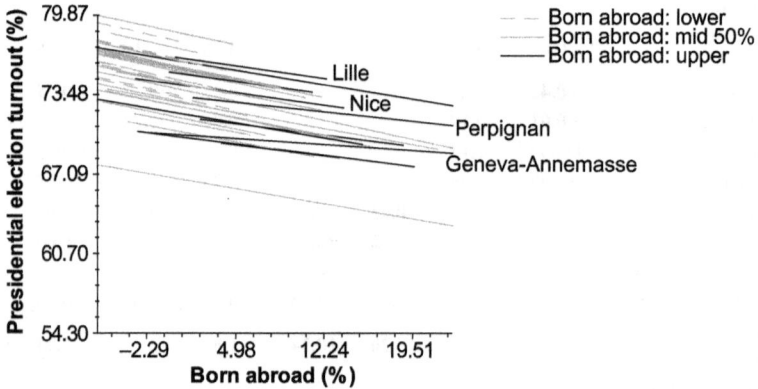

**c) Population density, by commune and population by metropolitan area**

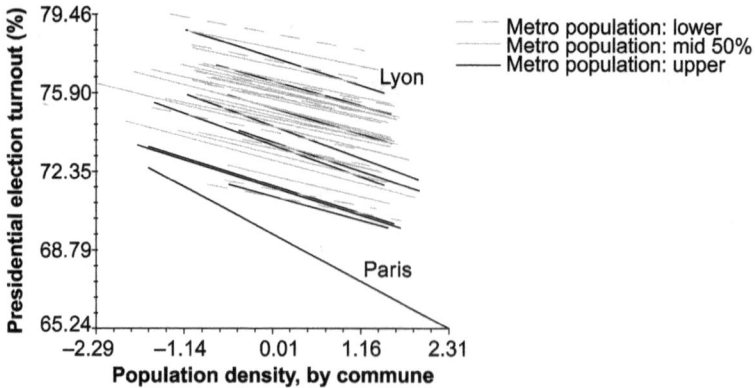

*Figure 5.3: Metropolitan variations in effects on presidential election turnout (randomised slopes by metropolitan area)*

The models affirm the importance of several contextual variables. In both the multilevel and the ordinary least squares models, local population density emerged as one of the strongest predictors of lower turnout (in the full hierarchical linear model, $B = -1.27$, $p<0.001$). Metropolitan size compounds this effect ($p<0.01$). More homeownership corresponded to significantly higher turnout even with the demographic variables included ($B = 0.03$, $p<.01$). When demographic variables were controlled, occupational heterogeneity had a stronger but more volatile positive effect ($B = 1.84$, $p<0.05$).

Other dimensions of the local context had surprising effects contrary to our expectations. Work on social capital from the United States suggests commuting or residential mobility should lead to higher voting turnout (e.g. Putnam 2000). In France, rather than undermine engagement in national politics, both commuting and residential mobility are in fact linked to higher levels of participation (in the full model, $B = -0.03$, $p<0.01$, and $B = -0.02$, $p<0.01$, respectively[7]). Although suggested in some of the Swedish results (Lidström 2005; also see Chapter 9 in this volume), this unusual finding may be linked to the extraordinary fragmentation of French metropolitan communes. Where metropolitan residents rarely live and work in the same municipality, mobility appears to have engaged citizens to participate more actively in elections.

Local political dynamics and the institutional conditions of communal elections also make a significant difference in national turnout rates. Social diversity, as measured by the Simpson Index, tends to promote turnout ($B = 1.84$, $p<0.05$). Political diversity, on the other hand, has an opposite effect. The less fragmented the local party landscape, as measured by the Laakso-Taagepera Index (Laakso and Taagepera 1979), the stronger the national electoral turnout (in the full model, $B = -0.26$, $p<0.01$). Solidaristic dynamics rather than competitive ones drive participation rates. The local election rules that give local voters in the smallest communes more choice in their selection of candidates also promote higher turnout rates in national elections. Communes with populations from 2,500 to 3,500 turn out significantly more than other places in national elections ($B = 0.55$, $p<0.05$). This relationship is even stronger for communes with populations under 2,500 ($B = 1.18$, $p<0.001$).

Final models with randomised metropolitan and regional variables enabled more detailed exploration of how the multilevel local effects differ by metropolitan regions (see Table 5.2). By allowing the slopes of the regression lines for each metropolitan area to vary, this model shows that the effects of higher education on turnout differ in several of the metropolitan regions with the highest overall levels of education (see Figure 5.3(a)). Within such metropolitan regions as Toulouse, Rennes and Grenoble, where higher educated residents have clustered, a metropolitan effect from an educated electorate boosts turnout across the board. Within these metropolitan areas, higher education makes significantly less difference for national election turnout than elsewhere. A similar flattening of municipal differ-

---

7.  Note that the variables, in fact, measure non-commuting and residential stability; hence the negative values.

*Table 5.3: Municipal election turnout, first round 2001*

| | Compositional | | Contextual | | Full linear | | Full randomised | | Final randomised | |
|---|---|---|---|---|---|---|---|---|---|---|
| | B | t | B | t | B | t | B | t | B | t |
| Intercept | 99.47 | 12.94 | 99.53 | 12.79 | 99.53 | 12.92 | 73.38 | 103.36 | 73.77 | 90.78 |
| *Metro level* | | | | | | | | | | |
| Eastern border region | 1.59 | 1.75 | 2.08 | 1.95 | 1.59 | 1.63 | 1.21 | 1.02 | 1.21 | 1.02 |
| South | **5.98** | **4.82** | **6.19** | **3.81** | **5.96** | **3.99** | **2.66** | **1.98** | **2.67** | 1.98 |
| Post-secondary education | −0.02 | −0.19 | −0.01 | −0.07 | −0.02 | −0.14 | | | | |
| Foreign-born | **−0.43** | **−3.29** | **−0.46** | **−2.81** | **−0.43** | **−2.88** | | | | |
| Population (log) | **−4.14** | **−3.23** | **−4.10** | **−2.57** | **−4.16** | **−2.85** | | | | |
| *Cross-level* | | | | | | | | | | |
| Post-secondary education | | | | | | | **0.01** | **2.77** | **0.01** | 2.80 |
| Foreign-born | | | | | | | 0.00 | 0.10 | | |
| Population (log) | | | | | | | **1.74** | **8.48** | **1.74** | 8.48 |
| *Local level* | | | | | | | | | | |
| Post-secondary education | 0.03 | 1.04 | | | **0.06** | **3.14** | **−0.15** | **−2.13** | **−0.15** | −2.16 |
| Foreign born | −0.95 | −11.39 | | | −0.22 | −7.53 | −0.27 | −4.60 | −0.26 | −9.07 |
| Age 60 or more | 0.17 | 5.46 | | | 0.04 | 1.71 | 0.02 | 0.96 | 0.02 | 0.97 |
| Median income | −0.001 | −6.65 | | | −0.001 | −6.05 | −0.0005 | −4.39 | −0.0005 | −4.93 |
| Unemployment | −0.64 | −6.27 | | | −0.30 | −9.96 | −0.27 | −8.67 | −0.27 | −8.73 |
| Homeowners | | | **0.09** | **9.01** | **0.05** | **4.99** | **0.06** | **5.80** | **0.06** | 5.83 |
| Non-commuters | | | **−0.03** | **−2.42** | **−0.05** | **−4.49** | **0.01** | **−2.90** | **−0.03** | −2.90 |
| Residential stability | | | **−0.05** | **−4.73** | **−0.03** | **−2.30** | **−0.05** | **−3.70** | **−0.05** | −3.70 |
| Housing after 1975 | | | **−0.03** | **−5.23** | **−0.04** | **−5.29** | **−0.37** | **−4.65** | **−0.04** | −4.65 |
| Occupational diversity | | | **−3.57** | **−4.53** | **−4.11** | **−3.36** | **−2.94** | **−2.36** | **−2.93** | −2.36 |
| Population density (log) | | | **−6.70** | **−31.02** | **−5.37** | **−21.93** | **−16.05** | **12.43** | **−16.07** | −12.43 |
| Political diversity | | | **−0.64** | **−8.00** | **−0.62** | **−7.07** | **−0.65** | **−7.48** | **−0.07** | −7.48 |
| Population 2,500–3,500 | | | 0.42 | 1.07 | 0.38 | 0.98 | 0.40 | 1.06 | 0.41 | 1.06 |
| Population under 2,500 | | | **3.67** | **11.66** | **3.61** | **11.63** | **3.58** | **11.62** | **3.58** | 11.64 |
| Chi-square | 888 | | 1468 | | 1206 | | 2537 | | 2549 | |
| D.f. (Metropolitan) | 36 | | 36 | | 36 | | 39 | | 39 | |
| (Local) | 6304 | | 6768 | | 6297 | | 6297 | | 6299 | |
| p-value | 0 | | 0.00 | | 0.00 | | 0.00 | | 0.00 | |
| Reliability est. | 0.931 | | 0.96 | | 0.95 | | 0.97 | | 0.97 | |

| | Compositional | Contextual | Full linear | Full randomised | Final randomised |
|---|---|---|---|---|---|
| Total variance explained | 37% | 48% | 52% | 47% | 47% |
| Metro variance explained | 49% | 38% | 48% | 14% | 14% |
| Local variance explained | 35% | 49% | 53% | 54% | 54% |
| Estimator | −2.13 | −2.21 | −2.03 | −2.03 | −2.03 |

*Notes:* For boldface coefficients, $p<0.05$.

ences takes place in the metropolitan areas with more foreign-born residents (see Figure 5.3(b)). In a number of the metropolitan regions with the highest proportions of foreign-born residents (e.g. Lille, Nice, and Annemasse on the Swiss border), larger numbers of residents born abroad make less of a difference for turnout at the local level than in other metropolitan areas. Finally, municipal population density has a more negative effect on national turnout in the largest metropolitan regions (see Figure 5.3(c)). This effect may simply reflect the greater range of density in these settings. It may also be traced back to the solidary dynamics of small metropolitan communities, which are more exposed to national media and party campaigns than peripheral regions.

The same models are even more effective in accounting for municipal election turnout. The hierarchical linear models account for up to 53 per cent of the local variance in municipal election turnout, along with 48 per cent of the variance between metropolitan areas. In these elections, metropolitan and local spatial contexts clearly matter more for turnout than the demographic composition of localities. Although the town types alone account for 1 per cent more of the variation in municipal turnout in the ordinary least squares models than the compositional variables (29 per cent, as opposed to 28 per cent), the contextual and full models account for 20 to 27 per cent more.

In the multilevel analysis, the contextual model explains 49 per cent of the variation compared to 35 per cent for the compositional model (see Table 5.3). Numerous individual contextual variables bear a stronger relationship to municipal turnout than to presidential turnout, including homeownership (B = 0.05, $p<0.01$), density (B = −5.37, $p<0.001$), and local political homogeneity (B = −0.62, $p<0.001$).

Although both commuting and residential stability exert similar effects to those in national elections, a third indicator of ties to local communities now demonstrates the expected effect. Larger proportions of new housing in a community emerge as a significant predictor of lower municipal election turnout (B = −0.04, $p<0.01$).

The compositional variables still account for the same overall proportion of the local variance as in the presidential election, and add 4 per cent to the variance explained in a full linear model. With all other influences controlled, higher-income communities voted even less consistently in municipal elections than in presidential

**a) Higher education, by commune and metropolitan area**

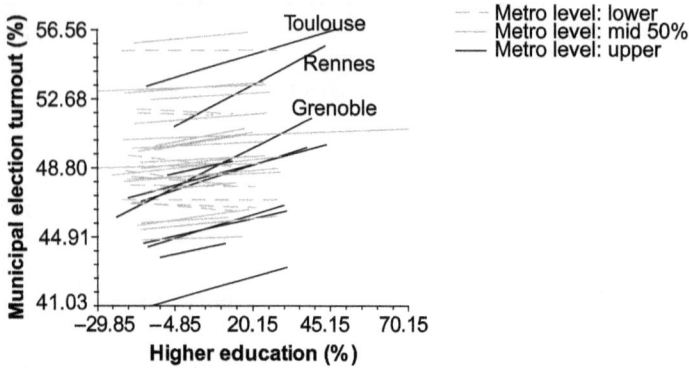

**b) Population density, by commune and metropolitan area**

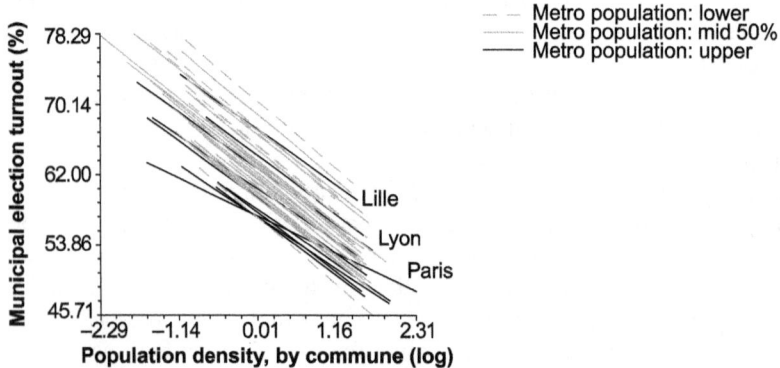

*Figure 5.4: Municipal turnout rates, by commune and by metropolitan area (randomised slopes by metropolitan areas)*

elections (p<0.001 compared to p<0.05). Two indicators that generally correspond to concentrated disadvantage, foreign-born residents (B = −0.22, p<0.001) and unemployment rates (B = −0.30, p<0.001), also contribute more strongly and consistently to lower municipal turnout than in the presidential election. Higher education retains a positive influence on local turnout (B = 0.06, p<0.05), but only at the local level; at the metropolitan level, this variable has no significant influence.

Regional and metropolitan influences affect municipal turnout more consistently than presidential turnout. In contrast with presidential voting, regional variations retain their significance regardless of the other variables included. Local turnout in the southern region remains markedly higher than elsewhere across the entire range of models (p<0.01). The eastern border region also exhibits higher turnout (p<0.10), except in the models with randomised metropolitan predictors.

As randomised models demonstrate, the directions as well as the strength of

*Table 5.4: Models of differential between presidential and municipal turnout*

| | Compositional | | Contextual | | Full linear | | Full randomised | |
|---|---|---|---|---|---|---|---|---|
| | **B** | **t** | **B** | **t** | **B** | **t** | **B** | **t** |
| Intercept | −10.37 | −1 | −10.31 | −1.44 | −10.42 | −1.55 | 3.86 | 6.16 |
| *Metro level* | | | | | | | | |
| Eastern border region | **−2.12** | **−2.90** | **−2.50** | **−2.79** | **−2.12** | **−2.50** | **−2.11** | **−2.30** |
| South | **−5.03** | **−4.62** | **−5.20** | **−3.80** | **−5.03** | **−3.89** | **−3.38** | **−3.25** |
| Post-secondary education | **0.26** | **2.43** | **0.26** | **2.18** | **0.26** | **2.32** | | |
| Foreign-born | 0.07 | 0.70 | 0.09 | 0.63 | 0.08 | 0.58 | | |
| Population (log) | 1.18 | 0.77 | 1.15 | 0.86 | 1.19 | 0.94 | | |
| *Cross-level* | | | | | | | | |
| Post-secondary education | | | | | | | **−0.01** | **−4.91** |
| Foreign born | | | | | | | 0.01 | 1.93 |
| Population (log) | | | | | | | **−2.45** | **−13.00** |
| *Local level* | | | | | | | | |
| Post-secondary education | 0.03 | 1.12 | | | 0.00 | −0.03 | **0.33** | **5.19** |
| Foreign born | **0.52** | **8.90** | | | 0.05 | 1.85 | 0.03 | 0.51 |
| Age 60 or more | **−0.17** | **−4.65** | | | −0.04 | −1.70 | −0.13 | −0.61 |
| Median income | **0.001** | **3.62** | | | **0.0004** | **4.78** | **0.0003** | **3.24** |
| Unemployment | **0.26** | **4.27** | | | **0.06** | **2.20** | 0.02 | 0.74 |
| Homeowners | | | **−0.03** | **−3.53** | **−0.03** | **−2.68** | **−0.04** | **−4.18** |
| Non-commuters | | | 0.01 | 0.53 | **0.02** | **2.12** | 0.00 | −0.36 |
| Residential stability | | | 0.02 | 1.68 | 0.01 | 1.02 | **0.04** | **3.24** |
| Housing after 1975 | | | **0.05** | **8.91** | **0.05** | **6.56** | **0.04** | **5.56** |
| Occupational diversity | | | **8.77** | **12.04** | **5.95** | **5.25** | **4.17** | **3.65** |
| Population density (log) | | | **4.60** | **23.01** | **4.09** | **18.06** | **19.19** | **16.18** |
| Political diversity | | | **0.31** | **4.21** | **0.36** | **4.40** | **0.40** | **5.02** |
| Population 2,500–3,500 | | | **0.20** | **0.55** | **0.18** | **0.50** | **0.11** | **0.31** |
| Population under 2,500 | | | **−1.81** | **−6.23** | **−1.80** | **−6.25** | **−1.79** | **−6.33** |
| Chi-square | | 1210 | | 1565 | | 1465 | | 1165 |
| D.f. (Metropolitan) | | 36 | | 36 | | 36 | | 39 |
| (Local) | | 6304 | | 6766 | | 6295 | | 6295 |
| p-value | | 0 | | 0.00 | | 0.00 | | 0.00 |
| Reliability est. | | 0.932 | | 0.95 | | 0.95 | | 0.96 |
| Total variance explained | | 28% | | 34% | | 39% | | 38% |
| Metro variance explained | | 44% | | 37% | | 44% | | 27% |
| Local variance explained | | 25% | | 33% | | 38% | | 40% |
| Estimator | | −2.04 | | −2.15 | | −1.98 | | −1.97 |

*Notes:* For boldface coefficients, p<0.05.

local effects are closely linked to metropolitan and regional differences. In several respects, the cross-level effects are the opposite of those for presidential election turnout. The community effects from higher education differ among metropolitan areas with different levels of education. In the metropolitan areas with the greatest concentrations of more educated residents, local milieus of intensified voter mobilisation produced higher municipal turnout rates (see Figure 5.4(a)). In the metropolitan areas of Grenoble, Rennes and Toulouse, the local turnout in the most educated municipalities was more pronounced than in other metropolitan regions. In these same metropolitan settings, local presidential election turnout rates were more uniform than in the other metropolitan regions. In several metropolitan areas with overall low levels of higher education, the most educated communities turned out less frequently in the municipal elections.

Metropolitan size had contrary cross-level effects in the municipal election from those in the presidential election (see Figure 5.4(b)). The demobilising effects of the most massive French metropolitan concentrations appeared to overshadow the local effects from the decline of community with rising population density in individual metropolitan towns. Particularly in metropolitan Paris, municipal turnout not only averaged lower than anywhere else, but declined less with rising density. In the national election, lower density had a stronger mobilising effect in metropolitan areas like Paris and Lyon than elsewhere.

The turnout gap between the presidential and local elections thus derives from an interrelated assortment of institutional, local and metropolitan effects (see Table 5.4). Contextual variables have the biggest delocalising effects. They explain a third of the overall variation in the differential between presidential and municipal election turnout, and when added to the demographic model account for 13 per cent more. Two variables directly linked to urbanised concentrations, population density ($B = 4.09$, $p<0.001$) and occupational diversity ($B = 5.95$, $p<0.001$), exert the strongest impact on delocalisation. Local political diversity, based on party performance in the presidential election, also contributes significantly to the turnout gap ($B = 0.36$, $p<0.001$), so does new housing ($B = 0.05$, $p<0.01$). The distinctive electoral rules and practices of the smallest communes limit the gap ($B = -1.80$, $p<0.001$), as does homeownership ($B = -0.03$, $p<0.05$). The southern and eastern border regions also mobilised more consistently in elections at both levels.

The most consistent demographic source of delocalised participation is socio-economic privilege in a community. The distinct effects from higher education and median income reveal significant variations in these influences. Metropolitan communities with higher median incomes generally mobilised more in the presidential election than in the municipal election ($B = 0.0004$, $p<0.001$). Higher education fostered delocalisation consistently at a metropolitan scale ($p<0.05$), but not at a local scale. As randomised variables demonstrated, the turnout gap narrowed in more educated communities within metropolitan concentrations of the educated. Concentrations of the disadvantaged, which contributed to lower turnout in both local and national elections, had significant but less robust delocalising effects (for unemployment: B =0.06, p<0.05; for the foreign born population: B = 0.05, p<0.10).

In a country with well-established national parties, national media and a national set of election rules, it is to be expected that electoral participation would remain largely uniform even in the wake of metropolitanisation. In France, however, metropolitanisation has brought about a national landscape of local settings with modest but systematic differences in electoral participation. In the low-density suburbs that are now absorbed into metropolitan regions, and particularly in regions with stronger clientelist traditions, inherited rural practices have continued to foster strong local and national voter turnout. In the most urbanised settings, the decline in voter turnout has been most pronounced. Here, and in most of the more privileged metropolitan communities, disengagement from local elections exceeds the disengagement from national elections. Further regressions, using the municipal typology, show that delocalisation in the urban concentrations goes further than what the multilevel models predicted.[8] In the presidential election, these tests also show significantly stronger mobilisation in poor minority suburbs and more demobilisation in affluent suburbs. Although these findings may reflect the specific circumstances that propelled Le Pen and the National Front into second place in the presidential election of 2002, the more general implications are also clear. Many of the local and metropolitan influences that decisively shaped turnout in these elections have undoubtedly also been at work in other recent French elections.

## New partisan cleavages and metropolitanisation

Metropolitanisation has also played a major, but mostly unexamined, role in the shifting party cleavages in France. Since the 1970s, as in other European countries, new parties have emerged. On the right, the 2002 election exemplified how the National Front under Jean-Marie Le Pen capitalised on such issues as immigration and Europe to win consistent support from up to 20 per cent of the national electorate. On the left, the Greens and a number of smaller, more radical parties increasingly replaced the French Communist Party as alternatives to the Socialist Party. Interests and distinct local cultures common to metropolitan communities influence the formation of new political configurations.

In several ways, new interests and orientations emerging from metropolitan areas could foster new lines of political cleavages (see Chapter 1 in this volume). Although many of these influences are well established in Anglo-Saxon countries, they remain less elucidated in France. This analysis draws on partisan indices created according to the IMO protocol to measure economic, cultural and transnational issues and voter self-placement. Along with testing a range of specific hypotheses

---

8. Both regressions of the municipal types along with the full ordinary least squares models, and further tests of the types against the residuals from the full hierarchical linear models, confirm these effects (see Tables WA.5.1, WA.5.2 and WA.5.4).

about partisan voting, the analysis examines whether partisan preferences are connected to the spatial characteristics of metropolitan and local contexts. Beyond the demographic composition of communities, contextual models incorporate the crucial economic and physical asset of homeownership (Gilderbloom *et al.* 1984; Kingston *et al.* 1984). Commuting, new housing, residential mobility, economic diversity and population density each capture dimensions of local consumption interests that could affect partisan orientations. Local contextual conditions like these could also be related to the cultural divergences that have given rise to the new cleavages (Clark and Hoffmann-Martinot 1998).

Regression models of demographic composition include social and economic measures of privilege and disadvantage in communities (median income, higher education, unemployment), along with age. The influx of immigrants, measured here by the number of local residents born abroad, has been demonstrated to promote ethno-nationalistic voting in France (e.g. Chalard 2006). Tests of the demographic variables at the metropolitan scale enable analysis of regional and cross-level effects that might condition local influences.

### Overall tendencies

In 2002, both the traditional parties and the newer, smaller parties drew disproportionate support from different types of metropolitan places (see Figure 5.5). The traditional right, led by the *Rassemblement pour la République* (RPR) under Jacques Chirac, won the vote in the urban concentrations as well as in other types of towns. They drew on the affluent suburbs as their strongest bases of support, and outperformed all other parties by a substantial margin in the middle-class and low-density suburbs. The small market liberal party of Alain Madelin also drew its strongest support from the affluent suburbs. In 2007, under the banner of Chirac's Union for a Popular Movement, Nicolas Sarkozy won decisively on the basis of agendas linked to suburban interests, values and lifestyles: privatisation, civil service cutbacks, immigration restrictions and tougher law enforcement.

The total votes for socialist Lionel Jospin and former socialist Jean-Pierre Chevenement in 2002 reflected an unusually low point for the moderate left. Support for the Socialist Party and its allies concentrated in the urban concentrations, where the total votes for the moderate left ranged nearly five points higher in the urban than in any other type of community. Although the municipal averages for other types fell within a range of 5 per cent, support ranged lowest in the low-density and middle-class communities. In both types of poor communities, which historically had furnished critical constituencies for victorious socialist candidates, the party finished third behind both the extreme right and the traditional right.

Both the extreme left and the new right drew their strongest support from these localities. The National Front of Le Pen and the smaller National Republican Movement under Bruno Mégret had gained the most from the Socialist losses. In the poor minority communities, the extreme right nearly exceeded the average vote for the traditional right; in poor non-minority communities, it did almost as well. In these same settings, the multiple candidates on the far left had clearly

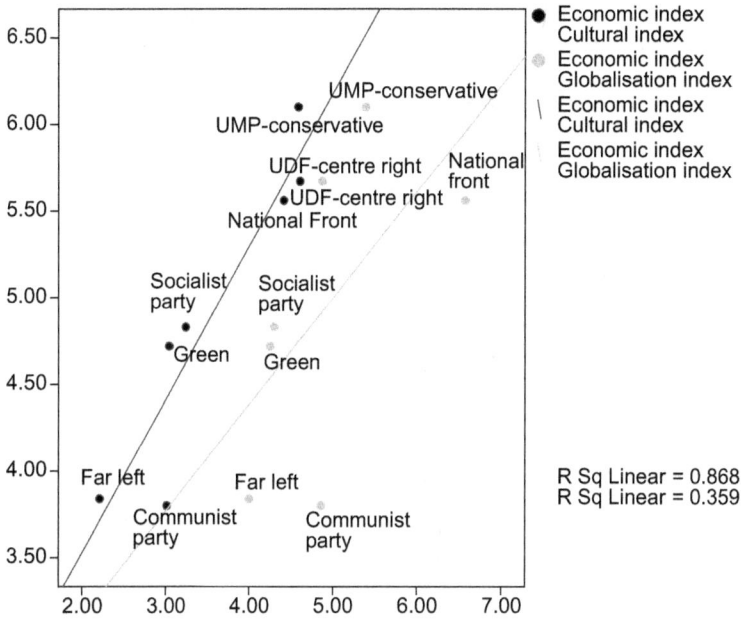

*Figure 5.5: Party positions by left-right self-placement and by indices for economic issues, cultural issues and globalisation*

drawn away part of the Socialist vote. In the poor non-minority communities, support for the far left approached that for the moderate left.

To analyse the relationship between these party configurations and metropolitan places more systematically, the standardised protocol of the IMO project for assigning partisan preferences to communities was employed. This portion of the analysis draws on the French National Election Survey of 2002 for voter self-placement, and surveys of party voters from 1996 to 2004 for indices of economic ideology, cultural values, and attitudes toward globalisation and multiculturalism (see Table 5.5). The separate indices enable examination of community sources of partisan support along each of these distinct dimensions of party competition.[9]

The preferences these indices revealed resembled patterns shown since the 1990s in the French party system (e.g. Kitschelt 1994, 1996; Kriesi *et al.* 2006). Party positions on the economic and cultural scales proved to be largely similar (see Figure 5.5). The main contrast between these indices and the scale for voter self-placement was the position of National Front supporters slightly to the left of the two traditional right or centre-right parties, the UMP and the UDF. Comparison with the globalisation index, however, shows distinctive configurations across the

9. See Chapter 14 (the Methodological Appendix to this volume) for the questions used to compile these indices.

*Table 5.5: Party placement by voter preferences (self-placement, economic, cultural and globalisation indices)*

| | Party Manifesto −50 (left) to +50 (right) | Voter Self-Placement 1 (left) to 10 (right) | Party Voter Identification 1 (left) to 10 (right) | Economic Index (1 left) to 10 right) | Cultural Index (1 left) to 10 right) | Globalisa-tion Index 1 (left) to 10 right) |
|---|---|---|---|---|---|---|
| Far left | | 3.68 (Besancenot) | 1.85 (Besancenot) | 3.87 | 2.21 | 4.01 |
| | | 3.55 (Laguiller) | 2.08 (Laguiller) | | | |
| | | 3.75 (Gluckstein) | 3.64 (Gluckstein) | | | |
| Communist Party | −17.5 | 2.83 | 3.25 | 3.83 | 3.01 | 4.95 |
| Socialist Party | −16.09 | 3.53 | 3.15 | 4.85 | 3.24 | 4.24 |
| | | 4.83 (Chevenement) | 3.95 (Chevenement) | | | |
| Green | −12.78 | 3.7 | 3.14 | 4.74 | 3.04 | 4.21 |
| UDF – Centre Right | 7.2 | 6.19 | 5.75 | 5.72 | 4.61 | 4.84 |
| UDF – Centre Right (Madelin) | | 6.72 | 5.85 | 6.03 | 4.58 | 4.84 |
| UMP – Conservative | −8.92 | 7.06 | 6.61 | 6.15 | 4.59 | 5.41 |
| National Front (Le Pen) | 27.56 | 6.92 | 7.66 | 5.40 | 4.42 | 6.69 |
| National Republican Movement (Megret) | | 9 | 8.48 | 5.63 | 4.57 | 6.69 |

*Notes:* Party Voter Identification indicates average placement of party by survey respondents voting for that party. Party manifesto left-right scale from 2002 Legislative elections. Voter self-placement and Party Voter Identification from Comparative Study of Electoral Systems data (May 2002). Economic Index compiled of eight items from European Values Survey (1999–2000), International Social Survey Program (1998, 1999). Cultural Index composed from ten items in European Values Survey (1999–2000), International Social Survey Program (1998, 2003). Globalisation index composed from sixteen items in International Social Survey Program (2004).

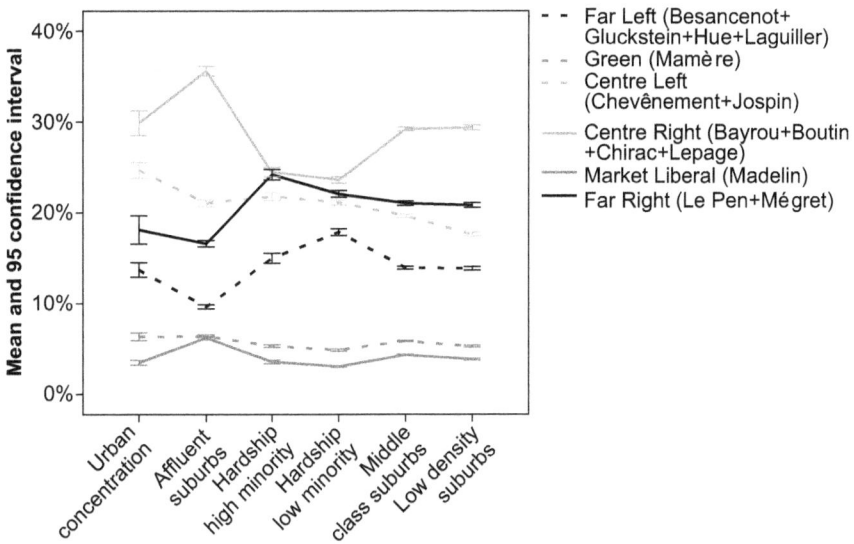

*Figure 5.6: Vote by presidential candidate in first round 2002, by type of commune*

political spectrum. The National Front now stood far to the right. The Socialists, Greens and traditional right parties converged toward similarly moderate positions. The Communists moved to the right of the moderate left parties, while the other extreme-left parties remained only slightly to the left.

The analysis relies on the performance of each party in a community to attribute an overall ideological position on each index for each locality. Three of the four indices bring out a clear ideological opposition between the affluent and low-density suburbs on the right, and the urban concentrations and poor low minority suburbs on the left (see Figures 5.6 and 5.7). Middle-class and poor minority suburbs divide more evenly between these two orientations. The patterns are broadly consistent with the polarisation hypothesised by Sellers and Walks (see Chapter 1 in this volume) between consumption interests and cultural values in urban concentrations and different types of suburbs. The economic and cultural indices skew to the left in terms of voter self-placement in the low-density suburbs, and more to the right in the other types. Ordinary least squares regressions of the town types confirm these influences (see Table WA.5.3). In ordinary least squares regressions, these types account for 5 per cent of variation in local voter self-placement, 14 per cent of variation in the economic dimension of partisanship and 9 per cent in the cultural dimension.

Metropolitan cleavages on globalisation, influenced strongly by support for the National Front and the Communist Party, diverged from this pattern. The poor minority suburbs averaged furthest to the right along this dimension, followed by the low-density suburbs, and the middle-class suburbs. The affluent suburbs, the most right-leaning in all of the other indices, shifted decisively to the left. regional

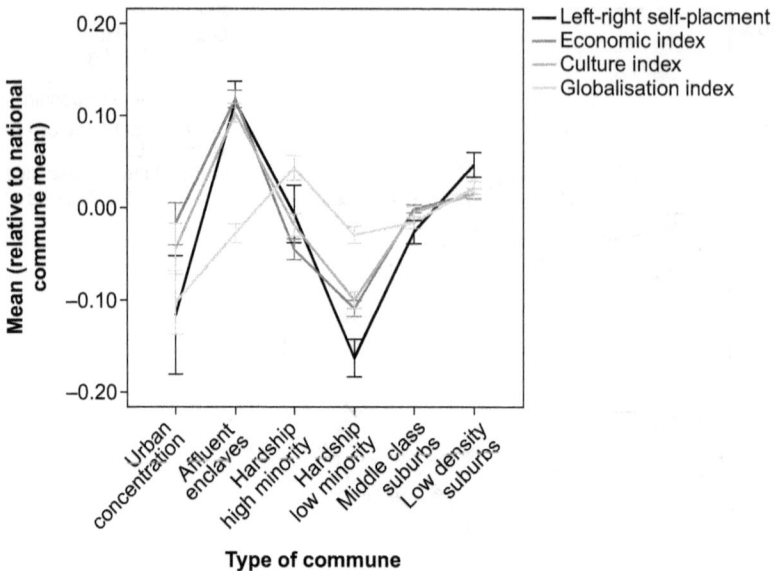

Figure 5.7: Indices of partisanship, by type of commune (adjusted by national mean)

Urban concentrations replaced poor low-minority suburbs as the furthest left on this scale. A distinct cleavage around cosmopolitanism opposes communities that derive economic advantages from globalisation to disadvantaged places facing influxes of immigrants.

In ordinary least squares regressions, the types accounted for only 2 per cent of the variation in this globalisation index. A full 40 per cent of the variance in extreme right support and 41 per cent of the variance in the index itself occurred between metropolitan regions. The extreme right received significantly stronger support in the eastern industrial and mining regions, the south and other parts of the country with concentrations of immigrants. By contrast, just under a quarter (24 per cent) of the local variance in support for the major traditional left and right parties occurred between metropolitan areas. Support for the Greens and the market liberal party of Madelin proved more uniform; more than 80 per cent of the variation in support for both parties occurred within rather than between metropolitan areas. Economic and cultural orientations also varied more within metropolitan regions (72 and 65 per cent respectively).

### Examining multilevel variation

Even as French partisan alignments remain largely nationalised, multivariate analysis demonstrates systematic influences from the local and metropolitan settings where voters live. Hierarchical linear models proved crucial to analyse these cleavages, and to capture the relations between local, metropolitan and regional influences. The models point to the spatial contexts of metropolitan and local set-tings as important determinants of local partisan preferences.

As with turnout, alternative tests compared models of demographic composition with models based on places as territorial contexts. Combined linear models and models with randomised metropolitan variables incorporated both compositional and contextual variables.[1] In both ordinary least squares regressions and multilevel analysis, these models consistently explained two times or more of the overall variation than models based on the town types. Although models of local demographic composition accounted for more of the variation than models of local contextual variables, metropolitan and local spatial characteristics proved at least as critical for a full explanation. Spatial contextual influences explain variations that the demographic composition of local electorates could not, and provide alternative explanations for most of the compositional effects. Effects from such components of local demographic composition as income, education and nationality also differ systematically by metropolitan area and region.

Multilevel analysis again provided the fullest account of these layered metropolitan, regional and local influences (see Table 5.6).[2] A contextual model of left-right self-placement accounted for half of the local variation explained by a model based on demographic composition (12 per cent, compared to 24 per cent). However, the contextual variables boosted the variation explained in the full model by 6 per cent over the compositional model (to 30 per cent).

A number of consistent relationships in these models reappeared through-out the models of partisan preferences. Despite the correlation between income and education, these two measures of socio-economic privilege bore contrast-ing relationships to voting on the left-right scale. Local median income emerged as one of the most consistent demographic predictors of voting for the right (in the full model, $B = 0.00004$, $p<0.001$).[3] Beyond this strong local effect, a logged version of the variable proved to be the most powerful linear predictor of support for the right at the metropolitan level ($p<0.05$). As tests with a randomised version of this vari-able show, intensified support for the right among higher income communities was especially strong in the richest metropolitan areas such as Paris, Lyon, Marseille or Grenoble (see Figure 5.8(a)). Here, where more of the wealthiest citizens cluster and more residential sorting by income often takes place, higher-income communities have developed particularly strong preferences for the right. The wealthy Paris sub-urb of Neuilly, where Nicolas Sarkozy served as mayor, exemplified the economic

1. Linear variables at metropolitan levels were again selected from a larger group of variables by backwards regression, supplemented by tests of permutations for the best alternative model that could be applied consistently for the various indices.

2. Ordinary least squares results (see Table WA5.4 in the Web Appendix, http://press.ecpr.eu/re-sources) demonstrated the significance of regional and metropolitan as well as local variations, but did not permit an examination of the relationships between these different levels of explana-tion.

3. Both the full linear regressions and the models with other compositional variables confirmed a significant bivariate correlation (0.255, $p<0$ .01).

*Table 5.6: Models of left-right self-placement for party voters, by commune*

| | Compositional | | Contextual | | Full linear | | Full randomised | | Final randomised | |
|---|---|---|---|---|---|---|---|---|---|---|
| | **B** | **t** | **B** | **t** | **B** | **t** | **B** | **t** | **B** | **t** |
| Intercept | −6.298 | −1.75 | −6.672 | −1.86 | −6.290 | −1.75 | 5.334 | 115.92 | 5.335 | 115.94 |
| *Metro level* | | | | | | | | | | |
| Eastern border region | 0.106 | 1.69 | 0.113 | 1.82 | 0.106 | 1.69 | **0.210** | **3.21** | **0.210** | **3.20** |
| South | 0.166 | 1.57 | 0.168 | 1.59 | 0.166 | 1.57 | **0.192** | **2.57** | **0.189** | **2.53** |
| Median income(log) | **3.044** | **3.22** | **3.143** | **3.33** | **3.042** | **3.22** | | | | |
| Foreign born | 0.010 | 1.04 | 0.009 | 0.89 | 0.010 | 1.04 | | | | |
| Post-secondary education | −0.015 | −1.65 | −0.015 | −1.67 | −0.015 | −1.65 | | | | |
| *Cross-level* | | | | | | | | | | |
| Post-secondary education | | | | | | | **−0.001** | **−4.09** | **−0.001** | **−4.13** |
| Foreign born | | | | | | | **0.002** | **3.24** | **0.002** | **3.25** |
| Median income (log) | | | | | | | **0.0004** | **3.07** | 0.0004 | 3.02 |
| *Local level* | | | | | | | | | | |
| Post-secondary education | **−0.003** | **−5.49** | | | **−0.004** | **−6.08** | **0.019** | **3.44** | **0.019** | **3.49** |
| Foreign born | **−0.011** | **−12.68** | | | 0.001 | 0.73 | **−0.011** | **−2.20** | **−0.011** | **−2.25** |
| Age 60 or more | **0.010** | **14.48** | | | **0.006** | **7.09** | **0.006** | **7.47** | **0.007** | **9.64** |
| Median income | **0.00004** | **6.09** | | | **0.00004** | **12.14** | **−0.001** | **−2.98** | **−0.001** | **−2.93** |
| Unemployment | **−0.008** | **−2.64** | | | **−0.002** | **−2.07** | −0.001 | −0.59 | | |
| Homeowners | | | **0.005** | **12.63** | **0.003** | **7.54** | **0.002** | **4.77** | **0.002** | **4.83** |
| Non-commuters | | | **0.006** | **14.64** | **0.006** | **13.30** | **0.005** | **10.84** | **0.005** | **10.88** |
| Residential stability | | | **−0.001** | **−2.47** | **−0.003** | **−6.76** | **−0.003** | **−7.25** | **−0.003** | **−7.17** |
| Housing after 1975 | | | **−0.001** | **−5.26** | 0.000 | −0.94 | 0.000 | −1.13 | | |
| Occupational diversity | | | 0.015 | 0.48 | **−0.096** | **−2.09** | -0.085 | −1.85 | −0.085 | −1.85 |
| Population (log)-logdens | | | **−0.076** | **−10.63** | **−0.102** | **−12.84** | **−0.108** | **−13.26** | **−0.110** | **−13.86** |
| Chi-square | 2283 | | 2244 | | 2480 | | 103 | | 102 | |
| D.f. (Metropolitan) | 36 | | 36 | | 36 | | 40 | | 39 | |
| (Local) | 6304 | | 6769 | | 6298 | | 6298 | | 6300 | |
| p-value | 0 | | 0 | | 0 | | 0 | | 0 | |
| Reliability est. | 0.981 | | 0.979 | | 0.984 | | 0.979 | | 0.979 | |
| Local variance explained | 24% | | 12% | | 30% | | 34% | | 34% | |
| Metro variance explained | 33% | | 33% | | 33% | | 8% | | 8% | |
| Total variance explained | 28% | | 20% | | 31% | | 24% | | 24% | |
| Estimator | 101 | | −373 | | 328 | | 440 | | 452 | |

*Notes:* For boldface coefficients, p<0.05.

assets, consumption interests and traditionalist orientations that reinforced suburban support for the established French right. In several of the least affluent metropolitan areas, by contrast, wealthier towns voted more for the left.

The most educated communities generally voted for the left. Although this relationship only emerged with median income controlled, it persisted throughout the linear models of voter self-placement and the partisan indices. Supplementing the strong local effect (B= −0.004, p <0 .01), the metropolitan rate of higher education fell barely short of a 0.10 significance. The randomised coefficients revealed this effect to be strongest in the university and high-tech service centres of Grenoble, Montpellier and Toulouse, but also strong in the largest metropolitan areas (see Figure 5.8(b)). In these regions, highly-educated workers clustered in distinctive types of localities distinguished less by wealth and more by consumption interests and local cultures supportive of left parties. Support for the Greens and for extreme left parties other than the Communists often ranged higher in these settings. In metropolitan areas lacking these concentrations of higher education, such as Limoges, towns with more educated local electorates often stand out as more conservative than the metropolitan average.

Other demographic variables also registered significant effects. Communities with older residents favoured the right (B = 0.006, p<0.01). Unemployment reinforced support for the left, even beyond the effects of income (B = −0.002, p<0.05). High proportions of immigrants made only a significant difference for left-right self-placement when the contextual variables were not taken into account. Randomised metropolitan versions of this variable showed that its local effects hinged on the size of the metropolitan immigrant presence (see Figure 5.8(c)). Only in the metropolitan areas with the largest proportions of immigrants, such as Nice, Nimes and Montpellier, did municipalities with the largest local concentration of immigrants vote strongly for the right.[4] In regions with smaller proportions of immigrants, including Ile de France, but also Brittany, concentrations of immigrants generated stronger support for left parties.

Beyond these metropolitan cross-level effects, local contextual influences contributed significantly to the explanation of left-right differences. Variables for logged population density (B = −0.10, p<0.001) and occupational diversity (B = −0.096, p<0.05) emerged as stronger predictors of left voting than any of the local demographic variables. Homeownership exerted the same conservative effect on the partisan orientations of communities in France as in Anglo-Saxon countries (B = 0.003, p<0.01). As in a number of other European contexts, the dormitory and commuter towns of French metropolitan areas also provided stronger, more consistent support for left parties than the outlying metropolitan communities (B = 0.006, p<0.01). Left support also ranged higher among metropolitan places with greater residential stability (B = −0.003, p<0.01), a result consistent with a significant but slight bivariate correlation (0.072, p<0.05). This result could reflect

---

4.    The one clear exception is the border metropolis of Annemasse-Geneva, where longstanding links to Switzerland have fostered a cosmopolitan local culture.

**a) Median income, by commune and by metropolitan average (logged)**

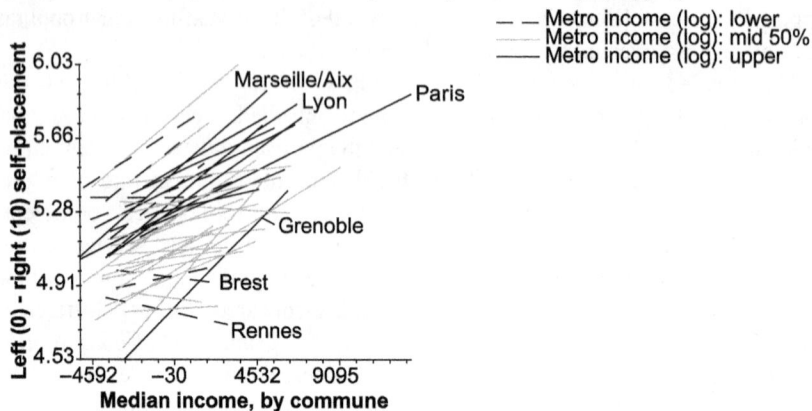

**b) Higher education, by commune and by metropolitan average**

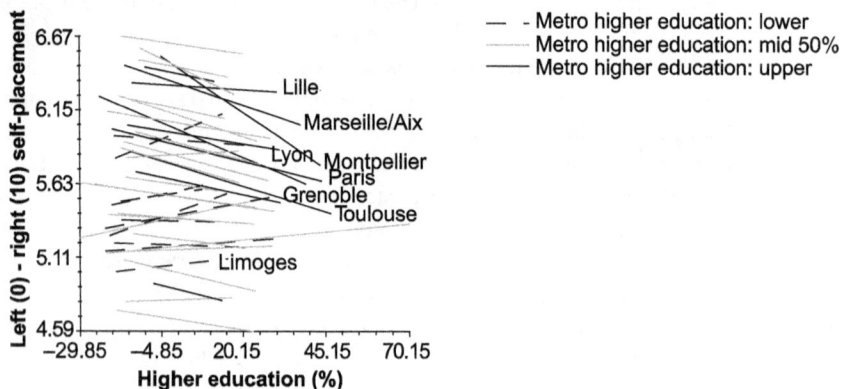

**c) Per cent born abroad, by commune and by metropolitan area**

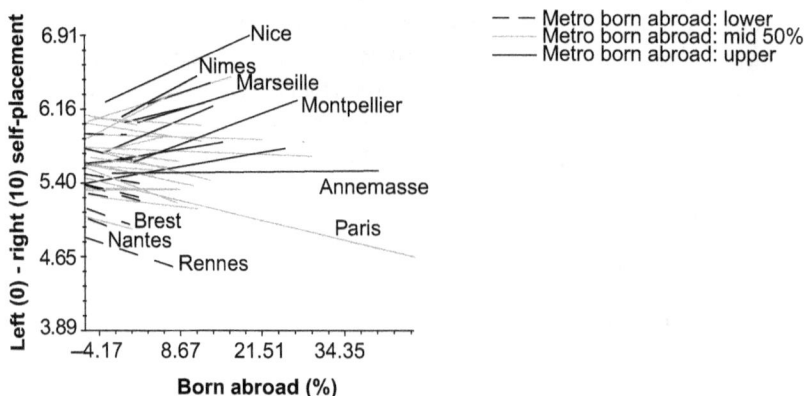

*Figure 5.8: Metropolitan and commune-level effects on left-right self-placement index*

greater support for the right among those middle-class and affluent voters who participated in the recent exodus from urban concentrations.

Parallel models of the economic and cultural indices confirmed nearly all these results (see Table 5.7). The models accounted most fully for community preferences along the economic dimension, explaining 40 per cent of the overall variance in local economic ideology. Indicators of metropolitan and communal median income proved even more powerful as predictors of economic conservatism than as predictors of voter self-placement on the right. Economic interests and the preferences being generated by them appear to have been especially important to metropolitan influences on partisan preferences.

As the municipal typology suggested, positions toward globalisation and cosmopolitanism departed from these consistent patterns. Although most of the variables retained a similar coefficient and significance as for the other indices, metropolitan income fell below statistical significance as a predictor of positions on the globalisation index. Instead, effects similar to the 'racial threat' hypothesis found in the US literature accounted for most of the variation (e.g. Giles and Herz 1994; Lubbers and Scheepers 2002). With or without the other metropolitan-level variables, support for the ethno-nationalist right rose with the proportion of immigrants in a community. Opposition to globalisation and cosmopolitanism also concentrated among the socio-economically disadvantaged communities where immigrants presented more direct economic competition to French workers. Unemployment, a strong determinant of left voting in the other indices, reversed the sign of its coefficient to become a significant predictor of voting for the right.

Additional tests demonstrated further effects from local and metropolitan influences. The distinct types of places highlighted in the municipal typology accounted for variations in partisan preferences even beyond what the full models of continuous variables could explain.[5] Metropolitan constituencies clearly mattered for the electoral coalition that maintained the traditional French right in power throughout the first decade of the twenty-first century. In 2002, the right won support from communities similar to those that provided a critical margin to George W. Bush in the United States: higher-income enclaves, low-density exurban communities, places with strong interests in protecting property assets and metropolitan areas with less educated electorates. These homogenous, low-density communities were the same ones that mobilised most consistently in local and national elections. If the moderate left managed to retain support in the

---

5. Both ordinary least squares models and models of residuals from the multilevel models demonstrate these additional effects (see Tables WA.5.3, WA.5.4). Affluent suburbs, low-density suburbs and also high, poor minority suburbs each provide significantly stronger support for the Right along the economic and cultural dimensions as well as left-right self-placement. Residuals from the multilevel linear regressions for the globalisation index point to an even stronger contextual effect in the hardship minority and low density suburbs. Both types of communes registered significantly stronger support for the right. Although the affluent suburbs had provided stronger support for the economic and cultural indices of voting for the right, no such support appeared for the rightist position on the globalisation index.

Table 5.7: Economic, cultural and globalisation indices

| | Economic index | | | | Cultural index | | Globalisation index | | | | | |
|---|---|---|---|---|---|---|---|---|---|---|---|---|
| | Full linear | | Full randomised | | Full linear | | Full linear | | Full randomised | | Final randomised | |
| | B | t | B | t | B | t | B | t | B | t | B | t |
| Intercept | -0.088 | -0.10 | 5.159 | 319.94 | -0.481 | -0.41 | 1.649 | 0.79 | 5.108 | 214.77 | 5.070 | 168.49 |
| *Metro level* | | | | | | | | | | | | |
| Eastern border region | 0.005 | 0.24 | 0.042 | 2.06 | 0.003 | 0.17 | 0.076 | 2.08 | 0.123 | 3.84 | 0.084 | 2.51 |
| South | 0.040 | 1.47 | 0.080 | 3.37 | 0.047 | 1.36 | 0.056 | 0.90 | 0.113 | 2.99 | | |
| Median income(log) | 1.354 | 5.90 | | | 1.450 | 4.71 | 0.922 | 1.68 | | | | |
| Foreign born | -0.002 | -0.96 | | | -0.001 | -0.40 | 0.012 | 2.03 | | | 0.013 | 3.57 |
| Post-secondary education | -0.014 | -0.75 | | | -0.002 | -0.82 | -0.008 | -1.50 | | | | |
| *Cross-level* | | | | | | | | | | | | |
| Post-secondary education | | | 0.000 | -3.33 | | | | | 0.000 | -3.62 | | |
| Foreign born | | | 0.001 | 3.75 | | | | | 0.000 | 3.01 | 0.001 | 3.62 |
| Logauinc | | | 0.000 | 5.02 | | | | | 0.000 | 2.76 | | |
| *Local level* | | | | | | | | | | | | |
| Post-secondary education | 0.003 | 5.52 | 0.011 | 4.48 | 0.003 | 9.87 | -0.006 | -18.27 | 0.002 | 1.07 | -0.005 | -17.14 |
| Foreign born | 0.001 | 0.97 | -0.006 | -2.96 | 0.001 | 3.21 | 0.000 | -0.63 | -0.002 | -1.37 | -0.005 | -2.31 |
| Age 60 or more | 0.004 | 8.50 | 0.004 | 11.62 | 0.004 | 11.53 | -0.001 | -2.16 | -0.001 | -1.66 | -0.001 | -1.94 |
| Median income | 0.000 | 7.68 | -0.001 | -4.93 | 0.000 | 10.66 | 0.000 | 9.75 | 0.000 | -2.66 | 0.000 | 8.50 |
| Unemployment | -0.003 | -2.60 | -0.002 | -4.44 | -0.003 | -6.87 | 0.001 | 2.81 | 0.002 | 3.60 | 0.001 | 2.33 |
| Homeowners | 0.001 | 3.98 | 0.001 | 4.18 | 0.001 | 5.96 | 0.001 | 7.36 | 0.001 | 4.80 | 0.001 | 5.52 |
| Non-commuters | 0.003 | 12.49 | 0.003 | 15.17 | 0.003 | 16.66 | 0.001 | 6.71 | 0.001 | 4.61 | 0.001 | 4.61 |
| Residential stability | -0.001 | -3.56 | -0.001 | -7.30 | -0.001 | -5.79 | -0.001 | -6.14 | -0.001 | -5.90 | -0.001 | -5.92 |
| Housing after 1975 | 0.000 | -0.58 | 0.000 | -1.16 | 0.000 | -1.06 | 0.000 | -1.32 | 0.000 | -1.68 | -0.003 | -2.01 |
| Occupational diversity | 0.000 | -0.01 | 0.011 | 0.57 | -0.002 | -0.13 | -0.051 | -2.51 | -0.053 | -2.58 | -0.049 | -2.41 |
| Population (log)-logdens | -0.043 | -6.12 | -0.047 | -14.19 | -0.046 | -5.49 | -0.044 | -12.46 | -0.048 | -13.08 | -0.044 | -12.29 |

| | Economic index | | Cultural index | Globalisation index | | |
| --- | --- | --- | --- | --- | --- | --- |
| | Full linear | Full randomised | Full linear | Full linear | Full randomised | Final randomised |
| Chi-square | 1735 | 149.8 | 2376 | 4151 | 347.5 | 5190 |
| D.f. (Metropolitan) | 36 | 39 | 36 | 36 | 39 | 39 |
| (Local) | 6297 | 6297 | 6298 | 6298 | 6298 | 6300 |
| p-value | 0 | 0 | 0 | 0 | 0 | 0 |
| Reliability est. | 0.973 | 0.986 | 0.971 | 0.990 | 0.986 | 0.99 |
| Local variance explained | 40% | 44% | 34% | 36% | 39% | 37% |
| Metro variance explained | 40% | −16% | 38% | 29% | 17% | 29% |
| Total variance explained | 40% | 27% | 36% | 33% | 28% | 33% |
| Estimator | 6024 | 6164 | 5459 | 5408 | 5496 | 5479 |

*Notes:* For boldface coefficients, p<0.05.

central cities and contest the middle-class suburbs, it remained confined to urban constituencies and service centres with concentrations of highly-educated voters. The shift to the right on the globalisation index, evident in voting for the far left parties as well as the National Front, undermined support for the moderate left in poor communities and in regions with higher immigration. In 2008, Nicolas Sarkozy drew from Le Pen's bases of support to win a solid majority for Chirac's party.

## Conclusion

In France, metropolitan areas now shape both contemporary configurations of partisanship and patterns of political participation. If the shift toward neoliberal policy agendas with suburban backing has been less evident than in Anglo-Saxon countries, many of the same interests, value orientations and participatory trends have emerged from the metropolitan transformation.

As the networks of rural villages that dominated the French landscape since the Middle Ages have become absorbed into expanding metropolitan regions, new territorial constituencies have emerged to reinforce majorities for the traditional French right. Affluent localities and metropolitan regions now harbour the strongest support for market liberalism and traditional conservatism, as well as for economic and other forms of trans-nationalisation. Central cities, the most urbanised areas and centres of higher education serve as core constituencies for the culturally liberal, internationalist and moderate left. Marginalised, disadvantaged suburbs and regions with recent histories of immigration, although still close to the left on other economic and cultural issues, proved to be susceptible to the appeals of the extreme right, anti-immigrant National Front in 2002. These metropolitan variations in partisanship are more than simply accidents of demographic composition. Influences from community characteristics account for variations in partisan preferences that demography cannot, and provide alternative or partial explanations for another portion. Even such demographic predictors of partisanship as income and education differ in their effects according to the contexts of different metropolitan regions.

Among the determinants of electoral participation, influences rooted in similar metropolitan contexts across the country now largely overwhelm regional differences as well. Differences in community characteristics are especially powerful predictors of voter turnout in municipal elections, and also influence national election turnout. In the low-density, lower-income and middle-class communities of metropolitan peripheries, rural clientelist and participatory traditions continue to foster higher, more uniform rates of electoral participation. Patterns of electoral mobilisation have favoured the low density, more homogenous localities where the right performed the best. Homeownership and lower settlement density have promoted both local and national electoral mobilisation. In contrast, metropolitan electoral demobilisation has most often disadvantaged the urbanised, diverse and disadvantaged strongholds of the left. In socio-economically stressed localities and dense urban concentrations, local participation also falls significantly below participation in national elections. Although affluent communities and larger metropolitan regions have disengaged from local elections, these areas have mobilised nationally to maintain the traditional right in power. In all these ways, metropolitanisation has decisively shaped patterns of electoral participation and partisan contestation in France.

## Bibliography

Abrial, S., Cautrès, B. and Mandran, N. (2003) 'Turnout and abstention at multi-level elections in France', Working Paper, Centre d'Informatisation des Données Socio-Politiques, Grenoble, France.

Blais, A. (2004) 'Where does turnout decline come from?', *European Journal of Political Research*, 43(2): 221–36.

Bréchon, P. and Cautrès, B. (1987) 'L'inscription sur les listes électorales: indicateur de socialisation ou de politisation', *Revue Francaise de Science Politique*, 37(4): 502–25.

Campbell, D. (2006) *Why We Vote*, Princeton: Princeton University Press.

Cavailhès, J., Peeters, D., Sékeris, E. and Thisse, J.-F. (2002) 'La Ville périurbaine', Université de Franche-Comté, Centre d'économie et sociologie appliquées à l'agriculture et aux espaces ruraux, Working Paper.

Chalard, L. (2006) 'Le vote d'extrê, e droite dans l'aire métroplitaine marseillaise', *Espaces-temps.net*, retrieved 23rd August 2008 at http://espacestemps.net/document2101.html.

Clanché, F. (2003) 'La participation électorale au printemps 2002. De plus en plus de votants intermittents', *INSEE-Première*, janvier, 877: 1–4.

Clark, T. N. and Hoffmann-Martinot, V. (eds) (1998) *The New Political Culture*, Boulder: Westview.

Dalton, R. (2008) *Citizen Politics,* Washington DC: Congressional Quarterly Press.

Fischel, W. A. (2001) *The Homevoter Hypothesis*, Cambridge MA: Harvard University Press.

Flanagan, S. (1980) 'National and local voting trends: cross-level linkages and correlates of change', in Steiner, K., Krauss, E. S. and Flanagan, S. (eds) *Political Opposition and Local Politics in Japan*, Princeton: Princeton University Press' 131–84.

Frandsen, A. G. (2002) 'Size and electoral participation in local elections', *Environment and Planning C: Government and Policy*, 20(6): 853–69.

Gilderbloom, J. I. and Markham, J. P. (1995) 'The impact of homeownership on political beliefs', *Social Forces*, 73: 1589–607.

Giles, M. W. and Hertz, K. (1994) 'Racial threat and partisan identification', *American Political Science Review*, 88(2): 317–26.

Gimpel, J. G., Morris, I. L. and Armstrong, D. R. (2004) 'Turnout and the local age distribution: examining political participation across space and time', *Political Geography*, 23(1): 71–95.

Goerres, A. (2005) 'Grey voting power on the rise? How the transition from middle to old age influences turnout in Europe', paper presented at the 55th Political Studies Association Annual Conference, 4–7 April 2005, University of Leeds.

Hoffmann-Martinot, V. (1992) 'La participation aux élections municipales dans les villes françaises', *Revue Francaise de Science Politique*, 42(1): 3–35.

— (2005) 'Towards an Americanization of French metropolitan areas?', in

Hoffmann-Martinot, V. and Sellers, J. M. (eds), *Metropolitanization and Political Change*, Wiesbaden: Verlag für Sozialwissenschaften.

Hoffmann-Martinot, V., Rallings, C. and Thrasher, M. (1996) 'Comparing local electoral turnout in Great Britain and France: more similarities than differences?', *European Journal of Political Research*, 30th September 1996: 241–57.

Julien, P. (2003) 'L'évolution des périmètres des aires urbaines 1968–1999', in Pumain, D. and Mattei, M. -F. (eds) *Données urbaines 4*, Paris: Anthropos: 11–20.

Kesselman, M. (1967) *The ambiguous consensus; a study of local government in France*, New York: Knopf.

Kingston, P. W., Thompson, J. L. P. and Eichar, D. M. (1984) 'The politics of homeownership', *American Politics Quarterly*, 12(2): 131–50.

Kitschelt, H. (1994) *The Transformation of European Social Democracy*, Cambridge University Press.

— (1996) *The Radical Right in Western Europe: A Comparative Analysis*, Ann Arbor: University of Michigan Press.

Kriesi, H., Grande, E., Lachat, R., Dolezal, M., Bornschier, S. and Frey, T. (2006) 'Globalization and the transformation of the national political space: six European countries compared', *European Journal of Political Research*, 45: 921–56.

Laakso, M. and Taagepera, R. (1979) 'Effective number of parties: a measure with application to Western Europe', *Comparative Political Studies*, 12: 3–27.

Lidström, A. (2005) 'Commuting and citizen participation in Swedish city-regions', *Political Studies*, 54(4): 865–88.

Lubbers, M. and Scheepers, P. (2002) 'French Front National voting: a micro and macro perspective', *Ethnic and Racial Studies*, 25(1): 120–49.

Morlan, R. L. (1984) 'Municipal vs. national election voter turnout: Europe and the United States', *Political Science Quarterly*, 99: 457–70.

Nevers, J. -Y. (2002) 'Electoral Participation and Local Democracy in French Rural Areas', Paper Presented at American Political Science Association Annual Meeting, Chicago, IL.

Niemi R. G. and Barkan, J.D. (1987) 'Age and Turnout in New Electorates and Peasant Societies', *American Political Science Review*, 81(2): 583–88.

Oliver, J. E. (2000) 'City size and Civic Involvement in Metropolitan America', *The American Political Science Review*, 94(2): 361–73.

— (2001) *Democracy in Suburbia*, Princeton: Princeton University Press.

Péguy, P. -Y. (2000) 'Analyse économique des configurations urbaines et de leur étalement', Ph.D dissertation, Université de Lyon.

Putnam, R. (2000) *Bowling Alone*, New York: Touchstone.

Rosenstone, S. J. (1982) 'Economic adversity and voter turnout', *American Journal of Political Science*, 26(1): 25–46.

Siegfried, A. (1913) *Tableau politique de la France de l'Ouest sous la Troisième République*, Paris: Armand Collin.

Squire, P., Wolfinger, R. E. and Glass, D. P. (1987) 'Residential mobility and voter turnout', *American Political Science Review*, 81(1): 45–66.

Tiberj, V. (2004) 'Vers une citoyenneté plurielle? Le rôle de l'origine ethnique dans l'intégration politique des 15–24 ans', Paris: Notes et Etudes du CEVIPOF, 43 p. Online. Available /www.cevipof.msh-paris.fr/ publications/ notes_etudes/VT_ehnicit.pdf

Verba, S. and Nie, N. H. (1972) *Participation in America: Political Democracy and Social Equality*, New York: Harper & Row.

# Appendix

*Table A5.1: Independent variables*

| | |
|---|---|
| Eastern border region | Location in eastern border region (1,0) |
| South | Location in region along Mediterranean Sea or Spanish border (1,0) |
| Post-secondary education | Per cent of adult population with baccalaureate or higher education, 1999 |
| Foreign born | Per cent of population born abroad, 1999 |
| Population (log) | Metropolitan population (logged), 1999 |
| Age 60 or more | Per cent of population aged 60 or more, 1999 |
| Median income | Median per capita communal income, 1999 |
| Unemployment | Per cent of workforce unemployed, 1999 |
| Homeowners | Per cent of households owning primary residence, 1999 |
| Noncommuters | Per cent of workers not commuting to another commune to work, 1999 |
| Residential stability | Per cent of population living in the same commune in 1990 and 1999 |
| Housing after 1975 | Per cent of primary residences built after 1975, 1999 |
| Occupational diversity | Simpson index of three occupational groups (lower status (employees and workers), middle status (intermediary jobs), and higher status (higher managers, professionals), 1999 |
| Population density (log) | Persons per square kilometre (logged), 1999 |
| Political diversity | Political diversity index, Presidential first round Partisan fragmentation/homogeneity, Presidential first round election 2002 (Laakso-Taagepera index) |
| Population 2,500–3,500 | Communes with voter choice of candidates on list (Communal population 2,500 to 3,500, 1999) |
| Population under 2,500 | Communes with no requirement of a party list (Communal population under 3,500, 1999) |

# Chapter Six | The Metropolitan Bases of Political Cleavage in Switzerland

*Daniel Kübler, Urs Scheuss and Philippe Rochat*

## Introduction[1]

The distinction between rural and urban areas is usually emphasised as one of the crucial factors for the explanation of Swiss politics. Indeed, tense relationships between cities and the countryside during long historical periods in Switzerland resulted in a persistent political cleavage between urban and rural areas. The effects of this founding cleavage are still felt in multiple ways. On the one hand, the quest for a balance of power between progressive urban and conservative rural areas was the main drive in Swiss constitutional history in the early nineteenth century (Masnata and Rubatell 1991; Kölz 1992). The resulting federalist system is geared towards the protection of cultural and regional minorities and, until today, provides the increasingly circumscribed rural population with decisive political influence. On the other hand, distinct voter-preferences in the cities and the countryside have been a constant of Swiss politics ever since, in elections (Lutz and Selb 2007) as well as in referendum voting (Trechsel 2007). The mobilisation of these preferences by political actors resulted in the organisation of the urban-rural cleavage, thereby contributing to the structuring of the Swiss party system (Ladner 2004).

According to data collected in the 2000 population census, only 26.7 per cent of the population live in rural areas, whereas the vast majority (73.3 per cent) live in places that are to be considered as urban, i.e. cities and metropolitan areas (Schuler *et al.* 2005). This ongoing process of metropolitanisation raises new questions with respect to the urban-rural divide. In terms of governance, relations between urban and rural areas have become tenser, as the former have started to challenge the political influence that the latter enjoys in the Swiss federal state (Kübler *et al.* 2003). The rural-urban divide will therefore continue to haunt inter-governmental relations and federalism in Switzerland.

Nevertheless, as metropolitan areas have become the dominant form of human settlement in this country, the rural regions increasingly turn into residual spaces. We can therefore argue that the traditional urban-rural distinction will become less and less significant as a determinant for political behaviour.

The interesting question, then, is whether new territorial patterns of political

1. This chapter is based on research conducted for the National Centre of Competence in Research, Challenges to Democracy in the 21st Century, at the University of Zurich. The authors are grateful to Hanspeter Kriesi for thorough and constructive criticism of earlier drafts.

behaviour have emerged *within* the urbanised area of this country, and how they can be explained. The goal of this chapter is to answer this question. Referring to the common theme of this volume, the analysis is guided by what we called the metropolitanisation of politics thesis. Our goal is to assess to what extent patterns of political behaviour within Swiss metropolitan areas can be explained not only by compositional differences, but by the genuine characteristics of the spatial context in which citizens dwell. The chapter follows the research framework defined by the International Metropolitan Observatory (IMO) project and presented in the introductory chapter of this volume. We start with outlining the territorial dynamics of Swiss metropolitan areas and summarise the findings in a five-fold typology of municipalities within metropolitan areas. The next section implements the ecological approach to analyse metropolitan effects on political behaviour. We use exploratory as well as regression techniques to analyse the compositional and contextual determinants of municipal-level data on turnout of national and local elections, as well as on partisanship. The conclusion summarises the findings and discusses their implications, both for understanding Swiss politics and for the *problématique* raised by the IMO programme. Technical details on data and variables used in the analysis are given in the Chapter 14.

## The socio-spatial structure of metropolitan Switzerland

The process of metropolitanisation in Switzerland has been ongoing throughout the twentieth century. It has produced a pattern of spatial organisation that is similar, in many respects, to the situation found in most other industrialised countries. Today, Switzerland is clearly dominated by its metropolitan areas, which provide the living space for nearly three quarters of its inhabitants and are the main motors of the Swiss economy. Similarly, the growth of Swiss metropolitan areas has mainly taken place as a growth in surface area, i.e. by spatial expansion and urban sprawl, resulting in a decrease in the average population density of urban settlements. Swiss metropolitan areas are clearly dominated by the suburbs, where the population outnumbers that of the core city by a ratio of three to one. In institutional terms, the lack of territorial reforms or the failure of attempts to amalgamate municipalities – especially in the second half of the twentieth century – has resulted in increasing geopolitical fragmentation of Swiss metropolitan areas. In the light of international comparative data (Hoffmann-Martinot and Sellers 2005), the degree of geopolitical fragmentation of Swiss metropolitan areas indeed appears to be one of the highest in Europe. The seven Swiss metropolitan areas under scrutiny illustrate these general observations quite well (see Table 6.1).

### Typology of core and suburban municipalities

Metropolitan growth has led to spatial differentiation within metropolitan areas and notably to socio-economic segregation. However, as we have argued previously (Kübler and Scheuss 2005), socio-economic disparities in Swiss metropolitan areas cannot be described entirely by the differences between core cities and

*Table 6.1: Characteristics of Swiss metropolitan areas under scrutiny (data for 2000)*

|          | Overall population | Overall number of municipalities | Population outside core city (%) | Density (inhabitants per hectare) | Index of geopolitical fragmentation |
|----------|--------------------|----------------------------------|----------------------------------|-----------------------------------|-------------------------------------|
| Zurich   | 1,080,728          | 132                              | 66.3                             | 9,95                              | 3.6                                 |
| Basle    | 731,167            | 127                              | 77.2                             | 9,95*                             | 4.4*                                |
| Geneva   | 645,608            | 131                              | 72.4                             | 10,32*                            | 4.2*                                |
| Bern     | 349,096            | 43                               | 63.2                             | 7,25                              | 3.3                                 |
| Lausanne | 311,441            | 70                               | 59.9                             | 9,97                              | 5.6                                 |
| Lucerne  | 196,550            | 17                               | 69.7                             | 9,94                              | 2.9                                 |
| Lugano   | 136,032            | 77                               | 80.5                             | 5,85*                             | 27.1*                               |

*excluding foreign municipalities in cross-border metropolitan areas

suburban locations. They follow a more complex pattern that sets apart the core city and the poor suburbs on the one hand and the middle class, affluent, and low density suburbs on the other hand.

The socio-economic differentiations within the suburban belt of Swiss metropolitan areas are well captured by the typological approach developed in the common research protocol. According to this protocol, the 482 municipalities located in the seven metropolitan areas under scrutiny[2] were classified into five types: urban concentrations, poor suburbs, middle-class suburbs, affluent suburbs and low-density suburbs (see Chapter 14, the Methodological Appendix, for a description of the procedure). A range of indicators sets apart these five types of metropolitan locations, thereby allowing us to discern the main spatial patterns of socio-economic differentiation in Swiss metropolitan areas (see Table 6.2).

On the one hand, this typology of municipalities within metropolitan areas encompasses geographical and morphological dimensions. First, it shows that metropolitan areas differ according to the spatial organisation (distances) of the municipal types. Low-density suburbs are those locations at the greatest distance from the centre, while the middle-class suburbs are a step closer to the centre. Poor and affluent suburbs are closer still to the centre, except in the metropolitan areas of Basle and Lausanne, where middle-class suburbs are on average closer to the centre than poor and affluent ones. Interestingly, there is no clear-cut correlation between the size of a metropolitan area (population) and the average distance from the centre of low-density suburbs, highlighting differences between metropolitan areas regarding the degree of urban sprawl.

---

2.  Data on the foreign municipalities, i.e. those municipalities pertaining to one of the cross-border metropolitan areas (Basle, Geneva, Lugano) but located in Germany, France or Italy, were not available. Hence, only municipalities located within Switzerland were included in the subsequent analysis.

*Table 6.2: Characteristics of types of metropolitan municipalities (means, data for 2000)*

| | N of municipali- ties | Population (sum) | Hard- ship index | Foreign born (%) | Eco- nomic diversity index | Resi- dents under 18 years (%) | Resi- dents aged over 65 (%) | Dis- tance from centre (km) | Single family housing (%) |
|---|---|---|---|---|---|---|---|---|---|
| *Types of municipality* | | | | | | | | | |
| Urban concentration | 7 | 1,047,399 | 57.3 | 35.3 | 0.887 | 14.8 | 12.3 | 0 | 4.0 |
| Poor suburbs | 119 | 952,162 | 50.7 | 29.2 | 0.848 | 20.1 | 8.8 | 9.7 | 20.6 |
| Middle-class suburbs | 119 | 502,624 | 35.6 | 21.1 | 0.830 | 20.8 | 8.1 | 9.7 | 36.8 |
| Affluent suburbs | 119 | 274,148 | 24.5 | 18.3 | 0.822 | 22.3 | 6.7 | 9.5 | 47.1 |
| Low-density suburbs | 118 | 232,904 | 28.1 | 17.1 | 0.817 | 24.1 | 5.4 | 19.1 | 45.6 |
| *Metropolitan areas* | | | | | | | | | |
| Zurich | 132 | 1,080,728 | 30.8 | 19.8 | 0.824 | 21.2 | 6.0 | 14.0 | 32.1 |
| Basle | 74 | 479,308 | 34.5 | 17.7 | 0.822 | 21.6 | 7.4 | 13.8 | 46.2 |
| Geneva | 74 | 471,314 | 32.3 | 32.3 | 0.843 | 24.1 | 7.0 | 13.4 | 42.3 |
| Berne | 43 | 349,096 | 31.6 | 11.2 | 0.790 | 21.1 | 6.7 | 11.3 | 31.2 |
| Lausanne | 70 | 311,441 | 35.8 | 21.0 | 0.834 | 23.3 | 7.1 | 10.9 | 33.0 |
| Lucerne | 17 | 196,550 | 38.0 | 17.2 | 0.825 | 23.2 | 6.6 | 6.5 | 23.8 |
| Lugano | 72 | 120,800 | 46.9 | 26.9 | 0.859 | 19.0 | 10.7 | 6.7 | 41.7 |
| Total | 482 | 3,009,237 | 35.1 | 21.8 | 0.830 | 21.7 | 7.3 | 11.8 | 37.0 |

Secondly, it shows that metropolitan areas display territorial differences in density and that this is related to the nature of the housing stock. Single-family housing is very important in affluent and low-density suburbs, as well as in middle-class and poor suburbs, but notably less so in central cities, where economic (less demand) and spatial restrictions (construction density) are more important.

On the other hand, the five types of municipalities also vary with respect to a number of socio-economic aspects. The general distribution of the socio-economic hardship composite index indicates the existence of a general pattern across all metropolitan areas, in spite of slight differences in the level of deprivation between them. Core cities show the highest values of socio-economic hardship. They are even more distressed than the poor suburbs, which come second. No clear distinction can be made, however, between middle-class suburbs and low-density suburbs. As expected, the lowest level of socio-economic hardship is found in affluent municipalities. This general pattern also holds true if we consider the proportion of foreign-born residents, which can be taken as a measure for the presence of immigrants. The largest proportions of residents born abroad are found in the core cities, followed by poor and middle-class suburbs. Affluent and low-density suburbs have the lowest proportion of foreign-born residents.

Besides these intra-metropolitan differences, notable differences also exist between metropolitan areas. Geneva stands out as the metropolitan area with the highest proportion of foreign-born residents, a fact that reflects Geneva's traditional role as a prime location for international organisations and businesses with a higher number of expatriates. The lowest proportion of foreign residents is found in Bern, which certainly relates to it being the more nationally-oriented capital.

Thirdly, economic diversity is, as expected, higher in core cities than in the rest of the metropolitan areas, thereby reflecting the functional differentiation and the economic centrality of core cities within metropolitan areas. Poor suburbs are somewhat more diverse economically speaking, but not as much as core cities. There are almost no differences between middle-class, affluent and low-density suburbs, which all show the least economic diversity and thereby appear as rather homogenous entities.

Differences across metropolitan areas are mainly due to differences between their core cities, as well as to differences between the language regions, where German-speaking metropolitan areas display less economic diversity than those located in the French-speaking or the Italian-speaking part of the country. Interestingly, middle-class, affluent and low-density suburbs across all metropolitan areas show similar low economic diversity – this reflects the strong presence of white-collar workers employed in the service sector in these places.

Fourthly, the indicator for the presence of families (the proportion of inhabitants under eighteen years old) shows that the number of families increases when moving from the central cities outwards to the metropolitan fringe. Indeed, the proportion of families is lowest in core cities and highest in low-density suburbs, with poor, middle-class and affluent suburbs in between. This undoubtedly reflects the higher availability of family housing in the metropolitan fringe. If families with young children tend to concentrate in the outskirts of metropolitan areas, the reverse is also true. Indeed, the proportion of retired people steeply decreases as when moving from the core cities to poor, middle-class, affluent and low-density suburbs. There is a negative correlation between the proportions of retired people and residents under eighteen years old, which also points to a spatial differentiation of potential demands vis-à-vis the welfare state in different metropolitan locations: services for the elderly in central locations, schooling and childcare on the outskirts. With respect to inter-metropolitan variations, Lugano clearly stands out as the metropolitan area with the highest proportion of retired residents. This reflects a Swiss 'sun-belt effect', i.e. retirees from north of the Alps move south for the milder climate that is found there.

## The political ecology of Swiss metropolitan areas

The image of rough mountains, bucolic villages and cows on green hills promoted by the Swiss tourist industry could not be more contrasted to the socio-economic reality in Switzerland. Indeed, the vast majority of the population in this country lives in metropolitan areas, characterised by the internal socio-economic and spatial differentiations described above. Can the metropolitanisation hypothesis thus be corroborated in the Swiss context? As we will show in the remainder of this chapter, the characteristics of metropolitan locations do indeed shape political behaviour. Our analysis focuses on the 482 municipalities located in the seven metropolitan areas under scrutiny. We use municipal-level data of local elections (two elections held around the year 2000), as well as of the 1999 and 2003 elections to the lower chamber of the national Parliament.[3] The aim is to single out the effect of compositional variables pointing towards territorially uniform political behaviour, compared to contextual variables indicative of genuine spatial effects. Nevertheless, our approach also controls for differences in political behaviour that can be assumed to exist between metropolitan areas in Switzerland. Indeed, as Caramani (2004: 116) has shown, political behaviour in Switzerland is territorially more heterogeneous than in other Western European countries. The particularities of the processes of state formation and nation building in a culturally divided society have produced a complex territorial pattern of cleavages. Political parties in Switzerland have historical roots in different regions of the country. These legacies can still be felt today and manifest themselves mainly as differences between the party systems of different cantons (Ladner 2004). As most of the metropolitan areas under scrutiny are located predominantly in one particular canton, taking metropolitan area differences into account allows us to control for these regional effects.

### *Turnout analysis: metropolitanisation and the delocalisation of political participation*

The psephology of Switzerland has been propelled by the fact that turnout in national elections is in decline since the mid-twentieth century – compared to other Western European countries, Switzerland has one of the lowest turnout levels for national elections. In the Swiss national elections held since the 1980s, turnout oscillated around an average of 45 per cent, roughly 25 percentage points lower than in other Western European countries during the same period (Linder 2005: 67). Similar to the findings in other countries, value change, party dealignment and individualisation are quoted as explanatory factors for the decline of electoral participation in Switzerland over time. With respect to the low absolute levels of turnout, it has been argued that the Swiss political system

---

3.  Municipal-level data on turnout and party voting in national elections was obtained from the Swiss Statistical Office and is available for all 482 municipalities. Data on turnout of local elections is not centrally available in Switzerland and was compiled for the purpose of this article. The data collection took place in the context of a research seminar held by the authors at the University of Zurich in the autumn and spring terms of 2007/2008. A request to provide local electoral as well as additional data was sent to all the 482 municipalities under scrutiny in this project. Data was delivered mostly on paper and had to be entered manually into the database. Out of 482 metropolitan municipalities under scrutiny, 314 provided data on local elections and are included in this analysis (see Table A.6.1.in the Appendix to this chapter). The authors are grateful to all the participants in the research seminar for precious help in this Herculean endeavour.

features a set of institutional conditions that reduce the political salience of national elections (Lutz and Selb 2007: 419). The rules of consensus democracy have resulted in a remarkable stability of the multiparty coalition in power at the national level, thereby limiting the potential impact of parliamentary elections on the direction of national politics. Additionally, the extensive instruments of direct democracy provide citizens with frequent opportunities to exert influence beyond parliamentary elections.

In contrast to national electoral turnout, much less is known about turnout in elections at the local level, mainly for reasons of data availability. Data on local elections in Switzerland are not centrally collected, nor are such data available from statistics' offices in the cantons. Additional difficulties stem from the fact that municipal elections are held in different years across cantons, sometimes even across municipalities within the same canton. Based on data gathered via surveys of municipal governments, the pioneering work of Ladner and Millner found that turnout in local elections is, in general, not significantly lower than turnout in national elections. They argue that, due to high municipal autonomy, 'participating in Swiss local elections is, less than elsewhere, an election of the "second order" […]' (1999: 237).

As levels of turnout in national elections vary considerably across cantons, research on electoral turnout in Switzerland has focused on contextual conditions that operate at the cantonal level (Wernli 2001; Bühlmann and Freitag 2006). Some of these differences can be explained by variations in the participatory culture between cantons, insofar as the electorate of cantons with a high level of direct democracy more frequently turns out also in national elections. Party behaviour also plays a role, insofar as strategic coordination between parties – frequent in smaller cantons – reduces the level of party competition and, in turn, affects turnout negatively. Finally, cultural differences are also emphasised insofar as the strength of Catholicism prevailing in a canton also has a positive influence on turnout in national elections – a fact that is explained by clientelistic links between the Christian Democratic Party and catholic voters.

Whereas the effect of the cantonal context on turnout is quite well established by existing research, there are only very few scholars who have focused on the influence of municipal-level variables on electoral turnout. These studies mostly examined the effect of contextual variables at the municipal level on turnout in municipal elections. Ladner and Millner (1999: 244), for instance, found evidence for the 'decline-of-community model' according to which political participation in anonymous cities is lower than in smaller towns because citizens are less integrated into community life. Indeed, local electoral turnout is negatively associated with a municipality's size in population. Additionally, they found the presence of a high number of parties, as well as proportional rule (as opposed to majority rule) to be positively associated with local electoral turnout, with both these effects being particularly significant in smaller municipalities (1999: 249). Results from research using other sources for data on local turnout are consistent with these findings. Zingg and Benz (2003), who collected official data on local elections in the canton of Zurich, found average levels of turnout in local elections to be higher than turnout in national elections, and showed that the size of a municipality plays a role for local turnout (turnout decreases when population increases). In addition, they showed that factors measuring a locally-oriented lifestyle of the population (i.e. various measures of residential and spatial non-mobility) also positively influence local turnout. Based on multilevel analysis of survey data, Ladner and Bühlmann's recent contributions (Bühlmann 2006; Ladner and Bühlmann 2007) made it possible to single out individual-level from municipal-level contextual determinants on (self-declared) electoral participation in national and local elections. They found only limited influence of contextual determinants on electoral participation. In their analyses, individual determinants such as age, education, party and associational membership, duration of residence, as well as housing status are significant predictors for turnout in both national and local elections. However, they did not find any municipal contextual variables to have significant effects on electoral turnout.[4]

### Metropolitanisation and turnout in national and local elections

The influence of metropolitanisation on turnout has not been systematically assessed by electoral research in Switzerland to date. The subsequent analysis examines this aspect by focusing on the relationships between spatial dynamics in metropolitan areas as affecting municipal-level contexts and turnout in local and national elections. The analysis confirms previously published evidence in several respects (see Figure 6.1). First, it shows the importance of the electoral rule for turnout levels in local government elections. Municipalities that elect their governments according to proportional rule tend to have a higher turnout compared with those electing by majority rule. Secondly, turnout in local elections is higher (in municipalities with proportional rule) or nearly as high (for municipalities with majority rule) as turnout in national elections. Ladner and Millner's general statement about the importance of local elections in Swiss politics can thus be confirmed for the metropolitanised space in this country.

A closer look at local and national electoral turnout reveals that not only the levels of turnout, but also the differences between levels of local and national turnout vary according to the types of metropolitan municipalities (see Figure 6.1). Turnout levels in both national and local elections are generally low in core cities and poor suburbs, but higher in middle-class, low-density and affluent suburbs. The picture gets more complex if we consider the differences between local and national turnout according to types of municipalities. In core cities, there is only a small difference between levels of turnout in local and national elections. In poor and middle-class suburbs, turnout in local elections is lower (when majority rule is

---

4. The list of contextual commune-level variables tested for by Ladner and Bühlmann (2007: 219/220) included the following: population of the commune, language-region, proportion of retired residents, distribution of income, tradition of participation, party-polarisation, electoral rule (proportional versus majoritarian), size of the municipal executive, institutional organisation (parliament or local citizen assembly), and fiscal income.

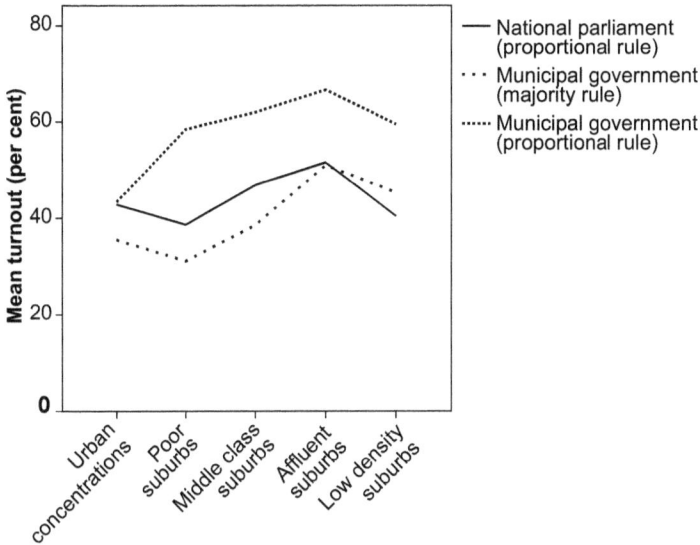

*Figure 6.1: Election turnout in types of municipalities of Swiss metropolitan areas*

*Notes:* All results are controlled for metropolitan area effects. National and municipal election turnouts are averaged over two consecutive elections before and after 2000 to smoothen short-term variances. Number of cases for local elections: 314 (majority rule: 222 / proportional rule: 92).

used) respectively higher (when proportional rule is used) than turnout in national elections. But in affluent and low-density suburbs, turnout in local elections is higher than turnout in national elections, independent from the electoral rule used in local elections. In these suburbs, located mostly at the outer fringe of metropolitan areas, the electorate seems to put stronger emphasis on local elections than on national elections. If we consider that the various types of municipalities reflect different degrees of functional integration of metropolitan places, this result then suggests that metropolitanisation leads to a delocalisation of political behaviour. Whereas the electorate in core cities is less locally oriented than in the suburban zones of a metropolitan area, local orientation is particularly strong in affluent and low-density suburbs at the outskirts of a metropolitan area.

The multivariate analysis of turnout levels in national and local elections allows a further differentiation of this overall picture. Five different regression models were estimated for both dependent variables:

(1) a baseline model was estimated, comprising the control variables (dummies for metropolitan areas, and a dummy for the use of proportional rule in local elections) and the municipal types;

(2) a model that focuses on the compositional variables,

(3) a model that focuses on contextual variables.

*Table 6.3: Determinants of national and local turnout (OLS regression)*

| | Turnout in national elections | | | Turnout in local elections | | |
|---|---|---|---|---|---|---|
| | Composi-tional | Contex-tual | Combined model | Composi-tional | Contex-tual | Combined model |
| (Constant) | **41.066** | **40.237** | **28.413** | **31.732** | **58.255** | **51.719** |
| | (4.222) | (10.060) | (9.945) | (8.474) | (17.647) | (18.986) |
| Bern MA | 1.248 | −0.398 | 0.997 | −2.635 | −4.394 | −3.987 |
| | (1.107) | (1.126) | (1.094) | (3.731) | (3.610) | (3.657) |
| Lucerne MA | **4.013** | 1.769 | **3.611** | 2.285 | *−2.398* | 4.157 |
| | (1.619) | (1.579) | (1.630) | (2.669) | (1.610) | (2.973) |
| Basle MA | 0.072 | **−4.952** | −1.315 | 0.871 | −2.398 | −0.361 |
| | (0.915) | (0.912) | (0.941) | (1.716) | (1.610) | (1.833) |
| Lugano MA | **3.220** | **−3.230** | 1.843 | **26.174** | **10.662** | **17.477** |
| | (1.162) | (1.200) | (1.553) | (3.355) | (3.351) | (3.913) |
| Lausanne MA | **−7.085** | **−8.014** | **−7.337** | −0.015 | **−5.509** | −3.644 |
| | (0.981) | 0.986) | (1.047) | (2.582) | (2.487) | (2.719) |
| Geneva MA | **−7.699** | **−4.300** | **-6.063** | **8.867** | **4.546** | **6.300** |
| | (1.287) | (0.990) | (1.388) | (2.381) | (1.654) | (2.579) |
| Socio-economic status | **0.129** | | **0.118** | 0.123 | | 0.120 |
| | (0.040) | | (0.041) | (0.084) | | (0.085) |
| Hardship index | **−0.133** | | **−0.201** | −0.124 | | −0.075 |
| | (0.056) | | (0.065) | (0.116) | | (0.134) |
| Foreign born | −0.018 | | −0.030 | −0.212 | | −0.084 |
| | (0.062) | | (0.063) | (0.118) | | (0.118) |
| Perc. manufact. occupation | **−0.190** | | −0.097 | 0.230 | | 0.142 |
| | (0.072) | | (0.076) | (0.147) | | (0.159) |
| Per cent under 18 | 0.163 | | **0.324** | 0.243 | | 0.267 |
| | (0.119) | | (0.127) | (0.228) | | (0.243) |
| Per cent retirees | **0.705** | | **0.405** | 0.096 | | −0.390 |
| | (0.174) | | (0.177) | (0.317) | | (0.333) |
| Distance to the centre | | **0.000** | **0.000** | | 0.000 | 0.000 |
| | | (0.000) | (0.000) | | (0.000) | (0.000) |
| Homeownership | | **0.121** | −0.020 | | **0.257** | *0.185* |
| | | (0.050) | (0.049) | | (0.096) | (0.102) |
| Single-family housing | | **0.102** | 0.041 | | −0.082 | −0.124 |
| | | (0.043) | (0.040) | | (0.087) | (0.090) |
| New housing | | *−0.064* | −0.033 | | *−0.105* | *−0.133* |
| | | (0.035) | (0.035) | | (0.063) | (0.070) |
| Pop. growth 1970-2000 | | **−1.865** | **−2.217** | | −0.910 | −1.615 |
| | | (0.476) | (0451) | | (0.961) | (1.004) |
| Residential stability | | −0.047 | 0.053 | | 0.070 | 0.095 |
| | | (0.065) | (0062) | | (0.113) | (0.117) |
| Out-commuting | | **−0.107** | **−0.087** | | **−0.185** | **−0.219** |
| | | (0.040) | (0.038) | | (0.069) | (0.072) |
| Population (Ln) | | **−1.428** | **−1.520** | | **−3.367** | **−3.289** |
| | | (0.463) | (0.429) | | (0.874) | (0.872) |
| Density (Ln) | | **1.510** | **1.278** | | −0.033 | 0.230 |
| | | (0.507) | (0.491) | | (0.887) | (0.950) |

|  | Turnout in national elections | | | Turnout in local elections | | |
|---|---|---|---|---|---|---|
|  | Composi-tional | Contex-tual | Combined model | Composi-tional | Contex-tual | Combined model |
| Econ. diversity | | **21.407** | **28.117** | | 19.569 | 23.606 |
| index | | (7.921) | (7.998) | | (14.317) | (15.683) |
| Proportional rule | | | | **7.596** | **8.882** | **9.106** |
| (local) | | | | (2.809) | (2.679) | (2.657) |
| Adjusted R² | 0.372 | 0.342 | 0.471 | 0.650 | 0.692 | 0.701 |
| N | 479 | 477 | 474 | 311 | 312 | 309 |

*Notes*: Table entries are unstandardised regression coefficients, standard errors in parentheses, significance for boldface coefficients, $p<0.05$; for italicised coefficients, $p<0.10$.

(4) a combined model that includes compositional and contextual variables; and

(5) a model that also includes the municipal types.

However, for lack of space, results are reported only for the compositional, the contextual and the combined models (see Table 6.3).

The estimation of the baseline model allows us to confirm some stable effects of the control variables that have also been established by previous research. First, the use of proportional rule at the municipal level clearly increases turnout in local elections. Secondly, significant differences were found between the various metropolitan areas: turnout in national elections is lower in the French-speaking parts of the country (the Geneva and Lausanne metropolitan areas) and higher in the Lugano metropolitan area, which is predominantly catholic. Turnout in local elections is significantly higher in the two predominantly Catholic metropolitan areas of Lucerne and Lugano, but also in the Geneva metropolitan area. And, confirming the bivariate results, turnout for both national and local elections is higher in affluent suburbs, and turnout in local elections is higher in low-density suburbs.

The estimation of the other models allows us, first, to discuss the relative importance of compositional as opposed to contextual variables. National election turnout is better explained by the compositional model (37.2 per cent of the observed variance) than by the contextual model (34.2 per cent). Nevertheless, contextual predictors remain significant even if compositional variables are controlled for in the full model.

As the combined model shows, national election turnout is positively influenced by compositional variables such as general socio-economic status, the absence of hardship, the presence of elderly citizens and families, but also by contextual variables such as distance from the centre, the absence of population growth, low rates of commuting, small population size, high population density as well as high economic diversity. For local elections the contextual model has more explanatory power (69.2 per cent of the observed variance) than the compositional model (65 per cent), and none of the compositional variables has a significant effect. As the combined model shows, the determinants of local election turnout in Swiss metropolitan areas are essentially contextual. More precisely, municipalities in which new housing has been built, that have large proportions of commuters and that are large in size tend to have lower levels of turnout in local elections. Homeownership however has a positive effect on turnout in local elections.

Contextual features therefore affect turnout mainly in local elections, but also in national elections. Metropolitanisation dynamics change these contextual features in a way that affects turnout negatively. Indeed, metropolitanisation implies the intensification of commuter movements, leads to population growth, requires the building of new housing, and results in a larger population of suburban municipalities, which are, however, less densely populated. We can therefore assume that metropolitanisation as territorial development depresses electoral participation in general, but particularly so participation in local elections. The results of the multivariate analysis therefore corroborate the bivariate results, namely that the metropolitanisation process will reinforce delocalised patterns of political participation.

## Partisanship: the suburban sources of Swiss international isolationism

There is obviously a strong relevance of the four classic cleavages identified by Lipset and Rokkan (1967) for understanding the structure of the political space in Switzerland. Historically, these classic cleavages – religion vs. secularism, centre vs. periphery, workers vs. owners, and urban vs. rural – adequately explain the main lines of division between the four major parties in Switzerland, even though there is some overlap (Linder 2005: 86ff.). The Liberal Party (*Freisinnig Demokratische Partei* (FDP)) mobilises a secular, urban and liberal right. The Christian Democratic Party (*Christlichdemokratische Volkspartei* (CVP)) traditionally appeals to a (mainly Catholic) religious electorate and defends the interests of the periphery. The Social Democrats (*Sozialdemokratische Partei* (SP)) defends workers' interests and a strong central state. The Swiss People's Party (*Schweizerische Volkspartei* (SVP)) originally mobilised agrarian interests and is now oriented towards the right. However, the emergence of new parties, such as the Greens in the 1980s, but also the changing electoral basis of the traditional parties, has made clear that some of these four classic cleavages have lost their structuring power in the Swiss political space. While the classic left-right cleavage based on the socio-economic divide between workers and owners continues to structure the political space in Switzerland, value changes have stimulated the emergence of new lines of political conflict (Hug and Sciarini 2002).

Some of these new lines are strongly mobilised by political parties. In particular, there is an important line of division separating those who advocate openness towards the international realm from others who adhere to values related to national traditions and sovereignty. It has been argued that the socio-structural basis of this second conflict relates to a differentiation in terms of winners and losers of globalisation: 'The likely winners include entrepreneurs and qualified employees in sectors open to international competition as well as all kinds of cosmopolitan citizens. The expected losers, by contrast, include entrepreneurs and qualified employees in traditionally-protected sectors, all unqualified employees and citizens who strongly identify themselves with their national community'

(Kriesi *et al.* 2006: 922). One particular party, the Swiss People's Party (SVP) has successfully mobilised this division since the early 1990s and produced a major transformation of the Swiss party system (Kriesi *et al.* 2005). The political position advocated by the SVP was mainly a clear opposition to Switzerland's integration into the European Union, as well as a strong emphasis on traditional values and national identity, including resistance against immigration. The key success factor of the SVP was its ability to monopolise this position of opposing the opening up of Switzerland towards the outside world in general, and the European Union in particular. By the turn of the millennium, the SVP became the strongest party and managed to nearly treble its share of votes between the elections of 1991 (roughly 11 per cent) and 2007 (29 per cent). In the process, the other parties have been compelled to position themselves with respect to the SVP. This indicates the existence of a cleavage between integration and demarcation (*'Öffnung und Abgrenzung'*) with regards to globalisation, a factor that is increasingly organised into the party system as all parties are forced to take sides on this issue.

Much has been written about the ways in which the rise of this new cleavage between globalisation losers and globalisation winners has affected Swiss politics (Ladner 2004; Kriesi *et al.* 2005). Interestingly however, little has been said regarding the spatial patterns of this new cleavage. This is all the more astonishing, given the historical roots of the SVP in agrarian interests and small rural businesses. How can the rise of the SVP during the 1990s be explained against this background? Ladner (2004: 384) contents himself with the observation that the intensity of the rural-urban cleavage is on the decrease, and that the rise of the SVP in recent years has nothing to do with the traditional rural-urban cleavage in terms of its agrarian socio-structural basis. In contrast, Kriesi *et al.* (2005: 53) show that the distinction between rural or urban electorates is a significant predictor for the SVP's electoral probability at the national level: the rural electorate tends to vote more in favour of the SVP than the urban one. However, this can only be part of the story, as the rise of the SVP at the national level has also taken place in urban regions. Recent analysis of the transformation of the political space in Switzerland has remained silent on the territorial dimensions of this process. We would argue that even if the rural-urban divide empirically shows some significant explanatory power in the analysis of political and electoral behaviour, it is much too crude a measure to allow closer understanding of the links between territorial developments and political structures in this country, especially with respect to the most peculiar change in recent Swiss politics – namely the rise of the SVP as the main national-conservative party opposed to globalisation.

In addition to the traditional opposition between left-right, as well as the new and intensifying conflict regarding globalisation processes, an additional line of division separates those who adhere to an individualistic ethos from others who emphasise traditional norms with respect to moral issues such as homosexuality, abortion, divorce, euthanasia, etc. (Hug and Sciarini 2002). While there is evidence for a socio-structural basis for this line of division – the weakening importance of religion and the decrease of religiosity in modern societies has reinforced cultural and moral libertarianism – a closer analysis of party voting suggested that this cleavage is not very strongly mobilised in the Swiss party system. Indeed, individuals' positions on these issues showed no significant relationship to their party affiliation (Brunner and Sgier 2002). Hence, it is not obvious to what extent diverging opinions on cultural values and morality issues currently can be considered a structuring cleavage in the Swiss political space to the same extent as the left-right opposition or the conflict between integration and demarcation with respect to globalisation processes.

For the analysis of partisanship in the Swiss context, it is therefore important to locate party voting with respect to the two major structuring cleavages ('left versus right'; 'openness versus isolationism in globalisation issues'), as well as to the third potential line of division ('cultural libertarianism versus conservatism). Following Kriesi *et al.* (2005: 273ff.), we used the data from the 1999 and 2003 Swiss Electoral Studies (Selects) to identify voter positions on left-right economic issues and globalisation issues. Unfortunately, the Selects post-election surveys do not include questions on moral issues that would have allowed us to calculate voters' positions with respect to cultural libertarianism or conservatism. We used data from the International Social Survey Programme 2002, as well as from the European Social Survey 2004, in order to calculate party affiliates' position on cultural issues.[5] There are, of course, several methodological problems to mixing sources of data – collected in different years – for the calculation of these indices. However, a comparison of the left-right self-placement of voters in the different surveys suggest that the data can be considered to measure positions accurately – except in the case of parties where there were only few respondents (see Table 6.4).

A closer look on the position scales of the four major parties represented in the Swiss government (SVP, SPS, FDP and CVP) shows that the positions on left-right economic issues reflect the familiar picture of the SPS on the left, the CVP in the middle, and the SVP and the FDP on the right. Regarding globalisation issues, the SPS is most in favour of international integration, the SVP most opposed, whereas CVP and FDP are located in between these two positions. However, party affinities in Switzerland are not significantly related to positions on cultural issues. Following the common research protocol, the subsequent analysis will neverthe-less focus on all four indices of partisanship: left-right self placement, voter positions on left-right economic issues, on globalisation issues, as well as on cultural issues.

### Spatial patterns of electoral behaviour in Swiss metropolitan areas

A bivariate analysis of partisanship in the 482 municipalities under scrutiny suggests important political disparities between the five types of metropolitan municipalities.

In terms of party voters' left-right self-placement, municipalities of Swiss

---

5.  ISSP 2002 and ESS 2004 were the only general population surveys conducted in Switzerland to include respondents' opinions on cultural and morality issues as well as party affiliations. (The Swiss questionnaire of the 1998 ISSP on religion did not ask for party affiliation.)

*Table 6.4: Party positions based on survey results*

| | Position of voters who voted for party (Source: Selects 1999 and 2003) | | | | | | Position of people with self-declared party affiliation (Source: ISSP 2002 and ESS 2004) | |
|---|---|---|---|---|---|---|---|---|
| | Left-right self-placement (0 [left] to 10 [right]) | | Position on economic issues (1 [left] to 3 [right])[a] | | Position on globalisation issues (0.5 [open] to 3 [isolation])[a] | | Position on cultural issues (1 [liberal] to 5 [conservative])[a] | Left-right self-placement (0 [left] to 10 [right]) |
| | 1999 | 2003 | 1999 | 2003 | 1999 | 2003 | ISSP 2002/ESS 2004 | ESS 2004 |
| Freisinnig demokr. Partei (FDP) | 6.08 | 6.09 | 2.70 | 2.66 | 1.84 | 1.61 | 2.45 | 6.06 |
| Christlichdemokr. Volkspartei (CVP) | 5.74 | 5.57 | 2.24 | 2.35 | 1.89 | 1.49 | 2.60 | 5.42 |
| Sozialdemokr. Partei (SPS) | 3.15 | 3.10 | 1.75 | 1.77 | 1.55 | 1.37 | 2.55 | 3.23 |
| Schweizerische Volkspartei (SVP) | 6.70 | 6.95 | 2.54 | 2.46 | 1.97 | 1.84 | 2.43 | 6.96 |
| Liberale Partei der Schweiz (LPS) | 7.05 | 7.06 | 3.26 | 3.19 | 1.88 | 1.35 | 1.86 | 6.76 |
| Landesring der Unabhängigen (LdU)[b] | 4.50 | 4.00 | 2.20 | 3.00 | 1.71 | 1.58 | | |
| Evangelische Volkspartei (EVP) | 5.28 | 5.30 | 2.03 | 2.00 | 1.63 | 1.31 | 3.03 | 5.10 |
| Partei der Arbeit (PdA)[b] | 1.95 | 0.67 | 1.39 | 2.33 | 1.46 | 1.22 | 2.69 | 3.13 |
| Solidarités[b] | 2.08 | 2.00 | 1.58 | 1.00 | 1.41 | 0.83 | | |
| Grüne Partei der Schweiz (GPS) | 2.98 | 3.13 | 1.84 | 1.80 | 1.42 | 1.26 | 2.69 | 3.08 |
| Schweizer Demokraten (SD)[b] | 7.40 | 7.33 | 2.20 | 2.33 | 1.88 | 1.50 | 2.25 | 9.00 |
| Eidgenössisch Demo. Union (EDU)[b] | 6.50 | 6.40 | 2.27 | 2.09 | 1.44 | 1.44 | 4.21 | 5.92 |
| Freiheitspartei der Schweiz (FPS)[b] | 9.50 | 2.00 | 2.50 | 1.00 | 2.00 | 1.00 | | |
| Lega dei Ticinesi (lega)[b] | 6.37 | 5.00 | 2.41 | 2.50 | 1.68 | 2.50 | | |
| OTHER[c] | 4.85 | 5.06 | 2.05 | 2.16 | 1.60 | 1.47 | 2.79 | 5.00 |

*Notes*: a = For the operationalisation of party positions, see Table A.6.1.in the Appendix to this chapter. b = Small number of respondents voting for this party in survey (n<15) and were attributed to category 'Other'. c = Category 'other' includes voters for LdU, PdA, Solidarités, SD, FPS, lega, as well as other, non-specified parties.

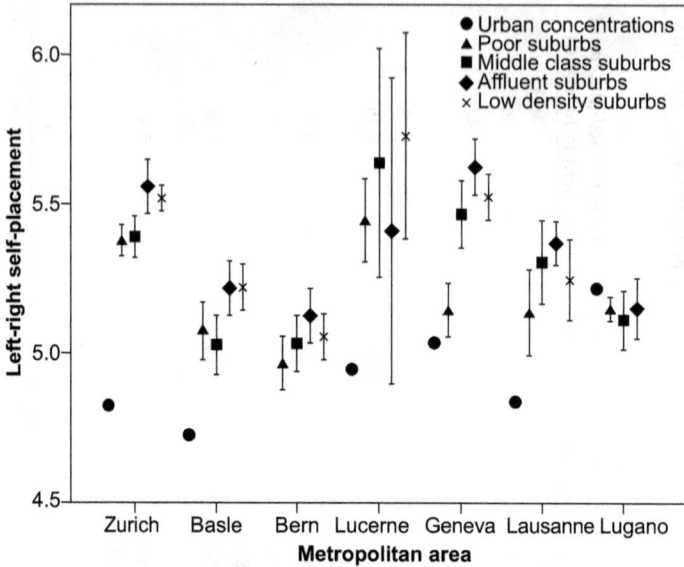

*Figure 6.2: Left-right self-placement in types of municipalities and metropolitan areas (elections 1999 and 2003; means and 95 per cent confidence intervals)*

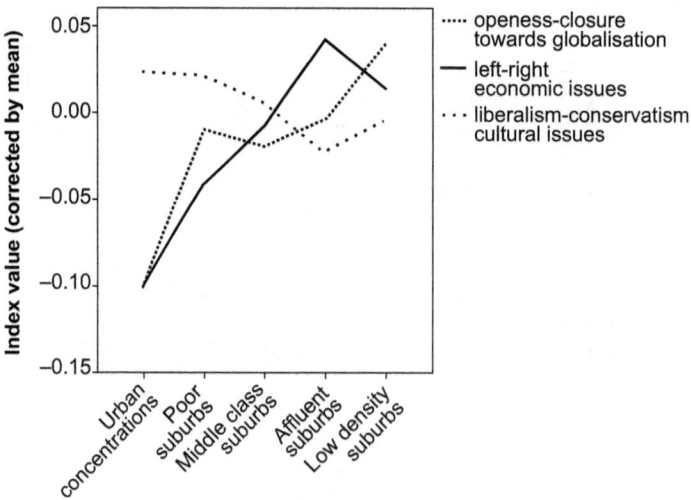

*Figure 6.3: Municipal positions on economic left-right and globalisation issues (means for national elections 1999 and 2003), as well as cultural issues (means for national election 2003)*

*Notes:* Values reflect mean position index values of municipalities. The index value for municipal positions on the three issues was corrected by the mean to improve graphic presentation.

Number of cases = 482 (urban concentrations: 7, poor suburbs: 119, middle-class suburbs: 115, affluent suburbs: 118, low-density suburbs: 118).

metropolitan areas show a distinct pattern, both within and across metropolitan areas (see Figure 6.2). Except in the Lugano metropolitan area, voters in the urban concentrations clearly lean more towards the left than those living in the suburban belt. However, there are also differences between suburban electorates. Voters in affluent and low-density suburbs lean more towards the right than those in middle-class and poor suburbs.

The municipal positions regarding the three-dimensional indices show that territorial dynamics in Swiss metropolitan areas affect partisanship in a very fine-grained way (see Figure 6.3). With respect to the economic conflict between work-ers and owners, core city electorates clearly vote in favour of strong state policies, those in affluent suburbs favour market solutions, whereas those in poor, middle-class and low-density suburbs adopt a position in between. Regarding the more recent globalisation cleavage, the electorate of core cities is more in favour of in-ternational integration than the electorate of suburban municipalities. With respect to the opposition between cultural libertarianism and conservatism, the affluent suburbs stand out as having an electorate that is more in favour of libertarianism.

An interesting threefold pattern of partisanship emerges. First, core cities stand out with their preference for redistribution and international integration, reflect-ing the classical leftist and cosmopolitan character of the electorate found there. Secondly, while the electorate of the four other types of municipalities is in gener-al more critical towards international integration, preferences regarding left-right economic issues, as well as cultural issues differ across types of municipalities. In poor, middle-class and low-density suburbs, there is a stronger preference for redistribution, combined with a stance against international integration and in fa-vour of cultural conservatism. This denotes (xenophobic) preferences for national conservatism — mobilised mainly by the SVP. In affluent suburbs, preferences against international integration and against redistribution but in favour of cultural libertarianism denote a tendency towards right-wing liberalism, based generally on the emphasis of individual freedom and a sceptical view of state regulatory intervention — be it national or international. These results therefore confirm our earlier estimates about the existence of a threefold spatial differentiation of voter preferences within Swiss metropolitan areas that emerged from the analysis of mere party votes (Kübler and Scheuss 2005: 225).

The multivariate analyses allow us to differentiate these findings (see Table 6.5 and Table 6.6; for restrictions of space, results are reported only for the com-positional, the contextual and the combined models). Estimations of the baseline models confirm that there are important differences between the seven metropoli-tan areas under scrutiny. Regarding left-right voting, the electorates living in the metropolitan areas of Bern, Basle, Lausanne and Lugano lean more to the left, those living in the Lucerne area prefer the right, while Geneva and Zurich (the reference category) are located in the middle of this spectrum. The picture is simi-lar for the economic issue dimension: voters in the Bern, Basle, Lausanne and Lugano metropolitan areas prefer parties that advocate strong state policies, while those in the Lucerne, Geneva and Zurich metropolitan areas are more in favour of market liberalism. Openness to globalisation processes is significantly stronger

*Table 6.5: Determinants of partisanship – left-right self-placement and economic index (OLS regression)*

| | Left-right self-placement index (municipal position, average 1999 and 2003 elections) | | | Economic left-right index (municipal position, average 1999 and 2003 elections) | | |
|---|---|---|---|---|---|---|
| | Composi-tional | Contextual | Combined model | Composi-tional | Contextual | Combined model |
| (Constant) | 5.162 | 0.5130 | 5.163 | 2.128 | 2.188 | 2.154 |
| | (0.145) | (0.326) | (0.338) | (0.042) | (0.104) | (0.099) |
| Bern MA | −0.324 | −0.392 | −0.289 | −0.045 | −0.079 | −0.036 |
| | (0.038) | (0.036) | (0.037) | (0.011) | (0.012) | (0.011) |
| Lucerne MA | *0.108* | 0.082 | **0.168** | **0.078** | **0.060** | *0.102* |
| | (0.055) | (0.050) | (0.055) | (0.016) | (0.016) | (0.016) |
| Basle MA | −0.331 | −0.374 | −0.364 | −0.043 | −0.075 | −0.053 |
| | (0.031) | (0.029) | (0.032) | (0.009) | (0.009) | (0.009) |
| Lugano MA | **−0.169** | **−0.423** | **−0.446** | 0.019 | **−0.065** | **−0.054** |
| | **(0.041)** | **(0.039)** | **(0.053)** | (0.012) | **(0.012)** | **(0.016)** |
| Lausanne MA | −0.113 | −0.238 | −0.217 | 0.081 | 0.049 | 0.055 |
| | (0.034) | (0.031) | (0.035) | (0.010) | (0.010) | (0.010) |
| Geneva MA | 0.015 | −0.019 | −0.117 | 0.113 | 0.126 | 0.075 |
| | (0.044) | (0.032) | (0.046) | (0.013) | (0.010) | (0.014) |
| Socio-economic status | 0.001 | | **0.003** | **0.002** | | **0.002** |
| | (0.001) | | (0.001) | (0.000) | | (0.000) |
| Hardship index | −0.010 | | −0.003 | −0.003 | | −0.001 |
| | (0.002) | | (0.002) | (0.001) | | (0.001) |
| Foreign born | **0.006** | | **0.011** | **0.002** | | **0.004** |
| | (0.002) | | (0.002) | (0.001) | | (0.001) |
| Per cent with a manufacturing occupation | 0.011 | | **0.005** | **0.003** | | 0.001 |
| | (0.002) | | (0.037) | (0.001) | | (0.001) |
| Per cent under age 18 | 0.006 | | −0.007 | 0.002 | | −0.002 |
| | (0.004) | | (0.004) | (0.001) | | (0.001) |
| Per cent retirees | 0.010 | | 0.008 | **0.005** | | **0.004** |
| | (0.006) | | (0.006) | (0.002) | | (0.002) |
| Distance to the centre | | 0.000 | 0.000 | | −2.5E-7 | 8.58E-7 |
| | | (0.000) | | | (0.000) | (0.000) |
| Homeownership | | **0.004** | **0.006** | | **0.001** | **0.001** |
| | | (0.002) | (0.000) | | (0.001) | (0.000) |
| Single-family housing | | −0.001 | **−0.003** | | *0.001* | 0.000 |
| | | (0.001) | (0.001) | | (0.000) | (0.000) |
| New housing | | *0.002* | **0.003** | | 0.000 | *0.001* |
| | | (0.001) | (0.004) | | (0.000) | (0.000) |
| Population growth 1970–2000 | | **−0.036** | **−0.036** | | *−0.009* | **−0.011** |
| | | (0.015) | (0.015) | | (0.005) | (0.005) |

| | Left-right self-placement index (municipal position, average 1999 and 2003 elections) | | | Economic left-right index (municipal position, average 1999 and 2003 elections) | | |
|---|---|---|---|---|---|---|
| | Compositional | Contextual | Combined model | Compositional | Contextual | Combined model |
| Residential stability | | −0.001 (0.002) | 0.002 (0.002) | | **−0.001** **(0.001)** | 0.001 (0.001) |
| Out-commuting | | −0.001 (0.001) | 0.000 (0.000) | | −0.001 (0.000) | 0.000 (0.000) |
| Population (Ln) | | **−0.069** (0.015) | **−0.080** (0.015) | | **−0.014** (0.005) | **−0.020** (0.004) |
| Density (Ln) | | **0.028** (0.016) | −0.011 (0.017) | | **0.016** (0.005) | −0.002 (0.005) |
| Econ. diversity index | | **0.729** (0.257) | 0.401 (0.274) | | **0.226** (0.082) | 0.086 (0.080) |
| Adjusted R² | 0.481 | 0.526 | 0.579 | 0.668 | 0.626 | 0.719 |
| N (number of cases) | 474 | 472 | 469 | 479 | 477 | 474 |

*Notes:* Table entries are unstandardised regression coefficients, standard errors in parentheses, significance for boldface coefficients, $p<0.05$; for italicised coefficients, $p<0.10$.

in the metropolitan areas of Bern, Basle, Lugano, Lausanne and Geneva than in Lucerne or Zurich. With respect to cultural issues, the electorates in the Lausanne, Geneva and Lucerne metropolitan areas are less conservative; those in the Bern and Lugano metropolitan are more conservative, Lucerne or Zurich being located in the middle. These differences between the metropolitan areas can plausibly be explained by the differences between the cantonal party systems in which these various metropolitan areas are located. While the Liberal Party has strongholds in the protestant urban centres of Geneva, Lausanne and Basle; Lucerne and Lugano are located in predominantly Catholic cantons, which are traditional strongholds of the Christian Democrats. And the canton of Zurich is the place where the Swiss People's Party had its first electoral successes with isolationism. The baseline model also confirms the political differences between the five municipal types identified in the bivariate analysis. Electorates of the core cities have stronger preferences for the left, favour strong state policies over market liberalism and are not as isolationist as those of all the other types of municipalities. However, their electorates are also more culturally conservative than those in middle-class and affluent suburbs.

With respect to the metropolitanisation thesis, the interesting question is whether ideological differences between metropolitan municipalities are linked to the contextual characteristics of these places, or whether they can be explained merely by compositional characteristics. The results of the compositional, the contextual and the combined models suggest a differential answer to these questions. With respect to left-right voting, the explanatory power of the contextual model (52.6 per cent of the observed variance) is superior to that of the compositional model (48.1 per cent). In addition, the combined model shows that spatial charac-

*Table 6.6: Determinants of partisanship – cultural index and globalisation index (OLS regression)*

| | Globalisation openness-isolation index (municipal position, average of 1999 and 2003 national elections) | | | Cultural liberalism-conservatism index (municipal position, average 1999 and 2003 national elections) | | |
|---|---|---|---|---|---|---|
| | Compositional | Contextual | Combined model | Compositional | Contextual | Combined model |
| (Constant) | 1.706 (0.018) | 1.649 (0.040) | 1.682 (0.043) | 2.621 (0.020) | 2.541 (0.052) | 2.585 (0.050) |
| Bern MA | −0.058 (0.005) | −0.057 (0.004) | −0.054 (0.005) | 0.008 (0.005) | 0.031 (0.006) | 0.010 (0.005) |
| Lucerne MA | 0.000 (0.007) | 0.001 (0.006) | 0.005 (0.007) | −0.018 (0.008) | −0.008 (0.008) | −0.025 (0.008) |
| Basle MA | −0.051 (0.004) | −0.050 (0.004) | −0.054 (0.004) | 0.001 (0.004) | 0.019 (0.005) | 0.008 (0.005) |
| Lugano MA | −0.036 (0.005) | −0.064 (0.005) | −0.068 (0.007) | 0.009 (0.006) | 0.037 (0.006) | 0.036 (0.008) |
| Lausanne MA | −0.056 (0.004) | −0.072 (0.004) | −0.069 (0.005) | −0.057 (0.005) | −0.048 (0.005) | −0.046 (0.005) |
| Geneva MA | −0.044 (0.006) | −0.065 (0.004) | −0.062 (0.006) | −0.087 (0.006) | −0.105 (0.005) | −0.072 (0.007) |
| Socio-economic status | −6.427E-5 (0.000) | | 0.000 (0.000) | −0.001 (0.000) | | −0.001 (0.000) |
| Hardship index | −0.001 (0.000) | | 0.000 (0.000) | 0.001 (0.000) | | 0.000 (0.000) |
| Foreign born | 0.000 (0.000) | | 0.000 (0.000) | −0.002 (0.000) | | −0.002 (0.000) |
| Per cent with a manufacturing occupation | 0.001 (0.000) | | 0.001 (0.000) | −0.001 (0.000) | | 0.000 (0.000) |
| Per cent under 18 | 0.000 (0.001) | | −0.001 (0.001) | −0.001 (0.001) | | −0.001 (0.001) |
| Per cent retirees | −0.001 (0.001) | | 0.000 (0.001) | −0.004 (0.001) | | −0.003 (0.001) |
| Distance to the centre | | 1.91E-7 (0.000) | 4.86E-8 (0.000) | | 5.171E-7 (0.000) | −1.8E-8 (0.000) |
| Homeownership | | 0.001 (0.000) | 0.001 (0.000) | | −0.001 (0.000) | −0.001 (0.000) |
| Single-family housing | | −0.001 (0.000) | −0.001 (0.000) | | −0.001 (0.000) | −3.5E-5 (0.000) |
| New housing | | 0.000 (0.000) | 0.000 (0.000) | | 0.000 (0.000) | 0.000 (0.000) |
| Population growth 1970–2000 | | −0.002 (0.002) | −0.001 (0.002) | | 0.002 (0.002) | 0.002 (0.002) |
| Residential stability | | 0.000 (0.000) | 0.000 (0.000) | | 0.001 (0.000) | 0.000 (0.000) |
| Out-commuting | | 0.000 (0.000) | 0.000 (0.000) | | 0.000 (0.000) | 9.05E-5 (0.000) |

| | Globalisation openness-isolation index (municipal position, average of 1999 and 2003 national elections) | | | Cultural liberalism-conservatism index (municipal position, average 1999 and 2003 national elections) | | |
|---|---|---|---|---|---|---|
| | Composi- tional | Contextual | Combined model | Composi- tional | Contextual | Combined model |
| Population (Ln) | | −0.007 | −0.008 | | 0.002 | 0.005 |
| | | (0.002) | (0.002) | | (0.002) | (0.002) |
| Density (Ln) | | −0.002 | −0.004 | | −0.008 | 0.001 |
| | | (0.002) | (0.002) | | (0.003) | (0.002) |
| Economic. | | 0.077 | 0.051 | | −0.034 | 0.035 |
| diversity index | | (0.031) | (0.035) | | (0.041) | (0.040) |
| Adjusted $R^2$ | 0.576 | 0.632 | 0.640 | 0.793 | 0.748 | 0.807 |
| N (number of cases) | 479 | 477 | 474 | 474 | 472 | 469 |

Notes: Table entries are unstandardised regression coefficients, standard errors in parentheses, significance for boldface coefficients, $p<0.05$; for boldface italicised coefficients, $p<0.10$.

teristics of municipalities are not explained away when compositional features are taken into account.

Left-right self-placement is influenced by both compositional and contextual variables. Right voting is associated with socio-economic status, the presence of immigrants, the percentage of residents with a manufacturing occupation, as well as homeownership. Left voting is linked to population size, population growth, as well as single-family housing. These results show that left-right voting in Swiss metropolitan areas is clearly related to spatial characteristics of the places in which voters live.

The three-dimensional indices allow a quite fine grained analysis of these more general patterns of left-right party voting (see Table 6.5 and Table 6.6). These are also influenced by a combination of compositional and contextual variables, although not all three in the same way. With respect to the economic issue dimension, the explanatory power of the compositional model (66.8 per cent of the observed variance) is superior to that of the contextual model (62.6 per cent). Similarly, the position on cultural issues is better explained by the compositional model (79.3 per cent) than by the contextual model (74.8 per cent). Interestingly though, the reverse is true for the position on globalisation issues, which is better explained by the contextual model (63.2 per cent) than by the compositional model (57.6 per cent). This suggests that the globalisation cleavage, as one of the prominent lines of division in contemporary Swiss politics, seems to be particularly related to territorial characteristics of the places in which people live.

In addition, the results in the combined model show that contextual variables are significant predictors on all three indices of partisanship, even if compositional variables are controlled for. With respect to the economic-issue positions (see Table 6.5), we find that preference for market liberalism is associated with compositional variables such as high socio-economic status, high proportion of foreign-born inhabitants, as well as high proportion of retirees. But contextual variables also play a role: the proportion of owner-occupied housing increases voting for market liberal parties, while population growth and population size is associated with preference for state-based policies.

With respect to the globalisation issue (see Table 6.6), the analysis shows that isolationism is associated with only one compositional variable, namely the proportion of residents aged 18 or lower. The main determinants for the position of the municipal electorate on globalisation issues indeed refer to the spatial characteristics of a municipality. Voting for isolationist parties increases with large proportions of owner-occupied housing, single-family housing, new housing, as well as small population size and low population density. This result also suggests that isolationism, and hence the rise of the SVP that mobilises this position, is closely associated with the metropolitanisation process, which has indeed produced patterns of settlement with precisely these characteristics.

Municipal positions with respect to cultural issues are also associated with compositional as well as contextual variables (see Table 6.6). On the compositional level, cultural conservatism in a municipality increases with high socio-economic status and, interestingly, strong presence of manufacturing occupation, but decreases with high proportions of foreign-born residents and retirees. Regarding the contextual predictors, cultural conservatism is associated with large proportions of owner-occupied housing, as well as with population size (the larger the municipality, the more conservative is its electorate). This is partly consistent with the findings from the typology-analysis that culturally-libertarian voters concentrate in affluent municipalities.

### Conclusion

Metropolitanisation made progress in Switzerland during the twentieth century and metropolitan areas are now the dominant pattern of human settlement in this country. Political behaviour in Swiss metropolitan areas remains heavily influenced by the cantonal and wider regional context in which these metropolitan areas are located. Hence, Caramani's (2004) finding of a relatively low degree of nationalisation of politics in Switzerland is reflected in the significant differences between the seven Swiss metropolitan areas analysed in this chapter. However, these regional and cantonal differences are only one part of the story. Indeed, the analyses presented in this chapter showed that the spatial differentiation related to metropolitanisation dynamics is an additional stratum that overlies the traditional territorial heterogeneity of political behaviour in Switzerland.

We found a clear place-effect on electoral participation – a finding that suggests two kinds of consequences of the metropolitanisation process on political participation. On the one hand, the territorial dynamics of metropolitanisation influence the contextual characteristics of municipalities in a way that is likely to reinforce the decline of electoral turnout. Epitomised mainly by urban sprawl, the metropolitanisation process in Switzerland is likely to increase the overall number of commuters and will lead to population growth in small municipalities at the outskirts of metropolitan areas. Both these factors – commuting and population size – have been shown to depress turnout in national and local elections. On the other hand, the place-effect on electoral turnout operates more strongly for local elections than for national elections. This means that turnout in local elections is likely to be more strongly depressed by metropolitan territorial transformations than is the case for turnout in national elections. As former rural villages or peripheral places at the outskirts are drawn into the metropolitan functional sphere of influence, the focus on local politics will weaken in the process. This is plausibly the causal mechanism behind the 'turnout-gap', i.e. the disparity between high(er) local turnout and low(er) national turnout, differentiated across types of municipalities within a metropolitan area. Whereas behaviour in national and local politics seems to be similar in core cities, these two spheres appear to be increasingly decoupled as one moves to the outskirts of the metropolitan area, with citizens in low-density suburbs being the most 'localised'. As metropolitan integration proceeds, however, these differences are likely to disappear.

Regarding partisanship, the analyses of left-right voting presented in this chapter also suggest the existence of a strong relationship between the territorial structuring of a metropolitan area and political behaviour therein. Drawing on party voters' positions with respect to the two currently most important political conflicts (economic issues and issues of globalisation), as well as a third minor division line (the opposition between libertarianism versus conservatism on moral and cultural issues), the results suggest the existence of a threefold pattern of political differentiation within Swiss metropolitan areas:

- the electorate of core cities votes in favour of strong state policies and is open to globalisation processes;
- voters in affluent suburbs emphasise market liberalism, are opposed to redistributive state interventions, and critical towards international integration; and
- poor, middle-class and low-density suburbs are also in favour of international demarcation, but more in favour of redistributive state interventions and cultural conservatism.

The political landscape of Swiss metropolitan areas presents a threefold division between cosmopolitan and left-wing core-cities, nationally-conservative poor, middle-class and low-density suburbs, and liberal affluent suburbs.

As the multivariate analyses have shown, these differentiations are not mere accidents of socio-demographic composition. The significant influence of contextual variables on the municipality's position in this three-dimensional space of partisanship suggests that there is also a place-effect on partisanship. Interestingly, this place-effect has turned out to be more dominant for voters' position on globalisation issues than for their positions on economic or cultural issues. More particularly, the analysis has shown that the dynamics of metropolitan transformation in Switzerland have shaped the contextual characteristics of municipalities in a way that reinforces isolationism. It is therefore plausible to hypothesise that the electoral success of the SVP – as the single most important feature of recent political change in Switzerland – can be explained, at least in part, by the ongoing metropolitanisation process. Indeed, metropolitanisation transforms territorial characteristics of Swiss municipalities in a way that turns them into a fertile ground for the isolationist programme advocated by this party.

In conclusion, the analyses presented in this chapter provide strong evidence in support of the 'metropolitanisation of politics' thesis. There is indeed a relationship between the territorial structure of a metropolitan area and political behaviour therein. Swiss metropolitan areas are characterised by lines of political division that not only follow lines of metropolitan territorial differentiation, but that are also structured by these and can hence be considered as metropolitan sources for political cleavages in this country.

## Bibliography

Brunner, M. and Sgier, L. (2002) 'Le nouvel individualisme' in S. Hug and P. Sciarini (eds) *Changement de valeurs et nouveaux clivages politiques en Suisse*, Paris: L'Harmattan, 135–78.

Bühlmann, M. (2006) *Politische Partizipation im Kommunalen Kontext. Der Einfluss Lokaler Kontexteigenschaften auf Individuelle Politisches Partizipationsverhalten*, Bern: Haupt.

Bühlmann, M. and Freitag, M. (2006) 'Individual and contextual determinants of electoral participation', *Swiss Political Science Review*, 12(4): 13–47.

Caramani, D. (2004) *The Nationaliziation of Politics*, Cambridge: Cambridge University Press.

Hoffmann-Martinot, V. and Sellers, J. M. (eds) (2005) *Metropolitanisation and Political Change*, Opladen: Verlag für Sozialwissenschaften.

Hug, S. and Sciarini, P. (2002) *Changement de Valeurs et Nouveaux Clivages Politiques en Suisse*, Paris: L'Harmattan.

Kölz, A. (1992) *Neuere Schweizerische Verfassungsgeschichte: ihre Grundlinien vom Ende der Alten Eidgenossenschaft bis 1848*, Bern: Sämpfli.

Kriesi, H., Grande, E., Lachat, Dolezal, M., Bornschier, S. and Frey, T. (2006) 'Globalisation and the transformation of the national political space: six European countries compared', *European Journal of Political Research*, 45: 921–25.

Kriesi, H., Lachat, R., Selb, P., Bornschier, S. and Helbling, M. (eds) (2005) *Der Aufstieg der SVP. Acht Kantone im Vergleich*, Zürich: NZZ Verlag.

Kübler, D., Schenkel, W. and Leresche, J. -P. (2003) 'Bright lights, big cities? Metropolisation, intergovernmental relations and the new Federal urban policy in Switzerland', *Swiss Political Science Review*, 9(1): 35–60.

Kübler, D. and Scheuss, U. (2005) 'Metropolitanisation and political change in Switzerland', in V. Hoffmann-Martinot and J. M. Sellers (eds) *Metropolitanisation and Political Change*, Opladen: Verlag für Sozialwissenschaften, 211–30.

Ladner, A. (2004) *Stabilität und Wandel von Parteien und Parteiensystemen. Eine vergleichende Analyse von Konfliktlinien, Parteien und Parteiensystemen in den Schweizer Kantonen*, Wiesbaden: Verlag für Sozialwissenschaften.

Ladner, A. and Bühlmann, M. (2007) *Demokratie in den Gemeinden*, Chur: Rüegger.

Ladner, A. and Millner, H. (1999) 'Do voters turn out more under proportional than majoritarian systems? The evidence from Swiss communal elections', *Electoral Studies*, 18: 235–50.

Linder, W. (2005) *Schweizerische Demokratie. Institutionen, Prozesse, Perspektiven*, Bern: Haupt.

Lipset, S. M. and Rokkan, S. (1967) 'Cleavage structures, party systems and voter alignments: an introduction', in S. M. Lipset and S. Rokkan, (eds) *Party Systems and Voter Alignments*, New York: The Free Press, 1–64.

Lutz, G. and Selb, P. (2007) 'The national elections in Switzerland', in U. Klöti, P. Knoepfel, H. Kriesi, W. Linder, Y. Papadopoulos, and P. Sciarini, (eds) *Handbook of Swiss Politics*, Zurich: NZZ Libro: 405–33.

Masnata, F. and Rubatell, C. (1991) *Le Pouvoir Suisse 1291–1991. Séduction démocratique et répression suave*, Lausanne: Editions de l'Aire.

Schuler, M., Dessemontet, P. and Joye, D. (2005) *Die Raumgliederungen der Schweiz*, Neuchâtel: Bundesamt für Statistik.

Trechsel, A. (2007) 'Popular votes', in U. Klöti, Knoepfel, P., Kriesi, H., Linder, W., Papadopoulos, Y. and Sciarini, P. (eds) *Handbook of Swiss Politics*, Zurich: NZZ Libro: 435–61.

Wernli, B. (2001) *Contraintes Institutionnelles, Influences Contextuelles et Participation aux Élections Fédérales en Suisse*, Bern: Haupt.

Zingg, E. and Benz, M. (2003) 'Mobilität, Wahlbeteiligung und Sozialkapital in Schweizer Gemeinden', *Schweizerische Zeitschrift für Politikwissenschaft*, 9(2): 59–87.

# Appendix

*Table A6.1: Definition of variables*

| Variable name | Definition | Cases with missing values |
|---|---|---|
| *Dependent variables* | | |
| National election turnout | National Council, average of the elections 1999 and 2000 | 0/482 |
| Local election turnout | Election turnout for the municipal executive election | 168/482 |
| Left-right voting | Sum of percentages of votes for parties, multiplied with voter self-placement on the left-right scale | 5/482 |
| Position on economic issues | Sum of percentage of votes for parties, multiplied with voter position on economic left-right issue (mean for 1999 and 2003 National Council election) | 5/482 |
| Openness-isolation towards globalisation | Sum of percentage of votes for parties, multiplied with voter position on globalisation (mean for 1999 and 2003 National Council election) | 5/482 |
| Liberalism-conservatism on cultural issues | Sum of percentage of votes for parties, multiplied with voter position on cultural issues (mean for 1999 and 2003 National Council election) | 5/482 |
| *Independent variables municipality-level* | | |
| Foreign born | proportion of foreign-born residents when place of birth is known | 0/482 |
| SES Hardship | summary index: $\sum(100*(x_i-x_{imin})/(x_{imax}-x_{imin}))/5$ where: <br> x1: proportion of people with low socio-economic status <br> x2: proportion of unemployed people <br> x3: proportion of people with low education profile <br> x4 proportion of people in residences where number of rooms is smaller than number of occupants <br> x5: proportion of retired people | 0/482 |
| SES Generally | summary index: $\sum(100*(x_i-x_{imin})/(x_{imax}-x_{imin}))/3$ where: <br> x1: proportion of people with university degree <br> x2: median income <br> x3: proportion of heads of household with higher education (higher professional education, applied sciences university, university) | 0/482 |

| Variable name | Definition | Cases with missing values |
|---|---|---|
| Manufacturing occupation | proportion of occupied people working in the 2nd sector | 0/482 |
| Simpson Index of Economic Diversity | percentage of maximum value of the Simpson index (Simpson index=$1-\Sigma p_i^2$, where p stands for the proportion of occupied people in three socio-professional categories; maximum value: Simpson index when all p= 1/number of categories) | 0/482 |
| Residents under 18 years | proportion of people under 18 years of age | 0/482 |
| Retirees | proportion of retired people | 3/482 |
| Single-family housing | proportion of residences that are single-family houses | 0/482 |
| Ln (Density) | natural logarithm of population/municipality's surface | 0/482 |
| Out-commuting | proportion of occupied people working in another municipality than municipality of residence | 0/482 |
| Distance to the centre | geographic distance from a municipality's centre to the centre of metropolitan area's core city in metres: $sqrt((x_1 - x_2)^2 + (y_1 - y_2)^2)$, where x and y indicate coordinates of geographic centres | 5/482 |
| New housing | proportion of dwellings built during the last 20 years (without renovations) | 0/482 |
| Owner-occupied housing | proportion of houses occupied by owners | 0/482 |
| Stability of residence | proportion of population living in the same municipality during the last five years | 0/482 |
| Ln (population) | natural logarithm of population size | 0/482 |
| Population growth | population growth rate: $(x_{10} - x_t)/xt$, where: $x_t$: population size in year t $x_{10}$: population in year t+10 | 0/482 |
| Proportional rule | Election rule for the election of the municipal executive, where: 0: majority rule 1: proportional rule | 168/482 |

*Sources:* coordinates of the municipalities' geographical centres: Institute for Transport Planning and Systems (ETH Zurich); median income: Federal Tax Administration; local election turnout: Internet sites of the cantons of Basle-Country (www.bl.ch), Geneva (www.ge.ch), Lucerne (www.lu.ch) and Ticino (www.ti.ch) and data collection by the authors; all other data: Swiss Federal Statistical Office.

# Chapter Seven | Does Political Ecology Matter? Voting Behaviour in German Metropolitan Areas

*Melanie Walter-Rogg[1]*

## Introduction

As a result of the enduring process of suburbanisation in the development of popu-lation and enterprises, metropolitan areas have become more and more relevant in Germany, similar to the patterns known from other industrialised nations (Walter-Rogg 2005). For a long time, the spatial phenomenon of suburbanisation was sole-ly observable in the western part of Germany. However, with the unification in 1989 and the adaptation of the free market economy, the suburbanisation started in eastern Germany as well. For political scientists, the question of the political impact of these suburbanisation processes is especially important. What happens in society when communes spread over their administrative boundaries and the functional complexity between core cities and suburbs is steadily rising? With the slogan 'place matters', researchers in the United States and Canada addressed a growing process of suburbanisation coupled with social polarisation and changes in the political orientations and behaviour of the citizens (Hirsch 1968; Greer and Greer 1976; Dreier *et al.* 2001; Sellers 2004).

The political ecology approach has been a breath of fresh air in the last decades as part of the new research direction in metropolitan governance. Therefore, we want to analyse within this contribution the political impact of suburbanisation in Germany. Is the nationalisation thesis correct that national political cleavages dominate political contests and party structures at every electoral scale, or can a difference in or between metropolitan areas be observed? In the latter case, we have to modify the nationalisation thesis with respect to our empirical results. With that aim, the German research team compiled a data set with various demographic and socio-economic indicators on the level of the communes. This was an ambi-tious task because such a data set did not yet exist. Five federal states have made it possible to analyse a broad range of relevant indicators for our research question.

1.  The author would like to thank the Thyssen Foundation for financing the German International Metropolitan Observatory (IMO) research project, the Federal Office for Building and Regional Planning (FOBP) for providing the current definition of metropolitan areas and the Statistical Office of Baden-Wuerttemberg for coordinating the IMO Data Set. Furthermore, I feel strongly indebted to Philip König and Martin Sojer for major contributions to the supervision of data collection and to my colleague Daniel Kübler for his contribution to the multilevel analyses.

These units of analysis comprise the metropolitan area of Berlin with the capital city, and fourteen metropolitan areas in West Germany (Baden-Wuerttemberg and Rhineland-Palatinate) and six in East Germany (Brandenburg and Saxony).

As we could show in the first IMO volume (Walter-Rogg 2005), the differentiation between these two parts of the country is important for the subject of metropolitanisation and political change, and surely for socio-demographic and socio-economic differences. Faced with the data available in Germany, it is necessary to confine the analysis of political participation in metropolitan areas to electoral behaviour. Statistics for other participatory possibilities, such as initiatives or referenda, are not systematically collected and in some federal states not even counted by the statistical offices.

In general, psephology is one of the best developed disciplines of empirical political research. Even though increasing evidence is given 'that voting is not just a function of factors internal to the individual, but also factors external to the individual' (Eriksson 2005: 2), most theories and models of empirical psephology abandon the spatial dimension. This non-consideration is regarded as an important deficit in existing models when it comes to explaining electoral behaviour. Moreover, the political ecology is a useful extension of the today's dominance of individual-oriented explanatory concepts (Falter and Winkler 2005: 133). To analyse the consequences of political ecology for political behaviour, the IMO research group decided to follow Orfield's reflections (2002) in his well-known book *American Metropolitics – the new suburban reality*. The author proposed to distinguish between various communal types in the analysis of metropolitan areas. Consequently for the analysis of suburbanisation and its political impact in Germany, our research questions are the following:

(1) To what extent does the socio-political structure of the community/metropolitan area affect the community's/metropolitan area's voter turnout and the political orientation?

(2) Do voting patterns vary by different communal types and what is the relative importance of community variables and metropolitan variables with regard to voting patterns at the local level?

So the aim of this contribution is fourfold: First, we present the current definition of metropolitan areas given by the FOBP, the available data set and the units of analysis. In a second step we look at explanatory concepts of electoral behaviour to develop relevant hypothesis for the empirical analysis. Thirdly, we develop our research design including the presentation of operational concepts for the independent and dependent variables. And finally, the main and last objective is a description of electoral behaviour in national and local elections in various communal types and a multilevel analysis of the relative importance of community variables in an intra-metropolitan and inter-metropolitan perspective.

## Definition of German metropolitan areas

This chapter is based on a definition of metropolitan areas published by the Federal Office for Building and Regional Planning (FOBP) in 2004,[2] which was created in the 1950s by Boustedt. This definition takes a central municipality and its surroundings as socio-economic units. In the current version, big core cities with more than 500,000 inhabitants and small core cities with more than 100,000 inhabitants make up the core of a metropolitan area (FOBP 2004). As a result, there are eighty German metropolitan areas, five of which do not meet the inhabitant breakpoint of the IMO definition. Fifty-eight of the eighty metropolitan areas feature four different settling zones (core, core area, inner and outer commuter area); most of these are located in the Ruhr area. Due to the high density of municipalities and inhabitants in this big area, it is possible that a core city has no other settling zones because the citizens of these communes commute to another city in this area. For our research question that addresses voting behaviour in different settling areas, this makes no difference. Rather is it necessary to know if a municipality is located in the core or in the periphery of a metropolitan area.

Figure 7.1 illustrates the current definition of metropolitan areas in Germany, where 41 per cent of 12,428 communes and 73 per cent of the population are located in eighty metropolitan areas. Compared to the FOBP definition in 2002 (Walter-Rogg 2005), 960 communes, or 7 per cent, disappeared in the process of territorial reform – especially in Eastern Germany (Walter-Rogg 2010).

All in all, the settlement structures in both parts of the country are quite diverse – 62 per cent of the eastern population live in outer commuter areas or rural areas and 20 per cent in core cities. A smaller number of people live in core areas or inner commuter areas. Thus, there is a population gap between the core cities and the rural areas. In West Germany, people concentrate much more in and around core cities and less in outer commuter or rural areas (see Table 7.1).

## Data set and units of analysis

For the analysis of the consequences of political ecology for the political behaviour in metropolitan areas, the IMO research group followed Orfield's approach to distinguish between suburbs that refer to various demographic and socio-economic indicators. Hence, the primary aim for our research team was to consider all seventy-five metropolitan areas that meet the inhabitant breakpoint of the IMO definition in Germany. Unfortunately, the available statistical data

---

2.   Three definitions of metropolitan areas were available in Germany: areas based on the concept of Boustedt (1970), agglomeration and urbanised areas as a part of the regional typology of the FOBP, and agglomeration areas defined by the Ministerial Conference on Regional Planning (MKRO). These definitions refer to the same two indicators but are weighted unequally: commuter complexity and settlement structure such as density or centrality. Boustedt's concept seemed to be more adequate for two reasons: first, the definition reflected the actual urban sprawl, which transgresses traditional territorial boundaries; secondly, this definition offered a possibility of analysing a wide range of areas.

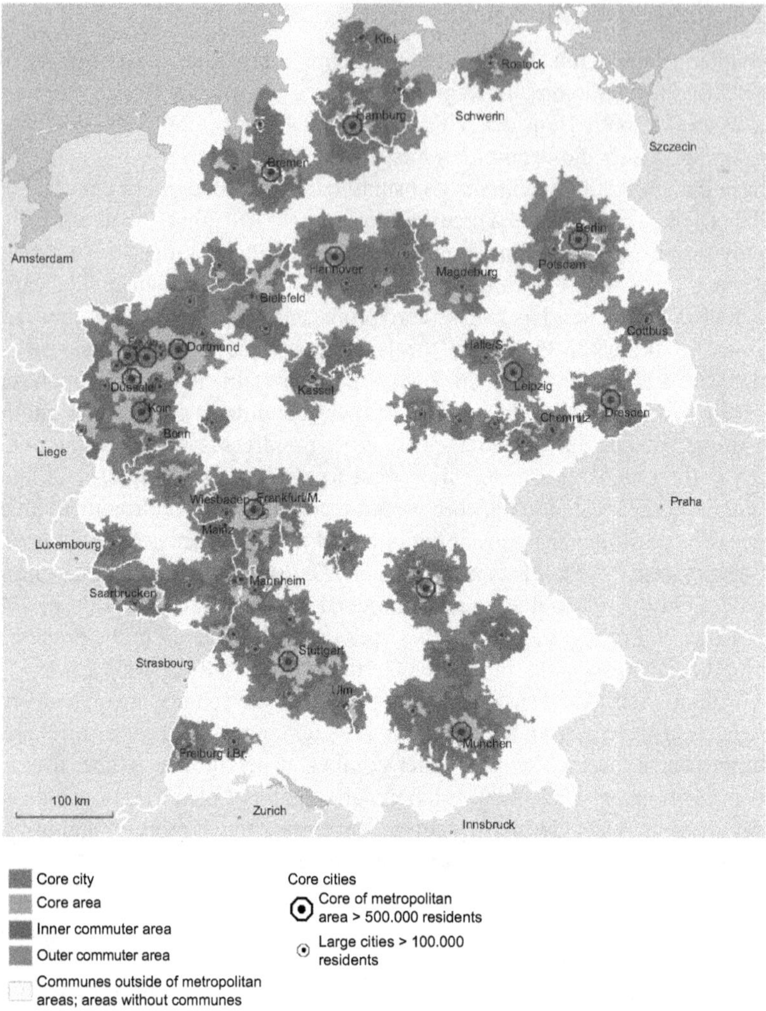

Core city
Core area
Inner commuter area
Outer commuter area
Communes outside of metropolitan
areas; areas without communes

Core cities
Core of metropolitan
area > 500.000 residents
Large cities > 100.000
residents

*Figure 7.1: German metropolitan areas 2004*

*Notes:* core areas = density daily population (daily population = population - commuter out of the city + commuter to the city) > 500 or a positive commuter balance (surplus commuter to the core area, 50% commuter to the core city); inner commuter area = at least 50% commuter to one or more core areas; outer commuter area = 25% to under 50% commuter to one or more core areas.

*Source:* Federal Office for Building and Regional Planning (2006).

rendered this intention impossible. The collection of indicators on the level of communes was an ambitious task. Due to the federal structure, sixteen statistical offices collect data for the federal states and their municipalities. Not all indicators are available for each federal state, and the available information can vary in different respects. Hence, the creation of a common data set with all required independent and dependent IMO variables was not feasible.

*Table 7.1: Metropolitan area definition in 2004*

| | Number of municipalities | % | West Germany | % | East Germany | % |
|---|---|---|---|---|---|---|
| Big core city >500,000 inhabitants | 12 | 0.1 | 12 | 0.1 | 0 | 0.0 |
| Small core city >100,000 inhabitants | 68 | 0.6 | 56 | 0.7 | 12 | 0.3 |
| Core city | 80 | 0.6 | 68 | 0.8 | 12 | 0.3 |
| Core area | 526 | 4.2 | 464 | 5.5 | 62 | 1.6 |
| Inner commuter area | 2,318 | 18.7 | 1,885 | 22.2 | 433 | 11.0 |
| Outer commuter area | 2,212 | 17.8 | 1,584 | 18.6 | 628 | 16.0 |
| Metropolitan area | 5,136 | 41.3 | 4,001 | 47.1 | 1,135 | 28.9 |
| Rural area | 7,292 | 58.7 | 4,500 | 52.9 | 2,792 | 71.1 |
| Total | 12,428 | 100.0 | 8,501 | 100.0 | 3,927 | 100.0 |

*Notes:* Commuter status 30.06.2004; municipality status 31.12.2004.
*Source:* Federal Office for Building and Regional Planning (2004).

Nevertheless, it was possible to analyse a broad range of indicators for five federal states. These units of analysis comprise fourteen metropolitan areas in West Germany (Baden-Wuerttemberg, Hesse) and seven in East Germany (Berlin, Brandenburg and Saxony) (see Table A7.1 in the Appendix to this chapter). As can be seen in the first IMO volume (Walter-Rogg 2005), the differentiation between these two parts of the country is important for the subject of metropolitanisation and political change, and surely for demographic and socio-economic differences.[3]

Starting with this dataset of twenty-one metropolitan areas and 2,452 municipalities, we employed a variant of the hierarchical factor analytic procedure prescribed to create a typology of municipalities (see Table WA7.1 in the Web Appendix).[4] For each of the hardship variables (unemployment rate, living space per capita, university degree and local tax rates), an index was computed to standardise municipal ratios calculated from data between 0 and 100. Based on the various computed indices, a hardship index was constructed. All in all, the specifications of the IMO protocol worked well with our data base. An overview of the indicators of the typology confirms our procedural method to separate

---

3. Since we restricted our considerations to five federal states, we have to consider two aspects. First, that nine metropolitan areas outreach their respective federal state and therefore, these communes are not in the following analysis. But for the multilevel analysis, we need indicators for the whole metropolitan area. In these cases, the calculation is based on all communes of the metropolitan area, preconditioned that this indicator is also available in the neighbouring federal state. Second, there are 24 communes in Baden-Wuerttemberg and Hesse where the citizenry is commuting to a metropolitan area outside of the respective federal state. These municipalities were also excluded in the following steps. Additionally, the metropolitan area of Offenbach am Main has a total population of less than 200,000 inhabitants. Following the IMO definition we also omitted these communes.

4. See Table WA7.1 and all other Web Appendixes WA07, http://press.ecpr.eu/resources.

*Table 7.2: German typology of municipalities*

| | West Germany | | | | East Germany | | | |
| | Baden-Wuerttemberg | | Hesse | | Berlin-Brandenburg | | Saxony | |
| | N | % | N | % | N | % | N | % |
|---|---|---|---|---|---|---|---|---|
| Urban concentrations | 19 | 1.7 | 8 | 2.0 | 4 | 0.9 | 7 | 1.3 |
| Low-density suburb | 139 | 12.5 | 54 | 13.4 | 42 | 10.0 | 29 | 5.6 |
| Affluent suburbs | 137 | 12.4 | 28 | 7.0 | 30 | 7.1 | 36 | 6.9 |
| Middle-class suburbs | 191 | 17.2 | 72 | 17.9 | 18 | 4.3 | 82 | 15.8 |
| Poor suburbs | 89 | 8.0 | 52 | 12.9 | 57 | 13.5 | 72 | 13.9 |
| Metropolitan areas | 575 | 51.8 | 214 | 53.2 | 151 | 35.8 | 226 | 43.5 |
| Rural areas | 534 | 48.2 | 188 | 46.8 | 271 | 64.2 | 293 | 56.5 |
| Total | 1109 | 100.0 | 402 | 100.0 | 422 | 100.0 | 519 | 100.0 |

*Source:* IMO Data Set 2003.

the municipalities in West and East Germany[5] (see Table WA7.2 in the Web Appendix).[6] As assumed for some European countries under the IMO protocol, the differentiation between poor and minority suburbs did not occur in Germany. The final result consists of five types of localities in metropolitan areas in both parts of Germany. For information, we also add rural areas to our comparative analysis, but not for the further steps.

The available demographic and socio-economic indicators differ more or less between the two parts of the country and the different communal types (see Tables A7.2(a) and (b) in the Appendix to this chapter). Additionally, the two typologies of municipalities indicate some variations between the analysed federal states (see Table 7.2). First, only 4 per cent of the communes in the metropolitan area of Berlin-Brandenburg are classified as middle-class suburbs and only 6 per cent of the communes in Saxony as low density suburbs. The federal state of Baden-Wuerttemberg is known as being relatively wealthy, so it is less surprising that this state indicates a number of affluent suburbs above average and a number of poor suburbs below average. A second disparity shows that in East Germany many

---

5. Berlin was assigned to East Germany, because the metropolitan area it belongs to consists of the core city of Berlin and ninety-one communes in Brandenburg.

6. Due to the fact that the population density in the western federal states is much higher than in the eastern ones, the category 'low-density suburbs' ends up with more than nearly triple the amount than the eastern category (181 vs. 66 population per km[2]). The distinction referring to the hardship index is not so high, but nevertheless exists. Whereas in West Germany the hardship starting point for 'affluent suburbs' is 22, that of 'middle-class suburbs' 50; these values are higher in East Germany with 35 and 61 respectively.

more communes are located in rural areas compared to West Germany. Whereas more than half of the number of municipalities in Baden-Wuerttemberg and Hesse are situated in metropolitan areas, there are only 36 per cent in Brandenburg and 44 per cent in Saxony. Considering these differences in the typology of localities between West and East, we assume some impact by this regional variable in the empirical analyses. Therefore, all descriptive statistics will be differentiated and all calculations will be controlled for this regional difference.

### Theoretical concepts and hypotheses

#### Explanatory concepts of general electoral behaviour

The research question of this comparative international metropolitan project is very ambitious, namely how the place of residence fits into the complex interplay of sociological and institutional, as well as local and national determinants of voter turnout and decisions. The first problem for handling this question is that theory-based reflections or empirical studies on local or metropolitan electoral behaviour barely exist. Thus broad theoretical concepts to explain national electoral voting have to be transferred to the respective local metropolitan level, e.g. the social-structural approach or the socio-economic model of political participation (Verba and Nie 1972; also see Chapter 1 in this volume). Next to several individual-based reflections, two macro concepts exist: the institutional and the geographical or ecological approach. The first one holds institutional arrangements like the design of voting rights responsible for electoral behaviour.

Due to their own tradition and political culture, the sixteen German federal states feature different local constitutions and voting rights. Up to 1989, these rights have been dominated, with the exception of Baden-Wuerttemberg and Bavaria, by the principle of a closed party list system. After 1990, some federal states introduced vote splitting and cumulating,[7] well known from Baden-Wuerttemberg and Bavaria. Although the local election rights in Germany feature a broad variation,[8] it is less reasonable to control the impact of local voting rights in our analysis. This is because some of the metropolitan areas link two Laender with more or less variation in local voting rights and also we had to reduce our analysis to five federal states. All in all, the variance of institutional settings between Baden-Wuerttemberg and Rhineland-Palatinate (West Germany), and Brandenburg and Saxony (East Germany) is too low for such an analysis. In particular, all four territorial states feature similar voting rights with respect to vote splitting and cumulating. Therefore, we expect relative uniformity in the local

---

7.  In this case the voter has several votes he can split up for different parties or boost certain candidates by cumulating the votes on their ticket. Generally, the party appoints the ranking of candidates on their list, which is presented to the voter. If the voter gives his voice to a certain party, the ranking decides on the composition of the local council and not the electorate (Gabriel and Walter-Rogg 2003: 145).

8.  See the overview at: http://wahlrecht.de/kommunal.

voting results considering the existing voting rules in the analysed federal states.

The geographical or ecological approach seems to be more adequate for our research questions. This method has a long tradition and was particularly used by geographers (e.g. Siegfried 1913; Wright 1932). The focal point of former research was on the category's continuity and stability, therefore the researcher analysed longitudinal electoral results. On this basis, they identified political regions, regional political cultures or regional fixed socio-moral settings. The interest of the newer ecological approach is the connection of social structure, regional contexts and electoral behaviour (Falter and Winkler 2005: 119). In Germany, scientists paid little attention to the political ecology approach for a long time. Nowadays, this approach pursues several aims. The main one is congruent with our research question: how can territorial variation in electoral behaviour be explained? In this regard, the most frequent determinants under scrutiny are economic and occupational structure, urbanisation and ethnic composition of geographical units (Falter and Winkler 2005: 109).

In the first IMO contribution, the analyses of the National Election Study 2002 gave some hints of the relevance of place for the explanation of political attitudes and behaviour. Indeed, patterns of orientations like 'party identification', 'candidate preference in national election', 'political ideology' or behaviour like 'national election vote', 'participation in traffic blockades' respectively 'participation in violent or authorised demonstrations' tend to vary – not very strongly, but significantly – in function of communal types. For this second IMO contribution, we collected several demographic, socio-economic and electoral data for the metropolitan areas in Germany. Therefore, the question is, does the available macro data confirm the results of the National Election Study?

In the past, researchers debated intensively, which of these theoretical approaches is most suitable for the explanation of electoral behaviour. In modern empirical research they are deemed compatible and are often used simultaneously, with the exception of the political ecology approach. For the development of manageable models, most researchers just assume the homogeneity of space. This non-consideration is regarded as an important deficit of existing models when it comes to explaining electoral behaviour. Moreover, the political ecology approach is a useful extension of today's dominance of individual-oriented explanatory concepts (Falter and Winkler 2005: 133).

### *Explanatory concepts of the interplay between local and national political participation*

With regard to the overall thoughts about the explanation of political behaviour, the IMO research group developed hypotheses referring to the relationship between local and national electoral turnout and voter preferences in metropolitan areas. The question is: do we expect similar or different results for the dependent variables in Germany regarding the extensive theoretical reflections and empirical results in North America and other European countries? Those German studies that exist tend to be rather limited in scope as they usually focus on single cases and thus neglect more systematic and longitudinal approaches. Therefore, only few trends have been identified so far.

With regard to our analysis, it appears most important to note that the turnout trends in German elections from 1946 to 2005 confirm the idea that the level of participation differs for the various layers of the political system. Turnout rates are always high for the German Bundestag, lower for the states and local parliaments and lowest for the European Parliament (Walter-Rogg 2007). Reif (1984: 247) mentioned reasons of importance regarding electoral turnout: 'Turnout at SOE (second-order election), regularly lower than FOE (first-order election) turnout, reflects the relevance and weight of difference SOE, i.e. reflects how much there is perceived to be at stake'. In her study of 114 German local elections from 1951 to 2008, Vetter confirmed that the time lag between national and local election dates has a weak but significant impact on the level of local turnout: 'The nearer the local election is to the date of the national one, the higher the local turnout rate' (Vetter 2009: 794, translation by MWR).

Only few electoral studies have attempted to systematically compare voting patterns in national and local German elections. The inevitable time lags between national and local elections constitute one of the major obstacles in this regard. As Gabriel (1997) points out, it is almost impossible to distinguish between systemic and situational determinants of local voting behaviour, especially if the big political picture in a country undergoes change between the national and local election days. Generally speaking, there is no broad consensus on what exactly differentiates local and national electoral behaviour. Instead of an overarching theoretical framework, there are only a few hypotheses, of which some point to particularities of local voting behaviour, whereas others do not. Löffler and Rogg (1991) and Gabriel (1997) have shown that local elections form a system on their own and tend to follow their own rules. On the local level, candidates are said to play a stronger role, whereas political affiliations seem to partly lose their importance (Czarnecki 1992: 19ff.; Eith 1997). Additionally, the divergent institutional settings and electoral codes add complexity to the picture.

Other authors, like Kevenhörster (1983), do not believe in distinct local voting patterns. Instead, they argue that local elections merely reflect the greater political game that is played on the national field. However, Gabriel's 1994 electoral analysis of local and national voting decisions in Baden-Wuerttemberg challenges Kevenhörster's view. In a rather stable national context, he indeed witnessed substantive differences between the two political layers with regard to voter turnout and voting decisions. More so, if the local party system does not exactly reproduce the national one and the local political culture mitigates the effects of party orientation (Gabriel 1997: 150). Comparing issue orientations in local and national elections, Busch (1997) came to the opposite conclusion in his study. He saw party affiliations as the vital force behind voting decisions in national as well as local elections. The arguments of both perspectives can be summarised in the thesis of Reif (1983: 246), which is that one of the main reasons for different or similar political pictures in local and national elections is the time lag between these two occasions: '[...] the time that has passed since the last FOE (first-order election) is the crucial variable structuring SOE (second-order election) results'.

Consequently, we control the following hypotheses for the dependent variables referring explicitly to the German situation, aside the number of hypotheses the IMO group formulated for the empirical part in general (see Chapter 1 in this volume):

H1: Turnout at local elections is lower than turnout at national elections in Germany.

H2: The thesis of nationalisation is correct; therefore no difference in the results of local and national German elections is observable.

H3: The thesis of nationalisation has to be modified; therefore a difference in the results of local and national German elections is observable.

H4: The thesis of metropolitanisation is correct; therefore a difference in the electoral results in and between German metropolitan areas is observable (place matters).

H5: The thesis of metropolitanisation has to be modified; therefore no difference in the electoral results in and between German metropolitan areas is observable (place does not matter).

### Research design

The general mode of electoral research is based on the individual level and combines it with some macro determinants such as voting rights or regional location. The political and social ecology of voter decisions is seldom analysed in detail. Critics argue, however, that instead of treating the individual as atomised, researchers should also consider the social surrounding in which the individual is embedded and its potential impact upon individual political behaviour (Books and Prysby 1988: 211; see also Eriksson 2005: 2). However, the best research design would be a combination of all relevant factors, but this requires a complex collection of micro and macro data for the particular geographical units. In the German case, it was very ambitious to compile macro data on the level of municipalities. Data protection means that information on social or economic characteristics is only available at the county or agglomeration level. Hence, we had to collect all indicators for the analysis of the impact of ecology indicators for national and local electoral behaviour on the community level and had to factor out individual resources or political orientations for individual voting behaviour. Figure 7.2 illustrates the research design for our analysis.

### The independent variables

The multilevel analysis requires a differentiation between independent variables on level 1 and level 2. For level 1, we furthermore distinguish between compositional and contextual variables – the former deals with the demographic makeup, the latter deals with spatial influences. The survey literature has established a number of demographic characteristics that make individuals more likely to vote than

**Geographical/ecological determinants (collective in living area)**
**Institutional determinants (voting right in living area)**

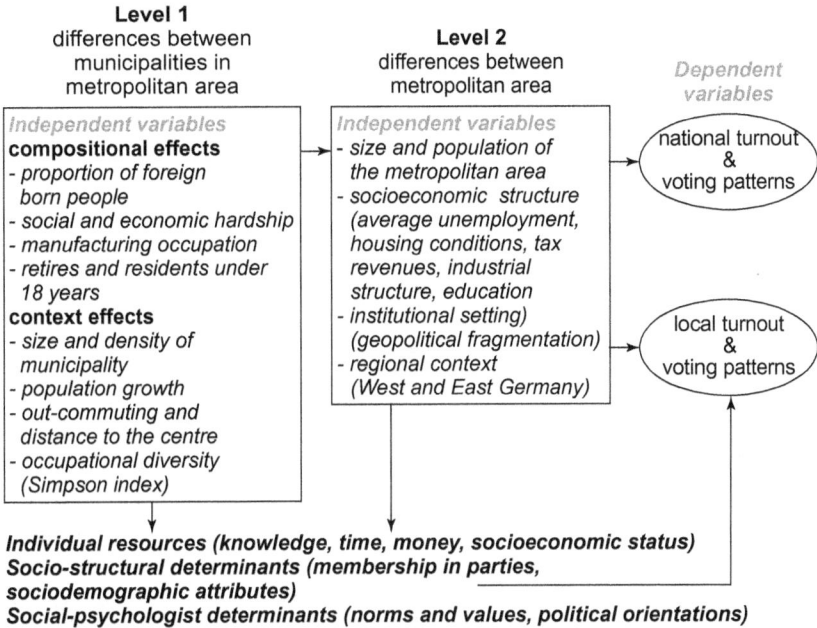

**Level 1**
differences between
municipalities in
metropolitan area

**Level 2**
differences between
metropolitan area

*Dependent variables*

*Independent variables*
**compositional effects**
- proportion of foreign
  born people
- social and economic hardship
- manufacturing occupation
- retires and residents under
  18 years

**context effects**
- size and density of
  municipality
- population growth
- out-commuting and
  distance to the centre
- occupational diversity
  (Simpson index)

*Independent variables*
- size and population of
  the metropolitan area
- socioeconomic structure
  (average unemployment,
  housing conditions, tax
  revenues, industrial
  structure, education
- institutional setting)
  (geopolitical fragmentation)
- regional context
  (West and East Germany)

national turnout
&
voting patterns

local turnout
&
voting patterns

**Individual resources (knowledge, time, money, socioeconomic status)**
**Socio-structural determinants (membership in parties,**
**sociodemographic attributes)**
**Social-psychologist determinants (norms and values, political orientations)**

*Figure 7.2: Research design for the analysis of political behaviour in German metropolitan areas*

others, independent of their living place. Our lower-level units are the individual spatial units (municipality), i.e. the scale at which the electoral data is aggregated. In this line of argumentation, researchers could show that communities with higher incomes and higher levels of education vote more frequently (Verba *et al.* 1978; Oliver 2000). Places where people face the greatest social disadvantages generally vote less. Communities with more disadvantaged ethnic or racial groups and immigrants also generally vote less frequently than others (Hill and Leighly 1999). Places with older citizens have generally voted more frequently than those with younger ones (Gimpel *et al.* 2004; Goerres 2005). So we assume that the following variables: foreign born, social and economic hardship, level of education, manufacturing occupation, retirees and residents under eighteen years, have some impact on electoral differences between the municipalities of different communal types in one metropolitan area (intra-metropolitan perspective). On the other hand, numerous hypotheses have already been adduced to account for the ways national and local electoral participation differ among places. Thus, we shall check the effects of context with reference to the following variables: size and density of the municipality, population growth, out-commuting, distance to the centre and occupational diversity.

For level 2, with an inter-metropolitan perspective, we calculated the average numbers of the indicator size, population, unemployment, housing conditions, local tax revenues, industrial structure and highest status occupational group for each of the twenty-one metropolitan areas, including communes located outside the four territorial states. Additionally, we wanted to analyse the institutional setting, such as fragmentation, concentration or polarisation of each metropolitan area, and the regional context of West and East Germany. But we have to consider that multivariate analysis needs sensitivity toward multicollinearity between the independent variables. Principal component analysis enabled a closer look of these relations. The result is a six-factor solution for West Germany and a four-factor solution for East Germany (see Table WA7.1 in the Web Appendix). Multicollinearity between compositional indicators is not really high in either part of the country. Regarding the effects of context as well as the combination of compositional and contextual effects, however multicollinear effect made it necessary to exclude some variables from the regression analysis.

## The dependent variables

For the measurement of electoral turnout and voting patterns, we refer back to the national election of the German Bundestag in 2002 and to the last local election in the five Laender before the year of 2003.[9] Before we can map voter preferences in the metropolitan areas under scrutiny, the operational concepts that allow a sensible classification of voter preferences on the basis of party votes need to be specified.

### Cleavages and voter preferences

After the formation of the Kaiserreich in 1871, the political mobilisation of the party system and individual voting behaviour in Germany were mainly influenced by a cultural (religion) and a social-economic (class) cleavage. The other two cleavages mentioned by Lipset and Rokkan (1967) – centre/periphery and rural/urban – were also present, but less prominent (Gabriel and Keil 2005: 590). Kriesi et al. (2006) analysed the German cleavage structure in 1976 and stated that the two main conflicts were hardly related to each other. In their assessment, the cultural dimension was marked by a strong opposition between support for cultural liberalism, on the one hand, and support for a strong army and a restrictive budgetary policy, on the other. Similar to Pappi (1984), they see a triangular structure of the three main parties, where the Social Democrats support cultural liberalism, environmental protection and the welfare state and oppose budgetary rigour and a reinforcement of the army. In contrast, the Liberals support cultural and economic liberalism, but are more distant from environmental protection.

---

9.   In Berlin and Brandenburg this aim was slightly complicated. In the city state of Berlin, elections for the district assembly are organised in twelve districts; therefore we have to use the average number of turnout rate and the average voting decisions for the whole city. In four cities of Brandenburg (Potsdam, Cottbus, Frankfurt an der Oder, Brandenburg an der Havel), local elections refer to the county council and not to the city council.

The Christian Democrats are also closer to economic liberalism than to a strong welfare state and respect cultural liberalism. In their analyses of recent German elections in the 1990s, Kriesi and his colleagues find changes mainly in the cultural cleavage. As a result, they see immigration as a new salient issue and more consensual support for the army, for budgetary rigour, culture and environmental protection. In their view, these changes indicate convergence among the traditional major parties. New parties, namely the Greens and the PDS have emerged around positions that redefine the cleavages (Kriesi *et al.* 2006: 299).

Thus, the cultural and class cleavages are still important in Germany today, but with different consequences for the Western and Eastern parts and a different shape of the cultural cleavage. The party system in the new Laender is formally the same as the one in the old Laender, but not in its empirical shape.

> Contrary to West Germany the party of the democratic socialism (PDS) is an important component of the Eastern party system. The Green party only plays a minor role, both as party organisation and as part of the elected state or local parliaments. These patterns are very similar for the Liberal party (FDP), although they hold much more party members in East Germany than the Green party (Crow 2001: 243).

The party system of the old federal states is stamped by the cleavage structure existing before the domination of the national socialists. In the former GDR, this tradition was interrupted between 1933 and 1989. During this period, no relationships between social groups and political parties could exist, and thus a different influence of cleavages for individual voting behaviour in East Germany was given. Next to the diverse relationship between social characteristics and party choice, Dalton and Bürklin (1995, 1996: 198) refer to the different demographic and socio-economic composition of both parts of the country as a second reason for the various effects of cleavages for the voting behaviour.

With respect to the religious dimension of the cultural cleavage, currently there are the secular-oriented parties SPD, FDP, the Greens and the PDS; representing religious norms and values are the CDU and the CSU. This pattern corresponds to the political loyalties of voters with secular and religious orientations. But the process of secularisation reduced the voter base with religious (mainly Catholic) orientations during the last decades. The number of Catholics as well as the share of churchgoers has declined (Gluchowski *et al.* 2002). Nevertheless the religious cleavage still has shaping power, in both parts of the country. Although a completely different religious denomination and commitment exists in East Germany[10] and with it different prerequisites for the cultural cleavage, researchers have observed a certain similarity between the voting behaviour in West and East Germany: Catholics vote more often for the Christian Democrats than Protestants (Gabriel and Keil 2005: 595).

---

10. Whereas in West Germany more than 80 per cent of the population have a church relationship, this figure is only one third in East Germany (Dalton and Bürklin 1995, 1996: 198).

Kriesi *et al.* also suggest that the 1990s have seen the emergence of a new conflict between losers and winners of the globalisation processes, thereby leading to a further differentiation and new meaning of the original cultural and socioeconomic conflict dimensions. The authors view this new conflict as rooted in socioeconomic structures. Entrepreneurs and qualified employees in sectors open to international competition as well as all kinds of cosmopolitan citizens are seen as winners. Entrepreneurs and qualified employees in traditionally protected sectors, all unqualified employees and citizens who strongly identify themselves with their national community are seen as losers (Kriesi *et al.* 2006: 922).

## *Analysis of partisanship*

For the analysis of partisanship in the German context, it is therefore important to locate party voting with respect to the major structuring cleavages. But following the IMO protocol, we also want to test the relevance of potential new conflicts. There are various solutions for this aim. A first possibility is to classify voters on the basis of positions taken by the political parties they voted for. One generally accepted method is the use of party manifesto data (Budge *et al.* 2001; Klingemann *et al.* 2006), which allows a positioning of political parties on the left-right dimension. Indeed, results for the positioning of single parties on the left-right dimension yields a picture that is quite congruent with previous knowledge (see Table A7.3(a) in the Appendix to this chapter). However, for two reasons the application of the party manifesto data is not useful. First, the information disallows any classification for the Republicans and other parties in Germany; secondly, for the new cleavages it is doubtful if the same procedure allows a meaningful classification of party positions with respect to globalisation issues. Therefore, we prefer to use the left-right self-placement of party voters surveyed in post-election studies for our analyses, as well as voter positions on left-right issues. All in all, the operationalisation of voting patterns covers four measures of left-right wing location. Namely, the left-right self-placement of voters based on the European Social Survey 2002/2003 and 2004/2005, as well as on party voter positions on culture, economic and globalisation issues. Following the IMO protocol, it is useful to distinguish between different policy dimensions of the left-right orientation of party voters. For instance, support for fiscally-conservative (right-wing in economic terms) policies may be expected in wealthy urban concentrations and affluent suburbs. But more support for socially-conservative (right-wing in social terms) policies may be expected in low-density suburbs at a greater distance from the centre (See Chapter 1).

We built our indexes on the basis of post-electoral surveys analysing answers of supporters of political parties (see Table A7.4 in the Appendix to this chapter and Chapter 14, the Methodological Appendix). Figure 7.3 uses the example of results for Green Party voters to demonstrate the need to differentiate left-right self-placement along various policy dimensions.[11] The positions for cultural

---

11. The correlation results of the left-right self-placement and the different issue positions also

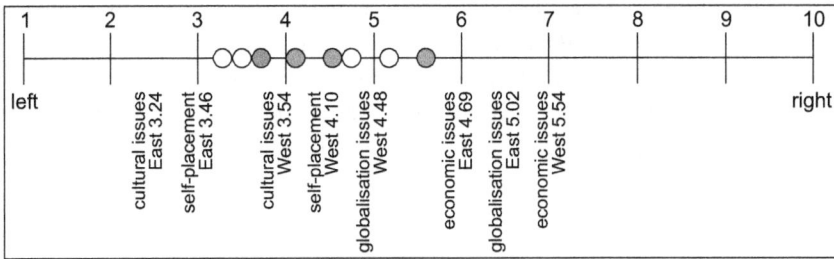

*Figure 7.3: Left-right self-placement for voters of the Green party (Alliance 90/ The Greens)*

*Source*: Left-right self-placement of voters: ESS 2002/2003 and 2004/2005; positions on culture, economic and globalisation issues based on Green Party voter responses draws on post-electoral surveys and questions.

issues are further left than the classical left-right self-placement of the Green Party voters would indicate. The positions for economic and globalisation issues are otherwise less to the left and more liberal than the left-right self-placement. With the exception of the globalisation issue – where Eastern Green Party voters support more nationalism than their Western counterparts – the Green voters in East Germany consistently adopt a more left position than the Green voters in West Germany.

The same pattern occurs for most positions adopted by the five major parties represented in the German Bundestag, with two exceptions: the Western PDS voters place themselves clearly more left support more for state control on economic issues than the Eastern PDS voters. The overall position on left-right economic issues reflects the far left position of PDS voters (preference for state control) and the voters of FDP and Christian democrats (preference for free market), whereas the voters of the Green Party and the SPD are located in between these two positions. Regarding cultural issues, the PDS and the Green Party voters are most in favour of social liberalism and the Christian Democrats for social conservatism, whereas the voters of SPD and FDP are in between. In relation to globalisation issues, the five government parties do not differ very much. The globalisation process is most likely supported by voters of the Green Party, while nationalism is most likely supported by the voters of CDU/CSU; the other three parties are in between these two positions.

The units of analysis for the following sections of this chapter are not the different party voters but the aggregate position of the municipality. For this reason it is necessary to state whether the mean voter orientation in a municipality

---

punctuated this procedure. With the exception of globalisation issue positions, which show – especially in East Germany – a very high correlation with the classical left-right self-placement, the measurements are relatively independent from each other (see Table A7.3(b) in the Appendix to this chapter).

is more left or right – generally and regarding cultural, economic and globalisation issues. Following the IMO protocol, we only refer to issue positions on the national level. The local parties in the federal state of Germany differ too much to be assigned consistent party voter positions. Another problem is the participation of the nonpartisan Free Voter Associations, which can hardly be classified in this manner, in local elections.

## Political participation in metropolitan areas

Traditionally, local government has been regarded as the place where public participation in the political process may be organised most efficiently and hence where the ideal of an open and responsive government may be more readily achieved (Gabriel and Eisenmann 2005). As a consequence of the widespread suburbanisation process, the local unit has expanded to a metropolitan space, which has to be differentiated into various communal types. The theoretical assumptions and empirical results of metropolitan research in North America indicate an interrelationship between living area and political behaviour. When it comes to the implications of suburbanisation for political participation, the research outline given in the introduction of Chapter 1 to this volume displays – theoretically as well as empirically – wide disagreement. Now we will examine the patterns of national and local turnout as well as of national voting decisions in the German metropolitan areas and see if they show uniformity (thesis of nationalisation) or diversity (thesis of metropolitanisation), or as some might say: 'tell me where you live, and I will tell you (if) how you vote'.

### *Uniformity or diversity of voter turnout and decisions in German metropolitan areas*

In a first step, this contribution briefly compares mean values for voter turnout and decisions observable at the community level of our sample. This helps to clarify whether, following variations in the type and structure of communities, different voting patterns become apparent. Despite the well-known pre-eminence of socio-economic and institutional determinants in Germany, 'place' seems in some cases to matter for the community's political behaviour and orientations. Indeed, the question where or, more precisely, in which kind of community one lives has a strong effect on the local voter turnout in West Germany (eta 0.52, see Table 7.3(a)) and a moderate impact on the other dependent variables under scrutiny (eta values between 0.12 and 0.35).[12] This is the case, if we use the means of each municipality for the partisanship results. All in all, the total amounts of variance

---

12. See the variance analyses for the positions on economic, culture and globalisation issues in post-election survey in Table WA7.3 in the Web Appendix, http://press.ecpr.eu/resources.

for the partisanship variables are very low.[13]

To simplify the interpretation, we add further information to the overview of voting decisions in the national election 2002 and last local elections since 2003 (see Table 7.3(b)), namely the percentage differences of votes between left parties (PDS, Greens, SPD) and liberal and conservative parties (FDP, CDU, CSU, NPD, REP) in the communal types. The negative signs indicate a more or less majority of left parties; positive signs indicate a majority of liberal and right parties. The alternative operationalisation indicates no change for the national model, but change for the local model. Using the first measurement, we see a clear underestimation of the impact of metropolitanisation and a distinct higher variance between the communal types. This is caused by a greater number of parties at the local level and a greater share of those party groups summarised in the category 'other parties'. The consequence is a higher variance in the dependent variable – 'voting decision last local election since 2003' – and a more valid answer to the question of whether people in metropolitan areas vote for those parties in Germany that are more left, liberal or right.

It is worthwhile noting that the pattern and the strength of that relationship between place and politics is far from being uniform. As a rule of thumb, the socio-economic structure of the community seems to be associated more strongly with the voter turnout than with the political orientation (eta ranging from 0.20 to 0.52 compared to 0.12 to 0.43 for voting decisions). Furthermore, the influence of metropolitan political ecology seems to be slightly higher in local elections than in national ones.

In the North American discussion, affluent suburbs are seen as the stronghold of modern conservatism. If we take a closer look at our findings, we also find some support for this contention in Germany. Affluent suburbs do indeed tend to be 'more conservative', i.e. tend to vote for parties to the right compared to urban concentrations, especially on the national level and in East Germany. Differences between affluent and middle-class suburbs are however smaller than expected. In national elections, together with low-density suburbs, affluent communities seem to generate a greater voter turnout than other metropolitan communities. This would – to a certain extent – back up Oliver's findings (2000), who claimed that affluent suburbs, because their size is likely to be smaller, bring about stronger social networks, thereby lowering the barriers for political participation. One could argue that the same is true for low-density suburbs, where a more rural structure might also lead to greater social and political integration.

The most interesting insight these preliminary analyses allow us to grasp is, that in more than twenty years since German reunification, regional trends persist. The overall participation in East Germany remains lower than in the Western Laender and there a stronger preference for the political left – especially

---

13. Standard deviations range from 0.03 to 0.24 in West Germany and from 0.04 to 0.72 in East Germany.

*Table 7.3(a): Turnout in national election 2002 and last local election since 2003*

**Turnout in national election 2002**

| | West Germany | | East Germany | |
|---|---|---|---|---|
| | % | N | % | N |
| Urban concentrations | 78.8 | 27 | 73.3 | 11 |
| Low density suburbs | 81.1 | 193 | 72.6 | 71 |
| Affluent suburbs | 82.8 | 165 | 73.5 | 63 |
| Middle class suburbs | 81.5 | 263 | 73.5 | 100 |
| Poor suburbs | 80.3 | 141 | 71.3 | 129 |
| Total | 81.4 | 789 | 72.6 | 374 |
| eta | *0.32* | | *0.20* | |

| ANOVA | West Germany | | | | | East Germany | | | | |
|---|---|---|---|---|---|---|---|---|---|---|
| | sum of squares | df | variance | f | sign. | sum of squares | df | variance | f | sign. |
| Between groups | 721.75 | 4 | 10% | 21.53 | 0.000 | 363.96 | 4 | 4% | 3.97 | 0.004 |
| Within groups | 6571.95 | 784 | 90% | | | 8459.03 | 369 | 96% | | |
| total | 7293.69 | 788 | | | | 8822.98 | 373 | | | |

**Turnout in last local election since 2003**

| | West Germany | | East Germany | |
|---|---|---|---|---|
| | % | N | % | N |
| Urban concentrations | 50.2 | 27 | 49.9 | 11 |
| Low density suburbs | 62.9 | 192 | 61.0 | 70 |
| Affluent suburbs | 60.0 | 165 | 56.4 | 63 |
| Middle class suburbs | 55.9 | 263 | 57.2 | 99 |
| Poor suburbs | 56.0 | 141 | 54.8 | 128 |
| Total | 58.3 | 788 | 56.7 | 371 |
| eta | *0.52* | | *0.28* | |

| ANOVA | West Germany | | | | | East Germany | | | | |
|---|---|---|---|---|---|---|---|---|---|---|
| | sum of squares | df | variance | f | sign. | sum of squares | df | variance | f | sign. |
| Between groups | 8498.02 | 4 | 27% | 72.83 | 0.000 | 2326.34 | 4 | 8% | 7.47 | 0.000 |
| Within groups | 22839.54 | 783 | 73% | | | 28513.21 | 366 | 92% | | |
| Total | 31337.56 | 787 | | | | 30839.54 | 370 | | | |

*Notes:* for boldface eta coefficients, p<0.05; for boldface italicised eta coefficients, p<0.01.
*Source:* voter turnout: IMO Data Set 2003.

Table 7.3(b): *Voting decision national election 2002 and last local election since 2003 (mean left-right self placement in post-election survey and percentage difference between left and liberal/right parties)*

*Voting decision national election 2002 (mean left-right self-placement in post-election survey and percentage difference between left and liberal/right parties)*

| | West Germany | | | East Germany | | |
|---|---|---|---|---|---|---|
| | **Mean** | % | N | **Mean** | % | N |
| Urban concentrations | 5.30 | -4.7 | 27 | 4.72 | -27.1 | 11 |
| Low-density suburbs | 5.49 | 10.4 | 193 | 4.87 | -16.6 | 71 |
| Affluent suburbs | 5.43 | 6.4 | 165 | 4.86 | -17.0 | 63 |
| Middle class suburbs | 5.38 | 1.6 | 263 | 4.92 | -11.8 | 100 |
| Poor suburbs | 5.39 | 1.5 | 141 | 4.85 | -18.8 | 129 |
| Total | 5.42 | 4.5 | 789 | 4.87 | -16.5 | 374 |
| eta | **0.28** | **0.27** | | **0.18** | **0.18** | |

| ANOVA | sum of squares | df | variance | f | sign. | sum of squares | df | variance | f | sign. |
|---|---|---|---|---|---|---|---|---|---|---|
| Between groups | 1.75 | 4 | 8% | 16.79 | 0.000 | 0.58 | 4 | 3% | 3.03 | 0.018 |
| Within groups | 20.40 | 784 | 92% | | | 17.61 | 369 | 97% | | |
| Total | 22.14 | 788 | | | | 18.19 | 373 | | | |

Table 7.3(b): Continued

*Voting decision last local election since 2003 (left-right self-placement in post-election survey and percentage difference between left and liberal/right parties)*

| | West Germany | | | East Germany | | |
|---|---|---|---|---|---|---|
| | Mean | % | N | Mean | % | N |
| Urban concentrations | 5.52 | 25.6 | 27 | 5.06 | −7.8 | 11 |
| Low-density suburbs | 5.55 | 57.8 | 183 | 6.05 | 46.1 | 70 |
| Affluent suburbs | 5.57 | 59.1 | 164 | 5.46 | 15.9 | 63 |
| Middle-class suburbs | 5.51 | 32.8 | 263 | 5.68 | 16.0 | 99 |
| Poor suburbs | 5.49 | 29.3 | 141 | 5.71 | 15.2 | 128 |
| Total | 5.53 | 43.3 | 778 | 5.70 | 20.7 | 371 |
| eta | *0.12* | *0.36* | | *0.30* | *0.43* | |

| ANOVA | variance (self-placement/ difference) | sum of squares | df | f | sign. | variance (self-placement/ difference) | sum of squares | df | f | sign. |
|---|---|---|---|---|---|---|---|---|---|---|
| Between groups | 2%/13% | 0.65 | 4 | 2.92 | 0.021/0.000 | 9%/18% | 16.97 | 4 | 8.94 | 0.000 |
| Within groups | 98%/87% | 43.21 | 773 | | | 91%/82% | 173.64 | 366 | | |
| Total | | 43.86 | 777 | | | | 190.61 | 370 | | |

*Notes:* For boldface eta coefficients, p<.05; for boldface italicised eta coefficients, p<.01.

*Source voting decision:* European Social Survey, means of 2002/2003 and 2004/2005. Originally used scale was: 0 to 10 scale where 0 meant extreme left, 10 extreme right, but for better comparability we have converted it to a 1–10 scale.

in national elections – is observable. Metropolitan patterns, as described above, do exercise their influence in some cases under scrutiny, but seem to be part of the more general divide between the West and the East. These findings concur with our first IMO contribution, which highlighted the distinct gap between West and East settlement structures (Walter-Rogg 2005). These results also confirm the thesis of psephology whereby Germany has different electorates in both parts of the country (Eith 1997; Dalton and Bürklin 1996; Arzheimer and Falter 1998). If we take all this into account, these intra-metropolitan comparisons clarify the importance of a community's socio-economic background for its voter turnout and decisions. This impact appears to be higher when local issues are at stake, which reinforces the contention that local voting patterns are not merely a duplication of national ones, but obey their own rules.

For the type of multivariate analysis not only intra-metropolitan, but inter-metropolitan differences in political participation and partisanship are important as well. In the United States there is a polarisation between 'red' (Republican) and 'blue' (Democratic) Americas. Chapter 2 of this volume shows that metropolitan areas reflect these regional contrasts, as well as the distinctive propensities of metropolitan areas themselves. Following the results of various electoral studies in Germany, we see a two-party system in the Western part, with polarisation between the Christian Democrats (CDU) and Social Democrats (SPD), and a three-party system in the Eastern part, with polarisation between these two parties and the PDS (Crow 2001: 243). This again validates our approach to separate the analyses for West and East Germany. It is a matter of whether all of the variations in participation and partisanship occur similarly within rather than between metropolitan areas. An analysis of variance that compares metropolitan and local variations in the dependent variables shows the extent of the difference for Germany (see Table 7.3(a) and 7.3(b)).

The variation in national and local turnout varies between 4 per cent and 27 per cent between metropolitan areas referring to the different political levels in the two parts of Germany. Among the fourteen metropolitan areas in West Germany, 8 per cent of the variation in national partisanship and 2 per cent (left-right self-placement) respectively and 13 per cent (percentage difference between left and liberal/right parties) in local partisanship ran between metropolitan areas rather than within them. Among the seven metropolitan areas in East Germany, this partisanship variation is only 3 per cent on the national level and 9 per cent (left-right self-placement) respectively 18 per cent (percentage difference between left and liberal/right parties) on the local level.

Following the IMO protocol, the focus of the following analyses will be the national level. In doing this we have to consider that the variation between metro-politan areas for the other three dependent variables positions on cultural, economic and globalisation issues are distinctly higher in West Germany than in East Germany (see Table WA7.3 in the Web Appendix). For all the dependent variables, a huge amount of the variance occurs within metropolitan areas. But in each case, the variance between groups is important enough to attain clear statistical significance.

Ordinary least squares regressions confirmed different pictures for national and local elections as well as for West and East Germany (see Table WA7.4(a) to WA7.6 in the Web Appendix). For both parts of the country, the analyses for the national level indicate albeit to different degrees – lower turnout rates in urban concentrations, poor and low-density suburbs, and higher turnout in affluent suburbs.[14] In contrast, the participation for the last local election since 2003 is distinctly lower in urban concentrations and distinctly higher in low-density suburbs. In the old federal states the turnout rate is clearly higher in affluent suburbs and slightly higher in poor suburbs, whereas in the new federal states the local rate is clearly lower in poor suburbs and slightly lower in affluent suburbs. In West Germany, the communal types accounted for 27 per cent of the variation in the last local election, but only 9 per cent for the national election 2002. In East Germany, the communal types have lower explanatory power for these two dependent variables with 7 per cent of the variation in the last local election and only 3 per cent in the national election 2002.

The models for the electoral margins of the parties in the national election are also more powerful in West Germany than in East Germany, but in local elections the communal types explain more (17 per cent) of the Eastern variation. Although ordinary least squares regressions confirmed numerous hypotheses, they did not allow full exploration of the clear regional and metropolitan variations. Because hierarchical linear models provided the most complete accounts, the following discussion will focus on these results.

### Multilevel explanation of voter turnout and decisions in German metropolitan areas

The preliminary findings encouraged us to take a closer look at the interplay of local and metropolitan structural variables via multilevel modelling.[15] To do so, we selected those communities that are part of a metropolitan area and created a multilevel file that brought together their socio-economic structure with a number of structural characteristics of the metropolitan areas in which the communities are rooted in. In fact, multilevel modelling seems particularly appropriate to capture the political reality of metropolitan areas. Localities do not exist in a political and socio-economic vacuum, but are embedded in a larger socio-economic context that is likely to influence local voting patterns.

Our presentation unfolds in two steps. First, we will successively develop multilevel models for all dependent variables. Starting from empty models, which

---

14. The models used as a reference point of middle-class suburbs, which were excluded fin order to avoid a linear dependency between the five dummy variables of communal types (see Treiman 2009).

15. The multilevel analyses were conducted with Stata.

estimate the dependent variable over all level-1 and level-2 units, we will introduce the effects of context as well as cross-level effects. The latter are designed to reveal the regional differences between the Eastern and Western metropolitan areas. Because of the limited number of fourteen metropolitan areas in the West and seven in the East, it is impossible to separate the multilevel models for both parts of the country. Therefore, we use a regional dummy variable on the metropolitan level.

Secondly, we shall briefly summarise the most important and common findings of our multilevel tests.[16]

### Political ecology – national and local voter turnout

All in all, for national and local turnout the contextual model fits better than the compositional model (see Table 7.4). But the full model is in each case better than the other models. Our first model tries to identify the principal determinants for the national voter turnout as observable on the community level. Contrary to the findings for local voter turnout we see significantly lower participation in East Germany (73 per cent) than in West Germany (82 per cent). In addition, the concentration of a metropolitan area is relevant for all three models. The less consolidated the metro area, the higher the local participation. Stable compositional effects are given for the variables 'SES hardship' and 'residents over 65 years'. The lower the hardship index and the number of retirees, the higher is the participation in national elections. In both turnout models the share of foreign-born residents decreases political participation in the compositional model, but the effect disappears in the full model. Two contextual variables have a negative impact on national voter turnout: size and distance to the centre. The share of out-commuters and the stability of residence have a slightly positive effect.

In the case of local voter turnout, the regional differentiation is not relevant. The participation in the last local election since 2003 is relatively low in both parts of the country, namely 58 per cent in the West and 57 per cent in the East. But two other variables on the metropolitan level influence the participation in local elections: fragmentation and concentration. The less fragmented and the more concentrated the metropolitan area, the higher is the local turnout rate. A stable influence is given – in the compositional as well as in the full model – by number of families and retirees in a municipality. The more families and retirees, the higher is the local voter turnout. Furthermore we can see three stable contextual effects – population size and suburbanisation are counterproductive and the stability of residence slightly productive for local participation. Increasing size and density have a negative impact and increasing population growth has a positive impact for local voter turnout.

---

16. Due to the fact that the variables 'manufacturing occupation' and 'economic diversity' indicate a relatively high number of non-responses, they were excluded from the multilevel analyses.

*Table 7.4: Determinants of national and local election turnout (multilevel model)*

| | National election turnout 2002 | | | | | | Local election turnout | | | | | |
| | Compositional model | | Contextual model | | Full model | | Compositional model | | Contextual model | | Full model | |
| | coeff. | s.e. | coeff. | s.e. | coeff. | s.e. | coeff. | s.e. | coeff. | s.e. | coeff. | s.e. |
|---|---|---|---|---|---|---|---|---|---|---|---|---|
| Constant | *92.72* | 11.59 | *81.94* | 10.96 | *82.83* | 10.78 | *49.68* | 16.75 | *108.70* | 17.64 | *95.39* | 16.90 |
| *Local level* | | | | | | | | | | | | |
| *Compositional effects* | | | | | | | | | | | | |
| Foreign born (%) | *-0.181* | 0.024 | | | -0.011 | 0.026 | *-0.541* | 0.048 | | | -0.014 | 0.045 |
| SES Hardship (index) | *-0.096* | 0.012 | | | *-0.086* | 0.011 | *-0.089* | 0.023 | | | *0.070* | 0.020 |
| University degree (%) | *-3.34E-9* | 1.44E-9 | | | -3.45E-9 | 2.56E-9 | -3.71E-9 | 3.26E-9 | | | *-8.16E-9* | 4.44E-9 |
| Residents under 18 years (%) | -0.106 | 0.062 | | | -0.062 | 0.063 | *1.017* | 0.124 | | | *0.237* | 0.109 |
| Residents over 65 years (%) | *-0.387* | 0.046 | | | *-0.101* | 0.046 | 0.175 | 0.092 | | | *0.229* | 0.080 |
| *Contextual effects* | | | | | | | | | | | | |
| Population (ln) | | | *-0.502* | 0.163 | -0.088 | 0.170 | | | *-4.097* | 0.276 | *-3.644* | 0.295 |
| Density (ln) | | | 0.052 | 0.150 | -0.211 | 0.155 | | | *-1.051* | 0.254 | *-1.247* | 0.270 |
| Stability of residence (1993-2003) | | | *0.036* | 0.007 | *0.021* | 0.008 | | | *0.046* | 0.013 | *0.042* | 0.015 |
| Out-commuting (%) | | | *0.093* | 0.011 | *0.109* | 0.011 | | | -0.009 | 0.018 | 0.020 | 0.020 |
| Distance to the centre (index) | | | *-0.804* | 0.141 | *-0.613* | 0.145 | | | -0.196 | 0.240 | -0.170 | 0.251 |
| *Metropolitan level* | | | | | | | | | | | | |
| Eastern Germany metro | *-9.610* | 1.820 | *-8.497* | 1.712 | *-8.462* | 1.669 | -0.244 | 2.629 | -2.528 | 2.756 | -1.711 | 2.611 |
| Metropolitan population | -0.051 | 0.598 | -0.320 | 0.568 | -0.293 | 0.547 | 0.139 | 0.843 | 0.081 | 0.912 | 0.118 | 0.850 |
| Fragmentation (Zeigler Brunn) | -0.948 | 0.611 | -1.054 | 0.580 | -0.952 | 0.559 | -0.787 | 0.868 | *-1.918* | 0.932 | *-1.837* | 0.871 |

| | National election turnout 2002 | | | | | | Local election turnout | | | | | |
| | Compositional model | | Contextual model | | Full model | | Compositional model | | Contextual model | | Full model | |
| | coeff. | s.e. | coeff. | s.e. | coeff. | s.e. | coeff. | s.e. | coeff. | s.e. | coeff. | s.e. |
| Concentration (Herfindahl) | **−12.810** | 5.616 | ***14.490*** | 5.330 | ***−13.460*** | 5.138 | −10.720 | 7.944 | **−19.420** | 8.560 | **−18.120** | 7.985 |
| Polarisation | 0.163 | 0.143 | 0.073 | 0.135 | 0.139 | 0.131 | −0.072 | 0.204 | −0.087 | 0.218 | −0.040 | 0.204 |
| *Variance components* | | | | | | | | | | | | |
| Local level | **7.878** | 0.341 | **6.698** | 0.283 | **6.698** | 0.283 | ***30.781*** | 1.336 | ***19.205*** | 0.813 | ***18.693*** | 0.812 |
| Metropolitan area-level | ***3.822*** | 1.284 | ***3.456*** | 1.146 | ***3.198*** | 1.066 | **7.253** | 2.609 | **8.856** | 2.945 | ***7.614*** | 2.572 |
| −2 log likelihood | −2693.7 | | −2729.9 | | −2558.44 | | −3417.27 | | −3322.33 | | −3146.66 | |
| Variance explained (pseudo R²) | 65.6% | | 70.1% | | 72.3% | | 32.4% | | 48.8% | | 52.2% | |
| Local level | 20.7% | | 54.4% | | 37.5% | | 26.9% | | 54.4% | | 55.6% | |
| Metropolitan area-level | 82.0% | | 35.0% | | 85.0% | | 45.7% | | 35.0% | | 43.9% | |
| N local level | 1086 | | 1138 | | 1083 | | 1083 | | 1136 | | 1081 | |
| N metropolitan area-level | 21 | | 21 | | 21 | | 21 | | 21 | | 21 | |

*Notes*: Table entries are unstandardised maximum likelihood (IGLS) estimates with estimated standard errors. For italicised coefficients, $p<0.10$; for boldface coefficients, $p<0.05$; for boldface italicised coeffients, $p<0.01$.

## Political ecology and decisions in national elections

After dealing with voter turnout, we turn our attention to voting decisions (see Table 7.5). Contrary to the first two models, the unstandardised coefficients are incredibly low; therefore, the level of explained variance is not reliable in the partisanship models. Standardised coefficients would surely minimise the problem, but are not intended by the IMO report. So the following model interpretation refers mainly to the given signs and significance levels of the variables and only to the full models of the multilevel analyses. The overall picture of the four dependent variables of voting decisions illustrates the stable importance of three compositional effects (SES Hardship, number of families, number of retirees), three contextual effects (population size, suburbanisation, stability of residence) and of the regional difference between East and West Germany. Referring to the specific operationalisation of the four dependent variables, the effects of the independent variables have the following implications with regards to content.

For the left-right self-placement in national elections, we see that municipalities with a high rate of families and retirees and increasing stability of residence vote more right. Density and population growth in the communities increase the preference for left parties. And Eastern communities vote more for left parties than Western communities. Regarding the left-right positions of economic issues, the patterns are very similar to the former models apart from the effect of the socio-economic hardship, which is now stable, and the population growth, which is now not relevant. Municipalities with a high hardship index and population density increase are rather in favour of state control in economic issues. Contrary to that, municipalities with a high rate of families or retirees rate are in favour of a free market model. In this model, the regional difference on the metro level is also relevant. Thus, communities in the new Eastern Laender support more state control than communities in the old Western Laender, which prefer a free market.

With regard to cultural issue positions, the multilevel analysis indicates some interesting interconnections. The higher the socio-economic hardship and the more families and retirees in a community, the more support there is for social conservatism. Also, density, population growth and the share of out-commuting in the communities increase the support for cultural liberalism. This confirms the classic suburbanisation thesis: when people live in urban concentrations, it is more likely that they have liberal orientations; when people live in the suburbs, it is more likely that they have conservative orientations. It is not necessarily a consequence of duration, but a consequence of social segregation. The one and only metro effect is the same as the regional difference: communities in the new Eastern Laender display more cultural liberalism than Western municipalities.

Concerning issues of globalisation, compositional influence is given by the level of hardship, the number of families and retirees, the rate of out-commuting and the distance to the centre. The more socio-economic hardship, families and retirees in a municipality, the more support there is for nationalism. The contextual variables of population growth, density, out-commuting and distance to the centre make a difference: the greater the population growth, density and out-commuting

*Table 7.5: Determinants of left-right self-placement in national elections (1 left to 10 right), position on economic (1 state control to 10 free market), cultural (1 social liberalism to 10 social conservatism) and globalisation issues nationally (1 support globalisation to 10 support nationalism)*

| | Left-right self-placement Full model | | Economic issues Full model | | Cultural issues Full model | | Globalisation issues Full model | |
|---|---|---|---|---|---|---|---|---|
| | coeff. | s.e. | coeff. | s.e. | coeff. | s.e. | coeff. | s.e. |
| Constant | *6.037* | 0.745 | *5.810* | 0.143 | *4.907* | 0.243 | *5.531* | 0.261 |
| *Local level variables* | | | | | | | | |
| *Compositional effects* | | | | | | | | |
| Foreign born (%) | −0.001 | 0.001 | −2.90E-4 | 0.000 | −0.001 | 0.001 | −2.27E-4 | 3.88E-4 |
| SES Hardship (index) | 0.001 | 0.000 | *−4.32E-4* | 1.03E-4 | *0.001* | 2.06E-4 | *0.001* | 1.68E-4 |
| University degree (%) | 0.000 | 1.05E-10 | −0.000 | 0.000 | −0.000 | 0.000 | 0.000 | 0.000 |
| Residents under 18 years (%) | *0.019* | 0.003 | *0.002* | 0.001 | *0.010* | 0.001 | *0.010* | 0.001 |
| Residents over 65 years (%) | *0.007* | 0.002 | *0.001* | 4.21E-4 | *0.004* | 0.001 | *0.003* | 0.001 |
| *Contextual effects* | | | | | | | | |
| Population (ln) | *−0.019* | 0.007 | −0.001 | 0.002 | *−0.011* | 0.003 | *−0.012* | 0.003 |
| Density (ln) | *−0.031* | 0.006 | *−0.007* | 0.001 | *−0.009* | 0.003 | *−0.005* | 0.002 |
| Stability of residence (1993–2003) | *0.002* | 0.000 | *0.001* | 7.68E-5 | *0.001* | 1.54E-4 | 8.10E-6 | 1.26E-4 |
| Out-commuting (%) | −0.001 | 0.001 | −1.84E-5 | 1.03E-4 | *−0.001* | 2.06E-4 | *−0.001* | 1.69E-4 |
| Distance to the centre (index) | 2.86E-4 | 0.006 | −0.002 | 0.001 | 0.003 | 0.003 | **0.006** | 0.002 |
| *Metropolitan area level variables* | | | | | | | | |
| Eastern Germany metro | *−0.371* | 0.116 | *−0.995* | 0.022 | *−1.037* | 0.038 | *0.399* | 0.041 |
| Metropolitan population | −0.010 | 0.039 | −0.003 | 0.007 | −0.006 | 0.013 | −0.002 | 0.014 |
| Fragmentation (Zeigler Brunn) | −0.009 | 0.040 | −0.004 | 0.007 | −0.013 | 0.013 | −0.010 | 0.014 |
| Concentration (Herfindahl) | −0.379 | 0.364 | −0.071 | 0.069 | −0.192 | 0.117 | −0.183 | 0.127 |
| Polarisation | −0.012 | 0.009 | −0.002 | 0.002 | −0.002 | 0.003 | −0.001 | 0.003 |
| *Variance components* | | | | | | | | |
| Local level | *0.016* | 0.005 | *0.005* | 0.00002 | *0.002* | 0.00009 | *0.001* | 0.00006 |
| Metropolitan area-level | *0.010* | 0.000 | *0.000* | 0.000 | *0.0001* | 0.001 | *0.002* | 0.0006 |
| −2 log likelihood | | 889.35 | | 2518.44 | | 1768.39 | | 1980.01 |

| | Left-right self-placement Full model | Economic issues Full model | Cultural issues Full model | Globalisation issues Full model |
|---|---|---|---|---|
| Variance explained (pseudo R2) | 77.7 % | n/a | n/a | n/a |
| Local level | 66.9 % | n/a | n/a | n/a |
| Metropolitan area-level | 80.7 % | n/a | n/a | n/a |
| N local level | 1083 | 1083 | 1083 | 1083 |
| N metropolitan area-level | 21 | 21 | 21 | 21 |

*Notes:* Table entries are unstandardised maximum likelihood (IGLS) estimates with estimated standard errors. For italicised coefficients, p<0.10; for boldface coefficients, p<0.05; for boldface italicised coeffients, p<0.01.

in a community, the more support there is for the globalisation process. The greater the distance to the centre, the more support for nationalism. On the metropolitan level, people in the East are more likely to support nationalism than globalisation compared to the people living in the West.

## Overview and conclusion

If we view all the evidence gathered by our multilevel modelling, a complex and intriguing picture emerges. First, it is encouraging to observe that place matters. Given the sheer weight individual socio-economic and psychological variables have in the process of determining one's vote, it must be seen as a success that our structural variables capture quite well what is going on in the metro ballots. Therefore, the thesis of metropolitanisation can be confirmed for Germany, with the proviso that the real impact varies greatly between national to local elections and between how much a community turns out and how it actually votes. Our models were more powerful for explaining why communities collectively vote than for analysing whether they prefer left, right or centrist parties. Furthermore, the influence of metropolitan political ecology seems to be slightly higher in local elections than in national ones. Additionally, we have to keep in mind that all our results translate to collective preferences only. Given the current data constraints, we are some way from building a multilevel model that would incorporate individual, community and metropolitan variables in order to determine their relative weight.

Secondly, there is something like a truly metropolitan pattern of voter turnout and decisions. Most of our results provide support for the idea that size and democracy are intimately linked. Voter turnout is highest in communities whose size is below average. It can easily be assumed that these smaller political units manage to create substantial networks of social and political integration, thereby affecting the distribution of individual resources positively. Eventually, this seems to increase the overall participation. With regard to the political colour of a community, affluent, middle-class and low-density suburbs clearly are more likely to vote in favour of conservative parties, whereas the urban concentrations appear to be strongholds of the left.

Thirdly, our empirical results more or less confirmed the hypotheses developed by the IMO research group. Contextual as well as compositional effects help to explain voter turnout and electoral behaviour in our metropolitan areas. It is observable that the suburbanisation process has a political impact. The partisanship analysis indicate that high population density and population growth in the communities increase a preference for economic positions on the left, and support for cultural liberalism and the globalisation process. Simultaneously, and this is shown by the turnout analysis, the suburbanisation process leads to a delocalisation (the local voter turnout is mainly influenced by contextual variables, more so than the national voter turnout) and to a general political disengagement (the national voter turnout is also influenced by contextual effects).

Fourthly, taking into account the regional difference between East and West Germany distinctly increases the explanatory power of our models. This translates into two realities. On the one hand, when it comes to issues as complex as voting, it makes no sense to consider communities on their own, but to see them embedded in a larger socio-economic context, an influence that is yet to be fully explored. On the other hand, the divide between East and West Germany continues to mark political life in the metropolis. Most relationships between independent and dependent variables are somehow moderated by the difference between East and West. The voters in the new German Laender vote more to the left, trust the state more regarding economic issues, are more liberal in cultural issues, but are less open-minded towards the globalisation process.

Finally, the fact that different determinants affect local and national voting patterns brings us back to the initial controversy about the 'autonomy' of local elections. In the light of our findings, we tend to believe that truly local issues are mainly affected by structural local variables and the 'close (metropolitan) context'.

Obviously, our design does not allow for any speculations about metropolitan or locality effects on individual predictors of voter turnout and decisions. Nevertheless, the natural next step seems to be to bridge that divide by building ambitious multilevel models that account for individual, local and metropolitan variables. The obstacles we confronted in constructing our database for this chapter lead us to believe that in Germany this endeavour may most likely take the form of detailed case studies, in which we combine micro-political knowledge with macro-political innovation.

What shall the answer be to our slogan 'Tell me where you live, and I'll tell you if (how) you vote'? At the beginning of this chapter, we asked to what extent the socio-political structure of a community affects the community's voter turnout and the voting decisions in German metropolitan areas. We can affirm that political ecology matters – moderately, but certainly. The political ecology of the metropolis, in particular the interaction between metropolitan and local variables, does affect the level of participation and to a lesser extent the decisions taken on an election day. This trend may not be as strong as in the United States, but to discover new valid predictors in a field as well explored as electoral studies is incentive enough to travel further down this road.

## Bibliography

Arzheimer, K. and Falter, J. W. (1998) 'Annäherung durch Wandel? Das Ergebnis der Bundestagswahl 1998 aus Ost-West-Perspektive', *Aus Politik und Zeitgeschichte* 48/B52: 33–43.

Books, J. and Prysby, C. (1988) 'Studying contextual effects on political behaviour: a research inventory and agenda', *American Politics Quarterly*, 16: 211–38.

Boustedt, O. (1970) 'Zum Konzept der Stadtregionen. Methoden und Probleme der Abgrenzung von Agglomerationsräumen', *Raum und Bevölkerung – Forschungsberichte des Ausschusses' Raum und Bevölkerung' der Akademie für Raumforschung und Landesplanung* 10.

Budge, I., Klingemann, H. -D., Volkens, A., Bara, J., Tannenbaum, E., Fording, R., Hearl, D., Hee Min, Kim, McDonald, M. and Mendes, S. (eds) (2001) *Mapping Policy Preferences: Estimates for Parties, Electors, and Governments 1945–1998*, Oxford: Oxford University Press.

Busch, M. (1997) 'Politische Themen und Wahlverhalten', in O. W. Gabriel, F. Brettschneider and A. Vetter (eds) *Politische Kultur und Wahlverhalten in einer Großstadt*, Opladen: Westdeutscher Verlag, 181–201.

Crow, K. (2001) 'Regionen und Wahlen. Eine ökologische Wahlanalyse für Sachsen-Anhalt 1990–1998', in B. Boll and E. Holtmann (eds) *Parteien und Parteimitglieder in der Region*, Opladen: Westdeutscher Verlag, 235–85.

Czarnecki, T. (1992) *Kommunales Wahlverhalten. Die Existenz und Bedeutsamkeit kommunaler Determinanten für das Wahlverhalten. Eine Empirische Untersuchung am Beispiel Rheinland-Pfalz*, München: Minerva.

Dalton, R. J. and Bürklin, W. (1995) 'The two German electorates: the social bases of the vote in 1990 and 1994', *German Politics and Society*, 13: 75–99.

— (1996) 'The Two German Electorates', in Dalton, R. J. (ed.) *Germans Divided. The 1994 Bundestag Elections and the Evolution of the German Party System*, Oxford/Washington, D.C.: Berg.

Dreier, P., Mollenkopf, J. and Swanstrom, T. (2001) *Place Matters: Metropolitics for the Twenty-First Century*, Lawrence, Kansas: University of Kansas Press.

Eith, U. (1997) 'Kommunales Wahlverhalten in Ost- und Westdeutschland', in O. W. Gabriel (ed.) *Politische Orientierungen und Verhaltensweisen im vereinigten Deutschland*, Opladen: Leske + Budrich, 377–400.

Eriksson, K. (2005) *Local Political Participation in Context – Does place of residence matter?* Paper presented at the ECPR Joint Sessions in Granada.

Falter, J. W. and Winkler, J. R. (2005) 'Wahlgeographie und Politische Ökologie', in J. W. Falter and H. Schoen (eds) *Handbuch Wahlforschung*, Wiesbaden: Verlag für Sozialwissenschaften, 107–33.

FOBP, 2004: Definition on metropolitan areas had been generated and provided by the Federal Office for Building and Regional Planning, www.bbr.bund.de, 01.05.2006.

Gabriel, O. W. (1997) 'Kommunales Wahlverhalten: Parteien, Themen und Kandidaten', in O. W. Gabriel, Brettschneider, F. and Vetter, A. (eds) *Politische Kultur und Wahlverhalten in einer Großstadt*, Opladen: Westdeutscher Verlag, 147–68.

Gabriel, O. W. and Eisenmann, S. (2005) 'Germany: a new type of local government?', in B. Denters and L. E. Rose (eds) *Comparing Local Governance – Trends and developments*, Houndmills: Palgrave Macmillan, 119–38.

Gabriel, O. W. and Keil. S. (2005) 'Wählerverhalten', in O. W. Gabriel and E. Holtman (eds) *Politisches System der Bundesrepublik Deutschland, 3. Auflage*, München: Oldenbourg, 575–621.

Gabriel, O. W. and Walter-Rogg, M. (2003) 'Kommunale Demokratie', in E. Jesse and R. Sturm (eds) *Demokratien des 21. Jahrhunderts im Vergleich. Historische Zugänge, Gegenwartsprobleme, Reformperspektiven*, Opladen: Leske + Budrich, 139–71.

Gimpel, J. G., Morris, I. L. and Armstrong, D. R. (2004) 'Turnout and the local age distribution: examining political participation across space and time', *Political Geography*, 23/1, 71–95.

Gluchowski, P., Graf, J. and Wilamowitz-Moellendorf, U. von (2002) 'Sozialstrukturelle Grundlagen des Parteienwettbewerbs in der Bundesrepublik Deutschland', in O. W. Gabriel, O. Niedermayer and R. Stöss (eds) *Parteiendemokratie in Deutschland*, Wiesbaden: Westdeutscher Verlag, 181–203.

Goerres, A. (2005) 'Grey Voting Power on the Rise? How the transition from middle to old age influences turnout in Europe', Paper presented at the 55th Political Studies Association Annual Conference, 4–7th April, University of Leeds.

Greer, A. and Greer, S. (1976) 'Suburban political behaviour: a matter of trust', in B. Schwartz (ed.) *The Changing Face of the Suburbs*, Chicago: University Press, 203–20.

Hill, K. Q. and Leighly, J. E. (1999) 'Racial diversity, voter vurnout, and mobilising institutions in the United States', *American Politics Quarterly*, 27, 275–95.

Hirsch, H. (1968) 'Suburban voting and national trends: a research note', *Western Political Quarterly*, 21/3, 508–14.

Kevenhörster, P. (1983) 'Kommunalwahlen – Instrument bürgerschaftlicher Einflussnahme auf die Kommunalpolitik?' in O. W. Gabriel (ed.) *Bürgerbeteiligung und kommunale Demokratie*, München: Minerva, 157–72.

Klingemann, H. -D., Volkens, A., Bara, J., Budge, I. and McDonald, M.D. (2006) *Mapping Policy Preferences II: Comparing 24 OECD and 24 CEE countries 1990–2003*, Oxford: Oxford University Press.

Kriesi, H., Grande, E., Lachat, R., Dolezal, M., Bornschier, S. and Frey, T. (2006) 'Globalisation and the transformation of the national political space. Six

European countries compared', *European Journal of Political Research*, 45: 921–56.

Lipset, S. M. and Rokkan, S. (1967) 'Cleavage structures, party systems and voter alignments: an introduction', in S. M. Lipset and S. Rokkan (eds) *Party Systems and Voter Alignments*, New York: The Free Press, 1–64.

Löffler, B. and Rogg, W. (1991) 'Kommunalwahlen und kommunales Wahlverhalten', in T. Pfizer, T. and H. -G. Wehling, H (eds) *Kommunalpolitik in Baden-Württemberg*, 2nd edn, Stuttgart et al.: Kohlhammer, 108–24.

Oliver, J. E. (2000) 'City size and civic involvement in metropolitan America', *American Journal of Political Science*, 94: 361–73.

Orfield, M. (2002) *American Metropolitics - the new suburban reality*, Washington D.C.: Brookings Institution Press.

Pappi, F. U. (1984) 'The West German party system', *West European Politics*, 7/1: 7–26.

Reif, K. (1984) 'National electoral cycles and European elections 1979 and 1984', *Electoral Studies*, 3. Jg./Heft 3: 244–55.

Sellers, J. M. (2004) *The Suburbanised Metropolis and Politics: Is There a U.S. Model?* Paper presented at the IMO meeting in Bordeaux, 9–10th January.

Siegfried, A. (1913) *Tableau politique de la France de l'Quest sous la Troisième République*, Paris: Slatkine.

Treiman, D. J. (2009) *Quantitative Data Analysis. Doing social research to test ideas*, San Francisco: Jossey-Bass.

Verba, S. and Nie, N. H. (1972) *Participation in America*, Chicago: University of Chicago Press.

Verba, S. and Nie, N. H., Kim, J. -O. (1978) *Participation and Political Equality: A Seven Nation Comparison*, New York: Cambridge University Press.

Vetter, A. (2009) 'Alles nur timing? Kommunale Wahlbeteiligung im Kontext von Bundestagswahlen und Wahlen zum Europäischen Parlament', *Zeitschrift für Parlamentsfragen*, Heft 4: 788–808.

Walter-Rogg, M. (2005) 'Metropolitan areas and political impact in Germany', in V. Hoffmann-Martinot and J. M. Sellers (eds.) *Metropolitanisation and Political Change*, Wiesbaden: Verlag für Sozialwissenschaften, 87–122.

—— (2007) 'Legitimacy of various political levels in Germany and Europe', in K. Pähle and M. Reiser (eds.) *Lokale politische Eliten und Fragen der Legitimation*, Baden-Baden: Nomos, 129–55.

—— (2010) 'Multiple choice: the persistence of territorial pluralism in the German Federation', in H. Baldersheim and L. E. Rose (eds.) *Territorial Choice: the politics of boundaries and borders*, Houndmills: Palgrave Macmillan, 138–59.

Wright, J. K. (1932) 'Sections and national growth: an atlas of the historical geography of the United States', *Geographical Review*, 22: 353–60.

# Appendix

*Table A7.1: Metropolitan areas and units of analysis*

| | Number of municipalities in metro area | Population 2003 | % of population federal state | % of population total metro area | Number of municipalities in total metro area | Population 2003 in total metro area |
|---|---|---|---|---|---|---|
| Baden-Wuerttemberg | | | | | | |
| Stuttgart | 226 | 3,110,427 | 29.1 | 100.0 | 226 | 3,110,427 |
| Freiburg im Breisgau | 69 | 592,180 | 5.5 | 100.0 | 69 | 592,180 |
| Heilbronn | 54 | 522,166 | 4.9 | 100.0 | 54 | 522,166 |
| Ulm | 47 | 325,820 | 3.0 | 62.8 | 64 | 518,469 |
| Heidelberg | 39 | 459,605 | 4.3 | 100.0 | 41 | 468,236 |
| Karlsruhe | 37 | 812,510 | 7.6 | 79.6 | 97 | 1,020,410 |
| Mannheim | 18 | 532,802 | 5.0 | 64.5 | 39 | 826,270 |
| Reutlingen | 31 | 329,079 | 3.1 | 100.0 | 31 | 329,816 |
| Pforzheim | 28 | 316,382 | 3.0 | 100.0 | 28 | 316,811 |
| Villingen-Schwenningen | 26 | 230,803 | 2.2 | 100.0 | 26 | 231,025 |
| Metro areas in BW | 575 | 7,231,774 | 67.7 | 67.6 | | |
| Metro areas outside BW | 2 | 5,880 | | 0.1 | | |
| Rural areas | 534 | 3,454,911 | 32.3 | 32.3 | | |
| Total | 1111 | 10,692,565 | | | | |
| Units of analysis | 1109 | 10,686,685 | 100.0 | | | |
| Hesse | | | | | | |
| Frankfurt am Main | 114 | 2,466,444 | 43.2 | 88.3 | 166 | 2,799,901 |
| Kassel | 48 | 620,662 | 10.9 | 98.7 | 49 | 628,254 |
| Darmstadt | 36 | 551,300 | 9.6 | 100.0 | 36 | 552,567 |
| Wiesbaden | 16 | 431,271 | 7.5 | 92.9 | 69 | 466,335 |
| Metro areas in Hesse | 214 | 4,069,677 | 71.2 | 66.8 | | |
| Metro areas outside Hesse | 22 | 231,149 | | 3.8 | | |
| Offenbach am Main (excluded from analysis <200.000 inhab.) | 2 | 146,084 | | 2.4 | | |

| | Number of municipalities in metro area | Population 2003 | % of population federal state | % of population total metro area | Number of municipalities in total metro area | Population 2003 in total metro area |
|---|---|---|---|---|---|---|
| Rural areas | 188 | 1,645,162 | 28.8 | 27.0 | | |
| Total | 426 | 6,092,072 | | | | |
| Units of analysis | 402 | 5,714,839 | 100.0 | | | |
| Berlin-Brandenburg* | | | | | | |
| Berlin | 92 | 4,333,567 | 72.9 | 99.8 | 94 | 4,343,480 |
| Potsdam | 15 | 335,038 | 5.7 | 100.0 | 15 | 335,817 |
| Cottbus | 44 | 357,283 | 6.0 | 100.0 | 44 | 358,405 |
| Metro areas in BB | 151 | 5,025,888 | 84.4 | 84.2 | | |
| Metro areas outside BB | 2 | 9,913 | | 0.2 | | |
| Rural areas | 271 | 931,604 | 15.6 | 15.6 | | |
| Total | 424 | 5,967,405 | | | | |
| Units of analysis | 422 | 5,957,492 | 100.0 | | | |
| Saxony | | | | | | |
| Dresden | 86 | 1,122,933 | 26.1 | 100.0 | 86 | 1,122,933 |
| Chemnitz | 61 | 631,864 | 14.7 | 100.0 | 61 | 630,743 |
| Leipzig | 53 | 866,554 | 20.2 | 90.6 | 72 | 956,557 |
| Zwickau | 26 | 316,103 | 7.4 | 99.4 | 27 | 317,926 |
| Metro areas in Saxony | 226 | 2,937,454 | 68.3 | 66.8 | | |
| Metro areas outside Saxony | 20 | 91,826 | | 3.1 | | |
| Rural areas | 293 | 1,365,645 | 31.7 | 30.1 | | |
| Total | 539 | 4,394,925 | | | | |
| Units of analysis | 519 | 4,303,099 | 100.0 | | | |

*Notes:* *The federal state of Brandenburg and the city state of Berlin were merged, because the metropolitan area of Berlin consists of the city of Berlin and 92 communes in Brandenburg.

*Source*: IMO Dataset 2003 of five federal states in Germany.

*Table A7.2(a): Characteristics of communal types in West and East Germany (all data from 2003)*

| | Density population per km² | | Unemployment rate % | | Local taxes per capita | | Living space per capita | | SES generally (university degree) % | | Distance to the centre* index | | Population growth index 1993-2003 | |
|---|---|---|---|---|---|---|---|---|---|---|---|---|---|---|
| | West | East | West | East | West | East | West | East | West | East | West | East | West | East |
| Urban concentrations | 1,492 | 1,378 | 10.9 | 20.5 | 455 | 294 | 39.6 | 38.4 | 12.9 | 14.3 | 1.5 | 1.6 | 103.6 | 92.4 |
| Low-density suburb | 117 | 43 | 16.8 | 45.1 | 198 | 187 | 43.2 | 37.3 | 5.9 | 7.2 | 3.6 | 3.7 | 104.5 | 103.9 |
| Affluent suburbs | 492 | 536 | 9.0 | 21.9 | 370 | 318 | 42.9 | 37.2 | 11.1 | 11.9 | 2.8 | 2.9 | 106.6 | 115.6 |
| Middle-class suburbs | 590 | 313 | 11.4 | 26.3 | 292 | 208 | 41.9 | 36.0 | 9.9 | 10.8 | 2.7 | 3.3 | 106.1 | 107.1 |
| Poor suburbs | 416 | 285 | 16.2 | 37.6 | 226 | 142 | 40.9 | 35.6 | 6.6 | 8.2 | 3.1 | 3.5 | 104.9 | 103.5 |
| eta | **0.66** | **0.59** | **0.41** | **0.60** | **0.21** | **0.27** | **0.33** | **0.29** | **0.57** | **0.56** | **0.60** | **0.54** | **0.15** | **0.23** |
| Metropolitan areas | 453 | 323 | 13.1 | 32.7 | 279 | 200 | 42.2 | 36.4 | 8.7 | 9.5 | 3.0 | 3.3 | 105.5 | 106.0 |
| Rural areas | 175 | 123 | 13.6 | 42.4 | 246 | 147 | 43.9 | 37.2 | 5.4 | 7.7 | 5.0 | 5.0 | 103.9 | 97.1 |
| eta | **0.41** | **0.33** | **0.04** | **0.28** | **0.06** | **0.15** | **0.26** | **0.12** | **.43** | **0.30** | **0.88** | **0.87** | **0.12** | **0.26** |
| Total | 320 | 205 | 13.3 | 38.4 | 264 | 168 | 43.0 | 36.9 | 7.1 | 8.5 | 4.0 | 4.3 | 104.8 | 100.6 |

*Notes*: The first five variables are relevant for the settlement typology. All steps of typology are based on the statistical method of lowest 25th (low-density/poor suburbs) or top 25th quartile (affluent suburbs). For boldface coefficients, p<0.05.

* The FOBP published a variable which is based on kilometre to the centre but contains only categorical information: 1 core city, 2 core area, 3 inner commuter area, 4 outer commuter area, 5 rural areas.

Table A7.2(b): Characteristics of communal types in West and East Germany (all data from 2003)

| | Out-commuting % | | Foreign born % | | People under 18 years % | | Retired people % | | Manufacturing occupation % | | SES hardship summary index | | Economic diversity Simpson index | |
|---|---|---|---|---|---|---|---|---|---|---|---|---|---|---|
| | West | East | West | East | West | East | West | East | West | East | West | East | West | East |
| Urban concentrations | 57.9 | 44.9 | 15.2 | 4.7 | 17.7 | 14.0 | 17.3 | 21.2 | 36.0 | 26.6 | 15.2 | 57.1 | 0.57 | 0.62 |
| Low-density suburb | 79.6 | 84.9 | 5.4 | 1.8 | 21.6 | 16.5 | 16.6 | 18.2 | 53.3 | 35.9 | 5.4 | 68.5 | 0.66 | 0.45 |
| Affluent suburbs | 84.6 | 78.4 | 8.0 | 1.9 | 20.5 | 15.9 | 15.9 | 19.2 | 51.3 | 36.7 | 8.0 | 54.3 | 0.61 | 0.56 |
| Middle-class suburbs | 78.3 | 75.3 | 10.3 | 1.6 | 19.8 | 15.4 | 16.4 | 20.1 | 47.3 | 37.5 | 10.3 | 63.3 | 0.55 | 0.53 |
| Poor suburbs | 79.0 | 78.2 | 9.3 | 2.0 | 20.5 | 15.6 | 16.5 | 19.3 | 51.2 | 35.0 | 9.3 | 69.5 | 0.58 | 0.51 |
| eta | 0.37 | **0.48** | **0.49** | **0.25** | **0.37** | **0.29** | **0.12** | **0.23** | **0.15** | **0.13** | **0.72** | **0.71** | **0.28** | **0.39** |
| Metropolitan areas | 79.4 | 77.7 | 8.6 | 1.9 | 20.4 | 15.7 | 16.4 | 19.4 | 49.9 | 35.9 | 53.4 | 64.6 | 0.60 | 0.52 |
| Rural areas | 73.9 | 78.7 | 5.7 | 1.7 | 21.4 | 15.8 | 17.3 | 20.0 | 53.8 | 37.9 | 53.7 | 70.1 | 0.61 | 0.48 |
| eta | **0.20** | 0.04 | **0.33** | 0.05 | **0.19** | 0.03 | **0.16** | **0.09** | **0.08** | 0.06 | 0.02 | **0.37** | 0.05 | **0.17** |
| Total | 76.7 | | 7.2 | 1.8 | 20.9 | 15.8 | 16.8 | 19.7 | 51.7 | 37.1 | 53.6 | 67.9 | 0.60 | 0.50 |

Notes: For boldface coefficients, p<0.05.

Table A7.3(a): Positions of parties and voters in Germany

| | Party manifestos | Position of party voters in national election 2002 or respondents with party affiliation | | | | | | | | |
|---|---|---|---|---|---|---|---|---|---|---|
| | | Left-right self-placement 1 left to 10 right[b] | | | Position on culture issues 1 social socialism to 10 social conservatism[c] | | Position on economic issues 1 state control to 10 free market[d] | | Position on globalisation issues 1 support globalisation to 10 support nationalism[e] | |
| | Left-right position 1 left to 10 right[a] | Germany | West | East | West | East | West | East | West | East |
| Party of the democratic socialism (PDS) | 4.15 | 3.17 | 2.18 | 3.29 | 4.06 | 3.12 | 3.87 | 4.21 | 5.41 | 5.50 |
| Green Party (Alliance 90/The Greens) | 4.39 | 3.95 | 4.10 | 3.46 | 3.54 | 3.24 | 5.54 | 4.69 | 4.48 | 5.02 |
| Social democrats (SPD) | 5.29 | 4.43 | 4.51 | 4.06 | 4.70 | 3.66 | 5.41 | 4.52 | 5.39 | 5.70 |
| Free Democratic Party (FDP)/Free voter associations | 5.23 | 5.73 | 5.59 | 5.87 | 4.71 | 3.89 | 6.36 | 5.06 | 5.30 | 5.67 |
| Christian Democrats (CDU/CSU) | 6.51 | 6.29 | 6.50 | 6.08 | 5.36 | 4.34 | 5.84 | 4.88 | 5.86 | 6.12 |
| Republicans (REP) | n/a | 8.13 | 7.87 | 8.20 | 4.51 | 3.22 | 5.14 | 4.08 | 6.82 | 7.05 |
| Other party | n/a | 5.76 | 4.87 | 7.60 | 4.90 | 3.52 | 5.19 | 4.54 | 6.82 | 8.55 |
| Non voter | — | 5.20 | 5.48 | 5.13 | 4.56 | 3.86 | 5.13 | 4.44 | 6.04 | 6.14 |
| All respondents | — | 5.16 | 5.30 | 4.79 | 4.81 | 3.81 | 5.53 | 4.57 | 5.64 | 5.87 |

| Party manifestos | Position of party voters in national election 2002 or respondents with party affiliation | | | | | | | |
| --- | --- | --- | --- | --- | --- | --- | --- | --- |
| | Left-right self-placement 1 left to 10 right[b] | | Position on culture issues 1 social socialism to 10 social conservatism[c] | | Position on economic issues 1 state control to 10 free market[d] | | Position on globalisation issues 1 support globalisation to 10 support nationalism[e] | |
| Left-right position 1 left to 10 right[a] | Germany West | East | West | East | West | East | West | East |

Notes: n/a not available.

Source a: Party Manifesto Data Set from Klingemann et al. 2006. Originally used scale was: −100 to +100 scale where −100 meant extreme left, +100 meant extreme right, but for better comparability we have converted it to 1–10 scale.

Source b: European Social Survey, means of 2002/2003 and 2004/2005. Originally used scale was: 0 to 10 scale where 0 meant extreme left, 10 extreme right, but for better comparability we have converted it to 1–10 scale.

Sources c, d and e: Different post-election surveys, for operationalisation and index construction, see Chapter 14, the Methodological Appendix.

Table A7.3(b): Correlation of the left-right self-placement and the different issue positions

| | West Germany | | | East Germany | | |
| --- | --- | --- | --- | --- | --- | --- |
| | Left-right-placement | Culture issues | Economic issues | Left-right-placement | Culture issues | Economic issues |
| Culture issues | 0.560 | | | 0.258 | | |
| Economic issues | 0.562 | 0.426 | | −0.092 | 0.755 | |
| Globalisation issues | 0.707 | 0.536 | −0.115 | 0.912 | 0.090 | −0.426 |

*Table A7.4: Variable definitions*

| Variable name | Definition | Missing values |
|---|---|---|
| *Dependent variables* | | |
| National election turnout | National Council (German Bundestag), election of 2002 | 3/1163 |
| Local election turnout | Election turnout for the last local election since 2003 | 7/1159 |
| Left-right voter self-placement | ESS, means of 2002/2003 and 2004/2005, 1 (left) to 10 (right)-scale | 3/1163 |
| Left-right party position on cultural issues on economic issues on globalisation issues | Party positions on culture, economic and globalisation issues based on voter responses draws on the following post-electoral surveys and questions (see Chapter 14, the Methodological Appendix). For the indexes the different scales were recoded in same directions and standardised in a 1 to 10-scale. Then the sum of percentage of votes for parties was multiplied with the voter position on culture, economic and globalisation left-right issues in each municipality: | 3/1163 |

$$Pos_i = \frac{posPDS * votesPDS,i}{votes_i} + \frac{posGreen * votesGreen,i}{votes_i} + \frac{posSPD * votesSPD,i}{votes_i} + \frac{posFDP * votesFDP,i}{votes_i} + \frac{posCDU/CSU * votesCDU/CSU,i}{votes_i} + \frac{posREP * votesREP,i}{votes_i} + \frac{posOther * votesOther,i}{votes_i}$$

where pos = issue position and i = municipality

| | | |
|---|---|---|
| *Independent variables commune-level, socio-Demographic/compositional variables (level 1)* | | |
| Foreign born | Proportion of foreign-born people | 56/1110 |
| SES Hardship | Summary index: $\sum(100*(x_i-x_{imin})/(x_{imax}-x_{imin}))/4$ where: x1: proportion of unemployed people (not available in Baden-Wuerttemberg for communes with less than 5,000 inhabitants); x2: proportion of people with high education profile; x3: proportion of living space per capita x4: proportion of local tax rates | 2/1164 |
| University degree | Proportion of employees paying social insurance with university degree | 7/1159 |
| Manufacturing occupation | Proportion of employees paying social insurance and working in the 2nd sector (not available in the federal state of Hesse, N = 402) | 273/893 |
| Retirees | Proportion of retired people | 25/1141 |
| Residents under 18 years | Proportion of people under 18 years of age | 25/1141 |
| *Independent variables commune-level, spatial/context variables (level 1)* | | |
| Ln(Population) | Natural logarithm of population size | 0/1166 |
| Ln(Density) | Natural logarithm of population/commune's surface | 0/1166 |
| Stability of residence | Population growth rate: $(x_{10}-x_t)/x_t$, where $x_t$: population size in year t and $x_{10}$: population in year t+10 | 0/1166 |
| Out-commuting | Proportion of occupied people working in another commune than commune of residence | 28/1138 |
| Distance to the centre | Communal types defined by the FOBP in 2004: Core city, core area, inner and outer commuter area. The typology based on a matrix of commuting and distance to the core city | 0/1166 |

| Variable name | Definition | Missing values |
|---|---|---|
| Simpson index of economic diversity | Simpson index (not available in the federal state of Hesse, $N = 402$). This index allows us to measure the diversity among occupational groups (agriculture and forestry, manufacturing, provision of services) by using the formula: $\sum p_i^2$ where $p_i$ is $n_i/N$. The index ranges from 0 to 1, the closer to 1 the less diverse the working community | 273/893 |

*Independent variables metropolitan-level (level 2)*

| | | |
|---|---|---|
| Eastern Germany metros | Regional differences between West and East Germany | 0/14 |
| Metropolitan population | Population size of metropolitan area | 0/14 |
| Growth of residence | (Population 2003 – population 1993) * 100 of metropolitan area | 0/14 |
| Manufacturing | Proportion of labour force employed in manufacturing industry and construction of metropolitan area (not available in the federal state of Hesse) | 4/14 |
| Fragmentation (Zeigler-Brunn) | Number of municipalities per 10,000 inhabitants/percentage of core city population over metropolitan area population (see Zeigler/Brunn 1980) | 0/14 |
| Concentration (Herfindahl) | Sum of squared local shares of the total metropolitan population (see Herfindahl 1950). The higher the numbers, the more consolidated the metropolitan structure is, and the lower the numbers, the more fragmentation occurs. Index = $\sum p_i^2$, where p: metropolitan commune's population share | 0/14 |
| Polarisation (Nathan-Adams index) | Composite city-suburb hardship disparity index according to Nathan and Adams (1976, 1989), based on the following indicators: a) proportion of population without a job; b) proportion of employees paying social insurance with university degree; c) proportion of living space per capita; d) proportion of local tax rates | 0/14 |

*Sources:* Definition, indicators and data on metropolitan areas had been generated and provided by the Federal Office for Building and Regional Planning for the Institute of Social Science at the University of Stuttgart; survey data: www.gesis.org/en/institute/.

# Chapter Eight | The Political Ecology of the Spanish Metropolis – Place, Socio-Economic and Regional Effects

*Clemente J. Navarro[1]*

Since the transition to democracy in Spain, territory has been a constant influence on the electoral behaviour of citizens. The classic distinction between city and countryside has always been a main factor explaining electoral mobilisation, as the rural electorate consistently turns out in greater numbers than urban dwellers to vote. It is also common to refer to Spain as a case of political regionalism; multiple studies confirm that nationalisation and regionalism are both important influences on the Spanish political system.

A growing majority of Spanish citizens now live in metropolitan areas. Accumulating evidence demonstrates that variations within and between these settings are shaping national patterns of electoral behaviour. Since the first elections at the end of the 1970s, for instance, turnout has regularly been lower in big cities. At the same time, urban centres are places where fluctuations in turnout are common. At the beginning of the 1990s, these territories swung their electoral support from the main left-wing party (Partido Socialista) toward the main right-wing one (Partido Popular). The important variations among metropolitan municipalities go beyond the difference between core city and suburbs. Contextual factors like size, density and population growth as well as socio-economic differences help to explain the variations in electoral behaviour that survey analysis and (more rarely) ecological analysis have shown. Metropolitanisation could be promoting socio-political variations among metropolitan areas, as well as the emergence of new intra-metropolitan cleavages (Hoffmann-Martinot and Sellers 2007).

This chapter analyses the influence of these socio-economic and contextual factors on Spanish election turnout (local and national), and on the different socio-political orientations of metropolitan communities there. Specifically, the results of three elections held during the period of 1996 to 2004 for the 1,053 municipalities included in thirty metropolitan areas will be studied. Together, these municipalities contain 64 per cent of the Spanish population. Through examination of the impact of contextual and compositional factors on electoral behaviour in these municipalities, the analysis will consider whether internal variations within and between metropolitan areas have altered nationalisation and regionalism that comprise the main territorial patterns in the Spanish political system.

---

1. The author is grateful to Cristina Mateos for her support in data search, and to Jefferey M. Sellers for his ideas and constructive criticisms of a previous version.

The first section of the chapter outlines basic features of metropolitan areas in Spain and the considerable variations among them. The second section explores metropolitan influences on local and national turnout. The third section analyses the four indices created for this study based on dimensions of partisan competition to explain the diversity of socio-political orientations among metropolitan municipalities. The results are summarised in the last section.

## Metropolitan Spain – diversity and regional differences

The development of metropolitan areas in Spain has taken place in two historical phases. Its origin traces back to rural emigration in the 1950s and 1960s toward economically more dynamic urban areas in the north and east. This process gave rise to a concentration of the population in urban regions around major cities, especially in rapidly-growing industrial belts. Large core cities and industrial dormitory communities comprised the main morphology of metropolitan areas. Since the 1990s, in a second phase, the suburbanisation process brought about a certain inversion of this tendency (Recaño 2006; Alba and Navarro 2007). This process expanded the territorial scope of metropolitan areas and the profile of the inhabitants in the metropolitan periphery. Alongside traditional industrial municipalities, suburbanisation has given rise to new residential spaces with younger households of a higher socio-economic status, as well as the metropolitan integration of rural municipalities through commuting (Leal 2006; Indovina 2007).

Despite the existence of this phenomenon and its recognition in the Spanish Constitution (1978), no official definition of metropolitan areas exists based on municipal interdependency or commuting. Until 2001, the census did not include any information that would facilitate the application of such criteria. Using this new information, several methods were employed to identify metropolitan areas in Spain. This study uses the classification of Feria (2008).[2] Following the International Metropolitan Observatory (IMO) protocol, we have chosen thirty metropolitan areas with over 200,000 inhabitants.[3] These areas differ widely according to population size, population concentration patterns, and socio-economic polarisation between core cities and their suburbs (see Table 8.1). Socio-economic differences between them manifest the disparities in regional development in Spain between the northern and eastern areas and the central and southern areas (as demonstrated in the metropolitan average municipal hardship index).

---

2. In this work, metropolitan areas are defined by: commuting (which has to be 20 per cent of the active population and no less than 1,000 workers), the existence of territorial continuity among municipalities in the metropolitan area, and a population over 100,000 inhabitants. Other proposals for defining the boundaries of metropolitan areas exist, but these only focus on a handful of specific metropolitan areas. This gives rise to a group of forty-six metropolitan areas. Other analyses use less restrictive criteria, which give rise to a greater number of metropolitan areas, as well as a wider extension of them (Boix 2007) or they define 'urban areas' using socio-demographic criteria without taking into consideration municipal interdependency by means of commuting (Spanish Ministry of Housing 2005).

3. Some smaller areas have been added as they really constitute 'multi-nuclear' (two or more central cities) areas according to Feria (2008): Marbella and Malaga, Alicante-Elche-Benidorm, Oviedo-Gijón-Avilés.

*Table 8.1: Basic characteristic of Spanish metropolitan areas*

| Metropolitan areas | No of munici- palities | Total population | Popula- tion in core city (%) | Geopoliti- cal fragmen- tation | Con- centra- tion | Polari- sation | Hard- ship |
|---|---|---|---|---|---|---|---|
| Madrid-Alcalá de Henares | 172 | 5,625,837 | 52.24 | 5.85 | 0.28 | 0.89 | 0.34 |
| Barcelona-Sabadell | 131 | 4,404,599 | 34.14 | 8.71 | 0.13 | 0.89 | 0.30 |
| Valencia | 74 | 1,594,762 | 46.30 | 10.02 | 0.22 | 1.00 | 0.33 |
| Sevilla | 49 | 1,369,708 | 49.98 | 7.16 | 0.26 | 1.16 | 0.51 |
| Bilbao | 93 | 1,131,564 | 30.93 | 26.57 | 0.12 | 0.86 | 0.31 |
| Oviedo-Gijón-Avilés | 28 | 871,859 | 30.56 | 10.51 | 0.17 | 1.03 | 0.40 |
| Málaga-Marbella | 29 | 1,000,900 | 52.39 | 5.53 | 0.30 | 1.10 | 0.50 |
| Palmas G. Canarias | 18 | 709,191 | 50.04 | 5.07 | 0.28 | 1.07 | 0.47 |
| Zaragoza | 31 | 684,490 | 89.83 | 5.04 | 0.81 | 0.81 | 0.29 |
| Cádiz-Jerez | 7 | 602,809 | 30.40 | 3.82 | 0.19 | 0.96 | 0.50 |
| Vigo-Pontevedra | 41 | 704,541 | 39.77 | 14.63 | 0.18 | 1.20 | 0.43 |
| Murcia-Cartagena | 14 | 728,694 | 50.88 | 3.78 | 0.23 | 1.11 | 0.42 |
| Granada | 46 | 496,288 | 48.49 | 19.11 | 0.24 | 1.13 | 0.45 |
| Palma de Mallorca | 20 | 470,000 | 71.02 | 5.99 | 0.52 | 0.77 | 0.28 |
| Coruña | 23 | 463,339 | 51.02 | 9.73 | 0.28 | 1.13 | 0.39 |
| Donosti | 27 | 431,696 | 41.32 | 15.14 | 0.21 | 1.04 | 0.33 |
| Sta. Cruz Tenerife | 13 | 430,858 | 43.74 | 6.90 | 0.29 | 1.08 | 0.46 |
| Valladolid | 28 | 395,258 | 80.09 | 8.84 | 0.65 | 0.87 | 0.32 |
| Santander | 29 | 388,734 | 46.49 | 16.05 | 0.25 | 0.92 | 0.35 |
| Alicante-Benidorm-Elche | 17 | 725,721 | 39.21 | 5.97 | 0.24 | 0.98 | 0.36 |
| Córdoba | 5 | 327,788 | 93.99 | 1.62 | 0.88 | 1.24 | 0.55 |
| Tarragona | 29 | 316,638 | 35.73 | 25.63 | 0.22 | 0.87 | 0.30 |
| Castellón | 20 | 305,651 | 48.31 | 13.54 | 0.27 | 0.92 | 0.30 |
| Pamplona | 25 | 294,843 | 62.39 | 13.59 | 0.40 | 0.90 | 0.29 |
| Vitoria | 19 | 238,114 | 91.07 | 8.76 | 0.83 | 0.65 | 0.22 |
| Huelva | 11 | 224,645 | 63.34 | 7.73 | 0.42 | 1.12 | 0.51 |
| Algeciras | 6 | 213,737 | 47.47 | 5.91 | 0.32 | 1.08 | 0.52 |
| León | 20 | 203,400 | 64.36 | 15.28 | 0.44 | 0.99 | 0.31 |
| Santiago Compostela | 18 | 201,332 | 44.80 | 19.96 | 0.23 | 1.07 | 0.39 |
| Almeria | 9 | 241,046 | 69.00 | 5.41 | 0.52 | 1.07 | 0.47 |
| Mean | 35.06 | 859,934 | 53.31 | 10.55 | 0.35 | 0.99 | 0.36 |

*Note:* Concentration: Herfindahl index of population concentration among municipalities. Fragmentation: Zeigler-Brunn index of geopolitical fragmentation among municipalities. Polarisation: Nathan-Adams index of central city/suburban hardship. For methods and sources see Hoffmann-Martinot and Sellers 2007.

*Table 8.2: Typology of municipalities in Spanish metropolitan areas*

| | Urban concentra-tions | Hardship suburbs | Middle-class suburbs | Low-density suburbs | Affluent suburbs | Total | F (*) |
|---|---|---|---|---|---|---|---|
| Population | **306,270** | 15,100 | 11,410 | **2,570** | 5,710 | 24,5000 | 113.10 |
| Density | **3,630** | 730 | 880 | **30** | 350 | 790 | 36.95 |
| Distance to the centre | **3.83** | 12.16 | 12.50 | **34.91** | 13.50 | 14.14 | 100.68 |
| SES Hardship | 0.40 | **0.49** | 0.35 | 0.36 | **0.24** | 0.36 | 597.93 |
| Low socio-economic status (0,1) | 0.28 | **0.44** | 0.26 | 0.31 | **0.19** | 0.29 | 178.79 |
| Unemployment | 0.24 | **0.30** | 0.17 | 0.19 | **0.13** | 0.19 | 112.89 |
| Low educational status | 0.22 | **0.41** | 0.22 | 0.34 | **0.13** | 0.25 | 192.57 |
| House living space | **0.85** | **0.81** | 0.73 | 0.62 | **0.52** | 0.70 | 243.66 |
| Immigration (%) | 3.41 | 2.17 | 3.03 | 3.23 | 3.46 | 2.97 | 4.57 |
| Population growth: 1991–01 (%) | 2.71 | 7.92 | 27.66 | 18.86 | 75.25 | 31.72 | 19.06 |
| <19 years (%) | 20.52 | 22.26 | 20.64 | 18.93 | 20.80 | 20.87 | 12.43 |
| >64 years (%) | 14.94 | 16.33 | 15.75 | 22.08 | 15.17 | 16.25 | 26.54 |
| Occupational diversity | 0.61 | 0.58 | 0.57 | 0.55 | 0.57 | 0.58 | 14.18 |

*Notes:* F = Snedecor F, all significant, $p < 0.05$.

Alongside these differences, major divergences characterise municipalities within metropolitan areas. In order to analyse these 'place differences', munici-palities have been classified into five types according to the common IMO meth-odology (see Table 8.2). Thus, territorial variables differentiate between urban concentrations and low-density suburbs. The hardship index, a composite socio-economic variable, clearly distinguishes affluent, middle-class and high-hardship (or poor) suburbs. Urban concentrations come closer to poor suburbs with regard to their socio-economic status, but above all are characterised by high occupa-tional diversity. The socio-economic composition of low-density suburbs situates them between affluent enclaves and middle-class suburbs. These are basically small towns which maintain such characteristics of rural areas as fewer occupants per home, a higher proportion of elderly people and a low level of occupational diversity, despite commuting patterns that link them to the metropolitan area.[4]

---

4.   Although we have applied the difference between minority hardship and non-minority hard-ship suburbs, the percentages of immigrant population are not so different compared to other types of municipalities to have to justify their differentiation (see Table 8.2). In fact, this is the

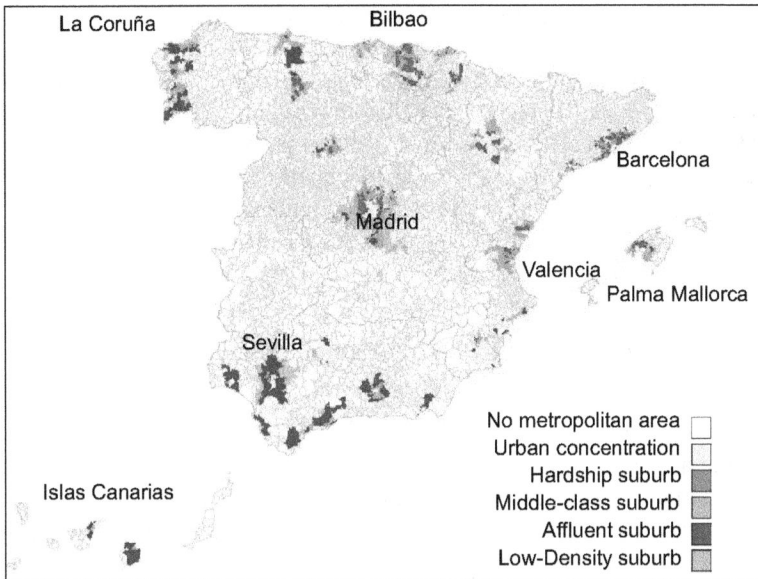

*Figure 8.1: The territorial distribution of municipalities types inside and among metropolitan areas*

These local variations occur between metropolitan areas as well as within them (see Figure 8.1). The types that demonstrate these variations can be localised according to regional development patterns. Affluent suburbs are most prevalent in northern and eastern metropolitan areas (especially in Catalonia, the Basque Country, and Navarra as well as in Madrid). Poor suburbs are concentrated in metropolitan areas of central and southern Spain (Andalusia, Canary Islands or Galicia). Interrelated metropolitan and municipal differences of this kind are crucial to understanding the political ecology of metropolitan Spain.

These differences are closely related to the regional territorial cleavages that distinguish the Spanish political system (Linz and Montero 1999).[5] Compared to other European countries, the regionalisation of the Spanish political system reflects a traditional cleavage between the national centre and the periphery (Caramani 2004). It is common to refer to different 'electoral Spains' depending

---

worst discriminating variable amongst municipalities. Correlations among these variables have a medium level (around 0.35). There exist some patterns among them according to the principal components factor analysis: distance, density, and older people vs. size, commuting, population growth, and young people vs. old people, commuting and university vs. hardship index, distance and immigration vs. commuting, occupational diversity vs. manufacturing workers (these are the main components of the factors that explain around 80 per cent of the variance).

5. With the aim of maintaining the same style throughout the book, we shall speak of regions and regional parties when referring to 'autonomous communities' (their political and administrative denomination) and nationalist parties.

on the election support that regional political parties receive (Pallarés 1994). In this regard, the four regions of Canarias, Cataluña, País Vasco, and Navarra stand out. In these regions, a regionalist party usually obtains strong support in national elections, as well as the highest number of votes in regional ones. In order to consider these regional effects on metropolitan political ecology, two variables are included in the following analyses: 'regionalist territories', to indicate those metropolitan areas that stand out because of a regional cleavage (Canary Islands, Catalonia and Basque Country)[6] and the average development level in metropolitan areas, measured by the hardship index.

### Metropolitan electoral participation – communitarian and regional variations

Survey analysis has been the method of choice for examining electoral turnout in Spain, but a number of ecological analyses demonstrate territorial and compositional patterns.[7] Existing accounts indicate that electoral mobilisation depends on political factors related to the circumstances of each election and changes in the mobilising capacity of political parties, in particular left-wing parties (Font 1995; Delgado 1997; Boix and Riba 2000, Barreiro 2001). This analysis, drawing on ecological data from several elections, focuses on local factors that are more or less constant over time.

Despite fluctuations over time, turnout in national elections has always been higher than in local ones (see Figure 8.2). This delocalised tendency is usually explained by the greater importance voters attach to national elections. Local elections tend to reflect the national opinion climate, as voters use them to validate or repudiate the governing party. Municipal elections in Spain have therefore assumed the character of second-order elections, especially in big cities (Delgado 1997).

Previous studies in Spain have identified a number of contextual and compositional influences on electoral participation. As in other countries, turnout is lower in larger municipalities, especially in municipal elections (Justel 1995; Font 1995). Delocalised participation is particularly characteristic of large municipalities, where the national political climate is a stronger mobilising factor (Delgado 1997). A study of municipalities with over 50,000 inhabitants showed a more educated population to be the main compositional predictor of voter mobilisation,

---

6. There are other regions where support for regionalist parties is significant, such as in Galicia, for instance, and more recently, Aragon, as well as Andalucía in former elections. But in these cases, the support is lower than in the four regions under scrutiny, especially when dealing with national elections, which will be analysed here. In fact, the average of regionalist vote among metropolitan municipalities in Galicia is around 10 per cent, being around 4 per cent in Andalucía and Aragon. This percentage is more than 30 per cent in 'regional territories' defined here.

7. Although the latter have tended to focus on regional and provincial comparisons, some municipal comparisons exist, such as a study carried out on local and national elections in cities with a population of over 50,000 inhabitants (Justel 1995), a study of the two great metropolitan areas of Madrid and Barcelona (Font 1992), or studies of local elections that point to the size of the municipality as fundamental (Delgado 1997; Capó 1991; Vallés and Sánchez 1994).

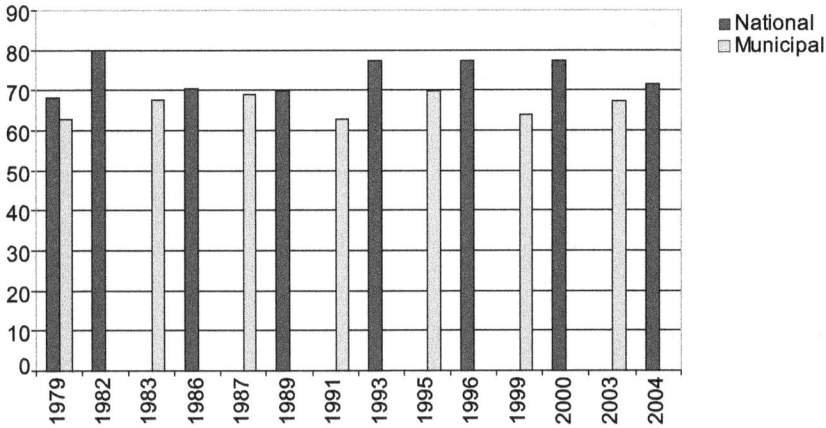

*Figure 8.2: Electoral participation in national and municipal elections, 1979–2004*

Source: Electoral Statistics, Ministerio del Interior, Gobierno de España.

followed by a larger active population, a larger percentage in the industrial sector and the presence of elderly people. Concentrations of immigrants, who tend to be less integrated into society, depress turnout (Font 1992). Although socio-economic status generally contributes to participation, its explanatory power averages less than other factors and varies widely (Justel 1995; Font 1995).

### Place effects on turnout: municipal variations according to the kind of elections

The average turnout in the different types of metropolitan municipalities from 1991 to 2004 manifests these established patterns.[8] The lowest levels of participation appear among urban concentrations, the highest among low-density suburbs. In municipal elections, demobilisation within large municipalities widens the range of variation between these extremes. In low-density suburbs, voter turnout for municipal elections averages higher than in national elections. This localised pattern of electoral participation contrasts in particular with urban concentrations, but also with the other three types of municipalities (see Figure 8.3). Among affluent, middle-class and poor suburbs, the variations are consistent with a positive relationship between the socio-economic level and participation but within a much

---

8.  As can be seen in Figure 8.2, electoral turnout in this period has been fairly stable, with the sole exception of municipal elections in 1995. This was the very first time that foreigners from other European countries living in Spain could vote in municipal elections, although it would really appear that the mobilisation that year was entirely due to the influence of exogenous political factors. In fact, the most mobilised with regard to 1991 were the residents in large cities (Delgado 1999), although in general, turnout in municipal elections is greater in the rural environment (Delgado 1997).

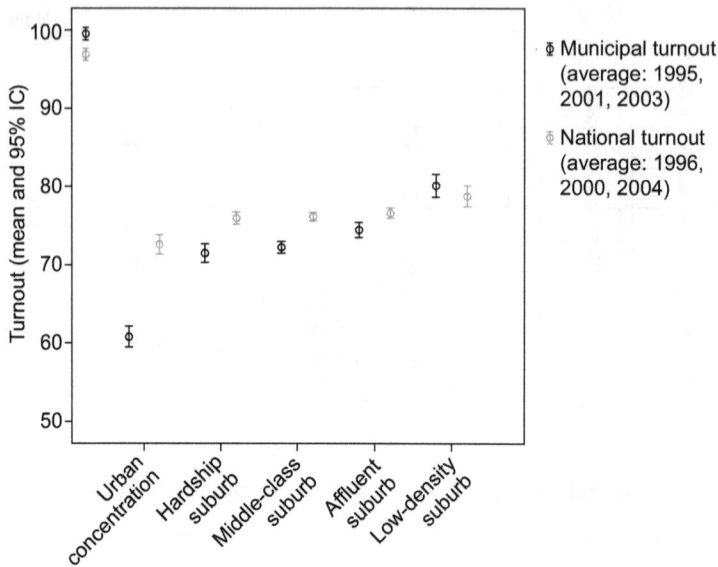

*Figure 8.3: Metropolitan municipalities and turnout*

more limited range. The 'turnout gap' between national and municipal elections remains similar for all three types (6 per cent), but doubles in urban concentrations (up to 13 per cent) and reverses among low-density suburbs.[9]

The differences among types of municipalities suggest that turnout depends more on territorial than on compositional influences. The demobilisation in urban concentrations in municipal elections aggravates this tendency. The municipal types account for more of the variance in municipal election turnout (16 per cent, according to the ANOVA analysis) than in national election turnout (4 per cent).

Municipal elections thus manifest an ecological pattern consistent with the classic thesis of the loss of community (Verba and Nie 1976). Urbanism leads to demobilisation. A contrary thesis of urban mobilisation accounts for part of the turnout in national elections. Urban voters, who do not usually participate in municipal elections, now vote. Above all, the activities of mobilising agents, such as parties and elites, may be more intense in large cities and temporarily contingent political influences can predominate over socio-economic or contextual ones. Therefore, among metropolitan municipalities 'small is beautiful' in local elections, but 'large is lively' in national elections (Kelleher and Lowery 2008).

---

9.  The application of variance homogeneity tests (b-Tuckey) shows that poor, middle-class and affluent suburbs constitute a homogeneous group as opposed to urban concentrations, on the one hand, and low-density suburbs on the other in national and local elections.

### The contextual and compositional bases of turnout – regionalism and the communitarian character of local participation

Regression analyses including contextual and socio-economic variables confirm these territorial and socio-economic effects, and permit a more precise specification of how they work (see Table 8.3).[10] In national elections, turnout increases with more populous municipalities, with more educated residents and with a more dependent population (Justel 1995). Urbanism is important, but the socio-demographic composition of municipalities is also a main factor. In municipal elections, territorial factors take on added importance. Beyond effects from size and population growth, demobilisation increases when more residents commute, a pattern that indicates suburbanisation.

Municipal social heterogeneity also emerges as a significant predictor. Turnout increases with greater occupational diversity, confirming a classic class conflict thesis over social solidaristic effects. Yet turnout falls when the proportion of immigrants increases. Rather than mobilise voters through ethnic conflict or racial threat, ethnic or racial diversity remains a source of demobilisation, even as disenfranchised minorities themselves remain too small in number to account fully for this effect.[11]

Population size is a common factor in explaining local and national election turnout. Compositional traits (education, dependent population or ethnic diversity) play a role along with contextual traits (occupational diversity, commuting and population growth). In both types of elections, occupational diversity promotes turnout whereas cultural diversity (immigration) inhibits it. A regional effect is also present in local and national elections. Turnout averages lower in less socio-eco-nomically developed metropolitan areas, especially in the 'regionalist territories' (see Table 8.3, Model 5). As measured by the increase in variance explained from previous models, this regional effect appears to be greater in national elections.

This analysis confirms that a variety of contextual effects limit the nationalisation of electoral mobilisation. How these effects occur depends on the type of elections. Based on the variance explained in separate OLS models, the contextual variables account for more of the variation in municipal turnout, while compositional factors better explain the variation in national turnout (see Web Appendix WA8 for these models). The regional effect is less significant in municipal elections (see Table 8.3).

---

10. In fact, the models that include quantitative variables explain the differences in turnout among municipalities better than the model that includes the typology of municipalities (Model 1 in analyses included in the Web Appendix WA08). All calculated models have been included in the Web Appendix WA8, http://press.ecpr.eu/resources. Only those necessary to show the main results have been included in the text.

11. Literature about the effect of 'social composition' on political participation shows conflicting hypotheses and striking results, for instance: local solidaristic effect (Eagles and Erfle 1989) vs. conflict among social groups (Oliver 2001). Racial diversity is also viewed as a factor affecting participation (Huckfeld 1986; Rubenson 2004), as well as a factor without influence on participation (Oliver 2001). About 'social composition' effects on political activism in Spain, cf. Navarro (2011).

*Table 8.3: Metropolitan participation in national and municipal elections (OLS regression models)*

| | National combined (Model 4) Coeff. (s.e.) | Local combined (Model 4) Coeff. (s.e.) | National full (Model 5) Coeff. (s.e.) | Local full (Model 5) Coeff. (s.e.) |
|---|---|---|---|---|
| Constant | **54.916** (5.285) | **92.578** (6.233) | **61.438** (4.628) | **104.992** (6.051) |
| *Compositional* | | | | |
| Young people (<19 years) | **0.986** (0.008) | **0.526** (0.095) | **0.720** (0.075) | **0.329** (0.096) |
| Old people (>64 years) | **0.539** (0.063) | **0.283** (0.075) | **0.373** (0.056) | 0.132 (0.072) |
| Immigration (%) | −0.015 (0.053) | **−0.144** (0.062) | **−0.097** (0.047) | **−0.182** (0.059) |
| Hardship Index | −1.985 (2.843) | −2.404 (3.352) | 5.359 (2.906) | −0.257 (4.257) |
| University (%) | **0.101** (0.040) | 0.027 (0.048) | **0.184** (0.036) | **0.104** (0.046) |
| Manufacturing (%) | 0.030 (0.024) | 0.008 (0.028) | **0.092** (0.022) | **0.072** (0.027) |
| *Contextual* | | | | |
| Municipal size (ln) | **−1.276** (0.231) | **−4.262** (0.273) | **−1.662** (0.202) | **−5.002** (0.271) |
| Municipal density (ln) | −0.185 (0.178) | 0.327 (0.210) | **−0.557** (0.156) | −0.010 (0.201) |
| Distance to the centre (km) | 0.006 (0.014) | 0.010 (0.016) | 0.017 (0.012) | 0.021 (0.017) |
| Out-commuting (%) | −0.011 (0.015) | **−0.073** (0.018) | −0.003 (0.013) | **−0.050** (0.017) |
| Population growth (1991-2001) (%) | 0.000 (0.002) | -0.003 (0.002) | -0.002 (0.002) | **−0.005** (0.002) |
| Occupational diversity (Simpson) | 2.911 (4.802) | **14.619** (5.650) | **14.015** (4.226) | **22.928** (5.346) |
| *Metropolitan* | | | | |
| Region | | | **−6.594** (0.363) | **−5.432** (0.467) |
| Metropolitan Hardship Index | | | **−17.727** (3.511) | **−11.553** (4.461) |
| $R^2$ | 0.214 | 0.524 | 0.404 | 0.589 |

*Notes:* For boldface coefficients, $p < 0.05$.

*Metropolitan and municipal variations of turnout – on ecological limits to nationalisation*

Multilevel analysis replicates the OLS models with greater precision (see Table 8.4). The multilevel models add a variable for population concentration in metropolitan areas, as the size of metropolitan cities appeared to be important in explaining election turnout. The results reaffirm the importance of local contextual factors and the demobilising regional effect in national elections. In municipal elections, the regional effect falls short of statistical significance. In national elections, this effect appears to be more closely related to regional politics than to socio-economic differences among metropolitan areas. The regionalist territories mobilise less in national elections, but regions with lower socio-economic status do not.

The multilevel models confirm that local context matters, particularly in municipal elections. Municipal size, population growth and immigration are demobilising factors, as is commuting in the case of municipal elections. Occupational heterogeneity has the expected mobilising effect in municipal elections. A bigger university-educated population and a higher percentage of workers from the industrial sector also stimulate participation, but in neither of the two types of elections does local socio-economic hardship exert significant influence.[12] Local factors (contextual or compositional) explain municipal participation somewhat better than national participation. The variance explained by the 'contextual model' is always higher than for the 'compositional model', but somewhat more so for municipal elections.[13]

Electoral mobilisation is more closely linked to integration into local life than to socio-economic differences among communities. The contrasts in voter participation stem from factors that affect opportunities to take part in the social and political life of a community. A smaller community invites greater participation, regardless of the differences among metropolitan areas or the contrasts between rich and poor communities. Residential mobility and ethnic diversity also limit opportunities for local social integration. 'Communitarian' influences of this kind

---

12. Previous studies have also shown that education and size are key explanatory factors, rather than other features of socio-economic structure (Font 1995). This analysis again demonstrates the demobilising effects of cultural diversity (immigration) and commuting, and the mobilisation produced by occupational heterogeneity.

13. For municipal elections, the explained variance at municipal level is around 18 per cent for compositional variables, and around 49 per cent for contextual ones. In the case of national elections, these figures are 25 per cent and 28 per cent respectively (see models in the Web Appendix WA8, http://press.ecpr.eu/resources). For the last model, these figures contrast with previous regression results where compositional factors explain more variance than contextual ones. In OLS regression analysis the effect of socio-economic differences among regions is not controlled, meanwhile multilevel analysis 'distinguished' this metropolitan (level 2) effect from the compositional effect at municipal level (above all, the hardship index on both levels). In fact, the hardship index effect disappears when metropolitan variables are included in regression analysis (see Table 8.3) and the final multilevel analysis reducing the explanatory capacity of compositional factors at municipal level. In other words, OLS regression 'hides' a metropolitan effect.

*Table 8.4: Metropolitan participation in national and municipal elections (multilevel models)*

|  | National turnout | Municipal turnout |
|---|---|---|
|  | Coefficient (s.e.) | Coefficient (s.e.) |
| Constant | **54.442**<br>(13.346) | **85.418**<br>(16.800) |
| *Compositional* |  |  |
| Young people (<19 years) | **0.373**<br>(0.077) | **0.229**<br>(0.095) |
| Old people (>64 years) | **0.256**<br>(0.052) | **0.198**<br>(0.063) |
| Immigration (%) | **−0.161**<br>(0.047) | **−0.279**<br>(0.056) |
| Hardship Index | 4.419<br>(2.533) | −1.077<br>(3.099) |
| University (%) | **0.198**<br>(0.032) | **0.085**<br>(0.039) |
| Manufacturing (%) | **0.080**<br>(0.022) | **0.078**<br>(0.026) |
| *Contextual* |  |  |
| Municipal size (ln) | **−1.532**<br>(0.181) | **−4.306**<br>(0.223) |
| Municipal density (ln) | **−0.290**<br>(0.143) | 0.112<br>(0.175) |
| Distance to the centre (km) | −0.004<br>(0.012) | 0.005<br>(0.015) |
| Out-commuting (%) | −0.014<br>(0.012) | **−0.075**<br>(0.015) |
| Population growth (1991–2001) (%) | **−0.004**<br>(0.001) | **−0.004**<br>(0.001) |
| Occupational diversity (Simpson) | 6.775<br>(3.728) | **16.484**<br>(4.557) |
| *Metropolitan* |  |  |
| Size (ln) | 1.232<br>(0.854) | 0.844<br>(1.079) |
| Concentration | 2.629<br>(3.596) | 0.139<br>(4.531) |
| Metropolitan Hardship Index | −5.814<br>(8.474) | 105.000<br>(10.651) |
| Region | **−6.493**<br>(1.569) | **−2.966**<br>(1.979) |

| | National turnout | Municipal turnout |
|---|---|---|
| *Variance components* | | |
| Metropolitan | 11.621 | 18.565 |
| Municipal | 13.909 | 20.730 |
| *Explained variance* | | |
| Metropolitan | 0.423 | 0.233 |
| Municipal | 0.328 | 0.484 |
| Metropolitan (N) | 30 | 30 |
| Municipal (N) | 1053 | 1053 |
| Deviance | 5861.137 | 6259.852 |

*Notes:* For boldface coefficients, p<0.05.

are strongest in municipal elections.[14] There, political contestation in communities with diverse occupations also drives turnout to a higher level. Weaker local ties among resident commuters discourage voting in municipal elections, but not in national elections. At the national level, the more limited contextual effects stem from population concentration, from residential mobility and from regionalist socio-political differences.

Local and regional contextual effects of this kind can make communities more or less susceptible to shifts in the political climate between elections, or to nationalising influences from party mobilisation and the mass media. If national events and agents are present throughout the country, then municipalities with lower community integration (such as urban concentrations) might be expected to be more open to influence from them. In this way, local, predominantly contextual differences, have produced divergent local impacts from common nationalising influences.

Overall, suburbanisation in Spain has, in many respects, produced precisely the opposite of the ecology of civic decline claimed by Putnam (2000) for the United States. As closer examination of the US case has confirmed (see Chapter 2 of this volume), suburban settlement there promotes higher voter turnout in comparison to the most urbanised communities. Rather than general effects from suburbanisation itself, the systematic divergences among Spanish municipalities have generated the most important metropolitan effects on election turnout. Electoral mobilisation is linked to differences in opportunities for integration into the social,

---

14. An additional analysis – regressing the town types against the residuals of the multilevel analysis – shows no effect regarding national turnout. However, the typology explains around 0.7 per cent of variance for municipal elections (adjusted $R^2=0.007$): the lowest coefficient is for low-density suburbs and poor suburbs, the highest for affluent and middle-class suburbs (urban concentration as reference category).

civic and political life of metropolitan communities. 'Small is beautiful' for both national and local elections in metropolitan Spain, and in some respects 'large is lively' for national ones.

### The socio-spatial structure of 'cleavages' in Spanish metropolitan areas – contextual variations and socio-economic cleavage

In Spanish political society, socio-economic, territorial and religious cleavages exist. The first two, built on legacies from earlier industrial and national revolutions (Lipset and Rokkan 1967), influence election preferences most strongly (Montero 1996; Linz and Montero 1999).[15] Persistent debates over the 'class vote' in Spain have rarely questioned its centrality to political life (Torcal and Chibber 1995; González 1996, 2009; Cainzos 2001), but rather its relation to other factors like age and political mobilisation.

Cleavages between centre and periphery comprise another central aspect of Spanish political society (Linz and Montero 1999). Easily discernible differences in territorial identification explain why regionalist parties receive considerable electoral support in certain areas (Pérez and Bonet 2006). Regions where the centre versus periphery cleavage is important can easily be distinguished from those without significant regionalist options (Montero 1996; Lago 2002). This difference is measured in this analysis by a dichotomous 'regional territory' variable that assigns a positive value to regions where regionalist parties are important. The clear pattern of contextual variation in these regions does not depend solely on social composition, but also on a cultural cleavage that is both ethnic and territorial (Giner and Moreno 1990). Socio-economic and religious cleavages bear a close relation to the left-right ideological distinction that customarily best explains election preferences in Spain.[16] Regionalist parties occupy both sides of this ideological continuum.

Employing the IMO common methodology, four indices have been computed by means of nationwide survey analysis. These indices use the average position of voters for different parties to place each party in relation to the cleavages discussed above. In addition to a left-right ideological index on a 1–10 scale based on the self-placement of party voters, an economic index to measure preferences for state intervention or markets, a cultural index to tap differences between liberal or non-

---

15. As far as the religious cleavage is concerned, it is indeed true that a historical conflict between Catholicism and secularisation exists in Spain, and debate is rife over the institutional role of the Church, in the terms used by Lipset and Rokkan (1967), to define this cleavage. Since the democratic transition, however, political parties have not used this question as a central argument in election disputes, focusing more on socio-economic issues. Thus, its role in the orientation of electoral preferences has been virtually negligible and fluctuated over time (Montero 1996). It has depended mainly on the extent to which parties have included issues related to moral values directly linked to the Catholic religion in electoral strategies (Calvo and Montero 2002; Montero, Calvo and Martínez 2008).

16. There is a vast literature about the importance of the left-right scale in election preferences in Spain.

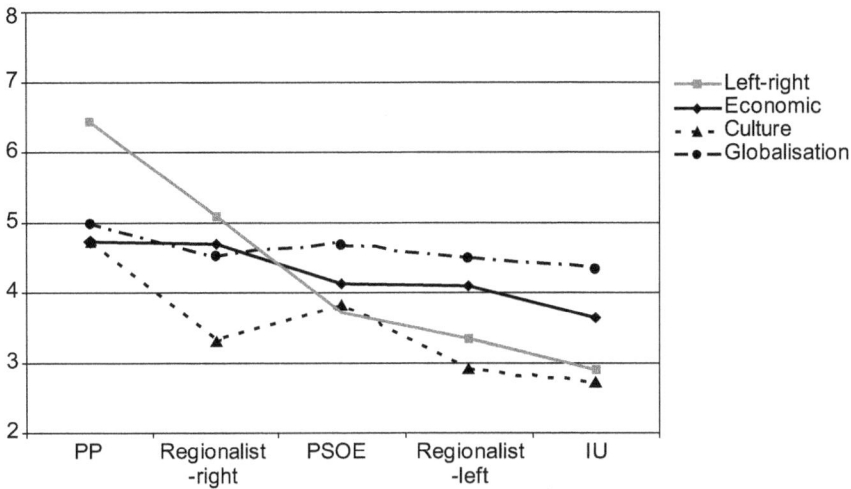

*Figure 8.4: Parties and socio-political orientations (indexes)*

traditional values and traditional or conservative values, and a globalisation index to assess attitudes toward immigration, nationalism and the European Union are included (see Figure 8.4).[17]

Ideological polarisation between left and right is readily apparent. Along the economic index, voters for each party occupy a similar position to their self-placement along a left-right scale. Support for state intervention on the left juxtaposes support for the market on the right. Along the cultural and globalisation indices, voters for the centre-right regionalist parties occupy a somewhat different position. They demonstrate greater social liberalism and more acceptance of globalisation than either of the main national parties (Popular Party and Socialist Party), although less than left-wing regionalist ones and minority left-wing parties (United Left, the former Communist Party).[18] To a certain extent, the regionalist cleavage is organised more around socio-cultural questions than around socio-economic ones.

Once the indices for municipalities are calculated, two patterns of municipal

17. The surveys and items used appear in Chapter 14, the Methodological Appendix, as well as index definitions. Regionalist parties have been grouped under 'centre-right' (CiU, PNV, UPN and CC) and 'centre-left' (PSA, CHA, EA, HB, IC-EV, ERC and BNG). Main right-wing national party (PP) and main right-wing regionalist party in Navarra (UPN) present a single one candidacy for the national elections analysed. Given the low number of voters for regionalist parties interviewed in the nationwide surveys used to compile these indices, the scores for these parties have to be taken with a certain caution.

18. Pérez and Bonet (2006) show that votes for centre-right regionalist parties in the general elections in 2004 depend above all on the centre-periphery cleavage; meanwhile socio-economic or religious factors are less important (cf. also Somuano 2002). Party manifesto data as well as World Values Survey data affirm that regionalist parties are more liberal in cultural issues than the two big parties.

socio-political orientations emerge. Outside the regionalist territories, similar municipal variations along all four indices indicate a common left-right axis. In regionalist territories, municipal variations along the socio-cultural dimensions measured by the cultural and globalisation indices diverge from patterns in the economic index and voter self-placement. This divergence between dimensions of partisanship that are similar in the rest of the country is critical to the regionalist cleavage.

### Place effects on socio-political orientations – a specific pattern of suburbanisation?

Municipal typological analysis suggests that community preferences differ more along the economic dimension than along those based on cultural beliefs, globalisation or self-placement. The typology accounts for 16 per cent of the variation in the economic index, but only 6 per cent for the other measures. The differences correspond to what might be inferred from socio-economic differences between the types. On the far left lie the poor suburbs and on the right the affluent enclaves, but also the low-density suburbs. Socio-economic differences can easily account for significant variations in the economic index. Poor suburbs depend on state intervention, while affluent suburbs prefer the market option. The variations in both the cultural and globalisation indices differ in ways that contextual influences will explain. Social conservatism and opposition to globalisation average highest among low-density suburbs and lowest among affluent suburbs.

Two main axes of ideological variation distinguish the types of municipalities. The first, expressed in the economic index, differentiates between municipalities with different socio-economic composition. The second axis reflects a divergence between two suburban patterns: low-density suburbs harbour classic right-wing social and economic conservatism (economic and social), while suburbs with higher socio-economic status embrace economic, but not social conservatism. Three distinct configurations of socio-political orientations appear in different types of municipalities:

1. The 'classic left' in poorer municipalities supports state intervention and social liberalism, and accepts globalisation.
2. The 'classic right' in low-density suburbs embraces markets together with social conservatism, and opposes globalisation.
3. The market individualism or 'new political culture' of affluent suburbs advocates markets alongside social liberalism and globalisation (Clark and Hoffmann-Martinot 1998; Clark and Rempel 1997).

Most affluent suburbs, however, are situated in regionalist territories (see Figure 8.5). Thus, the distinctive pattern in this type of municipality is due to not only the economic and cultural interests characteristic of new middle-class suburbanisation (Sellers 1999), but also to the importance of the regionalist cleavage in these territories. Indeed, the regionalist cleavage seems to concentrate in this type of municipality.

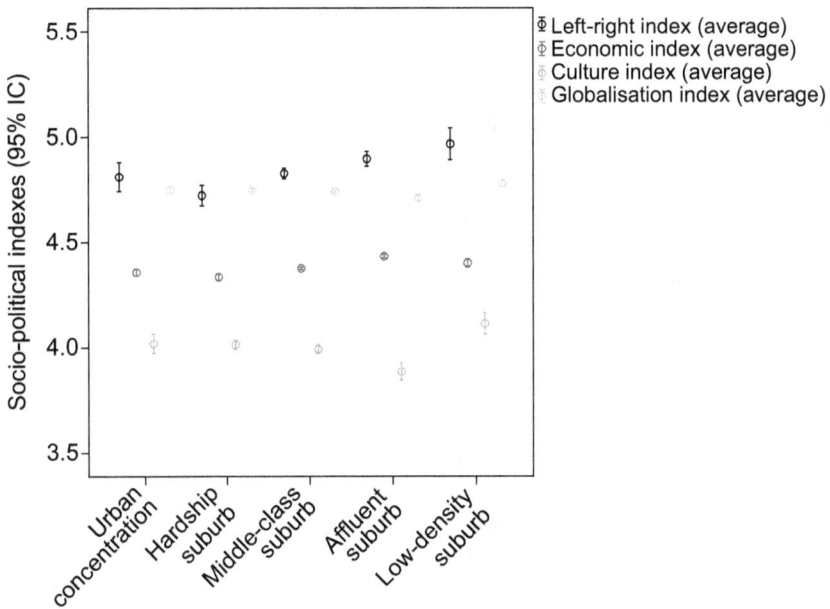

*Figure 8.5: Socio-political orientations among metropolitan municipalities (mean 0, 10-scales (ANOVA analysis))*

In regionalist territories, the difference between the percentage of votes for regionalist parties and the votes for non-regionalist ones (overall, −3 per cent) diverges starkly among municipalities according to their socio-economic status. Support for regionalist parties concentrates in affluent suburbs (18 per cent), followed by low-density suburbs (7 per cent). It falls off precipitously in middle-class suburbs (−9 per cent), hardship suburbs (−34 per cent) and urban concentrations (−39 per cent). This pattern remains similar whether the regionalist parties are aligned with the centre-right or with the left.[19]

Therefore, regional cultural cleavages cut across the more general divisions among municipalities according to economic ideology. Municipalities with similar socio-economic composition share similar economic ideologies, but diverge by region in orientations toward culture and globalisation.

---

19. In particular, the differences in ideological polarisation between regionalist parties are positive for any type of municipalities, but greater depending on socio-economic status: affluent suburbs (18), low-density suburbs (19), middle-class suburbs (13), hardship suburbs (14), and urban concentrations (9).

### The contextual and compositional patterns of socio-political orientations

Municipal level regression models affirm the importance of socio-economic differences for explaining these variations, especially the hardship index (see Table 8.5). This effect is common to all four dimensions of socio-political orientations. The lower is the socio-economic level, the stronger the tendency to the left; the greater the support for government intervention, the more liberal the cultural and the less resistance to globalisation. The presence of industrial workers and the size and/or density of urban concentrations also strengthen support for the left. These variables identify a clear intra-metropolitan cleavage between suburbs with higher

Table 8.5: The patterns of socio-political orientations among metropolitan municipalities – contextual and compositional factors (OLS regression)

| | Left-Right Index Contextual (Model 3) Coeff. (s.e.) | Economic Index Combined (Model 4) Coeff. (s.e.) | Cultural Index Combined (Model 4) Coeff. (s.e.) | Globalisation Index Combined (Model 4) Coeff. (s.e.) |
|---|---|---|---|---|
| Constant | 5.782 (0.271) | 4.590 (0.069) | 4.442 (0.225) | 4.901 |
| *Compositional* | | | | |
| Young people (<19 years) | 0.000 (0.004) | −0.005 (0.001) | 0.020 (0.003) | 0.006 (0.001) |
| Old people (>64 years) | 0.010 (0.003) | 0.001 (0.001) | 0.010 (0.003) | 0.003 (0.001) |
| Immigration (%) | 0.010 (0.003) | 0.001 (0.001) | 0.009 (0.002) | 0.003 (0.001) |
| Hardship Index | −1.107 (0.146) | −0.293 (0.037) | −0.409 (0.121) | −0.135 (0.037) |
| University (%) | 0.003 (0.002) | 0.002 (0.001) | −0.006 (0.002) | −0.002 (0.001) |
| Manufacturing (%) | −0.010 (0.001) | −0.001 (0.000) | −0.009 (0.001) | -0.003 (0.000) |
| *Contextual* | | | | |
| Municipal size (ln) | 0.034 (0.012) | −0.004 (0.003) | 0.046 (0.010) | 0.013 (0.003) |
| Municipal density (ln) | 0.046 (0.009) | 0.005 (0.002) | 0.039 (0.008) | 0.012 (0.002) |
| Distance to the centre (km) | 0.001 (0.001) | 0.001 (0.000) | 0.000 (0.001) | 0.000 (0.000) |
| Out-commuting (%) | −0.001 (0.001) | 0.000 (0.000) | −0.001 (0.001) | 0.000 (0.000) |
| Population growth (1991–2001) (%) | 0.000 (0.000) | 0.000 (0.000) | 0.000 (0.000) | 0.000 (0.000) |
| Occupational diversity (Simpson) | −1.068 (0.246) | 0.028 (0.063) | −1.348 (0.205) | −0.420 (0.062) |
| R² | 0.274 | 0.370 | 0.249 | 0.245 |

*Note:* Significant coefficients in bold (p<0.05).

hardship and larger urban working-class populations and those places with higher socio-economic status.

Contextual influences suggested by the municipal typology also play a role with these cleavages. Characteristics of rural peripheral towns, such as distance from urbanised centres, older residents, lower education levels and greater occupational homogeneity, contribute to economic and social conservatism. Among affluent and middle-class suburbs attitudes toward culture and globalisation diverge from economic preferences. Greater integration into commuting networks, more diverse occupational structures and higher levels of education predict preferences for markets over the state, and also for non-traditional values and globalisation. Although models including only socio-economic variables usually explain more variation, contextual models account for much of the same differences. In a combined model with the socio-economic variables, contextual predictors add between 1.5 per cent and 8 per cent to the overall variance explained (see models in the Web Appendix WA8).

The inclusion of regional differences in the models generates the expected results (see Table 8.6). Social liberalism and the acceptance of globalisation increase among metropolitan areas with a lower socio-economic level. The regional variable has a positive or conservative relationship to the economic index, and no net significance for left-right self-placement. The 'regionalist territories' combine non-traditional values and acceptance of globalisation with support for the market and a more right-wing profile. The addition of the regional variable increases the explained variance in both socio-cultural indices by 8 to 10 per cent, but detracts from the overall explanatory power of the model for the economic index (compare Tables in the Web Appendix WA8).

### Metropolitan and municipal variations of socio-political orientations – local socio-economic differentiation and cultural regionalism

Multilevel analysis confirms and elaborates upon the results of the above section (see Table 8.7). Municipal characteristics explain more of the variation in each of the four indices than regional differences. Multilevel models reaffirm the importance of socio-economic differences at the municipal level, as demonstrated by the hardship index. Regionalism also has the expected influence on the socio-cultural indices (cultural and globalisation). Three main findings emerge from this analysis.

First, socio-economic resources and the proportion of industrial workers differentiate municipalities along the liberalism versus conservatism continuum. As in the OLS analysis, models with compositional variables account for more of the variation than contextual models (see models in Tables WA8.6(a)–(d) of the Web Appendix). The models confirm an intra-metropolitan cleavage along the left-right ideological continuum, as well as the economic, social and globalisation orientations linked to it. A common socio-economic model accounts for much of these variations among the municipalities within metropolitan areas throughout Spain.

*Table 8.6: The regional effect on socio-political orientations (OLS regressions)*

|  | Left-Right Index Full Model 5 coeff. (s.e.) | Economic Index Full Model 5 coeff. (s.e.) | Cultural Index Full Model 5 coeff. (s.e.) | Globalisation Index Full Model 5 coeff. (s.e.) |
|---|---|---|---|---|
| Constant | **5.978** (0.254) | **4.548** (0.067) | 4.789 (0.153) | **5.004** (0.047) |
| *Local: compositional* | | | | |
| Young people (<19 years) | **−0.013** (0.004) | **−0.003** (0.001) | −0.002 (0.002) | −0.001 (0.001) |
| Old people (>64 years) | 0.002 (0.003) | **0.002** (0.001) | −0.002 (0.002) | -0.001 (0.001) |
| Immigration (%) | **0.008** (0.003) | 0.001 (0.001) | **0.005** (0.002) | **0.002** (0.00) |
| Hardship Index | −**1.041** (0.159) | **−0.332** (0.042) | **−0.222** (0.096) | **−0.086** (0.029) |
| University (%) | **0.006** (0.002) | **0.002** (0.001) | −0.001 (0.001) | 0.000 (0.000) |
| Manufacturing (%) | **−0.006** (0.001) | **−0.001** (0.000) | **−0.004** (0.001) | **−0.001** (0.000) |
| *Local: contextual* | | | | |
| Municipal size (ln) | 0.019 (0.011) | -0.001 (0.003) | **0.021** (0.007) | **0.006** (0.002) |
| Municipal density (ln) | **0.031** (0.009) | **0.007** (0.002) | **0.014** (0.005) | **0.004** (0.002) |
| Distance to the centre (km) | **0.002** (0.001) | **0.001** (0.000) | 0.001 (0.000) | 0.000 (0.000) |
| Out-commuting (%) | 0.000 (0.001) | 0.000 (0.000) | 0.000 (0.000) | 0.000 (0.000) |
| Population growth (1991-2001) (%) | 0.001 (0.000) | 0.000 (0.000) | 0.000 (0.000) | 0.000 (0.000) |
| Occupational diversity (Simpson) | **−0.634** (0.232) | −0.047 (0.061) | **−0.626** (0.139) | **−0.201** (0.043) |
| *Metropolitan* | | | | |
| Region | **−0.253** (0.020) | **0.044** (0.005) | **−0.422** (0.012) | **−0.128** (0.004) |
| Metropolitan Hardship Index | −0.183 (0.192) | 0.096 (0.051) | **−0.484** (0.116) | **−0.131** (0.035) |
| $R^2$ | 0.372 | 0.410 | 0.659 | 0.655 |

*Note:* For boldface coefficients, $p<0.05$.

*Table 8.7: Socio-political orientations among metropolitan municipalities: socioeconomic, contextual and regional factors (multilevel analysis)*

| | Left-Right Index coeff. (s.e.) | Economic Index coeff. (s.e.) | Cultural Index coeff. (s.e.) | Globalisation Index coeff. (s.e.) |
|---|---|---|---|---|
| Constant | **6.472** (0.902) | **4.728** (0.228) | **4.996** (0.501) | **5.084** (0.151) |
| *Local: compositional* | | | | |
| Young people (<19 years) | −0.004 (0.003) | **0.002** (0.001) | **−0.008** (0.002) | −0.002 (0.001) |
| Old people (>64 years) | **0.005** (0.002) | **0.002** (0.001) | −0.001 (0.001) | −0.001 (0.001) |
| Immigration (%) | **0.005** (0.002) | **0.002** (0.001) | **0.003** (0.001) | 0.001 (0.001) |
| Hardship Index | **−0.888** (0.113) | **−0.285** (0.031) | **−0.142** (0.071) | **−0.054** (0.022) |
| University (%) | **0.008** (0.001) | **0.002** (0.001) | 0.001 (0.001) | 0.001 (0.001) |
| Manufacturing (%) | **−0.005** (0.001) | **−0.002** (0.001) | **−0.002** (0.001) | **−0.002** (0.001) |
| *Local: contextual* | | | | |
| Municipal size (ln) | **−0.031** (0.008) | **−0.014** (0.002) | 0.006 (0.005) | 0.001 (0.001) |
| Municipal density (ln) | 0.001 (0.006) | 0.001 (0.001) | 0.001 (0.001) | 0.001 (0.001) |
| Distance to the centre (km) | 0.001 (0.001) | 0.001 (0.001) | **0.002** (0.001) | **0.002** (0.001) |
| Out-commuting (%) | **−0.002** (0.001) | **−0.002** (0.001) | **−0.002** (0.001) | **−0.002** (0.001) |
| Population growth (1991-2001) (%) | 0.001 (0.001) | −0.001 (0.001) | 0.001 (0.001) | 0.001 (0.001) |
| Occupational diversity (Simpson) | **−0.323** (0.166) | −0.013 (0.046) | **-0.397** (0.105) | **−0.115** (0.032) |
| *Metropolitan* | | | | |
| Size (ln) | −0.032 (0.059) | −0.009 (0.015) | −0.021 (0.033) | −0.008 (0.009) |
| Concentration | −0.245 (0.246) | −0.096 (0.062) | −0.011 (0.136) | −0.011 (0.041) |
| Metropolitan Hardship Index | −0.311 (0.563) | −0.044 (0.142) | −0.244 (0.314) | −0.082 (0.095) |
| Region | −0.131 (0.139) | **0.059** (0.027) | **−0.339** (0.060) | **−0.104** (0.018) |
| *Variance components* | | | | |
| Metropolitan | 0.058 | 0.004 | 0.017 | 0.002 |
| Municipal | 0.023 | 0.002 | 0.011 | 0.001 |
| Explained variance | | | | |
| Metropolitan | 0.073 | 0.267 | 0.518 | 0.546 |
| Municipal | 0.171 | 0.283 | 0.419 | 0.608 |
| Metropolitan (N) | 30 | 30 | 30 | 30 |
| Municipal (N) | 1053 | 1053 | 1053 | 1053 |
| Deviance | −556.964 | −3243.706 | −1522.41 | −3987.427 |

*Note:* For boldface coefficients, p<0.05.

Secondly, contextual influences linked to suburbanisation explain a further portion of the variation, and provide an alternative account for part of the compositional influences. Lower commuting rates and smaller populations are linked to stronger preferences for markets over the state. Greater distance from the centre, lower commuting rates and occupational homogeneity – all foster stronger socio-cultural conservatism as measured by the cultural and globalisation indices.

Thirdly, suburban conservatism is strongest in Spanish metropolitan municipalities that are smaller, more socially homogenous and less integrated into metropolitan life (such as the low-density suburbs). The same communitarian characteristics that foster higher turnout rates in these metropolitan municipalities have also cultivated this type of political conservatism.[20]

As in the analysis of participation, multilevel models are particularly helpful for clarifying how regional influences work. 'Regionalist territories' show a marked tendency towards the right and an even stronger pro-market preference, but stronger cultural liberalism and support for globalisation. The pattern corresponds to what we previously called 'market individualism' and is especially pronounced in the cultural dimension. Tests for cross-level effects between location in the regionalist territories and contextual variables for size, distance and commuting, as well as for the hardship index, confirm the distinctiveness of the regionalist territories (see Tables 8.8(a) and (b)).

Surprisingly, the relationship between the hardship index and the four partisan indices tends to be reversed, as are relationships with municipal size and commuting. In the regionalist territories, suburbs with higher socio-economic status are less conservative than the same kinds of suburbs in metropolitan areas where regionalist parties are not present. This difference in the orientations of affluent suburbs is primarily due to the regionalist cleavage. Rather than a general pattern of market individualism, this pattern reflects a tendency specific to one type of municipality in regionalist territories.

Multilevel analysis thus further elucidates the specificity we have already encountered in regionalist territories. Not only are there differences between regions and metropolitan areas, but also differences in the patterns among municipalities within different regions. The regionalist cleavage itself is primarily evident in the more affluent suburbs of regionalist territories. In comparison with their counterparts in non-regionalist territories, these affluent communities are conspicuous in their strong support for the regionalist parties. If regionalist territories represent an 'eccentric model' with respect to the predominant Spanish metropolitan political ecology, this 'eccentricity' concentrates in the affluent enclaves of metropolitan areas within those territories.[21]

---

20. In fact, for all the World Values Survey waves carried out in Spain, municipal size correlates very positively to post-materialist change indices, even when checking them against socio-demographic and income variables.

21. Further OLS regressions showed that the typology of municipalities does not explain the remaining multilevel residuals. The explained variance is not greater than 0.001 for any of the socio-political orientations.

*Table 8.8(a): The intra-metropolitan character of regionalism (multilevel analysis)*

|  | Left-Right Index | Economic Index | Cultural Index | Globalisation Index |
|---|---|---|---|---|
|  | coeff. (s.e.) | coeff. (s.e.) | coeff. (s.e.) | coeff. (s.e.) |
| Constant | **6.535** (0.865) | **4.664** (0.237) | **5.320** (0.443) | **5.179** (0.134) |
| *Local: compositional* | | | | |
| Young people (<19 years) | −0.004 (0.003) | **0.002** (0.001) | **−0.008** (0.002) | **−0.002** (0.001) |
| Old people (>64 years) | 0.004 (0.002) | **0.003** (0.001) | **−0.002** (0.001) | −0.001 (0.001) |
| Immigration (%) | **0.004** (0.002) | **0.002** (0.001) | 0.001 (0.001) | 0.001 (0.001) |
| Hardship Index | **−1.040** (0.124) | **−0.257** (0.033) | **−0.443** (0.073) | **−0.145** (0.022) |
| University (%) | **0.009** (0.001) | **0.022** (0.001) | 0.001 (0.001) | 0.001 (0.001) |
| Manufacturing (%) | **−0.005** (0.001) | **−0.002** (0.001) | **−0.002** (0.001) | −0.002 (0.001) |
| *Local: contextual* | | | | |
| Municipal size (ln) | **−0.030** (0.009) | **−0.010** (0.002) | −0.010 (0.005) | **−0.003** (0.001) |
| Municipal density (ln) | 0.003 (0.007) | -0.001 (0.001) | **0.009** (0.004) | **0.003** (0.001) |
| Distance to the centre (km) | **0.002** (0.001) | 0.001 (0.001) | **0.002** (0.001) | **0.002** (0.001) |
| Out-commuting (%) | **−0.003** (0.001) | **−0.002** (0.001) | **−0.002** (0.001) | **−0.002** (0.001) |
| Population growth (1991–2001) (%) | 0.001 (0.001) | 0.001 (0.001) | 0.001 (0.001) | 0.001 (0.001) |
| Occupational diversity (Simpson) | **−0.320** (0.166) | −0.029 (0.044) | **−0.333** (0.097) | **−0.096** (0.030) |
| *Metropolitan* | | | | |
| Size (ln) | −0.033 (0.865) | −0.008 (0.016) | −0.025 (0.029) | −0.009 (0.009) |
| Concentration | −0.244 (0.058) | −0.093 (0.064) | 0.028 (0.120) | -0.016 (0.036) |
| Metropolitan Hardship Index | −0.288 (0.539) | −0.057 (0.147) | −0.167 (0.028) | −0.060 (0.084) |
| Region | −0.233 (0.134) | **0.183** (0.037) | **−0.926** (0.072) | **−0.277** (0.022) |

*Note:* For boldface coefficients, p<0.05.

*Table 8.8(b): The intra-metropolitan character of regionalism (multilevel analysis)*

|  | Left-Right Index coeff. (s.e.) | Economic Index coeff. (s.e.) | Cultural Index coeff. (s.e.) | Globalisation Index coeff. (s.e.) |
|---|---|---|---|---|
| *Cross level interactions (metropolitan\*local )* | | | | |
| Region\*municipal size | 0.006 (0.010) | **−0.012** (0.003) | **0.039** (0.005) | **0.011** (0.001) |
| Region\*distance | −0.001 (0.001) | −0.001 (0.001) | −0.001 (0.001) | −0.001 (0.001) |
| Region\*municipal HSES | **0.497** (0.194) | −0.030 (0.052) | **0.736** (0.113) | **0.225** (0.035) |
| *Variance components* | | | | |
| Metropolitan | 0.052 | 0.004 | 0.014 | 0.001 |
| Municipal | 0.027 | 0.002 | 0.097 | 0.001 |
| *Explained variance* | | | | |
| Metropolitan | 0.154 | 0.214 | 0.627 | 0.647 |
| Municipal | 0.222 | 0.255 | 0.531 | 0.681 |
| Metropolitan (N) | 30 | 30 | 30 | 30 |
| Municipal (N) | 1053 | 1053 | 1053 | 1053 |
| Deviance | −543.773 | −3243.508 | −1652.298 | −4101.638 |

*Note:* For boldface coefficients, $p<0.05$.

## The political ecology of the Spanish metropolis – places, socio-economic differences and regions

The Spanish metropolitan political ecology is primarily articulated around intra-metropolitan cleavages. In both election turnout and partisan preferences, differences among municipalities exceed those among metropolitan areas. The patterns of municipal variation can be explained by various combinations of contextual and socio-economic factors, as well as by effects from the regionalist cleavage. Which of these factors are most important depends on the type of political behaviour analysed (see Table 8.9).

Contextual variables linked to a 'communitarian pattern' account for the largest portion of the variations in turnout. Greater community integration, associated with smaller size, less commuting, more social homogeneity and greater isolation from metropolitan dynamics, promotes a higher level of electoral participation. Conversely, larger size, greater social heterogeneity and more integration into metropolitan commuting networks foster lower election turnout. This pattern is similar for both municipal and national elections. In some national elections, higher turnout in larger urban centres appears to qualify this effect. These settings provide

*Table 8.9: The political ecology of Spanish metropolitan areas*

|  | Electoral participation | Socio-political orientations ('cleavages') |
|---|---|---|
| Main pattern | Intra-metropolitan and contextual: 'communitarian vote' | Intra-metropolitan and socio-economic: the socio-economic differences among municipalities |
| Main contextual variations | Urban concentrations (delocalised) vs. low-density suburbs (localised) | The 'regional effect': the 'centre vs. periphery' cleavage |
| Other contextual variations | The 'regional effect': a more localised participation in local elections | The intra-metropolitan ecology of regionalism: 'affluent suburbs' |

supportive conditions for the agents highlighted in the classic accounts of electoral mobilisation as well as in the specific literature on the Spanish case. The diversity, density and other features linked to urbanisation furnish more favourable contexts for engagement with issues beyond the scope of local politics. The smaller and more homogeneous 'communities' which make up the low-density suburbs vote consistently, but appear more resistant to these exogenous mobilising forces.

Overall, suburbanisation has promoted electoral participation. Although commuting inhibits turnout, most characteristics of suburban communities contribute to higher rates of participation. A suburbanite is more likely to vote than their urban counterpart. This is all the more likely if the municipality where they reside retains features of a communitarian character: social homogeneity, lower density, fewer ties to the urban centre and, to a certain extent, an upper to middle-class socio-economic status. Seen through the lens of electoral participation in Spain, suburbanisation does not destroy, but rather appears to strengthen 'political community'. Citizens in the metropolitan areas of regionalist territories generally participate less in national elections than other metropolitan citizens.

Electoral preferences reveal an intra-metropolitan cleavage that is rooted in socio-economic status, but demonstrates significant contextual variations. The latter mainly take the form of interrelated regional and local effects. Metropolitan Spain manifests a common socio-economic cleavage that is evident in voter self-placement on the traditional left-right scale, and in liberal and conservative positions on economic and social issues. Many of the same communitarian influences that have fostered higher levels of participation in Spanish suburbs are also linked to local preferences for the parties of the right. Suburbanisation may therefore be laying the foundations for more consistent electoral mobilisation on the right than on the left.

In the regionalist territories, the divergent preferences for cultural liberalism and globalisation represent the most striking exception to this national pattern of partisan preferences. Although commonly assumed to be regional rather than local or metropolitan in nature, these regional variations are actually directly linked to suburbanisation. Within regionalist territories, municipalities with higher socio-economic status express by far the strongest support for the distinctive economic and socio-cultural orientations of regionalist parties. These differences are not simply regional variations, but also local variations within the metropolitan areas of regionalist territories. In Spain, support for regionalism itself is rooted in consistent intra-metropolitan cleavages.[22]

Suburbanisation has introduced new major variations in socio-political orientations that have significance for regional and national politics. More research will be necessary to explain why support for the regionalist parties concentrates in affluent suburbs, and why suburbanisation accentuates regionalist cleavages. In this and other ways, metropolitan diversity has increasingly become the rule that structures electoral behaviour and preferences in Spain.

---

22. Despite the low number of interviewees used to calculate the indices of regionalist parties, the election results leave no doubt about the concentration of regionalist cleavage in this type of metropolitan municipality. Dummies for individual regions showed the phenomenon to be concentrated in Catalonia and the Basque country.

## Bibliography

Alba, C. and Navarro, C. (2007) 'L'emergence du fait métropolitain en Espagne', in V. Hoffmann-Martinot and J. M. Sellers (eds) *Politique et Métropole. Une comparaison internationale*, Paris: CNRS Editions, 153–72.

Barreiro, B. (2001) 'Los determinantes de la participación en las elecciones españolas de marzo de 2000: el problema de la abstención en la izquierda', Working paper 171, Instituto Juan March.

Boix, R. (2007) 'Concepto y delimitación de áreas metropolitanas: una aplicación a las áreas metropolitanas de España', *Seminario sobre Las grandes áreas metropolitanas españolas en perspectiva comparada*, Fundación centro de Estudios Andaluces. Sevilla, 11 de Abril.

Boix, C. and Riba, C. (2000) 'Las bases sociales y políticas de la abstención en las elecciones generales españolas: recursos individuales, movilización estratégica e instituciones electorales', *Revista Española de Investigaciones Sociológicas*, 90: 95–128.

Cainzos, M. (2001) 'La evolución del voto clasista en España, 1986–2000', *Zona Abierta*, 96–97: 91–172.

Calvo, K. and Montero, J. R. (2002) 'Cuando ser conservador ya no es un problema: religiosidad, ideología y voto en las elecciones generales de 2000', *Revista Española de Ciencia Política*, 6: 17–56.

Capó, J. (1991) 'Elecciones municipales, pero no locales', *Revista Española de Investigaciones Sociológicas*, 56: 143–65.

Caramani, D. (2004) *The Nationalisation of Politics*, Cambridge, Cambridge University Press.

Clark, T. N. and Hoffmann-Martinot, V. (1998) *The New Political Culture*, Boulder, Co.: Westview Press.

Clark, T. N. and Rempel, M. (1997) *Citizen Politics in Post-industrial Societies*, Boulder, Co.: Westview Press.

Delgado, I. (1997) *El Comportamiento Electoral Municipal Español, 1979–1995*, Madrid: CIS.

—— (1999) 'Resultados electorales y orientación del voto en los comicios municipales de 1995', *Revista Española de Investigaciones Sociológicas* 86: 247-273.

Eagles, M. and Erfle, S. (1989) 'Community cohesion and voter turnout in English parliamentary constituencies', *British Journal of Political Science*, 19(1): 115–25.

Feria, J. M. (2008) 'Un ensayo metodológico de definición de las áreas metropolitanas en España a partir de la variable residencia-trabajo', *Investigaciones geográficas*, 46: 49–68.

Font, J. (1992) 'La abstención electoral en las grandes ciudades, Madrid y Barcelona', *Revista Española de Investigaciones Sociológicas*, 58: 123–39.

—— (1995) 'La abstención electoral en España: certezas e interrogantes', *Revista Española de Investigaciones Sociológicas*, 71/72: 11–37.

Giner, S. and Moreno, L. (1990) 'Centro y periferia: la dimensión étnica de la sociedad española', in S. Giner (ed.) *España. Sociedad y Política*, Madrid: Espasa Calpe, 169–98.

González, J. J. (1996) 'Clases, ciudadanos y clases de ciudadanos. El ciclo electoral del pos-socialismo (1985–94)', *Revista Española de Investigaciones Sociológicas*, 74: 45–76.

—    (2009) 'Voto estructural, racional y mediatizado en las elecciones generales españoles de 1996, 2000 y 2004', *Revista Internacional de Sociología* 67(2): 285-307.

Hoffmann-Martinot, V. and Sellers, J. M. (2007) 'La métropolisation de la politique', in V. Hoffmann-Martinot and J. M. Sellers (eds) *Politique et métropole. Une comparaison internationale*, Paris: CNRS Editions, 216–33.

Huckfeldt, R. (1986) *Politics in Context*, New Cork: Agathon Press.

Indovina, F. (2007) *La ciudad de baja densidad*, Barcelona: Diputación de Barcelona.

Justel, M. (1995) *La abstención electoral en España, 1977–1993*, Madrid: CIS.

Kelleher, C. A. and Lowery, D. (2008) 'Central city size, metropolitan institutions and political participation', *British Journal of Political Science*, 39: 59–92.

Lago, I. (2002) 'Cleavages y umbrales: las consecuencias políticas de los sistemas lectorales autonómicos, 1980–2000', *Revista Española de Ciencia Política*, 7: 131–58.

Leal, J. (2006) 'Distribución del espacio residencial y localización de la población española', in J. A. Fernández Cordón and J. Leal (eds) *Análisis Territorial de la Demografía Española, 2006*, Madrid: Fundación Fernando Abril Martorell, 451–87.

Linz, J. and Montero, J. R. (1999) 'The party system in Spain: old cleavages and new challenges', Working paper 138, Instituto Juan March.

Lipset, S. M. and Rokkan, S. (1967) *Party Systems and Voter Alignments*, New York: Free Press.

Montero, J. R. (1996) 'Elecciones y comportamiento electoral: dimensiones, factores y reglas', in J. Tusell, E. y Lamo de Espinosa, R. Pardo (eds) *Entre dos siglos. Reflexiones sobre la democracia española*, Madrid: Alianza, 181–226.

Montero, J. R., Calvo, K. and Martínez, A. (2008) 'El voto religioso en España y Portugal', *Revista Internacional de Sociología*, 51: 19–54.

Navarro, C. J. (2011) *Comunidades locales y participación política en España*, Madrid, CIS.

Oliver, J. E. (2001) *Democracy in Suburbia*, Princeton: Princeton University Press.

Pallarés, F. (1994) 'Las elecciones autonómicas en España (1980–1992)', in P. Del Castillo (ed.) *Comportamiento Político y Electoral*, Madrid: CIS, 151–220.

Pérez, S. and Bonet, E. (2006) 'Identidades regionales y reivindicación de autogobierno. El etnorregionalismo en el voto a partidos nacionalistas en Bélgica, España y Reino Unido', *Revista Española de Ciencia Política*, 15: 123–61.

Putnam, R. (2000) *Bowling Alone*, New York: Touchstone Publishers.

Recaño, J. (2006) 'Migraciones internas y distribución espacial de la población española', in J. Leal (ed.*) Informe sobre al situación demográfica en España. 2004*, Madrid: Fundación Fernando Abril Martorell, 187–229.

Rubenson, S. J. (2004) 'The effect of racial heterogeneity on electoral and non-electoral political participation in American cities', Annual Meeting of the Midwest Science Political Association, Chicago, IL.

Sellers, J. M. (1999) 'Public goods and the politics of segregation', *Journal of Urban Affairs*, 21(2): 237–62.

Spanish Ministry of Housing (2005) *Atlas Estadístico de las Áreas Urbanas en España*, Madrid, Spanish Ministry of Housing.

Somuano, M. F. (2002) 'Voto nacionalista en España: explicación desde diferentes perspectivas teóricas', *Foro Internacional, XL*, (3): 572–98.

Torcal, M. and Chibber, P. (1995) 'Elites, cleavages y sistema de partidos en una democracia consolidada: España 1986–1992', *Revista Española de Investigaciones Sociológicas*, 69: 7–38.

Vallés, J. M. and Sánchez, J. (1994) 'Las elecciones municipales en España entre 1979 y 1991: balance provisional', in P. Castillo (ed.) *Comportamiento político y electoral*, Madrid: CIS, 365-383.

Verba, S. and Nie, N. H. (1976) *Participation in America*, New York: Harper and Row, Publishers.

# Appendix

*Table A8.1: Definition of variables*

| Level | Name | Definition |
|---|---|---|
| Metropolitan | Region | Regional territories (Canarias, Cataluña, País Vasco, Navarra) (Sources: Montero, 1996) |
| | Hardship Index | Average of municipalities HSES indexes in the metropolitan area |
| | Concentration | Herfindahl index (Hoffmann-Martinot and Sellers 2007) |
| | Fragmentation | Zeigler-Brunn index (Hoffmann-Martinot and Sellers 2007) |
| | Polarisation | Nathan-Adams Dissimilarity index (Core city HSES/ Metropolitan municipalities HSES) (Hoffmann-Martinot and Sellers 2007) |
| Municipal: Compositional | Young people | Proportion of inhabitants under 18 years |
| | Old people | Proportion of inhabitants up to 64 years |
| | Immigration | Proportion of foreign-born inhabitants |
| | Hardship Index | Summary index of $((Xi-Xmin)*100)/(Xmax-Xmin)$ where: |
| | | x1: Proportion of inhabitants with low socio-economic status (manual workers) |
| | | x2: unemployment rate |
| | | x3: proportion of inhabitants with low educational level |
| | | x4: living space (household size/household surface) |
| | University | Proportion of inhabitants with university degree |
| | Manufacturing | Proportion of occupied population in the II Economic Sector |
| Municipal: Contextual | Municipal size (ln) | Number of inhabitants (natural logarithm) |
| | Municipal density (ln) | Inhabitants/municipality's surface (natural logarithm) |
| | Distance to the centre (km) | geographic distance from municipality to the core city (Km) |
| | Out-commuting | Proportion of inhabitants |
| | Population growth | Population growth rate (1991–2001) |
| | Occupational diversity | Simpson diversity index: $1-Sum(pi^2)$ where pi are five occupational groups: |
| | | owners and employers, managers and professionals, non-manual workers, manual workers |
| Municipal: Elections: | National turnout | |
| | Municipal turnout | |
| | Left-Right Index | % votes weighted by parties position in left-right scales (National Post-electoral Elections) |

| Level | Name | Definition |
|---|---|---|
| | Economic index | % votes weighted by parties economic position (ISSP and ESV surveys) |
| | Cultural index | % votes weighted by parties cultural position (ISSP and EVS surveys) |
| | Globalisation index | % votes weighted by parties globalization position (ISSP and EVS surveys) |

*Sources*: Census data – National Statistic Institute, Gobierno de España; Electoral Statistics – Ministerio del Interior, Gobierno de España.

Parties position: Left-right scale – Post-electoral surveys, Centro de Investigaciones Sociológicas, Gobierno de España (1996: CIS2210; 2000: CIS2384; 2004: CIS2559)

Other indexes: see Chapter 14, Methodological Appendix in this volume.

# Chapter Nine | Metropolitan and Political Change in Sweden

*Daniel Kübler and Henry Bäck*

## Introduction

Metropolitan areas are characterised by centrifugal forces producing dispersed patterns of actors and activities. These patterns can be described along a number of dimensions. Three of those important dimensions are the spatial, the social and the political dimensions (Bäck 2005). In this chapter, we investigate how in particular the spatial and social dimensions are related to patterns of electoral behaviour in the three Swedish metropolitan areas of Stockholm, Göteborg and Malmö.

Among the advanced industrial countries examined in this volume, Sweden has maintained comparatively low rates of metropolitanisation and suburbanisation (Bäck 2005). Mostly dominated by the Social Democratic Party in the post-war period, Swedish governments have built up one of the world's most generous social welfare systems (Esping-Andersen 1990). Thanks to comprehensive welfare state arrangements, Sweden has been a relatively egalitarian society throughout the twentieth century. Territorial sorting according to lifestyles and consumption interests remains limited. In this national setting of relatively high territorial homogeneity, metropolitan spatial contexts might be expected to have less effect on political behaviour than in other countries.

In the early 1990s, economic crisis, globalisation and European Union membership have put the Swedish model of welfare capitalism under pressure. Reforms implemented by the first post-war, centre-right government (between 1991 and 1994), but also by subsequent Social Democratic governments have weakened the Swedish welfare state. In the first decade of the twenty-first century, the electoral victory of a centre-right alliance appears to mark a critical juncture in Swedish politics and a watershed for the future development of the Swedish model (Miles 2010).

Against this background, the analyses in this chapter discuss the metropolitanisation of politics thesis in the Swedish context. We pay particular attention to the links between territorial structure and political change in Sweden's metropolitan areas. Following the common research protocol, we will first examine the socio-economic and spatial structuring of the three major Swedish metropolitan areas. We then turn to analysing political behaviour, i.e. turnout in municipal and national elections, as well as the partisan orientations of municipal electorates, before we discuss the spatial pattern of electoral change in parliamentary elections between 1991 and 2010. In the conclusion, we explore the relationships between the processes of metropolitan and political change in Sweden as the country has entered the twenty-first century.

## The socio-spatial structure of the three Swedish metropolises

As in other industrialised nations, urbanisation in Sweden steadily increased over the course of the twentieth century. While approximately half of the Swedish population lived in rural areas before World War II, the population share of urban areas rose steeply to more than 80 per cent in 1970. Since then, the growth of Sweden's urban population was quite moderate: 84 per cent of the population lived in localities classified as urban in the year 2000, and in 2010, 85 per cent of Sweden's 9.42 million inhabitants lived in an urban environment (Statistics Sweden 2011: 3). Similarly, the development of large metropolitan areas has remained relatively limited. There are only three metropolitan areas with populations above 200,000 – namely Stockholm (1.66 million inhabitants), Göteborg (0.78 million) and Malmö (0.38 million) – and roughly a third of the overall population of the country lives there. However, since the 1970s the national population has concentrated increasingly in these three metropolitan areas (Bäck 2005: 121).

As in other Nordic countries, extensive territorial reforms have been carried out in Sweden's local government system in the mid-twentieth century. This is why today Swedish municipalities are generally large in size and why core cities in the metropolitan areas account for over half of the metropolitan population. The figures for the three metropolitan areas of Stockholm, Göteborg and Malmö (see Table 9.1) show that geopolitical fragmentation is indeed quite low. Nevertheless, all three metropolitan areas have been characterised by ongoing suburbanisation since the 1970s. Only in Malmö has the annual growth rate of the core city recently overtaken that of the suburban area.

By international standards, social segregation – particularly in the form of spatial clustering among low resource households – has been relatively limited in Sweden's metropolitan areas (Vogel 1992). Andersson *et al.* (2010) argue that, on the one hand, the generous Swedish welfare state arrangements have kept

*Table 9.1: Characteristics of three main metropolitan areas in Sweden (data for 2002)*

|                                                      | Stockholm | Göteborg | Malmö   |
| ---------------------------------------------------- | --------- | -------- | ------- |
| Overall population                                   | 1,666,513 | 781,622  | 382,271 |
| Population in core city                              | 45.5%     | 60.7%    | 69.4%   |
| Number of core city districts                        | 18        | 21       | 10      |
| Annual growth rate of core city (1990–2003)          | 1.0%      | 0.8%     | 1.1%    |
| Number of suburban municipalities                    | 21        | 9        | 6       |
| Annual growth rate suburban area (1990–2003)         | 1.3%      | 1.2%     | 0.7%    |
| Geopolitical fragmentation*                          | 0.290     | 0.210    | 0.263   |

*Notes:* *Zeigler Brunn index: number of municipalities per 10,000 inhabitants divided by the core city's share of the overall metropolitan population.
*Source:* Bäck (2005).

income disparities low while, on the other hand, Sweden's national government has implemented a broad range of anti-segregation policies. Tax equalisation among municipalities helps to maintain equal levels of municipal services in spite of different tax bases. Nationwide housing and land-use policies aimed at producing socially-mixed neighbourhoods were implemented from the mid-1970s onwards. A strategy of 'refugee dispersal' was put into practice in the mid-1980s to counteract further spatial concentration of immigrants in areas where there were already high proportions of ethnic minorities. Finally, a new area-based urban policy formulated in the late 1990s aimed to promote economic and social development in deprived neighbourhoods of the metropolitan areas of Stockholm, Göteborg and Malmö.

From the 1980s onwards, however, income differences between households have increased. Capital revenues among middle and high income earners as well as growing returns from educational investments in the service sector have contributed to this process. These income differences have translated into socio-economic segregation, and a widening polarisation between rich and poor metropolitan localities. Simultaneously, some of the anti-segregation policies were dismantled or relaxed by the centre-right government of the early 1990s, and recent reforms 'such as the dismantling of an active housing policy as well as education reforms have made it difficult for planning authorities to counteract segregation processes' (Andersson et al. 2010: 5). Although Sweden remains a country with relatively small economic disparities, socio-economic segregation is increasing in Swedish metropolitan areas, and it has a strong ethnic character.

As the maps in Figure 9.1 illustrate, this growing socio-economic differentiation is closely related to spatial differentiation in political behaviour. The top row of maps distinguishes five equally large categories of municipalities by their values on an index of socio-economic status (SES), summarising measures of income, education and unemployment. The municipalities with the highest SES are represented with the lightest shade of grey, while the lowest ranking (fifth) is black. The middle row of maps represents turnout in the 2002 local election, with the highest participation (above 82.5 per cent) in light grey and those with lowest participation (below 75 per cent in black). Finally the lowermost maps display the cumulative percentage of votes in the 2002 municipal elections for socialist parties (i.e. the Social Democrats and the Left Party) with the lowest share (below 31.9 per cent) in light grey and the highest share (above 45 per cent) in black.

As the national metropolis, the Stockholm region (left column) has experienced the most extensive process of suburbanisation and population sorting. The central city there has retained a large concentration of affluent residents. In doing so, it has maintained a higher average socio-economic status, comparatively moderate electoral participation and a mixed socialist vote. Closer inspection reveals a concentration of four to five relatively affluent municipalities located north east of the core city. There the average socio-economic status is high, levels of turnout are high and support for socialist parties is low. The industrial Malmö region (the right-hand column) presents in many respects an inverse picture.

In all three maps, low socio-economic status, low electoral participation and

| Stockholm | Göteborg | Malmö |
|-----------|----------|-------|

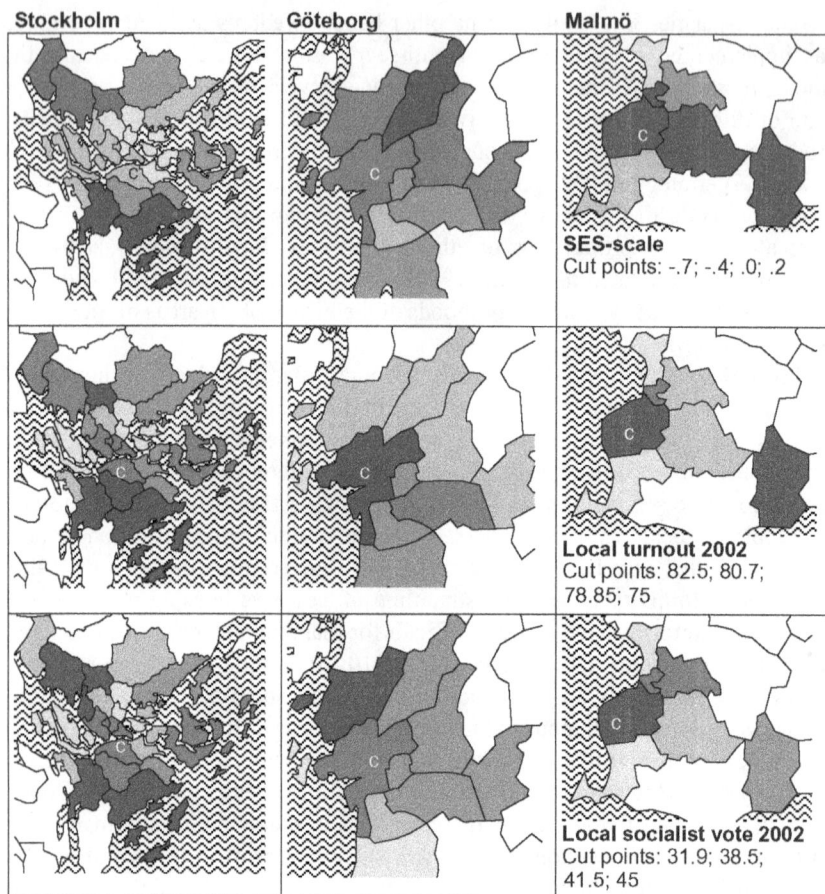

**SES-scale**
Cut points: -.7; -.4; .0; .2

**Local turnout 2002**
Cut points: 82.5; 80.7; 78.85; 75

**Local socialist vote 2002**
Cut points: 31.9; 38.5; 41.5; 45

*Figure 9.1: Social structure and electoral behaviour in local elections in the municipalities of Swedish metropolitan areas*

*Note:* C = Core cities

high support for socialist parties in the core city contrast with the predominant pattern in the surrounding localities. In the service centre of Göteborg, the core city is characterised by comparatively moderate socio-economic status, but similarly low electoral participation and strong support for socialist parties. Metropolitan localities around Göteborg generally evince less spatial sorting and more similar socio-economic profiles.

The internal differentiation of the Swedish metropolitan areas is also captured by the fivefold typology of metropolitan localities constructed according to the common research protocol (see Table 9.2).[1] Urban concentrations comprise the core cities of the three metropolitan areas. They are very large in terms of population

---

1.    See the Appendix A9.1 to this chapter for details on the construction of the typology.

*Table 9.2: Characteristics of types of municipalities in three Swedish metropolitan areas (Stockholm, Göteborg, Malmö), data for 2002*

| | | Urban concentrations | Poor suburbs | Middle-class suburbs | Affluent enclaves | Low-density suburbs | Total |
|---|---|---|---|---|---|---|---|
| Number of municipalities | N | 3 | 6 | 16 | 6 | 8 | 39 |
| Population | Mean | 499,516 | 36,563 | 39,347 | 47,408 | 24,809 | 72,574 |
| Density (inh./km²) | Mean | 2,266 | 265 | 755 | 949 | 120 | 695 |
| SES score (income and education) | Mean | 0.055 | −1.793 | −0.231 | 2.397 | −0.593 | −0.119 |
| Per cent foreign born | Mean | 20.6 | 15.5 | 12.2 | 13.0 | 10.6 | 13.1 |
| Per cent under 18 | Mean | 19.0 | 24.4 | 24.3 | 24.1 | 26.4 | 24.3 |
| Per cent retirees | Mean | 19.8 | 17.4 | 17.6 | 19.9 | 15.8 | 17.7 |
| Per cent unemployed | Mean | 4.5 | 3.0 | 2.1 | 1.7 | 1.7 | 2.3 |
| Distance to centre in km | Mean | | 23.5 | 16.7 | 13.3 | 35.2 | 21.4 |
| Per cent single family housing | Mean | 16.7 | 55.5 | 55.5 | 50.8 | 65.7 | 53.9 |
| Per cent commuting | Mean | 19.8 | 63.0 | 66.1 | 70.0 | 66.2 | 62.8 |

size, have a high share of multi-family dwellings and are, therefore, very densely populated. The proportions of foreign born inhabitants approach 20 per cent in all three core cities, well above the overall mean. In the Stockholm metropolitan area, the socio-economic status of the core city is higher than average; in Göteborg and Malmö it is lower.

The thirty-six suburban municipalities were classified into the four remaining types. Six municipalities were classified as poor suburbs – three in the Malmö metropolitan area, two in Stockholm and one in Göteborg.[2] They represent the quartile of municipalities with very low socio-economic status. Opposite these, six municipalities in the highest quartile of socio-economic status were classified as affluent suburbs. Five of these suburbs were located in the Stockholm area, one in Malmö and none in Göteborg. Among those municipalities in the two middle quartiles of socio-economic status, eight sparsely populated municipalities located

2. An application of the original protocol devised the additional category of poor minority suburbs. However, as there was only one Swedish municipality in this category, it was merged with the poor suburb category for the subsequent analyses in this chapter.

on the outskirts of the metropolitan areas were classified as low-density suburbs. The remaining sixteen municipalities were classified as middle-class suburbs.

The distribution of the various types of suburban municipalities across the three metropolitan areas gives a good idea of the general character of the three metropolitan areas. Typical of Stockholm is the over-representation of affluent suburbs (located north east of the core city) and the underrepresentation of poor suburbs. Malmö is at the other end of the scale, with few affluent enclaves and a high number of poor suburbs. Göteborg is situated in the middle, with rather few affluent suburbs, average proportions of poor and middle-class suburbs, but a large number of low-density suburbs. In sum, Stockholm is relatively wealthy; Malmö is a poor but compact metropolitan area; and Göteborg is socially average and spatially spread.

## Explaining electoral turnout in Swedish metropolises

In international comparison, electoral turnout in Sweden is high. Moreover, turnout levels in Swedish national (parliamentary) elections and municipal elections have remained closer than elsewhere. Municipal elections in Sweden are held on the same day as national elections and traditionally are highly-politicised contests between the national parties (Morlan 1984: 463). The slightly lower level of municipal election turnout is largely attributable to differences in the electorate. Whereas only Swedish citizens are entitled to vote in national parliamentary elections, the electorate of municipal elections also includes foreigners (residents from European Union or other Nordic countries, as well as long-term residents from other countries) whose participation in the political process is substantially lower (Bäck and Soininen 1998). Consistent with the known effects of the electoral law specificities (Blais *et al.* 2003) as well as the high degree of territorial homogeneity in Sweden, turnout levels in the three metropolitan areas under scrutiny do not differ substantially from average rates for the rest of the country (see Table 9.3).

Among the metropolitan municipalities themselves, the variation in turnout between averages for the different types is also considerably narrower than in the other countries in this study. The means for the types differ by 9 per cent in municipal elections and only 5 per cent in parliamentary elections (see Figure 9.2). An analysis of variance nonetheless demonstrates some variations that are statistically significant. In urban concentrations and poor suburbs, turnout is significantly lower than average. In the affluent suburbs, it is significantly higher than average. Turning to multivariate techniques, the subsequent analyses seek to explain these differences. In the light of the overall research *problématique* of this volume, we will pay particular attention to distinguishing explanatory factors linked to the socio-demographic composition of the electorate (in terms of socio-economic status, age, employment sector, and migration) from factors that refer to the spatial context of the localities in which people live (municipality size, population density, proportion of single family housing, proportion of commuters, and location within the metropolitan area).

*Table 9.3: Turnout (in %) parliamentary and municipal elections in Sweden and in the three metropolitan areas, 1991–2010*

| Year of election | Parliamentary elections (all of Sweden)* | Parliamentary elections (in three metropolitan areas) | Municipal elections (all of Sweden)* | Municipal elections (in three metropolitan areas) |
|---|---|---|---|---|
| 1991 | 86.7 | 88.8 | 84.3 | 85.9 |
| 1994 | 86.8 | 88.5 | 84.4 | 85.7 |
| 1998 | 81.4 | 83.4 | 78.6 | 80.6 |
| 2002 | 80.1 | 82.5 | 77.9 | 80.2 |
| 2006 | 82.0 | 84.3 | 79.4 | 82.0 |
| 2010 | 84.6 | 86.5 | 81.6 | 83.6 |

*Source: * = Statistical Yearbook of Sweden 2011 (www.scb.se).*

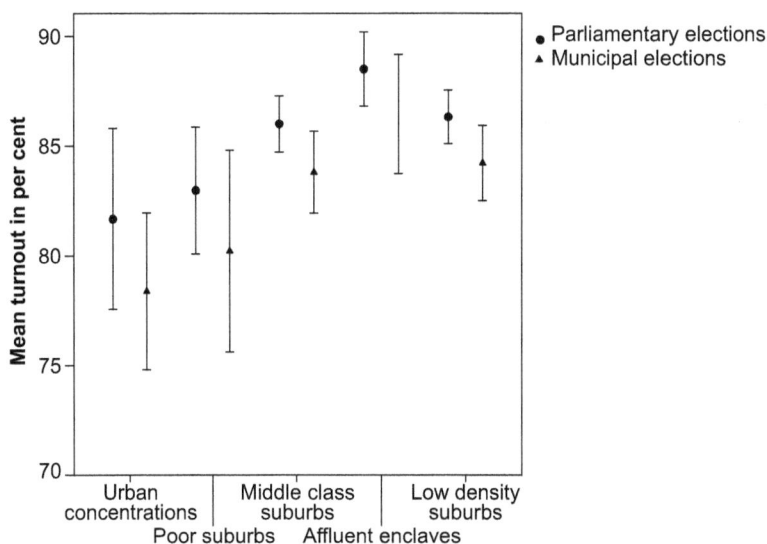

*Figure 9.2: Average turnout in parliamentary and municipal elections (1991 to 2010) according to municipal types in three Swedish metropolitan areas (means and 95 per cent confidence intervals)*

### Turnout in municipal elections

For the analysis of municipal turnout, the availability of data at the level of the core city districts[3] enabled the number of units of analysis to be increased to a total of eighty-five (forty-nine core city districts plus thirty-six suburban municipalities). Following the same procedure as for the suburban municipalities, the core city districts were classified into affluent, middle-class and poor districts. The latter category was further subdivided to distinguish poor districts with a strong immigrant presence from other poor districts.

Beyond the importance of the types of municipalities, bivariate correlation analysis suggests that local turnout in municipal elections is related both to compositional and contextual variables (see Table 9.4). In order to single out the effects of these variables, five OLS regression models were estimated, with dummies controlling for differences in turnout levels between the three metropolitan areas. In a first model (see Table WA9.1 in the Web Appendix[4]), only the types of districts and/or municipalities were entered. This 'typological' model explains 67.5 per cent of the variance and confirms previous observations, namely that electoral turnout is lower in poor localities and higher in affluent suburbs, and explains nearly 70 per cent of the observed variance. A second model that estimated coefficients for the compositional variables proved more powerful, accounting for more than 95 per cent of the observed variance (see Table 9.4). A third model based only on the contextual variables provided an alternative explanation for just over half of this variation, or 51.6 per cent of the overall variance.

The fourth, combined model confirms that many of the effects captured by the contextual model can be explained away when compositional variables are taken into account. The combined model shows that turnout in municipal elections is positively related to socio-economic status, to the presence of households with children and to the proportion of retirees. It is lower in municipalities with larger proportions of foreign-born citizens. Even with all of these demographic factors included, however, this model showed turnout to decrease with population size. In a fifth model (see Table WA9.1 in the Web Appendix), dummies for the types of municipalities were added back in order to test for type-based contextual effects not captured by the continuous variables. In addition to the significant predictors from the fourth model, an additional dichotomous variable for the poor localities with a high proportion of immigrants showed turnout to be especially depressed there.

Compositional variables clearly explain more of the variation in municipal

---

3.  City districts were introduced in the core cities of the three metropolitan areas in the 1990s as a device of political decentralisation. In Stockholm, there are eighteen city districts, twenty-one in Göteborg and ten in Malmö. City districts are governed by neighbourhood committees (so-called urban district councils) appointed by the city councils. City districts are primarily responsible for the provision of social welfare services, and considerable parts of city budgets (some three-quarters) have been decentralised. For an analysis of urban political decentralisation in large Scandinavian cities, see Bäck et al. (2005).

4.  See this table and all other Web Appendixes WA09, http://press.ecpr.eu/resources.

*Table 9.4: Determinants of electoral turnout in three Swedish metropolitan areas – municipal elections*

| | Bivariate | OLS regression models (unstandardised coefficients and standard errors) | | |
| | Pearson correlation | Compositional model | Contextual model | Combined model |
|---|---|---|---|---|
| (Constant) | | **72.035** (2.001) | **92.836** (10.962) | **77.195** (3.692) |
| Stockholm MA | 0.095 | −0.619 (0.605) | **6.822** (1.859) | 0.024 (0.782) |
| Göteborg MA | −0.070 | **−2.295** (0.549) | 0.993 (1.754) | **−2.059** (0.576) |
| Socio-economic status | **0.599** | **1.348** (0.157) | | **1.344** (0.196) |
| Per cent foreign born | **−0.930** | **−0.521** (0.021) | | **−0.459** (0.042) |
| Per cent manufact. occupation | 0.065 | 0.019 (0.019) | | 0.027 (0.019) |
| Per cent under 18 | −0.005 | **0.485** (0.049) | | **0.366** (0.104) |
| Per cent retirees | **0.218** | **0.195** (0.052) | | **0.211** (0.054) |
| Distance to the centre | *0.205* | | **−0.436** (0.112) | −0.027 (0.038) |
| Per cent single-family housing | **0.591** | | **0.239** (0.040) | 0.032 (0.023) |
| Per cent commuting | **−0.384** | | -0.086 (0.094) | −0.021 (0.031) |
| Population (Ln) | **−0.430** | | **−2.052** (0.739) | **−0.512** (0.232) |
| Density (Ln) | **−0.407** | | 1.115 (1.049) | 0.334 (0.356) |
| Adjusted $R^2$ | | 0.954 | 0.516 | 0.957 |
| N | 85 | 85 | 85 | 85 |

*Notes:* For boldface coefficients, $p<0.05$; for italicised coefficients, $p<0.10$.

election turnout across localities in Swedish metropolitan areas than contextual variables. Nevertheless, the negative effects of municipality size and of the immigrant concentration point to spatial influences beyond demographic makeup, and other contextual variables offer alternative explanations for part of the variation.

### Turnout in parliamentary elections

For turnout in parliamentary elections, data is not available by core city districts. The analysis therefore remains limited to the thirty-six suburban municipalities and the three core cities. Bivariate correlations again suggest a simultaneous influence of compositional and contextual variables on turnout in parliamentary elections (see Table 9.5). In order to single out these influences, four[5] OLS regression models were estimated. In the first model (see Table WA9.2 in the Web Appendix, http://press.ecpr.eu/resources), only the types of municipalities were entered as independent variables alongside the dummies controlling for differences across the three metropolitan areas. This model explains 54.7 per cent of the observed variance and confirms previous observation from the typological analysis. The electorates of core cities and poor suburbs vote in fewer numbers in parliamentary elections, whereas the electorate of affluent suburbs shows a higher level of turnout. A second model estimates the influence of compositional variables (see Table 9.5).

The percentage of variance this model explains (86.2 per cent) is far higher than that of the typological model. Socio-economic status and the proportion of households with children exert clear positive effects on turnout in parliamentary elections, whereas the presence of immigrants depresses parliamentary turnout within municipalities. The third model based on the contextual variables explains over half the variation as well, but less than either the types or the compositional model. In the final combined model, the significant contextual effects fall out altogether once the compositional variables are taken into account. Thus, parliamentary election turnout in a municipality is positively affected by large proportions of inhabitants with high socio-economic status, as well as by large proportions of households with children. It is negatively related to the proportion of foreign-born residents. None of the contextual influences survive as a significant effect once these others are taken into account.

This result must be understood in light of the narrow variation in parliamentary election turnout among Swedish metropolitan municipalities. Within this limited range, socio-demographic structures are quite decisive. Analysis of the slightly greater turnout variation in municipal elections points to stronger contextual effects, most notably for population size. Compared to other countries, however, place-based effects on electoral turnout in Swedish metropolitan areas remain

---

5.   Due to the limited number of cases, the estimation of models with a large number of predictors becomes critical. This is why we refrained from estimating the fifth model controlling for type-based effects, as was done for municipal election turnout.

*Table 9.5: Determinants of electoral turnout in three Swedish metropolitan areas –
parliamentary elections*

| | Bivariate | OLS regression models (unstandardised coefficients and standard errors) | | |
|---|---|---|---|---|
| | Pearson correlation | Compositional model | Contextual model | Combined model |
| (Constant) | | **74.832** (5.794) | **75.008** (12.764 | **70.286** (11.549) |
| Stockholm MA | −0.078 | −0.030 (0.888) | **2.747** (1.328) | 0.363 (1.133) |
| Göteborg MA | 0.078 | −0.297 (0.631) | 1.416 (1.149) | 0.024 (0.689) |
| Socio-economic status | **0.534** | **1.249** (0.233) | | **0.992** (0.311) |
| Per cent foreign born | **−0.731** | **−0.307** (0.048) | | **−0.326** (0.081) |
| Per cent manufact. occupation | n/a | n/a | n/a | n/a |
| Per cent under 18 | **0.431** | **0.385** (0.116) | | *0.330* (0.195) |
| Per cent retirees | 0.245 | 0.146 (0.164) | | 0.137 (0.197) |
| Distance to the centre | 0.075 | | **−0.136** (0.063) | −0.023 (0.038) |
| Per cent single-family housing | 0.567 | | **0.157** (0.030) | 0.016 (0.031) |
| Per cent commuting | 0.395 | | 0.025 (0.047) | 0.034 (0.029) |
| Population (Ln) | −0.410 | | 0.709 (0.863) | 0.160 (0.574) |
| Density (Ln) | −0.185 | | 0.995 (0.617) | 0.291 (0.413) |
| Adjusted R² | | 0.862 | 0.532 | 0.860 |
| N | 39 | 39 | 39 | 39 |

*Notes:* For boldface coefficients, p<0.05; for italicised coefficients, p<0.10.

modest at best.

## Party voting in Swedish metropolitan areas

Sweden's party system is largely structured around the left-right dimension. This
has been observed in various contexts such as voters' attitudes, patterns of voters' partisan change and intra-parliamentary coalition behaviour (Bäck 2008).
The main outlines of this system were established in the early twentieth century
around five major parties: the conservative Moderates, the Liberals, the Centre
Party (originally an agrarian party), the Social Democrats and the Left Party (the

*Table 9.6: Party positions based on survey results (partisanship indices)*

| | Left-right self-placement (1 [left] to 10 [right]) | | Position on economic issues ( 0 [state] to 10 [market]) | Position on globalisation issues (0 [open] to 10 [isolation]) | Position on cultural issues (0 [liberal] to 10 [conservative]) |
|---|---|---|---|---|---|
| Years of Survey | 2002 | 2006 | 1998–2003 | 1998–2003 | 1998–2003 |
| Left Party (V) | 1.9 | 1.4 | 4.0 | 2.3 | 4.2 |
| Social Democratic Party (SAP) | 3.4 | 3.7 | 4.6 | 2.8 | 4.7 |
| Green Party (MP) | 3.6 | 3.5 | 4.8 | 2.9 | 4.1 |
| Centre Party (C) | 5.8 | 6.4 | 5.0 | 3.7 | 4.8 |
| People's Party Liberals (FP) | 6.4 | 7.3 | 4.0 | 2.3 | 4.2 |
| Christian Democrats (KD) | 7.0 | 7.7 | 5.4 | 4.8 | 4.7 |
| Moderate Party (M) | 7.4 | 8.7 | 6.5 | 2.9 | 4.6 |
| Sweden Democrats (SD) | n/a | 9.2 | n/a | n/a | n/a |

*Sources:* Comparative Study of Electoral Systems (2002 and 2006), European Value Study (3rd wave 1999/2000), International Social Survey Programme (1998, 2002 and 2003).

For the breakdown of issue positions, see Chapter 14, the Methodological Appendix, in this volume.

former Communist Party). During the last decades of the twentieth century, the emergence of the Christian Democrats and the Greens altered this constellation. In the first decade of the twenty-first century, the rise of the nationalist Sweden Democrats has established the 'new populist right' (Kriesi *et al.* 2008) as a persistent presence in the Swedish party system (Loxbo 2010).

Partisanship indices computed on the basis of party voters' self-placement on the left-right scale as well as on a range of policy issues (see Table 9.6) provide a clearly differentiated picture of the Swedish parties' ideological positions.

With respect to the left-right dimension or attitudes in economic policy (state versus market), a clear distinction runs between the Left Party, the Social Democrats and the Greens, on the one hand, and the Centre Party, the Liberals, the Christian Democrats and the Moderates, on the other hand. This division has long served as the foundation of Swedish 'block politics'. The divide between the socialist block (the Left Party plus the Social Democrats) and a non-socialist block (the Liberals, the Moderates, the Centre Party and the Christian Democrats) has been closely connected to class cleavages in society.

The positions of party voters on globalisation issues indicate that an additional political division that is not directly related to economic ideology and class politics has emerged in the Swedish party system. Supporters of the Left Party and the Liberal Party clearly exhibit a more positive attitude towards globalisation and ethnic diversity than supporters of the other parties. Supporters of the

Centre Party or the Christian Democrats are particularly critical of globalisation processes. Cultural issues related to the choice between liberalism and traditionalism divide supporters of the various parties less.[6] Relative positions of different party supporters on these issues nonetheless follow a largely similar ordering from left to right as along the globalisation dimension.

Understanding the metropolitan sources of these dimensions can shed new light on what has all the appearances of a watershed moment in Swedish politics. Throughout the twentieth century, the Social Democrats dominated Swedish politics. Since the end of World War II, the 1991 to 1994 interlude of a centre-right coalition was the only period when the Social Democrats were not in charge of the government. This has changed in the new millennium. The 2006 elections saw the victory of the centre-right parties who inflicted a historical defeat on the Swedish Social Democrats. The centre-right government renewed its success in the 2010 election. For the first time in post-war Swedish history, the Social Democrats were excluded from government for more than one term of office.

### *The metropolitan sources of partisanship*

Like the other Nordic countries, Sweden is characterised by a vertically-integrated party system. The parties that participate in national elections are also those that dominate politics at the sub-national level, i.e. counties and municipalities. Although independent local parties do increasingly compete in Swedish municipal elections, voters' support for these lists is generally quite low. It has been shown that local voting in Sweden is to a large extent determined by national politics (Thomsen 1998). National and sub-national elections are held on the same day in Sweden, and this synchronism tends to obscure the importance of local politics: 'many voters are simply not very interested in local politics and thus vote like they would do in national elections' (Thomsen 1998: 338). Municipal-level results of the elections to the national parliament thus capture the essence of metropolitan patterns of partisanship in Sweden.

On the basis of the partisanship indices and the share of votes that each party obtained, we can calculate the average 'ideological centre of gravity' (Gross and Sigelman 1984) for each municipality. A breakdown by types of municipalities is shown in Figure 9.3. An analysis of variance shows that the variation across municipal types is significant for the left-right self-placement index, the economic index, as well as the globalisation index, but not for the cultural index. The affluent suburbs stand out, with an electorate that tends to vote more to the right and is more favourable to liberal free market positions. Among local attitudes towards globalisation, the more ethno-nationalist stance of the poor suburbs is also distinctive.

What factors account for the relations between these types and the ideological positions of municipal electorates? Given the importance of left-right block

---

6. Note that the more limited differences are partly an artefact of the failure to separate out preferences of voters for the Swedish Democrats in the surveys used to estimate party positions on cultural issues.

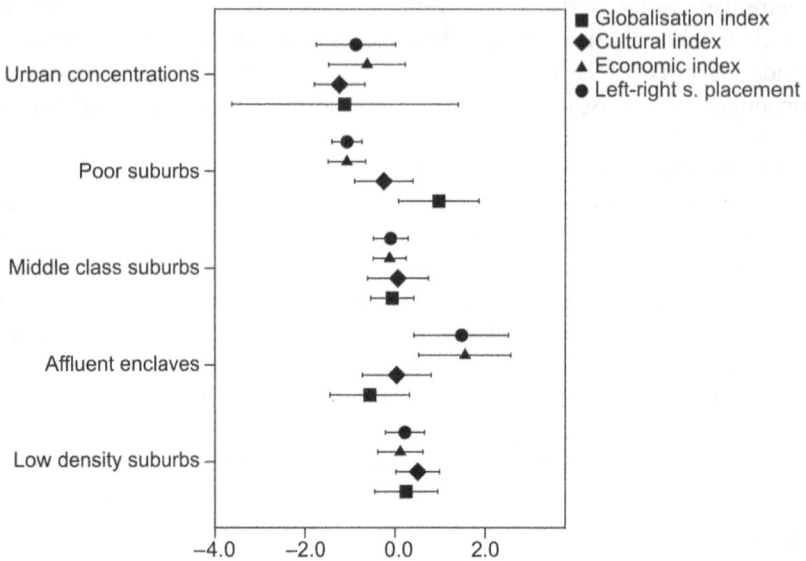

*Figure 9.3: Mean position of voters in types of municipalities according to partisanship indices and vote shares of parties in parliamentary elections 2002 (means and 95 per cent confidence intervals)*

politics and class-based cleavages in Sweden (Svallfors 1995), one would expect that the socio-demographic influences captured by the compositional variables would be sufficient to explain the partisan orientations of a municipal electorate. Especially for the left-right scale or for attitudes toward policy choices between the state and markets, socio-economic status in particular should be determinative. It is much less clear, however, whether the compositional or the contextual factors can be expected to influence the partisan orientations with respect to socio-cultural and globalisation issues.

In fact, even on the left-right scale (see Table 9.7), contextual factors linked to the property assets and lifestyles associated with single-family houses play a role alongside demographic composition. Significant bivariate relationships with the local ideological centre of gravity for both types of factors suggest this relationship and multivariate analyses confirm it. The compositional variables do play a stronger overall role than contextual influences, accounting for all but 4.4 per cent of the variance explained in the combined model. In the compositional model, municipalities with higher socio-economic status, fewer foreigners, more families with children and more retirees all vote significantly more for the right. A purely contextual model, nonetheless, accounts for 44.5 per cent of the overall variation. In this model, localities with more single-family housing and greater population density support the right more.

In the combined model, multicollinearity appears to undermine the significance of most compositional and contextual factors. Compositional effects from socio-economic status and contextual effects from single family housing remain robust across the different models. If class remains a powerful predictor of municipal partisanship, the property assets and consumption interests linked to residence clearly play a significant role.

The same variables play almost exactly the same role in explaining the position of municipal electorates on the role of the market versus the state (see Table 9.7). Compositional factors, notably socio-economic status, favour pro-market voting. Place-based effects, most notably higher proportions of single-family housing, also correspond to pro-market positions. In the service-based Göteborg metropolitan area, as Sellers and Walks hypothesise (see Chapter 1 in this volume) support for statist policies is also generally stronger.

Predictors for a municipal electorate's positions on globalisation issues point to an even stronger relationship with factors beyond local class composition (see Table 9.8). All the contextual variables except commuting manifest significant bivariate relationships with the globalisation index. In the multivariate analysis, the contextual model explains a larger part of the observed variance (57.8 per cent) than the compositional model (49 per cent). Although socio-economic status is positively related to global cosmopolitanism, several contextual influences are also robust. Municipal electorates are more critical towards globalisation in smaller municipalities and in those located towards the outskirts of a metropolitan area.

As in France, Switzerland and the United States, peripheral exurban zones and poor suburbs have provided the most fertile metropolitan ground for parties opposed to globalisation and ethnic diversity. This pattern confirms the more general metropolitan bases of support for right-wing populist parties mobilised around anti-immigration policies and isolationism. In the metropolitan areas of Göteborg and Stockholm, as might be expected in centres of post-industrial business and administrative services (see Chapter 1 in this volume), support for cosmopolitan positions is generally higher than in the industrial centre of Malmö. Although multicollinearity with other variables cancels out these effects in the full combined model, backward regression confirms them.

Positions on cultural issues vary less among Swedish parties, but metropolitan contextual factors are clearly important to these differences as well (see Table 9.8). Bivariate analysis points to significant correlations between the cultural index and all the contextual variables except commuting. As with the globalisation index, multivariate analysis shows contextual variables to have more explanatory power than compositional variables. Although the compositional model explains 50.8 per cent of the observed variance, the contextual model explains essentially all of the 71.6 per cent variance accounted for in the full model.

In the compositional model cultural liberalism is associated with high socio-economic status and high proportions of immigrants in a municipality, while cultural conservatism increases with larger proportions of retirees and families with children. These compositional effects disappear in the full model alongside several significant contextual factors. The contextual variables show cultural conservatism to be associated with two features of suburban lifestyles (see Chapter 1 in this

Table 9.7: Determinants of partisanship in Swedish metropolitan municipalities – left-right self-placement index and economic index (parliamentary elections 2002)

| | Left-right self-placement | | | | Economic issues index | | | |
|---|---|---|---|---|---|---|---|---|
| | Bivariate | OLS regression models (unstandardised coefficients and standard errors) | | | Bivariate | OLS regression models (unstandardised coefficients and standard errors) | | |
| | Pearson correlation | Compositional | Contextual | Combined model | Pearson correlation | Compositional | Contextual | Combined model |
| (Constant) | | 3.260 (0.779) | 3.399 (1.678) | 3.963 (1.327) | | 4.795 (0.300) | 4.375 (0.740) | 4.645 (0.539) |
| Stockholm MA | 0.212 | 0.220 (0.119) | 0.476 (0.175) | 0.221 (0.130) | 0.291 | 0.029 (0.046) | 0.172 (0.077) | 0.044 (0.053) |
| Götenburg MA | −0.148 | −0.024 (0.085) | 0.096 (0.151) | 0.013 (0.079) | −0.292 | −0.078 (0.033) | −0.030 (0.067) | −0.073 (0.032) |
| Socio-economic status | 0.764 | 0.162 (0.030) | | 0.202 (0.036) | 0.828 | 0.083 (0.012) | | 0.092 (0.014) |
| Per cent foreign born | −0.437 | −0.023 (0.006) | | −0.001 (0.009) | −0.326 | −0.008 (0.002) | | −0.002 (0.004) |
| Per cent under 18 | 0.227 | 0.050 (0.016) | | 0.000 (0.022) | 0.145 | 0.016 (0.006) | | 0.002 (0.009) |
| Per cent retirees | 0.301 | 0.051 (0.022) | | 0.030 (0.023) | 0.297 | 0.012 (0.008) | | 0.012 (0.009) |
| Distance to the centre | 0.026 | | −0.008 (0.008) | 0.003 (0.004) | −0.066 | | −0.004 (0.004) | 0.000 (0.001) |
| Per cent single-family housing | 0.331 | | 0.021 (0.006) | 0.012 (0.004) | 0.206 | | 0.008 (0.002) | 0.004 (0.001) |
| Per cent commuting | 0.280 | | −0.002 (0.006) | −0.003 (0.003) | 0.255 | | 0.000 (0.003) | 0.000 (0.001) |

| | Left-right self-placement | | | | Economic issues index | | | |
| | Bivariate | OLS regression models (unstandardised coefficients and standard errors) | | | Bivariate | OLS regression models (unstandardised coefficients and standard errors) | | |
| | Pearson correlation | Compositional | Contextual | Combined model | Pearson correlation | Compositional | Contextual | Combined model |
|---|---|---|---|---|---|---|---|---|
| Population (Ln) | -0.194 | | -0.061 (0.113) | -0.016 (0.066) | -0.082 | | 0.003 (0.050) | 0.022 (0.027) |
| Density (Ln) | 0.063 | | **0.232** (0.081) | 0.042 (0.047) | 0.149 | | **0.078** (0.036) | -0.004 (0.019) |
| Adjusted R² | | 0.829 | 0.445 | 0.873 | | 0.856 | 0.388 | 0.882 |
| N | 39 | 39 | 39 | 39 | 39 | 39 | 39 | 39 |

*Notes:* For boldface coefficients, p<0.05; for italicised coefficients, p<0.10.

Table 9.8: Determinants of partisanship in Swedish metropolitan municipalities, measured by globalisation and cultural indices (parliamentary elections 2002)

| | Globalisation index | | | | | Cultural index | | | |
| | Bivariate Pearson correlation | OLS regression models (unstandardised coefficients and standard errors) | | | | Bivariate Pearson correlation | OLS regression models (unstandardised coefficients and standard errors) | | |
| | | Compositional | Contextual | Combined model | Backward stepwise | | Compositional | Contextual | Combined model |
|---|---|---|---|---|---|---|---|---|---|
| (Constant) | | 4.365 (0.103) | 4.614 (0.111) | 4.636 (0.176) | 4.605 (0.054) | | 2.159 (0.297) | 3.204 (0.271) | 3.121 (0.448) |
| Stockholm MA | -0.489 | -0.008 (0.016) | -0.046 (0.012) | -0.030 (0.017) | -0.040 (0.010) | | 0.144 (0.046) | 0.074 (0.028) | 0.125 (0.044) |
| Götenburg MA | 0.139 | -0.021 (0.011) | -0.022 (0.010) | -0.015 (0.010) | -0.020 (0.009) | | 0.117 (0.032) | 0.112 (0.024) | 0.145 (0.027) |
| Socio-economic status | -0.537 | -0.014 (0.004) | | -0.006 (0.005) | -0.006 (0.003) | -0.263 | -0.027 (0.011) | | -0.007 (0.012) |
| Per cent foreign born | -0.392 | -0.001 (0.001) | | 0.001 (0.001) | | 0.461 | -0.006 (0.002) | | 0.004 (0.003) |
| Per cent under 18 | 0.271 | 0.003 (0.002) | | -0.003 (0.003) | | -0.101 | 0.015 (0.006) | | -0.008 (0.008) |
| Per cent retirees | 0.061 | 0.005 (0.003) | | 0.000 (0.003) | | -0.580 | 0.025 (0.008) | | 0.006 (0.008) |
| Distance to the centre | 0.445 | | 0.001 (0.001) | 0.001 (0.001) | 0.001 (0.001) | 0.419 | | 0.002 (0.001) | 0.000 (0.001) |
| Per cent single-family housing | 0.547 | | 0.000 (0.000) | 0.001 (0.000) | | 0.423 | | 0.003 (0.001) | 0.005 (0.001) |
| Per cent commuting | 0.202 | | 0.000 (0.000) | 0.000 (0.000) | | 0.648 | | -0.003 (0.001) | -0.002 (0.001) |
| Population (Ln) | -0.613 | | -0.013 (0.008) | -0.015 (0.009) | -0.013 (0.004) | 0.169 | | -0.060 (0.018) | -0.056 (0.022) |
| Density (Ln) | -0.476 | | 0.007 (0.005) | 0.009 (0.006) | 0.008 (0.004) | -0.527 | | 0.054 (0.013) | 0.041 (0.016) |
| Adjusted R² | | 0.490 | 0.587 | 0.624 | 0.648 | | 0.508 | 0.715 | 0.716 |
| N | 39 | 39 | 39 | 39 | 39 | 39 | 39 | 39 | 39 |

Notes: For boldface coefficients, p<0.05; for italicised coefficients, p<0.10.

volume), single-family housing and smaller municipalities. A further association with lower commuting rates suggests that it is stronger in more sheltered suburban settings. With the control for population size included, however, it is also stronger in more densely populated suburbs. Local electorates in metropolitan Stockholm and Göteborg, although more supportive of cosmopolitan parties than in greater Malmö, also vote significantly more in favour of culturally-conservative positions.

Two straightforward conclusions flow from these findings. On the one hand, the compositional predictors of left-right self-placement and economic ideology in Sweden's metropolitan areas demonstrate a clear logic of metropolitan partisan divisions. Positive attitudes to state intervention and redistribution decrease with higher levels of education and income. As an important contextual variable with independent effects, however, the nature of the housing stock also plays a role in partisan variations. Single-family houses are typically owner-occupied assets, and the suburbs where they predominate feature many of the same aspects that favour more privatised lifestyles as in other countries. Even in the more homogeneous metropolitan context shaped by the Swedish welfare state, right-wing parties that advocate lower taxes and other pro-market policies have found new territorial constituencies in metropolitan communities of single-family homes. Even if this contextual influence amounts to a place-related element in the class base of Swedish block politics, its ecological effect occurs independently of income, education and occupation. Critical dimensions of twenty-first century Swedish politics, moreover, are more place-based than class-based. Electorates in large and wealthy municipalities located close to the centre of the metropolitan areas are cosmopolitan and culturally liberal. Ethnonationalism and cultural conservatism thrive in suburban settings on the outskirts of the metropolitan areas, where sprawl, deprivation and institutional fragmentation have grown.

### *The metropolitan bases of electoral swings*

Place effects described above have played a role in the recent swing to the right in Swedish national elections. Figure 9.4 shows the development of the share of votes for the centre-right block (the cumulated percentage of votes for the Moderates, the Centre Party, the Liberal Party and the Christian Democrats) in relationship to the share of votes for the socialist block (the cumulated percentages of votes for the Social Democrats and the Left Party), over the six elections from 1991 to 2010. A value above zero means that the votes for the centre-right block exceeded those for the socialist block, whereas a value below zero indicates that the majority of voters supported the socialist block rather than the centre-right block.

With respect to the types of municipalities, the graphs in Figure 9.4 illustrate the earlier findings that support for the centre-right block is highest in affluent enclaves and above average in low density as well as middle-class suburbs, whereas the electorate of urban concentrations and poor suburbs vote clearly more for socialist parties. The development of the graphs over time shows that the electoral swing in favour of the centre-right block has been part of a general wave that is not confined to any particular type of municipality. However, only in

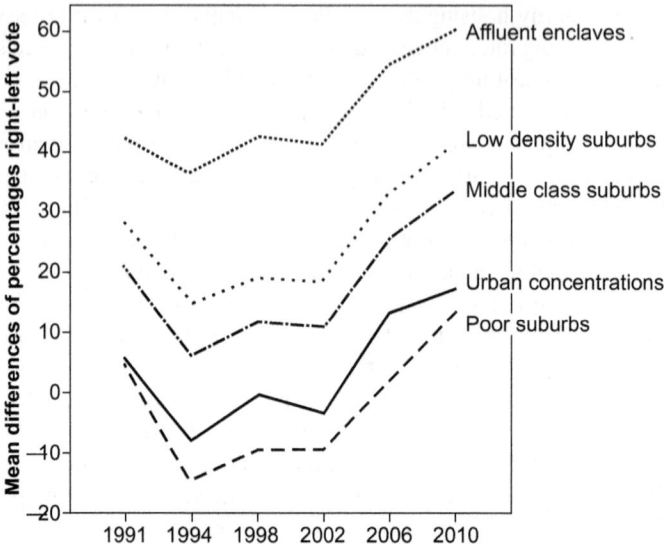

*Figure 9.4: Difference of voters' support of the centre-right (Moderates, Centre Party, Liberal Party and Christian Democrats) and the left (Social Democrats and Left Party) according to types of municipalities, parliamentary elections 1991 to 2010*

the urban concentrations and the poor suburbs did the majority of votes actually change from centre-right to socialist (between 1991 and 1994) and back (between 2002 and 2006). The swing in these two types of municipalities was decisive for the overall result, as urban concentrations and poor suburbs account for nearly 60 per cent of the overall metropolitan population and therefore outnumber the population of the other municipalities.

This suggests that developments in the core cities and the poor suburbs were the key to the socialist parties' electoral defeat in the first decade of the new millennium. In the poor suburbs, the socialists were weakened not only by the centre-right parties, but very much by the rise of the Swedish Democrats. This new nationalist, anti-immigrant, pro-market party managed to more than double its share of votes between the 2002 and 2010 elections (from 3.8 per cent to 9.7 per cent). The emergence of the new populist right in Sweden's metropolitan areas seems to have taken place mainly in the poor suburbs. Characterised by a combination of low socio-economic status and a high proportions of immigrants, as well as a rather peripheral location in the metropolitan area, they have provided a particularly fertile ground for the Sweden Democrats' combination of nationalist and culturally-conservative ideology.

The electoral swing from left to right in the 2006 parliamentary election has been viewed as a sea change in Swedish politics (Miles 2010). A closer analysis of the factors associated with the increase of the votes for centre-right parties at the municipal level, between the 2002 and the 2006 elections, yields further

*Table 9.9: Determinants of electoral swing in Swedish metropolitan municipalities, measured by the difference of the share of votes for parties of the centre-right bloc and the left bloc between the 2002 and 2006 parliamentary elections*

| | Bivariate | OLS regression models (unstandardised coefficients and standard errors) | | |
| | Pearson correlation | Compositional | Contextual | Combined model |
|---|---|---|---|---|
| (Constant) | | **30.091** | −6.220 | −14.691 |
| | | (13.109) | (13.926) | (23.283) |
| Stockholm MA | **0.448** | −1.652 | 0.156 | 0.819 |
| | | (2.010) | (1.449) | (2.285) |
| Götenburg MA | **−0.614** | **−5.041** | **−5.185** | **−5.517** |
| | | (1.427) | (1.254) | (1.389) |
| Socio-economic status | 0.123 | 0.444 | | -0.461 |
| | | (0.505) | | (0.626) |
| Per cent foreign born | 0.234 | −0.077 | | −0.276 |
| | | (0.109) | | (0.163) |
| Per cent under 18 | −0.079 | −0.382 | | 0.030 |
| | | (0.263) | | (0.392) |
| Per cent retirees | −0.252 | *−0.681* | | 0.083 |
| | | (0.370) | | (0.397) |
| Distance to the centre | −0.082 | | −0.068 | −0.053 |
| | | | (0.069) | (0.077) |
| Per cent single-family housing | −0.239 | | −0.020 | −0.065 |
| | | | (0.032) | (0.062) |
| Per cent commuting | 0.032 | | 0.061 | 0.095 |
| | | | (0.051) | (0.059) |
| Population (Ln) | 0.254 | | **2.103** | **2.949** |
| | | | (0.942) | (1.157) |
| Density (Ln) | 0.087 | | **−1.843** | **−1.740** |
| | | | (0.673) | (0.832) |
| Adjusted R² | | 0.340 | 0.480 | 0.470 |
| N | 39 | 39 | 39 | 39 |

*Notes:* For boldface coefficients, $p<0.05$; for italicised coefficients, $p<0.10$.

interesting insights into its dynamics (see Table 9.9). Bivariate correlations are only significant for the metro region dummies: in the Göteborg metropolitan area, this increase has been less pronounced than in the other two metropolitan areas. The multivariate regression models show that the contextual model has more explanatory power (48 per cent of the variance explained) than the compositional model (34 per cent of the variance explained).

As the combined model shows, the weak effect of the proportion of retirees in the compositional model is explained completely away once the contextual variables are taken into account. The increase in votes for parties of the centre-right block bears an unmistakeable positive relation to population size and a negative one with population density. It is not significantly related to socio-economic status or any other socio-demographic variables. It would require closer investigation to ascertain which constituencies within the largest metropolitan municipalities most decisively turned to the centre-right block, but the effect of density indicates a further significant shift to the right in the peripheral suburban areas where more pro-market and more ethno-nationalist views were already stronger. These place-based patterns show that metropolitan influences made a difference both for the emergence of the far right, and for the growing strength of the centre-right.

## Conclusion

Socio-economic status remains important to explain patterns of electoral behaviour in Sweden's three metropolitan areas. Along with the comparatively small variations in electoral turnout, differences in social class and other demographics account for most of the local variations in left-right voting as well as positions on economic ideology. However, patterns of political behaviour in these metropolitan areas are also to a certain extent place-based. Besides income, education and age, housing and other aspects of the places in which people live influence not only how often, but especially for whom, Swedish metropolitan residents vote. Ideological positions toward cultural liberalism versus tradition and toward cosmopolitanism versus ethnonationalism have become even more strongly associated with place-related contextual factors than with the socio-demographic composition of metropolitan communities.

The analyses in this chapter thus provide empirical evidence for the metro-politanisation of politics in the Swedish context. A core-city effect is clearly discernible. As a group, citizens of core cities vote left, share more positive attitudes towards state intervention, and demonstrate more openness towards globalisation and greater cultural liberalism. Outside the centre, suburban communities characterised by large proportions of single-family housing tend to favour neoliberal economic policies, endorse anti-globalisation sentiments and support cultural traditionalism. In conjunction with a high proportion of immigrants and low socio-economic status, the suburban space has furnished particularly favourable conditions for the recent rise of the populist right in Swedish politics.

In Sweden, as elsewhere, the neoliberal agenda seems firmly rooted in suburbia. It would certainly be an exaggeration to attribute the centre-right's recent electoral victories only to territorial influences. Analysts of the 2006 parliamentary elections (Aigus 2007) argue that the shift from a left to a right majority is a result of a decades-long battle of ideas over the Swedish model of the welfare state, and reflects an embrace of individualism and the free-market economy among the public in general. The analyses of this chapter indicate that any such process has been closely linked to metropolitanisation and segregation in the largest urban regions. The territorial sources of support for the right in these metropolitan settings would appear decisive for its current electoral advantage.

These ongoing metropolitan processes and their political effects hold critical implications for the future of partisan competition in Sweden. Metropolitanisation presents a major challenge for the Social Democrats, a party long regarded as Sweden's 'natural party of government' (Aigus 2007: 585). So long as the Social

Democrats continue to look solely to their roots in the core cities, metropolitanisation and the continued growth of suburbs will make it more and more difficult for them to regain their hegemonic position in Swedish politics.

Recent political and policy changes in Sweden are likely to accelerate these metropolitan shifts. We have seen that, in an international comparative perspective, Swedish metropolitan areas remain limited in extent and relatively homogenous in spatial terms. Generous welfare state arrangements as well as substantial anti-segregation policies have limited metropolitan spatial sorting and its effects. Although the current centre-right government has partly built its electoral success on promises to maintain the welfare state, it has proceeded with the dismantling of anti-segregation measures and parts of the welfare state that reinforced them (Andersson *et al.* 2010). In a general context of increasing income disparities, these policy changes are likely to accelerate the ongoing processes of socio-spatial differentiation within Swedish metropolitan areas. As segregation increases, so will polarisation between rich and poor metropolitan neighbourhoods. The ethnic character of current segregation dynamics in Sweden assures that high immigrant densities in poor suburbs and neighbourhoods will persist. Future trajectories of spatial development in Sweden's metropolitan areas are thus bound to produce more of the affluent and low-density communities that favour neoliberal agendas, and reinforce the poor immigrant concentrations that have spurred the growth of the new populist right.

The shifting national electoral majorities, the consequent changes in territorial and welfare policies, and the increasing socio-economic differentiation of Swedish metropolitan areas can be understood as mutually-reinforcing processes. In the Swedish case, the links between them provide a telling example of the close relationship between metropolitan and political change.

# Bibliography

Aigus, C. (2007) 'Sweden's 2006 parliamentary election and after: contesting or consolidating the Swedish model?', *Parliamentary Affairs*, 60: 585–600.

Andersson, R., Bråmå, Å. and Holmqvist, E. (2010) 'Counteracting segregation: Swedish policies and experiences', *Housing studies*, 25: 237–56.

Bäck, H. (2005) 'Communication, cohesion and coordination. Metropolitan regions in Sweden,' in V. Hoffmann-Martinot and J. M. Sellers (eds) *Metropolitanization and Political Change,* Wiesbaden: Verlag für Sozialwissenschaften, 119–140.

Bäck, H. E. (2008) 'Intra-party politics and coalition formation – Evidence from Swedish local government', *Party Politics*, 14: 71–89.

Bäck, H. and Soininen, M. (1998) 'Immigrants in the political process', *Scandinavian Political Studies*, 21: 29–50.

Bäck, H., Gjelstrup, G., Helgesen, M., Johansson, F. and Klausen, J. E. (2005) *Urban Political Decentralisation: Six Scandinavian cities*, Wiesbaden: Verlag für Sozialwissenschaften.

Blais, A., Massicotte, L. and Dobrzynksa, A. (2003) *Why is Turnout Higher in Some Countries than in Others?* Ottawa: Elections Canada.

Esping-Andersen, G. (1990) *The Three Worlds of Welfare Capitalism*, Cambridge, Polity Press.

Gross, D. A. and Sigelman, L. (1984) 'Comparing party systems. A multi-dimensional approach', *Comparative Politics*, 16: 463–79.

Kriesi, H., Grande, E., Lachat, R., Dolezal, M. and Bornschier, S. (2008) *West European Politics in the Age of Globalization*, Cambridge: Cambridge University Press.

Loxbo, K. (2010) 'The impact of the radical right: lessons from the local level in Sweden, 2002–2006', *Scandinavian political studies*, 33: 295–315.

Miles, L. (2010) 'Making mischief with Swedish models: reflections on contemporary Swedish politics', *Scandinavica*, 49: 65–84.

Morlan, R. L. (1984) 'Municipal vs. national election voter turnout: Europe and the United States', *Political Science Quarterly*, 99: 457–70.

Statistics Sweden (2011) *Localities 2010*, Stockholm: Statistics Sweden.

Svallfors, S. (1995) 'The end of class politics? Structural cleavages and attitudes to Swedish welfare policies', *Acta Sociologica*, 38: 53–74.

Thomsen, S. R. (1998) 'Impact of national politics on local elections in Scandinavia', *Scandinavian Political Studies*, 21: 325–45.

Vogel, J. (1992) 'Urban segregation in Sweden, housing policy, housing markets and the spatial distribution of households in metropolitan areas', *Social Indicators Research*, 27: 139–55.

# Appendix

*Table A9.1: Variable description*

| Variable | Definition |
|---|---|
| Socio-economic status | Summarises measures of education (percentage of residents with tertiary education) and income |
| Foreign born residents | Percentage of residents born abroad |
| Under 18 | Percentage of residents aged less than 18 years |
| Retirees | Percentage of residents with old age pensions |
| Unemployment | Percentage of active population on unemployment benefits |
| Distance to centre | Distance to the core city by car |
| Commuting | Per cent of working population commuting to work in another municipality |
| Single-family housing | Percentage of dwellings in single-family houses |
| Population (Ln) | Logged number of inhabitants |
| Density (Ln) | Logged number of residents per square kilometre |

# Chapter Ten | The Delocalised Homo Politicus – the Political Ecology of Polish Metropolitan Areas

*Paweł Swianiewicz*

## Introduction[1]

This chapter analyses the political behaviour of citizens of twenty-one Polish metropolitan areas.[2] Is it different from the behaviour of Polish people living outside of metropolitan areas? If so what are the differences? And what are the factors influencing the variation within metropolitan areas?

In performing this empirical study we meet several difficulties, availability of data being only one of them.[3] It is not very easy to refer to theories stemming from earlier empirical investigations. For obvious reasons, Polish empirical studies of electoral behaviour do not have a very long tradition. No real elections took place between World War II and the fall of Communism in 1989, so there was not much to investigate. There are several studies of elections after 1989 (for example Raciborski 2004; Grabowska 2004; Szczerbiak 2003), but most of them pay minimal attention to geographical (locational) or community dimensions of electoral behaviour. Instead, they concentrated on classic socio-demographic variables such as age, education or levels of individual wealth. There are also some interesting (although not very numerous) empirical studies on spatial variations in political behaviour (Bartkowski 2003, Herbst 2005, Zarycki 1996, 2002, 2003; Swianiewicz 2003), but they rarely refer to local government elections; nor do they pay any special attention to metropolitan areas. If metropolitan areas are noticed at all in these studies, the interest of researchers is generally limited to pointing out specific features of election results in the largest cities (usually identified with high education levels, low unemployment and high levels of relative wealth). But the situation in suburban municipalities has hardly attracted any attention.

Difficulties in performing this empirical study are also related to the use of the common theoretical framework and hypotheses developed for cross-national

---

1. I want to express my thanks to Professor Jerzy Bartkowski and Julita Łukomska for their invaluable help in the struggle with multilevel modeling calculations.

2. For the discussion of the definition of metropolitan areas, see Swianiewicz and Klimska (2005).

3. Sources of data used in quantitative analysis: BDR (Bank of Regional Data managed by Central Statistical Office – GUS) 1994–2005; PKW (Polish National Electoral Commitee); ISS (International Social Survey) 2002; TRC (Tocqueville Research Centre in Budapest, implementing research project funded by LGIS/OSI) 2003: Ministry of Finance – median income 2002, and National Census data 2002.

analysis in the International Metropolitan Observatory (IMO) project. As we explained in our earlier report (Swianiewicz and Klimska 2005), processes of suburbanisation in Polish metropolitan areas are relatively recent, and are generally limited to the largest ones, i.e. mainly Warszawa, Poznań or Gdańsk. Many of the hypotheses developed in the IMO protocol seem to be rooted in a 'poor city – rich suburb' paradigm. However, as we argued elsewhere (Swianiewicz and Klimska 2005), the Polish reality is better described by 'rich city – poor suburb' or, in some cases, 'rich city – sandwich suburbs', i.e. a mosaic of affluent and poor suburban municipalities. Moreover, common IMO hypotheses often imply homogenous community characteristics, while Polish suburban municipalities are usually relatively large and internally diversified units. In Polish metropolitan areas, it is hard to find municipalities that do not contain a mixture of smaller upper-class, middle and lower-class neighbourhoods. Moreover, in spite of recent metropolitan growth, socio-spatial segregation is still relatively low, and there is often a mixture of different social strata found within single neighbourhoods, even if these are small. Similarly, as a consequence of annexation that was common until the 1980s, central cities have wide geographical boundaries, resulting in a mixture of inner city and suburb-type housing within the same central city municipality.

Finally, while classic left-right distinctions may also be problematic for many other countries, they are even less meaningful in Poland. The political arena is very unstable and there are different parties competing in almost every election. Quite often this instability applies even to major national political parties. The most extreme example is perhaps the situation in the 2001 parliamentary election, when both parties of the previous governing coalition (AWS and UW) failed to pass the 5 per cent threshold and fell apart soon afterwards. There are more examples of rapid growth or decrease of electoral support for various parties; it is not possible to conduct an analysis based on mean support for certain parties over a longer period – simply because there are different parties to be considered every time. Neither are the positions on the left-right spectrum very clear. In the Polish public discourse, 'left' and 'right' is identified with the social rather than with the economic dimension. There are also examples of parties that locate themselves in the centre or on the right, but which are seen as left-wing by the majority of public opinion.

In the context of community dimensions, local elections should be especially interesting for us. But it is next to impossible to conduct an analysis of local elections based on parties, because parties are almost absent in most local governments. Polish local government has the lowest ratio of party membership in Europe, both among councillors and local mayors (Fallend et al. 2006). The non-partisan character applies notably to small and mid-size municipalities, but it is also present in some of the large cities. We will describe this phenomenon in more detail below, but here we simply want to emphasise that these features of Polish local government complicates comparisons with countries characterised by highly partisan local government.

The instability of the party system makes it difficult to use in this analysis averages taken from a few subsequent elections. Nevertheless, we try to base the analysis on such central tendencies in order to exclude the impact of semi-random, one-time fluctuations in political behaviour.

## Polish metropolitan areas – spatial and demographic dimensions

As elsewhere, metropolitan areas have been playing an increasingly important role in the economic and social life in Poland. On the basis of the definitional criteria used in the common research protocol (Swianiewicz and Klimska 2005), a set of twenty-one metropolitan areas with a population over 200,000 were identified for 2002. Together, they make up 42 per cent of the overall population of the country. Economic activities in Poland are concentrated in these metropolitan areas and, as a consequence, levels of economic wealth are clearly higher in metropolitan areas than in the rest of the country.

As we have shown in an earlier context (Swianiewicz and Klimska 2005), processes of suburbanisation in Polish metropolitan areas are relatively recent, and are generally limited to the largest ones, i.e. mainly Warszawa, Poznań and Gdańsk. Before the political events of 1989, the spatial development of Polish metropolitan areas was influenced by limitations imposed on migration within the country – limiting the possibility of moving to the larger cities, especially to Warsaw – as well as by centrally-planned housing estates removed from the city centre, a characteristic of the socialist city. Since the political transformation of 1989, metropolitan areas have grown in population, especially in the peripheries of major cities, as well as in suburban zones, where new private housing was developed. Some of the core cities – such as Warsaw – have even lost population in this period.

As a consequence of annexation, which was common until the 1980s, central cities usually have wide geographical boundaries. Compared with other countries, the core cities' share of the overall metropolitan population is therefore quite high, and the suburban municipalities are also quite large in size. Hence, Polish metropolitan areas are characterised by relatively low levels of geopolitical fragmentation (see Table 10.1). Given the large size of core cities and suburban municipalities in Poland's metropolitan areas, municipal units are generally internally diverse. In core cities, there is usually a mixture of inner city and suburban-type housing. And it is hard to find suburban municipalities that are not a mixture of smaller upper-class, middle-class and lower-class neighbourhoods.

With respect to their internal differentiation, metropolitan areas in Poland do generally not correspond to the 'chocolate city, vanilla suburb' picture found elsewhere, particularly in North America. Instead, the Polish reality is better described by 'vanilla city, chocolate suburb' or, in some cases, 'vanilla city, sandwich suburbs' (with a mosaic of affluent and poor suburban municipalities). In spite of recent metropolitan growth, socio-spatial segregation is still relatively low, and there is often a mixture of different social strata found within single neighbourhoods, even if these are small. Nevertheless, demographic patterns have changed in Poland's metropolitan areas since the 1990s, and socio-spatial inequalities have increased. While most of the new problem areas – depreciated parts of inner

*Table 10.1: Characteristics of Polish metropolitan areas (data for 2002)*

| | Overall population | Number of municipalities | Population in core city (%) | Geopolitical fragmentation |
|---|---|---|---|---|
| Katowice | 2,708,744 | 51 | 28.02 | 0.82 |
| Warszawa | 2,582,169 | 52 | 65.38 | 0.31 |
| Krakow | 1,366,261 | 40 | 55.45 | 0.53 |
| Gdansk | 1,214,953 | 31 | 62.27 | 0.41 |
| Lodz | 1,129,189 | 23 | 69.53 | 0.29 |
| Wroclaw | 956,467 | 23 | 66.82 | 0.36 |
| Poznan | 846,497 | 18 | 68.18 | 0.31 |
| Bydgoszcz | 751,151 | 22 | 77.55 | 0.38 |
| Szczecin | 674,542 | 13 | 61.54 | 0.31 |
| Lublin | 564,180 | 19 | 63.52 | 0.53 |
| Rybnik | 505,798 | 19 | 31.99 | 1.41 |
| Bialystok | 426,234 | 13 | 68.43 | 0.45 |
| Czestochowa | 392,876 | 16 | 63.85 | 0.64 |
| Kielce | 347,931 | 13 | 60.88 | 0.61 |
| Radom | 346,129 | 12 | 66.18 | 0.52 |
| Rzeszow | 345,571 | 15 | 46.24 | 0.94 |
| Bielsko Biala | 325,288 | 11 | 54.67 | 0.62 |
| Walbrzych | 256,031 | 12 | 50.67 | 0.93 |
| Olsztyn | 241,262 | 8 | 71.49 | 0.46 |
| Tarnow | 224,339 | 8 | 53.30 | 0.67 |
| Opole | 211,952 | 8 | 61.02 | 0.79 |

*Notes:* Zeigler-Brunn index – number of communes per 10,000 inhabitants divided by the central city's share of the overall metropolitan population expressed as per cent.

cities or old housing estates – are actually found within core cities, there is also a deepening division between rich enclaves and poor neighbourhoods in the suburban zone. This differentiation is captured by the fivefold typology of metropolitan municipalities that has been constructed on the basis of the common research protocol (see Table 10.2):

(1) *Urban concentrations* comprise the twenty-one core cities, five additional cities in the polycentric metropolitan areas of Gdansk, Katowice and Bydgoszcz, plus six other major urban centres[4] in the metropolitan areas of Upper Silesia around Katowice. They are generally quite large, densely

---

4. Municipalities are classified as such if they have a population of more than 100,000 or are larger than half of the core city's population.

populated, characterised by high proportions of residents with a university education, high rates of unemployment, average social hardship, as well as demographic stability.

(2) *Low-density suburbs* are classified as such on the basis of an index composed of three variables: population density, new housing per capita in the 2001–5 period, (minus) weighted by the size of metro area distance from the central city. In every metropolitan area the suburbs in the lowest quartile of this index are classified in this category.

(3) *Affluent suburbs* group the quartile of the remaining suburbs with the lowest hardship index in each metropolitan area.

(4) *Poor suburbs* are defined as the quartile of the remaining suburbs with the highest hardship index in each municipality.

(5) *Middle-class suburbs* are a residual category, grouping the suburbs that were neither classified as low density, affluent or poor.

Such a definition of types of municipalities implies that both low density and affluent/poor terms are applied as relative to the situation in a given metropolitan area. In other words, what is, for example, an 'affluent suburb' in one metro area might be less affluent than an 'average suburb' in another (richer) metropolitan area.

*Table 10.2: Characteristics of types of metropolitan municipalities (data for 2002)*

| | | Urban concentrations | Affluent suburbs | Poor suburbs | Middle-class suburbs | Low-density suburbs | Total |
|---|---|---|---|---|---|---|---|
| N | | 32 | 69 | 80 | 149 | 97 | 427 |
| Population | Mean | 320,371 | 16,526 | 13,347 | 18,624 | 12,190 | 36,816 |
| | SD | 311,441 | 13,957 | 14,132 | 14,750 | 10,789 | 116,968 |
| Inhabitants /km² | Mean | 2,059 | 405 | 231 | 435 | 128 | 444 |
| | SD | 640 | 458 | 517 | 665 | 112 | 705 |
| University education (%) | Mean | 14.91 | 11.35 | 4.98 | 7.46 | 5.21 | 7.67 |
| | SD | 5.02 | 5.45 | 1.62 | 2.64 | 1.99 | 4.38 |
| Unemployment (%) | Mean | 20.59 | 17.30 | 21.60 | 18.82 | 20.38 | 19.58 |
| | SD | 4.10 | 4.56 | 5.95 | 4.26 | 6.25 | 5.32 |
| Distance to centre in km | Mean | 2.03 | 13.47 | 19.87 | 16.30 | 27.95 | 18.09 |
| | SD | 4.55 | 6.93 | 8.30 | 7.29 | 9.830 | 10.43 |
| Hardship index | Mean | 54.68 | 55.50 | 72.62 | 64.56 | 70.90 | 65.31 |
| | SD | 7.41 | 9.87 | 6.09 | 6.44 | 7.01 | 9.66 |
| Demographic Stability index | Mean | 33.89 | 7.13 | 42.57 | 27.73 | 48.01 | 32.26 |
| | SD | 16.61 | 36.30 | 26.66 | 26.30 | 18.75 | 29.47 |

## The political ecology of the Polish metropolis

Is political behaviour in metropolitan areas in any way different from that of citizens living in the remaining parts of the country? Are there any specific rules determining interest in politics or party politics in and around the biggest cities, or is it possible to explain metropolitan political ecology by the same factors that may be found in electoral studies conducted for the whole country?

In exploring the political ecology of the twenty-one Polish metropolitan areas under scrutiny, we are focusing on two main aspects of political behaviour:

(1) participation in politics, measured by turnout in local and national elections; and

(2) the political preferences of citizens, measured by support for individual political parties in national elections.

In order to facilitate international comparisons, we will not examine support for single parties, but use indices allowing the location of parties on internationally-comparable scales of political issues. In addition, by analysing local elections we check to what extent local government in Polish metropolitan areas is dominated by party politics.

### Analysis of turnout

As in many other countries, voters in Poland participate more in national than in local (municipal) elections. With the exception of the 2006 local elections, the turnout in parliamentary elections was always significantly higher than turnout in the nearest local elections (see Table 10.3). But how is this pattern related to metropolitanisation? Is political participation in metropolitan areas in any way different from that of citizens in remaining parts of the country? Are there specific rules determining interest in politics or party politics in and around the biggest cities, or does the political ecology of these places follow the same patterns found by electoral studies conducted for the whole country?

There are indeed reasons to expect differences in the willingness to vote between municipalities located in metropolitan areas and municipalities located

*Table 10.3: Average turnout in per cent in local and national elections in Poland*

|  | Local elections | National (parliamentary) elections |
|---|---|---|
| 1989–1990 | 42 (1990) | 62 (1989) |
| 1993–1994 | 33 (1994) | 51 (1993) |
| 1997–1998 | 47 (1998) | 48 (1997) |
| 2001–2002 | 44 (2002) | 46 (2002) |
| 2005–2006 | 46 (2006) | 41 (2005) |

in the rest of the country. More particularly, we expect local election turnout to be lower in metropolitan municipalities. Many citizens, especially in suburban areas are weakly connected to their municipality. Many of them have roots elsewhere because they moved in relatively recently. Also, their daily life is not very much connected to their municipal surroundings. They commute to the core city, consume public services in various places of the metropolitan area, so why should they be especially interested in local government issues in their municipality of residence, with which not much binds them, neither emotionally nor 'functionally'? They may be more interested in metro-wide services, which cannot be provided by their municipality, so they distance themselves from opaque and functionally split local governments (Hoffmann-Martinot and Sellers 2005). But at the same time, they may be more inclined to vote in national elections. Metropolitan areas are inhabited by voters who are (more often than in other parts of the country) affluent and educated, and they potentially have good access to information on national politics. These are all factors, which according to classic sociological models of voting (e.g. Lipset 1981), may positively influence turnout in elections.

In addition, we hypothesise that the difference between interest in national and local politics will be especially high in large metropolitan areas. This hypothesis follows the observation of Preteceille (2000: 92ff.) in his analysis of the French situation, finding that in municipalities of equal size, abstention in local elections was distinctly higher in the greater Paris region, suggesting a distinctive effect of the size of the metropolitan area on political behaviour in local elections. In large metropolitan areas, local government structures are more likely to be opaque to the citizen, thereby reducing interest in local politics. Independent of size, this effect can also stem from geopolitical fragmentation, as high fragmentation of local government structures adds to opaqueness and additionally depresses turnout in local elections.

A number of other possible predictors for turnout in local and national elections are associated with the characteristics of individual municipalities. We expect the turnout gap between national and local elections to be especially high in affluent metropolitan municipalities (i.e. with a low hardship index). Voters in these communities vote more often in national elections, and at the same time they are more often 'de-rooted' (their life-style involves satisfying various needs in different places of the metro area), so their interest in local elections is lower than average. In municipalities with a high hardship index, we expect lower turnout levels in general, since there is a well-known tendency for social and political exclusion of communities with lower social status. In addition, we expect a positive correlation between the level of education and level of turnout – education is connected to higher economic status and it enables easier access to information on politics. As has been shown elsewhere in Poland and in several other countries (Swianiewicz 2002; Rose 2002), we expect size to affect interest in local politics – in small municipalities there is more incentive for participation because a single individual vote will 'weigh more'; also, contacts between councillors and citizens are closer and politicians are more accountable to their local communities (Denters 2002). We also expect that turnout in local elections will be higher in municipalities where urban sprawl is not so extensive, i.e. in communities that are more demographically stable and more distant from the central city. Finally, the electoral rules in Poland can also be hypothesised to play a role. Whereas in municipalities below 20,000, majority rule is used for local elections, proportional rule is used in municipalities above this threshold – proportional rule is generally seen to increase electoral participation.

Potential factors explaining turnout in national elections are not exactly the same as for local elections. As in local elections, turnout is supported by demographic stability, low hardship (affluence of local community) and the level of education. However, the impact of the size of municipality is more complicated. The spatial distribution of economic status in Poland is such that one may expect higher interest in national politics in larger municipalities. This is true for nationwide data, but not necessarily for metropolitan areas. Since in Poland, the central city areas are usually more affluent than suburban municipalities, one may expect positive correlation between size and turnout in national elections if all metropolitan areas are considered. But this relationship may not be confirmed if we limit our analysis to suburban zones only, where there is no relationship between size and affluence of communities. Thus size can be expected to matter as an explanatory variable for turnout in local elections, but not necessarily in national elections.

We must also acknowledge that factors determining turnout may vary according to different elections. To minimise the impact of one-time distortion factors, we take into account the average from several subsequent elections. For turnout in local elections, we take the average of the local elections from 1994, 1998 and 2002. For turnout in national elections, averages are taken from parliamentary elections in 1993, 1997, and 2001.

Is political participation different in metropolitan municipalities from that in municipalities located in other parts of the country? Figure 10.1 shows that elec-

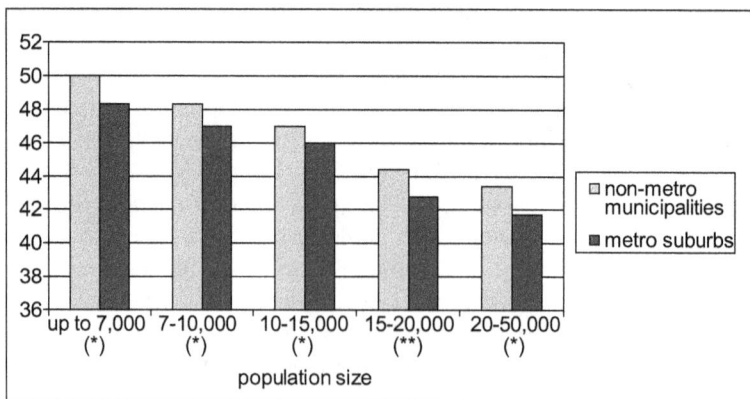

*Figure 10.1: Turnout in local elections (means from 1994, 1998 and 2002 elections), metropolitan municipalities and non-metropolitan municipalities*

*Notes:* (*) difference significant on 0.05 level, (**) difference significant on 0.01 level, (***) difference significant on 0.001 level.

toral turnout in local government elections is lower in metropolitan municipalities than in non-metropolitan municipalities of comparable size.

When we compare turnout in national (parliamentary) elections, the pattern is reversed – turnout is higher in metropolitan municipalities than in non-metropolitan municipalities of comparable size. This tells us that lower participation in local elections found in metropolitan municipalities is not a result of a lower interest in politics in general, but suggests specific features of local politics in metropolitan areas. As shown in Figure 10.2, if we take into account results of the most recent (2005) parliamentary elections, the difference between metro and non-metro areas becomes very significant. Does the time of observation matter? This claim is confirmed by turnout in national referenda. In the 1997 referendum (on the Polish constitution), turnout in the metropolitan suburbs was marginally higher than in other regions, but the difference was hardly statistically significant. However, six years later in the 2003 EU accession referendum, citizens of metropolitan areas were voting much more often than citizens of similar size municipalities outside the largest agglomerations (difference significant at the 0.001 level). Finally, the same pattern can be observed in presidential elections. The difference between metro and non-metro municipalities was insignificant in 1995 and 2000, but became significant in the 2005 elections. It may indicate that Polish metropolitan areas have recently become 'more metropolitanised', i.e. in a few years there may have been an increase in those features of political behaviour related to theories of metropolitanisation than was the case in the previous decade.

We start with checking how turnout varies according to the fivefold typology of metropolitan municipalities (see Figure 10.3). In local elections, the only significant difference is between urban concentrations and all remaining types – citizens in the central areas of cities are less willing to take part in local government elec-

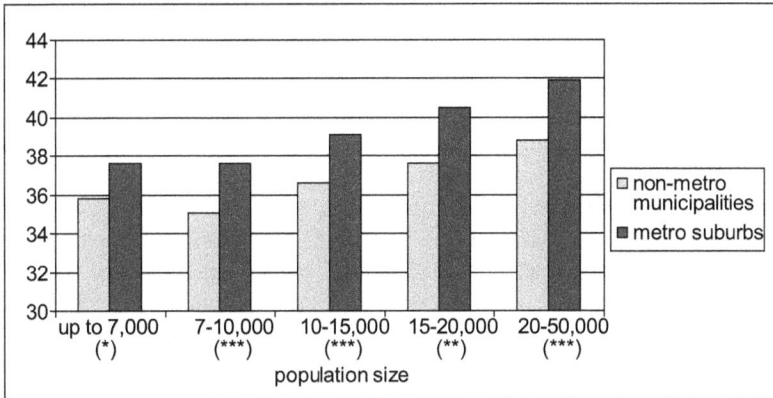

*Figure 10.2: Turnout in 2005 parliamentary elections, metropolitan municipalities and non-metropolitan municipalities*

Notes: (*) difference significant on 0.05 level, (**) difference significant on 0.01 level, (***) difference significant on 0.001 level.

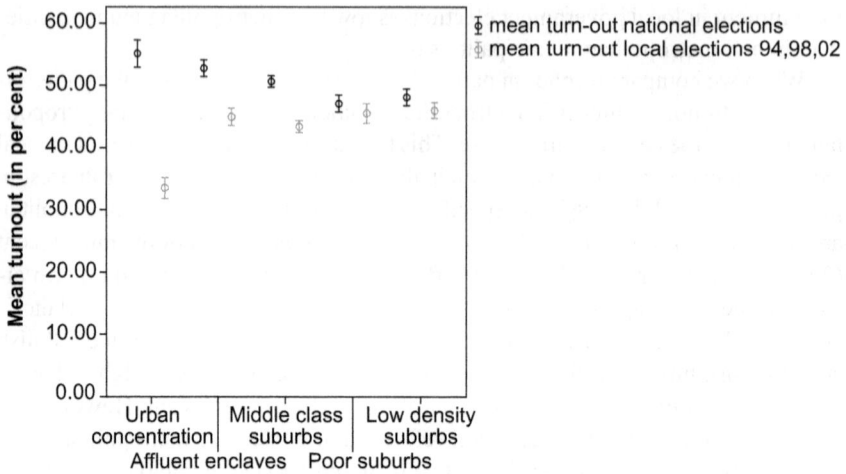

*Figure 10.3: Electoral turnout in local elections (means for municipal elections 1994, 1998, 2002) and national elections (means for Parliamentary elections 1993, 1997, 2001) by municipal types*

tions. In the case of national elections, the pattern is reversed – central city areas have a significantly higher turnout than any other type of suburban municipalities. If we consider the suburban zones, the highest participation in national voting is characteristic for the most affluent communities – it is significantly higher than in poor suburbs and low-density (and more distant from metro centres) peripheral urban suburbs.

Looking at potential predictors affecting turnout in local and national elections, as well as the gap between national and local election turnout, a bivariate analysis yields some interesting insights (see Table 10.4). As expected, local election turnout is lower (and therefore the turnout gap, i.e. delocalisation, is higher) in large metropolitan areas – but it is not affected by geopolitical fragmentation of metropolitan areas. Municipal level variables are also significantly correlated to electoral turnout. Interestingly though, they do not work in the same direction for turnout in local as in national elections. While local election turnout decreases with size of the municipality, the contrary is true for national elections. The more a municipality is distant to the centre of the metropolitan area, the lower the turnout in national elections, while it is higher in local elections. Municipal hardship is associated to lower turnout in national elections, but parallels higher turnout in local elections. The percentage of residents with a university education is associated with higher turnout in national election, but the reverse is true with respect to local elections. Demographic stability, however, did not play a role, as it is correlated neither to local election turnout nor to national election turnout.

These results suggest that the ecological pattern behind local electoral turnout is very different from the one that is behind national electoral turnout. But some of the dependent variables are inter-connected, for example education and size or hardship and distance from the centre. Therefore, an improved test of our

*Table 10.4: Correlations between turnout levels (local and national elections) in municipalities of Polish metropolitan areas and independent variables (Pearson correlation coefficients)*

| | Turnout in local elections (means 1994, 1998 and 2002 elections) | Turnout in national elections (means of 1993, 1997 and 2001 parliamentary elections) | Turnout gap (difference between turnout in national and local elections) |
|---|---|---|---|
| *Metro level variables* | | | |
| Metropolitan population (ln) | **−0.103** | 0.029 | **0.103** |
| Geopolitical fragmentation | −0.012 | 0.093 | 0.081 |
| *Municipal level variables* | | | |
| Municipal population (log) | **−0.610** | **0.349** | **0.741** |
| Distance to centre | **0.247** | **−0.249** | **−0.381** |
| Hardship index | **0.205** | **−0.448** | **−0.505** |
| University education (%) | **−0.343** | **0.263** | **0.472** |
| Demographic stability | 0.000 | −0.065 | −0.049 |

*Note:* For boldface coefficients, $p < 0.05$.

hypotheses is provided by a multivariate analysis with all seven explanatory variables considered simultaneously. Multilevel regression analysis shows that turnout in both local and national elections is influenced by variables that relate to the socio-demographic composition of a municipality, as well as by variables that relate to the nature of their spatial context. More precisely, local election turnout is depressed by social hardship, by municipal size, as well as by population density, but increases with demographic stability (see Table 10.5). Participation of a municipality's voters in national elections is also depressed by social hardship and increases with demographic stability, but the effect of municipal size is opposite: the larger a municipality, the higher the turnout in national elections, thereby confirming the results of the bivariate analysis (see Table 10.6). The analyses also show that both for local and national turnout, the compositional and contextual variables explain away the effects of the types of municipalities. Due to methodological constraints – the number of metropolitan areas in the dataset is too limited – a significant effect of neither size of the overall metropolitan area, nor its geopolitical fragmentation can be confirmed in the multivariate analysis.

## Metropolitanisation and the role of parties in local government

In Poland, political parties play a reduced role in local politics. Compared with other European countries, Polish local governments indeed have the lowest ratio of

Table 10.5: Predictors of turnout in local elections (means for 1994, 1998 and 2002 elections) in municipalities of Polish metropolitan areas (multilevel regression)

| | | Municipal types (model 1) | | Compositional (model 2) | | Contextual (model 3) | | Combined (model 4) | | Combined with types (model 5) | |
|---|---|---|---|---|---|---|---|---|---|---|---|
| | | B | t | B | t | B | t | B | t | B | t |
| Constant | | 34.395 | 1.248 | 48.417 | 14.197 | 75.642 | 15.051 | 107.039 | 18.451 | 109.310 | 18.910 |
| Municipal | Affluent suburbs | 11.025 | 1.331 | | | | | | | -3.162 | 1.909 |
| | Middle-class suburbs | 9.314 | 1.228 | | | | | | | -2.773 | 1.907 |
| | Poor suburbs | 11.156 | 1.301 | | | | | | | -1.741 | 2.112 |
| | Low-density suburbs | 11.763 | 1.273 | | | | | | | -2.184 | 2.175 |
| | University education (%) | | | -0.001 | 0.000 | | | 0.000 | 0.000 | 0.000 | 0.000 |
| | Hardship index | | | 0.021 | 0.040 | | | -0.217 | 0.046 | -0.228 | 0.058 |
| | Municipal size (ln) | | | | | -3.706 | 0.370 | -4.831 | 0.398 | -4.453 | 0.425 |
| | Distance to centre | | | | | -0.021 | 0.032 | 0.035 | 0.033 | 0.033 | 0.039 |
| | Population density | | | | | -0.000 | 0.000 | -0.001 | 0.000 | -0.001 | 0.000 |
| | Demographic stability | | | | | -0.002 | 0.011 | 0.028 | 0.013 | 0.019 | 0.014 |
| Metropolitan | Metropolitan population (ln) | | | -0.323 | 0.954 | 0.346 | 1.052 | -0.549 | 1.242 | -0.417 | 1.254 |
| | Geopolitical fragmentation | | | -1.221 | 2.830 | 0.511 | 3.152 | -0.414 | 3.695 | -0.122 | 3.717 |
| Variance components | Metropolitan | 5.877 | 2.697 | 6.662 | 3.277 | 9.207 | 3.754 | 13.195 | 5.172 | 13.262 | 5.251 |
| | Municipal | 32.956 | 2.350 | 36.515 | 2.579 | 23.546 | 1.668 | 21.706 | 1.542 | 21.831 | 1.571 |
| Explained variance | Pseudo R2 | 0.186 | | 0.095 | | 0.313 | | 0.268 | | 0.264 | |
| N | Metropolitan | 21 | | 21 | | 21 | | 21 | | 419 | |
| N1 | Municipal | 421 | | 427 | | 425 | | 425 | | 21 | |

Note: For boldface coefficients, p<0.05.

Table 10.6: Predictors of turnout in national elections (means for 1993, 1997 and 2001 elections) in municipalities of Polish metropolitan areas (multilevel regression)

| | | Municipal types (model 1) | | Compositional (model 2) | | Contextual (model 3) | | Combined (model 4) | | Combined with types (model 5) | |
|---|---|---|---|---|---|---|---|---|---|---|---|
| | | **B** | **t** | **B** | **t** | **B** | **t** | **B** | **t** | **B** | **t** |
| Constant | | **53.558** | 1.407 | **80.994** | 24.720 | 23.738 | 23.411 | **94.512** | 25.148 | **87.775** | 25.064 |
| Municipal | Affluent suburbs | **-4.860** | 1.091 | | | | | | | 1.265 | 1.676 |
| | Middle-class suburbs | **-7.331** | 1.006 | | | | | | | 1.534 | 1.677 |
| | Poor suburbs | **-10.560** | 1.066 | | | | | | | 0.0887 | 1.859 |
| | Low-density suburbs | **-9.517** | 1.042 | | | | | | | -0.000 | 0.000 |
| | University education (%) | | | **0.000** | 0.000 | | | -0.000 | 0.000 | -0.000 | 0.000 |
| | Hardship index | | | -0.400 | 0.030 | | | **-0.547** | 0.0421 | **-0.508** | 0.052 |
| | Municipal size (ln) | | | | | 1.313 | 0.380 | **0.712** | 0.355 | **0.856** | 0.373 |
| | Distance to centre | | | | | -0.487 | 0.033 | **0.066** | 0.030 | **0.075** | 0.348 |
| | Population density | | | | | 0.001 | 0.000 | 0.000 | 0.000 | 0.000 | 0.000 |
| | Demographic stability | | | | | -0.026 | 0.11 | **0.061** | 0.012 | **0.057** | 0.012 |
| Metropolitan | Metropolitan population (ln) | | | -0.769 | 1.743 | 0.6366 | 1.654 | -1.680 | 1.749 | -1.589 | 1.731 |
| | Geopolitical fragmentation | | | 3.147 | 5.209 | 4.317 | 4.954 | 0.692 | 5.224 | 1.062 | 5.162 |
| Variance components | Metropolitan | **23.616** | 8.072 | **28.512** | 10.109 | **25.040** | 9.077 | **28.409** | 10.046 | **27.660** | 9.791 |
| | Municipal | **22.064** | 1.569 | **18.899** | 1.330 | **24.608** | 1.741 | **17.215** | 1.222 | **16.754** | 1.203 |
| Explained variance | Pseudo R2 | 0.138 | | 0.105 | | 0.063 | | 0.139 | | 0.161 | |
| N | Metropolitan | 21 | | 21 | | 21 | | 21 | | 21 | |
| N1 | Municipal | 421 | | 427 | | 425 | | 425 | | 419 | |

Note: For boldface coefficients, p<0.05.

party membership both among councillors and mayors (Fallend *et al.* 2006). This reflects the general weakness of Polish national parties (Mair and van Biezen 2001) and the low levels of trust shown by voters towards political parties (Domański 2005). This has resulted in politicians attempting to avoid using party labels, even though they might in fact be closely connected to a political party (Swianiewicz 2003). The non-partisan character of local politics is more pronounced in small and mid-size municipalities, but there are also some large cities where parties have a relatively reduced role in the local political arena.

Against this background, we hypothesise that the role of political parties in local politics is more pronounced, the more a municipality has been transformed by metropolitanisation. The metropolitanisation process leads to a transformation of municipalities in different respects, paralleling a loss of citizens' roots in the local community. Consequently, they do not know local politicians personally, so the rational decision during the local elections is to refer to clichés of national politics. In a metropolitan environment, voters will be more likely to refer to political parties they know from the national political arena, even when selecting local councillors. Therefore, we expect that the role of political parties in local politics is more important in municipalities that are located in large metropolitan areas, closer to the core city, and show lower levels of demographic stability as a consequence of migration. In addition, we also expect that population size of a municipality leads to a more pronounced role by political parties in local politics, as the electoral rule differs with municipal size. In municipalities with fewer than 20,000 citizens, elections are based on a majoritarian, first-past-the post system. In larger municipalities, proportional rule is used, thereby increasing the likelihood of electoral lists of candidates presented by political parties.

An exploration of data on party membership of local councillors and mayors in the municipalities of Polish metropolitan areas shows that, overall, less than a fifth of mayors and less than a third of all local councillors are in fact members of a political party (see Table 10.7). Even in the urban concentrations – mainly the core cities – where the role of parties could be expected to be particularly prominent, more than half (in 2002) and almost half (in 2006) of the elected mayors were not members of a political party. The percentage of partisan councillors is strongly diversified between core cities across metropolitan areas. In some cases, such as Warsaw, all councillors have clear party affiliations, while, in contrast, there are two cities in which the proportion of partisan councillors is lower than 40 per cent (Rzeszów 36 per cent and Gdynia 39 per cent). In both cases, the mayor is also formally independent and a large group of councillors were elected from 'his' committee, i.e. drawing on the high personal reputation of their leader. In core cities of metropolitan areas, councils are much more likely to be partisan than their (directly elected) mayors. In 2002, almost two-thirds of councillors – and in 2006 more than four in five councillors – were elected from party lists in the core cities. But it still means that over 30 per cent in 2002 and almost 20 per cent of councillors in 2006 were elected from lists of local committees that were unaffiliated to any national parties. Quite often the names of committees refer to the name of a popular candidate for mayor.

*Table 10.7: Percentage of councillors and mayors in local government of Polish metropolitan areas who are a member of a political party (2002 and 2006 local elections), according to type of municipality*

|  | Councillors | | Mayors | |
| --- | --- | --- | --- | --- |
|  | 2002 | 2006 | 2002 | 2006 |
| Urban concentrations | 67 | 81 | 27 | 50 |
| Affluent suburbs | 13 | 15 | 10 | 3 |
| Poor suburbs | 16 | 17 | 18 | 8 |
| Average suburbs | 17 | 19 | 9 | 9 |
| Low-density suburbs | 19 | 17 | 20 | 9 |
| Overall mean | 26 | 30 | 17 | 16 |

*Source:* own calculations based on data from the Polish Electoral Committee.

The more general picture is that the role of parties in local politics is clearly higher in urban concentrations than in all other types of metropolitan municipalities. Interestingly, however, the affluent suburbs are those that have the lowest allocation of partisan mayors. It seems that in these better-off communities, it is more likely that strong local leaders run for office and are elected on the basis of their personal popularity rather than on the basis of partisan loyalty.

The multivariate analysis confirms the importance of variables measuring the spatial context of a municipality for the explanation of the partisan character of local politics. Indeed, not only population size and density of a municipality, but also its location within a metropolitan area as well as demographic stability, significantly influence the ratio of non-party members among the local councillors (see Table 10.8). More precisely, local councillors not affiliated to political parties are more likely to be voted for in smaller and less densely populated municipalities. Demographics and distance to the centre are also associated with party membership of local councillors, but in a counter-intuitive way: the proportion of independent local councillors increases with distance from the centre and demographic stability, but these relationships are only marginally significant. Similarly, the overall size of the metropolitan area is shown to have a positive effect on the proportion of independent local councillors. This can be explained by the fact that larger metropolitan areas also tend to have a larger number of small municipalities, where the proportion of independent councillors is high.

## Analysis of partisanship

The classic distinction between left and right political positions is obviously one of the most widely used scales to measure voter preferences. However, as the theory of a New Political Culture suggests, this distinction may be inadequate in some countries (Clark and Hoffmann-Martionot 1998; Clark and Lipset 1991). The usefulness of the left-right distinction seems particularly questionable in Poland,

Table 10.8: Predictors of percentage of independent local councillors (local elections 2002) in municipalities of Polish metropolitan areas (multilevel regression)

| | | Municipal types (model 1) | | Compositional (model 2) | | Contextual (model 3) | | Combined (model 4) | | Combined with types (model 5) | |
|---|---|---|---|---|---|---|---|---|---|---|---|
| | | B | t | B | t | B | t | B | t | B | t |
| Constant | | **42.488** | 3.689 | **51.045** | 34.039 | **85.697** | 35.946 | **60.551** | 41.665 | **58.495** | 42.831 |
| Municipal | Affluent suburbs | **43.790** | 4.057 | | | | | | | **7.701** | 6.585 |
| | Middle-class suburbs | **40.131** | 3.744 | | | | | | | **7.604** | 6.547 |
| | Poor suburbs | **40.749** | 3.968 | | | | | | | **7.416** | 7.228 |
| | Low-density suburbs | **36.978** | 3.881 | | | | | | | **4.733** | 7.453 |
| | University education (%) | | | -0.000 | 0.000 | | | -0.000 | 0.000 | -0.000 | 0.000 |
| | Hardship index | | | -0.115 | 0.115 | | | 0.077 | 0.152 | 0.002 | 0.187 |
| | Municipal size (ln) | | | | | **-8.521** | 1.245 | **-6.492** | 1.377 | **-5.623** | 1.468 |
| | Distance to centre | | | | | -0.216 | 0.108 | -0.286 | 0.113 | -0.227 | 0.133 |
| | Population density | | | | | **-0.005** | 0.001 | **-0.005** | 0.001 | **-0.006** | 0.001 |
| | Demographic stability | | | | | **-0.128** | 0.036 | **-0.123** | 0.044 | **-0.098** | 0.046 |
| Metropolitan | Metropolitan population (ln) | | | **2.709** | 5.081 | **5.814** | 14.445 | **6.066** | 12.655 | **5.374** | 12.255 |
| | Geopolitical fragmentation | | | 2.222 | 6.586 | 2.463 | 7.402 | 2.588 | 7.631 | 2.572 | 7.510 |
| Variance components | Metropolitan | **36.292** | 18.168 | 29.607 | 18.335 | 41.716 | 21.042 | **43.812** | 23.108 | **40.671** | 22.498 |
| | Municipal | **306.537** | 21.828 | **316.797** | 22.398 | **268.116** | 19.010 | **261.884** | 18.670 | **262.832** | 18.999 |
| Explained variance | Pseudo R2 | 0.215 | | 0.207 | | 0.291 | | 0.300 | | 0.305 | |
| N | Metropolitan | 21 | | 21 | | 21 | | 21 | | 21 | |
| N1 | Municipal | 421 | | 427 | | 425 | | 425 | | 419 | |

Note: Significant coefficients in bold (p<0.05).

as in other countries of Central and Eastern Europe, where the political arena is still in the transformation stage. Grabowska (2004: 247ff.) argues that the cleavage between post-communist and anti-communist political groups tends to blur the classic left-wing spectrum. Moreover, the Polish party system is very volatile and it rarely happens that the same political party retains the same level of power in two subsequent elections. The instability of the Polish party system makes it difficult to analyse averages between subsequent elections. But, nevertheless, we base our analysis on central tendencies in order to exclude the impact of semi-random, one-time fluctuations in partisanship.

But even if we analyse the variation of voting not for individual parties, but for wider groups of parties identified with the left and right wing of the political spectrum, the picture is not much clearer. This is due to the fact that, in Poland, the distinction between left and right is only to a small extent based on the differences in party programmes, and more on historical roots in the pre-1989 political establishment or the Solidarity opposition. Although Grabowska (2004) argues that the historical nature of the left-right dimension can also be observed in several countries of Western Europe (e.g. in Ireland), it seems that this dimension is especially strong in Poland.

This is why a two-dimensional left-right classification of Polish parties has been used in Polish political studies (e.g. Raciborski 1997; Markowski 2001). It distinguishes an economic dimension of the left-right scale, referring to the relation between the state and the private sector – plus the role of redistribution of wealth – as well as a cultural dimension of the left-right scale, referring to the tensions between culturally-liberal positions and cultural conservatism. For the subsequent analysis, we follow the procedure defined in the common IMO research protocol and locate parties according to the mean positions of their voters on a range of political issues, as measured in post-electoral surveys. More precisely, we distinguish four different indices to measure parties' political positions (see Table 10.9):

(1) a left-right index based on voter self-placement;[5]
(2) an index of economic left-right issues reflecting positions on issues such as redistribution, economic policy and the relationship between the public and the private sector;
(3) an index of cultural conservatism, referring to party voters' position on moral issues such as family life, abortion or homosexuality; and
(4) an index reflecting positions with respect to issues of globalisation.[6]

While the positions of party voters on cultural issues are similar to positions on globalisation issues (i.e. culturally-conservative persons tend to oppose global

---

5. Numbers reflect the mean of left-right self-placement of respondents of the International Social Survey (ISS) who declared having voted for this party in the last election.

6. The exact construction of the indices is given in Chapter 14, the Methodological Appendix of this volume.

*Table 10.9: Political position indices for major parties in Poland*

| | Left-right self-assessment of party voters (1 'left' to 10 'right') | Party voters' positions on economic issues (1 'left' to 10 'right') | Party voters' position on cultural issues (1 'liberal' to 10 'conservative') | Party voters' position on globalisation issues (1 'open' to 10 'closed') |
|---|---|---|---|---|
| SLD (Left Democratic Alliance – post-communists) | 4.02 | 3.80 | 6.32 | 4.93 |
| PSL (Polish Peasant Party) | 5.45 | 3.55 | 6.76 | 5.24 |
| Samoobrona (Self-defence) | 5.48 | 3.13 | 7.1 | 5.49 |
| UW (Union of Freedom) | 6.09 | 5.27 | 5.57 | 4.63 |
| PO (Civic Platform) | 6.99 | 4.83 | 6.36 | 4.52 |
| PiS (Law and Justice) | 7.14 | 4.59 | 6.45 | 4.91 |
| LPR (League of Polish Families) | 7.28 | 3.78 | 7.37 | 5.37 |
| AWS (Electoral Action Solidarity) | 7.34 | 4.33 | 6.95 | 5.02 |
| PWN (Polish National Fellowship) | n/a | n/a | n/a | 4.00 |
| German Minority Party | n/a | n/a | n/a | 5.16 |
| PUG (Polish Economic Union) | n/a | n/a | n/a | 4.95 |
| Other parties | n/a | n/a | n/a | 4.79 |

*Note:* *1–10 scale, where 1 means extreme left, 10 extreme right.

*Sources:* International Social Survey Programmes 2002 and 2004, Polish subsamples.

openness and international integration), positions on left-right economic issues point in the opposite direction of what is known from observations of Western European countries. Indeed, there is a clear negative correlation between 'leftism' on economic issues and cultural 'leftism' (i.e. culturally-liberal positions) or globalisation 'leftism' (i.e. openness towards immigrants and international integration). Voters who are 'conservative' on economic issues (e.g. who are in favour of a small public sector) are often liberal on cultural issues (e.g. in favour of equal treatment of homosexuals) and open towards globalisation (e.g. in favour of EU integration). This highlights the difficulty in defining the left-right orientation of political behaviour in the Polish context. Party positions based on voters' left-right self-assessment are more strongly correlated with opinions on economic than on cultural or globalisation issues, but this correlation is not very strong. Thus, the economic, cultural and – to a lesser extent – globalisation indices for party positions are more meaningful than the left-right self-placement scale. The latter will thus be omitted from the subsequent analysis.

### Metropolitan patterns of partisanship

Observations from other countries suggest that support for right-wing positions is greater in low-density metropolitan municipalities that are more distant from the centre of the city. In Poland, however, we may also expect the opposite relationship. Due to the geographical distribution of poverty and wealth in Polish metropolitan areas where the central areas of cities and their adjacent suburbs are better off than suburban municipalities on the outer fringe, one may expect more support for right-wing parties in the suburbs that are closer to the centre and in the actual central areas of the cities. With respect to the economic left-right index, support for fiscally-conservative policies (right-wing in economic terms) may be expected in wealthy central areas and rich suburbs. But with respect to the cultural and globalisation indices, more support for socially-conservative and isolationist orientations may be expected in the low-density suburbs.

Based on parties' scores on the three indices (position on economic left-right issues, cultural issues, and globalisation issues), average issue positions were calculated for each municipality on the basis of the municipal level of electoral support in the 1997 and 2001 elections to the national parliament. An exploration of municipal issue positions shows that voters tend to have distinct political orientations according to the different types of metropolitan municipalities (see Figure 10.4). Voters in urban concentrations and (to a smaller extent) affluent suburbs display support for right-wing positions on economic issues, as well as culturally-liberal positions and openness towards globalisation. At the other extreme, we have low-density suburbs, at far distance from the centre, whose voters support leftist positions on economic issues, are more culturally conservative and are critical with respect to globalisation.

An analysis of correlations between municipal issue positions and compositional and contextual variables allows further differentiation of this overall picture (see Table 10.10). A very strong correlation is found between municipal issue posi-

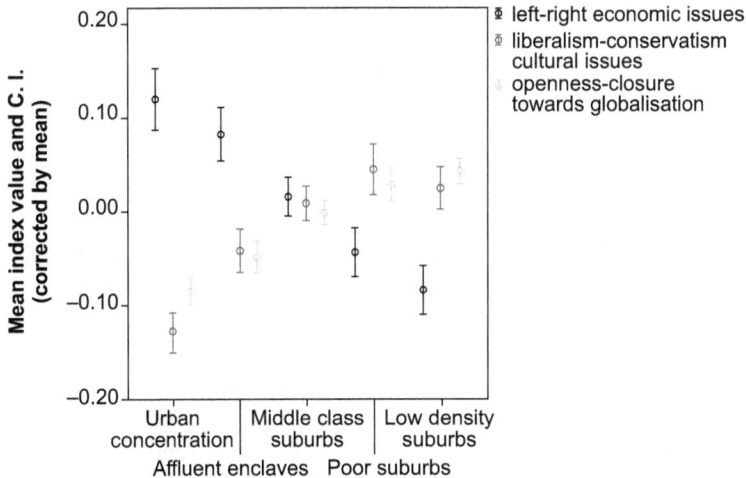

*Figure 10.4: Average communal issue positions on economic, cultural and globalisation issues (means for national elections 1997 and 2001)*

tions and the hardship index. Voters in less affluent municipalities are more leftist in their opinions on economic issues, but they are more culturally conservative and display more isolationist attitudes with respect to globalisation. Not surprisingly, the correlation with the level of education points in the opposite direction: municipalities with a higher proportion of university-educated inhabitants are more right wing on economic issues and, simultaneously, more liberal on cultural issues and more open towards globalisation. As social hardship is usually lower in municipalities located closer to the metro core, it is not surprising that correlations between municipal issue positions and the distance to the centre are similar to those of the hardship index.

To control for such spurious correlations, multilevel regression analyses were performed in order to estimate the influence of various independent variables on municipal voters' positions:

- on left-right economic issues (see Table 10.11);
- on the cultural liberalism-conservatism scale (see Table 10.12); and
- with regard to their attitudes towards globalisation (see Table 10.13).

What these analyses show, first of all, is that both compositional and contextual variables determine the political preferences of voters in Polish metropolitan municipalities. More precisely, the multivariate analysis confirms that political preferences are clearly related to social hardship. With respect to positions on economic issues, the results show that the higher social hardship is in a municipality, the stronger the preferences of this municipality's voters for left positions (e.g. redistributionist interventions of the state – see Table 10.11). With respect to positions on cultural issues or attitudes towards globalisation, the opposite is true: the higher the hardship is in a municipality, the more likely are its voters to support culturally-conservative positions (see Table 10.12) or ethnocentrism and international isolation (see Table 10.13).

The strong influence of social hardship on municipal issue positions points towards socio-demographic causes of political preferences. Nevertheless, the multilevel models also show that contextual variables play a role, even if compositional variables are controlled for (see Table 10.11). More precisely, we find that municipal size and demographic stability are associated with a particular position on the left-right economic spectrum: the larger a municipality, and the more it is characterised by migration flows, the more this municipality's voters tend to support right-wing positions. This can be explained by the fact that, in Polish metropolitan areas, wealth is often more present in the central areas of cities, which are characterised both by large size and demographic instability. The analysis also shows that, even if we control for the influence of compositional and contextual variables, voters living in affluent enclaves are still more likely to support right-wing positions on economic issues. Looking at the cultural and globalisation issue positions, we also find contextual variables play a role: voters in larger and more densely-populated municipalities that are characterised by migration flows tend to support culturally-liberal positions (see Table 10.12) and openness towards

*Table 10.10: Correlations between municipal issue positions (mean of 1997 and 2001 national parliamentary elections) and independent variables (Pearson correlation coefficients)*

| | Left-right economic issues (1 left, 10 right) | Cultural liberalism-conservatism (1 liberal, 10 conservative) | Attitudes towards globalisation issues (1 openness, 10 isolation) |
|---|---|---|---|
| *Metro-level variables* | | | |
| Metropolitan population (ln) | **0.254** | **−0.166** | **−0.317** |
| Geopolitical fragmentation | 0.097 | −0.028 | **−0.062** |
| *Municipal level variables* | | | |
| University education (%) | **0.244** | **−0.259** | **−0.268** |
| Hardship index | **−0.615** | **0.504** | **0.607** |
| Municipal population (log) | **0.431** | **−0.398** | **−0.473** |
| Population density | **0.387** | **−0.413** | **−0.473** |
| Distance to centre | **−0.268** | **0.202** | **0.225** |
| Demographic stability | **−0.358** | **0.440** | **0.452** |

*Note:* For boldface coefficients, $p<0.05$.

globalisation (see Table 10.13). In addition, the more a municipality is distant from the metro core, the more its voters tend to favour cultural conservatism (see Table 10.12) and international demarcation (see Table 10.13). This suggests that, while the electorate's position on the left-right dimension is closely related to the nature of economic assets present in a municipality, the electorate's positions on cultural or globalisation issues seems to be more closely linked to the lifestyles or traditions of particular types of metropolitan places of living.

Hence, besides the influence of compositional variables – most importantly, social hardship – on the political preferences of citizens in Polish metropolitan areas, these results suggest that such preferences are also place-related, i.e. shaped by the specific spatial context of metropolitan municipalities.

Again, this observation can be illustrated by drawing the political preference map of two major metropolitan areas in Poland: Warsaw (see Figure 10.5) and Wrocław (see Figure 10.6). In the Warsaw metropolitan area, the most economically right-wing areas are three affluent upper- and middle-class suburbs (Podkowa Leśna, Izabelin and Michałowice) followed by two suburban municipalities that are a mixture of middle-class housing for affluent commuters and the location of numerous small and mid-size enterprises (Józefów and Łomianki). These five suburban municipalities are followed by Warsaw. In general, economically right-wing communities prevail close to Warsaw (especially in the richer, western side of the metropolitan area) while the more economically left-wing are in the more distant and eastern part of the area. In the Wrocław metropolitan area, the most economically right-wing area is the core of the city itself, followed by some of the communities located next to city borders. In both metro areas, the most culturally-

*Table 10.11: Predictors of municipal positions on the left-right economic index (based on municipal level results to the national parliamentary elections 1997 and 2001) in Polish metropolitan areas (multilevel regression)*

| | | Municipal types (model 1) | | Compositional (model 2) | | Contextual (model 3) | | Combined (model 4) | | Combined with types (model 5) | |
|---|---|---|---|---|---|---|---|---|---|---|---|
| | | **B** | t | **B** | t | **B** | t | **B** | t | **B** | t |
| Constant | | **4.207** | 0.025 | **4.515** | 0.324 | **3.351** | 0.367 | **3.966** | 0.339 | **3.880** | 0.348 |
| Municipal | Affluent suburbs | **-0.048** | 0.020 | | | | | | | **0.078** | 0.032 |
| | Middle-class suburbs | **-0.110** | 0.018 | | | | | | | 0.061 | 0.032 |
| | Poor suburbs | **-0.163** | 0.019 | | | | | | | 0.055 | 0.035 |
| | Low-density suburbs | **-0.207** | 0.019 | | | | | | | 0.016 | 0.036 |
| | University education (%) | | | **0.000** | 0.000 | | | -0.000 | 0.000 | 0.000 | 0.000 |
| | Hardship index | | | **-0.008** | 0.000 | | | **-0.004** | 0.000 | **-0.004** | 0.000 |
| | Municipal size (ln) | | | | | **0.027** | 0.006 | **0.023** | 0.006 | **0.029** | 0.007 |
| | Distance to centre | | | | | **-0.002** | 0.000 | -0.001 | 0.000 | -0.000 | 0.000 |
| | Population density | | | | | 0.000 | 0.000 | 0.000 | 0.000 | 0.000 | 0.000 |
| | Demographic stability | | | | | **-0.001** | 0.000 | **-0.000** | 0.000 | **-0.000** | 0.000 |
| Metropolitan | Metropolitan population (ln) | | | 0.004 | 0.022 | 0.035 | 0.025 | 0.015 | 0.023 | 0.009 | 0.023 |
| | Geopolitical fragmentation | | | 0.076 | 0.067 | 0.129 | 0.077 | 0.095 | 0.068 | 0.097 | 0.069 |
| Variance components | Metropolitan | **0.007** | 0.002 | **0.004** | 0.001 | **0.006** | 0.002 | **0.004** | 0.001 | **0.004** | 0.001 |
| | Municipal | **0.007** | 0.000 | **0.007** | 0.000 | **0.006** | 0.000 | **0.006** | 0.000 | **0.006** | 0.000 |
| Explained variance | Pseudo R² | 0.870 | | 0.870 | | 0.855 | | 0.988 | | 0.878 | |
| N | Metropolitan | 21 | | 21 | | 21 | | 21 | | 21 | |
| N1 | Municipal | 420 | | 426 | | 425 | | 425 | | 419 | |

*Note*: For boldface coefficients, p<0.05.

*Table 10.12: Predictors of municipal positions on cultural liberalism-conservatism index (based on municipal level results of national parliamentary elections 1997 and 2001) in Polish metropolitan areas (multilevel regression)*

| | | Municipal types (model 1) | | Compositional (model 2) | | Contextual (model 3) | | Combined (model 4) | | Combined with types (model 5) | |
|---|---|---|---|---|---|---|---|---|---|---|---|
| | | **B** | t | **B** | t | **B** | t | **B** | t | **B** | t |
| Constant | | **6.488** | 0.024 | **6.204** | 0.413 | **6.815** | 0.388 | **6.454** | 0.387 | **6.533** | 0.395 |
| Municipal | Affluent suburbs | **0.075** | 0.015 | | | | | | | -0.009 | 0.023 |
| | Middle-class suburbs | **0.122** | 0.014 | | | | | | | 0.011 | 0.023 |
| | Poor suburbs | **0.151** | 0.015 | | | | | | | 0.009 | 0.026 |
| | Low-density suburbs | **0.139** | 0.015 | | | | | | | 0.001 | 0.027 |
| | University education (%) | | | **-0.000** | 0.000 | | | -0.000 | 0.000 | -0.000 | 0.000 |
| | Hardship index | | | **0.004** | 0.000 | | | **0.002** | 0.000 | **0.001** | 0.000 |
| | Municipal size (ln) | | | | | **-0.025** | 0.004 | **-0.020** | 0.004 | **-0.020** | 0.005 |
| | Distance to centre | | | | | -0.001 | 0.000 | **-0.002** | 0.004 | **-0.001** | 0.000 |
| | Population density | | | | | -0.000 | 0.000 | **-0.000** | 0.000 | **-0.000** | 0.000 |
| | Demographic stability | | | | | **0.001** | 0.000 | **0.001** | 0.027 | **0.001** | 0.000 |
| Metropolitan | Metropolitan population (ln) | | | 0.005 | 0.029 | 0.003 | 0.027 | 0.014 | 0.027 | 0.012 | 0.027 |
| | Geopolitical fragmentation | | | 0.017 | 0.087 | -0.039 | 0.082 | -0.025 | 0.080 | -0.024 | 0.082 |
| Variance components | Metropolitan | **0.009** | 0.003 | **0.008** | 0.002 | **0.007** | 0.002 | **0.006** | 0.002 | **0.007** | 0.002 |
| | Municipal | **0.004** | 0.000 | **0.004** | 0.000 | **0.003** | 0.000 | **0.003** | 0.000 | **0.003** | 0.000 |
| Explained variance | Pseudo $R^2$ | 0.110 | | 0.204 | | 0.312 | | 0.343 | | 0.328 | |
| N | Metropolitan | 21 | | 21 | | 21 | | 21 | | 21 | |
| N1 | Municipal | 420 | | 426 | | 425 | | 425 | | 419 | |

*Note:* For boldface coefficients, $p < 0.05$.

Table 10.13: Predictors of municipal positions on the globalisation-isolation index (based on municipal level results of national parliamentary elections 1997 and 2001) in Polish metropolitan areas (multilevel regression)

| | | Municipal types (model 1) | | Compositional (model 2) | | Contextual (model 3) | | Combined (model 4) | | Combined with types (model 5) | |
|---|---|---|---|---|---|---|---|---|---|---|---|
| | | B | t | B | t | B | t | B | t | B | t |
| Constant | | **4.937** | 0.015 | **4.922** | 0.210 | **5.575** | 0.183 | **5.234** | 0.190 | 5.315 | 0.197 |
| Municipal | Affluent suburbs | **0.038** | 0.011 | | | | | | | **-0.044** | 0.016 |
| | Middle-class suburbs | **0.079** | 0.010 | | | | | | | -0.027 | 0.016 |
| | Poor suburbs | **0.106** | 0.011 | | | | | | | -0.029 | 0.018 |
| | Low-density suburbs | **0.123** | 0.010 | | | | | | | -0.013 | 0.019 |
| | University education (%) | | | **-0.000** | 0.000 | | | **0.000** | 0.000 | -0.000 | 0.000 |
| | Hardship index | | | **0.004** | 0.000 | | | **0.002** | 0.000 | **0.002** | 0.000 |
| | Municipal size (ln) | | | | | **-0.019** | 0.003 | -0.017 | 0.003 | **-0.021** | 0.003 |
| | Distance to centre | | | | | 0.000 | 0.000 | -0.000 | 0.000 | **-0.000** | 0.000 |
| | Population density | | | | | **-0.001** | 0.000 | **-0.000** | 0.000 | **-0.000** | 0.000 |
| | Demographic stability | | | | | **0.001** | 0.000 | **0.001** | 0.000 | **0.000** | 0.000 |
| Metropolitan | Metropolitan population (ln) | | | -0.014 | 0.014 | -0.026 | 0.012 | -0.015 | 0.013 | -0.013 | 0.013 |
| | Geopolitical fragmentation | | | -0.036 | 0.044 | -0.078 | 0.038 | -0.058 | 0.038 | -0.059 | 0.039 |
| Variance components | Metropolitan | **0.002** | 0.000 | **0.001** | 0.000 | **0.001** | 0.000 | **0.001** | 0.000 | **0.001** | 0.000 |
| | Municipal | **0.002** | 0.000 | **0.002** | 0.000 | **0.001** | 0.000 | **0.001** | 0.000 | **0.001** | 0.000 |
| Explained variance | Pseudo $R^2$ | 0.205 | | 0.374 | | 0.482 | | 0.509 | | 0.505 | |
| N | Metropolitan | 21 | | 21 | | 21 | | 21 | | 21 | |
| N1 | Municipal | 420 | | 426 | | 425 | | 425 | | 419 | |

Note: For boldface coefficients, $p<0.05$.

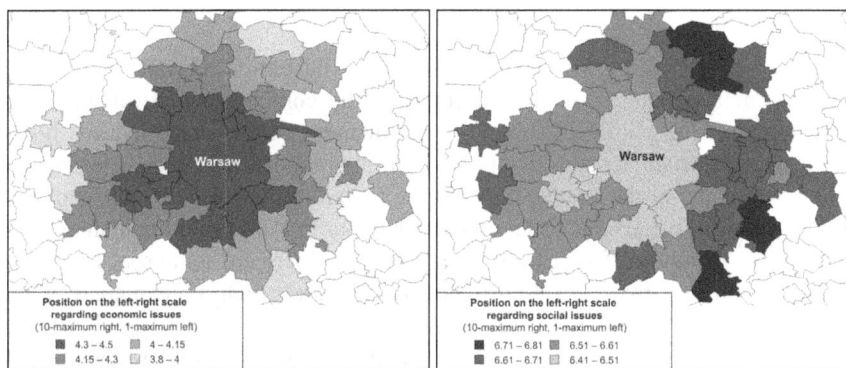

*Figure 10.5: Municipal issue positions on left-right economic issues (left map) and on cultural liberalism-conservatism (right map) in the Warsaw metropolitan area (drawing on the 1997, 2001 and 2005 national parliamentary elections)*

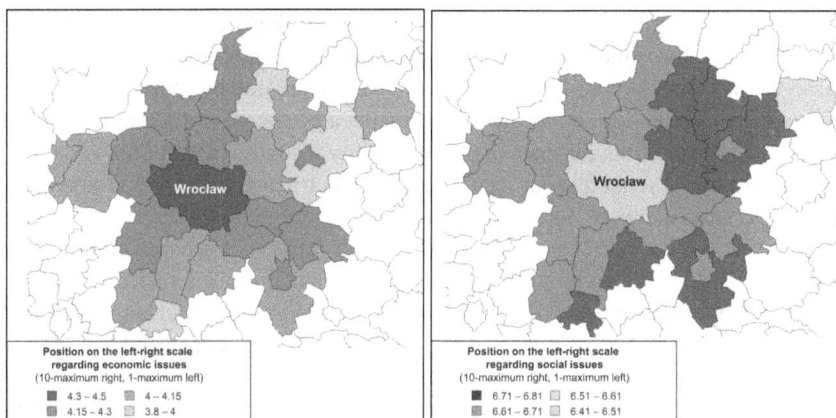

*Figure 10.6: Municipal issue positions on left-right economic issues (left map) and on cultural liberalism-conservatism (right map) in the Wroclaw metropolitan area (drawing on the 1997, 2001 and 2005 national parliamentary elections)*

conservative communities are those that are the most economically leftist. Thus, the 'visual analysis' of the maps confirms the impact of distance from the metro centre. The most culturally-liberal ('left') municipalities in the Warsaw metro area are the affluent municipality of Podkowa Leśna (famous for the high proportion of the 'bohema' living there), followed by Warsaw city and other affluent suburbs of the western edge of the metro area: Michałowice and Milanówek. In the Wrocław metropolitan area, the most culturally-liberal municipality is the core city itself.

## Conclusions

The analysis set out in this chapter provides an illustration relevant to the more general metropolitanisation thesis providing the common analytical thread to this volume. The political ecology of Polish metropolitan areas indeed shows some specific characteristics compared with the rest of the country's territories. Moreover, some of the results highlight the importance of place for the explanation of political behaviour. The political behaviour in Polish metropolitan areas is not subject to rules different from other areas, but there are some specific points that distinguish it from the circumstances outside these metropolitan areas. What are the differences that we have noted?

The analysis in this chapter confirms that location in metropolitan areas matters for some aspects of political behaviour. Turnout in local elections is systematically lower, while turnout in national elections is systematically higher in metropolitan municipalities compared with municipalities of similar size located outside metropolitan areas. But the hypotheses explaining the variation of turnout across metropolitan municipalities were only partially confirmed. Most of the significant factors refer to individual municipalities. Turnout in local elections is depressed by social hardship, municipality size, population and demographic instability. The turnout in national parliamentary elections is also depressed by social hardship and demographic instability, but positively influenced by the size of a municipality. A (positive) impact of the distance of a municipality from the metropolitan core was found only for national turnout. Features of the metro area itself seem to be much less important. We have not found any impact of the geopolitical fragmentation index or of the overall size of the metropolitan areas. Citizens of metropolitan areas may be called *homo politicus*, since they are more interested in politics than residents of other parts of the country (with higher turnout in national voting than towns of a similar size elsewhere). Perhaps this difference can be related to specific features of a metropolitan population – they are more affluent on average and more educated. At the same time their interest in politics is *delocalised* – they are more interested in national politics, but seldom in local politics. Turnout in local elections is lower in metropolitan municipalities than elsewhere. Moreover, internal variation within metropolitan areas suggests that 'the more metropolitan' the nature of a municipality, the less 'localised' its political behaviour therein. For example, in municipalities that are closer to the core cities, we find higher proportions of local councillors who are affiliated with political parties. Similarly, lower turnout in local elections is found in municipalities that have lower levels of demographic stability, i.e. that have a higher proportion of 'fresh' migrants – another typical phenomenon for metropolitanised suburbs.

The analysis of explanatory factors for the varying role of political parties in local politics of metropolitan municipalities showed the importance of municipal size and population density. To some extent, this result is due to the different sociological characteristics of small communities and also to the electoral system, which in Poland is majoritarian in municipalities with fewer than 20,000 citizens, but it turns to proportional in larger jurisdictions. Demographic stability also matters – voters in stable communities tend to vote for known personalities, while in a more unstable communities of migrants, there is an 'escape' to ideological clichés and vote for parties. To a smaller extent, distances from the core city also matter. In municipalities that are more distant from the core city, communities are 'less metropolitan', the social bonds of local community are stronger, people know more about individual (independent) candidates and are more inclined to vote for them rather than for parties.

Finally, investigation into the variations of political preferences of citizens in municipalities has been complicated due to the difficulties with the dependent variable. Nevertheless, the three indices measuring support for positions on issues, such as the left versus right on economic issues, cultural liberalism versus conservatism, and, to a lesser extent, openness versus isolationist attitudes with respect to globalisation, also proved meaningful in the Polish context. These analyses have shown that compositional variables – most importantly social hardship – play a role in determining voters' preferences, but there are also contextual variables that retain explanatory power. The fact that municipal size, population density and demographic stability are significantly associated with the position taken by municipal voters on issues also highlights the connection to place with regard to political preferences in the Polish context.

**Bibliography**

Bartkowski, J. (2003) *Tradycja i polityka: wpływ tradycji kulturowych polskich regionów na współczesne zachowania społeczne i polityczne*, Warszawa: Wydawnictwo Żak.

Clark, T. N. and Hoffmann-Martinot, V. (1998) *The New Political Culture*, Boulder, Colorado: Westview.

Clark, T. N. and Lipset, S. M. (1991) 'Are social classes dying?', *International Sociology*, 6(4): 397–410.

Denters, B. (2002) 'Size and political trust: evidence from Denmark, the Netherlands, Norway and the United Kingdom', *Environment and Planning: Government & Policy*, 20(6): 793–812.

Domański, H. (2005) 'Państwo to nie my', *Polityka*, 49(2533): 94–5.

Fallend, F., Ignits, G. and Swianiewicz, P. (2006) 'Divided loyalties? Mayors beetween party representation and local community interests', in H. Bäck, H. Heinelt and A. Magnier (eds) *The European Mayor: Political leaders in the changing context of local democracy*, Opladen: Verlag für Sozialwissenschaften, 245–71.

Grabowska, M. (2004) *Podział postkomunistyczny: społeczne podstawy polityki w Polsce po 1989 roku*, Warszawa: Scholar.

Herbst, J. (2005) *Oblicza społeczeństwa obywatelskiego*, Warszawa: Fundacja Rozwoju Społeczeństwa Obywatelskiego.

Lipset, S. M. (1981) *Political Man: The Social Basis of Politics*, Baltimore: The Johns Hopkins University Press.

Mair, P. and Van Biezen, I. (2001) 'Party membership in twenty European democracies 1980–2000', *Party Politics*, 7(1): 5–21.

Markowski, R. (2001) 'Party system institutionalization in new democracies: Poland – a trend-setter with no followers', in P. G. Lewis (ed.) *Party Development and Democratic Change in Post-Communist Europe: The first decade*, London: Frank Cass, 55–77.

Preteceille, E. (2000) 'Segregation, class and politics in large cities', in: A. Bagnasco and P. Le Gales (eds) *Cities in Contemporary Europe*, Cambridge: Cambridge University Press, 74–98.

Raciborski, J. (1997) *Polskie wybory; zachowania wyborcze społeczeństwa polskiego w latach 1989–1995*, Warszawa: Scholar.

— (2004) 'Zachowania wyborcze Polaków', in M. Marody (ed.) *Wymiary życia społecznego: Polska na przełomie XX i XXI wieku*, Warszawa: Scholar, 22–51.

Rose, L. (2002) 'Municipal size and local non-electoral participation: findings from Denmark, the Netherlands, and Norway', *Environment and Planning: Government & Policy*, 20(6): 829–51.

Swianiewicz, P. (2002) *Consolidation or Fragmentation? The size of local governments in Central and Eastern Europe*, Budapest: Open Society Institute.

— (2003) 'Partisan cleavages in local governments in Poland after 1990', in T. Zarycki and G. Kolankiewicz (eds) *Regional Issues in Polish Politics, London: School of Slavonic and East European Studies*, University College London, Occasional Papers No. 60: 179–201.

Swianiewicz, P. and Klimska, U. (2005) 'Polish metropolitan areas: vanilla centres, sandwich suburbs', in: V. Hoffmann-Martinot and J. M. Sellers (eds) *Metropolitanization and Political Change*, Opladen: Verlag für Sozialwissenschaften, 303–34.

Szczerbiak, A. (2003) 'Chaos out of order? Polish parties' electoral strategies and bases of support', in T. Zarycki and G. Kolankiewicz (eds) *Regional Issues in Polish Politics*, London: School of Slavonic and East European Studies, University College London, Occasional Papers No. 60: 133–57.

Zarycki, T. (1996) *Nowa przestrzeń społeczno-polityczna Polski*, Warszawa: Europejski Instytut Rozwoju Regionalnego i Lokalnego, Uniwersytet Warszawski.

— (2002) *Region Jako Kontekst Zachowań Politycznych*, Warszawa: Scholar.

— (2003) 'The regional dimension of the Polish political scene', in T. Zarycki and G. Kolankiewicz (eds) *Regional Issues in Polish Politics*, London: School of Slavonic and East European Studies, University College London, Occasional Papers No. 60: 239–62.

# Chapter Eleven | The Political Ecology of Czech Metropolitan Areas – is there a Post-Communist Metropolitan Model?

*Tomáš Kostelecký, Daniel Čermák and Jana Vobecká*

## Introduction[1]

The first signs of metropolitanisation on the territory of the contemporary Czech Republic trace back to the interwar period, when the country experienced a wave of rapid economic development. The largest cities that served as cores of administrative, commercial and industrial activities grew quickly, and substantial suburban development took place in the adjacent regions (Musil *et al.* 2002). Pre-war expansion of Czech metropolitan areas took place under the conditions of a market economy and a democratic system of government, as Czechoslovakia remained one of the few European countries of the time in which democracy remained stable. The Nazi occupation of 1939 abruptly changed the conditions of governance and metropolitan development, and the subsequent war deeply affected both the population and physical structures of cities. The Communist regime that gained power in 1948 had an even deeper long-term impact, as the new rulers radically altered the political and economic system of the entire country. For almost forty years the 'natural' development of metropolitan areas was obstructed by a powerful and omnipresent planning system. All political freedoms, including free and competitive elections on both national and local levels, were abolished. Following the general Communist Party strategy of equalisation, planners designed both physical and population structures of cities and their hinterlands. State control over housing construction suppressed the population growth of the largest cities; strict land-use planning and land protection policies halted the development of suburban settlement.

After the collapse of the Communist rule in 1989, a comprehensive transformation of metropolitan areas and their politics took place. Several major changes took place nearly simultaneously. Free and competitive elections were re-established at the local level; market principles were reintroduced into the housing market; and laws were changed to enable foreign trade, foreign investment and foreign immigration. As the party system had been gradually established (Kostelecký 2002), both party politics (Mansfeldová 1998, 2004; Linek and Mansfeldová 2006) and

1.  This text was made possible because of a research grant from the Grant Agency of the Czech Academy of Sciences IAA700280802 and the Fulbright-Masaryk Fellowship.

voting behaviour (Matějů and Vlachová 1998; Vlachová 2001) were thoroughly studied by sociologists and political scientists. At the same time, the metropolitanisation process itself was studied in detail, mostly by social geographers (Sýkora 2005; Ouředníček 2007; Novák and Sýkora 2007; Sýkora and Ouředníček 2007; Sýkora 2009). Little attention has been paid to the relations between the process of metropolitanisation on one hand, and its political consequences on the other.

This chapter aims to fill this gap. It scrutinises the factors underlying the electoral participation and political preferences in metropolitan areas in the Czech Republic. The first part sketches an overview of these areas, examining the variations between municipalities in metropolitan areas, and identifies and describes five different types of municipalities. The second part measures and compares the intra-metropolitan and inter-metropolitan variations of electoral participation and political preferences. The third part concentrates in detail on the effects of social composition and spatial/contextual factors on these variations in local electoral behaviour.[2]

## Metropolitan areas in the Czech Republic

Neither an official definition of metropolitan areas, nor any metropolitan administrative units exists in the Czech Republic. Following the International Metropolitan Observatory (IMO) Protocol, we have delineated territories of metropolitan areas on the basis of commuting patterns from suburban zones to the largest Czech cities (for details see Kostelecký and Čermák 2004). This exercise confirmed a relatively low level of metropolitanisation in the Czech Republic. In a country with ten million inhabitants living in over 6,000 independent municipalities, only the four largest metropolitan areas counted more than 200,000 inhabitants. The basic characteristics of the metropolitan areas of Prague, Pilsen, Brno and Ostrava are summarised in Table 11.1.

Czech metropolitan areas vary widely, e.g. by area, population size and the level of geopolitical fragmentation. The Prague metropolitan area has as many inhabitants as the other three metropolitan areas combined; it is the only Czech metropolitan area with its total population exceeding one million. The number of municipalities within individual metropolitan areas also varies substantially. While the Prague metropolitan area is made up of almost 200 municipalities, Ostrava metropolitan area consists of only 54 municipalities. Population density in both the Prague and Ostrava metropolitan areas exceeds 750 inhabitants per square kilometre, while population density in the metropolitan area of Pilsen is as low as 232 inhabitants per square kilometre. Despite their differences, Czech metropolitan areas also have something in common: with the partial exception of Ostrava, they all have a large core city and relatively underdeveloped suburban areas. In these areas, a large number of rapidly growing, but still very small, suburban

---

2.    The chapter relies on data from the 2001 census, and on electoral data from the period 1990–2002. Detailed analyses use results from local and parliamentary elections in 2002.

*Table 11.1: Czech metropolitan areas under study*

| | Population size | Area (km²) | Population density | Number of municipalities |
|---|---|---|---|---|
| Prague metropolitan area *from which* | 1,343,179 | 1,788 | 751 | 198 |
| *Prague core city* | *1,169,106* | *496* | *2,357* | *1* |
| *Suburban zone* | *174,073* | *1,292* | *135* | *197* |
| Pilsen metropolitan area *from which* | 233,690 | 1,009 | 232 | 82 |
| *Pilsen core city* | *165,259* | *125* | *1,322* | *1* |
| *Suburban zone* | *68,431* | *884* | *77* | *81* |
| Brno metropolitan area *from which* | 514,869 | 1,393 | 370 | 133 |
| *Brno core city* | *376,172* | *230* | *1,636* | *1* |
| *Suburban zone* | *138,697* | *1,163* | *119* | *132* |
| Ostrava metropolitan area *from which* | 671,947 | 883 | 761 | 54 |
| *Ostrava core city* | *316,744* | *214* | *1,480* | *1* |
| *Suburban zone* | *355,203* | *669* | *531* | *53* |

*Source:* Own calculations based on Census 2001, Czech Statistical Office.

communes are typical. The Ostrava metropolitan area presents an exception to this pattern. Here the historical development of local coal mining and steel industries gave birth to several secondary industrial centres around the core city.

The structure and strength of the local economy in these metropolitan areas varies widely. The Prague and Ostrava metropolitan areas represent two divergent trajectories that metropolitan economic development has followed since 1989. The service-based metropolitan area of Prague has witnessed an economic boom since the beginning of the 1990s, accompanied by low levels of unemployment (ranging between 2 and 5 per cent during the whole period) and salaries exceeding 130 per cent of the national average. Over the same period, the Ostrava metropolitan area underwent a painful restructuring process caused by the rapid decline of its heavy industries. Consequently, the unemployment rate climbed to 13 per cent, while the traditionally high wages earned in heavy industries substantially declined in relative terms. The economic trajectories of Brno and Pilsen were ranged between the boom in Prague and the decline in Ostrava. Both metropolitan areas of Brno and Pilsen traditionally served as centres of engineering, food processing and tex-tile industries. These metropolitan areas underwent painful restructuring, but the diversity of the local economies and availability of highly-qualified local labour helped to attract new investment. Thus, Brno and Pilsen have not enjoyed the same economic conditions as Prague, but they have been much better than in Ostrava.

The differences between Czech metropolitan areas are substantial, and so too are the intra-metropolitan variations. The differences between the core cities and suburbs and the variation between the suburbs themselves are noticeable. Generally, five different types of municipalities can be identified in the Czech metropolitan areas. The first type – urban concentrations – is represented by the core cities – Prague, Pilsen, Brno, and Ostrava plus the city of Havířov, a secondary centre of the Ostrava metropolis. The remaining four types of metropolitan municipalities – low-density suburbs, poor suburbs, affluent suburbs, and middle class suburbs – are all suburban ones.[3]

Low-density suburbs have low population density. In the Czech context, low population density is a consequence of a relatively large historical municipal area (that includes farmland and forests) surrounding very small settlements. Rather than the outcome of low-density housing development, as is frequently the case in North America, these suburbs result from no development at all. Czech low-density communities are basically rural communes whose inhabitants have undergone suburbanisation of life styles, not communities created by new housing and out-migration from the cities. Poor, middle-class and affluent suburbs were distinguished on the basis of the socio-economic characteristics of their inhabitants, measured by a general socio-economic index calculated from various indicators of social hardship and socio-economic status.[4] More detailed information about the municipalities of five different types is set out in Table 11.2.

It is clear from Table 11.2 that aspects of all four types of suburban municipality differ radically from the municipalities belonging to urban cores. All suburban municipalities are generally much smaller in terms of population size and area. Similarly, the population density of suburban municipalities is substantially lower than that of the urban cores. Low-density suburbs feature the lowest population density. Affluent suburbs have somewhat higher population density than the poor and the middle-class suburbs, partly due to more intensive housing construction in wealthier communities. All types of suburban municipalities contain a much higher share of people living in single-family homes than municipalities of the urban core.

Different types of metropolitan municipality vary substantially in socio-economic composition. The share of the poor households is highest in the urban concentrations, but is almost at the same level in the poor suburbs. It is substantially lower in both the middle-class and the affluent suburbs. The poverty rate in the low-density suburbs is somewhat higher than in the middle-class suburbs, but not as high as in the poor suburbs. A similar pattern can be found in the unemployment rate or the level of overcrowding. The share of the population aged over sixty-five is lowest in the affluent suburbs and highest in the low-density suburbs, but this particular difference is not very substantial. The share of people with university

3.   We experimented with more possible classifications of suburban municipalities. The final typology, however, was based solely on density and the socio-economic differences between various suburbs. The low share of visible minorities and immigrants in the population of Czech metropolitan areas prevents us from identifying specific minority suburbs.

4.   The percentage of poor households, the unemployment rate, population with a low education, percentage of university graduates, the percentage of people older than 65 years, and per capita revenue of municipalities from personal taxes paid by local citizens.

*Table 11.2: Means of selected variables by types of municipalities in 2001*

| | | Core districts | Suburban districts | | | |
|---|---|---|---|---|---|---|
| | | Urban concentrations | Low-density suburbs | Poor suburbs | Middle-class suburbs | Affluent suburbs |
| Number of municipalities | | 5 | 93 | 75 | 190 | 101 |
| Population total | | 2,113,136 | 28,378 | 165,053 | 284,942 | 172,176 |
| Average population size | | 422,627 | 305 | 2,200 | 1,500 | 1,704 |
| Area total | km² | 1.097 | 946 | 653 | 1617 | 796 |
| Average size of area | km² | 219 | 10 | 9 | 9 | 8 |
| Average Population density | per km² | 1,894 | 31 | 144 | 146 | 209 |
| Poor households* | % | 5.0 | 3.6 | 4.1 | 2.3 | 1.4 |
| Unemployment rate | % | 11.8 | 6.8 | 10.1 | 7.2 | 5.1 |
| Housing overcrowding | Person/rooms | 1.00 | 0.90 | 0.94 | 0.90 | 0.84 |
| Population 65 + | % | 14.4 | 15.3 | 14.9 | 14.7 | 14.0 |
| University educated | % | 13.5 | 5.3 | 3.1 | 6.1 | 11.1 |
| Increase in the share of university educated between 1991 and 2001 | Percentage. points | 2.2 | 2.4 | 1.0 | 2.2 | 4.4 |
| Single-family homes | % | 14.7 | 89.5 | 90.2 | 88.5 | 85.0 |
| Immigrants/visible minorities (Ukrainians, Vietnamese, Roma) | % | 0.50 | 0.52 | 0.26 | 0.29 | 0.45 |
| Annual tax revenue* from personal income | CZK per capita | 3,483 | 1,148 | 1,176 | 1,221 | 1,318 |

*Note:* Data with asterisks are from 2003.

*Source:* Author's calculations, based on data from the Czech Statistical Office and the Ministry for Labor and Social Affairs.

education[5] varies considerably among the five identified types of metropolitan municipality. It is highest in the urban cores, but almost as high in affluent suburbs. In contrast, the percentage of university-educated people is substantially lower in the middle-class suburbs and the low-density suburbs, and very low in the poor suburbs. Moreover, it is clear from the data describing changes in educational attainment between 1991 and 2001 that the figure for those who are highly educated rose at a very different pace. By far the largest increase in the proportion of those attending university took place in the affluent suburbs – a clear sign of the ongoing process of suburbanisation in its most classical form. The share of immigrants and visible minorities remained at the same very low level in all observed types of metropolitan municipality, suggesting that local concentrations of poverty in the Czech Republic have not (yet) connected with immigration.

---

5.  Only people with completed a master's degree were considered as 'university educated' by the 1991 and 2001 population censuses in the Czech Republic.

Financial variations among the types of municipalities are somewhat counter-intuitive. The per capita annual tax revenue from income taxes is much higher in the urban concentrations than in any type of suburban communes, including the affluent suburbs. The explanation, however, is quite straightforward. Municipalities in the Czech Republic do not have a right to impose their own local taxes; they only share tax revenues that are collected by the state. Both the rates of income tax and the distribution of tax-money collected by the state for individual municipalities are at the discretion of the national parliament. As a consequence, differences in per capita revenues from personal income tax among individual municipalities do not necessarily reflect variation in incomes, and have no direct relation to the political decisions of local political representatives. Rather, they depend on the formula used for the distribution of the nationally-collected income taxes. The formula for municipal revenue from income taxes is based mostly on the population size of a municipality, and to some extent on the number of self-employed and employees in the municipality. Larger municipalities are strongly favoured by this formula and generally receive higher per capita revenue from taxes. When comparing the tax revenues per capita between different types of suburban communities, the population size factor is not so important. Hence, as one might expect, tax revenues are highest in affluent suburbs and lowest in poor suburbs. However, the differences among suburbs are not especially dramatic.

Basic information about political behaviour of voters in five types of metropolitan municipalities is summarised in Table 11.3. Over the observed period from 1990–2002, turnout in local elections was generally much lower in the municipalities of the urban core than in the suburban communities. The differences among the various types of suburban municipality in this respect remained modest. In all types of communities, the changes in turnout over time were very similar: the sharp decrease in turnout between 1990 and 1998 was followed only by minor changes between 1998 and 2002. Over the time, the turnout in urban core municipalities decreased the fastest. Consequently, the gap between turnout in the urban cores and the suburban municipalities of all types widened. The affluent suburbs represented the only type of municipality where a slight increase in turnout was observable between 1998 and 2002.

The picture is somewhat similar when one looks at turnout in the national elections. The municipalities of the urban core always registered lower turnout than the other four types. The difference in participation between the urban concentrations and the suburban communities, however, remained substantially smaller throughout the entire period. This difference was very small in 1990, increased substantially in 1992, then decreased again. What is more interesting, however, is the rising variation among the suburban communities of different types. While turnout in suburban communes of all four types was virtually the same in 1990 and still very similar in 1992 and 1996, since the 1998 election the difference between turnout in affluent municipalities and the poor ones increased: voters in affluent communes voted at higher rates than those in the poorer suburbs.

In the election years of 1990, 1998 and 2002, local and national elections held within the same calendar year enabled us to compare national and local turnout

*Table 11.3: Mean turnout in the local and national elections and mean values of indexes of political orientation\* by type of municipality*

| Type of Municipality | | Core districts | Suburban districts | | | |
|---|---|---|---|---|---|---|
| | | Urban concentrations | Low-density suburbs | Poor suburbs | Middle-class suburbs | Affluent suburbs |
| *Local elections – turnout* | | | | | | |
| 1990 | % | 66.0 | 86.1 | 84.3 | 84.5 | 83.0 |
| 1994 | % | 54.3 | 79.3 | 73.4 | 74.3 | 73.9 |
| 1998 | % | 34.7 | 69.3 | 60.8 | 61.6 | 59.9 |
| 2002 | % | 31.8 | 68.7 | 60.4 | 59.2 | 60.5 |
| *National elections – turnout* | | | | | | |
| 1990 | % | 95.6 | 97.7 | 98.0 | 97.8 | 97.7 |
| 1992 | % | 79.8 | 91.8 | 90.3 | 90.2 | 90.3 |
| 1996 | % | 72.7 | 83.0 | 80.2 | 81.8 | 81.2 |
| 1998 | % | 71.8 | 81.0 | 75.7 | 78.4 | 79.8 |
| 2002 | % | 56.2 | 64.1 | 60.4 | 63.5 | 65.9 |
| *Difference national turnout – local turnout* | | | | | | |
| 1990 | % | 29.6 | 11.6 | 13.7 | 13.3 | 14.7 |
| 1998 | % | 37.1 | 11.7 | 14.9 | 16.8 | 19.9 |
| 2002 | % | 24.4 | -4.6 | 0.0 | 4.3 | 5.4 |
| *Political attitudes – economic dimension* | | | | | | |
| 1996 | index | 5.01 | 4.96 | 4.92 | 4.98 | 5.13 |
| 1998 | index | 5.21 | 5.13 | 5.03 | 5.16 | 5.33 |
| 2002 | index | 5.02 | 4.88 | 4.90 | 5.00 | 5.16 |
| *Political attitudes – cultural dimension* | | | | | | |
| 1996 | index | 4.47 | 4.51 | 4.68 | 4.56 | 4.49 |
| 1998 | index | 4.56 | 4.61 | 4.75 | 4.65 | 4.55 |
| 2002 | index | 4.67 | 4.66 | 4.73 | 4.69 | 4.66 |
| *Political attitudes – globalisation dimension* | | | | | | |
| 1996 | index | 6.01 | 6.00 | 6.06 | 6.02 | 6.01 |
| 1998 | index | 6.07 | 6.10 | 6.12 | 6.09 | 6.05 |
| 2002 | index | 6.15 | 6.15 | 6.16 | 6.15 | 6.12 |
| *General political preferences – self-placement on the left-right axis* | | | | | | |
| 1996 | index | 5.87 | 5.82 | 5.73 | 5.87 | 6.08 |
| 1998 | index | 5.92 | 5,81 | 5.69 | 5.87 | 6.14 |
| 2002 | index | 5.57 | 5.49 | 5.38 | 5.56 | 5.89 |

*Notes:* \*Political orientation is measured by three aggregate indexes measuring three dimensions of voters' political attitudes and by voters' self-placement on the political left-right axis. The values of indexes: economic dimension (1 = extreme state control, 10 = extreme free market), cultural dimension (1 = extreme social liberalism, 10 = extreme social conservatism), globalisation dimension (1 = extreme support for globalisation, 10 = extreme nationalism), political self-placement (1 = extreme left, 10 = extreme right).
*Source:* Author's calculations, based on data from the Czech Statistical Office.

closely for individual municipalities. In urban cores, the comparison highlighted clear evidence of delocalisation. In each of these elections, local election turnout in these settings fell dramatically below the turnout in the national elections. In suburban municipalities, the difference between national and the local election turnout remained much smaller, but was still substantial in the 1990 and 1998 elections. In the 2002 elections, the difference among these municipalities practically disappeared. Generally, the gap between turnout in national and local elections ranged from being the highest in affluent suburbs to somewhat smaller in the middle-class and poor suburbs. In low-density suburbs, by contrast, turnout in local elections was higher than in national elections. In these settings, as in similar types of suburbs in such countries as France and Switzerland as well as in Poland, small population size and a stable population appear to add to the building of local community and the fostering of voters' interest in local elections.

In order to avoid dealing separately with electoral preferences of multiple political parties, we generalised voters' political preferences to the form of three different indices measuring the variability along different dimensions of political conflicts – economic, cultural and globalisation/nationalism. The values of each index vary from 1 to 10. For each municipality, we calculated the value of the three indices that measured the position of an average municipal voter who participated in the parliamentary elections in 2002.[6] Similarly, we constructed an index of average overall ideological self-placement based on the self-placement of voters for individual parties on the left-right scale.

The data on the ideological orientations of voters living in different types of metropolitan municipality tell a different story about local variations from what the turnout data revealed. Regardless of the method of measurement, no clear difference emerged between the political preferences of urban and suburban voters. Differences in overall political attitudes among the various types of metropolitan municipality also remained generally smaller than the differences in electoral participation. Nor did the partisan orientations of communities change much over the observed period. The indices designed to tap distinct dimensions of political orientations revealed a somewhat more colourful picture. Statistically significant differences among communities marked the economic dimension of political attitudes. Voters in affluent suburbs consistently inclined more towards free-market positions than voters in poor and low-density suburbs. On the other hand, only statistically insignificant differences separated different types of municipality in the attitudes of the voters towards the cultural dimension of political conflict. Hardly any variations separated the types in community attitudes toward globalisation and nationalism.

Beside three indices of political attitudes, we also measured the political

---

6. The surveys and items used for the construction of indices are described in Chapter 14, the Methodological Appendix, as well as the position of main Czech political parties measured by individual indices. The values of the respective indices in each municipality were calculated as weighted averages. The ideological position of individual political parties was weighted by the actual shares of votes obtained by individual parties in the election in the respective municipality.

ideology of voters by their self-placement on the left-right political scale. Because this is closely related to attitudes on economic issues in the Czech context, it was not surprising that voters in affluent suburbs considered themselves more to the right than voters in other types of municipality. For similar reasons, voters in the poor suburbs placed themselves mostly to the left.

## Local and regional variation in metropolitan political behaviour

Since the reintroduction of competitive elections in the Czech Republic in the early 1990s, a number of authors have repeatedly confirmed the surprisingly stable voting patterns at the regional level over time (Jehlička and Sýkora 1991; Kostelecký 1996; Sokol 2003). Spatial patterns of electoral participation have repeated consistently over time, as have the voting patterns for political parties in each subsequent national election. Regional differences in political orientation of voters as measured by their position within ideological space have remained even more stable than the voting patterns for individual parties (Kostelecký 2002). Generally, voters in Bohemia, the Western part of the Czech Republic, have consistently supported fiscal conservatives who push for free market policies, low taxes and less state regulation in the economy. Fiscally-conservative parties have performed the strongest in the most prosperous, mainly urban regions of Bohemia, including the metropolitan areas of Prague and Pilsen. Voters in Moravia, the eastern part of the country, have generally tended to support the left. Within Moravia, the rural region of southern Moravia, an area with the highest share of Roman Catholics, has remained the electoral stronghold of the socially-conservative Christian Democracy.

A more detailed picture of the inter-metropolitan variations in electoral behaviour and the changes over time appears in Table 11.4. This illustrates the generally low – and even decreasing – level of inter-metropolitan differences in electoral participation. In 2002, inter-metropolitan variance accounted for only about 8 per cent of the total variance in local election turnout, and less than 3 per cent of the total variance in parliamentary turnout. The data on general political preferences of voters based on the results of national elections tell a different story. Although political preferences also vary more within metropolitan areas than between them, the inter-metropolitan variation is substantial and increases over time. Depending on the year, it comprises a fourth to a third of the total variance. A more detailed view of the political preferences and turnout in the 2002 parliamentary elections (supplemented by the level of education) in four Czech metropolitan areas are provided in Figure 11.1.

The inter-metropolitan differences in partisan preferences are unmistakeable. Municipalities in the Prague metropolitan area clearly lean more towards the right than any other Czech metropolitan area. Neither voter turnout nor the level of education follows this pattern. The maps also highlight the similar patterns of spatial diversity in all four metropolitan areas. In Pilsen, Brno, and Ostrava, inhabitants of the central city areas have on average a higher level of education and incline towards the right, but their participation in the parliamentary elections is lower than the participation of inhabitants of respective suburbs.

*Table 11.4: Analysis of inter-metropolitan variance in turnout and general political preferences, local and national elections, 1990–2002*

| Year of election | 1990 | 1992 | 1994 | 1996 | 1998 | 2002 |
|---|---|---|---|---|---|---|
| *National elections – turnout* | | | | | | |
| F | 8.40 | 12.30 | | 3.82 | 1.71 | 3.95 |
| Significance | 0.000 | 0.000 | | 0.010 | 0.165 | 0.008 |
| Inter-metropolitan variance as a percentage of total variance | 10.37 | 13.36 | | 1.50 | 1.36 | 2.83 |
| *Local elections – turnout* | | | | | | |
| F | 21.42 | | 11.39 | | 12.54 | 7.51 |
| Significance | 0.000 | | 0.000 | | 0.000 | 0.000 |
| Inter-metropolitan variance as a percentage of total variance | 25.09 | | 10.11 | | 14.57 | 8.39 |
| *National elections – general political preferences* | | | | | | |
| F | n/a | n/a | | 44.3 | 70.5 | 63.1 |
| Significance | | | | 0.000 | 0.000 | 0.000 |
| Inter-metropolitan variance as a percentage of total variance | | | | 23.3 | 25.7 | 33.9 |

*Notes:* General political preferences in municipalities were measured by the results of the respective national elections weighted by the self-placement on the left-right axis of voters of individual parties. Results of 1990 and 1992 national elections were not analysed due to the unclear political position of the high proportion of existing political parties.

In the Prague metro area, inhabitants of the central city have higher education, participate less and display similar political preferences in comparison with inhabitants of surrounding suburbs. Comparing across the suburban municipalities alone, one can observe a somewhat different pattern. Those with higher levels of education also incline more towards support for the right. Unlike their central city counterparts, however, suburbs supporting the right also turn out to vote more than suburbs supporting the left. As these communities continue to grow, they are likely to provide stronger, more consistent bases of mobilisation for parties of the right than central cities.

| | Education 2001 | Parliamentary turnout 2002 (%) | Political preference of the Right – parliamentary elections 2002 (%) |
|---|---|---|---|
| P R A G U E | | | |
| P I L S E N | | | |
| B R N O | | | |
| O S T R A V A | | | |
| Cut points: | 3  4  5  7  9  12 | 57  60  62  65  67  71 | 24  28  31 34  38  44 |

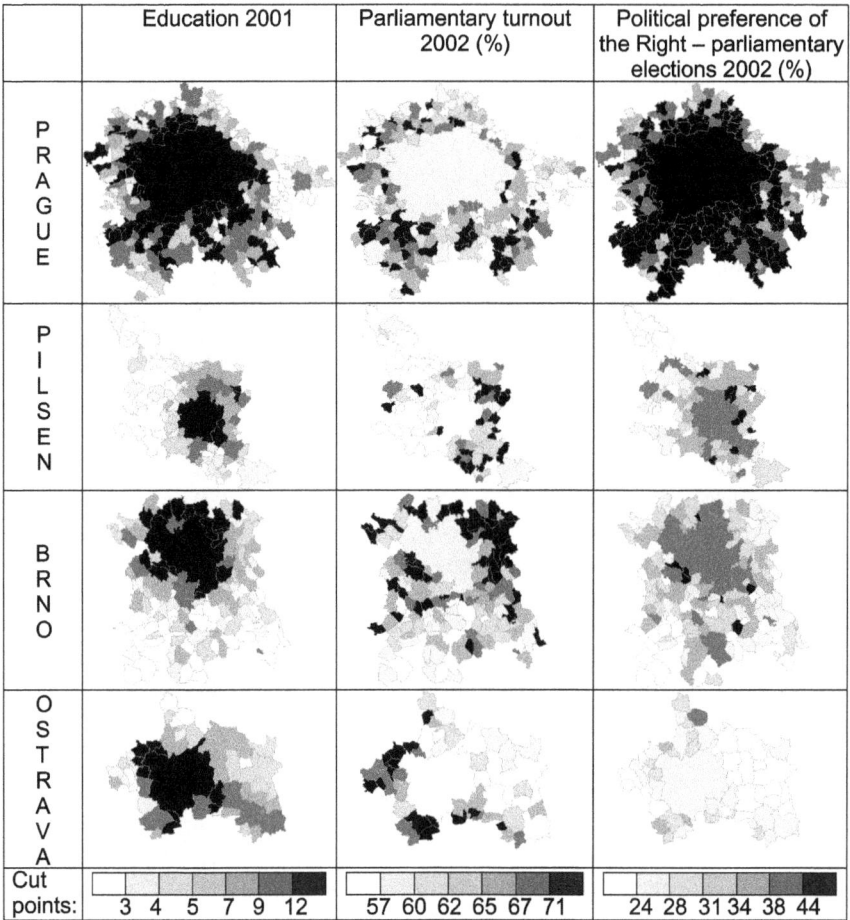

*Figure 11.1: Education, parliamentary turnout, and political preferences of the right in municipalities in Czech metropolitan areas*

## Explaining spatial variations in metropolitan political behaviour: compositional and contextual influences

To date, very little of the available literature has examined the relationship between political behaviour and place in the Czech Republic. In an analysis of voting patterns from the first free post-Communist parliamentary election in 1990, Blažek and Kostelecký (1991) found that a number of structural factors accounted for spatial differences in both participation rate and the voting support for the parties. In a comparison of support for parties in the 1990 parliamentary elections with support for their pre-Communist predecessors, Jehlička and Sýkora (1991) found remarkable continuity in voting behaviour and party identification despite almost fifty years without competitive elections. Both papers, however, concentrated on the regional level and used the administrative districts as units of observation. In rare cases, researchers have analysed voting patterns using the data from individual municipalities. Daněk (1993) analysed Moravian voting patterns in parliamentary elections to examine the links between political affiliation and ethnic identification. In a later study of political behaviour in borderland regions, Daněk (2002) compared areas formerly dominated by the German population and resettled after 1946, with areas where the Czech population had remained stable. Kostelecký (1993) analysed results from the parliamentary election of 1990 in municipalities with more than 5,000 inhabitants. A typology of cities and towns by electoral results showed that both the population size of a city and its geographical location were important influences on local voting behaviour. Residents of larger cities tended to support parties of the right, although they voted less often. Residents of smaller cities favoured the left, and voted more frequently. However, differences among groups of cities located in different regions tended to overshadow these effects from differences in population size.

Kostelecký and Kroupa (1996) and Kostelecký (1996, 2007), in studies of local elections between 1990 and 2002, showed the size of municipalities, as measured by population, to have especially strong effects on political behaviour. The larger is the municipality, the lower is the participation rate and the stronger the inclination to vote for right-oriented parties. In small villages, active party members were rarer than in larger municipalities. In most of the smallest municipalities, political parties were not able to take place in the local elections at all. Consequently, ad hoc lists of independent candidates dominated local elections.

Finally, Kostelecký and Čermák (2003) employed representative surveys to test the influence of territorially specific factors on the political orientations of voters. Of the four model regions in this analysis, two corresponded approximately to the metropolitan areas of Prague and Ostrava. The spatial context was defined at the regional level of administrative districts rather than at the local level of individual municipalities or city neighbourhoods. The analysis found contextual and compositional factors to be of similar importance. Political values, attitudes, and electoral behaviour depended both on the personal characteristics of respondents (class, age, gender, education, marriage status) and on the territorial context in which respondents lived (the average unemployment rate, the share of those with a university education, and the share of Catholics in the district of residence).

The multivariate analyses that follow undertake several more detailed tests of the sources of metropolitan and local variations in voting behaviour. First, the models provide a more detailed assessment of whether the types of municipalities are good predictors of political behaviour. Secondly, an analysis that employs continuous variables aims to identify the most relevant factors underlying the variations in local voting behaviour within the four Czech metropolitan areas.[7] Finally, this analysis will enable us to assess whether the variations in municipal voting behaviour can

7. Independent variables and their definitions are provided in Table A11.2 in the Appendix to this chapter.

be explained solely by the demographic composition of municipalities, or whether effects from the spatial context of metropolitan municipalities are also at work. A purely compositional explanation would confirm the nationalisation of Czech electoral behaviour. Significant contextual influences would indicate that causes rooted in the spatial characteristics of metropolitan places are also at work.

Employing similar statistical models, we analysed electoral turnout and the partisan preferences of voters. In both cases, the dependent variables refer to the results of elections in 2002, while independent variables refer mostly to data from the 2001 census. Separate ordinary least squares regression models for each of the four metropolitan areas were developed to explain the variation in each dependent variable.[8] Model 1 employed the types of suburban municipalities as dummy variables in a baseline model. Model 2 used compositional variables as the independent variables, and Model 3 included only contextual variables. Model 4 included both compositional and contextual variables in a full model.[9] Comparison of results from the four models allowed us to estimate the relative contribution of the compositional versus contextual variables, as well as the combined collinear effects from both types of variables.

### Electoral turnout

We analysed turnout separately in the local election (see Table 11.5(a) and Table 11.5(b)) and turnout in the national election in 2002 (see Table 11.6(a) and Table 11.6(b)). Generally speaking, the models explaining turnout in various metropolitan areas were relatively similar. Although differences among the models of electoral participation for individual metropolitan areas emerged, the similarities were most striking. Such results were not very surprising because the variation in electoral participation occurred within metropolitan areas, rather than between them.

Municipal types explained part of intra-metropolitan variation in local turnout. In all cases, however, models that employed continuous independent variables performed better. Contextual factors primarily drove variation in local election turnout. In all four metropolitan areas, models using only these variables were more successful than those employing only the compositional variables. The single most important independent variable was the log of the municipal population. Population size proved a strong predictor of lower turnout in all four metropolitan areas, an effect that did not diminish when the full models took compositional variables into account. Consistent with the strong parallel effect in Poland, and similar ones in Western democracies, this finding gives support to the decline-of-community thesis in Czech electoral practice – the larger the municipality,

---

8.  The small number of metropolitan areas in the Czech Republic did not allow the use of multilevel modelling.

9.  We also experimented with combined models that included municipal types as dummy variables, compositional and contextual variables. The results of this type of modelling were not included into tables because such models did not increase the percentage of explained variability. Moreover, such models suffered from the problem of multicollinearity among independent variables.

Table 11.5(a): OLS regression models explaining turnout in local election in municipalities of the Prague and Pilsen metropolitan areas in the Czech Republic, 2002

| | Prague metropolitan area | | | | | | | | Pilsen metropolitan area | | | | | | | |
| --- | --- | --- | --- | --- | --- | --- | --- | --- | --- | --- | --- | --- | --- | --- | --- | --- |
| | Model 1 | | Model 2 | | Model 3 | | Model 4 | | Model 1 | | Model 2 | | Model 3 | | Model 4 | |
| | Beta | Sig. | Beta | Sig. | Beta | Sig. | Beta | Sig. | Beta | Sig. | Beta | Sig. | Beta | Sig. | Beta | Sig. |
| (Constant) | | 0.001 | | 0.000 | | 0.000 | | 0.000 | | 0.006 | | 0.006 | | 0.000 | | 0.002 |
| *Types of suburbs* | | | | | | | | | | | | | | | | |
| Affluent suburbs | **1.030** | **0.023** | | | | | | | **0.565** | **0.037** | | | | | | |
| Poor suburbs | **0.527** | **0.053** | | | | | | | **0.606** | **0.025** | | | | | | |
| Middle-class suburbs | **0.954** | **0.034** | | | | | | | **1.019** | **0.030** | | | | | | |
| Low-density suburbs | **1.173** | **0.002** | | | | | | | **1.389** | **0.004** | | | | | | |
| *Compositional* | | | | | | | | | | | | | | | | |
| Identity | | | −0.009 | 0.909 | | | −0.005 | 0.943 | | | −0.081 | 0.453 | | | −0.040 | 0.664 |
| Hardship | | | **−0.244** | **0.026** | | | **−0.348** | **0.001** | | | −0.260 | 0.071 | | | −0.164 | 0.243 |
| Education | | | −0.188 | 0.081 | | | 0.081 | 0.439 | | | **−0.430** | **0.003** | | | −0.119 | 0.381 |
| Manufacturing | | | −0.020 | 0.796 | | | 0.096 | 0.298 | | | **−0.253** | **0.031** | | | −0.173 | 0.403 |
| Families with kids | | | −0.050 | 0.576 | | | 0.085 | 0.319 | | | 0.068 | 0.626 | | | 0.053 | 0.660 |
| Old | | | −0.003 | 0.971 | | | 0.087 | 0.290 | | | **0.446** | **0.002** | | | 0.242 | 0.065 |
| *Contextual* | | | | | | | | | | | | | | | | |
| Economic diversity | | | | | **−0.149** | **0.020** | −0.140 | 0.113 | | | | | −0.138 | 0.115 | 0.022 | 0.912 |
| Family houses | | | | | −0.025 | 0.751 | −0.102 | 0.240 | | | | | **0.277** | **0.021** | 0.127 | 0.408 |
| Log population size | | | | | **−0.477** | **0.000** | **−0.640** | **0.000** | | | | | **−0.456** | **0.000** | **−0.503** | **0.001** |
| Population growth | | | | | 0.020 | 0.758 | −0.143 | 0.093 | | | | | −0.108 | 0.219 | −0.104 | 0.280 |
| R Square | 0.161 | | 0.037 | | 0.242 | | 0.331 | | 0.184 | | 0.269 | | 0.491 | | 0.524 | |
| Adjusted R Square | 0.143 | | 0.006 | | 0.226 | | 0.294 | | 0.140 | | 0.209 | | 0.464 | | 0.455 | |
| S.E. of the estimate | 10.445 | | 11.253 | | 9.925 | | 9.481 | | 11.788 | | 11.307 | | 9.306 | | 9.386 | |

Note: For boldface coefficients, p<0.05.

Table 11.5(b): *OLS regression models explaining turnout in local election in municipalities of the Brno and Ostrava metropolitan areas in the Czech Republic, 2002*

| | Brno metropolitan area | | | | | | | | Ostrava metropolitan area | | | | | | | |
| | Model 1 | | Model 2 | | Model 3 | | Model 4 | | Model 1 | | Model 2 | | Model 3 | | Model 4 | |
| | Beta | Sig. | Beta | Sig. | Beta | Sig. | Beta | Sig. | Beta | Sig. | Beta | Sig. | Beta | Sig. | Beta | Sig. |
| (Constant) | | 0.000 | | 0.004 | | 0.000 | | 0.000 | | 0.000 | | 0.000 | | 0.000 | | 0.010 |
| **Types of suburbs** | | | | | | | | | | | | | | | | |
| Affluent suburbs | 0.983 | 0.003 | | | | | | | 1.007 | 0.000 | | | | | | |
| Poor suburbs | 1.422 | 0.002 | | | | | | | 0.830 | 0.007 | | | | | | |
| Middle-class suburbs | 1.455 | 0.003 | | | | | | | 1.029 | 0.003 | | | | | | |
| Low-density suburbs | 1.208 | 0.000 | | | | | | | | | | | | | | |
| **Compositional** | | | | | | | | | | | | | | | | |
| Identity | | | -0.055 | 0.498 | | | -0.085 | 0.246 | | | 0.095 | 0.418 | | | 0.205 | 0.053 |
| Hardship | | | -0.313 | 0.008 | | | -0.266 | 0.023 | | | -0.922 | 0.000 | | | -0.179 | 0.276 |
| Education | | | -0.314 | 0.009 | | | -0.112 | 0.360 | | | -0.377 | 0.007 | | | 0.088 | 0.526 |
| Manufacturing | | | 0.081 | 0.357 | | | 0.423 | 0.011 | | | 0.147 | 0.164 | | | 0.411 | 0.026 |
| Families with kids | | | 0.024 | 0.811 | | | -0.071 | 0.483 | | | 0.311 | 0.032 | | | 0.116 | 0.303 |
| Old | | | 0.339 | 0.001 | | | 0.219 | 0.023 | | | 0.261 | 0.043 | | | 0.082 | 0.424 |
| **Contextual** | | | | | | | | | | | | | | | | |
| Economic diversity | | | | | -0.021 | 0.781 | -0.343 | 0.028 | | | | | -0.087 | 0.257 | -1.999 | 0.052 |
| Family houses | | | | | 0.116 | 0.251 | -0.091 | 0.410 | | | | | 0.302 | 0.047 | 1.126 | 0.267 |
| Log population size | | | | | -0.424 | 0.000 | -0.456 | 0.000 | | | | | -0.659 | 0.000 | -3.598 | 0.001 |
| Population growth | | | | | -0.009 | 0.906 | 0.084 | 0.357 | | | | | -0.195 | 0.019 | -0.497 | 0.622 |
| R Square | 0.121 | | 0.199 | | 0.260 | | 0.390 | | 0.249 | | 0.653 | | 0.766 | | 0.822 | |
| Adjusted R Square | 0.093 | | 0.161 | | 0.237 | | 0.340 | | 0.204 | | 0.609 | | 0.747 | | 0.780 | |
| S.E. of the estimate | 9.221 | | 8.869 | | 8.459 | | 7.867 | | 12.055 | | 8.447 | | 6.794 | | 6.337 | |

*Note:* For boldface coefficients, p<0.05.

*Table 11.6(a): OLS regression models explaining turnout in national election in municipalities of the Prague and Pilsen metropolitan areas in the Czech Republic, 2002*

| | Prague metropolitan area | | | | | | | | Pilsen metropolitan area | | | | | | | |
| | Model 1 | | Model 2 | | Model 3 | | Model 4 | | Model 1 | | Model 2 | | Model 3 | | Model 4 | |
| | Beta | Sig. | Beta | Sig. | Beta | Sig. | Beta | Sig. | Beta | Sig. | Beta | Sig. | Beta | Sig. | Beta | Sig. |
|---|---|---|---|---|---|---|---|---|---|---|---|---|---|---|---|---|
| (Constant) | | 0.000 | | 0.000 | | 0.000 | | 0.000 | | 0.000 | | 0.000 | | 0.000 | | 0.000 |
| *Types of suburbs* | | | | | | | | | | | | | | | | |
| Affluent suburbs | 0.430 | 0.352 | | | | | | | 0.240 | 0.429 | | | | | | |
| Poor suburbs | -0.018 | 0.949 | | | | | | | 0.008 | 0.978 | | | | | | |
| Middle-class suburbs | 0.157 | 0.734 | | | | | | | 0.297 | 0.553 | | | | | | |
| Low-density suburbs | 0.336 | 0.386 | | | | | | | 0.351 | 0.494 | | | | | | |
| *Compositional* | | | | | | | | | | | | | | | | |
| Identity | | | -0.101 | 0.136 | | | -0.165 | 0.012 | | | -0.037 | 0.704 | | | 0.010 | 0.908 |
| Hardship | | | -0.385 | 0.000 | | | -0.362 | 0.000 | | | -0.335 | 0.013 | | | -0.224 | 0.091 |
| Education | | | 0.058 | 0.530 | | | 0.161 | 0.094 | | | -0.030 | 0.817 | | | 0.279 | 0.031 |
| Manufacturing | | | 0.002 | 0.978 | | | -0.099 | 0.248 | | | -0.280 | 0.009 | | | -0.101 | 0.597 |
| Families with kids | | | -0.118 | 0.127 | | | -0.107 | 0.172 | | | -0.142 | 0.266 | | | -0.204 | 0.074 |
| Old | | | 0.184 | 0.023 | | | 0.233 | 0.002 | | | 0.326 | 0.010 | | | 0.144 | 0.226 |
| *Contextual* | | | | | | | | | | | | | | | | |
| Economic diversity | | | | | -0.085 | 0.216 | 0.090 | 0.265 | | | | | -0.287 | 0.003 | -0.114 | 0.532 |
| Family houses | | | | | 0.167 | 0.051 | -0.057 | 0.474 | | | | | 0.485 | 0.000 | 0.076 | 0.588 |
| Log population size | | | | | -0.119 | 0.163 | -0.426 | 0.000 | | | | | -0.028 | 0.829 | -0.450 | 0.002 |
| Population growth | | | | | 0.197 | 0.005 | 0.147 | 0.062 | | | | | -0.025 | 0.792 | 0.093 | 0.296 |
| R Square | 0.110 | | 0.270 | | 0.119 | | 0.425 | | 0.038 | | 0.379 | | 0.365 | | 0.580 | |
| Adjusted R Square | 0.091 | | 0.247 | | 0.100 | | 0.394 | | -0.012 | | 0.329 | | 0.332 | | 0.521 | |
| S.E. of the estimate | 6.267 | | 5.703 | | 6.234 | | 5.116 | | 7.870 | | 6.410 | | 6.395 | | 5.414 | |

*Note:* For boldface coefficients, p<0.05.

*Table 11.6(b): OLS regression models explaining turnout in national election in municipalities of the Brno and Ostrava metropolitan areas in the Czech Republic, 2002*

| | Brno metropolitan area | | | | | | | | Ostrava metropolitan area | | | | | | | |
|---|---|---|---|---|---|---|---|---|---|---|---|---|---|---|---|---|
| | Model 1 | | Model 2 | | Model 3 | | Model 4 | | Model 1 | | Model 2 | | Model 3 | | Model 4 | |
| | Beta | Sig. | Beta | Sig. | Beta | Sig. | Beta | Sig. | Beta | Sig. | Beta | Sig. | Beta | Sig. | Beta | Sig. |
| *(Constant)* | | *0.000* | | *0.000* | | *0.000* | | *0.000* | | *0.000* | | *0.025* | | *0.000* | | *0.037* |
| *Types of suburbs* | | | | | | | | | | | | | | | | |
| Affluent suburbs | 0.423 | 0.210 | | | | | | | 0.822 | 0.001 | | | | | | |
| Poor suburbs | 0.287 | 0.525 | | | | | | | 0.322 | 0.252 | | | | | | |
| Middle-class suburbs | 0.606 | 0.218 | | | | | | | 0.803 | 0.012 | | | | | | |
| Low-density suburbs | 0.391 | 0.246 | | | | | | | | | | | | | | |
| *Compositional* | | | | | | | | | | | | | | | | |
| Identity | | | 0.013 | 0.854 | | | -0.008 | 0.912 | | | -0.134 | 0.248 | | | 0.010 | 0.932 |
| Hardship | | | **-0.490** | **0.000** | | | **-0.459** | **0.000** | | | **-0.751** | **0.000** | | | **-0.109** | **0.536** |
| Education | | | -0.030 | 0.780 | | | 0.087 | 0.459 | | | -0.094 | 0.479 | | | 0.396 | 0.010 |
| Manufacturing | | | 0.045 | 0.574 | | | 0.280 | 0.079 | | | 0.127 | 0.224 | | | 0.420 | 0.034 |
| Families with kids | | | 0.089 | 0.322 | | | 0.017 | 0.861 | | | 0.119 | 0.396 | | | -0.045 | 0.708 |
| Old | | | **0.364** | **0.000** | | | **0.297** | **0.001** | | | 0.092 | 0.464 | | | 0.002 | 0.985 |
| *Contextual* | | | | | | | | | | | | | | | | |
| Economic diversity | | | | | -0.104 | 0.221 | -0.235 | 0.115 | | | | | -0.059 | 0.546 | -0.256 | 0.141 |
| Family houses | | | | | 0.131 | 0.242 | -0.085 | 0.423 | | | | | 0.276 | 0.153 | -0.114 | 0.545 |
| Log population size | | | | | -0.159 | 0.160 | **-0.308** | **0.002** | | | | | **-0.540** | **0.006** | **-0.675** | **0.000** |
| Population growth | | | | | 0.101 | 0.237 | 0.087 | 0.321 | | | | | -0.041 | 0.693 | 0.160 | 0.122 |
| R Square | 0.080 | | 0.349 | | 0.093 | | 0.435 | | 0.322 | | 0.662 | | 0.611 | | 0.796 | |
| Adjusted R Square | 0.052 | | 0.318 | | 0.064 | | 0.389 | | 0.282 | | 0.619 | | 0.580 | | 0.748 | |
| S.E. of the estimate | *6.091* | | *5.165* | | *6.050* | | *4.890* | | *5.865* | | *4.272* | | *4.487* | | *3.473* | |

*Note:* For boldface coefficients, p<0.05.

the less 'local' the local politics. In a large municipality, most voters do not personally know local politicians, and personal networks are of limited use in providing politically-relevant information. Thus, voters rely on the same type of impersonal information sources as in national elections. As local elections lose the attractiveness linked to personal familiarity, they become simply a 'second-order' version of national elections, and voter engagement falls.

Although turnout in national elections has remained higher than in local elections, many of the significant variations of turnout in national elections resemble those for local elections (see Table 11.6 (a) and (b)). Once more, models for various metropolitan areas demonstrate more similarities than differences. Models using continuous variables again perform better than models using municipal types.

In contrast with the predominantly contextual influences on participation in local elections, however, compositional variables play a much more important role as influences on national electoral participation. Turnout in the national election depends more on the social and demographic composition of the municipal population than on local spatial characteristics. The most significant compositional variables in the models are social hardship, education and the share of seniors. The logic of these influences is a simple matter of individual and household characteristics. Lower social hardship, greater education and an older population improve participation rates in national elections. The population size of the municipality remains important. Smaller municipal size remains a predictor of higher turnout in national elections, even when effects from other variables are held constant.

The contrasts suggest a systematic mobilisation of more privileged groups in national elections that is not present in local elections. Regressions of the difference between national and local turnout also showed an especially pronounced delocalisation of participation in the urban concentrations of all four metropolitan areas. The larger the municipality, the bigger the turnout gap between national elections and municipal elections.

### *Political preferences*

Finally, we analysed the effects of the same underlying factors on the political preferences of voters. We used four different dependent variables to measure community political preferences. Alongside estimates based on the self-placement of party voters on a left-right scale, three aggregate indices were calculated to capture attitudes towards economic, cultural, and globalisation/nationalist dimensions of political ideology. The results of the regression models explaining the political self-placement of voters on left-right scale are summarised in Table 11.7(a) and Table 11.7(b).

The first thing to notice is that the regression models explaining political self-placement vary more widely among the individual metropolitan areas than the regression models explaining turnout. This is not surprising – the inter-metropolitan variation in political preferences is substantially higher than inter-metropolitan variation in turnout. Greater variation in the relationship between the dependent variable and independent variables can also be expected, as regionally-specific factors alter the relationship between dependent and independent variables.

Again, models using continuous variables perform much better than models using types of municipality as dummy variables. Models based on the demographic composition of municipalities generally work better than models based solely on contextual factors. But with contextual variables added to compositional ones in the full models, the explanatory power generally increases substantially. The compounding effect of context on the compositional makeup of communities consistently influences local political orientations; not only who the voters are, but also where they live shapes the political orientation of a municipality.

Effects from the independent variables also vary from one metropolitan area to another. In the Prague metropolitan area, the most significant predictor of voting preferences is the composite indicator of social hardship. As one would predict, a higher level of hardship is associated with a reduced inclination to vote for the right. Self-placement to the right also increases with a higher level of education in a municipality. Stronger right orientations can also be found in municipalities with a larger share of single-family houses and a faster rate of population growth. All these relations are quite consistent with expectations that suburbanisation would strengthen the political right. In the Czech Republic, as elsewhere, higher education, lower levels of social hardship, greater proportions of single-family houses and more rapid population growth are all typical features of growing suburbs.

The metropolitan area of Pilsen appears somewhat different. There the most dominant explanatory factor in the models is socio-economic status as measured by education. As one would expect in the Czech context, the more educated communities incline towards the right. The index of hardship, however, has no significant effect on local political orientations in the Pilsen metropolitan area. Rather, the positive relationship between support for the right and the proportion of population below the age of nineteen indicates concentrations of support in communities where families have more children. Contextual measures of the share of people living in single-family houses and the size of municipalities predicted support for the right in a model that included only contextual variables. Alongside the compositional variables in the full model, however, the significance of these contextual variables disappeared.

The models explaining the political orientation of voters in the Brno metropolitan area exhibit similarities with both those in Prague and Pilsen. Local support for the right declines with higher levels of social hardship, as in Prague, but rises with the proportion of families with children, as in Pilsen. What is specific to the Brno metropolitan area is the somewhat higher support for the right in the municipalities with a higher proportion of older residents. This is a clear example of an effect from a regionally-specific factor. Many older residents of the Brno metropolitan area are Catholics, who tended to support the moderately right Christian Democrats, adding to the overall support for the right in many communities.

Patterns in the Ostrava metropolitan area diverge significantly from those in the other Czech metropolitan areas. The outcome of the modelling tells us the following story: in a metropolitan area that was mostly built by means of large-

Table 11.7(a): OLS regression models explaining political self-placement of voters on left-right scale in municipalities of the Prague and Pilsen metropolitan areas in the Czech Republic, 2002

| | Prague metropolitan area | | | | | | | | Pilsen metropolitan area | | | | | | | |
| | Model 1 | | Model 2 | | Model 3 | | Model 4 | | Model 1 | | Model 2 | | Model 3 | | Model 4 | |
| | Beta | Sig. | Beta | Sig. | Beta | Sig. | Beta | Sig. | Beta | Sig. | Beta | Sig. | Beta | Sig. | Beta | Sig. |
| (Constant) | | 0.000 | | 0.000 | | 0.000 | | 0.000 | | 0.000 | | 0.000 | | 0.000 | | 0.000 |
| *Types of suburbs* | | | | | | | | | | | | | | | | |
| Affluent suburbs | -0.043 | 0.921 | | | | | | | -0.081 | 0.778 | | | | | | |
| Poor suburbs | -0.432 | 0.097 | | | | | | | -0.367 | 0.175 | | | | | | |
| Middle-class suburbs | -0.466 | 0.280 | | | | | | | -0.349 | 0.460 | | | | | | |
| Low-density suburbs | -0.326 | 0.368 | | | | | | | -0.660 | 0.174 | | | | | | |
| *Compositional* | | | | | | | | | | | | | | | | |
| Identity | | | 0.115 | 0.055 | | | 0.114 | 0.071 | | | 0.041 | 0.671 | | | 0.062 | 0.531 |
| Hardship | | | **-0.554** | **0.000** | | | **-0.456** | **0.000** | | | -0.122 | 0.353 | | | -0.085 | 0.582 |
| Education | | | **0.182** | **0.027** | | | **0.206** | **0.028** | | | **0.556** | **0.000** | | | **0.505** | **0.001** |
| Manufacturing | | | 0.061 | 0.296 | | | 0.082 | 0.323 | | | 0.035 | 0.740 | | | -0.166 | 0.457 |
| Families with kids | | | 0.123 | 0.069 | | | 0.072 | 0.342 | | | **0.312** | **0.016** | | | **0.295** | **0.027** |
| Old | | | 0.097 | 0.172 | | | 0.053 | 0.472 | | | 0.211 | 0.090 | | | 0.131 | 0.344 |
| *Contextual* | | | | | | | | | | | | | | | | |
| Economic diversity | | | | | -0.075 | 0.238 | -0.040 | 0.611 | | | | | 0.006 | 0.955 | 0.239 | 0.263 |
| Family houses | | | | | **0.233** | **0.004** | **0.186** | **0.017** | | | | | **0.503** | **0.001** | 0.288 | 0.084 |
| Log population size | | | | | **0.337** | **0.000** | 0.114 | 0.141 | | | | | **0.559** | **0.000** | 0.167 | 0.303 |
| Population growth | | | | | **0.380** | **0.000** | 0.075 | 0.325 | | | | | -0.089 | 0.418 | -0.133 | 0.203 |
| R Square | 0.223 | | 0.436 | | 0.238 | | 0.460 | | 0.145 | | 0.385 | | 0.184 | | 0.428 | |
| Adjusted R Square | 0.207 | | 0.418 | | 0.222 | | 0.431 | | 0.101 | | 0.336 | | 0.142 | | 0.348 | |
| S.E. of the estimate | 0.308 | | 0.264 | | 0.305 | | 0.261 | | 0.330 | | 0.283 | | 0.322 | | 0.281 | |

Note: For boldface coefficients, p<0.05.

Table 11.7(b): OLS regression models explaining political self-placement of voters on left-right scale in municipalities of the Brno and Ostrava metropolitan areas in the Czech Republic, 2002

| | Brno metropolitan area | | | | | | | | Ostrava metropolitan area | | | | | | | |
| | Model 1 | | Model 2 | | Model 3 | | Model 4 | | Model 1 | | Model 2 | | Model 3 | | Model 4 | |
| | Beta | Sig. | Beta | Sig. | Beta | Sig. | Beta | Sig. | Beta | Sig. | Beta | Sig. | Beta | Sig. | Beta | Sig. |
| (Constant) | | 0.000 | | 0.000 | | 0.000 | | 0.000 | | 0.000 | | 0.000 | | 0.000 | | 0.010 |
| *Types of suburbs* | | | | | | | | | | | | | | | | |
| Affluent suburbs | -0.060 | 0.849 | | | | | | | 0.293 | 0.310 | | | | | | |
| Poor suburbs | -0.467 | 0.275 | | | | | | | 0.109 | 0.743 | | | | | | |
| Middle-class suburbs | -0.224 | 0.628 | | | | | | | 0.191 | 0.607 | | | | | | |
| Low-density suburbs | -0.505 | 0.113 | | | | | | | | | | | | | | |
| *Compositional* | | | | | | | | | | | | | | | | |
| Identity | | | 0.075 | 0.321 | | | 0.100 | 0.190 | | | 0.183 | 0.292 | | | 0.210 | 0.290 |
| Hardship | | | **-0.463** | **0.000** | | | **-0.400** | **0.001** | | | **-0.680** | **0.002** | | | -0.600 | 0.059 |
| Education | | | 0.163 | 0.137 | | | 0.103 | 0.414 | | | -0.160 | 0.420 | | | -0.223 | 0.399 |
| Manufacturing | | | 0.042 | 0.609 | | | 0.001 | 0.994 | | | 0.053 | 0.734 | | | -0.066 | 0.847 |
| Families with kids | | | 0.231 | 0.014 | | | 0.184 | 0.082 | | | 0.128 | 0.541 | | | 0.142 | 0.505 |
| Old | | | 0.144 | 0.106 | | | 0.176 | 0.076 | | | -0.057 | 0.761 | | | -0.183 | 0.347 |
| *Contextual* | | | | | | | | | | | | | | | | |
| Economic diversity | | | | | -0.050 | 0.545 | 0.032 | 0.843 | | | | | -0.072 | 0.604 | 0.078 | 0.800 |
| Family houses | | | | | **0.255** | **0.020** | 0.136 | 0.235 | | | | | 0.695 | 0.013 | **0.786** | **0.023** |
| Log population size | | | | | 0.400 | 0.000 | 0.260 | 0.013 | | | | | 0.246 | 0.364 | 0.489 | 0.109 |
| Population growth | | | | | **0.196** | **0.019** | 0.077 | 0.418 | | | | | -0.208 | 0.164 | -0.221 | 0.228 |
| R Square | 0.181 | | 0.307 | | 0.149 | | 0.346 | | 0.038 | | 0.245 | | 0.216 | | 0.353 | |
| Adjusted R Square | 0.155 | | 0.274 | | 0.123 | | 0.292 | | -0.020 | | 0.149 | | 0.152 | | 0.202 | |
| S.E. of the estimate | 0.298 | | 0.276 | | 0.304 | | 0.273 | | 0.276 | | 0.252 | | 0.251 | | 0.243 | |

Note: For boldface coefficients, p<.05.

*Table 11.8(a): OLS regression models explaining socially-conservative vote in municipalities of the Prague and Pilsen metropolitan areas in the Czech Republic, 2002*

| | Prague metropolitan area | | | | | | | | Pilsen metropolitan area | | | | | | | |
| | Model 1 | | Model 2 | | Model 3 | | Model 4 | | Model 1 | | Model 2 | | Model 3 | | Model 4 | |
| | Beta | Sig. | Beta | Sig. | Beta | Sig. | Beta | Sig. | Beta | Sig. | Beta | Sig. | Beta | Sig. | Beta | Sig. |
|---|---|---|---|---|---|---|---|---|---|---|---|---|---|---|---|---|
| *(Constant)* | | *0.000* | | *0.000* | | *0.000* | | *0.000* | | *0.000* | | *0.000* | | *0.000* | | *0.000* |
| *Types of suburbs* | | | | | | | | | | | | | | | | |
| Affluent suburbs | −0.303 | 0.528 | | | | | | | −0.060 | 0.843 | | | | | | |
| Poor suburbs | −0.294 | 0.309 | | | | | | | 0.045 | 0.876 | | | | | | |
| Middle-class suburbs | −0.401 | 0.403 | | | | | | | −0.054 | 0.914 | | | | | | |
| Low-density suburbs | −0.447 | 0.268 | | | | | | | 0.107 | 0.835 | | | | | | |
| *Compositional* | | | | | | | | | | | | | | | | |
| Identity | | | −0.072 | 0.342 | | | 0.011 | 0.887 | | | 0.080 | 0.509 | | | 0.067 | 0.589 |
| Hardship | | | **0.243** | **0.022** | | | 0.141 | 0.208 | | | −0.181 | 0.264 | | | −0.126 | 0.515 |
| Education | | | **0.257** | **0.015** | | | **0.311** | **0.008** | | | −0.207 | 0.196 | | | −0.093 | 0.618 |
| Manufacturing | | | **−0.183** | **0.015** | | | −0.152 | 0.144 | | | −0.083 | 0.520 | | | 0.239 | 0.395 |
| Families with kids | | | 0.011 | 0.894 | | | 0.135 | 0.156 | | | −0.177 | 0.260 | | | −0.118 | 0.476 |
| Old | | | 0.116 | 0.199 | | | 0.150 | 0.101 | | | 0.015 | 0.921 | | | 0.012 | 0.944 |
| *Contextual* | | | | | | | | | | | | | | | | |
| Economic diversity | | | | | −0.091 | 0.191 | 0.045 | 0.645 | | | | | −0.091 | 0.440 | −0.326 | 0.225 |
| Family houses | | | | | −0.018 | 0.836 | −0.003 | 0.972 | | | | | −0.023 | 0.884 | −0.117 | 0.571 |
| Log population size | | | | | **0.180** | **0.037** | 0.082 | 0.399 | | | | | −0.122 | 0.441 | −0.166 | 0.413 |
| Population growth | | | | | **−0.229** | **0.001** | **−0.309** | **0.001** | | | | | −0.129 | 0.279 | −0.325 | 0.746 |
| R Square | 0.038 | | 0.081 | | 0.098 | | 0.155 | | 0.029 | | 0.060 | | 0.039 | | 0.095 | |
| Adjusted R Square | 0.018 | | 0.051 | | 0.079 | | 0.109 | | −0.021 | | −0.015 | | −0.011 | | −0.032 | |
| *S.E. of the estimate* | *0.049* | | *0.048* | | *0.048* | | *0.047* | | *0.049* | | *0.049* | | *0.049* | | *0.049* | |

*Note:* For boldface coefficients, p<0.05.

*Table 11.8(b): OLS regression models explaining socially-conservative vote in municipalities of the Brno and Ostrava metropolitan areas in the Czech Republic, 2002*

| | Brno metropolitan area | | | | | | | | Ostrava metropolitan area | | | | | | | |
|---|---|---|---|---|---|---|---|---|---|---|---|---|---|---|---|---|
| | Model 1 | | Model 2 | | Model 3 | | Model 4 | | Model 1 | | Model 2 | | Model 3 | | Model 4 | |
| | Beta | Sig. | Beta | Sig. | Beta | Sig. | Beta | Sig. | Beta | Sig. | Beta | Sig. | Beta | Sig. | Beta | Sig. |
| *(Constant)* | | 0.000 | | 0.000 | | 0.000 | | 0.000 | | 0.000 | | 0.000 | | 0.000 | | 0.010 |
| *Types of suburbs* | | | | | | | | | | | | | | | | |
| Affluent suburbs | 0.123 | 0.712 | | | | | | | 0.182 | 0.511 | | | | | | |
| Poor suburbs | 0.555 | 0.217 | | | | | | | 0.467 | 0.148 | | | | | | |
| Middle-class suburbs | 0.447 | 0.360 | | | | | | | 0.632 | 0.080 | | | | | | |
| Low-density suburbs | 0.156 | 0.640 | | | | | | | | | | | | | | |
| *Compositional* | | | | | | | | | | | | | | | | |
| Identity | | | 0.077 | 0.330 | | | 0.091 | 0.237 | | | 0.141 | 0.357 | | | 0.148 | 0.411 |
| Hardship | | | -0.285 | **0.012** | | | **-0.255** | **0.038** | | | **-0.503** | **0.007** | | | **-0.832** | **0.005** |
| Education | | | -0.267 | **0.020** | | | **-0.265** | **0.040** | | | **-0.476** | **0.009** | | | **-0.649** | **0.009** |
| Manufacturing | | | 0.163 | 0.057 | | | 0.483 | 0.006 | | | 0.039 | 0.776 | | | -0.402 | 0.199 |
| Families with kids | | | **0.429** | **0.000** | | | **0.389** | **0.000** | | | **0.574** | **0.003** | | | **0.694** | **0.001** |
| Old | | | **0.321** | **0.001** | | | **0.296** | **0.004** | | | **0.349** | **0.038** | | | **0.396** | **0.028** |
| *Contextual* | | | | | | | | | | | | | | | | |
| Economic diversity | | | | | 0.079 | 0.350 | **-0.358** | **0.028** | | | | | 0.183 | 0.206 | 0.505 | 0.073 |
| Family houses | | | | | **0.391** | **0.001** | 0.146 | 0.210 | | | | | -0.062 | 0.826 | 0.085 | 0.780 |
| Log population size | | | | | **0.270** | **0.017** | **0.332** | **0.002** | | | | | -0.310 | 0.269 | 0.192 | 0.480 |
| Population growth | | | | | -0.071 | 0.406 | -0.057 | 0.549 | | | | | 0.219 | 0.156 | 0.025 | 0.878 |
| R Square | | 0.095 | | 0.254 | | 0.096 | | 0.331 | | 0.113 | | 0.410 | | 0.165 | | 0.469 |
| Adjusted R Square | | 0.066 | | 0.218 | | 0.068 | | 0.227 | | 0.060 | | 0.334 | | 0.097 | | 0.345 |
| S.E. of the estimate | | 0.087 | | 0.080 | | 0.087 | | 0.077 | | 0.053 | | 0.045 | | 0.052 | | 0.045 |

*Note:* For boldface coefficients, p<0.05.

Table 11.9(a): OLS regression models explaining anti-globalisation/nationalistic vote in municipalities of the Prague and Pilsen metropolitan areas in the Czech Republic, 2002

|  | Prague metropolitan area | | | | | | | | Pilsen metropolitan area | | | | | | | |
| --- | --- | --- | --- | --- | --- | --- | --- | --- | --- | --- | --- | --- | --- | --- | --- | --- |
|  | Model 1 | | Model 2 | | Model 3 | | Model 4 | | Model 1 | | Model 2 | | Model 3 | | Model 4 | |
|  | Beta | Sig. | Beta | Sig. | Beta | Sig. | Beta | Sig. | Beta | Sig. | Beta | Sig. | Beta | Sig. | Beta | Sig. |
| (Constant) |  | 0.000 |  | 0.000 |  | 0.000 |  | 0.000 |  | 0.000 |  | 0.000 |  | 0.000 |  | 0.000 |
| Types of suburbs |  |  |  |  |  |  |  |  |  |  |  |  |  |  |  |  |
| Affluent suburbs | 0.106 | 0.803 |  |  |  |  |  |  | 0.099 | 0.737 |  |  |  |  |  |  |
| Poor suburbs | 0.478 | 0.063 |  |  |  |  |  |  | 0.345 | 0.216 |  |  |  |  |  |  |
| Middle-class suburbs | 0.559 | 0.188 |  |  |  |  |  |  | 0.319 | 0.513 |  |  |  |  |  |  |
| Low-density suburbs | 0.401 | 0.262 |  |  |  |  |  |  | 0.551 | 0.271 |  |  |  |  |  |  |
| Compositional |  |  |  |  |  |  |  |  |  |  |  |  |  |  |  |  |
| Identity |  |  | -0.102 | 0.079 |  |  | -0.114 | 0.067 |  |  | -0.001 | 0.993 |  |  | -0.022 | 0.829 |
| Hardship |  |  | **0.498** | **0.000** |  |  | **0.430** | **0.000** |  |  | 0.000 | 0.997 |  |  | -0.044 | 0.780 |
| Education |  |  | **-0.273** | **0.001** |  |  | **-0.317** | **0.001** |  |  | **-0.591** | **0.000** |  |  | **-0.585** | **0.000** |
| Manufacturing |  |  | -0.049 | 0.385 |  |  | -0.059 | 0.470 |  |  | -0.049 | 0.651 |  |  | 0.136 | 0.553 |
| Families with kids |  |  | -0.111 | 0.093 |  |  | -0.094 | 0.205 |  |  | **-0.296** | **0.026** |  |  | **-0.288** | **0.036** |
| Old |  |  | -0.121 | 0.081 |  |  | 0.008 | 0.190 |  |  | -0.218 | 0.090 |  |  | -0.121 | 0.398 |
| Contextual |  |  |  |  |  |  |  |  |  |  |  |  |  |  |  |  |
| Economic diversity |  |  |  |  | 0.072 | 0.265 | -0.008 | 0.920 |  |  |  |  | -0.011 | 0.923 | -0.240 | 0.274 |
| Family houses |  |  |  |  | **-0.208** | **0.011** | **-0.163** | **0.032** |  |  |  |  | **-0.458** | **0.003** | -0.282 | 0.098 |
| Log population size |  |  |  |  | **-0.338** | **0.000** | -0.079 | 0.301 |  |  |  |  | **-0.446** | **0.004** | -0.078 | 0.637 |
| Population growth |  |  |  |  | **-0.352** | **0.000** | -0.013 | 0.865 |  |  |  |  | 0.116 | 0.303 | 0.166 | 0.121 |
| R Square | 0.247 |  | 0.466 |  | 0.214 |  | 0.481 |  | 0.090 |  | 0.340 |  | 0.138 |  | 0.397 |  |
| Adjusted R Square | 0.231 |  | 0.449 |  | 0.197 |  | 0.452 |  | 0.042 |  | 0.287 |  | 0.093 |  | 0.312 |  |
| S.E. of the estimate | 0.035 |  | 0.030 |  | 0.036 |  | 0.030 |  | 0.039 |  | 0.034 |  | 0.038 |  | 0.033 |  |

Note: For boldface coefficients, p<0.05.

*Table 11.9(b): OLS regression models explaining anti-globalisation/nationalistic vote in municipalities of the Brno and Ostrava metropolitan areas in the Czech Republic, 2002*

| | Brno metropolitan area | | | | | | | | Ostrava metropolitan area | | | | | | | |
| | Model 1 | | Model 2 | | Model 3 | | Model 4 | | Model 1 | | Model 2 | | Model 3 | | Model 4 | |
| | Beta | Sig. | Beta | Sig. | Beta | Sig. | Beta | Sig. | Beta | Sig. | Beta | Sig. | Beta | Sig. | Beta | Sig. |
|---|---|---|---|---|---|---|---|---|---|---|---|---|---|---|---|---|
| (Constant) | | 0.000 | | 0.000 | | 0.000 | | 0.000 | | 0.000 | | 0.000 | | 0.000 | | 0.010 |
| *Types of suburbs* | | | | | | | | | | | | | | | | |
| Affluent suburbs | 0.005 | 0.988 | | | | | | | −0.327 | 0.261 | | | | | | |
| Poor suburbs | 0.184 | 0.676 | | | | | | | −0.242 | 0.470 | | | | | | |
| Middle-class suburbs | 0.029 | 0.952 | | | | | | | −0.355 | 0.342 | | | | | | |
| Low-density suburbs | 0.371 | 0.260 | | | | | | | | | | | | | | |
| *Compositional* | | | | | | | | | | | | | | | | |
| Identity | | | −0.079 | 0.312 | | | −0.105 | 0.181 | | | −0.205 | 0.225 | | | −0.226 | 0.243 |
| Hardship | | | **0.464** | **0.000** | | | **0.403** | **0.001** | | | **0.752** | **0.000** | | | **0.709** | **0.023** |
| Education | | | −0.061 | 0.592 | | | 0.005 | 0.967 | | | 0.266 | 0.170 | | | 0.347 | 0.180 |
| Manufacturing | | | −0.076 | 0.373 | | | −0.093 | 0.597 | | | −0.060 | 0.689 | | | 0.126 | 0.705 |
| Families with kids | | | **−0.340** | **0.001** | | | **−0.291** | **0.008** | | | −0.282 | 0.168 | | | −0.307 | 0.142 |
| Old | | | **−0.232** | **0.013** | | | **−0.264** | **0.010** | | | −0.035 | 0.848 | | | 0.087 | 0.647 |
| *Contextual* | | | | | | | | | | | | | | | | |
| Economic diversity | | | | | 0.011 | 0.891 | 0.032 | 0.846 | | | | | 0.046 | 0.739 | 0.145 | 0.625 |
| Family houses | | | | | **−0.324** | **0.004** | −0.145 | 0.220 | | | | | **−0.606** | **0.029** | **−0.757** | **0.024** |
| Log population size | | | | | **−0.410** | **0.000** | **−0.311** | **0.004** | | | | | −0.113 | 0.675 | −0.466 | 0.116 |
| Population growth | | | | | −0.158 | 0.060 | −0.066 | 0.500 | | | | | 0.163 | 0.272 | 0.225 | 0.208 |
| R Square | 0.124 | | 0.254 | | 0.139 | | 0.306 | | 0.030 | | 0.288 | | 0.224 | | 0.387 | |
| Adjusted R Square | 0.097 | | 0.218 | | 0.112 | | 0.249 | | −0.029 | | 0.197 | | 0.161 | | 0.244 | |
| *S.E. of the estimate* | *0.044* | | *0.041* | | *0.044* | | *0.040* | | *0.038* | | *0.034* | | *0.035* | | *0.033* | |

*Note:* For boldface coefficients, p<0.05.

scale collective housing projects during the Communist era, and that underwent a deep economic decline after the breakdown of the regime, the most important predictor of the political orientation of voters is the share of people living in single-family houses. The more people that live in communities dominated by these homes, the stronger the local inclination toward the political right. Although the level of social hardship also predicts lower electoral support for the right, the relation is not strong enough to be considered statistically significant in all models. No other relationships were found to be significant.

A similar series of models analysed local variations in the dependent variables measuring economic, cultural and cosmopolitan or nationalist dimensions of partisan preferences. The political self-placement of communities and their economic attitudes are closely correlated. Regression models explaining the inter-municipal differences in the mean economic index generated results almost identical with those for self-placement on the left-right scale.

Social conservatism follows very different spatial patterns that also produce distinctive results from the regression models. As the numbers in Table 11.8(a) and Table 11.8(b) suggest, the regression models of variations in social conservatism were generally not very successful. Models using municipal types as dummy independent variables failed to work at all. Models employing only contextual variables explained less than 10 per cent of the variation. In the Prague and Pilsen metropolitan areas, none of the models were useful in explaining variation among municipalities. In Brno and Ostrava, models comprised of compositional independent variables proved somewhat more successful. There the models linked local social conservatism among voters to a larger share of families with children, a larger older population, a lower level of education, and a higher level of social hardship. This combination of independent variables corresponds to typical characteristics of the Czech Catholic population. Catholics tend to be older than the general population. Younger Catholic families have typically more children than the average Czech family. As a consequence from an overrepresentation of old people among Catholics, the general education level of Catholics remains lower than average. At the same time, Catholics have typically faced fewer social problems, lower unemployment, and hence a lower level of social hardship. Since a larger share of Catholics live in the eastern part of the Czech Republic, where the Brno and Ostrava metropolitan areas are located, Catholicism could explain why cultural conservatism follows these patterns in these two metropolitan areas.

The final set of regression analyses aims to explain variations in the average attitudes toward globalisation, nationalism and ethnic diversity among communities in Czech metropolitan areas (see Table 11.9(a) and Table 11.9(b)). As in the tests for cultural conservatism, models that used municipal types as the independent variable work poorly. However, the models containing continuous variables account for between 20 and 40 per cent of inter-municipal variation. Compositional variables measuring differences in the structure of local populations are again of more importance than contextual variables, but inclusion of the contextual variables generally improved the quality of the models. No independent variables attain statistical significance in all the models across all four metropolitan areas. Some variables, however, exert generally consistent effects. Support for nationalism rises with the level of social hardship, but tends to decline with rising levels of education, and with an increasing share of families with children in a municipality. A larger share of single-family houses and a larger population enhance municipal support for globalisation. The overall results suggest that the fear of effects from globalisation is most widespread among municipalities likely to suffer the most from its potential negative effects – the small municipalities with more public housing, less-educated inhabitants and already high levels of social hardship.

## Conclusions

Analysis of political behaviour in Czech metropolitan areas reveals some differences from metropolitan areas in those Western countries with long-standing traditions of democracy and a market economy, but these are accompanied by many similarities. As in other countries, the analysis identified five characteristic types of municipality: urban concentrations, low-density suburbs, poor suburbs, middle-class suburbs, and affluent suburbs. These types of metropolitan place differ systematically, both in their demographics and in their political behaviour. The key dividing line runs between the urban concentrations and the suburban types. Socio-economic and political divisions within metropolitan areas have long followed a more traditional European model than a North American one. The core cities remain generally richer and have a more educated population than the suburbs. The command economy and planning system under Communism reinforced this model, concentrating investment in the core cities and for more than four decades suppressing much of the potential suburbanisation.

The transition of political and economic regimes at the end of the 1980s dramatically changed the rules governing metropolitan development. As a consequence, suburbanisation became the most important socio-spatial process in the country after 1989. To date, the four suburban types do not differ dramatically, but the trends are clear, as the socio-economic differences among different types of suburbs have continued to deepen. The growing divide between affluent and poor suburbs reflects a classical North American pattern, which is also now widespread in Western Europe. Thus far, the main contrast with the majority of Western metropolises is the absence of municipalities with concentrations of poor minority populations in Czech metropolitan areas. Although immigration to the Czech Republic has grown, the mix of new immigrants has helped to prevent such spatial concentrations. Immigrant groups include predominantly workers from socio-economically and culturally similar countries such as Slovakia and the Ukraine, as well as professionals from the advanced countries of the West and traders and shopkeepers from economically-successful Asian communities.

The emerging socio-spatial differences within metropolitan areas affects electoral turnout. In both national and local elections, the inter-metropolitan variation in turnout tended to decrease over the observed period. Variation within metropolitan areas among the individual types of municipalities has grown. Spatial patterns of voter participation in national elections and local elections vary noticeably. In national elections, turnout in the core cities and the suburbs is generally similar, suggesting that motives for participation in national elections are not dominantly local. The statistical models indicate the key role of the compositional socio-economic indicators in explaining the relatively small variations in national election turnout. The greater is the economic success of municipalities and their inhabitants, the higher the turnout in parliamentary elections.

In local elections, however, as has also been the case in Poland (see Chapter 10), voters in the core cities participate dramatically less frequently than voters in the suburbs. The contextual variables rather than the socio-economic conditions, and especially the population size of municipalities, decisively influence the participation in the local elections. Delocalised politics was greatest in the core cities and the larger suburban municipalities with a higher share of newcomers. This de-localisation of politics in the urban centres is particularly pronounced in the two post-communist countries of this study, but also reflects tendencies evident in long-standing democracies.

The general political preferences of voters in metropolitan communities were measured by self-placement of voters on the left-right axis and by three indices aggregating voters' attitudes toward economic, cultural and globalisation/nationalism dimensions of political ideology. Political preferences among metropolitan communities basically followed the national trends over the observed period. The variation among metropolitan areas tended to increase over the time and was generally more pronounced in the case of voter turnout. Regional factors substantially affected these variations – a centre-periphery cleavage fostered different political preferences in Prague from those in the other metropolitan areas. Inhabitants of the core cities of the Czech metropolitan areas, and especially residents of Prague, are generally more educated and more affluent than inhabitants of suburban municipalities. Typical of Czech Republic, Poland and other post-communist countries, these concentrations of affluent voters remain strongholds of the right. In this sense, differences in political preferences of communities are mainly influenced by the socio-economic composition of their inhabitants, while the contextual features of the municipalities matter less. Analysis of the political preferences in suburban municipalities suggests that affluent suburbs are leaning towards the right as well. If the socially-selective migration of affluent voters to the affluent suburbs continues at the current pace, these suburbs may soon replace the core cities as the political stronghold of the right.

In the Czech context, self-placement on the left-right scale is closely correlated with attitudes towards economic issues. To be right-oriented means to be fiscally conservative, and to support free markets and small government. Among metropolitan municipalities, the inclination to the right increases with higher socio-economic status and rising home ownership. Following a similar logic, municipalities with a higher level of social hardship tend to incline more towards nationalism and against globalisation. In contrast to the situation in Hungary, Czech voters who consider themselves on the right are not necessarily socially conservative. Consequently, the spatial patterns of metropolitan support for social conservatism remain independent from the patterns of support for fiscal conservatism. Social conservatism is stronger in municipalities with larger Catholic populations.

The metropolitanisation of Czech society is undoubtedly changing the country's political landscape. The internationalisation of the Prague metropolitan area and its growing economic dominance over the other Czech metropolitan areas has deepened the regional variations with regard to the political preferences of Czech voters. Suburbanisation, combined with the social and economic diversification of suburban communities, has added an intra-metropolitan dimension to spatial variations in both political preferences and electoral participation. While the scope of change is still influenced by the egalitarian heritage that is specific to many post-communist countries, most of the trends in the Czech Republic closely resemble those observed in the metropolitan areas of the most developed countries.

## Bibliography

Blažek, J. and Kostelecký, T. (1991) 'Geografická analýza výsledků parlamentních voleb v roce 1990', *Sborník ČGS* 96 (1): 1–13.

Daněk, P. (1993) 'Communist landscapes of Moravia and Silesia (1925–1992)', *Scripta Fac.Brun*, 23(1): 9–24.

— (2002) *Geografické a strukturální předpoklady demokratické místní správy v pohraničí českých zemí*, thesis, Prague: Charles University, Faculty of Sciences.

Jehlička, P. and Sýkora, L. (1991) 'Stabilita regionální podpory tradičních politických stran v Českých zemích (1920–1990)', *Sborník ČGS*, 96(2): 81–95.

Kostelecký, T. (1993) *Geografie voleb jako součást politické geografie*, thesis, Prague: Charles University, Faculty of Science.

— (1996) 'The Results of the 1990 parliamentary elections in regional perspective', in H. D. Klingemann (ed.) Election handbook 1990 – Czechoslovakia, Poland, Hungary, Slovenia, Berlin: WZB.

— (2002) *Political Parties after Communism: Developments in East-Central Europe*, Washington, D.C.: Woodrow Wilson Center Press.

— (2007) 'Political parties and their role in local politics in the post-Communist Czech Republic', in F. Lazin, M. Evans, V. Hoffmann-Martinot and H. Wollman (2007) *Local Government Reforms in Countries in Transition: A global perspective*, Lanham, Maryland: Lexington Books, 106–21.

Kostelecký, T. and Čermák, D. (2003) 'Výběrová šetření a analýza agregátních dat – diskuse na téma použitelnosti různých přístupů v komparativních analýzách politického chování', *Sociologický časopis/Czech Sociological Review*, 39(4): 529–50.

— (2004) *Metropolitan Areas in the Czech Republic – Definitions, Basic Characteristics, Patterns of Suburbanisation and Their Impact on Political Behaviour*, Prague: Institute of Sociology, Sociologické studie/ Sociological Studies 04:3.

Kostelecký, T. and Kroupa, A. (1996) 'Party organization and structure at national level and local level in the Czech Republic since 1989', in P. Lewis (ed.) *Party Structure and Organisation in East-Central Europe*, Aldershot: Edward Elgar Publishing Ltd, 89–119.

Linek, L. and Mansfeldová, Z. (2006) 'The impact of the EU on the Czech party system', in P. Lewis and Z. Mansfeldová (eds) *The European Union and Party Politics in Central and Eastern Europe*, Houndmills, Basingstoke, Hampshire: Palgrave Macmillan, 20–39.

Mansfeldová, Z. (1998) 'The Czech and Slovak Republics', in Berglund, S., Hellén, T., and Aarebrot F. H. (eds) *The Handbook of Political Change in Eastern Europe*, Cheltenham, Northampton: Edward Elgar, 191–230.

— (2004) 'The Czech Republic', in S. Berglund, J. Ekman and F. Aarebrot (eds) *The Handbook of Political Change in Eastern Europe*. Second Edition, Cheltenham, Northampton: Edward Edgar, 223–53.

Matějů, P. and Vlachová, K. (1998) 'Values and electoral decisions in the Czech Republic', *Communist and Post-communist Studies*, 31(3): 249–69.

Musil, J., Horská, P and Maur, J. (2002) *Zrod velkoměsta. Urbanizace Českých zemí a Evropa*, Litomyšl: Paseka.

Novák, J. and Sýkora, L. (2007) 'A city in motion: time-space activity and mobility patterns of suburban inhabitants and structuration of spatial organisation in the Prague metropolitan area', *Geografiska Annaler B: Human Geography*, 89(2): 147–67.

Ouředníček, M. (2007) 'Differential suburban development in the Prague urban region', *Geografiska Annaler: Human Geography*, 89B(2): 111–25.

Sokol, P. (2003) 'Základní údaje volební geografie při volbách do Poslanecké sněmovny Parlamentu 2002', in L. Linek, L. Mrklas, A. Seidlová and P. Sokol (eds) *Volby do Poslanecké sněmovny 2002*, Prague: Institute of Sociology, 163–75.

Sýkora, L. (2005) 'Gentrification in post-communist cities', in R. Atkinson and G. Bridge (eds) *The New Urban Colonialism: Gentrification in a Global Context*, London, Routledge, 90–105.

— (2009) 'New socio-spatial formations: places of residential segregation and separation in Czechia', *TESG Tijdschrift voor economische en sociale geografie (Journal of Economic & Social Geography)*, 100(4): 417–35.

Sýkora, L. and Ouředníček, M. (2007) 'Sprawling post-communist metropolis: commercial and residential suburbanisation in Prague and Brno, the Czech Republic', in E. Razin, M. Dijst and C. Vázquez, C. (eds) *Employment Deconcentration in European Metropolitan Areas: Market Forces versus Planning Regulations*, Springer: Dordrecht, 209–33.

Vlachová, K. (2001) 'Party identification in the Czech Republic: inter-party hostility and party preference', *Communist and Post-communist Studies*, 34: 479–99.

## Appendix

*Table A11.1: Position of voters of the largest Czech parties in different dimensions of 'an ideological space' (average values of respective indexes)*

| Voters of: | Economic dimension | Cultural dimension | Globalisation dimension | Self-Place-ment on the Left-Right Axis |
|---|---|---|---|---|
| *Scale* | *1 = state control, 10 = free market* | *1 = social liberalism, 10 = social conservatism* | *1 = support globalisation, 10 = nationalism* | *1 = extreme left, 10 = extreme right* |
| Social Democratic Party | 4.61 | 4.56 | 6.28 | 4.65 |
| Civic Democratic Party | 6.25 | 4.22 | 5.98 | 7.84 |
| Communist Party | 3.84 | 4.90 | 6.49 | 2.79 |
| Christian Democratic Union | 5.05 | 6.19 | 6.11 | 6.87 |
| Other parties | 4.79 | 4.51 | 6.02 | 5.63 |
| All voters altogether | 5.13 | 4.63 | 6.14 | 6.05 |

*Source:* Authors' calculations based on data from European Value Survey 1999–2000, European Social Survey 2002, International Social Survey Program 1998, 1999, 2003, 2004.

*Table A11.2: Definitions of independent variables*

| Concept | Variable | Definition |
|---|---|---|
| *Socio-demographic compositional variables:* | | |
| Immigrants/visible minorities | Identity | % of Ukrainians, Vietnamese, and Romany in total population |
| Secondary sector | Manufacturing | % of labour force employed in manufacturing industry and construction |
| Socio-economic status | Education | % with university degree (of pop. aged 25 and more) |
| Disadvantage/ marginalisation | Hardship | Hardship index combining:<br>• % households with income lower than 1.2 multiple of subsistence level in 2003<br>• % unemployed in 2001<br>• % of population over 15 without completed secondary education number of persons per one living room as a measure of housing overcrowding |
| Presence of families/ family values | Families with kids | % of total population under age 19 |
| Ageing, aged, greying | Old | % of total population age 65 or older |
| *Spatial/contextual variables:* | | |
| Economic diversity | Economic diversity | The Simpson index of economic diversity distinguishing four sectors: agriculture, industry + construction, retail + transport, public employees |
| Security of tenure/ quality of housing | Family houses | % total population living in own family house |
| Population density | Log population density | Log of persons/km square in municipality |
| Population size of municipality | Log Population size | Log of population size of municipality |
| Population growth | Population growth | (Population 2001/population 1991)*100 |

*Note:* When the year is unspecified, the data are from population Census 2001.

# Chapter Twelve | Metropolitan Processes and Voting Behaviour in Israel

*Eran Razin and Anna Hazan*

## Introduction[1]

Unveiling how voting behaviour and political orientations vary within and between Israel's metropolitan areas provides a fundamental perspective on the political components of intra- and inter-metropolitan processes. Moreover, it provides insights on a potentially emerging democratic crisis associated with decreasing voter turnout, political fragmentation, eroding image and legitimacy of elected politicians – and, in some cases, intensification of voting behaviours based on kinship, ethnicity and religion. All of these processes are manifested at the local and metropolitan scale. This chapter has two objectives:

(1) To examine variations in local voting behaviour in Israel, discussing variations in turnout between local authorities and their interrelationships with metropolitan processes.

(2) To examine the political ecology of partisanship in Israel's metropolitan areas, i.e. political orientations in different local authorities, as revealed by voting patterns in national elections.

Our analysis of local elections identifies the determinants of voter turnout, party/list fragmentation of elected councils, and party/list composition (right-wing and religious parties, centre-left parties, Arab parties and non-partisan independent lists). It also examines over time changes in these indicators of voting behaviour. The study examines whether patterns of voter turnout and voting preferences in national elections diverge from those of local elections, and looks also at different scales of left-right political orientations at the national level. We seek to identify the manifestation of variations in voting behaviour in metropolitan space, assessing if place of residence is an explanatory variable of voting behaviour in Israel, or if inter-local variations in voting merely reflect socio-economic, demographic and ethno-religious attributes of particular local authorities.

Israel has four metropolitan areas: Tel Aviv, Haifa, Jerusalem and Beer Sheva (Razin and Hazan 2005). The Tel Aviv metropolis is Israel's dominant economic and cultural heart, consisting of nearly one half of Israel's population and economy. Haifa and Jerusalem are secondary metropolitan areas, Jerusalem being unique as Israel's capital city and as a bi-national metropolis. Beer Sheva is a smaller and

1.   The authors would like to thank Noga Buber and Ron Horne for their research assistance.

weaker peripheral metropolitan area. Given Israel's small size and short distances, it is somewhat superfluous to limit the analysis to the narrow definitions of these metropolitan areas. In fact, under a broad definition, the whole area of Israel, except for its most remote southern and north-eastern localities, can be divided into four regions, each defining a metropolitan sphere of influence. Using a broad definition of metropolitan regions also provides larger samples of local authorities, essential for statistical analysis. Our study thus covers all local authorities in Israel, except for those in rural regional councils, classified into four metropolitan regions.

Information was gathered at the local authority level. An analysis of aggregate variables at the local authority level rather than at the individual voter level (for example Walks 2004a) limits the ability to distinguish between various socio-economic and ethnic attributes that are highly correlated when measured as aggregates, and the ability to determine causality based on the results of a regression model. The aggregate level, however, enables the identification of finer spatial variations between local authorities, in addition to being based on real election results rather than on less reliable surveys.

The analysis includes the local elections held in 1998 and 2003 and the national elections held in 1999 and 2003,[2] as well as insights from the 2006 national elections. The data for both local and national elections excludes the rural regional councils (8.7 per cent of Israel's population). Local elections in regional councils, which include kibbutzim, moshavim and exurban settlements, differ from elections in urban local authorities (including those in small towns and exurban settlements that have an independent municipal status), in being non-partisan and majoritarian, rather than proportional.[3] The local elections data also exclude local authorities that did not hold elections in the particular year – 1998 or 2003 (elections at a different date can be caused by the resignation/death of the mayor or the early dissolution of a council of a malfunctioning local authority).

The analysis included the following dependent variables, representing voting behaviour and party orientation: voter turnout, percentage of votes for the following groups of parties: (1) right-wing and religious parties, (2) centre-left parties, and (3) Arab parties. Additional dependent variables for the local elections included the number of parties/lists per council member, the share of the largest party out of total number of council members, the share of the mayor's party out of the total number of council members, and the percentage of council members of immigrant parties and independent lists. In the case of the 2003 national elections, reference was also made to additional left-right scales based on economic and cultural ideologies and left-right self-placement.

The first part in the analysis was based on a classification of local authorities into seven types – central cities and six suburban categories, differentiating local authorities by population size, socio-economic status and minority (Arab)

2.  Only data for 2003 is presented in some tables, because data for 1998/1999 revealed very similar patterns.

3.  Councillors in regional councils represent specific rural localities rather than parties/lists.

population. Means of the dependent variables were compared for the seven types, providing insights on intra-metropolitan variations in voting behaviour and on the political ecology of Israeli metropolitan areas. Means of compositional and place-linked independent variables were also compared. Compositional variables included the Arab-Jewish distinction, several measures of socio-economic status, percentage of immigrants, percentage of children (up to age 18), and percentage of elderly (over age 60). Place-linked variables included population size, population density, distance from a metropolitan centre, Gini coefficient (representing income disparities and class heterogeneity of the population), rate of home ownership, and metropolitan region. Insights gleaned from the 2006 national elections, in which the traditional right-left divide in Israeli politics seemed to be falling apart, portending a shift in long-standing patterns of partisanship, also feature here.

The next part consists of multivariate analyses of variables expected to have a major influence on inter-local variations in voting patterns. Finally, based on the results of the OLS regression analyses, multilevel models were opted on two major dependent variables: voter turnout in the 2003 local elections, and percentage of votes for right wing and religious parties in the 2003 Knesset elections.

## National and local elections in Israel

### Israel's electoral system

Israel is a unitary state with only two levels of government: national and local. Except in the case of the rural regional councils, elections to both levels are proportional – elected members of the Knesset (Israel's legislature) and members of local authority councils formally represent party lists and not voters of a particular constituency. Debates on changing this system, at least partially, into majoritarian elections, in order to reduce fragmentation, instability and the immense bargaining power of small coalition parties, have led nowhere, largely because of possible implications on Jewish religious and ultra-religious parties. The divide between Jews and Arabs and across Jewish secular, religious and ultra-religious populations also presents risks for gerrymandering if majoritarian representation is applied. Increasing the election threshold also faced considerable opposition, and its increase from 1 per cent until 1988 to 1.5 per cent afterwards and to 2 per cent in 2006 had a limited impact on levels of fragmentation in the Knesset.

The alternative chosen in Israel was a move from a Knesset/council elected prime minister/mayor to a method of directly elected prime minister/mayor. Although considered successful at the local government level (see below), subsequent implementation of this system in the national elections of 1996 and 1999 led to unanticipated outcomes (Brichta 2001). Representation of parties of elected prime ministers became much smaller in the Knesset (Kenig et al. 2004), weakening the prime minister's and the government's influence there. Hence, the reform was scrapped at the national level and, in the 2003 elections, the method of a Knesset-elected prime minister was back, with some modifications.

Continued political instability, reflected by rapid turnover of ministers in most government ministries and the consistent inability of the Knesset to complete its four-year term,[4] led to renewed pressures for reform in 2006. Calls had been either for a presidential regime or alternative steps such as a further increase in the election threshold, integration of a regional element into the proportional election method and integration of party primaries into the main elections (IDI 2006; Megidor 2007). However, such proposals have not gained sufficient political support to be adopted.

### Local government elections in Israel and the evolving local democracy crisis

Legislation concerning local elections in Israel was reformed in 1975. The two major changes were the shift from a system of council-elected mayors to a system of directly elected ones and the separation of local elections from national elections. Direct elections immensely strengthened the power of mayors, diminishing their dependence on external power brokers, party nomination committees and party centres. National parties continued to play a role in local politics (except for the regional councils), but new dependencies emerged in the other direction – some runners in the party primaries for national elections sought the support of influential mayors to recruit votes (Torgovnik 2001). Moreover, in the triangle of power within local governments between elected mayors, elected council members and professional bureaucracy, the power tilted very much in favour of the mayors. Checks on the power of mayors at the local level have become rather weak. Council members are all but unable to vote the mayor out of power. Being unpaid, most of them lack the time and resources to monitor effectively municipal affairs, and those appointed by the mayor to a salaried position would obviously play a limited monitoring role. Municipal bureaucracies tend to be weaker than those of central government ministries. Bureaucracies tend to be stronger in larger cities, whereas in small local and regional councils, management of the municipality by the mayor can result in a 'one man show'. Nevertheless, local political cultures and norms of administration vary widely from one local authority to another, depending on the attributes of the local communities and on the character of the mayor.

Candidates running for council membership or for the mayor's position are of several types. Some represent national parties, whereas others head independent lists, although practically identified with a national party. Candidates of a third type are completely independent. Whereas party affiliation is sometimes a liability in the election campaign, the major advantage of mayors affiliated to national parties is in access to politicians at the central state level. Candidates may prefer running for independent lists when they are members of a national party that is unpopular in the specific locality, e.g. a Labour candidate running for mayor in a

---

4. Since the mid-1970s, nearly all Knesset elections were held early. Only in 1988 was the Knesset able to complete its full four-year term.

city dominated by Likud supporters (Torgovnik 2001). A party member may also run independently when the local party branch nominates another person as its candidate.

Separation of local elections from the national ones in 1978 (including a move to hold local elections every five years, instead of every four years) influenced voting behaviour considerably. The share of council members of independent lists in Jewish local authorities passed 10 per cent for the first time in 1978, growing rapidly in the 1990s, and reaching around 45 per cent in 1998 (Brichta 2001). Intended to encourage voters not to involve their political orientation at the national level in their local voting decision, the change was accompanied by an additional outcome – a sharp decline in voter turnout.

Voter turnout in Israel has traditionally been very high: over 80 per cent in the national elections and close to 80 per cent in the local elections (see Table 12.1). This is even more remarkable when taking into account that Israelis abroad cannot vote and that a substantial number of eligible voters practically do not live in Israel. The high turnout has partly been explained by deep rivalries over crucial issues at stake that concern the perpetual Israeli-Arab conflict. Voter turnout in local elections decreased somewhat in the post-1973 war elections, but the major drop occurred in 1978, when the local elections were held separately for the first time. Voter turnout stabilised between 1978 and 1998 at a level of 56 to 59 per cent, compared to 77 to 79 per cent in the national elections. The decrease in turnout could be partly attributed to the fact that local Election Day has taken place

*Table 12.1: Israel – voter turnout in local and national elections, 1950–2003*

|  | **Turnout local elections (%)** | **Turnout national elections (%)** |
| --- | --- | --- |
| 1950[1] | 79.6 | 86.9 |
| 1955 | 78.6 | 82.8 |
| 1959 | 79.0 | 81.6 |
| 1965 | 82.7 | 83.0 |
| 1969 | 79.0 | 81.7 |
| 1973 | 73.0 | 78.6 |
| 1978[1] | 57.3 | 79.2 |
| 1983[1] | 59.2 | 78.8 |
| 1989[1] | 59.5 | 79.6 |
| 1993[1] | 56.3 | 77.4 |
| 1998[1] | 57.4 | 78.7 |
| 2003[1] | 49.7 | 67.8 |
| 2006 |  | 63.5 |
| 2008[1] | 51.9 | 65.2 |

*Notes:* [1]Local elections did not take place together with the national elections. Turnout in the national elections refers to elections that took place up to two years before or after the national elections.

*Source:* Central Bureau of Statistics.

on an ordinary work day since 1993. An all-time low of 49.7 per cent voted in the 2003 local elections.

Voter turnout dropped even more sharply in the national elections of 2003 and 2006, stabilising at around 65 per cent in 2009 (see Table 12.1). This drop seems to indicate a long-term change in voting behaviour and a convergence of voter turnout rates with those common in most democracies. For example, a phenomenon of high voter turnout in the first local elections held after democratisation followed by a continuous decline in levels of participation in local elections has been observed in the Czech Republic (Kostelecky and Cermak 2005). Hence, the uniqueness of voting behaviour in Israel consisted, perhaps, of the persistence of a high turnout for so many years after independence.

The argument on an evolving local democracy crisis has also pointed to increasing fragmentation of municipal councils, partly a consequence of low voter turnout that gives disproportionate power to small well-organised groups. In extreme cases in Arab local authorities, each elected member represented a different party, in this case not because of low turnout, but because of kinship-based voting behaviour (Ghanem 2001). Disproportional representation of organised pressure groups makes the task of forming a stable coalition difficult. Indeed, in quite a few local authorities, including large cities, mayors faced a recalcitrant council or an even-numbered council, i.e. without a majority coalition (Shafat 1992). Such a phenomenon has been a product of the 1978 shift to a directly-elected mayor method without a complementary move from a proportionally-elected council into a majoritarian election, and seems to have intensified with the decreasing turnout and growing fragmentation of councils.

### The left-right divide in Israeli politics

Israeli politics at the national level was dominated by left-wing socialist parties, from pre-statehood years (the early 1930s) until 1977. The moderate left wing, led by the Labour party, traditionally formed a coalition with the large religious party. The much weaker right wing included both the political-nationalistic right, increasingly appealing to the lower classes, and an economic right, appealing to a segment of the middle class. Communists and Jewish ultra-religious parties were marginal.

The 'political upheaval' of 1977 revealed a new political alignment that remained rather stable until 2006, although the details of parties running for elections and the composition of coalitions changed frequently. The dominant power in Israeli politics subsequently became the right-wing religious block, mainly identified by its political-nationalistic views towards the Arab-Israeli conflict, but also by a more religious orientation than the centre-left block. Although having a solid electoral base among the Jewish lower classes, it also has increasingly tilted towards neoliberal economic ideology. The centre-left block was mainly distinguished by more moderate attitudes towards the Arab-Israeli conflict, and by a stronger support base among the secular middle class. Substantial variations in attitudes towards social and economic policy were evident within this block. A distinct Arab block was occasionally perceived as part of the centre-left block, particularly during the years of the Oslo peace process, but this association has diminished since 2000. The far-left has completely disappeared from Israeli politics. Far-right parties were occasionally represented in the Knesset, but the distinction between the far-right and the main right-wing religious block is often unclear.

Voter left-right self-placement reveals a sharp distinction between right wing and/or religious parties and centre-left parties along the lines described above. This is reflected also in the left-right cultural scale, referring to attitudes towards God, family values and women's work. Jewish religious and ultra-religious parties tilt to the right, whereas secular parties – Labour, Meretz and Shinui – tilt to the left. However, on the economic scale that measures support for neoliberal ideologies versus welfare state values, variations between different parties are small and inconsistent (see Figures A12.1 and A12.2 in the Appendix).

The party realignment that characterised Israeli politics for more than a quarter of a century destabilised in the 2006 elections. The core parties of both blocks suffered unprecedented setbacks, and the new Kadima party, formed by Ariel Sharon, could not have been easily classified as fitting one of the two old blocks. The prominence of the Arab-Israeli conflict as the major dividing political issue among Israel's Jewish population had somewhat diminished, while economic policies gained greater influence on voting decisions, leading to greater divisions among the working classes. However, the Arab-Jewish conflict has since regained its place as the prime issue on the public agenda.

## Major explanatory variables of voting behaviour

Compositional variables, including those relating to major societal divisions between Jews and Arabs, between non-ultra-orthodox and ultra-orthodox Jews, and between new immigrants and veteran Israelis, have a major role in shaping Israeli politics. Socio-economic status is another compositional explanatory variable, influencing voter turnout and inclination to vote for right wing, left wing or independent lists (in local elections). The Jewish lower class has long been identified with the right wing that represents a hard-line approach to the Arab-Israeli conflict. The religious and ultra-religious vote for their sectional parties, identified with the right wing since 1977 in terms of attitudes towards to the Arab-Israeli conflict. This strengthening link between religious and right-wing attitudes indicates that socio-economic status may be diminishing as a causal determinant of political orientation in Israel. Instead, ethnicity and religion have risen in importance. The Jewish lower classes contain a large component of Jews of Middle Eastern and North African origin – traditionally, they tend to take a more hard-line view of the Arab-Israeli conflict. Religious Jews that form the hard core of settlers in the West Bank and Gaza Strip vote right wing, and immigrants from the former USSR also tend to vote for parties on the right.

Local authority size has long been acknowledged as a contextual factor influencing voting behaviour in local elections. The more direct nature of local democracy in small local authorities could lead to higher voter turnout than in larger cities. In addition, independent candidates are more common in small local authorities, where local politics is less partisan in nature, and election campaigns are less costly and challenging organisationally. Such influences have been identified elsewhere, such as in the Czech Republic (Kostelecky and Cermak 2005).

The impact of contextual variables would traditionally be expected to be overshadowed by social composition. For example, the rate of home ownership in Israel (over 70 per cent of households) does not vary widely between local authorities. Only 6 per cent of households are social renters and 15 per cent are private renters (although central cities and locations popular among students have a greater share of private renters). The role of diversity at the local level remains unclear. In local authorities, where secular and ultra-religious Jews live together, one can expect the secular population to tilt towards the centre-left, better representing interests of the non-religious population. The question of whether proximity to Arabs in mixed cities such as Akko and Lod, or in the Galilee, increases the tendency of Jews to vote for right-wing parties is an interesting one. Such an effect is difficult to trace in a broad statistical analysis, being overshadowed by the extremely strong spatial correlation with socio-economic status.

Based on the experience of North American metropolitan areas, suburbanisation might be expected to be associated with greater political support for neo-liberalism, reflected in a tendency to vote for right-wing parties (Walks 2004b). According to Walks (2004a), suburbanisation influences lifestyle preferences that may affect voting behaviour. Dependence on privatised modes of consumption in the suburbs increases the support for liberal but exclusionary policies, associated with right-wing orientation, whereas inner cities have greater stakes in the left-wing associated welfare state.

The Israeli case, however, is likely to differ in this respect, where the right-left distinction refers primarily to attitudes towards the Arab-Israeli conflict. Higher socio-economic status is associated with the left wing, whereas support for the more hard-line right wing is solid in lower socio-economic status Jewish localities and among the religious population. Thus, suburban localities may be more characterised by right-wing orientation, particularly in the Tel Aviv and Haifa metropolitan areas, not because of middle-class suburban attitudes, but because of their relatively low socio-economic status (on average). Middle-class suburbanisation may strengthen left-wing voting. It should also be noted that a large segment of the suburban population, including the outer suburbs, actually lives in rather densely-populated neighbourhoods, thus not really experiencing the lifestyles and landscapes of a North American suburb (Gonen 1995).

## Inter-local variations – insights from a typology of cities and suburbs

Attributes of each of the seven types of Israeli local authorities (excluding the rural regional councils) are presented in Table 12.2. The four central cities of Israel's metropolitan areas are, on average, larger in population size than any type of suburban local authorities, but they are less densely-populated than other large cities of more than 100,000 inhabitants. Smallest and least dense are low-density

*Table 12.2: Israel – types of municipalities by selected demographic and socio-economic attributes, 2003[1] (unweighted means for local authorities)*

| | | Type of municipality | | | | | | | |
|---|---|---|---|---|---|---|---|---|---|
| | | Of those: | | | | | | | |
| | Urban concen-trations | Central cities | Other large cities[2] | Low-density suburbs | Minority suburbs[3] | Affluent suburbs[4] | Middle-class suburbs[5] | Poor suburbs[6] | Total |
| N | 14 | 4 | 10 | 44 | 70 | 13 | 30 | 26 | 197 |
| Population (thousands) | 216,1 | 377,2 | 151,6 | 6,0 | 11,6 | 37,4 | 26,9 | 24,3 | 30,6 |
| Population density[7] | 20,638 | 17,033 | 22,080 | 5,686 | 10,278 | 11,499 | 12,388 | 12,539 | 10,689 |
| Distance to centre (km) | 14.5 | 0 | 20.3 | 37.3 | 40.0 | 16.0 | 35.6 | 42.9 | 35.7 |
| % new immigrants[8] | 22 | 19 | 23 | 6 | 0 | 8 | 23 | 21 | 10 |
| % up to age 18 | 28 | 28 | 29 | 34 | 46 | 29 | 29 | 39 | 37 |
| % age 60 and over | 17 | 17 | 17 | 9 | 5 | 14 | 13 | 10 | 9 |
| Socio-economic index | 5.79 | 6.00 | 5.70 | 7.48 | 2.76 | 8.08 | 5.70 | 3.54 | 4.93 |
| Employment income inequality (Gini) | 0.44 | 0.47 | 0.42 | 0.43 | 0.34 | 0.43 | 0.39 | 0.38 | 0.38 |
| Homeowners (%) | 71 | 65 | 74 | 83 | 93 | 78 | 74 | 65 | 82 |

*Sources*: [1]Based on data of the Central Bureau of Statistics. The data excludes the rural regional councils. [2]Population of over 100,000. [3]Arab majority. [4]SES 8–10 (10 – highest). [5]SES 5–7. [6]SES 1–4. [7]Density per square km is measured out of the total residential built up area. [8]Immigrated to Israel since 1989.

suburbs – being defined by their exurban or low-density suburban nature. Poor suburbs, minority (Arab) suburbs and low-density suburbs are, on average, most distant from the central city of their metropolitan area.

Large cities, middle-class and poor suburbs have the highest proportions of new immigrants. The proportion of new immigrants is very low in affluent sub-urbs and in low-density suburbs and reaches zero in minority (Arab) localities. These variations are largely a product of variations in the availability of affordable housing, except for the case of Arab localities that are practically not a feasible residential choice for immigrant Jews.

Minority suburbs have an extremely young age pyramid. Poor non-minority suburbs, on the one hand, and low-density suburbs, on the other hand, also have a high proportion of children, whereas central cities and other large cities have the highest proportion of elderly. Affluent suburbs and low-density suburbs are characterised by highest levels of economic well-being, in contrast with poor suburbs and minority suburbs. The Gini coefficient representing class heterogeneity is highest in central cities, while being lowest in the poor minority suburbs, followed by poor (non-minority) suburbs.

## The metropolitan dimension of voting behaviour

Variations in voting behaviour in Israel are clearly manifested in metropolitan structure and have metropolitan implications, although it is difficult to identify more than a few specific influences of ecological characteristics of place that do not merely reflect the socio-economic and ethnic makeup of communities. The first section examines voter turnout in local municipal authorities and the question of how changes in the political ecology of the metropolis may manifest in council fragmentation, followed by analysis of Knesset elections. The second section examines the contextual effects on partisanship in local and Knesset elections. The third section examines the effect of the metropolitan context on political attitudes related to globalisation, sociocultural values, and political economy.

## Voter turnout

First, it is important to see how electoral participation maps on to the typology of city and suburban communities. Table 12.3 shows that voter turnout in local elections is lowest in central cities and is also low in other large cities. Meanwhile, the municipal councils of minority suburbs are most fragmented, largely because local elections in these localities represent competition of extended families over municipal resources. The mayor's party has a rather small share in the councils of the central cities. This share in the cities of Tel Aviv, Haifa and Beer Sheva was 13 per cent, 19 per cent and 16 per cent respectively in 2003. An exceptional rise in the share of the mayor's party in Jerusalem between 1998 and 2003 (from 10 to 29 per cent) is explained by the election of an ultra-religious mayor – the ultra-religious population of different sects tends to have high voter turnout and votes as a block according to the instructions of their religious leaders.

The share of municipal council members of independent lists is highest in minority suburbs, where these lists represent families, followed by low-density suburbs, where local politics are of a most non-partisan suburban nature, characterising also the rural regional councils not included in our study. The share of independent lists is lowest in central cities, followed by other large cities and by poor suburbs, which are still the domain of national parties (see Table 12.3).

The above variations between types of local authorities are evident also when metropolitan areas are examined separately. Variations in voting behaviour between types of local authorities were nearly identical in the Tel Aviv and Haifa metropolitan areas. Voter turnout here is lowest in the inner part of the metropolis and highest in the outer suburbs. The prime explanations for this spatial pattern are the smaller population size of local authorities in the outer parts and the large number of Arab local authorities in metropolitan fringe areas. Our initial

*Table 12.3: Israel – selected measures of the 1998 and 2003 local elections by type of municipality*

| Type of municipality | N | Voter turn-out | Share of mayor's party | % council members of right wing and religious parties | % council members of indepen-dent lists |
|---|---|---|---|---|---|
| *1998* | | | | | |
| Urban concentrations | 13 | 50.3 | 20 | 32 | 41 |
|    Central cities | 4 | 47.2 | 19 | 32 | 45 |
|    Other large cities | 9 | 51.7 | 20 | 31 | 40 |
| Low-density suburbs | 30 | 76.2 | 42 | 20 | 69 |
| Minority suburbs | 58 | 92.1 | 9 | 1 | 90 |
| Affluent suburbs | 13 | 64.7 | 33 | 19 | 46 |
| Middle-class suburbs | 26 | 66.7 | 30 | 29 | 48 |
| Poor (non-minority) suburbs | 20 | 73.0 | 21 | 43 | 41 |
| Total | 160 | 77.0 | 23 | 18 | 66 |
| *2003* | | | | | |
| Urban concentrations | 14 | 41.9 | 22 | 37 | 45 |
|    Central cities | 4 | 34.6 | 19 | 37 | 41 |
|    Other large cities | 10 | 44.9 | 24 | 37 | 46 |
| Low-density suburbs | 30 | 69.5 | 34 | 18 | 73 |
| Minority suburbs | 53 | 89.4 | 10 | 0 | 89 |
| Affluent suburbs | 13 | 53.9 | 33 | 16 | 62 |
| Middle-class suburbs | 27 | 58.8 | 30 | 30 | 59 |
| Poor suburbs | 19 | 66.8 | 24 | 42 | 47 |
| Total | 156 | 70.3 | 23 | 18 | 69 |

hypotheses points at a powerful explanation of two compositional variables – the Jewish-Arab distinction and socio-economic status – and one contextual variable – population size of the local authority – on variations in voting patterns between local authorities in Israel. One could argue, however, that the explanatory power of these variables conceals the impact of meaningful variables that are perhaps less easily measurable (and still unknown), but which could have a considerable causal effect on voting behaviour. Given the relatively small number of local authorities and multicollinearity problems, multivariate models that include a full array of variables may not produce reliable results. Thus our final (limited) models are those that fit best to each dependent variable, excluding non-significant variables and those that create multicollinearity problems.

### *Voter turnout in local elections – a substantial drop in large Jewish local authorities*

The major variable influencing turnout was found to be population size (see Table 12.4 and Table 12.5): voter turnout in large local authorities is lower than in small ones. The more direct nature of local democracy in small local authorities, stronger ties between citizens and those running for elections, as well as the fact that narrow personal interests could be affected more directly by election results in small local authorities, encourages people to vote. Another prominent factor is the Arab/Jewish distinction: voter turnout in Arab local authorities is much higher than among Jewish local authorities. Voter turnout in an average Arab local authority was around 90 per cent in 2003 compared to 60 per cent among Jewish local authorities, and no more than 42 per cent among Jewish local authorities with more than 100,000 inhabitants (see Table 12.4). Some Arab local authorities even had a voter turnout of over 96 per cent, in one case close to 98 per cent. However, in addition to indicating a well-developed civil society and awareness of local politics, these extremely high participation rates also represent competition by extended families over municipal resources – jobs and contracts (Mustafa 2010).

High voter turnout is associated with low economic status, even after controlling for the extremely high turnout in the low socio-economic status Arab local authorities (see Table 12.5). However, age structure was found to be a far more powerful explanatory variable of voter turnout in local elections. The proportion of young population had a strong positive influence on turnout in the 2003 local elections, and the proportion of elderly had a negative influence on turnout in the 1998 elections.

Although spatial variables were not significant in 2003, and were of minor significance in 1998, it is clear that the central cities in all four metropolitan areas had extremely low voter turnout. Tel Aviv had the lowest turnout of all local authorities in Israel in 2003 – 29 per cent. Haifa had the second lowest, and Beer Sheva and Jerusalem had the fifth and sixth lowest (the third and fourth lowest were Bat Yam and Holon – two inner suburbs of Tel Aviv). In all central cities, except for Jerusalem, voter turnout dropped considerably between 1998 and 2003.

It should be noted that multivariate models for both 1998 and 2003 had a very high explanatory power (adjusted $R^2$ of 0.88 and 0.91) and are mostly similar. This indicates sound and stable results concerning the major impact of compositional variables – age structure, the Arab/Jewish distinction and socio-economic status – and of one contextual variable – population size – on voter turnout. A problem of low and declining voter turnout thus characterises Jewish local authorities, mainly large cities and local authorities characterised by a relatively old and affluent population.

*Table 12.4: Israel – voter turnout in the 1998 and 2003 local elections by population sector and size[1]*

|  | 1998 | | 2003 | |
|---|---|---|---|---|
|  | **Voter turnout** | **N** | **Voter turnout** | **N** |
| Total | 77.0 | 160 | 70.3 | 156 |
| *Population sector* | | | | |
| Jewish[2] | 68.4 | 102 | 60.5 | 103 |
| Arab | 92.1 | 58 | 89.4 | 53 |
| *Population size* | | | | |
| Up to 10,000 | 84.5 | 76 | 79.0 | 61 |
| 10,001–20,000 | 82.3 | 28 | 78.6 | 29 |
| 20,001–30,000 | 75.8 | 16 | 70.7 | 20 |
| 30,001–50,000 | 64.4 | 20 | 61.1 | 19 |
| 50,001–100,000 | 60.6 | 9 | 54.3 | 13 |
| More than 100,000 | 49.4 | 11 | 41.9 | 14 |
| *Population size (excluding Arab localities)* | | | | |
| Up to 10,000 | 76.9 | 39 | 69.8 | 34 |
| 10,001–20,000 | 73.0 | 14 | 65.9 | 14 |
| 20,001–30,000 | 68.3 | 11 | 62.4 | 14 |
| 30,001–50,000 | 63.2 | 19 | 56.4 | 15 |
| 50,001–100,000 | 57.6 | 8 | 52.3 | 12 |
| More than 100,000 | 49.4 | 11 | 41.9 | 14 |

*Notes:* [1]The table includes unweighted means of local authorities in each category. [2]Including mixed local authorities with a Jewish majority.
*Source:* Based on data of Central Bureau of Statistics and the Ministry of Interior.

*Table 12.5: Israel – regression models of local authority characteristics explaining voter turnout in the 1998 and 2003 local elections[1]*

| Independent variables | Coefficients | |
|---|---|---|
|  | **1998** | **2003** |
| Ln (population) | *−0.352* | *−0.426* |
| SES – Mean including employment | *−0.232* | **−0.075** |
| Arab local authority | *0.256* | *0.302* |
| % young population (up to 18) |  | *0.399* |
| % elderly (age 60+) | *−0.305* |  |
| Population density | *−0.149* |  |
| Distance from metro centre | *−0.097* |  |
| Jerusalem metro[#] | **−0.065** |  |
| Adjusted $R^2$ | 0.88 | 0.91 |
| N | 148 | 141 |
| Adj. $R^2$ – compositional variables only[3] |  | 0.77 |
| Adj. $R^2$ – contextual variables only |  | 0.48 |

*Notes:* [1]The Table presents standardised regression coefficients and their significance. Only significant variables were kept in the final models due to multicollinearity in the smaller sample. For boldface coefficients, $p<0.05$; for boldface italicised coefficients, $p<0.01$. [#] Base category: Tel Aviv metro. [3] SES, Arab local authority, % young population.

## *Local government council fragmentation – not a new phenomenon*

Growing fragmentation of local government councils, partly as a consequence of declining voter turnout, is viewed as a problem in the functioning of local authorities in Israel. In some cases, mayors were elected with a very wide margin, but their parties won only few seats and formed small minorities in the councils, because supporters of the mayor gave their council vote to a different party representing their particular interests. Even in the city of Tel Aviv, the party of the popular mayor received only 11.4 per cent of the votes (four out of thirty-one seats), and the senior citizens party came out as the largest party with 16.7 per cent of the votes (six seats). In Arab local authorities, the mayor's party/list in some cases received no votes and no seats at all. This has usually been a consequence of deliberately planned voting behaviour aimed to secure another seat at the local council (when the mayor's party does not have any seats in a council of eleven members, for example, the mayor becomes a twelfth council member).

Our results indicate that in fact there was no change in levels of council fragmentation between 1998 and 2003. The average numbers of parties per council member grew insignificantly from 0.55 to 0.56 and the average share of the mayor's party in the council remained stable at 23 per cent. Hence the problem, to the extent that it is a problem, did not surface only in 2003, but practically emerged after the electoral reform of 1978.

The prime variable influencing council fragmentation in 2003 was the distinction between Arab and Jewish local authorities (see Table 12.6). Arab local authorities are characterised by very high levels of fragmentation – the average share of the mayor's party in the council of these local authorities reached only 10 per cent.

*Table 12.6: Israel – regression models of local authority characteristics explaining council fragmentation, 2003 local elections*

| | Dependent variables | |
|---|---|---|
| | The share of the mayor's party (% of council | % council members of independent |
| Independent variables | members) | parties/lists |
| Ln (population) | *−0.206* | |
| SES – Mean including employment | | *0.425* |
| Arab local authority | *−0.793* | *0.774* |
| Rate of home ownership | **0.253** | |
| Distance from metro centre | | **0.142** |
| Adjusted R$^2$ | 0.36 | 0.39 |
| N | 141 | 141 |
| Adj. R$^2$ – compositional variables only$^2$ | 0.28 | 0.38 |
| Adj. R$^2$ – contextual variables only | 0.05 | 0.01 |

*Notes:* The table presents standardised regression coefficients and their significance.
For boldface coefficients, $p < 0.05$; for boldface italicised coefficients, $p < 0.01$.

On average, about two-thirds of council members in an Israeli local authority are members of independent parties/lists, although some of these lists are unofficially linked to a national party, and persons running for the mayor's position as independent candidates could be active members of political parties. The proportion of independent council members slightly increased between 1998 and 2003, continuing a trend that gained momentum since 1978.

Again, the prime variable predicting the proportion of independent council members is the Arab-Jewish distinction: Arab local authorities had a much greater proportion of council members who are part of independent lists (see Table 12.6) – usually lists associated with extended families or segments of extended families. Another important explanatory variable is socio-economic status: the proportion of independent council members tended to be higher in local authorities characterised by high socio-economic status. This correlation is strongly evident only among Jewish local authorities. National parties – particularly right-wing and religious parties – are much more powerful in Jewish local authorities of low socio-economic status. Whereas on average 91 per cent of council members were members of independent lists in the most affluent local authorities in 2003, among the lowest socio-economic status Jewish local authorities, the figure was only 25 per cent. There was also a strong negative correlation between socio-economic status and votes for right-wing and religious parties in the local elections, running from 65 per cent of council members in the poorest local authorities in 2003 to zero in the wealthiest. Thus, in low socio-economic localities, where the parties still predominate, it is the right-wing parties that take most of the votes.

### Voter turnout in national elections – a different behaviour

Voting behaviour at the national level differs considerably from that at the local level, at least in the propensity to vote (see Table 12.7). While turnout in the national elections is also low in the central cities and other large cities, similar to local patterns, participation in the national elections is nonetheless much higher than in the local elections and does not vary that much among localities. Turnout in the suburbs also remains elevated in comparison with municipal elections (except for minority and/or Arab communities) demonstrating that Israel, like many developed nations, has been experiencing delocalisation. Voter turnout in local elections tends to be highest in minority suburbs, and it is high in low-density suburbs – due to the more direct nature of democracy in these small local authorities – and in poor non-minority suburbs – perhaps because these communities are more easily mobilised by party machines. However, in the national elections, turnout in minority suburbs is low, while being highest in low-density suburbs.

Not only is voter turnout much higher at the national level, but the factors influencing turnout differ as well. The Arab-Jewish distinction is a significant explanatory variable of voter turnout, but in a completely different direction than in the local elections. Arabs are characterised by a lower turnout than Jews in the national elections (see Table 12.8) and the gap between the two groups widened between 1998 and 2003 – mainly in light of Arab frustration associated with

*Table 12.7: Israel – selected measures of the 1999 and 2003 Knesset elections by type of municipality*

| Type of municipality | N | Voter turnout | National/local turnout differential |
|---|---|---|---|
| *1999* | | | |
| Urban concentrations | 14 | 77.9 | 27.3 |
|   Central cities | 4 | 75.7 | 28.5 |
|   Other large cities | 10 | 78.8 | 26.7 |
| Low-density suburbs | 43 | 85.6 | 8.1 |
| Minority suburbs | 70 | 77.8 | −13.4 |
| Affluent suburbs | 15 | 83.6 | 19.5 |
| Middle-class suburbs | 29 | 80.7 | 14.1 |
| Poor suburbs | 26 | 81.0 | 6.3 |
| Total | 197 | 80.8 | 3.6 |
| *2003* | | | |
| Urban concentrations | 14 | 66.8 | 24.9 |
|   Central cities | 4 | 64.7 | 30.0 |
|   Other large cities | 10 | 67.7 | 22.8 |
| Low-density suburbs | 44 | 77.2 | 7.5 |
| Minority suburbs | 70 | 63.1 | −25.0 |
| Affluent suburbs | 13 | 75.7 | 23.0 |
| Middle-class suburbs | 30 | 68.6 | 9.4 |
| Poor suburbs | 26 | 70.3 | 0.9 |
| Total | 197 | 69.1 | −1.3 |

*Notes:* National/local turnout differential – voter turnout in national elections minus voter turnout in local elections.

the second Intifada and the loss of influence of Arab members of the Knesset on policies and allocations at the national level. The regression model explaining the national/local voter turnout differential confirms that the Arab-Jewish distinction is a prime explanatory variable (see Table 12.9). Arabs have a far lower voter turnout in national than in local elections. The variation in voter turnout between different population groups is narrower at the national level than at the local level, and the regression models on voters turnout have much lower $R^2$ (see Table 12.9). The highest voter turnout is in the Jewish ultra-religious local authorities (see Table 12.8), but these are not included as a separate category in the multivariate analysis because of their small number.

Differences in the effects of metropolitan context on local and national voting behaviour are evident when modelled using linear regression (see Table 12.9). Socio-economic status influences voter turnout positively at national elections, but has the opposite impact in local elections. The impact of population size, Arab local authorities, and age structure on voter turnout works similarly in national and local elections: small populations and young age structures are associated with higher turnout. However, the concentration of young people, Arab local authori-ties, as well as distance from the centre, all decrease the gap between national and

*Table 12.8: Israel – selected voting patterns in the 2003 Knesset elections by population sector and socio-economic index of the local authority*

|  | Voter turnout | % votes for right wing & religious parties | % votes for centre-left parties | % votes for Arab parties | N |
|---|---|---|---|---|---|
| Total | 69.1 | 42 | 30 | 22 | 197 |
| *Population sector* | | | | | |
| Jewish | 72.0 | 59 | 36 | 1 | 123 |
| Jewish – ultra-religious | 85.7 | 92 | 3 | 0 | 4 |
| Arab | 63.1 | 10 | 23 | 62 | 70 |
| *Socio-economic index (excluding Arab localities)* | | | | | |
| 1–2 (lowest) | 71.5 | 78 | 13 | 0 | 2 |
| 3–4 | 67.8 | 74 | 18 | 2 | 23 |
| 5–6 | 69.7 | 68 | 27 | 1 | 39 |
| 7–8 | 75.1 | 51 | 44 | 0 | 45 |
| 9–10 | 75.8 | 31 | 64 | 0 | 14 |

*Note:* The table includes unweighted means of local authorities in each category. It does not include elections to rural regional councils.

*Source:* Based on data of the Ministry of Interior.

local turnout, whereas population size, homeownership and income diversity work to increase the turnout gap. To this end, the latter three variables, all of which are contextual variables, are demonstrated to augment the tendency toward delocalisation – similar to the observations made in a number of developed nations.

## Partisanship in national elections

Israel's many political parties can be categorised into three main groups in which alliances have tended to form: Arab parties, centre-left parties, and right-wing and religious parties. The way that support for these three groups of parties varies across the typology of urban and suburban municipalities can be seen in Table 12.10. The centre-left parties have stronger support in the inner parts of the metropolitan areas, particularly in the more affluent sectors (a close mapping shows, for instance, a concentration to the north in the city of Tel Aviv). The centre-left also enjoys considerable support in small 'islands' in suburban space – affluent albeit rather small suburbs and exurbs, and in lower-density suburbs. On the other hand, the right-wing/religious block is particularly strong in large and medium-sized cities, and in suburban space in lower- and middle-class cities. Right-wing parties receive their highest levels of support from poor non-minority suburbs. Arab parties are prominent mainly in Arab localities; all in the outer suburbs (see Figures A12.3a and A12.3b in the Appendix of this chapter for maps of partisanship in the 2003 Knesset elections).

Thus, the major variables influencing voting preferences at the national level were the Jewish-Arab distinction and socio-economic status. Indeed, given the

*Table 12.9: Israel – regression models of local authority characteristics explaining selected voting patterns in the 2003 Knesset elections*

| Variables included | Voter turnout | | National/local voter turnout differential[1] | |
|---|---|---|---|---|
| | Full | Limited | Full | Limited |
| SES – Mean income employment | 0.04 | *0.33* | 0.09 | |
| Immigrants (%) | −0.51 | | −0.00 | |
| Age under 19 (%) | 0.34 | *0.29* | 0.43 | *−0.19* |
| Age 60+ (%) | −0.10 | | −0.08 | – |
| Ln (population) | *−0.31* | *−0.25* | *−0.29* | *0.20* |
| Population density | 0.10 | | 0.08 | |
| Homeownership (%) | −0.03 | | −0.04 | *0.13* |
| Distance from metro centre | **−0.16** | *−0.19* | **−0.16** | **−0.08** |
| Gini coefficient | 0.13 | | 0.12 | *0.25* |
| Cars per household | 0.32 | | 0.32 | |
| Arab local authority | **−0.49** | *−0.45* | **−0.50** | **−0.54** |
| Tel Aviv metro | 0.05 | | 0.17 | |
| Jerusalem metro | 0.05 | | 0.10 | |
| Voter turnout | | | | |
| Adjusted R² | 0.41 | 0.38 | 0.88 | 0.88 |
| N | 166 | 166 | 166 | 146 |
| Adj. R² – compositional variables only[2] | | 0.33 | | 0.78 |
| Adj. R² – contextual variables only | | 0.10 | | 0.74 |

*Notes:* The table presents standardised coefficients. Full models are presented for the sake of comparison with other countries included in the book. [1]National elections turnout (%) minus local elections turnout. For boldface coefficients, $p<0.05$; for boldface italicised coefficients, $p<0.01$.

election results in a particular local authority, it is possible to predict with almost complete accuracy whether the authorities are Jewish or Arab, as well as their socio-economic status if they are Jewish.

OLS regression analysis demonstrates how compositional and contextual variables operate on partisanship in the Israeli Knesset (see Table 12.11).[5] Among Jewish local authorities, the higher the socio-economic status, the lower is the percentage of votes given to right-wing and religious parties and the higher the percentage of votes given to centre-left parties. The mean percentage of votes for right-wing and religious parties in 2003 was 78 per cent in the lowest socio-economic status Jewish local authorities and 31 per cent in the most affluent local authorities, whereas voting for the centre-left consistently climbed from 13 per

5.  An attempt to add the typology of municipalities into the multivariate models of voting preferences revealed that the fundamental compositional and contextual variables – SES, age and Jewish-Arab distinction – had greater explanatory power than the typology. The only dummy variable of the typology included in the final model was minority suburbs, distinguishing Arab local authorities; all others were dropped because of multicollinearity problems and inferior explanatory power compared with other variables.

*Table 12.10: Israel – selected measures of the 1999 and 2003 Knesset elections by type of municipality*

| Type of municipality | N | % votes for right-wing and religious parties | % votes for centre-left parties | % vote for Arab parties |
|---|---|---|---|---|
| *1999* | | | | |
| Urban concentrations | 14 | 59 | 34 | 1 |
| Central cities | 4 | 55 | 37 | 2 |
| Other large cities | 10 | 61 | 32 | 0 |
| Low-density suburbs | 43 | 49 | 44 | 0 |
| Minority suburbs | 70 | 15 | 20 | 61 |
| Affluent suburbs | 15 | 44 | 51 | 0 |
| Middle-class suburbs | 29 | 61 | 31 | 0 |
| Poor non-minority suburbs | 26 | 76 | 16 | 2 |
| Total | 197 | 42 | 29 | 22 |
| *2003* | | | | |
| Urban concentrations | 14 | 63 | 33 | 1 |
| Central cities | 4 | 57 | 37 | 2 |
| Other large cities | 10 | 65 | 32 | 0 |
| Low-density suburbs | 44 | 50 | 45 | 0 |
| Minority suburbs | 70 | 10 | 23 | 62 |
| Affluent suburbs | 13 | 47 | 50 | 0 |
| Middle-class suburbs | 30 | 65 | 31 | 0 |
| Poor suburbs | 26 | 76 | 16 | 2 |
| Total | 197 | 42 | 30 | 23 |

cent in the poorest local authorities to 64 per cent in the most affluent ones. Age structure is an important explanatory factor in national elections; in particular, a high proportion of elderly is associated with voting for centre-left parties (see Table 12.11).

Contextual variables that reveal significant effects on partisanship include population size and homeownership. However, although population size operated in the expected direction (i.e. in favour of centre-left parties and dampening support for right-wing and religious parties), the coefficients for homeownership contrasted with those derived from North American analysis – in this case, augmenting support for the left. This demonstrates that the effect of a variable such as homeownership remains context-dependent.

Location in the Jerusalem metropolitan area influenced the proportion of votes for the right-wing positively and the proportion of votes to the centre-left negatively. Jerusalem is considered a right-wing and religious city, surrounded by West Bank Jewish settlements that tilt towards the right. It is interesting to note that, unlike the typical image presented in the mainstream media, residence in a Jewish local authority on the periphery (the Beer Sheva region and/or northern Israel) does not increase the right-wing preferences of its voters. Indeed, it is low socio-

*Table 12.11: Israel – regression models of local authority characteristics explaining the proportion of votes for three major party groups in the 2003 Knesset elections*

| | Right wing and religious parties | | Centre-left parties | | Arab parties | |
|---|---|---|---|---|---|---|
| Variables included | Full | Limited | Full | Limited | Full | Limited |
| SES | *−0.39* | *−0.358* | *0.89* | *0.80* | −0.13 | |
| Immigrants (%) | 0.02 | | −0.01 | | 0.02 | |
| Age under 19 (%) | *−0.29* | | *0.42* | | 0.00 | |
| Age 60+ (%) | −0.11 | *−0.130* | *0.30* | *0.32* | −0.07 | |
| Ln (population) | *0.15* | | **0.17** | | 0.08 | **0.07** |
| Population Density | 0.06 | | −0.06 | | −0.02 | |
| Homeownership (%) | −0.06 | | 0.15 | *0.18* | 0.01 | |
| Distance to centre | −0.01 | | 0.09 | | −0.04 | |
| Gini Index | 0.03 | | 0.00 | | −0.04 | |
| Cars per HH | −0.14 | | 0.09 | | 0.11 | |
| Tel Aviv metro | **0.08** | | **−0.21** | **−0.11** | 0.01 | |
| Jerusalem metro | *0.13* | *0.093* | **−0.22** | **−0.17** | −0.02 | |
| Arab local authority | *−1.04* | *−1.157* | 0.09 | *0.32* | *0.88* | *0.95* |
| Adjusted R² | 0.87 | 0.86 | 0.51 | 0.57 | 0.87 | 0.87 |
| N | 166 | 166 | 166 | 166 | 166 | 166 |

*Notes:* The table presents standardised coefficients. For boldface coefficients, $p < 0.05$; for boldface italicised coefficients, $p < 0.01$.

economic status that gives these local authorities their right-wing orientation.[6]

The 1999 and 2003 national elections were held under completely different circumstances, yet the electoral patterns are remarkably similar. In 1999, criticism over the malfunctioning of Netanyahu's right-wing Likud government led to the victory of the left-wing Labour Party, committed to the Oslo process, led by Barak. In 2003, the Labour government had already collapsed, in part as a result of the outbreak of the second Intifada. For the first time in decades, the victory of the Likud, headed by Sharon, could be predicted with very high certainty, and support for the Labour Party fell more than ever before. Still, these results show that determinants of political orientations change little over time in Israel and the impact of socio-economic status on voting behaviour remained as strong as ever.

---

6.    Hierarchical linear models (HLM) predicting the percentage of votes for right-wing and religious parties in the 2003 Knesset elections (not shown) revealed a somewhat more substantial effect of the metropolitan area than those for voter turnout in local elections, but an absolute lack of interaction effects, thus confirming the validity of OLS regressions that disregard interaction effects between lower-level local authority attributes and higher-level metropolitan attributes. HLM models also confirmed the lack of interaction effects on turnout.

## Metropolitanisation and political attitudes

Political attitudes related to the different attitudinal axes identified in the introduction to this volume also vary by metropolitan context. Table 12.12 details the position of each of the urban community types with respect to left-right political self-placement, economic policy preferences, sociocultural values, and positions with respect to globalisation and international trade. Left-right self-placement of voters confirms the anticipated variations explained by class and ethnicity: poor Jewish suburbs lean most to the right; affluent suburbs and low-density suburbs lean to the left; and voters of Arab minority suburbs are most extreme in self-placing themselves on the left – obviously not voting for right-wing hardliners in the Arab-Jewish conflict.

Orientations toward the economic and globalisation indices vary little across locality types, although there is a clear correlation between them with minority suburbs and large cities leaning the most to the right (poor non-minority suburbs lean the most to the left on the economic index, while low-density suburbs lean the most to the left with respect to international policy). However, the interpretation of the globalisation index is particularly complex in Israel; it mixes loosely-related ideas of nationalism, free trade, and immigration policy agendas that have different meanings in Israel than elsewhere on the globe. On the cultural scale, minority suburbs clearly identify themselves by their distinct right-wing orientation, possessing the most traditional family values and religious orientations. Low-density and affluent suburbs, as expected, lean mainly to the left in their cultural orientation, as reflected by their voting patterns.

Regression models estimating community-level effects on the four indices reveal a mix of compositional and contextual influences (see Table 12.13). Models for the left-right index confirmed that right-wing self-placement characterised

*Table 12.12: Israel – selected left-right position indices by type of municipality, 2003 Knesset elections*

| Type of municipality | N | Left-right self-placement | Economic | Globalisation/ internationalism | Sociocultural |
|---|---|---|---|---|---|
| Central cities | 4 | 6.07 | 3.58 | 4.93 | 4.56 |
| Other large cities | 10 | 6.46 | 3.61 | 5.03 | 4.64 |
| Low-density suburbs | 44 | 5.72 | 3.51 | 4.74 | 4.36 |
| Minority suburbs | 70 | 3.02 | 3.62 | 5.26 | 5.29 |
| Affluent suburbs | 13 | 5.67 | 3.59 | 4.81 | 4.41 |
| Middle-class suburbs | 30 | 6.41 | 3.56 | 4.98 | 4.60 |
| Poor non-minority suburbs | 26 | 6.73 | 3.47 | 5.01 | 4.67 |
| Total | 197 | 5.04 | 3.56 | 5.02 | 4.79 |

*Notes:* The table presents mean indices for each type. The position of each party according to each left-right position index is presented in Figures A12.1 and A12.2 in the Appendix to this chapter.

poor non-minority local authorities and those in the Jerusalem metropolitan area, whereas Arab localities reveal the lowest right-wing orientation (an orientation primarily associated with a hard line on the Israeli-Arab conflict). Arabs, on the other hand, were most right-wing (traditional-conservative) in their cultural position. High socio-economic status and to a lesser extent old age composition, were associated with left-wing cultural orientations, whereas large cities culturally tilted more to the right-wing. The model predicting economic left-right positions had weak explanatory power, mainly because of low inter-local variation.

Of the contextual effects identified in the model, only population size and homeownership reveal any significant influence (distance to the centre has a significant effect on sociocultural values, but the effect is small and does not remain in the limited-variable model). Interestingly, population size is associated with moving voters to the right on all but the left-right self-placement index, suggesting perhaps a disconnection between the latter and the other indices. Homeownership, meanwhile, is associated with a positioning further to the right on the economic index, in line with results from a number of national studies reported in this volume. This provides further evidence that context does play a role, albeit limited and selective, in structuring Israeli political orientations.

*Table 12.13: Israel – regression models of local authority characteristics on four indices of political attitudes, in the 2003 Knesset elections*

| Variables included | Left-right | | Economic | | Globalisation | | Culture | |
|---|---|---|---|---|---|---|---|---|
| | All | Limited | All | Limited | All | Limited | All | Limited |
| SES | **−0.23** | *−0.31* | −0.004 | | **−0.30** | *−0.30* | **−0.41** | *−0.245* |
| Immigrants (%) | −0.02 | | 0.008 | | 0.01 | | 0.02 | |
| Age under 19 (%) | **−0.22** | **−0.13** | −0.23 | *−0.27* | −0.22 | | **−0.34** | |
| Age 60+ (%) | −0.06 | | −0.10 | | −0.26 | | **−0.26** | **−0.124** |
| Ln (population) | **−0.11** | **−0.09** | **0.26\*** | *0.23* | **0.21** | **0.18** | 0.14 | *0.184* |
| Population density | 0.05 | | 0.05 | | 0.05 | | −0.04 | |
| Homeownership (%) | −0.02 | | 0.21 | **0.23** | 0.05 | | 0.05 | |
| Distance to centre | −0.00 | | −0.05 | | −0.11 | | **−0.11** | |
| Gini index | 0.02 | | −0.07 | | -0.20 | | −0.05 | |
| Cars per HH | −0.12 | | 0.10 | | 0.04 | | 0.07 | |
| Arab local authority | **−1.01** | *−1.05* | 0.28 | *0.37* | **0.32** | *0.47* | *0.63* | *0.68* |
| Tel Aviv metro | 0.03 | | −0.16 | | −0.04 | | 0.01 | |
| Jerusalem metro | **0.09** | *0.09* | −0.12 | | 0.00 | | 0.01 | |
| Adjusted R² | 0.86 | 0.86 | 0.15 | 0.18 | 0.45 | 0.45 | 0.72 | 0.72 |
| N | 166 | 166 | 166 | 166 | 166 | 166 | 166 | 166 |

*Notes:* A high value of the position indexes indicates right-wing orientation. The table presents standardised coefficients. For boldface coefficients, p<0.05; for boldface italicised coefficients, p<0.01.

## The 2006 Knesset elections – a turning point?

It has been argued that the 2006 Knesset elections signified the breaking of the traditional right-left divide that dominated Israeli politics for three decades. The victory of the new Kadima party, not easily classified as right or left (but clearly right wing in its approach to the Israeli-Arab conflict), the unprecedented success of the retirees party, also not easily classified into a particular block, and the decline of traditional right-wing and left-wing parties, hint at such a change. In particular, it seemed that the neoliberal reforms initiated by Benjamin Netanyahu, when Minister of Finance, would lead to an unprecedented shift of the lower classes away from traditional right-wing parties.

However, the average measures for the different types of local authorities reveal that change has been less marked then perceived (see Table 12.14). Voter turnout was the lowest ever, but similar to 1999 and 2003, low-density suburbs and affluent suburbs had the highest turnout, whereas minority suburbs and central cities had the lowest. Voting for the right-wing and religious parties remained associated with low socio-economic status. This relationship seems to have strengthened, with only an average of 28 per cent in affluent suburbs voting for the right-wing parties, compared with 68 per cent in poor non-minority suburbs. The decline of the right-wing was particularly marked in affluent suburbs and in low-density suburbs, but much less so in poor suburbs. Voting for the centre-left was associated, as always, with high socio-economic status, while voting patterns for Kadima and the retirees resembled those of the centre-left – with the highest support received in affluent suburbs, followed by low-density suburbs. Thus, Kadima would appear to be making inroads into affluent and low-density suburbs, potentially laying the ground for a shift of these suburbs towards neoliberal policies and parties.

*Table 12.14: Israel – selected measures of the 2006 Knesset elections by type of municipality*

| Type of municipality | N | Voter turnout | % votes for right-wing and religious parties | % votes for centre-left parties | % votes for Kadima-retirees | % vote for Arab parties |
|---|---|---|---|---|---|---|
| Urban concentrations | 14 | | | | | |
|    Central cities | 4 | 57.2 | 44 | 22 | 29 | 2 |
|    Other large cities | 10 | 59.5 | 51 | 16 | 31 | 0 |
| Low-density suburbs | 40 | 70.1 | 38 | 25 | 34 | 0 |
| Minority suburbs | 73 | 57.8 | 7 | 19 | 8 | 65 |
| Affluent suburbs | 13 | 68.7 | 28 | 28 | 41 | 0 |
| Middle-class suburbs | 30 | 58.7 | 47 | 18 | 32 | 0 |
| Poor suburbs | 27 | 62.0 | 68 | 12 | 15 | 3 |
| Total | 197 | 61.8 | 32 | 20 | 22 | 25 |

## Conclusion

Our study reveals four major determinants of voting behaviour in Israel. The first is population size of the local authority – the only contextual variable that both markedly and consistently influences voting behaviour in Israel. Population size has a major influence on turnout in local elections and, to a lesser extent, in national elections. Larger cities are characterised by lower turnout, while the large central cities of Israel's metropolitan areas are characterised by particularly low levels of electoral participation.

Compositional variables are revealed as consistently important determinants of voting behaviour in Israel, at both local and national levels. A major compositional determinant is the distinction between Jewish and Arab local authorities. Arab local authorities are characterised by exceptionally high turnout in local elections, high levels of council fragmentation, and a high proportion of council members representing independent lists, which are associated with the prominence of extended families in voting behaviour. In national elections, Arabs tend to vote for Arab parties, but voter turnout is lower, reflecting lower levels of identification with the Israeli state. Concentrations of immigrants, meanwhile, have only limited affects on either turnout or partisanship in Israel.

Socio-economic status is another significant compositional variable, primarily a major determinant of left-right orientation: poor non-minority local authorities tend to vote for right-wing parties, including religious parties, whereas affluent areas vote centre-left. Independent lists are more prominent in the councils of local authorities characterised by high socio-economic status, whereas parties play a greater role in poor (Jewish) local authorities, where right-wing and religious parties usually predominate. As is the case in other countries, in more affluent places voter turnout tends to be relatively higher in national elections than in local ones, whereas the opposite is true for the poorer segments of society, including the Arab minority. Finally, age structure also has an independent effect. A young age structure is associated with higher turnout, whereas an older age structure increases the tendency to vote centre-left.

It should be noted that the proportion of ultra-orthodox Jews is probably a significant determinant of voting behaviour, as this group has a high voter turnout and votes almost unanimously for ultra-religious (right-wing) parties. However, the small number of local authorities with a high proportion of ultra-religious population precluded full inclusion of this variable in the analysis.

A number of contextual variables examined in this study, including density, distance from a metropolitan centre, class heterogeneity and rate of homeownership, reveal weaker and less consistent effects. Among these, homeownership was the one to demonstrate an effect in the expected direction (i.e. support for neoliberalism in relation to the index of economic policy preferences). However, at the same time, homeownership was found to operate against expectations (in augmenting support for centre-left parties). This suggests that the effects of such variables, and in turn of metropolitanisation, are highly dependent on both national context and the phase of development in evidence at the time of the study.

As to the political ecology of the Israeli metropolis, one remarkable independent effect concerns the right-wing orientation of Jerusalem and of the suburbs that are

West Bank settlements. This is obviously conditioned by the context of the Israeli-Arab conflict there. Otherwise, the political ecology of metropolitan areas largely reflects the determinants specified above, and the impact of these determinants on voting behaviour does not vary significantly from one metropolitan area to another. Central city areas are characterised by low voter turnout and centre-left orientation, associated with their large size, relatively high socio-economic status and old age structure.

Suburbs of the Israeli metropolis are, like those of many other nations, very heterogeneous. Their tendency to vote for right-wing and religious parties is associated with lower socio-economic status, rather than with a conservative orientation based on a suburban way of life. However, suburban space in Israel has experienced two major processes of change. First, a process of suburbanisation of the middle class has increased the centre-left orientation in particular suburban spaces, while suburbanisation leads to an increase in voter turnout, particularly in local elections. A second process concerns the incorporation of rapidly-growing Arab local authorities by the expanding metropolitan areas. This brings into metropolitan space a new diversity that will have effects for many years to come.

Despite remarkable stability in the determinants of voting behaviour, our results reveal a long-term trend of declining voter turnout. The trend is particularly pronounced in local elections, thus providing an indication of a growing deficit in local democracy (Hasson 2006), and a shift toward delocalisation. It has been observed that local election results in the 1990s have rewarded well-managed local authorities – unlike in previous decades, mayors who created large financial deficits were usually not re-elected (Brender 2003; Diskin and Eden 1999). However, recent election results have put a question mark on the continuation of this process – reflecting realities of the financial crisis and declining trust in elected mayors and council members.

The results suggest that migration from larger to smaller local authorities might increase voter turnout, as well as participation in the local democratic game. Thus, the publicly-promoted policy to amalgamate small local authorities in the name of efficiency and good governance may not work in favour of local democracy. However, a parallel trend of declining turnout seems to be emerging also at the level of national elections. Moreover, declining voter turnout is observed in all types of local authorities – large and small, affluent and poor, in both local and national elections – thus indicating a deeper socio-political process that is unlikely to be solved by manipulating the municipal map. Proposals such as changing the number of council members in the municipal councils, or introducing majoritarian elections of council members as a means of making them accountable directly to a particular constituency, have been raised. It is argued that they would reduce council fragmentation, while the latter proposal would possibly increase turnout through the more direct democracy associated with it. However, the root of the problem of declining turnout seems more fundamental and is evident also in other democracies – solutions involve deeper aspects of value change, education and perhaps the evolution of complementary modes of participation and deliberative democracy.

**Bibliography**

Brender, A. (2003) 'The effect of fiscal performance on local government election results in Israel, 1989–1998', *Journal of Public Economics*, 87: 2187–205.

Brichta, A. (2001) 'Changes in local government in Israel', in A. Brichta and A. Pedhzur (eds) *Elections to the Local Authorities in Israel – 1998: Continuity or Change?* Tel Aviv: Ramot-Tel Aviv University, 199–213. (Hebrew)

Diskin, A. and Eden, A. (1999) *The Rational Voter in the Municipal Elections in Israel*, Jerusalem: The Floersheimer Institute for Policy Studies (Hebrew).

Ghanem, A. (2001) 'Elections to Arab local authorities', in A. Brichta and A. Pedhzur (eds) *Elections to the Local Authorities in Israel – 1998: Continuity or Change?* Tel Aviv: Ramot-Tel Aviv University, 67–79. (Hebrew).

Gonen, A. (1995) *Between City and Suburb, Urban Residential Patterns and Processes in Israel*, Aldershot: Avebury.

Hasson, S. (ed.) (2006) *The Local Democratic Deficit, A Seeming Democracy?* Jerusalem: The Floersheimer Institute for Policy Studies (Hebrew).

IDI (2006) *Parliamentary Reform for a Stable Democracy – the Main Proposals of the Israel Democracy Institute*, Jerusalem: Israel Democracy Institute. Online. Available /www.idi.org.il/hebrew/article. asp?id=13122006142731 (Hebrew).

Kenig, O., Rahat, G. and Hazan, R. (2004) 'The adaptation and retreat from direct election of Prime Minister and their political outcomes', in A. Arian and M. Shamir (eds) *The Elections in Israel 2003*, New Brunswick, New Jersey: Transaction Publishers, 33–61.

Kostelecky, T. and Cermak, D. (2005) 'Metropolitanisation and political change in the Czech Republic', in V. Hoffmann-Martinot and J. M. Sellers (eds) *Metropolitanisation and Political Change*, Wiesbaden: Verlag für Sozialwissenschaften, 353–70.

Megidor, M. (2007) *Presidential Committee for the Assessment of Governance Structure, Citizens' Empowerment Centre in Israel*. Online. Available http://ceci.org.il/heb/commitee.asp (Hebrew).

Mustafa, M. (2010) 'Attributes of Arab local politics and the issue of leadership', in A. Haidar (ed.) *The Collapse of Arab Local Authorities: Suggestions for restructuring*, Jerusalem: Van Leer Institute and Hakibbutz Hameuchad, 76–104 (Hebrew).

Razin, E. and Hazan, A. (2005) 'Metropolitanization and political change in Israel', in V. Hoffmann-Martinot and J. M. Sellers (eds.) *Metropolitanization and Political Change*, Wiesbaden: Verlag für Sozialwissenschaften, 395–423.

Shafat, A. G. (1992) *Local Government, Legal Aspects, Past, Present and Future*, Jerusalem: Ministry of Interior (Hebrew).

Torgovnik, E. (2001) 'Parties and local elections – the end of the "historical tie"?', in A. Brichta and A. Pedhzur (eds) *Elections to the Local Authorities in Israel – 1998: Continuity or Change?* Tel Aviv: Ramot-Tel Aviv University, 31–47 (Hebrew).

Walks, R. A. (2004a) 'Place of residence, party preferences, and political attitudes in Canadian cities and suburbs', *Journal of Urban Affairs*, 26: 269–95.

— (2004b) 'Suburbanization, the vote, and changes in Federal and provincial political representation and influence between inner cities and suburbs in large Canadian urban regions, 1945–1999', *Urban Affairs Review*, 39: 411–440.

## Appendix

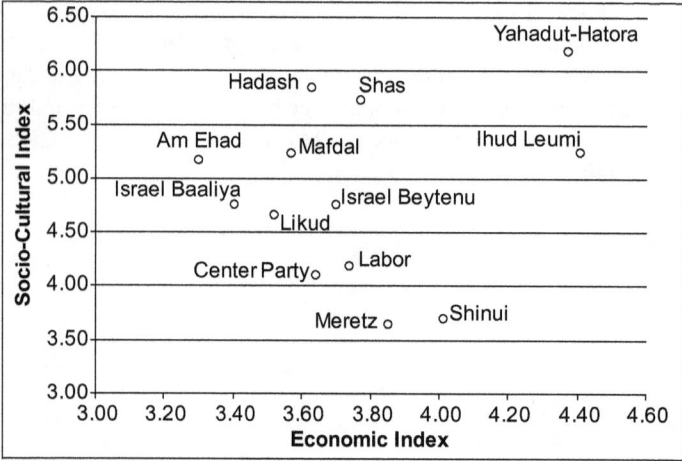

*Figure A12.1: Position of Israeli political parties on the sociocultural and economic indices, 2003*

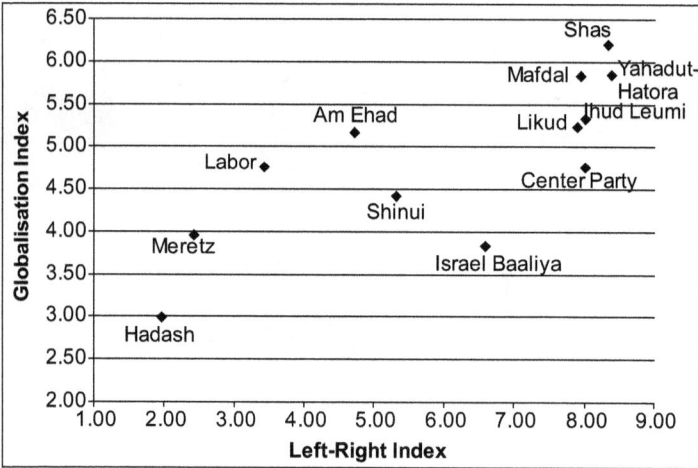

*Figure A12.2: Position of Israeli political parties on the left-right and globalisation indices, 2003*

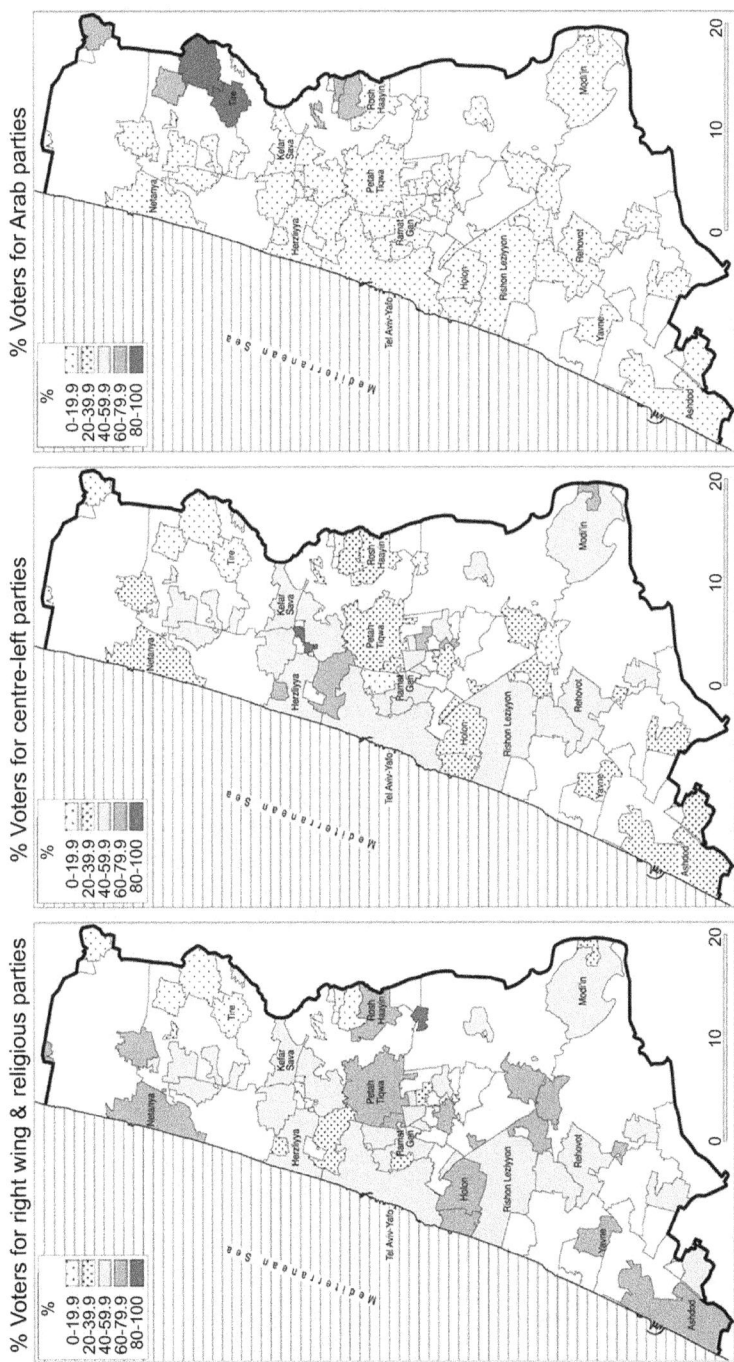

*Figure A12.3a: 2003 Knesset elections – Tel Aviv metropolitan area*

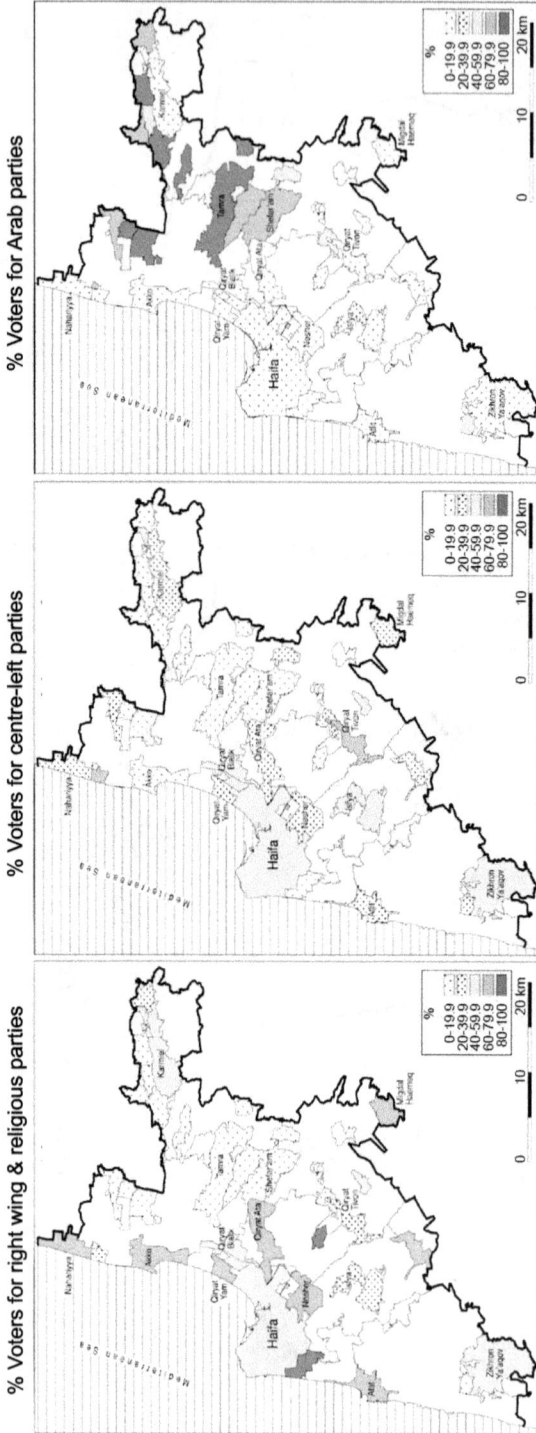

*Figure A12.3b: 2003 Knesset elections – Haifa metropolitan area*

# Chapter Thirteen | Conclusion – Metropolitan Sources of Political Behaviour

*Jefferey M. Sellers, Daniel Kübler, R. Alan Walks,*
*Philippe Rochat and Melanie Walter-Rogg*

## Introduction

With the advent of the twenty-first century, metropolitan areas have become the dominant form of human settlement. Regardless of the national historical differences in processes of urbanisation, a number of common elements now characterise metropolitan areas throughout the world. As areas of dispersed settlement, they stretch across a multiplicity of communities and jurisdictional boundaries. Flows of capital, labour, services and goods act as the glue that integrates communities across metropolitan territories. Metropolitan regions are embedded in national and transnational urban hierarchies. Some serve as economic or cultural centres for a nation or a continent; others specialise in particular kinds of activities that dominate the local economy.

This volume has investigated how the characteristics of metropolitan places influence political behaviour within and among their constituent communities. The results show the need to re-evaluate presumptions that have long stood at the core of thinking about the geography of modern elections and party systems. The *nationalisation* thesis, which emerged during the time of rapid industrialisation in Western Europe and North America, attempted to account for the earlier evolution of national political systems out of segmented territorial regions. In a nationalised system, electoral competition and contestation occur between national social and economic constituencies based on class, ethnicity or other identities, rather than between geographic places. If territorial variation persists, then it must be due to the social composition of those territories. In a nationalised political system, places are merely containers for the political behaviour of different social groups.

As diverse, expanding metropolitan regions have overwhelmed and supplanted old social identities based on the urban-rural divide, metropolitan territorial influences have emerged to call this view of political behaviour into question. Territorial variations within and between metropolitan regions now comprise a major influence on whether and how citizens vote. More than the result of random social and economic sorting, these variations are a product of metropolitan places themselves. Identical social groups living in metropolitan places with distinct interests and lifestyles behave in starkly different ways. When they reside in densely populated core cities, where economies of scale favour the collective provision of services, such as public transport or public day care, they tend to support programmes of state provision. When they reside in outlying low-density municipalities, where similar services are more difficult to coordinate collectively, the same groups support market provision and privatisation over state programs. Even when people can choose their place of residence, those choices remain a function of the alternatives embedded in existing metropolitan settlement structures. Living in one or another setting reinforces prevailing preferences. The metropolitan spatial context thus retains significant power to explain the political behaviour of a community.

The metropolitanisation thesis exemplifies a relationship between scales that is intrinsic to many other contemporary processes of global economic and social change, from transformations in capitalism (Gereffi and Korzeniewicz 1994) to post-modern cultural shifts (Inglehart and Welzel 2005). Although national and even global in its extent and impact, metropolitanisation has taken place at the local and regional scale. Within societies dominated by pervasive metropolitan patterns, parties of both the left and right have found new territorial electoral strongholds and new sources of advantage and disadvantage in the competition for votes. Influences from metropolitan places on electoral mobilisation have altered the balance of power among these electoral constituencies. Over the last twenty years, the cumulative impact of these territorial reconfigurations has been a persistent electoral advantage for the parties of the right, and for the neoliberal agendas they have increasingly advocated. Metropolitanisation has been a key factor in the rise and pervasive influence of neoliberalism.

Metropolitan territorial configurations pose challenges to the nationalisation thesis in several ways. Metropolitanisation has interposed a new set of intra-regional territorial divides. Rather than rooted in traditional regional differences, these place-based configurations of political consciousness are embedded in localities and neighbourhoods and in different metropolitan structures. Rather than remain divided into segmented, largely uniform regional cultures, metropolitan places are linked to each other through flows of commuting, consumption and markets. Among regions that have converged toward similar patterns of metropolitan structure, territorial divisions rooted in metropolitan life may also erode traditional regional differences in political culture. Even when metropolitanisation has had nationalising effects of this kind, it has supplemented or supplanted regional divides with metropolitan and local ones.

Metropolitan territorial effects are more contested than the regional party configurations that dominated earlier patterns of territorial variation (Caramani 2004). As metropolitan populations have grown and have come to account for the majority of the electorate throughout most developed countries, competition for suburban votes has drawn national parties from across much of the ideological spectrum toward neoliberal and culturally-conservative agendas. Even as these parties retain territorial strongholds in certain types of metropolitan places, competition for 'swing' communities has frequently produced volatile or mixed territorial patterns of metropolitan support.

Finally, nationalisation implies that national parties operate as vertically-integrated organisations, and that community behaviour in local elections follows patterns in national elections. Instead, a layered examination of metropolitan patterns reveals numerous multilevel dynamics in both electoral behaviour and the economic, social and spatial influences that shape it.

This chapter concludes this volume with a comparative multilevel analysis of these overarching patterns. The dataset we employ is compiled from the national datasets analysed in all the separate country chapters.[1] It includes 13,300 municipalities located in 175 metropolitan areas in eleven countries (see Table 13.1). Alongside analysis of the cross-national commonalities and differences, the integrated dataset enables an exploration of metropolitan influences that the smaller numbers of metropolitan areas did not permit in some of the country chapters. The first section of this chapter focuses on patterns of electoral turnout, the second on patterns of partisanship.

## Metropolitan patterns of electoral participation

Political participation is the foundation of democracy and participation in elections is perhaps the most fundamental act of democratic citizenship. Moreover, it is one of the most reliable and readily available empirical indicators of political behaviour. A first step towards unravelling the metropolitan determinants of political behaviour therefore consists of an analysis of turnout in local and national elections,[2] aggregated to the municipal level. Analysis of this dataset demonstrates clear limits to the nationalisation of electoral behaviour and the importance of systematic differences at the metropolitan and local levels to patterns of voting turnout.

### Nationalisation, localisation or fragmentation?

What cross-national political effects has metropolitanisation had? The pooled dataset of national and municipal results enables an analysis of the territorial heterogeneity of local participatory patterns at both municipal and national levels. In addition to uniformity, the nationalisation of politics implies integration of municipal elections into national electoral patterns. The comparison of municipal and national turnout rates provides the first rigorous cross-national test of this dimension of nationalisation.

---

1.   The compilation of this database was a Herculean task. In order to avoid misspecification of indicators across countries, the integrated database has been confined to only those variables that are identical in all the countries (see the procedures described in Chapter 14, the Methodological Appendix of this volume).

2.   Except for the US results, all the country data and analyses of turnout presented in this book are based on official electoral data. This means that the turnout rate is based on a comparison of the number of voters and the number of registered electors. In the US, voluntary voter registration leaves official tallies of eligible voters much less representative than in other countries. US turnout data here is based on census figures for the voting age population, who are naturalised or native-born citizens (see Chapter 2 in this volume).

*Table 13.1: Metropolitan municipalities/communities, metropolitan areas and countries in the overall sample*

| Country | Total number of metropolitan areas | Total number of municipalities/communities* | Type of municipalities/communities* | | | | | | |
|---|---|---|---|---|---|---|---|---|---|
| | | | Urban concentrations | Poor (hardship) suburbs | | Middle-class suburbs | Affluent suburbs | Low density suburbs |
| | | | | High minority | Low minority | | | |
| United States | 12 | 1.935 | 22 | 300 | 317 | 473 | 298 | 525 |
| Canada | 11 | 369 | 35 | 21 | 32 | 141 | 54 | 86 |
| United Kingdom | 20 | 394 | 135 | 14 | 17 | 150 | 39 | 39 |
| France | 42 | 6.774 | 50 | 331 | 843 | 2.298 | 539 | 2.713 |
| Switzerland | 7 | 482 | 7 | | 119 | 119 | 119 | 118 |
| Germany | 21 | 1.166 | 38 | | 270 | 363 | 231 | 264 |
| Spain | 30 | 1.053 | 51 | | 228 | 456 | 228 | 90 |
| Sweden | 3 | 39 | 3 | 1 | 5 | 16 | 6 | 8 |
| Poland | 21 | 427 | 32 | | 80 | 149 | 69 | 97 |
| Czech Republic | 4 | 464 | 5 | | 75 | 190 | 101 | 93 |
| Israel | 4 | 197 | 14 | 70 | 26 | 30 | 13 | 44 |
| Total | 175 | 13.300 | 392 | | 2.749 | 4.385 | 1.697 | 4.077 |

*Notes:* *In Canada and the United Kingdom, a lack of sufficient municipalities in many metropolitan regions required the substitution of electoral districts for the purposes of categorising communities. In some cases, the boundaries of such districts adhere to those of municipalities, but in many metros there are many more such districts than there are municipalities (indeed, in many cases there are only one or two municipalities for the entire metropolitan area).

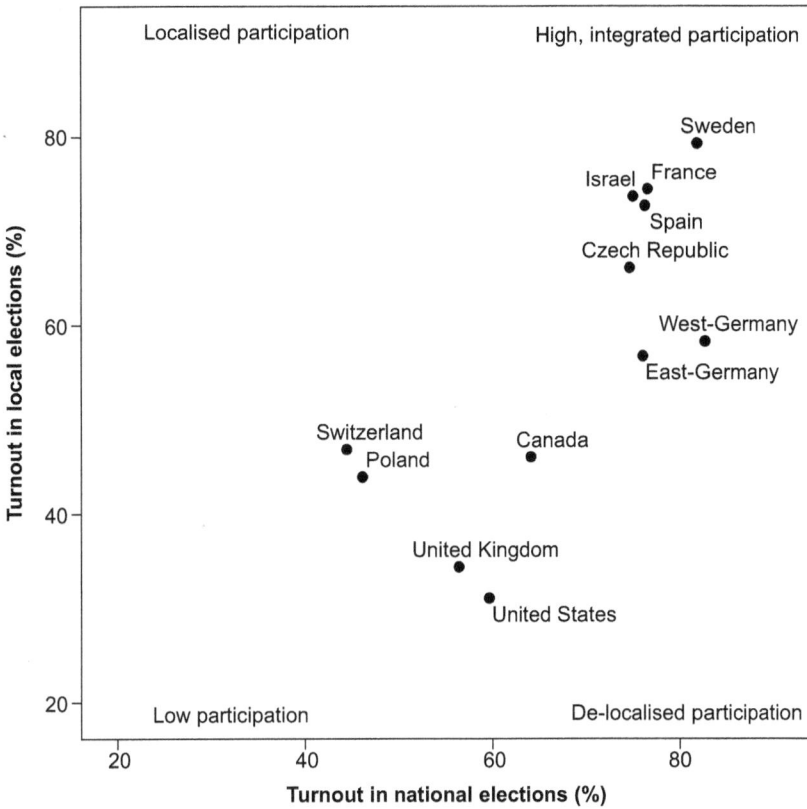

*Figure 13.1: Relations between national and local electoral participation, overall means by countries*

Comparison by country of the (unweighted) average turnout for the two types of elections (municipal and national) reveals striking differences in this dimension (see Figure 13.1). In several countries, high average participation in both types of elections leaves little doubt that there is strong national-local electoral integration. In Sweden, France, Israel and Spain, turnout rates for both types of elections average 70 per cent or higher. Since the electorate for municipal elections in Sweden includes all resident non-citizens, while in the other European Union countries all resident EU citizens, the convergence of turnout in these countries is all the more impressive.[3]

In other countries a national tendency toward delocalisation is clear. In the Anglo-American nations of the United States, Canada and the United Kingdom (albeit in the latter case, based on a much more limited London area sample), this

---

3. As a result, rules for non-voting by non-citizens correlated negatively with turnout in the pooled dataset and any independent effects from those rules could not be sorted out.

Table 13.2: Territorial heterogeneity of metropolitan turnout in municipal elections by country

| | Election(s) | S (Standard Deviation) | National S Post-WWII (Caramani 2005) | S² (Variance) | National S2 Post-WWII (Caramani 2005) | MAD: Mean Absolute Deviation | National MAD Post-WWII (Caramani 2005) | MSD: Mean Squared Deviation | National MSD Post-WWII (Caramani 2005) | IPR | Variability Coefficient | N |
|---|---|---|---|---|---|---|---|---|---|---|---|---|
| United States | 1996–2003 | 12.85 | | 165.07 | | 10.38 | | 164.97 | | 0.41 | 0.41 | 1606 |
| Canada | mid-2000s | 14.58 | | 212.48 | | 12.13 | | 210.96 | | 0.36 | 0.32 | 140 |
| Switzerland | 1996–2005 | 13.87 | 14.32 | 192.45 | 212.66 | 11.45 | 10.59 | 191.83 | 205.88 | 0.35 | 0.30 | 314 |
| Israel | 1999–2003 | 15.92 | | 253.48 | | 13.42 | | 252.01 | | 0.30 | 0.22 | 172 |
| East Germany | 1999–2003 | 9.13 | | 83.35 | | 7.48 | | 83.13 | | 0.26 | 0.16 | 371 |
| Poland | 1994–2002 | 6.82 | | 46.49 | | 5.44 | | 46.38 | | 0.25 | 0.16 | 445 |
| Czech Republic | 1994–2002 | 9.54 | | 90.93 | | 7.36 | | 90.74 | | 0.24 | 0.14 | 464 |
| France | 2001 | 9.73 | 3.40 | 94.58 | 11.82 | 7.83 | 2.56 | 94.57 | 11.69 | 0.23 | 0.13 | 6784 |
| Germany | 1999–2003 | 7.36 | 6.49 | 54.22 | 23.02 | 5.79 | 2.55 | 54.17 | 22.15 | 0.22 | 0.13 | 1159 |
| Spain | 1995–2003 | 8.80 | 6.01 | 77.49 | 36.68 | 7.26 | 4.48 | 77.42 | | 0.22 | 0.12 | 1049 |
| West Germany | 1999–2003 | 6.31 | | 39.82 | | 4.99 | | 39.77 | | 0.21 | 0.11 | 788 |
| United Kingdom | 2004 (London only) | 3.06 | 5.75 | 9.38 | 34.51 | 2.62 | 4.14 | 9.10 | 34.46 | 0.20 | 0.09 | 33 |
| Sweden | 1998–2002 | 4.46 | 1.54 | 19.89 | 2.91 | 3.47 | 1.21 | 19.38 | 2.81 | 0.15 | 0.06 | 39 |

Notes: For calculation of indices, see Caramani (2004, 2005). Indices from Caramani (2005: 307) based on Lower Chamber legislative elections.

Table 13.3: Territorial heterogeneity of metropolitan turnout in national elections by country

| | Election(s) | S (Standard Deviation) | Overall S Post-WWII (Caramani 2005) | S² (Variance) | Overall S² Post-WWII (Caramani 2005) | MAD: Mean Absolute Deviation | Overall MAD Post-WWII (Caramani 2005) | MSD: Mean Squared Deviation | Overall MSD Post-WWII (Caramani 2005) | IPR | Variability Coefficient | N |
|---|---|---|---|---|---|---|---|---|---|---|---|---|
| United States | 1996–2004 | 11.96 | | 142.98 | | 9.37 | | 142.90 | | 0.28 | 0.20 | 1841 |
| Poland | 1993–2001 | 6.98 | | 48.71 | | 5.74 | | 48.60 | | 0.25 | 0.15 | 445 |
| Switzerland | 1999–2003 | 6.72 | 14.32 | 45.12 | 212.66 | 5.41 | 10.59 | 45.03 | 205.88 | 0.25 | 0.15 | 482 |
| United Kingdom | 2001 (England + Wales) | 6.61 | 5.75 | 43.65 | 34.51 | 5.41 | 4.14 | 43.53 | 34.46 | 0.22 | 0.12 | 361 |
| Israel | 1999–2003 | 8.41 | | 70.72 | | 6.54 | | 70.36 | | 0.21 | 0.11 | 197 |
| Canada | 2006 | 5.01 | | 25.13 | | 3.85 | | 24.97 | | 0.17 | 0.08 | 156 |
| Spain | 1996–2004 | 5.83 | 6.01 | 33.95 | 36.68 | 4.52 | 4.48 | 33.92 | | 0.17 | 0.08 | 1052 |
| Czech Republic | 1996–2002 | 5.36 | | 28.73 | | 4.23 | | 28.66 | | 0.17 | 0.07 | 464 |
| France | 2001 | 5.51 | 3.40 | 30.41 | 11.82 | 4.32 | 2.56 | 30.40 | 11.69 | 0.17 | 0.07 | 6784 |
| *East Germany* | 1998–2002 | 5.08 | | 25.80 | | 4.26 | | 25.73 | | 0.17 | 0.07 | 373 |
| Germany | 1998–2002 | 4.80 | 6.49 | 23.01 | 23.02 | 3.63 | 2.55 | 22.99 | 22.15 | 0.15 | 0.06 | 1162 |
| Sweden | 1998–2002 | 3.54 | 1.54 | 12.50 | 2.91 | 2.74 | 1.21 | 12.18 | 2.81 | 0.13 | 0.04 | 39 |
| *West Germany* | 1998–2002 | 2.82 | | 7.94 | | 2.21 | | 7.93 | | 0.12 | 0.03 | 789 |

Notes: For calculation of indices, see Caramani (2004, 2005). Indices for France and US from Caramani (2005) based on Lower Chamber legislative elections.

delocalised pattern is most pronounced. Average national turnout rates in these countries have approached or exceeded 60 per cent, but local voter turnout rates ranging from 46 per cent (in Canada) to 31 per cent (in the United States) give rise to significant turnout gaps between the two scales of governance. More limited delocalisation is also present in West Germany.

The lower national and municipal turnout rates in Switzerland indicate a more general voter disengagement as well as limited national-local integration. This is the only nation that can truly be characterised as having a generally localised political culture, although sub-national and national electoral dynamics are becoming increasingly integrated (Selb 2006).

The three post-Communist territories, where a general disengagement from voting has also been noted (Kostadinova 2003), reveal some distinct patterns. In each, participation in one type of election or the other averages lower than in settled democracies with relatively similar systems of institutions. In East Germany, participation averages lower than in West Germany. In the Czech Republic, turnout in local elections is lower than in other countries with similarly stable party systems and high national turnout. In Poland, both national and local participation average relatively low.

A comparison of overall turnout rates in national and local elections already suggests important variations in the way that electoral institutions function. To further assess how these variations might be related to metropolitanisation and nationalisation, we turn our attention to how uniformly turnout rates vary among metropolitan territories. An established line of research focused on the territorial homogeneity of electoral behaviour across time and space has developed several indices for this purpose (Caramani 2005). Table 13.2 and Table 13.3 show calculations of six such indices for the metropolitan dataset by country: the standard deviation; the variance; the mean absolute deviation; the mean squared deviation; the variability coefficient, and the IPR index. The latter, based on the differences between the turnout rate in each municipality and the overall mean of turnout across all municipalities, takes into account the number and size of municipalities (see Table 13.2 and Table 13.3). For the purposes of illustration, Figure 13.2 displays the IPR values for turnout rates in local and national elections.

The six indices converge around similar results. Within most countries, they show significant variation in the electoral participation of metropolitan municipalities. In municipal elections, this territorial heterogeneity is especially pronounced. For every country analysed in Caramani (2004) except Switzerland, the metropolitan indices of variability in municipal election turnout range consistently higher than corresponding figures for national elections based on all national election districts (see Table 13.2). In France, Germany, Spain and Sweden, metropolitan municipal turnout varies more dramatically, producing index values at double or triple the national figures. Even in national elections, where turnout rates are generally more uniform (see Figure 13.2), the metropolitan indices in most of these countries are somewhat higher than those for all parliamentary constituencies in national elections (see Table 13.3). Only in two of the most territorialised countries, Spain and Switzerland, do slightly lower metropolitan indices of variability imply somewhat more uniform results among metropolitan localities than among national legislative districts.

The territorial heterogeneity of metropolitan voting propensities varies significantly among countries (see Figure 13.2). On one end of the spectrum, metropolitan communities in the United States, Switzerland, Israel and Canada reveal widely-differing turnout levels. The great variability in these countries is especially evident in local elections (see Table 13.2), but apparent even at the highest level of national elections (see Table 13.3). In the post-Communist countries, including (former) East Germany, tendencies toward nationalisation are also more qualified than in Western European countries. In Poland, the variability of turnout in national elections ranges considerably higher than in local elections. At the other end of the spectrum, the relatively homogeneous territorial distribution of turnout in Sweden and West Germany indicates more nationalised patterns of electoral participation.

National differences in institutions, from electoral systems to local government systems, account for much of the variation in municipal political behaviour. Despite the relatively small number of twelve countries, simple bivariate correlations between several explanatory variables at the country level and these national patterns point to numerous relationships that approach or exceed statistical significance (see Table 13.4). The predominance of metropolitan regions in national politics is strongly related to more general patterns of electoral participation, as dominant metropolitan constituencies mobilise in national elections at the expense of more marginal ones. National rates of metropolitanisation, measured here by the proportion of the national population residing in metropolitan areas with populations over 200,000 reveal the highest positive correlation with a large national-local turnout gap (at 0.513, $p<0.10$) (cf. Hoffmann-Martinot and Sellers 2005).

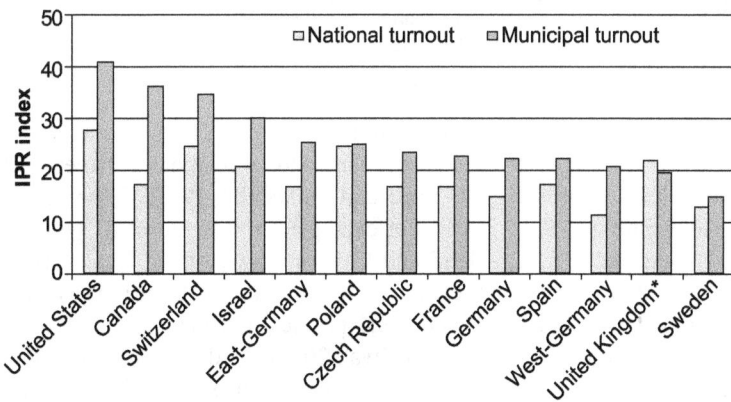

*Figure 13.2: Territorial heterogeneity of voter turnout (national and municipal elections) in the metropolitan areas of eleven countries (IPR index)*

*Note*: *Municipal turnout for greater London only.

*Table 13.4: Bivariate correlations of average local/municipal turnout with national institutions*

| | Average municipal turnout | Average national turnout | Average turnout gap | Municipal turnout IPR | National turnout IPR | Turnout gap IPR | N |
|---|---|---|---|---|---|---|---|
| National metropolitanisation | −0.214 | 0.151 | *0.513* | 0.267 | 0.093 | −0.275 | 12 |
| Civic localist local government (Sellers and Kwak 2011) | **−0.794** | **−0.636** | 0.484 | ***0.642*** | *0.558* | −0.381 | 11 |
| Nationalised local government (Sellers and Kwak 2011) | 0.429 | 0.368 | −0.232 | −0.477 | −0.406 | 0.291 | 11 |
| Local elitist local government (Sellers and Kwak 2011) | *−0.519* | 0.402 | −0.334 | −0.345 | −0.305 | 0.200 | 11 |
| Third wave of democratisation (Huntington 1993) | 0.128 | 0.031 | −0.159 | −0.223 | −0.039 | 0.264 | 12 |
| Proportional representation (national) | 0.478 | 0.161 | *−0.568* | −0.344 | −0.253 | 0.244 | 11 |
| Proportional representation (local council) | ***0.670*** | *0.575* | −0.361 | −0.498 | −0.530 | 0.212 | 11 |
| Election Day is rest day or holiday | ***0.733*** | 0.328 | **−0.770** | −0.468 | −0.381 | 0.299 | 11 |
| Easy voting index (Blais *et al.*) | 0.068 | −0.077 | −0.204 | −0.095 | −0.184 | −0.030 | 11 |
| Election Day registration | 0.063 | −0.016 | −0.121 | −0.126 | −0.184 | 0.012 | 11 |
| Compulsory registration | 0.287 | −0.055 | −0.531 | 0.017 | 0.022 | −0.005 | 11 |

*Notes*: Where N = 12, sample includes separate units for East and West Germany.
For italicised coefficients, $p < 0.10$; for boldface coefficients, $p < 0.05$; for boldface italicised coefficients, $p < 0.01$.

Especially in municipal elections, systematic effects derive from well-known differences in local government institutions and in relations between local and national politics (Morlan 1984; Page and Goldsmith 1987; Hesse and Sharpe 1991; Goldsmith and Page 2010). For example, in 'civic localist' systems, such as the United States, Switzerland and Canada, much of the local participation takes place outside of council elections; institutions for local governance differ widely among municipalities, and local politics and elections maintain fewer links to national politics (Sellers and Kwak 2011). As the consistently significant correlations demonstrate, this form of local governance is clearly associated with lower turnout at both levels of government, as well as greater spatial variation in turnout at both levels.

In contrast, 'local elitist' systems maintain stronger links between national and local politics, a factor that Morlan (1984) found to increase electoral mobilisation in local elections (the correlation is 0.503, p<0.10). In southern European countries like France and Spain, 'political localism' (Page 1991) has relied on local elected officials to represent local concerns within higher level governments. In countries such as Germany, the Czech Republic, and Israel, strong links between local and national party organisations account for vertical integration (Deschouwer 2003; Razin 1998). Such forms of integration are strongest in the relatively 'national-ised' local government system of Sweden (Sellers and Lidström 2007), where both national and local turnout in metropolitan localities are highest and most uniform.

Among other national institutions, proportional and mixed compensatory electoral systems have been shown to foster electoral participation to a significantly greater degree than first-past-the-post and majoritarian systems (Blais *et al.* 2003). In voting systems that are proportional, every vote has an effect on the result. Since even voters for small parties can expect their preferred party to gain at least some seats in the legislature, voter turnout under these systems should be higher. The direction of the correlations for average turnout is consistent with this hypothesis, but only proportional representation in local council elections correlates significantly with higher turnout (in local elections 0.643, and in national elections 0.601, both p<0.05). National rules of electoral administration also play a role. Turnout is higher when the electoral legislation facilitates the exercise of the right to vote (Blais *et al.* 2003). Holding elections on a public holiday correlates with both higher municipal turnout and a lower turnout gap.[4]

In the metropolitan areas in this study, the national integration of electoral participation rates remains limited. An overview of turnout means from all eleven countries in the dataset (see Figure 13.3) confirms considerable cross-national variations in degrees of nationalisation, especially in local elections. Whatever the effects from national institutions, the wide variations within countries often approach or exceed the range of differences among these national averages. Only in a few countries, notably Sweden and West Germany, do figures for municipal and national turnout cluster tightly around the overall mean. Only these countries can be considered to possess fully-integrated systems.[5]

---

4.  Blais *et al.* (2003) also construct an 'ease of voting' index that aggregates opportunities to vote by correspondence, in advance or by proxy. Facilitating voter registration either by making it obligatory, by making it possible to register on Election Day, or by making the government rather than individual citizens responsible for taking the initiative in registration can also raise the turnout rate. Although correlations demonstrated no statistically significant relationship between these conditions and the national turnout averages, the directions of the correlations generally corresponded to expectations.

5.  The scatter plots also reveal a variety of relationships between national and local turnout patterns, from the linear co-variation in Sweden (Pearson r = 0.98), to the much more limited relationships in the United States (r = 0.50), Poland (r = 0.109) and Israel (r = −0.009).

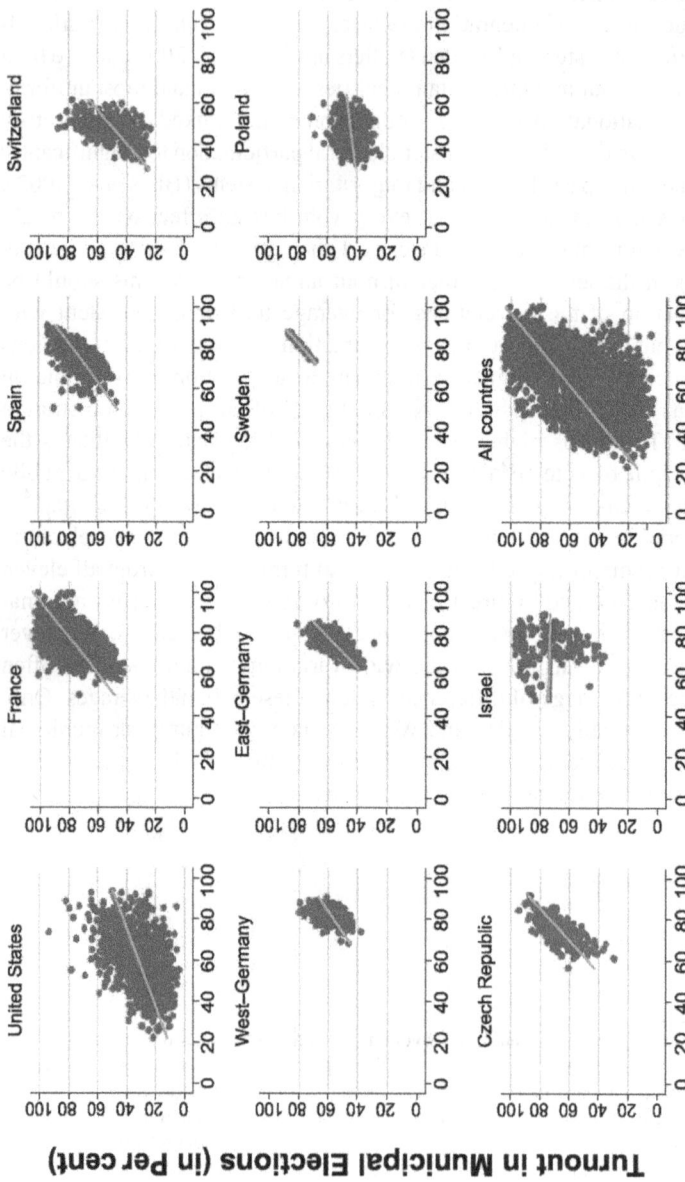

Figure 13.3: Turnout in national and municipal elections in metropolitan municipalities of ten countries (West Germany and East Germany as two separate countries)

*Table 13.5: Bivariate correlations of average local/municipal turnout with metropolitan structure*

| | | National turnout (average) | Municipal turnout (average) | Turnout gap |
|---|---|---|---|---|
| Metropolitan population (log) | | −0.152 | −0.404 | 0.464 |
| | N | 175 | 148 | 148 |
| Metropolitan population concentration (Herfindahl index) | | −0.079 | 0.054 | −0.191 |
| | N | 144 | 144 | 144 |
| Metropolitan geopolitical fragmentation (Zeigler-Brunn index) | | 0.199 | 0.329 | −0.261 |
| | N | 155 | 147 | 147 |
| Metropolitan socio-spatial polarisation (three-category Simpson Index) | | −0.125 | −0.539 | 0.339 |
| | N | 175 | 148 | 148 |
| City-suburban polarisation (aggregated Nathan Adams index) | | 0.083 | −0.175 | 0.480 |
| | N | 141 | 121 | 121 |
| Metropolitan affluence | | 0.023 | −0.067 | 0.063 |
| | N | 175 | 148 | 148 |

*Notes*: For boldface coefficients, $p < 0.05$; for boldface italicised coefficients, $p < 0.01$.

### Understanding multi-scalar spatial effects on turnout

Differences among metropolitan regions comprise one of the main sources of variations in turnout and help to account for a significant part of the differences among nations. In nearly every country in this study, the analyses have affirmed that higher population density and larger size reduce turnout in elections (see Table 13.5). Across the entire dataset, just as Preteceille (2000) found for France, larger metropolitan areas have lower voting rates. This effect is much stronger in municipal elections, where ties to a local community within the wider metropolis play a more crucial role in voter mobilisation.[6] Several other structural features of metropolitan areas also correlate intriguingly with local turnout rates (see Table 13.5). Metro-level correlations suggest that a lower turnout gap (between national and local participation rates) is linked to geopolitical fragmentation and possibly population concentration. The Zeigler-Brunn index of geopolitical fragmentation correlates significantly with national turnout, but even more strongly with municipal turnout, and therefore with a smaller turnout gap.[7] Socio-

---

6. A logged variable for metropolitan population correlates strongly (−0.409, p<0.01) with lower turnout in municipal elections, but just short of significantly (−0.146, p<0.10) with national election turnout. As the country analyses of the United States and France both found, the combined effect is an even stronger positive correlation with the gap between national and local electoral participation (0.474, p<0.01).

7. A related measure of total population concentration, the Herfindahl index, measures the overall population concentration among metropolitan municipalities. Although this index correlates

spatial diversity and polarisation also correlate significantly enough to bolster the case that metropolitan structure has independent effects on turnout. Metropolitan variations also comprise an important source of the cross-national differences. Fully 48 per cent of the variation in metropolitan polarisation, 45 per cent of the variation in metropolitan population concentration and 41 per cent of the variation in metropolitan geopolitical fragmentation occur between countries, rather than within them.

Decades of electoral research have, of course, shown election turnout to be influenced by a broad range of variables beyond the macro-institutional setting and the metropolitan context (Franklin 2004; Geys 2006). A full analysis of why communities vary in turnout must also take into account place-related variables describing the spatial contextual attributes of a community, as well as variables related to the motivation and resources of individual citizens to engage in the act of voting. To separate out these influences, analysis of the integrated dataset employed multilevel modelling techniques similar to those used in most of the country chapters.

### Predicting turnout in local elections

Participation in municipal elections is influenced by factors operating at all three scales of governance. According to a simple analysis of variance, the differences between countries that have traditionally been the focus of cross-national turnout comparisons leave 29 per cent of the variance unexplained. Since as much as 48 per cent of the variance between countries also corresponds to metropolitan and local variation, sub-national effects are likely at work beyond what this initial figure suggests. At least 25 per cent of the overall variance occurs at the municipal/community scale, and at least 6 per cent at the metropolitan scale. The country chapters have shown that municipal characteristics exert numerous influences on local election turnout and account for an important part of the variation in municipal election turnout within countries.

Multilevel regressions based on the pooled dataset enabled an encompassing test of national and metropolitan differences alongside others tested in the country chapters (see Table 13.6). After tests of alternative hierarchical and non-hierarchical models, we settled on a set of three-level hierarchical models that incorporated effects at the municipal (level 1), the metropolitan (level 2), and the national levels (level 3). The models thus fitted included a linear model, a model with cross-level interactions, and a combined model.[8] Metropolitan effects, combined with dichot-

---

weakly with either national or local turnout, it correlates significantly with a lower turnout gap. Although the correlation between this index and the Zeigler-Brunn index is significant (0.407, p<0.01), it remains low enough to permit independent effects from overall population concentration in some of the following models.

8.     At both the municipal and the metropolitan levels, the model included weights to correct the different numbers of municipalities and metropolitan areas in the country samples. Final variables for each model were selected through backward regression.

*Table 13.6: Multilevel regression analysis of municipal election turnout*

| | Linear model | | Cross-level effects | | Combined model | |
|---|---|---|---|---|---|---|
| | **B** | **t** | **B** | **t** | **B** | **t** |
| Intercept | **74.34** | **4.37** | **80.02** | **4.67** | **88.86** | **9.09** |
| *Country-level variables* | | | | | | |
| Metropolitanisation | −0.13 | −0.50 | −0.13 | −0.49 | | |
| Civic localism | | | | | **−55.62** | **−7.69** |
| Third-wave democracies | | | | | **−1.00** | **−0.45** |
| Election Day holiday | | | | | **−32.34** | **−3.75** |
| Ease of voting | | | | | **33.17** | **4.17** |
| Compulsory registration | | | | | **14.43** | **6.31** |
| *Metropolitan and cross-level variables* | | | | | | |
| Population concentration | **7.96** | **2.93** | **7.42** | **2.69** | **7.45** | **2.72** |
| Geopolitical fragmentation | **0.14** | **2.51** | **0.13** | **2.27** | *0.10* | *1.72* |
| Civic localism (country) | | | | | 0.76 | 2.51 |
| Socio-spatial polarisation | *−4.77* | *−1.76* | *−4.85* | *−1.77* | −3.85 | −1.42 |
| Metropolitan population (log) (metro) | *−0.82* | *−0.84* | *−1.70* | *−1.61* | −1.04 | −0.98 |
| Metropolitan affluence | −0.24 | −0.17 | −1.46 | −0.98 | −1.73 | −1.18 |
| *Municipal and cross-level variables* | | | | | | |
| Urban concentrations | **2.23** | **3.45** | **−31.23** | **−4.29** | **−33.14** | **−4.43** |
| Population concentration (metro) | | | **9.90** | **2.66** | **13.24** | **3.02** |
| Metropolitan population (log) (metro) | | | **4.65** | **3.76** | **5.47** | **4.18** |
| Metropolitan affluence (metro) | | | **8.79** | **3.39** | **8.33** | **3.00** |
| Affluent suburbs | −0.50 | −1.58 | **−3.83** | **−4.38** | 0.20 | 0.31 |
| Civic localism (country) | | | | | **4.15** | **4.49** |
| Third-wave democracies (country) | | | | | **1.51** | **2.59** |
| Compulsory registration (country) | | | | | **−1.84** | **−2.80** |
| Socio-spatial polarisation (metro) | | | **7.75** | **4.09** | | |
| Low-density suburbs | **0.61** | **1.98** | **0.62** | **1.99** | **0.72** | **2.32** |
| Municipal population (log) | **−10.05** | **−33.55** | **−7.84** | **−13.00** | **−8.11** | **−12.30** |

| | Linear model | | Cross-level effects | | Combined model | |
|---|---|---|---|---|---|---|
| | **B** | **t** | **B** | **t** | **B** | **t** |
| Geopolitical fragmentation (metro) | | | **−0.10** | **−3.45** | **−0.10** | **−3.30** |
| Metropolitan affluence (metro) | | | **−3.21** | **−3.30** | **−2.68** | **−2.43** |
| Poor non-minority suburbs | −0.30 | −1.21 | −0.37 | −1.51 | 0.46 | 0.87 |
| Metropolitan affluence (metro) | | | | | *−2.05* | *−1.74* |
| Poor minority suburbs | **−1.99** | **−3.14** | **−13.52** | **−5.24** | −0.39 | −0.47 |
| Metrpolitanisation (country) | | | **0.21** | **4.71** | | |
| Geopolitical fragmentation (metro) | | | | | **−0.17** | **−2.18** |
| Log likelihood | | −39192 | | −39159 | | −39132 |
| Reliability: Level one | | 0.97 | | 0.97 | | 0.96 |
| Level two | | 0.98 | | 0.98 | | 0.56 |
| Variance explained | | | | | | |
| Local | | 50% | | 51% | | 51% |
| Metropolitan | | 8% | | 9% | | 11% |
| National | | 15% | | 15% | | 98% |
| Total | | 23% | | 23% | | 83% |
| Deviance | | 78384 | | 78318 | | 78264 |
| Estimated parameters | | 43 | | 50 | | 58 |
| N: Local | | 12012 | | 12012 | | 12012 |

*Notes:* Coefficients are full maximum likelihood estimates in HLM3 with randomised error terms. For italicised coefficients, $p<0.10$; for boldface coefficients, $p<0.05$.

omous place variables for each of the different types of metropolitan municipalities/communities, accounted for 50–51 per cent of the local variance and 23 per cent of overall variance in turnout.

Certain structural and institutional features of metropolitan areas exert especially strong influences. The models point to a robust 'large is lively' effect (Kelleher and Lowery 2004). The more the population of a metropolitan area is concentrated in a small number of municipalities, the higher the turnout in local elections. Since the separate measure of metropolitan geopolitical fragmentation – the Zeigler and Brunn (1980) index – also raises municipal election turnout, the model provides simultaneous support for the countervailing 'small is beautiful' thesis. A significant cross-level variable in the full model shows that the latter effect is concentrated strongly in countries with civic localist local government systems.[9] These specific

---

9. Models in Table 13.6 and Table 13.7 exclude Canadian and UK data due to the absence of some

structural features of metropolitan areas overwhelmed influences from the other metropolitan variables that correlated with variations in turnout.

The multilevel models confirm important and consistent place effects from distinct types of suburban localities, even when national differences are taken into account. In all three models, the large negative effect from population size on municipal turnout overwhelms the other variables. Beyond this effect, municipal turnout is also consistently higher in low-density suburbs. Variables for cross-level interactions also show that the effect from municipal size depends partly on metropolitan structures. In more affluent and middle-class metropolitan areas, and in those with higher levels of geopolitical fragmentation, smaller communities also have disproportionately higher turnout rates than elsewhere. Each of these relationships extends beyond the United States, and beyond North America. Rather than products of a distinct national culture, they must be understood as global consequences of metropolitan settlement.

At the same time, many of the largest, most densely-populated and most central metropolitan communities have more lively and engaging municipal elections. As the dichotomous variable for urban concentrations demonstrates, municipal turnout in these settings averages significantly higher than their size would predict. The models with cross-level interactions indicate that this effect is confined to particular metropolitan contexts. Municipal election turnout in metropolitan urban centres is higher where the metropolitan population is more concentrated, bigger and/or more affluent. Beyond these settings, turnout in urban centres is significantly lower than their size alone would dictate.

Among affluent suburbs, the models reveal a surprising exception to the greater mobilisation that has generally been found among affluent voters. As the French and Polish analyses observed, the lower turnout of this type of community in municipal elections suggests a disengagement from local politics that has not been noted before. Yet the effect is inconsistent, and there are caveats. The affluent suburbs of civic localist countries, third-wave democracies, and the more-divided metropolitan regions turn out more often to vote. And where compulsory national voter registration laws are present, the differential in turnout rates between affluent suburbs and other communities diminishes.

Among poor suburbs, the effects from class-related differences are also inconsistent. Poor minority suburbs turn out to vote consistently less than elsewhere (at least in the first two models).[10] Only in more affluent metropolitan areas does the same effect hold in poor nonminority suburbs.

Institutional factors account for much of the differences in spatial-contextual effects across communities. Variables that capture cross-national differences in

---

metropolitan indicators for both, and the limited local turnout data for the UK. Models including the data from these two countries nonetheless confirmed strong civic localism effects.

10. The addition of national institutional differences to the third model eliminates this effect, except for a significantly lower turnout rate among poor minority concentrations located in more fragmented metropolitan regions.

institutions and politics raise the overall proportion of variance explained from 23 to 82 per cent. Although the small number of countries necessitates caution about making too many inferences from this result, we note that our sample includes a distribution of cases that span the range of institutional alternatives. Of these, the civic localism of the Anglo-American democracies and Switzerland exerts the strongest single direct effect. It produces unevenness in participation even as it depresses overall turnout, fostering higher participation in affluent suburbs but lower turnout in poor minority suburbs. Meanwhile, both ease of voting and compulsory registration raise turnout significantly, while interaction with other national-institutional variables produces a significant negative coefficient for the Election Day holiday.

Importantly, the full model with the national-institutional variables included serves to confirm the independence and significance of most effects at the metropolitan and local levels. Beyond what established sources of cross-national differences can explain, influences at these levels account for nearly a quarter of the overall variation in municipal turnout.

### Predicting participation in national elections

As Figure 13.1 showed, turnout rates in national elections are generally higher, and in some countries much higher, than in municipal elections. Although many of the same contextual factors account for variations in national and municipal turnout, there are also important differences linked to metropolitan and local characteristics. The more mobilised electorate of national elections is generally more biased in favour of affluent and middle-class municipalities and against more diverse, more polarised metropolitan areas. National levels of metropolitanisation also make a difference in promoting turnout in national elections that is not evident in municipal elections.

Metropolitan structure contributes in a largely similar way to national turnout as it does to municipal turnout, but with significant variations. Metropolitan population concentration fosters significantly higher voting rates, although the coefficients remain smaller and less significant than for municipal elections (see Table 13.7). Polarisation among metropolitan communities depresses national turnout even more strongly than it does municipal turnout. However, the positive effects from intergovernmental fragmentation on municipal election turnout disappear altogether in national elections. The large size that results from concentrated population thus fosters liveliness less in national elections than in municipal ones. The reduction in size that follows from metropolitan jurisdictional fragmentation, whatever its beauty is for municipal democracy, lacks any discernible influence on national electoral participation.[11]

---

11. It could be argued that the Zeigler-Brunn and Simpson indices measure a similar phenomenon that manifests itself at different scales of analysis. Thus municipal fragmentation, which is associated with socio-spatial polarisation among municipalities, has stronger effects at the municipal level, while polarisation among households more generally has stronger effects on national electoral participation.

*Table 13.7: Multilevel regression analysis of national election turnout*

| | Linear model | | Cross-level effects | | Combined model | |
|---|---|---|---|---|---|---|
| | **B** | **t** | **B** | **t** | **B** | **t** |
| Intercept | **49.07** | **3.56** | **47.77** | **3.46** | **101.59** | **10.93** |
| *Country-level variables* | | | | | | |
| Metropolitanisation | 0.26 | 1.18 | 0.30 | 1.38 | | |
| Civic localism | | | | | −46.94 | −6.34 |
| Third-wave democracies | | | | | −2.08 | −0.90 |
| Election Day holiday | | | | | *−31.69* | *−3.25* |
| Ease of voting | | | | | *27.06* | *3.04* |
| Election Day registration | | | | | −21.77 | −5.43 |
| Compulsory registration | | | | | −4.48 | −1.69 |
| *Metropolitan-level variables* | | | | | | |
| Population concentration | **5.24** | **2.43** | **3.61** | **1.59** | **5.58** | **2.53** |
| Geopolitical fragmentation | −0.03 | −0.71 | 0.05 | 0.91 | 0.02 | 0.30 |
| Socio-spatial polarisation | **−4.75** | **−2.17** | **−6.75** | **−2.97** | **−4.46** | **−1.98** |
| Metropolitan population (log) | 1.08 | 1.33 | 1.14 | 1.34 | 0.52 | 0.60 |
| Metropolitan affluence | 1.61 | 1.39 | 0.28 | 0.23 | 0.38 | 0.31 |
| *Municipal and cross-level variables* | | | | | | |
| Urban concentrations | 0.31 | 0.61 | −0.31 | −0.13 | −3.04 | −3.35 |
| Metropolitanisation (country) | | | **−0.12** | **−3.08** | | |
| Population concentration (metro) | | | **7.52** | **2.48** | | |
| Socio-spatial polarisation (metro) | | | **8.09** | **2.73** | | |
| Metropolitan affluence | | | **4.85** | **2.65** | **5.69** | **3.33** |
| Affluent suburbs | **1.40** | **4.39** | **−13.37** | **−3.55** | **2.97** | **6.14** |
| Metropolitanisation (country) | | | **0.05** | **2.05** | | |
| Civic localism (country) | | | | | **8.31** | **12.23** |
| Ease of voting (country) | | | | | **−6.60** | **−4.69** |
| Metropolitan population (log) (metro) | | | **2.10** | **3.26** | | |
| Low-density suburbs | **−1.26** | **−6.86** | **−16.89** | **−7.39** | **−10.11** | **−4.81** |
| Metropolitanisation (country) | | | **0.05** | **3.15** | | |
| Election Day holiday (country) | | | | | **−2.64** | **−4.66** |
| Population concentration (metro) | | | **3.76** | **2.93** | **3.50** | **2.80** |
| Ziegler-Brunn Index (metro) | | | **0.05** | **2.22** | **0.05** | **2.11** |
| Socio-spatial polarisation (metro) | | | **−2.54** | **−2.57** | **−2.25** | **−2.29** |
| Metropolitan population (log) (metro) | | | **2.22** | **6.50** | **1.92** | **6.31** |
| Municipal population (log) | **−3.02** | **−10.74** | **−2.32** | **−6.60** | **−2.97** | **−9.24** |
| Election Day registration (country) | | | | | **7.25** | **9.30** |

| | Linear model | | Cross-level effects | | Combined model | |
|---|---|---|---|---|---|---|
| | **B** | **t** | **B** | **t** | **B** | **t** |
| Geopolitical fragmentation (metro) | | | **−0.13** | **−4.06** | **−0.08** | **−3.00** |
| Poor non-minority suburbs | **−1.68** | **−7.74** | **5.66** | **2.12** | **−1.45** | **−7.44** |
| Civic localism (country) | | | | | **−4.07** | **−6.46** |
| Metropolitan population (log) (metro) | | | **−1.27** | **−2.80** | | |
| Poor minority suburbs | **−2.73** | **−7.11** | *7.30* | *1.67* | | |
| Metropolitanisation (country) | | | **−0.06** | **−2.30** | **3.50** | **0.93** |
| Civic localism (country) | | | | | **−3.83** | **−3.29** |
| Population concentration (metro) | | | 5.73 | 1.60 | | |
| Metropolitan population (log) (metro) | | | *−1.30* | *−1.78* | *−1.04* | *−1.67* |
| Log likelihood | −36308 | | −36257 | | −36186 | |
| Reliability: Level one | 0.98 | | 0.98 | | 0.98 | |
| Level two | 0.98 | | 0.98 | | 0.77 | |
| Variance explained | | | | | | |
| Local | 34% | | 34% | | 34% | |
| Total | 24% | | 26% | | 82% | |
| Deviance | 72617 | | 72515 | | 72371 | |
| Estimated parameters | 43 | | 59 | | 61 | |
| N | 12441 | | 12441 | | 12441 | |

*Notes:* Coefficients are full maximum likelihood estimates in HLM3 with randomised error terms. For italicised coefficients, $p<0.10$; for boldface coefficients, $p<0.05$.

At the level of local communities, the cross-country analysis of national participation rates identifies greater mobilisation among affluent and middle class communities than in municipal elections, on the one hand, and lower mobilisation among poor communities on the other. This is especially pronounced in civic localist countries and those scoring low on ease of voting scale (see Blais *et al.* 2003). This effect is furthermore linked to high levels of metropolitanisation and greater metropolitan size.

Unlike in municipal elections, moreover, both poor minority suburbs and poor nonminority suburbs experience significantly lower turnout rates. These communities are thus significantly under-represented in national electorates. For both types of disadvantaged communities, as the cross-level interactions demonstrate, these effects concentrate in civic localist countries, in larger metropolitan areas, and in countries with higher rates of metropolitanisation.

Municipal size has similar effects on national elections as it does on municipal elections, albeit on a more limited scale. However, there is a clear difference among low-density suburbs. The municipal elections are distinguished by significantly higher turnout rates than elsewhere, but these localities vote at significantly lower rates in national elections. This effect is especially pronounced in smaller, more polarised, less concentrated, and less geopolitically fragmented metropolitan areas, and in countries with lower levels of metropolitanisation.

With a few exceptions, the national-institutional influences on participation in national elections are more difficult to distinguish. However, there is a clear relationship with civic localism. This form of governance retains a significant association with lower overall national turnout, and with both higher rates in affluent suburbs and lower rates in poor and minority suburbs. Election Day registration has a negative relationship with national turnout as a result of multicollinearity with other national-institutional influences, but a positive cross-level relationship with larger municipalities.

Finally, the significance of greater metropolitanisation at the national scale points to a more general relationship between metropolitanisation and national patterns of electoral mobilisation. Analyses of metropolitan political influence in the national policy-making process of the United States have convincingly demonstrated how the growing power of affluent and middle-class suburbs over the twentieth century marginalised representatives from inner-city and disadvantaged communities (Mollenkopf 1983; Wolman and Marckini 1998). The results here suggest that these differentials in influence are a transnational consequence of metropolitanisation that is connected to differences in electoral mobilisation itself. Metropolitanisation raises national election turnout in affluent and low-density suburbs, and lowers it in urban concentrations and poor minority suburbs. These effects may come about partly through differences in the influence of representatives from these types of places on electoral laws, policies and other institutions. The effects from national metropolitanisation are clearly collinear with effects from the national institutional differences tested in the full model, and disappear when the institutional variables are included.

Metropolitanisation at the national scale thus has systemic consequences for the mobilisation of different types of metropolitan communities. In the most metropolitanised polities, affluent, middle class and low density suburbs mobilise more effectively than others to maintain their predominant position in the metropolitan electorate. On top of the difficulties that municipal size and urban density create for mobilisation, urban concentrations and poor suburbs face a growing numerical disadvantage in the national electoral competition to influence public policy.

## Metropolitanisation and electoral participation

The spread of metropolitan settlement has established systematic geographic variations in political participation. The predominant accounts of political nationalisation by Caramani (2004) have failed to recognise this complex re-territorialisation of politics. Older distinctions between urban and rural settlement, or between discrete territorial regions between countries, cannot capture the main lines of the resulting divisions within and between metropolitan areas. Numerous consequences from metropolitanisation, including increasingly uneven electoral participation in larger cities and divided, dispersed metropolitan regions, have undoubtedly contributed to the declining overall turnout levels in developed democracies over the last decades (Fuchs and Klingemann 1995). As the multilevel analysis of turnout has shown, a simple transnational typology of local places and metropolitan characteristics captures a remarkable proportion of the cross-national local variation.

A final question concerns the degree to which turnout patterns are simply a result of the social composition of the electorate that happens to live in distinct types of places, rather than consequences from the characteristics of places themselves. While the demographic composition of municipalities remains a major predictor of turnout rates, and in national elections can account for most of the explained variation in participation (see Table 13.7), the fine-grained analyses of the country chapters confirm that, indeed, it is features of the local and metropolitan spatial contexts that make much of the difference (see Table 13.8).

Contextual factors frequently predict municipal turnout better than demographic composition does, and provide alternative accounts to socio-economic characteristics for a further proportion of the variation. The country chapters confirm a variety of specific spatial effects:

- The negative effect of population size and/or population density on election turnout stands out as an overall result. In every country, turnout in at least one type of election falls with the population size or population density of a municipality. In eight of the eleven countries, this relationship holds for both national and local elections. The independent effects of population size and density alongside each other, where both are available and significant, confirm a clear 'small is beautiful' effect.

- In every European and North American democracy where homeownership was tested, it exerts a positive effect on turnout in elections at one or both levels beyond the effects of demographic composition.

- In four of the six countries where occupational diversity was tested, it had negative effects on turnout in elections at one or both levels. More economically-homogeneous communities generally turn out to vote more.

- The presence of commuters has diverse effects on turnout rates that are related to national differences in the social geography of cities. For example, in the United States and Sweden, the effect in local elections is negative whereas in both local and national elections in France and Spain, and in national elections in Germany, commuting is a significant predictor of higher turnout. The research from Canada suggests these differences derive partly from the way that social class interacts with the automobile dependence of places.

- Residential stability has a positive influence on election turnout in the United States and Poland, but negative effects in the United Kingdom and France. Its effects were generally more positive at the municipal level than at the national level.

- Electoral competition also has diverse effects on participation. For example, it has a positive effect in the United States but a negative one in France.

*Table 13.8: Influences on local/municipal-level turnout in local and national elections, overview of country results*

| | Israel 100% | | Germany 83% | | USA 78% | | UK 76% | | Canada 64% | | Spain 54% | | France 52% | | Poland 42% | | Switzerland 40% | | Sweden 32% | | Czech Rep. 28% | |
|---|---|---|---|---|---|---|---|---|---|---|---|---|---|---|---|---|---|---|---|---|---|---|
| | Loc | Nat | Loc | Nat | Loc | Nat | Loc | Nat | Loc | Nat | Loc | Nat | Loc | Nat | Loc | Nat | Loc | Nat | Loc | Nat | Loc | Nat |
| Metropolitanisation | 100% | | 83% | | 78% | | 76% | | 64% | | 54% | | 52% | | 42% | | 40% | | 32% | | 28% | |
| *Compositional variables at municipal level* | | | | | | | | | | | | | | | | | | | | | | |
| Socio-economic status | – | (+) | + | + | + | + | 0 | + | 0 | 0 | (+) | + | + | + | 0 | 0 | 0 | + | + | + | (–) | + |
| Hardship index | n/a | n/a | 0 | 0 | 0 | – | – | – | – | – | 0 | 0 | – | – | – | – | 0 | – | n/a | n/a | (–) | – |
| Foreign born residents | n/a | n/a | 0 | 0 | 0 | 0 | (+) | + | 0 | 0 | – | (–) | – | – | n/a | n/a | 0 | – | + | – | 0 | 0 |
| Old residents | (–) | 0 | + | 0 | + | + | 0 | + | 0 | 0 | + | + | 0 | 0 | n/a | n/a | 0 | + | + | 0 | (+) | + |
| Young residents | (+) | (+) | + | 0 | n/a | n/a | + | + | 0 | 0 | + | + | n/a | n/a | n/a | n/a | 0 | + | + | 0 | (+) | 0 |
| *Contextual variables at municipal level* | | | | | | | | | | | | | | | | | | | | | | |
| Homeownership | n/a | 0 | n/a | n/a | + | + | 0 | + | 0 | + | n/a | n/a | + | + | n/a | n/a | + | (+) | (+) | (+) | (+) | (+) |
| Residential stability | n/a | n/a | n/a | n/a | 0 | + | 0 | (–) | 0 | 0 | n/a | n/a | – | – | + | + | 0 | 0 | n/a | n/a | n/a | n/a |
| Out-commuting | n/a | n/a | 0 | + | (–) | 0 | 0 | 0 | (–) | 0 | – | 0 | + | + | n/a | n/a | – | – | 0 | 0 | n/a | n/a |
| Electoral competition | n/a | n/a | n/a | n/a | + | + | n/a | n/a | n/a | n/a | n/a | n/a | – | – | n/a | n/a | n/a | n/a | n/a | n/a | n/a | n/a |
| Population size | – | – | – | – | – | – | – | – | – | – | – | – | – | – | – | + | – | – | – | 0 | – | (–) |
| Population density | (–) | 0 | – | 0 | 0 | (+) | 0 | – | 0 | 0 | 0 | (–) | – | – | – | 0 | 0 | + | 0 | 0 | 0 | n/a |
| Economic diversity | n/a | n/a | – | – | 0 | – | – | – | – | 0 | + | (+) | – | + | n/a | n/a | 0 | + | n/a | n/a | 0 | 0 |

*Notes:* + = significant positive relation to turnout; – = significant negative relation to turnout; 0 = no significant relation to turnout; n/a = relation not tested in country study. Parentheses indicate significance in some but not all models.

Not only do these attributes of place matter, but the arrangement and structure of metropolitan areas make a large difference. For electoral participation in a metropolitan municipality, it matters whether that municipality is located in a metropolitan area in which the population is concentrated or dispersed, whether the institutional configuration is fragmented or consolidated, whether the socio-economic pattern is homogeneous or diverse, whether the metropolitan area is large or small, and whether it is affluent or not. Thus, metropolitanisation complicates the local 'small is beautiful' and other localised place effects on municipal election turnout with a variety of countervailing and reinforcing effects at intermediate scales.

Taken together, the results of the country studies and the pooled analysis provide compelling confirmatory evidence for metropolitanisation as an important source of variations in national and local political participation, and the pervasive gap between them. Beyond this turnout gap itself, the analysis has also revealed partly divergent ecological dynamics in national and local elections. Especially in local elections, but to an important and overlooked degree in national elections as well, features of metropolitan places themselves are critical to these dynamics. The continued expansion of metropolitan regions compounds and gives growing weight to the processes this analysis has revealed. The persistent divergences in turnout between metropolitan places ultimately skew patterns of competition between the parties these places support.

## Metropolitanisation and partisanship

Metropolitanisation has also transformed the geographic sources of partisan loyalties and, in turn, national strategies of partisan competition. In doing so, it has altered the nationalisation of partisan competition that took place with the decline of regionally-distinct party systems over the nineteenth and early twentieth centuries. Place-based partisan divergences that first emerged within large established metropolises are being mirrored in other metropolitan areas throughout national territories (Hoffmann-Martinot and Sellers 2005). Where similar contrasts within metropolitan areas have emerged in regions with traditionally-distinct partisan affiliations, the resulting regional convergence may seem to bring about a degree of nationalisation. Far from the disappearance of territory in national politics, however, metropolitan political divides represent a new, embedded source of territorial cleavages that are increasingly central to partisan competition.

Research on the nationalisation of party systems has devised a number of metrics to compare the territorial homogeneity of electoral support for political parties among countries and over time (see Table 13.9).[12] Applied to measure the

---

12. The IPR index (Caramani 2005: 300), already used to measure heterogeneity in turnout, is based on the differences between the share of the votes for each party in the municipality, weighted by the number and size of municipalities. The IPR varies between a minimum of zero, signifying a perfectly homogeneous distribution of partisan support, and one, indicating territorially-distinct concentrations of support for different parties. The cumulative standard deviation for party

*Table 13.9: Levels of territorial heterogeneity of party support in metropolitan municipalities/communities across eleven countries (national elections)*

| | Country | Year(s) of election | Cumulative S.D. | Overall S.D., 1990s (Caramani 2004) | IPR (weighted summary) | Overall weighted IPR, 1990s (Caramani 2004) | PSNS | Overall PSNS, 1980s and 1990s (Jones and Mainwaring 2003) |
|---|---|---|---|---|---|---|---|---|
| Nationalised | United States | 1996–2004 | 26.0 | | 0.32 | | 0.86 | 0.84 |
| | Sweden | 1998–2002 | 31.3 | 22.3 | 0.34 | 0.29 | 0.84 | |
| | Germany | 1998–2002 | 33.0 | 55.1 | 0.34 | 0.40 | 0.82 | |
| | West | | 21.0 | | 0.28 | | 0.89 | |
| | East | | 26.1 | | 0.32 | | 0.86 | |
| | Czech Republic | 1996–2002 | 42.3 | | 0.39 | | 0.78 | |
| | France | 2001 | 43.1 | 34.2 | 0.39 | 0.32 | 0.77 | |
| Territorialised | United Kingdom (England, Wales) | 2001 | 49.2 | 53.9 | 0.40 | 0.44 | 0.77 | |
| | Poland | 1993–2001 | 59.8 | | 0.46 | | 0.71 | |
| | Spain | 1996–2004 | 62.1 | 57.6 | 0.48 | 0.37 | 0.68 | |
| | Switzerland | 1999–2003 | 68.7 | 102 | 0.49 | 0.58 | 0.67 | |
| | Canada | 2006 | 68.9 | | 0.51 | | 0.66 | 0.72 |
| | Israel | 1999–2003 | 110.8 | | 0.64 | | 0.48 | |

*Notes:* PSNS = Party System Nationalisation Score US score from Jones and Mainwaring (2003) and IPR for France from Caramani (2004) based on Lower Chamber legislative elections, rather than presidential elections used for IMO dataset. Metropolitan figures calculated by legislative districts in the United Kingdom and Canada, by municipal units in all other countries.

territorial homogeneity of party support among the metropolitan communities in each country, these measurements correspond remarkably closely to national differences found in the literature on party-system nationalisation. Caramani's cut-off point for distinguishing nationalised from 'regionalised' or more territorialised systems[13] yields five countries in the first category and six in the second.

For the three clearly nationalised countries with comparative metrics (the

---

support is a measure of the dispersion of support of individual parties across municipalities within countries. The higher is the figure, the higher territorial heterogeneity of party support (Caramani 2005: 321). Similarly, the so-called Party System Nationalisation Score (PSNS) (Jones and Mainwaring 2003: 143) is based on the Gini coefficient and measures the equality of the share of votes for each party across municipalities, weighted by the overall size of each party. The PSNS varies from a minimum of zero, indicating perfectly unequal party support across municipalities, to a maximum of one, indicating perfectly equal party support across municipalities. The specific strengths and weaknesses of each of these indicators have been discussed elsewhere (Caramani 2005).

13. Since the metrics measure overall territorial heterogeneity, including sub-regional variation, it is misleading to employ 'regionalised' as the opposite of 'nationalised' (Carmani 2005: 300). Table 13.9 adapts Caramani's categories accordingly.

United States, Sweden and France), the indicators show slightly greater territorial heterogeneity among metropolitan localities than among national legislative districts. For most countries with major regional partisan differences, notably Switzerland, the United Kingdom, Germany and Canada, the overall metropolitan variation is less pronounced than that among national legislative districts. German metropolitan patterns proved sufficiently homogeneous to move that country into the nationalised category. In Germany, especially, and in Switzerland, metropolitan divisions have overlaid regional ones with elements of cross-regional standardisation. In countries with less stark historical regional divisions, metropolitan divisions appear to capture and even accentuate the overall levels of national territorial heterogeneity.[14]

Measures such as these from the nationalisation literature provide no way of sorting out territorial heterogeneity at the metropolitan and local scales from other variation. As noted in Chapter 1 in this volume, it is also important to understand how much of the variation in partisanship occurs within as well as between metropolitan areas (see Table 1.2 in Chapter 1). Comparison of the variance within and between metropolitan areas in the left-right partisanship index of the metropolitan dataset demonstrates the pervasive role of local variation in the overall patterns (see Figure 13.4). Although the eleven nations in our study display quite different mixes of regional and local variation, significant territorial variations are present in all of them. Most striking is the absence of purely regional heterogeneity. Among countries with high regional variation, such as Canada, Spain and Switzerland, the variations are instead multi-scalar. Partisan heterogeneity within the metropolitan areas of these countries is generally higher than in most of the other cases. Within Israel, the country with the greatest territorial variation, the largest component of that variation occurs within metropolitan areas.

The country chapters have already shown many of the ways patterns of party support differ systematically across metropolitan communities. This metropolitan heterogeneity has added new layers of complexity to previous patterns of political regionalism. In some cases, metropolitanisation has worked to reduce the importance of regionalism. In others, the interaction between the two has fostered new political allegiances and party relationships. If metropolitanisation has levelled some regional variations, it has reinforced others. It has entrenched new territorial divides and lines of partisan competition among communities and subcultures within metropolitan areas. Often, the metropolitan places with the most opposed partisan loyalties are located only a few minutes apart from each other. In all these respects, metropolitanisation has given rise to new forms of territorialisation.

---

14. Caramani also classified Switzerland into a separate group of highly-regionalised countries (Caramani 2004: 93). However, the metrics he reports for that country in the 1990s (Caramani 2004: 89), reflected in Table 13.9, do not place it in that category.

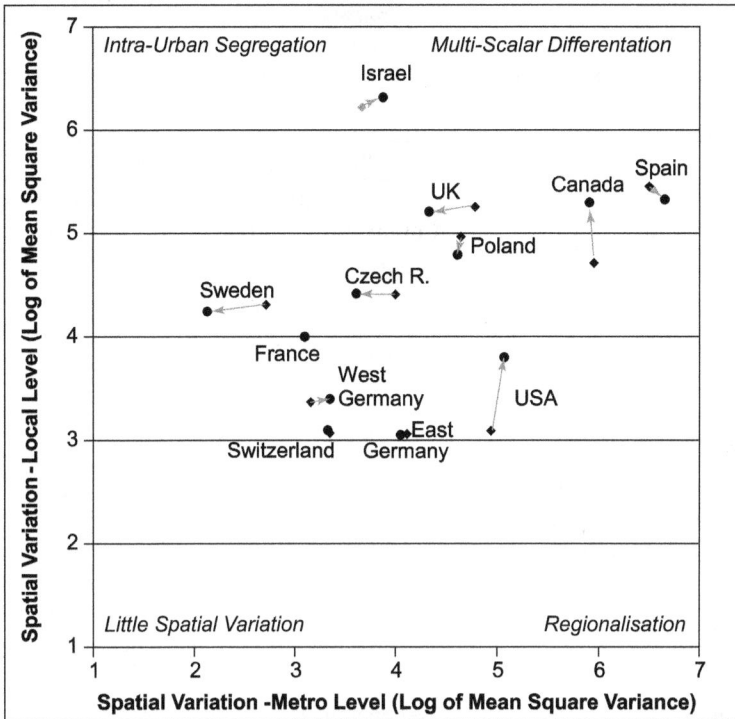

*Figure 13.4: Change in the level of local and metropolitan variation in partisanship over time*

*Note:* Variance reflects the variance decomposition as determined through ANOVA.

## Metropolitan patterns of party support – from nationalisation to metropolitanisation?

As in the analysis of turnout, cross-national comparison requires that local and metropolitan patterns of partisanship be considered against the backdrop of national political competition and other variations among countries. Parties can be interpreted as competing in a political marketplace for votes (Kitschelt 1994). The choices voters make remain constrained by the positions and candidates that the parties choose to offer. Increasingly, metropolitanisation has shaped this dual logic of partisan competition. Each of the main party families in developed and transitional democracies has found strongholds of support in specific types of metropolitan places. Despite the large differences between national party systems, a consistent metropolitan political ecology comprises part of the genealogical make-up of each party family.[15]

---

15. Definitions of party families follow the classification scheme in Kriesi et al. (2008). See Table A13.1 in the Appendix to this chapter.

*Table 13.10: Voter support for parties, grouped by party families and ideological issue position indices (standardised by countries) in metropolitan communities – proportions of variance between countries, metropolitan areas and municipalities (ANOVA)*

| | Percentage of variance between: | | |
|---|---|---|---|
| **Voter support** | **Countries** | **Metropolitan areas** | **Municipalities/ communities** |
| Far left parties (6/11 countries) | 47% | 14% | 39% |
| Green parties (8/11 countries) | 39% | 14% | 47% |
| Centre-left parties (11/11 countries) | 62% | 12% | 26% |
| Centre-right parties (11/11 countries) | 52% | 19% | 28% |
| Market liberal parties (10/11 countries) | 73% | 10% | 17% |
| Far right parties (5/11 countries) | 25% | 31% | 44% |
| Regionalist and ethnic parties (3/11 countries) | 15% | 55% | 30% |

The eleven countries of the dataset encompass a wide variety of national party systems, and reflect diverse national trends in contemporary electoral competition. The cross-sectional variations exemplify how the fortunes of different parties have fluctuated over time. The sample includes countries with, at the time of study, overall majorities to the left at the national level (Sweden, Germany, the United Kingdom and Poland), one country with a mixed-left majority (the Czech Republic), one country with a mixed-right majority (Switzerland), three countries with a right majority (France, Spain and Israel), and two countries (Canada and the United States) where the majority shifted from centre-left to right over the period under study.

Because of the distinctive origins and historical trajectories of national party systems, it should come as no surprise that the largest proportion of the variance in community support for most types of parties in our sample is explained by differences between countries (see Table 13.10). The analysis of variance, however, leaves equally little to question about the importance of variations within and between metropolitan areas. Indeed, for parties of both the far left and the far right, as well as 'Green' parties, regionalist and ethnic parties, support varies more at the sub-national level than between countries. For any type of party except for regionalist and ethnic parties, local differences within metropolitan areas comprise the greatest source of sub-national variation. These municipal-level differences make up between 17 per cent and 47 per cent of the overall variance. While local variations are especially decisive for the far left, the far right and the Greens, they still represent over a quarter of the overall variance in support for the centre-left and centre-right, and about 30 per cent of the variance in regionalist and ethnic party support.

Analysis of the metropolitan and local influences on the performance of party families reveals a clear relationship between each type of party and specific types of metropolitan places (see Table 13.11).[16] The most consistent bases of metropolitan support appear among the long-established parties of the moderate left and the far left. Moderate left parties rely on support from larger communities, poor suburbs and larger metropolitan areas in general. They perform consistently less well in affluent and low-density suburbs. In more affluent metropolitan areas, as well as those with stronger relations to the global economy, support for the moderate left has lagged.

The smaller far left parties have also performed better in poorer and more urbanised communities, but their profile most closely follows patterns of economic disadvantage. Poorer metropolitan areas with fewer minorities generally provide stronger support for the far left. At the local level, support for these parties has concentrated in poorer, more densely-populated communities, and outside affluent suburbs and metropolitan urban centres.

The newer family of Green parties, born of post-industrial cleavages that first emerged in the 1970s, has grown to occupy a distinctive metropolitan niche. Although largely an urban party like their counterparts on the left, with little basis of support in low-density suburbs, the Greens have thrived most in centres of educational and administrative services and high-tech employment (Sellers 1998). Much of their support has come from urban centres, especially the cores of the largest metropolitan areas, and from affluent suburbs only occasionally won by the moderate left. They have won a larger share of the vote in smaller metropolitan areas and those with larger proportions of affluent and middle-class communities, two types of regions where the moderate left has consistently underperformed.

On the right, there are also fairly consistent metropolitan patterns of support. Moderate right and market liberal parties, which have been the greatest proponents of neoliberal policies, rely most consistently on the affluent suburbs for support. Both are least likely to receive support from poor suburbs. There and in less diverse, less polarised metropolitan areas, moderate right parties have performed worst. They have also underperformed in the more populous localities and metropolitan areas. While low-density suburbs are more likely to vote for moderate right parties, they are less likely to vote for market liberals. The latter gather more of

---

16. As in the analysis of voter turnout, a series of three-level regression models compared the effects of variables of national, metropolitan influences on the performance of each type of party family in those countries where it had established a national presence. The regressions for each party began with linear baseline models, followed by models that incorporated cross-level influences selected through backwards regressions. Although small samples of countries limited the reliability of inferences at the country level, the models included controls for dominance of the left or the right in national elections, and for post-Communist or transitional democracies. Additional variables controlled for the local performance of other competing parties on the left or the right. For full regression results, see the Web Appendix WA13, http://press.ecpr.eu/resources.

*Table 13.11: Significant predictors of party voting in metropolitan municipalities/communities, by party family*

|  | Far left | Greens | Moderate left | Market liberal | Moderate right | Far right |
|---|---|---|---|---|---|---|
| *Metropolitan effects* | | | | | | |
| Airport passengers/ year (metro) | – | | (–) | + | | |
| Metropolitan population (log) (metro) | | (–) | + | | (–) | |
| Metropolitan affluence (metro) | | + | – | | | |
| Metropolitan polarisation (metro) | | | | | – | |
| Poor non-minority concentrations (metro) | + | | | | | + |
| Poor minority concentrations (metro) | | | | | | + |
| *Municipal effects* | | | | | | |
| Urban concentrations | (–) | (+) | | | | (–) |
| Affluent suburbs | (–) | + | – | (+) | + | (–) |
| Low-density suburbs | | – | – | – | + | |
| Municipal population (log) | + | | + | | (–) | |
| Poor non-minority suburbs | + | – | + | – | – | + |
| Poor minority suburbs | + | – | (+) | (–) | – | + |
| Maximum variance explained | | | | | | |
| Local | 17% | 8% | 35% | 31% | 35% | 31% |
| Overall | 48% | 19% | 49% | 35% | 18% | 45% |

*Notes:* Positive and negative signs represent direction of significant direct effects. Parentheses indicate significance in linear but not full equations. Boldface indicates $p<0.01$; otherwise $p<0.05$.

the vote among the more urbanised constituencies and in more globally-connected metropolitan areas.

Meanwhile, recently established far right parties, like the National Front of France, the Swiss People's Party or the Swedish Democrats, have built support around nationalist and often ethnocentric agendas. These appeals have gained the strongest support in communities and metropolitan areas with more marginal positions in the global economy. Support for the far right concentrates among poor suburbs, especially those with fewer minorities, and is generally stronger among metropolitan areas with larger concentrations of these poor suburbs. It is significantly lower in urban centres as well as in affluent suburbs.

### Metropolitan sources of left-right voting

The overall consequences of metropolitan political divisions can be gauged more systematically by means of the partisan ideological indices constructed in each country for each metropolitan locality. These indices employed partisan voting and the ideological preferences expressed by supporters for each party in national surveys so as to estimate the ideological 'centre of gravity' for each locality in the study (Gross and Sigelman 1984).

First, an index based on the self-placement of voters for each of the parties in contemporaneous surveys enabled an analysis of where each locality stands on the left-right spectrum. Second, three additional ideological indices were constructed using the issue positions of party voters on a pre-defined range of issues:

(1) political-economic (state-centred versus market-centred economic policies),

(2) sociocultural (cultural conservatism versus social liberalism), and

(3) globalisation and cosmopolitanism (openness to immigration and trade versus nationalism and ethnocentrism).[17]

These indices provide a more in-depth analysis of the distinct dimensions of partisanship and ideology.

Analysis of voter self-placement on the standard left-right scale highlights many of the most important general findings from the country studies (see Figure 13.5). Across the whole range of countries, distinct partisan cleavages are articulated among different types of metropolitan places. Regardless of the electoral outcome, urban centres and poor minority suburbs give stronger support to parties they perceive to be on the left than do other suburban places. In each country, the affluent and low-density suburbs harbour the strongest support for the right. Middle-class suburbs stand between these other types. They have consistently voted more for the right than the urban concentrations, but more for the left than either the low-density or the affluent suburbs.

Multilevel analysis of the full dataset generally confirms these patterns (see Table 13.12). A variable for the log of population demonstrates a strong, consistent relationship between size and left support, as does the dichotomous variable for poor minority suburbs. Affluent suburbs clearly maintain consistent bases of support for the right.[18]

---

17. The procedure for defining these ideological indices is described in the country chapters and summarised in Chapter 14, the Methodological Appendix. Positive coefficients in these models for each index indicate a more conservative position and negative coefficients greater support for the left. As we are more interested in variation between municipalities and metropolitan areas rather than countries, all four indices have been standardised at the country level, thereby setting the variance between countries to zero.

18. In models without the variable for size, urban concentrations emerged as a significant predictor of

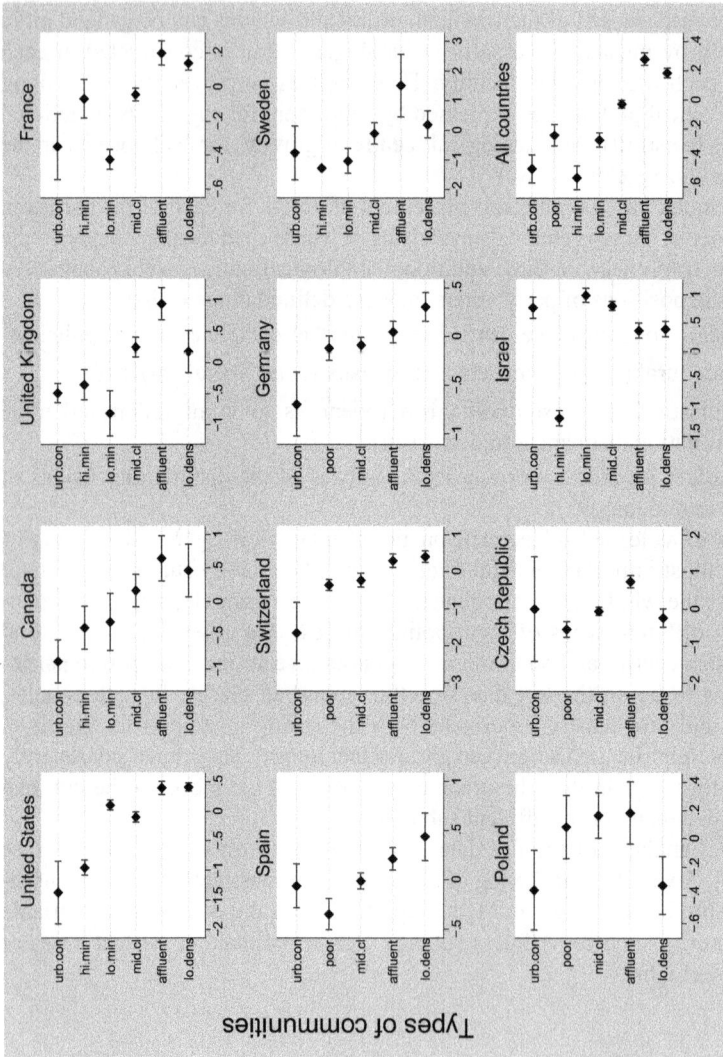

*Figure 13.5: Party support in metropolitan communities of eleven countries, measured by party voters' left-right self-placement, by type of locality (mean values and 95 per cent confidence intervals)*

*Table 13.12: Multilevel regression analysis of party support in metropolitan communities (left-right self-placement index and economic index)*

| | Party self-placement | | (Cross-level effects) | | Economic index | | (Cross-level effects) | |
|---|---|---|---|---|---|---|---|---|
| | **B** | **t** | **B** | **t** | **B** | **t** | **B** | **t** |
| Intercept | 1.15 | 1.32 | 0.51 | 0.56 | 0.07 | 0.08 | 0.35 | 0.43 |
| *Metropolitan effects* | | | | | | | | |
| Socio-spatial polarisation (metro) | 0.10 | 0.26 | −0.05 | −0.14 | −0.25 | −0.76 | −0.38 | −1.17 |
| Airport passengers/year (metro) | **0.07** | **2.87** | **0.05** | **2.32** | **0.07** | **3.32** | **0.07** | **3.17** |
| Metropolitan population (metro) | **−0.33** | **−1.98** | −0.20 | −1.16 | −0.19 | −1.27 | −0.25 | −1.62 |
| Metropolitan affluence (metro) | 0.24 | 1.07 | 0.23 | 1.03 | **0.72** | **3.65** | **0.80** | **4.01** |
| *Municipal and cross-level effects* | | | | | | | | |
| Urban centres | −0.16 | −1.10 | −0.14 | −0.97 | −0.02 | −0.11 | **3.01** | **4.04** |
| Metropolitanisation (country) | | | | | | | **−0.01** | **−2.33** |
| Metropolitan population (metro) | | | | | | | **−0.36** | **−2.91** |
| Affluent suburbs | **0.28** | **4.67** | **0.33** | **6.37** | **0.51** | **5.65** | −0.65 | −1.47 |
| Right wins (country) | | | | | | | **0.40** | **4.89** |
| Post-Communist (country) | | | **−0.27** | **−1.97** | | | | |
| Metropolitan population (metro) | | | | | | | **0.21** | **2.94** |
| Metropolitan affluence (metro) | | | | | | | **−0.36** | **−1.93** |
| Low-density suburbs | 0.09 | 0.99 | *−0.66* | *−1.84* | 0.05 | 0.56 | **−1.13** | **−3.04** |
| Post-Communist (country) | | | **−0.47** | **−3.61** | | | | |
| Metropolitanisation (country) | | | **0.01** | **2.48** | | | **0.01** | **3.51** |
| Metropolitan polarisation (metro) | | | **−0.42** | **−2.15** | | | **−0.54** | **−2.98** |
| Airport passengers/year (metro) | | | **−0.03** | **−2.11** | | | | |
| Metropolitan population (metro) | | | 0.12 | 1.69 | | | 0.12 | 1.90 |
| Municipal population (log) | **−0.23** | **−6.35** | 0.55 | 1.60 | −0.14 | −1.54 | **−0.24** | **−2.08** |
| Metropolitan polarisation (metro) | | | 0.35 | 2.01 | | | | |
| Airport passengers/year (metro) | | | 0.03 | 2.58 | | | 0.03 | 2.44 |
| Metropolitan population (metro) | | | −0.18 | −2.78 | | | | |
| Poor non-minority suburbs | −0.09 | −1.63 | **−0.48** | **−2.38** | **−0.21** | **−4.74** | 0.60 | 1.15 |
| Metropolitanisation (country) | | | 0.01 | 1.81 | | | 0.01 | 2.26 |
| Airport passengers/year (metro) | | | | | | | 0.05 | 3.38 |
| Metropolitan population (metro) | | | | | | | −0.25 | −2.57 |
| Poor minority suburbs | −0.56 | −3.00 | 4.12 | 7.23 | −0.37 | −3.38 | 2.45 | 3.57 |

| | Party self-placement | | (Cross-level effects) | | Economic index | | (Cross-level effects) | |
|---|---|---|---|---|---|---|---|---|
| | B | t | B | t | B | t | B | t |
| Metropolitanisation (country) | | | −0.03 | −5.34 | | | | |
| Metropolitan population (metro) | | | −0.42 | −4.68 | | | −0.46 | −4.12 |
| Log likelihood | −14438 | | −14365 | | −14736 | | −14708 | |
| Reliability: Level one | 0.98 | | 0.98 | | 0.97 | | 0.97 | |
| Level two | 0.00 | | 0.01 | | 0.04 | | 0.04 | |
| *Variance explained* | | | | | | | | |
| Local | 19% | | 19% | | 21% | | 21% | |
| Metropolitan | 5% | | 5% | | 14% | | 15% | |
| Deviance | 28876 | | 28731 | | 29472 | | 29415 | |
| Estimated parameters | 42 | | 88 | | 42 | | 85 | |
| N | 12843 | | 12843 | | 12797 | | 12797 | |

*Notes:* Coefficients are full maximum likelihood estimates in HLM3 with randomised error terms. For italicised coefficients, $p<0.10$; for boldface coefficients, $p<0.05$. Due to the standardisation of the dependent variable around the mean for each country, linear country variables were insignificant and are not shown here.

The multilevel analysis also reveals a number of significant predictors at wider scales. Greater integration of a metropolitan area into the global capitalist economy, measured here by the number of airport passengers,[19] generally works to the advantage of the right (model 1). As the model with cross-level interaction terms (model 2) shows, this effect also varies by type of locality. Larger metropolitan localities in more globalised metropolitan settings vote significantly less strongly for the left, while low-density suburbs give less support to the right.

A second set of multilevel influences stems from metropolitan settlement structures. Larger metropolitan areas and countries with more metropolitan patterns of settlement have experienced deeper ideological divides among different types of metropolitan communities. Larger metropolitan areas generally provide greater support for the left. Poor minority suburbs in these settings give the left even stronger support, while low-density suburbs align more strongly with the right.

Greater ethnic and income diversity at the metropolitan scale may mitigate the consequences of the deepening divides that metropolitanisation generally brings. Socio-spatial polarisation in a metropolitan area, a contextual feature related to aggregate ethnic and socio-economic diversity, exerts contrasting effects to those of other metropolitan variables. Low-density suburbs in spatially polarised settings give less support to the right, while the orientation to the left in larger suburbs stands out less.

voting for the left and low-density suburbs as a predictor of voting for the right.

19. Alternative measures for the number of international passengers, the volume of freight, and the volume of international freight, generated similar results.

Alongside these metropolitan influences, the multivariate tests of the country chapters reveal an array of local effects. These patterns represent far more than a reflection of the social and economic composition of these places (see Table 13.13); they differ substantially between older and younger capitalist democracies. In Western Europe and North America, where metropolitanisation is most advanced, population density or size emerges as one of the most consistent predictors of voting for the left. Only Sweden, the older democracy with the lowest level of metropolitanisation, departs from this trend. Homeownership also exerts clear, consistent effects. In every country where this variable was tested except for Israel, where distinct historical conditions apply, communities with more homeowners gave significantly greater support to the right.

Wherever metropolitanisation has absorbed the majority of the electorate into extended urban regions, distinct spatial cleavages have emerged. The right has drawn new support from voters with interests and orientations rooted in the suburban localities of homeowners, low-density settlement, concentrated privilege and links to the international marketplace. These are the metropolitan bastions of neoliberalism within the contemporary capitalist city. In eight of the eleven countries, communities with higher overall socio-economic status or income vote more for the right. In seven of the eleven, those communities containing more seniors also disproportionately support the right.

In contrast, the left has drawn support from both larger urbanised places and those with more renters, smaller families and more young adults. Although socioeconomic composition often proves multicollinear with contextual differences, it remains a major source of the intra-metropolitan variation. Minority or immigrant concentrations vote left with some degree of consistency (in eight of the eleven countries), and in every country except Germany, communities with greater socioeconomic hardship vote significantly more to the left (see Table 13.13).

Patterns in the two newer democracies of post-Communist Europe, the Czech Republic and Poland, differ from those in the other countries. In these countries, population density (and city size) predicts stronger support for the right rather than the left. State socialism there long prevented the emergence of housing markets outside the urban centres. As a result, metropolitanisation and suburban low-density settlement remain more limited than in older capitalist democracies. Within both party systems, legacies from the post-Communist transition have also produced a distinctive relationship between the economic and other dimensions of partisan ideology (Kreuzer and Pattai 2004). The resulting menu of partisan choices has enabled Czech and Polish cities to embrace marketisation, cultural liberalism and cosmopolitanism at the same time.

*Table 13.13: Significant predictors of voter self-placement in metropolitan municipalities/communities, by country: overview from country*

| | USA | Canada | UK | France | Switzerland | Germany | Spain | Sweden | Poland | Czech Rep. | Israel |
|---|---|---|---|---|---|---|---|---|---|---|---|
| Winning parties in study period | Mixed | Mixed/ Right | Left | Right | Mixed | Left | Mixed | Left | Left | Mixed/ Right | Right/ Centre |
| *Compositional variables at local-community level* | | | | | | | | | | | |
| Socio-economic status | + | + | + | + (income) − (educ.) | (+) | − | + | + | 0 | + | − |
| Hardship index | − | 0 | − | 0 | 0 | 0 | − | n/a | − | − | n/a |
| Foreign-born residents | − | 0 | 0 | (+) | + | 0 | + | (−) | n/a | 0 | 0 |
| Old residents | 0 | (+) | + | + | 0 | 0 | + | 0 | n/a | (+) | 0 |
| Young residents | n/a | 0 | + | n/a | 0 | + | 0 | 0 | n/a | (+) | − |
| *Contextual variables at local-community level* | | | | | | | | | | | |
| Homeownership | + | 0 | + | + | + | n/a | n/a | + | n/a | + | 0 |
| Residential stability | − | (−) | (−) | − | 0 | n/a | n/a | n/a | - | n/a | n/a |
| Out-commuting | (−) | (−) | 0 | − | 0 | 0 | − | (−) | n/a | n.a. | n/a |
| Population size | | n/a | n/a | n/a | − | 0 | − | 0 | + | + | − |
| Population density | − | (−) | − | − | 0 | − | 0 | (+) | 0 | n/a | 0 |
| Economic diversity | + | 0 | − | 0 | 0 | 0 | − | n/a | n/a | 0 | n/a |

*Notes*: + = positive relation to right self-placement; − = positive relation to left self-placement; 0 = no significant relation to left-right self-placement; n/a = relation not tested in country study. Parentheses indicate significance in some but not all models.

## Metropolitan influences on the dimensions of partisanship

As much of the literature on partisan competition since the 1970s in Western Europe has demonstrated, political parties no longer position themselves solely in relation to a one-dimensional left-right scale. Increasingly, cultural issues (Kitschelt 1994) and questions related to globalisation (Kriesi *et al.* 2006; Kriesi *et al.* 2008) now supplement long-standing economic questions about the relations between state and market as the defining issues in elections. For societies outside the developed West, the multi-dimensional character of partisan competition has been even more evident (Kreuzer and Pattai 2004). Three indices reveal how the partisan preferences of voters reflect positions on major dimensions of ideology (see Figure 13.6 and Chapter 14, the Methodological Appendix). The economic index captures issues directly linked to policy regarding the state and markets, including distributive questions about the welfare state. The sociocultural index derives from questions about domestic cultural issues such as religion, gender and familial authority. The globalisation index encompasses a broad range of issues linked to the general difference between cosmopolitanism and ethnonationalism. Although items in this last index overlap with cultural and economic issues, the index focuses solely on matters that are international in scope or that concern immigration and racial diversity.[20]

## The dimension of economic ideology

One of the most direct ways that metropolitanisation has created new bases of support for neoliberalism stems from economic interests in assets and consumption patterns linked to the places where metropolitan residents live (see Chapter 1 in this volume). In densely-populated urban settings, as in the traditional industrial city, economies of scale and proximity as well as limited property assets give residents more reason to support the collective provision of services by the welfare state. Suburban communities, by contrast, depend more on private property and individualised modes of service provision. As a result, residents of these communities look more to the markets and private solutions that are a hallmark of neoliberal ideology. Affluent or middle-class and lower-density suburban communities with more property assets, fewer opportunities for collective provision, and greater capacities for purchasing private services should be more prone toward neoliberal economic orientations (Dunleavy 1979; Walks 2006).

The index based on the economic ideology of party voters offers a calibrated test of these effects. As the discussion in the country chapters has shown, this index captures widespread opposition between support for markets and support for the welfare state. The typology of metropolitan localities provides a general view of the ways that similar types of municipalities compare in different countries (see Figure 13.6). Multilevel analysis enables us to test the patterns systematically, and to compare variance in the economic index with the overall variations in voter self-placement on the left-right scale (see Table 13.12, models 3 and 4).

The hypotheses about pro-market orientations apply most clearly to affluent and middle-class suburbs. As measured by the beta coefficients, affluent suburbs support pro-market parties nearly twice as strongly as they identify with the right on the ideological scale. Beyond this, the more that affluent and middle-class suburbs dominate a metropolitan area, the stronger is the average metropolitan support for market-friendly policies and parties. In accordance with expectations about the effects from increasing metropolitanisation, support for pro-market parties among affluent suburbs is especially pronounced in larger metropolitan areas. Where parties of the right have consistently won, moreover, these parties have performed especially well in the affluent suburbs.[21]

The multilevel models also largely confirm the findings of numerous country chapters that support for welfare-statist parties concentrates in the urban centres that

---

20. As the indices for different countries have in some instances employed different survey questions, comparison of the results requires caution about setting index values for each country directly alongside each other. For this reason, the pooled analysis again centres the sub-national variation in each index on the national mean values.

21. In an intriguing exception to this, the relationship between metropolitan affluence and pro-market voting is reversed in affluent suburbs.

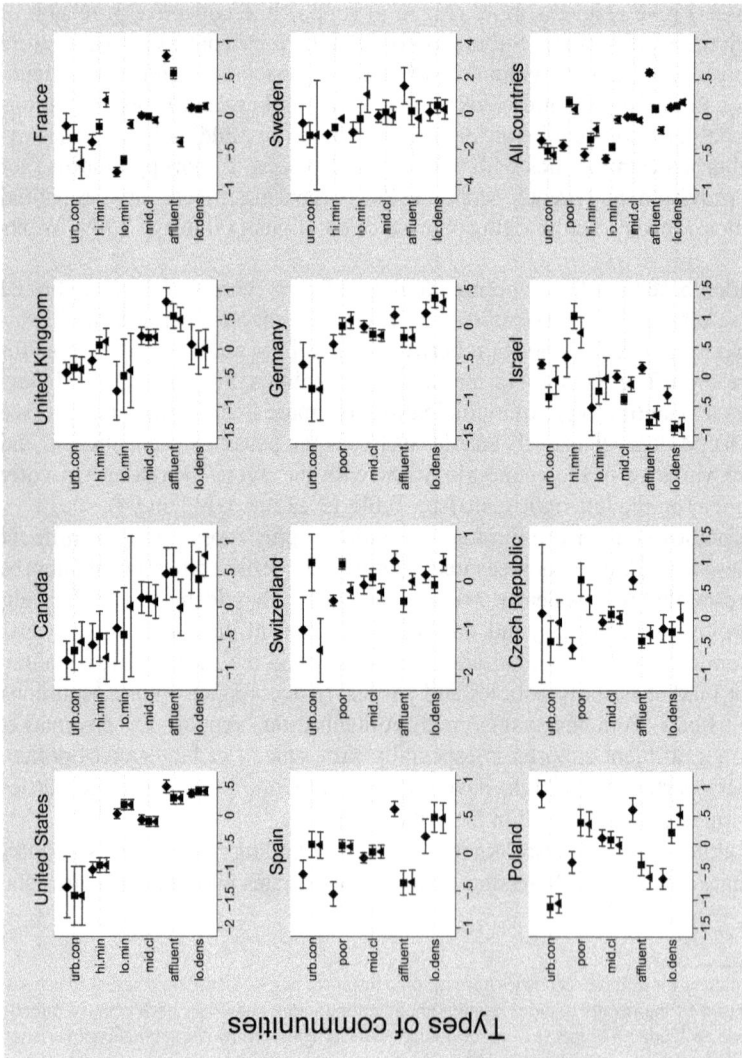

Figure 13.6: Party support in metropolitan communities of eleven countries, measured by party voter's position on issues related to economic policies, globalisation, as well as cultural issues by type of municipalities (issue indices standardised by country, mean values and 95 per cent confidence intervals)

also usually serve as centres of metropolitan public service provision. The effect attains statistical significance in larger metropolitan areas and in countries with higher rates of metropolitanisation. Everywhere but in Poland, the Czech Republic and Israel, urban centres vote more strongly for welfare-statist parties than the metropolitan average. In the United States, Canada and Switzerland, urban centres give stronger average support to pro-welfare state parties than do the poor suburbs.

In mature developed economies, sprawling metropolitan settlement clearly contributes to political support for neoliberal parties. The higher is the national level of metropolitanisation, the more low-density suburbs vote for these parties. Smaller metropolitan municipalities also disproportionately support pro-market parties, once effects from global connectivity are controlled for. The country chapters show these effects to operate independently of the consequences from socio-economic status, and to go beyond the occupational interests that have preoccupied theories of nationalisation and modernisation. In metropolitanised countries, numerous contextual variables linked to suburban lifestyles also predict stronger support for neoliberal policies:

- homeownership or single-family houses (in France, Sweden, Switzerland, the United Kingdom and the United States);
- lower density or population size (in France, Germany, Switzerland, the United Kingdom and the United States);
- housing or population growth (in Canada, Germany, Switzerland, the United Kingdom and the United States);
- residential mobility (in Canada, France and the United States); and
- commuting or driving to work (in Canada, the United Kingdom and at the metropolitan level in the United States).

Each type of poor suburb supports parties with more welfare-statist orientations. In both types of poor communities, these statist orientations increase with the size of metropolitan area. In more metropolitanised countries, however, the private property and private amenities of suburban places alter these effects. As the positive cross-level coefficient for these national contexts shows, many poor non-minority suburbs also harbour strong neoliberal countercurrents.

At the metropolitan scale, connectivity to the global economy, as well as over-all affluence, strengthens support for pro-market parties.[22] In metropolitan areas favoured by the globalised market economy, and in places with the more priva-tised suburban lifestyles, neoliberal leanings are strongest. In the most urbanised communities at or near the metropolitan core, interests in collective consumption and redistribution contribute to welfare-statist orientations.

---

22. This result is consistent with previous analyses of how favourable economic prospects in a glo-balised economy promote stronger market orientations among private professional workers (e.g. Kitschelt 1994). The territorial effect, however, suggests that perceptions of economic advantages from global connections extend beyond occupational or class effects. The cross-level model shows (model 4) that global connectivity of a metropolitan area fosters pro-market orientations, particularly in larger municipalities and in poor non-minority suburbs.

In the two post-Communist countries and in the distinctive metropolitan context of Israel, central cities remain bastions of neoliberal support. Here, and to a lesser degree in such Western European countries as France and Sweden, the continued attraction of urban centres for economic elites has altered the predominant patterns. Although class and demography remain of utmost importance to these patterns, they do not wholly dictate them. Suburban neoliberalism and the ideological polarisation surrounding it are thus also partly consequences of the differential effects of place.

### The cultural dimension

Contrasts between liberalism and conservatism in the social and culture sphere also play an important role in producing and defining metropolitan political cleavages. The index to test this dimension of partisan ideological competition generally captured preferences related to traditional attitudes toward religion, gender and parental authority.[23] By and large, the sociocultural dimension of political differences among localities reinforces the economic one (see Table 13.14). To focus analysis on how the two dimensions differ, our modelling of the culture index included the values of the economic policy index as an independent variable. These models therefore test whether the value of the sociocultural index for each type of community stands to the right (positive) or the left (negative) of its position on the economic index.

Values of the economic index account for nearly half (48 per cent) of the variation in sociocultural orientations. In countries with high rates of metropolitanisation, and where the right has dominated national elections, the correspondence between the two dimensions is the strongest. By comparison with economic ideology, analyses of the country chapters suggest somewhat less consistent metropolitan spatial patterns in the cultural index. However, several significant divergences also set the sociocultural dimension of metropolitan political ecology apart from the economic dimension.

One of the most striking contrasts appears in the most-educated, highest-income communities. In the affluent suburbs, comparatively liberal social and cultural attitudes accompany pro-market policy preferences. In ten of the eleven countries, these suburbs average less sociocultural conservatism than economic conservatism (see Figure 13.6; and in eight, such differences are significant at the 95 per cent confidence level). The tendency is especially pronounced in the post-Communist countries. As the multivariate tests presented in the country chapters confirmed, communities with higher socio-economic status in Germany, Switzerland, the Czech Republic and Poland have voted more strongly for pro-market policy platforms than for cultural conservatism.

---

23. Unfortunately, insufficient data for our eleven countries did not allow us to examine in enough detail the materialism/post-materialism aspects of socio-cultural changes in this cross-national study. This remains an objective for future analyses.

The sociocultural dimension also reinforces the advantage of the left in its urbanised strongholds. Post-materialist orientations in these settings comprise part of the challenge to traditional cultural values (see Chapter 1 in this volume). In the pooled analysis, significant urban support for the left emerges along the cultural dimension, even when it does not appear along the economic one (see Table 13.14). In larger metropolitan areas and in countries where the left has consistently won majorities, this relationship is significantly stronger.

Among the poor suburbs that support the left along the economic dimension, the analysis confirms a tendency for the cultural dimension to undermine left support. A cultural divide separates these suburbs from both the urban centres and the affluent suburbs. Poor suburbs generally support more conservative positions on the sociocultural dimension than on the economic one (see Figure 13.6). In every country but the United States, Canada and Sweden, the difference for at least one type of poor suburb exceeds the range between confidence intervals. The pooled regressions confirm this relationship for poor non-minority suburbs in countries where metropolitanisation is furthest advanced.[24]

Compared with the economic dimension, salience for the cultural dimension may give the right a slight net advantage in metropolitan voting. Where the right has dominated national elections, cross-level interactions with the economic index show that cultural conservatism has averaged significantly higher. Low-density suburbs also swing significantly conservative along the cultural dimension, once a cross-level variable controls for right majorities.

Throughout the older democracies, lower density or smaller size also emerged as the most consistent contextual predictor of cultural conservatism (in France, Germany, Sweden, Switzerland, the United Kingdom, the United States, and at the metropolitan level in Canada).[25]

Metropolitan differences over cultural issues both reinforce and modify the effects of the divisions linked to economic ideology. Cultural liberalism has furnished the left with bases of urban support that welfare statism does not, and enabled it to make inroads into some affluent suburbs. Cultural traditionalism has strengthened support for the right in low-density suburbs and beyond, and eroded support for the left in poor non-minority suburbs.

### The globalisation dimension

Rather than values linked to traditional culture, it is globalisation that marks the clearest new dimension of metropolitan cleavages that cross-cut economic ideology. Here the index incorporates a wide range of issues that partly overlap with both economic ideologies and traditional social values. The common thread among the issues in this index is attitudes toward diversity and cosmopolitanism, as ex-

---

24. A similar tendency among poor minority suburbs falls just short of statistical significance (p<0.10), except in metropolitan areas with larger proportions of poor non-minority suburbs.

25. Homeownership or single-family housing played a less consistent role, predicting cultural conservatism only in the United States, France and Sweden.

*Table 13.14: Multilevel regression analysis of party support (cultural index and globalisation indices) in metropolitan communities*

| | Cultural index | | (Cross-level effects) | | Globalisation index | | (Cross-level effects) | | (With ethnic diversity) | |
|---|---|---|---|---|---|---|---|---|---|---|
| | B | t | B | t | B | t | B | t | B | t |
| Intercept | 0.94 | 1.13 | 0.90 | 1.08 | 1.51 | 1.61 | 1.19 | 1.21 | 1.19 | 1.21 |
| *Metropolitan effects* | | | | | | | | | | |
| Socio-spatial polarisation (metro) | *0.06* | *0.17* | -0.07 | -0.19 | *0.68* | *1.72* | *0.74* | *1.86* | *0.70* | *1.76* |
| Airport passengers/year (metro) | *0.03* | *1.47* | 0.03 | 1.46 | *0.04* | *1.82* | *0.04* | *1.81* | *0.04* | *1.79* |
| Metropolitan population (log) (metro) | *-0.28* | *-1.77* | -0.25 | -1.61 | *-0.34* | *-1.87* | *-0.28* | *-1.47* | *-0.27* | *-1.44* |
| Metropolitan affluence (metro) | *0.35* | *1.62* | 0.40 | 1.80 | *-0.28* | *-1.17* | *-0.22* | *-0.93* | *-0.24* | *-0.98* |
| *Municipal and cross-level effects* | | | | | | | | | | |
| Urban concentrations | **-0.11** | **-2.70** | **-0.11** | **-2.86** | **-0.13** | **-2.25** | **-0.15** | **-2.67** | **-0.15** | **-2.75** |
| Affluent suburbs | **-0.13** | **-4.21** | **-0.08** | **-2.41** | **-0.28** | **-3.24** | 0.30 | 1.42 | 0.28 | 1.32 |
| Right wins (country) | | | -0.08 | -2.43 | | | **-0.51** | **-10.71** | **-0.52** | **-11.01** |
| Post-Communist (country) | | | -0.11 | -1.91 | | | | | | |
| Metropolitan population (log) (metro) | | | | | | | **-0.07** | **-2.06** | *-0.06* | *-1.94* |
| Low-density suburbs | 0.04 | 1.46 | **0.08** | **2.44** | **0.13** | **4.55** | **0.23** | **5.02** | **0.22** | **4.88** |
| Right wins (country) | | | -0.11 | -2.91 | | | | | | |
| Airport passengers/year (metro) | | | | | | | **-0.02** | **-2.88** | **-0.02** | **-2.78** |
| Municipal population | *-0.10* | *-1.87* | 0.21 | 1.41 | **-0.15** | **-2.55** | **0.64** | **2.52** | **0.65** | **2.59** |
| Left wins (country) | | | **-0.30** | **-6.56** | | | **-0.43** | **-4.40** | **-0.41** | **-4.17** |
| Right wins (country) | | | | | | | **-0.17** | **-3.50** | **-0.15** | **-3.07** |
| Metropolitanisation (country) | | | 0.00 | 1.95 | | | | | | |
| Metropolitan polarisation (metro) | | | 0.15 | 2.03 | | | | | | |
| Metropolitan population (log) (metro) | | | -0.08 | -3.12 | | | | | | |
| Poor non-minority suburbs | **0.09** | **2.40** | -0.11 | -1.14 | **0.16** | **3.60** | **-0.99** | **-3.71** | **-0.94** | **-3.41** |
| Metropolitanisation (country) | | | 0.00 | 2.18 | | | | | | |
| Airport passengers/year (metro) | | | | | | | **-0.03** | **-3.56** | **-0.03** | **-3.44** |

| | Cultural index | | (Cross-level effects) | | Globalisation index | | (Cross-level effects) | | (With ethnic diversity) | |
|---|---|---|---|---|---|---|---|---|---|---|
| | B | t | B | t | B | t | B | t | B | t |
| Metropolitan population (log) (metro) | *0.17* | *1.91* | 0.16 | 1.49 | 0.03 | 0.39 | **0.22** | **4.54** | **0.21** | **4.24** |
| Poor minority suburbs | | | | | | | **0.89** | **2.57** | **1.05** | **3.02** |
| Ethnic diversity (country) | | | | | | | | | **−0.79** | **−2.46** |
| Poor non-minority concentrations (metro) | | | | | | | **0.34** | **2.89** | **0.34** | **2.93** |
| Metropolitan polarisation (metro) | | | | | | | **0.66** | **1.88** | **0.84** | **2.29** |
| Metropolitan population (log) (metro) | | | | | | | **−0.18** | **−3.16** | **−0.18** | **−3.12** |
| Economic ideology | **0.52** | **4.03** | **−0.43** | **−2.04** | | | **−0.43** | **−2.60** | **−0.48** | **−2.77** |
| Right wins (country) | | | **0.57** | **6.69** | | | | | | |
| Left wins (country) | | | | | | | | | | |
| Metropolitanisation (country) | | | **0.01** | **4.87** | | | **−0.54** | **−4.70** | **−0.56** | **−4.64** |
| Metropolitan polarisation (metro) | | | −0.19 | −1.90 | | | **0.02** | **6.93** | **0.02** | **6.95** |
| Metropolitan affluence (metro) | | | | | | | **−0.19** | **−2.47** | **−0.20** | **−2.48** |
| Log likelihood | −1686 | | −1660 | | −11503 | | −11524 | | −11525 | |
| Reliability: Level one | 1.00 | | 1.00 | | 0.99 | | 0.99 | | 0.99 | |
| Level two | 0.09 | | 0.05 | | 0.02 | | 0.07 | | 0.08 | |
| Variance explained | | | | | | | | | | |
| Local | 89% | | 89% | | 42% | | 42% | | 42% | |
| Metropolitan | <1% | | <1% | | 4% | | 4% | | 4% | |
| Deviance | 3371 | | 3320 | | 23007 | | 23048 | | 23050 | |
| Estimated parameters | 89 | | 100 | | 142 | | 102 | | 103 | |
| N | 12814 | | 12814 | | 12813 | | 12813 | | 12813 | |

*Notes*: For italicised coefficients, p<0.10; for boldface coefficients, p<0.05. Due to the standardisation of the dependent variable around the mean for each country, linear country variables were insignificant and are not shown here.

pressed in opinions about international institutions and influences, immigration and multiculturalism. In the coding scheme, low values indicate cosmopolitanism and higher values ethnonationalism.[26] Because the established right and left parties often maintain similar positions on these issues, voting for such parties on the right as the French National Front and the Swiss People's Party, and such parties on the left as the French Communists and the Greens, exert disproportionate influence on this index.

The globalisation index captures a distinct geography of ideological variation from either the sociocultural values or economic ideology. The economic index accounts for 24 per cent of the variation in positions related to globalisation, only half the variation in cultural attitudes.[27] Compared with economic issues, emphasis on issues surrounding globalisation may provide a diffuse advantage to the left similar to the effects of cultural issues for the right. The negative cross-level interactions between effects from the local economic index and national left majorities indicate stronger left support along the globalisation dimension, and contrast with the positive cross-level interactions in the opposite direction in the models for the cultural index. In the more metropolitanised countries, however, neoliberal economic ideologies predict even stronger ethnonationalism. This effect is even greater than the impact on cultural conservatism.

Contrasts in wider regional and metropolitan contexts largely shape support for cosmopolitanism and ethnonationalism. Overall, both global connectivity and metropolitan polarisation and diversity are linked to slightly higher metropolitan levels of ethnonationalism ($p<0.10$). In localities where economic preferences are more welfare statist, however, metropolitan affluence generally fosters stronger cosmopolitanism. In countries as diverse as Israel, the United States, France and Poland, the largest, richest and best-educated metropolitan regions have generally given stronger support to more cosmopolitan parties. Among urban concentrations, larger localities and poor minority suburbs, metropolitan size has parallel cosmopolitan effects. Global connectivity reinforces cosmopolitanism in outlying low-density suburbs and poor non-minority suburbs, but has a contrary effect among poor minority suburbs. The country chapters also point to a variety of more specific regional and country-specific effects.[28]

Within metropolitan areas, the patterns are broadly consistent with the

---

26. Comparative data for all eleven countries did not enable precise tests of the territorial effects from industrial and occupational restructuring hypothesised in Table 1.5 of Chapter 1 in this volume. However, it is likely that our measures for metropolitan size, affluence and global connectivity partly capture effects from occupational clustering. Affluent and globally-connected metropolitan regions contain bigger post-industrial private business sectors. These sectors may help to account for more cosmopolitan, culturally liberal and neoliberal orientations there, especially in affluent suburbs.

27. Correspondence with the economic index averages higher in more metropolitanised countries but lower in more affluent metropolitan areas (see Table 13.14).

28. Border regions of France, as well as Jerusalem in Israel, smaller metropolitan regions in Poland, Malmö and Stockholm in Sweden, and central and southern regions of the United States, harbour more ethno-nationalist preferences.

hypotheses of Sellers and Walks (Chapter 1 in this volume) regarding the effects of diversity.[29] Larger places generally expose residents to more diversity, and the larger municipalities clearly support cosmopolitanism. This support is especially pronounced in larger metropolitan areas and in countries where the left has dominated national elections. Urban concentrations also support cosmopolitanism just as strongly as they do cultural liberalism. In every country except Spain, these places vote more for cosmopolitanism than most suburbs. However, urban cores are not the only territorial sources of cosmopolitan voting. Coefficients for the affluent suburbs demonstrate more than twice as strong an effect on the globalisation index (B = −0.28, p = 0.01) as on the cultural index (B = −0.13, p<0.01). In eight of the eleven countries, these suburbs give stronger average support to cosmopolitanism than they do to neoliberalism (see Figure 13.6). As the cross-level effects demonstrate, the cosmopolitan effect concentrates in larger metropolitan areas and in those countries where the right has consistently won national majorities.

At the opposite end of the spectrum, ethnonationalism demonstrates greater strength in the metropolitan places most distant from urban concentrations and minority concentrations. Low-density suburbs give stronger, more consistent support to ethno-nationalist parties than they do to cultural traditionalist ones. Ethno-nationalist leanings characterise these suburbs in every country except Israel, where social geographies of the outlying suburban areas reflect the distinctive history of Palestinian and Israeli settlement.

The majority in poor or poor non-minority suburbs typically retains some distance from minorities and immigrants, but may face competition with these groups for employment and services. In the multilevel models, the coefficient for these suburbs indicates a stronger relation to ethno-nationalist preferences (B = 0.16, p<0.01) than to traditionalism (B = 0.09, p<0.05).[30] In all eleven countries, ethno-nationalist preferences in these suburbs averaged higher on a standardised scale than neoliberal preferences. In six of the eleven countries, the margin between the two indices exceeded a confidence interval of 95 per cent. Location in more globally-connected metropolitan regions reverses this relationship, suggesting that the effects of globalisation are indeed multi-scalar. Meanwhile, inconsistent relationships with ethnonationalism among poor suburbs with concentrations of ethnic minorities suggest important interdependencies between national and local contexts.[31]

---

29. Due to data unavailability for all metropolitan areas and localities, tests of these hypotheses were confined to cross-sectional local and national variations. Full testing would require analysis of metropolitan and regional effects, as well as longitudinal data on patterns of immigrant settlement.

30. In four countries (Canada, the United Kingdom, Sweden, and Israel), ethnonationalism in these suburbs averaged stronger than cultural traditionalism.

31. Ethnic and racial diversity (measured here by the Fearon-Laitin index of ethnic fractionalisation) contributes in specific settings to cosmopolitan attitudes. In countries with greater levels of fractionalisation, such as Canada and the United States, poor minority suburbs provide greater support to cosmopolitan parties (model 5). Along with the effects hypothesised by Sellers and Walks (see Chapter 1 in this volume), this effect may stem from the greater weight of poor minori-

Orientations toward globalisation and multiculturalism bring out a separate dimension of partisan competition rooted in distinctive metropolitan divisions. This dimension has reinforced and broadened electoral advantages for cosmopolitan left parties, like the Greens, in urbanised communities and in larger, more affluent and, in some respects, more globalised metropolitan areas. In affluent suburbs, cosmopolitan parties have found new support. Among low-density suburbs and in less globalised metropolitan areas and regions, salience for this dimension has strengthened support for the right. In the poor suburbs, where economic affinities generally remain with the left, ethno-nationalist appeals have enabled the right to make new inroads.

### Metropolitanisation of partisan cleavages and competition

Throughout advanced industrial societies, and increasingly beyond them, the emerging context of metropolitan settlement has imposed a new political geography on partisan competition and ideology. Antiquated concepts like the urban-rural divide, or persistently relevant ones like social class, race and region, are inadequate to account for the resulting territorial lines of partisan competition.

The previous chapters in this book have explained the patterns within each country more fully. The more predominant metropolitan settlement has become, and the larger the metropolitan area, the more these types have taken on characteristic ideologies and partisan orientations (see Table 13.15). The partisan indices employed in this chapter offer the first comparative transnational overview of these widespread new patterns of partisan allegiances. The consistent metropolitan patterns that have already emerged from the country chapters are unmistakable here. Affluent, middle-class and low-density suburbs vote for market liberal and moderate right parties. More urbanised communities and poor minority suburbs vote for the left. The rise of the far right in poor and low-density suburbs and poorer, smaller metropolitan areas has expanded territorial constituencies for the right. Beyond the traditional strongholds of the left, the moderate left and especially the Greens have established new electoral bases in urbanised areas and, to a degree, in affluent and middle-class suburbs. Overall, metropolitan support for the left ranges higher in the largest metropolitan areas, on one hand, and in those more sheltered from the global economy on the other.

The country chapters have demonstrated that these electoral patterns are linked to such contextual features of metropolitan places as urban density and homeownership, as well as class and demographic composition. Indices based on distinct ideological dimensions of partisan competition reveal significant variations in these metropolitan territorial effects. Juxtaposed with each other

---

ties themselves in the local electorate of more diverse countries. In less fractionalised countries, such as France or Sweden, the stronger ethno-nationalist voting in the same type of suburbs probably reflects a backlash among the larger native ethnic majority. Smaller minorities also help to account for the positive relationship between minorities or immigrants and ethno-nationalist voting in countries such as the Czech Republic, Germany and Poland.

and with the findings of consistent metropolitan differences in voter turnout, the indices expose the different strategic imperatives that the left and the right now face in their attempts to win the increasingly pivotal votes of metropolitan areas.

All told, parties of right stand to gain the most from the ongoing metropolitanisation of politics. The gains are especially apparent for the neoliberal agendas that have been adopted with enthusiasm by many parties. New sources of support for marketisation have emerged in affluent, middle-class and low-density suburbs. The more globally connected and the more affluent a metropolitan area is, the stronger its ideological leaning toward neoliberal policies. Cultural conservatism has reinforced support for the right in many suburbs and smaller metropolitan areas and enabled it to make inroads into long-time leftist strongholds in poor non-minority suburbs. Ethnonationalism, often fuelled by new far-right parties, has enhanced and extended these bases of support. Along the globalisation dimension, the right has won greater support in low-density suburbs and in more polarised, more diverse metropolitan areas. Along both dimensions these gains have come at the cost of losses among culturally liberal, cosmopolitan affluent suburbs and urban cores, and they have occurred despite counter-currents from the growing diversity and social complexity of metropolitan areas.

For parties of the left, metropolitanisation creates a more limited set of opportunities. Left parties supporting welfare statist policies over neoliberal economic and social policies have drawn on bases of support that are increasingly inconsistent. Along the other dimensions of partisan competition, the left faces trade-offs that mirror those of the right. Green and other culturally-liberal parties have established solid bases of support in urban concentrations, in the larger localities of more extensive and diverse metropolitan areas, and in affluent suburbs. Cosmopolitanism has generally reinforced these strongholds. Gains in these areas for left parties have come at the cost of losses to traditionalist parties in poor and middle-class suburbs and to ethno-nationalist parties in poor suburbs, low-density suburbs, and in polarised metropolitan areas more generally.

Metropolitan patterns of electoral mobilisation have been even more decisive for the advantages of the right. The affluent and middle-class suburbs that have generally supported the right turn out at the highest rates in national elections (see Table 13.15). Among the large, urbanised communities where the left has won support through cultural liberalism and cosmopolitanism, voter participation rates are consistently and often dramatically lower than elsewhere. The persistent stronger electoral mobilisation among the suburban strongholds of the right typically biases electoral results in its favour.

Although parties of the left can and do win metropolitan majorities, the electoral logic growing out of metropolitanisation has favoured a gradual drift toward neoliberalism on the left as well as the right. Affluent and middle-class suburbs, and metropolitan areas integrated into global markets contain an ever-growing proportion of potential voters. The poor suburbs and urbanised communities that give the strongest support to welfare statist policies have mobilised much less than places supportive of neoliberalism. As the left has turned to cultural liberalism and especially cosmopolitanism, it has found new bases of support among affluent

*Table 13.15: Summary of selected results from pooled multilevel regressions*

| | Turnout | | | Left-right indices | | |
| --- | --- | --- | --- | --- | --- | --- |
| | Local | National | Self-placement | Economic | Cultural** | Globalisation** |
| *Intra-metropolitan* | | | | | | |
| Urban concentrations (UR) | Higher | | | | Left | Left |
| Municipal size (SZ) | Much Lower | Much lower | Left | (Left) | (Left) | Left |
| Poor minority suburbs (PM) | Lower | Lower | Left | Left | (Right) | |
| Poor non-minority suburbs (PN) | | Lower | | Left | Right | Right |
| Affluent suburbs (AF) | | Higher | Right | Right | Left | Left |
| Low-density suburbs (LO) | Higher | Lower | | | | Right |
| *Metropolitan and related cross-level effects** | | | | | | |
| Size (population, logged) | (Lower) | | Left | | (Left) | (Left) |
| | UR+ | AF+, LO+, PN- | (LO-R), SZ-R, PM-R | UR-L, AF-R, (LO-R), PN-L, PM-L | SZ-L | AF-L, SZ-L. PM-L |
| Global connectivity | --- | --- | Right | Right | | (Right) |
| | | | LO-L, SZ-R | SZ-R, PN-R | | LO-L, PN-L |
| Affluence | | | | Right | | |
| | UR+, SZ- | UR+ | | AF-L | | |
| Polarisation/diversity | (Lower) | Lower | | | | (Right) |
| | AF+ | UR+, LO- | LO-L, SZ-R | LO-L | SZ-R | PM-R |
| *Country and related cross-level effects** | | | | | | |
| Metropolitanisation | | | --- | --- | --- | --- |
| | | UR-, AF+, LO+, PM- | LO-R, (PN-R), PM-L | UR-L, LO-R, PN-R | (SZ-R), PN-R | |
| Postcommunist/New democracies | | | --- | --- | --- | --- |
| | | | AF-L, LO-L | | (AF-L) | |
| Right wins | --- | --- | --- | --- | --- | --- |
| | | | | AF-R | AF-L, LO-L | AF-L, SZ-L |
| Left wins | --- | --- | --- | --- | --- | --- |
| | | | | | SZ-L | SZ-L |

*Notes:* * = significant linear effects in first row, cross-level effects immediately below; ** = trends measured in relation to economic ideology. L = Favours Left; R = Favours Right; --- = not tested in models. Relationships in parentheses significant at p<0.10; all other relationships significant at p<0.05.

suburbs, cosmopolitan urban concentrations and large metropolitan areas. Many of these places are precisely the metropolitan settings where support for neoliberalism tends to be strongest. Those that harbour more support for welfare statist policy, such as the urban concentrations, mobilise less in elections. Metropolitan trends have thus given the left as well as the right electoral incentives to turn to neoliberal agendas. As an influence on partisan orientations, on voter participation and, ultimately, on electoral strategies, metropolitanisation is a pervasive driving force behind the rise and entrenchment of neoliberalism.

## Conclusion

In most advanced industrial societies, the growth of extended metropolitan regions into the predominant mode of settlement is already an established fact. The importance of these regions for economics and governance has increasingly become apparent. As the analyses of this book have demonstrated, metropolitanisation also has important consequences for political behaviour. Metropolitan contexts decisively shape whether citizens exercise the most fundamental political right of modern democratic citizenship and the ideological orientations they bring to this task. Especially in countries with metropolitan majorities, metropolitan patterns of local interests, institutions, and cultural orientations have replaced the urban-rural divide and the segmented regions of pre-industrial and industrial society with an increasingly-pervasive new political geography. Instead of the national uniformity among places predicted by the nationalisation thesis, metropolitanisation has embedded inter-related divergences in local electoral behaviour.

Analysis of voter turnout shows that differences in this most basic act of political participation vary in ways that trace back to local and metropolitan sources. Examination of these patterns casts new light on the role of voter participation in the layered governance of contemporary societies and in particular on the relationship between local and national electoral mobilisation. In conjunction with national institutions, metropolitan and local political subcultures have produced sometimes dramatically divergent patterns of electoral participation within the same country or even the same region. In this dimension of political behaviour, the systematic local and regional variations that metropolitanisation has introduced clearly contradict the thesis of nationalisation. In some places, such as the peripheral towns of metropolitan Switzerland and France, metropolitan patterns perpetuate traditional localised practices of political participation. In other places, such as the US and Polish urban regions, metropolitan settlement has produced a variegated geography of delocalised participation.

Partisan cleavages reflect much more than divisions between social classes, urban and rural areas, or regional ethnic traditions. They are also a result of the consumption interests, assets, and cultural practices arising from, and located in, distinct types of metropolitan places, and the different positions of metropolitan economies in the global economy. Throughout the advanced industrial world, suburbanisation and the variable patterns of metropolitan economic advantage and disadvantage have been much more than products of neoliberalism. They are drivers of the political dynamics that have embedded neoliberalism in party platforms and public policy around the world.

As a result of these trends, parties of the left now often compete for national power on terms that tend to favour the right. The affluent and middle-class metropolitan strongholds of the right make up growing proportions of national electorates. These places mobilise more consistently and more strongly than the more urbanised, more disadvantaged metropolitan strongholds of the left. The sources of new support for the left in urban concentrations and in affluent communities stem more from culturally-liberal or cosmopolitan values than from opposition to marketisation or privatisation. Voters in these places harbour either ambivalence or outright opposition toward welfare statist approaches in economic and social policy. Urbanised communities also turn out less often to vote. In poor and low-density suburbs, backlash from cultural liberalism and cosmopolitanism have further undermined support for the left. The resulting electoral incentives for both the left and the right have compounded the social and economic disadvantages of poor metropolitan communities with chronic underrepresentation in election campaigns and in public policy.

The widespread shift toward metropolitanisation provides both a powerful explanation for these convergent developments and a basis for understanding significant variations in them. The study of metropolitanisation also contributes in several broader ways to understanding how contexts shape political behaviour.

First, this study points to a layered dimension of political contexts that has rarely been examined systematically. One consistent conclusion has been that contextual effects at different scales depend on and interact with each other. The size of a community has different effects on turnout in a larger or a smaller metropolitan area. Urban cores can harbour leftist orientations in the largest metropolitan regions, but rightist orientations in more globally-connected or smaller metros. Metropolitan and local effects, as the analysis of election turnout showed, can also work in different ways under distinct national institutions. Analyses of such contextual factors as ethnic and racial diversity at a single scale have failed to capture these multilevel influences, which are often crucial to the operational significance of context.

Secondly, our study demonstrates the need to capture the increasingly-dynamic, contingent relations between territory and political behaviour. By definition, metropolitan areas are functionally interrelated to a degree that earlier, less integrated cities and regions were not. In the course of a single day's shopping or commuting to work and back, metropolitan citizens participate in the life of numerous communities. Metropolitan areas themselves are constantly changing, not only in territorial extent and in the porousness of their boundaries, but in the social, cultural and economic dynamics underlying political behaviour and ideology. The density of inter-metropolitan economic and social connections, including the quantum leap in capacities to transcend territory that the internet and other new media have made possible, adds to this dynamism. It should come as little surprise that some of the most significant contextual influences on metropolitan voting patterns reflect complex partisan swings among metropolitan constituencies rather than rigidly consistent territorial patterns.

This study represents the first systematic cross-national examination of metropolitanisation and its political consequences. Several types of inquiry remain necessary to further elaborate and test the analyses undertaken here, and as noted above, due to data limitations it has not been possible to test all of the conceptual relationships hypothesised in Chapter 1. At the macro level of the nation state, relationships between the metropolitanisation of society, culture and the economy, and the emergence of political divides within metropolitan regions remain to be probed more deeply. Comparative historical analysis of the trajectories in national policy and their links to metropolitan change, a connection that has already been drawn in work on the United States (e.g. Mollenkopf 1983; Dreier *et al.* 2001) remains necessary to account more fully for the transformations this research has revealed. At the micro level of citizens, more sophisticated approaches to analysis of cross-national surveys must be developed to account for the multi-layered contextual effects this study has revealed. Even the most elaborate national or cross-national surveys rarely sample on sufficiently detailed contextual factors to enable these to be tested in relation to individual attributes, as well as to each other. A further need persists for more intensive qualitative and quantitative investigation of metropolitan effects at the local level itself, including the scale of neighbourhoods. Community studies of this kind can provide some of the most crucial evidence about the links between individual and collective behaviour, as well as between the numerous layers of collective action.

The most powerful impetus to further advances in the study of metropolitan political behaviour is the gathering force of metropolitanisation itself. By the late twenty-first century, metropolitan areas are predicted to be the predominant form of settlement in every world region (United Nations 2009). As the examples in this volume suggest, metropolitan political ecologies outside of Western Europe and North America will bring about new and often distinctive variations on the themes elaborated here. Economic, cultural, and political divisions among metropolitan places will remain as fundamental a feature of politics as the city itself has long been.

## Bibliography

Airport Council International (2007) *World Air Traffic Report 2006*, Geneva: ACI Headquarters.

Blais, A., Massicotte, L. and Dobrzynksa, A. (2003) *Why is Turnout Higher in Some Countries than in Others?*, Ottawa, Elections Canada.

Caramani, D. (2004) *The Nationalization of Politics*, Cambridge: Cambridge University Press.

— (2005) 'The formation of national party systems in Europe: a comparative-historical analysis', *Scandinavian political studies*, 28: 295–322.

Deschouwer, K. (2003) 'Political parties in multi-layered systems', *European Urban and Regional Studies*, 10: 231–26.

Dreier, P., Mollenkopf, J. H. and Swanstrom, T. (2001) *Place Matters: Metropolitics for the twenty-first century*, Lawrence: University Press of Kansas.

Dunleavy, P. (1979) 'The urban basis of political alignment: social class, domestic property ownership, and state intervention in consumption interests', *British Journal of Political Science*, 9: 409–43.

Fearon, J. D. (2003) 'Ethnic and cultural diversity by country', *Journal of Economic Growth*, 8: 195–222.

Franklin, M. N. (2004) *Voter Turnout and the Dynamics of Electoral Competition in Established Democracies Since 1945*, Cambridge: Cambridge University Press.

Fuchs, D. and Klingemann, H. -D. (1995) 'Citizens and the state: a changing relationship?' in H. -D Klingemann and D. Fuchs (eds) *Citizens and the State,* Oxford: Oxford University Press.

Gereffi, G. and Korzeniewicz, M. (1994) *Commodity Chains and Global Capitalism*, Westport: Praeger.

Geys, B. (2006) 'Explaining voter turnout: a review of aggregate-level research', *Electoral Studies*, 25: 637–63.

Goldsmith, M. and Page, E. C. (eds) (2010) *Changing Government Relations in Europe. From localism to intergovernmentalism*, London: Routledge.

Gross, D. A. and Sigelman, L. (1984) 'Comparing party systems. A multidimensional approach', *Comparative Politics*, 16: 463–79.

Hesse, J. J. and Sharpe, L. J. (1991) 'Conclusions', in J. J. Hesse (ed.) *Local Government and Urban Affairs in International Perspective*, Baden-Baden: Nomos, 293–305.

Hoffmann-Martinot, V. and Sellers, J. M. (2005) 'Conclusion: the metropolitanization of politics' in V. Hoffmann-Martinot and J. M. Sellers (eds) *Metropolitanization and Political Change,* Opladen: Verlag für Sozialwissenschaften, 425–43.

Huntington, S. (1993) *The Third Wave: Democratization in the late twentieth century*, Norman, Oklahoma: University of Oklahoma Press.

Inglehart, R. and Welzel, C. (2005) *Modernization, Cultural Change and Democracy: The human development sequence*, Cambridge: Cambridge University Press.

Jones, M. P. and Mainwaring, S. (2003) 'The nationalization of parties and party systems: an empirical measure and an application to the Americas', *Party Politics*, 9: 139–66.

Kelleher, C. and Lowery, D. (2004) 'Political participation and metropolitan institutional contexts', *Urban Affairs Review*, 39: 720–57.

Kitschelt, H. (1994) *The Transformation of European Social Democracy*, Cambridge: Cambridge University Press.

Kostadinova, T. (2003) 'Voter turnout dynamics in post-Communist Europe', *European Journal of Political Research*, 42: 741–59.

Kreuzer, M. and Pattai, V. (2004) 'Political parties and the study of political development: new insights from the postcommunist democracies', *World Politics*, 56(4): 606–33

Kriesi, H., Grande, E., Lachat, R., Dolezal, M. and Bornschier, S. (2008) *West European Politics in the Age of Globalization*, Cambridge: Cambridge University Press.

Kriesi, H., Grande, E., Lachat, R., Dolezal, M., Bornschier, S. and Frey, T. (2006) 'Globalization and the transformation of the national political space: six European countries compared', *European Journal of Political Research*, 45: 921–25.

Lipset, S. M. and Rokkan, S. (1967) 'Cleavage structures, party systems and voter alignments: an introduction' in S. M. Lipset and S. Rokkan (eds) *Party Systems and Voter Alignments*, New York: The Free Press, 1–64.

Mair, P. and Mudde, C. (1998) 'The party family and its study', *Annual Review of Political Science*, 1: 211–229.

Mollenkopf, J. H. (1983) *The Contested City*, Princeton: Princeton University Press.

Morlan, R. L. (1984) 'Municipal vs. national election voter turnout: Europe and the United States', *Political Science Quarterly*, 99: 457–70.

Page, E. (1991) *Localism and Centralism in Europe*, Oxford: Oxford University Press.

Page, E. and Goldsmith, M. (eds) (1987) *Central and Local Government Relations*, London: Sage.

Preteceille, E. (2000) 'Segregation, class and politics in large cities', in P. Le Galès and A. Bagnasco (eds) *Cities in Contemporary Europe*, Cambridge, Cambridge University Press, 74–97.

Razin, E. (1998) 'The impact of decentralisation on fiscal disparities among local authorities in Israel', *Space and Polity*, 2: 49–69.

Selb, P. (2006) 'Multi-level elections in Switzerland', *Swiss Political Science Review*, 12: 49–75.

Sellers, J. M. (1998) 'Public goods and the politics of segregation: an analysis and cross-national comparison', *Journal of Urban Affairs*, 21: 237–62.

Sellers, J. M. and Kwak, S. -Y. (2011) 'State and society in local governance: lessons from a multilevel comparison', *International Journal of Urban and Regional Research*, 35: 620–43.

Sellers, J. M. and Lidstrom, A. (2007) 'Decentralization, local government, and the welfare state', *Governance – an International Journal of Policy and Administration*, 20: 609–32.

United Cities and Local Governments (2008) *First Global Report on Decentralization and Local Democracy*, Washington, DC, World Bank.

United Nations (2009) *World Urbanization Prospects. The 2009 revision,* United Nations, Department of Economic and Social Affairs, Population Division.

Walks, R. A. (2006) 'The causes of city-suburban political polarisation? A Canadian case study', *Annals of the Association of American Geographers*, 96: 390–414.

Wolman, H. and Marckini, L. (1998) 'Changes in central-city representation and influence in Congress since the 1960s', *Urban Affairs Review*, 34: 291–312.

Zeigler, D. J. and Brunn, S. D. (1980) 'Geopolitical fragmentation and the pattern of growth and need' in S. D. Brunn and J. O. Wheeler, J. O. (eds) *The American Metropolitan System: Present and future,* New York, John Wiley, 77–92.

# Appendix

## Party family classification

Following Lipset and Rokkan (1967), political parties can be seen to have formed around social cleavages, and parties that were mobilised on the same side of the same cleavage can be seen to constitute a separate party family. Typologies of party families given in the literature vary considerably (Mair and Mudde 1998: 223). There is, however, a common core of seven party families that also apply to party systems outside of Western Europe: far left (e.g. communist and ex-communist parties), greens, centre-left (e.g. social democrats), centre-right (e.g. Christian democrats), market liberals, far right (e.g. populist right), as well as regional and ethnic parties (e.g. regionalist and separatist parties). Parties in individual countries were classified into these seven party families by the authors of the country chapters (see Table A13.1).

*Table A13.1: Classification of national parties into party families*

| | Far left | Greens | Centre-left | Market liberal | Centre-right | Far right | Ethnic and regional parties | Others |
|---|---|---|---|---|---|---|---|---|
| United States | | | Democratic Party | | Republican Party | | | |
| Canada | | Green Party of Canada | NDP: New Democratic Party | Liberal Party of Canada | Conservative Party of Canada | | Bloc Québécois | Difference to 100% |
| United Kingdom | | | Labour Party | Liberal Democratic Party | Conservative Party | | Plaid Cymru SNP: Scottish National Party | GPEW: Green Party of England and Wales Others |
| France | LCR: Besancenot PT: Gluckstein PCF: Hue LO: Laguiller | LV: Mamère | MDC: Chevênement PS: Jospin | DL: Madelin | UDF: Bayrou FRS: Boutin RPR: Chirac CAP21: Lepage | FN: Le Pen MNR: Mégret | | CPNT: Saint-Josse PRG: Taubira |
| Switzerland | | GPS: Green Party of Switzerland | SPS: Social Democratic Party of Switzerland | FDP: Radical Democratic Party LPS: Swiss Liberal Party | CVP: Christian Democratic Party | SVP: Swiss People's Party | | All other small parties (LdU, EVP, CSP, PdA, FGA, SD, EDU, FPS, Lega, Sol.) |
| Germany | PDS: Party of Democratic Socialism | The Greens | SPD: Social Democratic Party of Germany | FDP: Free Democratic Party | CDU: Christian Democratic Union | | | Republicans NPD: National Democratic Party of Germany Others |

| | Far left | Greens | Centre-left | Market liberal | Centre-right | Far right | Ethnic and regional parties | Others |
|---|---|---|---|---|---|---|---|---|
| Spain | IU: United Left | | PSOE: Socialist Party | | PP: Popular Party | | RD: Regionalist Right; RI: Regionalist Left | Minorities |
| Sweden | V: Left Party | Green Party | SAP: Swedish Social Democratic Party | FP: Liberal People's Party; C: Centre Party | KD: Christian Democrats; M: Moderate Party | | | Difference to 100% |
| Poland | PPS: Polish Socialist Party; National Party of Retirees and Pensioners; Self-Defence of the Republic of Poland (Sambroona) | | SLD: Democratic Left Alliance; UP: Labour Union | UW: Freedom Union; KLD: Liberal Democratic Congress; UD: Democratic Union | PSL: Polish People's Party; AWS: Solidarity Electoral Action; PO: Civic Platform Independent Self-governing Trade Union 'Solidarity' Catholic Election Committee; BBWR: Non-Party Block for Supporting Reforms | PiS: Law and Justice; LPR: League of Polish Families; ROP: Movement for the Reconstruction of Poland; PC: Centre Agreement; KPN: Confederation for an Independent Poland | German Minority; NMGS: German Minority of Upper Silesia; RAS: Silesian Autonomy Movement | Social Alternative Movement; PWN: Polish National Community; PUG: Polish Economic Union; PL: Peasants Agreement; KDR: Coalition for the Republic Party 'X'; Others (Difference to 100%) |

| | Far left | Greens | Centre-left | Market liberal | Centre-right | Far right | Ethnic and regional parties | Others |
|---|---|---|---|---|---|---|---|---|
| Israel | | | Avoda (Labor party) Shinuy Am Echad Meretz | Likud | Israel Baaliya (Russian immigrants) Merkaz | Halchud Haleumi Mafdal (national religious) Yahadut Hatora (ultra-orthodox) Shas (ultra-religious) Ihud Leumi Israel Beitenu (Russian immigrants) | Balad Hadash Aravit Meuchedet | Difference to 100% |
| Czech Republic | KSCM: Communist Party of Bohemia and Moravia LB: Left Block | SZ: The Green Party | SDLSNS: Free Democrats-Liberal National Social Party CSSD: Czech Social Democracy DZJ: Pensioners for Social Security SDL: Party of the Democratic Left CMUS: Bohemian-Moravian Union of Centre CSNS: Czech National Social Party HA: Humanistic Alliance NH: New Movement SZR: Party of Common Sense SVOS: Party of Countryside-Unified Civic Forces CSD: Czech Social Democracy Movement SZJ: Party for Social Security SDS: Party of Democratic Socialism | ODS: Civic Democratic Party ODA: Civic Democratic Alliance US: Union of Freedom | DEU: Democratic Union KDU: Christian Democratic Union CP: Czech Right DL: Democratic League VPB: Choice for the Future NADEJE: Hope CZ: The Way of Change KDUUSDEU (coalition election '02) PB: Right Block | SPRRSC: Association for the Republic-Republican Party of Czechoslovakia NDS: National Democratic Party REPMS: Republicans of Miroslav Sladek REP: Republicans | MNS: Moravian National Party HSMS: Movement for Self-Governing Moravia and Silesia MDS: Moravian Democratic Party ROI: Romany Civic Initiative | NEZAV: Independents OK: Civic Coalition BPS: Balbin's Poetic Party AZDS: Action for Abolition of Senate SNK: Association of Independent Candidates |

*Table A13.2: Definition of variables*

| Name | Variable description | Source |
|---|---|---|
| *Country variables* | | |
| Metropolitanisation | Per cent living in metropolitan areas with over 200,000 population, early 2000s | Hoffmann-Martinot and Sellers 2005 |
| Civic localism | Local government system | Sellers and Kwak 2011 |
| Nationalised local government | Local government system | Sellers and Kwak 2011 |
| Local elitism | Local government system | Sellers and Kwak 2011 |
| Third-wave democracies | Democratisation from 1980s | Huntington 1993 |
| Proportional representation (national) | PR in national lower house elections | Blais *et al.* 2003 |
| Proportional representation (local council) | From country factsheets, World Report on Decentralisation and Local Democracy | United Cities and Local Governments 2008 |
| Election Day holiday | Election Day is holiday or rest day | Blasi *et al.* 2003 |
| Easy voting index | Multi-item index of measures to make voting easier | Blais *et al.* 2003 |
| Election Day registration | Voter registration permitted on Election Day | Blais *et al.* 2003 |
| Compulsory registration | All eligible voters automatically registered | Blasi *et al.* 2003 |
| Ethnic diversity | Fearon-Laitin index of ethnic diversity | Fearon 2003 |
| Right wins | Right wins all national elections during period | Own calculation |
| Left wins | Left wins all national elections during period | Own calculation |
| *Metropolitan variables* | | |
| Population concentration | Herfindahl index of population concentration by municipality | Calculated from country databases |
| Geopolitical fragmentation | Index measuring (1) municipalities per person, and (2) per cent population in central city | Zeigler and Brunn 1980 |
| Socio-spatial polarisation | Three-item Simpson index based on proportions of affluent suburbs, poor suburbs and others | Calculated from country databases |
| City-suburban polarisation | Multi-item Nathan-Adams index of central-city disadvantage relative to suburbs | Hoffmann-Martinot and Sellers 2005 |
| Metropolitan population (log) | Population as of early 2000s | From country databases |
| Metropolitan affluence | Proportion of municipalities classified as affluent or middle-class suburbs | Calculated from country databases |
| Poor non-minority concentrations (metro) | Proportion of municipalities classified as poor non-minority | Calculated from country databases |

| Name | Variable description | Source |
|------|---------------------|--------|
| Poor minority concentrations (metro) | Proportion of municipalities classified as minority | Calculated from country databases |
| Airport passengers/year (metro) | Total annual passengers for all airports in metropolitan area | Airport Council International 2007 |
| *Local variables* | | |
| Population (log) | Municipal population | From country databases |
| Urban concentrations | 1=yes, 0=no | From country databases |
| Affluent suburbs | 1=yes, 0=no | From country databases |
| Poor minority suburbs | 1=yes, 0=no | From country databases |
| Poor nonminority suburbs | 1=yes, 0=no (includes poor suburbs for countries without poor minority suburbs) | Calculated from country databases |
| Low-density suburbs | 1=yes, 0=no | From country databases |

# Chapter Fourteen | Methodological Appendix
*Jefferey M. Sellers and Philippe Rochat*

## Definition of metropolitan areas

The first task the International Metropolitan Observatory faced in the development of a methodological framework for this study was to arrive at a common protocol for the designation of metropolitan areas. In most countries with census definitions of metropolitan areas, the statistical basis for these definitions differed. National governments often applied more than one alternative definition; in a number of countries, there was no official metropolitan designation in use.

The final common protocol adopted official, nationally-specific definitions based mainly on economic or commuting ties as the baseline for the analysis. As metropolitan activity has expanded outward, functional definitions of this kind are necessary to capture effects from metropolitan dynamics beyond the built-up agglomerations. Although the precise functional criteria applied to the definitions in Canada, France, Germany, Sweden, Switzerland and United States differ, each definition is designed to capture a similar metropolitan territorial scope in a distinct national and regional setting. With the exception of the United States, where parts of metropolitan territories are not under municipal governments, municipalities comprised the units for designation of metropolitan boundaries.

In the Czech Republic, Poland, Spain and the United Kingdom, where official definitions were unavailable or did not take account of functional dynamics, new or altered definitions were devised, based mainly on commuting ties. Official Israeli designations were also partly revised to reflect actual functional relations among the local units.

Close examination revealed that cross-national differences in such formal criteria as commuting flows were closely linked to actual cross-national differences in metropolitan dynamics and structure. In France and Switzerland, for instance, where metropolitan commuter flows take place more around a single urban core, criteria for counting a municipality as part of a metropolitan region continue to stress commuting ties to the central city. In the United States, where metropolitan settlement in many regions is more dispersed among multiple nodes, the criteria allow lower levels of commuting to the central core. Instead, the US Census Bureau imposes additional criteria based on population density and growth rates. The criteria based on the low population densities in most of the United States, however, would not permit a clear differentiation of metropolitan boundaries in European regions with traditional rural settlement structures dominated by networks of rural villages.

*Table A.1: Official definitions*

| Country | Designation of metropolitan areas<br>*(Note: according to the IMO project assumptions, the population of a metropolitan area must be at least 200,000)* |
|---|---|
| United States | Definitions from the US Census Bureau from 1999:<br>*Metropolitan Statistical Area (MSA)* – designations centre on contiguous groups of counties, or in the case of New England states, of towns. The definition generally employs a multi-criteria standard that incorporates population density, urbanised settlement patterns, commuting, and in some instances population growth.<br>*Consolidated Metropolitan Statistical Area (CMSA)* – in addition to adjustments that have permitted metropolitan designations to reflect growing mobility, this overarching category has recently supplemented the standard definitions. It permits definitions that merge increasingly interconnected urban regions in the most urbanised parts of the country. The CMSAs (in this case: Atlanta, Detroit, Los Angeles, New York, Philadelphia and Seattle) encompass wider functional areas analogous to the French *aires urbaines* for the most of the largest metropolitan regions in the country. |
| Canada | Definition from Statistics Canada: the Canadian census uses the designation of census metropolitan areas (CMAs) to refer to geographical areas or territorial units comprised of an urban core and adjacent urban and rural municipalities, where there is a high level of economic and social integration with the urban core. The boundaries of CMAs are defined by using morphological and functional criteria, i.e. by using methods that consider population size, density and commuting models:<br>(1) The morphological approach is used to define the urban core, which consists of a central city, typically the oldest settlement within the metropolitan area.<br>(2) The population of a CMA (central city and its suburbs) must equal or exceed 100,000 inhabitants at its inception.<br>(3) The functional approach is used to determine the *municipalities that should be included in the CMA* based on the degree of integration, using data on home-to-work commuting between the municipalities and the central city. If at least half of the population living within a municipality contiguous to the metropolitan area commutes into the central city, or at least 25 per cent of the workforce is derived from those commuting out of the central city, the municipality is included within the boundaries of the CMA. |
| France | Metropolitan areas (*aires urbaines*) according to French Census Administration (INSEE) include:<br>(1) an urban area (*pôle urbain*) with at least 5,000 jobs;<br>(2) an exurban ring/commuter belt (*couronne périurbaine*), composed of rural communes or urban units in which at least 40 per cent of the active members work in the urban centre or in a secondary centre that is already attached to the urban centre by means of this criterion. |

| Country | Designation of metropolitan areas |
|---|---|
| | *(Note: according to the IMO project assumptions, the population of a metropolitan area must be at least 200,000)* |
| Switzerland | Definition of the Swiss Federal Statistical Office: |
| | (1) Metropolitan areas count at least 20,000 inhabitants and are formed by reuniting the territories of adjacent communes. |
| | (2) Each metropolitan area has a central zone, consisting of one core-commune (central city). |
| | (3) A commune is allocated to a metropolitan area if at least 1/6 of its commuting residents commute to the central zone. Additionally, a commune must fulfil three of the following five criteria: (i) continuity of the built-up environment with the core-commune, (no gaps of more than 200 metres); (ii) residential and job density in relationship to the constructible and agricultural area is greater than 10 per hectare; (iii) population increase in the preceding ten years was at least 10 per cent over the national average (for communes newly-attributed to a metropolitan area); (iv) at least 1/3 of professionally-active residents work in the central zone; and (v) the proportion of residents working in agriculture does not exceed the double of the national average. |
| Germany | Definition of the Federal Office for Building and Regional Planning (FOBP), 2006: |
| | (1) Core city: big core cities with more than 500,000 inhabitants and small core cities with more than 100,000 inhabitants. |
| | (2) Core area: high population density (density daily population >500, whereas daily population = population – commuter out of the city + commuter to the city) or a positive commuter balance (surplus commuter to the core area, 50 per cent commuter to the core city). |
| | (3) Inner commuter area: at least 50 per cent commuter to one or more core areas. |
| | (4) Outer commuter area: 25 per cent to under 50 per cent commuter to one or more core areas. |
| Sweden | Metropolitan areas according to the Swedish Association of Local Authorities (SALA): |
| | (1) Big cities: a municipality with more than 200,000 inhabitants. |
| | (2) Suburban municipality: more than 50 per cent of the resident population commutes to work in another municipality. The most common target must be a big city. |

*Table A.2: Modified official definitions*

| Country | Designation of metropolitan areas |
|---|---|
| | *(Note: according to the IMO project assumptions, the population of a metropolitan area must be at least 200,000)* |
| Poland | Combination of the UMP (Union of Polish Metropolises) definition for twenty-seven regions with a functional links analysis. The authors checked each analysed entity against the following criteria: |
| | (1) Population density (2002). |
| | (2) Balance of migration 1998–2002 'daily commuting' – because there are no official statistics on daily commuting the authors use an approximate estimation based on: *(the number of employed in the municipality + the number of adults whose main source of income is farming (1996)) / (the number of people of the productive age living in the municipality).* |
| | (3) These variables are weighted regionally because the population density and the number of variables used depend not only on the metropolitan/non-metropolitan character of the municipality, but also on some regional factors. The municipality located in the county neighbouring the major city is recognised as a metropolitan suburb if it fulfils at least two of the following three criteria: (i) balance of migration in 1998–2002 was not negative; (ii) population density is higher than third quartile for rural communities and mixed urban-rural municipalities in the given region; (iii) the ratio of the employed to productive age citizens is not higher than third quartile for the region. |
| | (4) Finally, metropolitan areas should be continuous in geographical space (i.e. a municipality 'cut off' by other municipalities does not fulfil the required criteria). |
| Israel | Based on the authors' own and statistical definitions there are four metropolitan areas with populations over 200,000 in Israel: Tel Aviv, Haifa, Jerusalem, and Beer Sheva. |
| | *Official definition for Tel Aviv and Haifa metropolitan areas:* according to the formal definition of Israel's Central Bureau of Statistics (CBS) a metropolitan area includes adjacent settlements that form a single functional entity in terms of economic, social and cultural linkages. The definitions are based on commuting patterns, volume of traffic and migration. Several Jewish settlements in the West Bank that are functionally an integral part of the Tel Aviv metropolitan area are excluded, because official spatial subdivisions of the CBS do not include areas that are not formally part of Israel. |
| | *Definitions of Jerusalem and Beer Sheva metropolitan areas based on authors' evaluations:* |
| | (1) *Jerusalem metropolitan area* – there is no formal definition of this metropolis. According to the authors, the Jerusalem metropolitan area includes two, perhaps three, distinct parts. The first consists of an area within the state of Israel (including annexed East Jerusalem). The second consists of Jewish settlements in the West Bank that functionally form part of the metropolis. The third consists of Palestine localities formally controlled by the Palestinian National Authority that geographically form an integral part of the metropolis, but functionally have very limited ties with the Israeli metropolis in recent years. |
| | (2) *Beer Sheva metropolitan area* – the definition of the CBS for the Beer Sheva metropolitan area is extremely broad and includes vast tracts of sparsely-populated desert. Because of that the authors used a narrower definition. |

*Table A.3: No official definition*

| Country | Designation of metropolitan areas *(Note: according to the IMO project assumptions, the population of a metropolitan area must be at least 200,000)* |
|---------|------------------------------------------------------------------------------------------------------------------------------------------------------|
| United Kingdom | Metropolitan areas as defined here involve all those conurbations with populations greater than 250,000. The central city municipality or municipalities of each metropolitan area is/are identified based on the boundaries of municipal settlement as at the beginning of the Second World War (see Chapter 4, Table 4.1). Parliamentary constituencies are then classified based on how they map onto these core municipalities: <br> (1) Inner cities – all parliamentary constituencies contained within (or mostly within) the boundaries of the municipalities are defined as belonging to the urban core/central city. Within Greater London, the inner city is defined as the inner-London boroughs. <br> (2) Suburbs – non-rural constituencies within the commuting shed of each inner core for whom the majority of the population lives within local authorities (boroughs or counties) located outside the boundaries of the central cities, and where at least half the population commutes into central municipalities for work. |
| Spain | Using the classification of Feria (2008) metropolitan areas are defined by: <br> (1) Commuting to the core – which has to be 20 per cent of the working population and no less than 1,000 workers. <br> (2) Existence of territorial continuity among municipalities included in the metropolitan area. <br> (3) Total population of metropolitan area over 100,000 inhabitants. |
| Czech Republic | Definition of metropolitan areas (including core cities, inner and outer suburban zones) by Kostelecký and Čermák (2005): <br> (1) Core cities – four core cities are analysed (Prague, Brno, Ostrava, Plzen) <br> (2) Inner suburban zone – all municipalities with more than 40 per cent of daily commuters to the core city. <br> (3) Outer suburban zone – all municipalities with 30 to 40 per cent of daily commuters to the core city. Municipalities with slightly less than 30 per cent of commuters are included in the outer suburban zone as well if it is necessary for keeping the spatial continuity of the covered suburban area. <br> *(Note: several larger industrial cities located east of Ostrava are included in the outer suburban zone of the Ostrava metropolitan region even if the share of commuters to Ostrava was lower.)* |

The many different variations on metropolitan patterns make it difficult to envisage a fully uniform cross-national definition, and in many countries the criteria for designation continue to shift with metropolitan dynamics. Definitions under the protocol, nonetheless, proved sufficiently broad to capture a similar range of characteristic metropolitan communities in each country, from central cities to exurbs.

## Typologies of municipalities

Following cluster and factor analysis of the characteristics of municipalities in several countries, a hierarchical factor analytical procedure was devised to classify metropolitan municipalities into six common categories. Each category captured a type of municipality that could be found in most, if not all of the countries. The types included urban concentrations, low-density suburbs, affluent suburbs, poor suburbs, minority suburbs (separated from other poor suburbs where possible), and middle-class suburbs.

This typology served two purposes. Most important, following the example of Orfield (2001), it provided an initial basis for analysing the variations in types of communities and the relation to partisanship and turnout. Beyond this, it also served as one among several tests of ecological effects on municipal electoral behaviour that could not be captured through demographic composition alone.

For classification the following steps are carried out:

1. *Urban concentrations:* first, the central cities were separated out in each metropolitan area. Additionally, a set of factors was used to separate out other essentially urban metropolitan towns:

    (a) All metropolitan municipalities with half or more of the population of the largest municipality were designated as urbanised core areas.

    (b) In addition, other large urban concentrations were placed in this category. These include places with over 100,000 inhabitants.

    (c) Localities with densities less than that of the central city were excluded from this type.

2. *Low density suburbs:* a factor based on density, new housing and (where available) distance from the centre was used to separate out low-density peripheral suburbs.

3. For the remaining towns, a factor based on the dimensions of socio-economic status derived from indicators for income, poverty, housing, education, unemployment, dependents, university education, highest status occupational group, and homeownership is used to separate out:

    (a) *Affluent suburbs:* the most privileged communities.

    (b) *Poor suburbs:* the least privileged communities. Where possible, this type has been subdivided into two distinct types:

        (i) *Poor minority suburbs:* a factor based on racial/ethnic diversity was used to separate out high minority or high immigrant concentrations from other poor communities. In the Czech Republic, Germany,

Poland, Spain, and Switzerland, this factor corresponded so closely with socio-economic status that no distinct poor minority suburbs could be distinguished. In Sweden, only one poor municipality fell within this category, but several inner city districts did. This type was only separated out for purposes of the country chapter in the analysis of municipal turnout (which used inner city districts and peripheral municipalities). It was employed in the pooled analysis.

(ii) *Poor suburbs (non-minority):* least privileged communities with low racial/ethnic diversity.

4. *Middle-class suburbs:* all remaining municipalities were placed in this category.

Cut-off points for the designation of communities in steps 2 and 3 varied with the patterns of distribution. As in the designation of metropolitan boundaries, cross-national differences in the most relevant measures as well as in concentrations of population, privilege and disadvantage required distinctions between similar types of places to be calculated using measures and cut-off points distinct to each country. Table A.4 summarises the principles used to distinguish the different types by country.

Table A.4: Derivation of municipal typology, by country

| Country | | Low-density suburbs | Affluent suburbs | Poor suburbs | Minority suburbs | Middle-class suburbs |
|---|---|---|---|---|---|---|
| United States | Factors | housing built since 1980, population density | affluence index through principle components analysis, based on per capita income, education, unemployment and poverty rates indicators for race, ethnicity and immigration | | | ... |
| | Separators | top quartile of housing built since 1980 and lower half of population density | municipalities above 80th percentile as measured in affluent index | bottom 30% as measured in affluent index that did not match the additional criteria for minority suburbs | bottom 30% as measured in affluent index and 10% or more foreign-born populations, 25% or more African-Americans or 25% or more Hispanic Americans | remaining municipalities |
| Canada | Factors | population density | high socio-economic status | low income, high proportion of the population facing hardship indicators for visible minorities and immigrants | | |
| | Separators | areas with population density significantly below the suburban average | suburban areas with combined index of average household income and high-status occupations >20% above the CMA average for the index | suburban areas with a hardship index >20% above the average AND average household incomes less than 90% of the CMA average below average proportion of visible minorities and immigrants | suburban areas with a hardship index >20% above the average AND average household incomes less than 90% of the CMA average above average proportion of visible minorities and immigrants | all remaining suburban constituencies |

| Country | | Low-density suburbs | Affluent suburbs | Poor suburbs | Minority suburbs | Middle-class suburbs |
|---|---|---|---|---|---|---|
| United Kingdom[1] | Factors | Population density | Socio-economic status, proportion of the population facing hardship | | proportions of visible minorities and/or immigrants | ... |
| | Separators | areas with population densities significantly lower than the metropolitan average | suburban areas with levels of socio-economic status 20% higher than metropolitan average, and levels of hardship approximately 20% below average | levels of disadvantage and hardship greater than 25% higher than metropolitan average,[2] proportion of visible minorities and/ or immigrants below metropolitan average | levels of disadvantage and hardship greater than 25% higher than metropolitan average,[2] proportion of visible minorities and/ or immigrants above metropolitan average | remaining suburban districts |
| France | Factors | density | factor using indicators for income and higher education | unemployment rate and minority status (measured by foreign-born population) | | ... |
| | Separators | 40th percentile or below | 90th or higher percentile | unemployment rates in the 70th percentile or higher and residents born abroad below 85th percentile | unemployment rates in the 70th percentile or higher and residents born abroad in the 85th percentile or higher | remaining municipalities |

1. Types of districts based on characteristics derived from the 2001 census at the level of parliamentary constituencies.
2. Metro average excluding Greater London conurbations (for Greater London conurbations: London average proportion foreign born).

| Country | | Low-density suburbs | Affluent suburbs | Poor suburbs | Minority suburbs | Middle-class suburbs |
|---|---|---|---|---|---|---|
| Switzerland | Factors | factor based on density, new housing, and distance to the centre | factor based on low education, retirees, unemployment, foreigners, low socio-economic status, non-Western European language, university education, highest status occupational group, and homeownership | | | |
| | Separators | third 25th percentile | third 33rd percentile | first 33rd percentile | n/a | in between first and third 33rd percentile |
| Germany[3] | Factors | population density | standardised hardship index based on unemployment rate, living space per capita, university degree, local tax rates | | | |
| | Separators | lowest quartile | top quartile | lowest quartile | n/a | in between lowest and top quartile |
| Spain | Factors | density and distance to the centre | two criteria: (1) socio-economic factor based on: low occupational status (% manual workers), unemployment rate, low educational status (% less than university) and living space (household members/household surface) (2) immigration: % population born abroad | | | |
| | Separators | lowest quartile of density and highest quartile of distance to the centre (simultaneously) | (1) socio-economic: highest quartile | (1) socio-economic: lowest quartile (2) immigration: <median | (1) socio-economic: lowest quartile (2) immigration: >median | (1) socio-economic: second and third quartiles |

3. In view of socio-economic differences in Western and Eastern Germany the author created a separate typology of communes for these two parts of the country.

| Country | | Low-density suburbs | Affluent suburbs | Poor suburbs | Minority suburbs | Middle-class suburbs |
|---|---|---|---|---|---|---|
| Sweden | Factors | factor of income and education, factor of density and distance to the centre | factor of income and education | factor of income and education, percentage born abroad | factor of income and education, percentage born abroad | factor of income and education, factor of density and distance to the centre |
| | Separators | medium socio-economic status, low density/long distance | high socio-economic status | low socio-economic status, low percentage born abroad | low socio-economic status, high percentage born abroad | medium socio-economic status, high density/short distance |
| Poland | Factors | index based on population density, new housing per capita (2001-2005), (minus) weighted by distance from the central city | hardship index based on Nathan and Adams concept using the sum of the standardised values of different indicators: level of unemployment 2002, level of education 2002 (proportion of residents with university degrees among all residents 15 years and older), housing conditions 2002 (number of rooms per capita), wealth of local population 2002 (average income of tax payer), and dependency index 2002 (proportion of population of non-productive age) | | | … |
| | Separators | lowest quartile | lowest quartile | highest quartile | n/a | remaining municipalities |

| Country | | Low-density suburbs | Affluent suburbs | Poor suburbs | Minority suburbs | Middle-class suburbs |
|---|---|---|---|---|---|---|
| Czech Republic | Factors | population density | socio-economic index through principal component analysis; indicators: percentage of poor households 2003, unemployment rate 2001, population with low (lower than secondary) education, percentage of university graduates, percentage of people older than 65 years, and per capita revenue of municipality from personal taxes paid by local citizens | | | ... |
| | Separators | lowest quintile | highest quartile | lowest quartile | n/a | remaining municipalities |
| Israel | Factors | | | | | |
| | Separators | | SES 8–10 (10 – highest) | SES 1–4 | Arab majority | SES 5–7 |

## Partisan ideological indices

Indices of partisan ideology were constructed on the basis of responses among voters for each party to questions about those issues in post-electoral or other contemporaneous surveys. Insofar as possible, the items employed in the indices came from a battery of identical questions posed in most of the countries in the study as part of the International Social Survey Program (ISSP) or the World Values Survey (WVS) from 1998 to 2003.[1]

The indices were designed to provide clear, cross-nationally equivalent metrics to assess the ideological propensities of the parties and, ultimately, the communities that voted for them. This purpose made formative indices more appropriate for the analysis than the reflective indices that have often been used in survey research (Inglehart and Welzel 2005). Questions chosen for each index captured a range of issues for which responses could be arrayed along the same general conceptual axis. In a formative index, each item measures a potentially different component of the common dimension. As a result, unlike a reflective index, this type of index cannot be constructed through a method based on correlations among item responses such as factor analysis (Diamantopoulos and Winklhofer 2001; Coltman et al. 2008). Indeed, a formative index requires no correlation among the individual items to be valid. Instead, items aggregated into each index were simply assigned equal weight and a standardised range.

Surveys and items used for the three dimensional indices in each country are shown in Tables A.5 to A.7.

---

1.  Exceptions were made for Switzerland and on some items for Poland, where low levels of party identification left sample sizes for some parties in these cross-national surveys too small to permit reliable inferences. For Canada, the indices employed later surveys more contemporaneous to the elections in the analysis. In all these cases, the questions employed remained similar if not virtually identical to those used to construct the indices in the other countries.

## Appendix

*Table A.5: Economic index*

| | | United States | Canada | United Kingdom | France | Switzerland | Germany | Spain | Sweden | Poland | Czech Republic | Israel |
|---|---|---|---|---|---|---|---|---|---|---|---|---|
| Competition good or harmful for people (Q54C) | WVS 1999/2000 | X | | X | X | | X | | X | | X | |
| State give more freedom or control firms more effectively (Q54D) | WVS 1999/2000 | | | X | X | | X | X | X | | X | |
| State should equalise income or provide incentives for individual effort (Q54E) | WVS 1999/2000 | | | X | X | | | | | | X | |
| Private or government ownership of business (Q54F) | WVS 1999/2000 | X | | X | X | | X | | | | X | |
| Government must reduce the differences in income | ISSP 1999 | X | | X | X | | X | X | X | | X | X |
| Rich people should pay more taxes | ISSP 1999 | X | | X | | | | X | X | | | X |
| The differences in income are too large | ISSP 1999 | X | | X | | | | X | X | | | X |
| Government should be responsible for providing job for people who want that | ISSP 1998 | X | | X | X | | X | X | X | | X | X |
| State should equalise incomes or provide incentives for individual effort | ISSP 1998 | X | | X | X | | X | X | X | | | X |
| Are you favourable to higher taxes on high incomes or are you favourable to lower taxes on high incomes? | SELECTS 1999/2003 | | | | | X | | | | | | |
| The role of the government is to minimise differences between rich and poor | ESS 2002 | | | | | | | | | X | | |

| | United States | Canada | United Kingdom | France | Switzerland | Germany | Spain | Sweden | Poland | Czech Republic | Israel |
|---|---|---|---|---|---|---|---|---|---|---|---|
| The role of the government is to secure jobs for everyone | ESS 2002 | | | | | | | | | X | |
| The role of the government is to secure minimal income for everyone | ESS 2002 | | | | | | | | | X | |
| The role of the private sector in the economy should be enlarged | 2003 Survey of Councillors | | | | | | | | | X | |
| Private sector is usually more efficient than public | 2003 Survey of Councillors | | | | | | | | | X | |
| Government should leave the economy entirely to private sector | CES 2006 | | X | | | | | | | | |
| Do you favour or oppose having some private hospitals in Canada? | CES 2006 | | X | | | | | | | | |
| How much should be done to reduce gap between the rich and the poor? | CES 2006 | | X | | | | | | | | |
| People who don't get ahead should blame themselves, not the system | CES 2006 | | X | | | | | | | | |
| The welfare state makes people less willing to look after themselves | CES 2006 | | X | | | | | | | | |
| Should the government spend more or less on welfare? | CES 2006 | | X | | | | | | | | |
| Should personal income taxes be increased or decreased or kept about the same as now? | CES 2006 | | X | | | | | | | | |
| Should corporate taxes be increased, decreased or kept about the same as now? | CES 2006 | | X | | | | | | | | |

*Table A.6: Cultural index*

| | | United States | Canada | United Kingdom | France | Switzerland | Germany | Spain | Sweden | Poland | Czech Republic | Israel |
|---|---|---|---|---|---|---|---|---|---|---|---|---|
| How important is God in your life? (Q33) | WVS 1999/2000 | X | | X | X | | X | X | X | | X | X |
| How important is religion in your life? (Q1F) | WVS 1999/2000 | X | | X | X | | X | X | X | | X | |
| Approve/disapprove of abortion if a couple doesn't want more children (Q50B) | WVS 1999/2000 | X | | | X | X | | X | X | | X | X |
| Working mom: pre-school child suffers | ISSP 2002 | X | X | X | X | X | X | X | X | X | X | X |
| Working mom: family life suffers | ISSP 2002 | X | X | X | X | X | X | X | X | X | X | X |
| Approval of a couple living together without marriage | ISSP 2002 | X | X | X | X | X | X | X | X | X | X | X |
| Divorce may be the best solution for marriage problems | ISSP 2002 | X | X | X | X | X | X | X | X | X | X | X |
| Sexual relations before marriage | ISSP 1998 | X | | X | X | | X | X | X | | | X |
| Sexual relations between two adults of the same sex | ISSP 1998 | X | | X | X | | X | X | X | | | X |
| Husband's job is to earn money while wife's job is to care about family | ISSP 1998 | X | | X | X | X | X | X | X | | X | X |
| Gays should be free to live their life as they think is best | ESS 2004 | | | | | X | | | | | | |
| Men should earn money while woman should stay at home | ESS 2002 | | | | | | | | | X | | |
| If only possible woman should stay at home | ESS 2002 | | | | | | | | | X | | |
| There should be sex education in school | ESS 2002 | | | | | | | | | X | | |
| Abortion should be allowed if only woman wishes so | ESS 2002 | | | | | | | | | X | | |
| Homosexual contacts are acceptable | ESS 2002 | | | | | | | | | X | | |

| | | United States | Canada | United Kingdom | France | Switzerland | Germany | Spain | Sweden | Poland | Czech Republic | Israel |
|---|---|---|---|---|---|---|---|---|---|---|---|---|
| Corporal punishment for children is sometimes necessary | ESS 2002 | | | | | | | | | | X | |
| Divorce should be easier | ESS 2002 | | | | | | | | | | X | |
| Acceptance for death sentence | ESS 2002 | | | | | | | | | | X | |
| Role of religion in life | ESS 2002 | | | | | | | | | | X | |
| Do you think it should be very easy for women to get an abortion? | CES 2006 | | X | | | | | | | | | |
| Do you favour or oppose the death penalty? | CES 2006 | | X | | | | | | | | | |
| Do you favour or oppose same-sex marriage? | CES 2006 | | X | | | | | | | | | |
| Only people who are legally married should be having children | CES 2006 | | X | | | | | | | | | |
| Society would be better off if more women stayed home with their children | CES 2006 | | X | | | | | | | | | |
| This country would have many fewer problems if there were more emphasis on family values | CES 2006 | | X | | | | | | | | | |
| In your life, would you say religion is very important? | CES 2006 | | X | | | | | | | | | |
| How much do you think should be done for women? | CES 2006 | | X | | | | | | | | | |

*Table A.7: Globalisation index*

| | | United States | Canada | United Kingdom | France | Switzerland | Germany | Spain | Sweden | Poland | Czech Republic | Israel |
|---|---|---|---|---|---|---|---|---|---|---|---|---|
| I would rather be a citizen of [country] than of any other country in the world | ISSP 2003 | X | | X | X | | X | X | X | X | X | X |
| People should support their country even if the country is in the wrong | ISSP 2003 | X | | X | X | | X | X | X | X | X | X |
| [Country] should limit the import of foreign products in order to protect its national economy | ISSP 2003 | X | | X | X | | X | X | X | X | X | X |
| Free trade leads to better products becoming available in [country] | ISSP 2003 | X | | X | X | | X | X | X | X | X | X |
| International organisations are taking away too much power from the [country nationality] government | ISSP 2003 | X | | X | X | | X | X | X | X | X | X |
| Increased exposure to foreign films, music, and books is damaging our national and local cultures | ISSP 2003 | X | | X | X | | X | X | X | X | X | X |
| It is impossible for people who do not share [country's] customs and traditions to become fully [country's nationality] | ISSP 2003 | X | | X | X | | X | X | X | X | X | X |
| Immigrants increase crime rates | ISSP 2003 | X | | X | X | | X | X | X | X | X | X |
| Immigrants are generally good for [country's] economy | ISSP 2003 | X | | X | X | | X | X | X | X | X | X |
| Immigrants take jobs away from people who were born in [country] | ISSP 2003 | X | | X | X | | X | X | X | X | X | X |

| | | United States | Canada | United Kingdom | France | Switzerland | Germany | Spain | Sweden | Poland | Czech Republic | Israel |
|---|---|---|---|---|---|---|---|---|---|---|---|---|
| Immigrants improve [country nationality] society by bringing in new ideas and cultures | ISSP 2003 | X | | X | X | | X | X | X | X | X | X |
| Children born in [country] of parents who are not citizens should have the right to become [country nationality] citizens | ISSP 2003 | X | | X | X | | X | X | X | X | X | X |
| Legal immigrants to [country] who are not citizens should have the same rights as [country nationality] citizens | ISSP 2003 | X | | X | X | | X | X | X | X | X | X |
| [Country] should take stronger measures to exclude illegal immigrants | ISSP 2003 | X | | X | X | | X | X | X | X | X | X |
| Benefits from being member of EU: EU Members | ISSP 2003 | | | | X | | | | X | | X | |
| [Country] should follow EU decisions, even if it does not agree with them | ISSP 2003 | | | | X | | | | X | X | X | |
| Do you think Switzerland should join the EU or stay away from EU? | SELECTS 1999/2003 | | | | | X | | | | | | |
| Do you think that foreigners in Switzerland should have equal chances compared to Swiss citizens? Or do you think Swiss citizens should have better chances? | SELECTS 1999/2003 | | | | | X | | | | | | |
| Immigrants make an important contribution to this country | CES 2006 | | X | | | | | | | | | |

| | | United States | Canada | United Kingdom | France | Switzerland | Germany | Spain | Sweden | Poland | Czech Republic | Israel |
|---|---|---|---|---|---|---|---|---|---|---|---|---|
| Immigrants take jobs away from other Canadians | CES 2006 | | X | | | | | | | | | |
| Too many recent immigrants just don't want to fit into Canadian society | CES 2006 | | X | | | | | | | | | |
| International trade creates more jobs in Canada than it destroys | CES 2006 | | X | | | | | | | | | |
| We should look after Canadians born in this country first and others second | CES 2006 | | X | | | | | | | | | |
| Which of the following do you identify with most: The world as a whole | CES 2006 | | X | | | | | | | | | |
| Only people who are Canadian citizens should be allowed to be members of a political party | CES 2006 | | X | | | | | | | | | |
| We have gone too far in pushing equal rights in this country | CES 2006 | | X | | | | | | | | | |
| Overall, free trade with the United States. has been good for the Canadian economy | CES 2006 | | X | | | | | | | | | |

*Notes:* CES = Canada Election Survey, WVS = World Values Survey, ESS = European Social Survey, ISSP = International Social Survey Programme, SELECTS = Swiss Electoral Study.

## Municipal ideological positions

Drawing on the partisanship indices, average issue positions of communal electorates were constructed on the basis of the percentage of votes for each party in a given commune. This portion of the analysis applies a formula developed by Gross and Sigelman (1984) to estimate the 'ideological centre of gravity' for a community.

For each municipality, this procedure applies the following formula:

$$Pos_i = \sum_{p=1}^{n} \frac{pos_p \cdot votes_{p,i}}{votes_i}$$

where:

        pos = issue position
        i = municipality
        p = party
        n = number of parties with votes in municipality i

The same procedure was employed to derive estimates of left-right self-placement for each municipality.

The resulting ideological estimates require important caveats for proper interpretation. As artefacts of both party performance in a community and the positions of the aggregated national electorate for the parties, they represent a mapping of wider patterns of party competition as well as the actual preferences of the local voters. To organise these elements and test the entire pathway of effects from metropolitanisation on voters, parties and axes of partisan competition, would require a much more complex research design than has thus far been attempted. Nevertheless, the current analysis is sufficient to show that the metropolitan patterns they have produced are now a fixture of contemporary politics.

## Bibliography

Coltman, T., Devinney, T. M., Midgley, D. F. and Venaik, S. (2008) 'Formative versus reflective measurement models: two applications of formative measurement', *Journal of Business Research*, 61: 1250–62.

Diamantopoulos, A. and Winklhofer, H. M. (2001) 'Index construction with formative indicators: an alternative to scale development', *Journal of Marketing Research*, 38: 269–77.

Feria, J. M. (2008) 'Un ensayo metodológico de definición de las áreas metropolitanas en España a partir de la variable residencia-trabajo', *Investigaciones geográficas*, 46: 49–68.

Gross, D. A. and Sigelman, L. (1984) 'Comparing party systems: a multidimensional approach', *Comparative Politics*, 16: 463–79.

Kostelecký, T. and D. Čermák (2005) 'Metropolitanization and political change in the Czech Republic', in V. Hoffmann-Martinot and J. M. Sellers (eds) *Metropolitanization and Political Change*, Wiesbaden: VS Verlag für Sozialwissenschaften, 353–70.

Inglehart, R. and Welzel, C. (2005) *Modernization, Cultural Change, and Democracy: The human development sequence*, New York: Cambridge University Press.

Orfield, M. (2001) *Metropolitics*, Washington: Brookings Institution Press.

Walks, R. A. (2005) 'City-suburban electoral polarization in Great Britain, 1950–2001', *Transactions of the Institute of British Geographers*, 30(4): 500–17.

# | Index